INTRODUCTION

Andrew Warren, Managing Director, Condé Nast Johansens Ltd.

There has been no better time to travel and stay throughout Great Britain & Ireland.

A more unsettled world has meant that travellers have stayed closer to home, creating an opportunity to rediscover the wonderful hospitality and welcome offered within their own region.

As you will see, our team of Regional Inspectors have once again been very busy and this edition of our Guide is a treasure trove of fabulous places, many of which we are pleased to recommend to you again and some that are new.

Please let us know of your experiences at our Recommendations, there are 'Guest Survey Forms' at the back of this Guide and on our website www.johansens.com where you can take advantage of some very attractive 'Special Offers'.

Above all, please remember to mention Johansens when you make an enquiry or reservation and again when you arrive. You will be especially welcome.

W0008051

THE CONDÉ NAST JOHANSENS PROMISE

Condé Nast Johansens is the most comprehensive illustrated reference to annually inspected, independently owned accommodation and meetings venues throughout Great Britain, Europe and North America.

It is our objective to maintain the trust of guide users by recommending by annual inspection a careful choice of accommodation offering quality, excellent service and value for money.

Our team of over 50 dedicated Regional Inspectors visit thousands of hotels, country houses, inns and resorts throughout 39 countries to select only the very best for recommendation in the 2004 editions of our Guides.

No hotel can appear unless it meets our exacting standards.

Condé Nast Johansens Guides

Recommending only the finest hotels in the world

As well as this Guide Condé Nast Johansens also publishes the following titles:

Recommended Country Houses, Small Hotels & Inns, Great Britain & Ireland

240 smaller more rural properties, ideal for short breaks or more intimate stays

Recommended Hotels, Europe & the Mediterranean

351 continental gems featuring châteaux, resorts and charming countryside hotels

Recommended Hotels, Inns & Resorts, North America, Bermuda, Caribbean, Mexico, Pacific

200 properties including many hidden properties from across the region

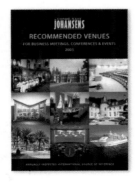

Recommended Venues for Business Meetings, Conferences and Events, Great Britain & Europe

230 venues that cater specifically for a business audience

When you purchase two Guides or more we will be pleased to offer you a reduction in the cost.

The complete set of Condé Nast Johansens Guides may be purchased as 'The Chairman's Collection'.

To order any Guides please complete the order form on page 487 or call FREEPHONE 0800 269 397

Hildon Ltd., Broughton, Hampshire SO20 8DQ, ☎ 01794 - 301 747, Fax 01794 - 301 718
e-mail: hildon@hildon.com – www.hildon.com

How to use this Guide

To find a hotel by location:

- Use the **county maps** at the front to identify the area of the country you wish to search.

- Turn to the relevant **county section** where hotels are featured alphabetically by location.

- Alternatively use the **maps** on pages 474–485 at the rear of the Guide. These maps cover all regions of Great Britain & Ireland and each hotel is marked.

There are over 61 properties which did not feature in our last (2003) edition and these are identified with a "NEW" symbol at the top of the page.

To find a hotel by its name or the name of its nearest town look in the indexes on pages 461–472.

The indexes also list recommended hotels by their amenities such as swimming pool, golf, etc.

If you cannot find a suitable hotel where you wish to stay, you may decide to choose one of **Condé Nast Johansens Recommended Country Houses, Small Hotels or Inns** as an alternative. These more intimate establishments are listed by place names on pages 432–436.

Once you have made your choice please contact the hotel directly. Rates are per room, including VAT and breakfast (unless stated otherwise) and are correct at the time of going to press but should always be checked with the hotel before you make your reservation. When making a booking please mention that Condé Nast Johansens was your source of reference.

We occasionally receive letters from guests who have been charged for accommodation booked in advance but later cancelled. Readers should be aware that by making a reservation with a hotel, either by telephone, e-mail or in writing, they are entering into a legal contract. A hotelier under certain circumstances is entitled to make a charge for accommodation when guests fail to arrive, even if notice of the cancellation is given.

All guides are obtainable from bookshops, or by calling Freephone 0800 269397, or by using the order coupons on pages 487–496.

Condé Nast Johansens

Condé Nast Johansens Ltd., 6-8 Old Bond Street, London W1S 4PH
Tel: +44 (0)20 7499 9080 Fax: +44 (0)20 7152 3565
Find Condé Nast Johansens on the Internet at: www.johansens.com
E-Mail: info@johansens.com

Publishing Director:	Stuart Johnson
P.A. to Publishing Director:	Fiona Galley
Hotel Inspectors:	Jean Branham
	Geraldine Bromley
	Robert Bromley
	Jules Dunkley
	Pat Gillson
	Marie Iversen
	Pauline Mason
	John O'Neill
	Mary O'Neill
	Fiona Patrick
	Liza Reeves
	John Sloggie
	David Wilkinson
	Helen Wynn
Production Manager:	Kevin Bradbrook
Production Controller:	Laura Kerry
Senior Designer:	Michael Tompsett
Editorial Manager:	Stephanie Cook
Copywriters:	Clare Barker
	Sasha Creed
	Norman Flack
	Debra Giles
	Rozanne Paragon
	Leonora Sandwell
Sales and Marketing Director:	Tim Sinclair
Promotions & Events Manager:	Adam Crabtree
Client Services Director:	Fiona Patrick
P.A. to Managing Director :	Siobhan Smith
Managing Director:	Andrew Warren

Copyright © 2003 Condé Nast Johansens Ltd.

Condé Nast Johansens Ltd. is part of The Condé Nast Publications Ltd.

ISBN 1 903665 13 2

Printed in England by St Ives plc
Colour origination by Graphic Facilities

Distributed in the UK and Europe by Portfolio, Greenford (bookstores). In North America by Casemate Publishing, Havertown (Bookstores).

Champagne for the Independently Minded

CHAMPAGNE
TAITTINGER
Reims

Condé Nast Johansens
preferred Champagne partner

2003 AWARDS FOR EXCELLENCE

The winners of the Condé Nast Johansens 2003 Awards for Excellence

The Condé Nast Johansens 2003 Awards for Excellence were presented at the Awards Dinner held at The Dorchester hotel, London, on November 11th, 2002. Awards were offered to those properties worldwide that represented the finest standards and best value for money in luxury independent travel. An important source of information for these awards was the feedback provided by guests who completed Johansens Guest Survey reports. Guest Survey forms can be found on page 488.

Most Excellent Country Hotel Award

DROMOLAND CASTLE – Co. Clare, Ireland, p348

"The unique experience offers guests an opportunity to stay in the most famous baronial castle in Ireland with stately halls and beautifully furnished bedrooms and suites."

Most Excellent London Hotel Award

ONE ALDWYCH – London, England

"A happening lobby - brilliant, contemporary interiors, down-to-earth service, cutting-edge technology and an interesting art collection at this great location."

Most Excellent Value for Money Award

HASSOP HALL – Derbyshire, England, p89

"The Chapman family have owned Hassop Hall since 1975 and are committed to the preservation of its outstanding heritage. Large bedrooms, comprehensive menus and beautifully maintained gardens joint with the theatrical room service renders Hassop as a first-class choice."

2003 AWARDS FOR EXCELLENCE

The winners of the Condé Nast Johansens 2003 Awards for Excellence

Most Excellent Service Award

KINFAUNS CASTLE – Perth, Scotland, p404

"Set in 26 acres of parklands overlooking the River Tay, the 16 suites reflect the quality, comfort and ambience one expects from a luxury country house - excellent service in this splendid grand castle."

Most Excellent Restaurant Award

PERCY'S COUNTRY HOUSE HOTEL & RESTAURANT
– Devon, England, p112

"Tina Bricknell Webb's contemporary country cuisine uses the very best local produce and home grown organic ingredients. The only chef in Devon to receive 4 RAC dining awards. Percy's Academy of Culinary Excellence has been set up for young people wishing to cultivate a career in the industry."

Most Excellent Spa Award

DANESFIELD HOUSE – Buckinghamshire, England p38

"This luxurious spa with a 20-metre pool, state-of-the-art gym and dedicated treatment and rest rooms is a sanctuary of calm with everything that is need to escape the stresses of daily life."

Knight Frank Award for Excellence & Innovation

MARTIN & JOY CUMMINGS, AMBERLEY CASTLE
– West Sussex, England p279

"Proprietors, Joy and Martin Cummings, have transformed this medieval fortress into a unique country castle hotel. They offer a warm, personal welcome and their hotel provides the ultimate in contemporary luxury."

2003 AWARDS FOR EXCELLENCE

The winners of the Condé Nast Johansens 2003 Awards for Excellence

The following award winners are featured within Condé Nast Johansens 2004 Guides to Country Houses – Great Britain & Ireland, Hotels & Spas – Europe & The Mediterranean, Hotels – North America & Caribbean. See page 2 for details.

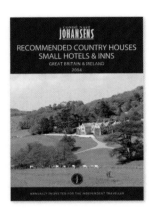

Most Excellent Country House Award
La Sablonnerie – Sark, Channel Islands

Most Excellent Traditional Inn Award
The Lamb Inn – Oxfordshire, England

Most Excellent Coastal Hotel Award
The White Horse – Norfolk, England

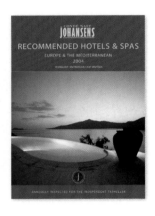

Europe: The Most Excellent City Hotel
Hôtel Plaza Athénée – Paris, France

Europe: The Most Excellent Countryside Hotel
Read's – Mallorca, Balearic Islands

Europe: The Most Excellent Waterside Hotel
Hotel Punta Est – Liguria, Italy

Europe: Best Value for Money Hotel
Hotel Giorgione – Venice, Italy

North America & Caribbean: Most Outstanding Hotel
Sutton Place Hotel – Illinois, USA

North America & Caribbean: Most Outstanding Inn
Fairview Inn – Mississippi, USA

North America & Caribbean: Most Outstanding Resort
Curtain Bluff – Antigua, Caribbean

North America & Caribbean: Special Award for Excellence
Vista Verde Guest Ranch – Colorado, USA

May we be of service?

Our experienced and focussed hotels team provides a range of high-quality services to both private hoteliers and corporate clients, operating with discretion, flexibility and professionalism to successfully bring together buyers, vendors and lenders.

Why else would we be Johansens only preferred property Agents?

London	020 7629 8171
Exeter	01392 493101
Leeds	0113 246 1533
Winchester	01962 850333
Edinburgh	0131 225 8171

The local office with a global network

Knight Frank

www.knightfrank.com

ENGLAND

Recommendations in England appear on pages 11-340

For further information on England, please contact:

Cumbria Tourist Board
Ashleigh, Holly Road, Windermere, Cumbria LA23 2AQ
Tel: +44 (0)15394 44444
Web: www.gocumbria.co.uk

East of England Tourist Board
Toppesfield Hall , Hadleigh, Suffolk IP7 5DN
Tel: +44 (0)1473 822922
Web: www.eastofenglandtouristboard.com

Visit Heart of England
Larkhill Road, Worcester, Worcestershire WR5 2EZ
Tel: +44 (0)1905 761100
Web: www.visitheartofengland.com

Visit London
Glen House, Stag Place, London SW1E 5LT
Tel: +44 (0)906 866 3344
Web: www.londontouristboard.com

Northumbria Tourist Board
Aykley Heads, Durham DH1 5UX
Tel: +44 (0)191 375 3000
Web: www.visitnorthumbria.com

North West Tourist Board
Swan House, Swan Meadow Road, Wigan, Lancashire WN3 5BB
Tel: +44 (0)1942 821 222
Web: www.visitnorthwest.com

Tourism South East England Tourist Board
The Old Brew House, Warwick Park, Tunbridge Wells, Kent TN2 5TU
Tel: +44 (0)1892 540766
Web: www.seetb.org.uk

Visit Southern England
40 Chamberlayne Road, Eastleigh, Hampshire SO50 5JH
Tel: +44 (0) 23 8062 5400
Web: www.visitsouthernengland.com

South West Tourism
Woodwater Park, Exeter, Devon EX2 5WT
Tel: +44 (0)870 442 0830
Web: www.westcountrynow.com

Yorkshire Tourist Board
312 Tadcaster Road, York, Yorkshire YO24 1GS
Tel: +44 (0)1904 707961
Web: www.ytb.org.uk
Yorkshire and North & North East Lincolnshire.

English Heritage
Customer Services Department , PO Box 569, Swindon SN2 2YP
Tel: +44 (0) 870 333 1181
Web: www.english-heritage.org.uk

Historic Houses Association
2 Chester Street, London SW1X 7BB
Tel: +44 (0)20 7259 5688
Web: www.hha.org.uk

The National Trust
36 Queen Anne's Gate, London SW1H 9AS
Tel: +44 (0)20 7222 9251
Web: www.nationaltrust.org.uk

or see **pages 437-440** for details of
local attractions to visit during your stay.

Images from www.britainonview.com

THE BATH PRIORY HOTEL AND RESTAURANT

WESTON ROAD, BATH, SOMERSET BA1 2XT

Directions: 1 mile west of the centre of Bath. Please contact the hotel for precise directions.

Web: www.johansens.com/bathpriory
E-mail: bathprioryhotel@compuserve.co.uk
Tel: 0870 381 8345
International: +44 (0)1225 331922
Fax: 01225 448276

Price Guide: (incl. full English breakfast)
double/twin from £260

Bath

Taunton   Yeovil

Standing in 4 acres of gardens, The Bath Priory Hotel is close to some of England's most famous and finest architecture. Within walking distance of Bath city centre, this Georgian, mellow stone building dates from 1835, when it formed part of a row of fashionable residences on the west side of the city. Visitors will sense the luxury as they enter the hotel; antique furniture, many superb oil paintings and objets d'art add interest to the 2 spacious reception rooms and the elegant drawing room. Well-defined colour schemes lend an uplifting brightness throughout, particularly in the tastefully appointed bedrooms. The classical style of Michelin-starred head chef, Robert Clayton, is the primary inspiration for the cuisine, served in 3 interconnecting dining rooms which overlook the gardens. An especially good selection of wines can be recommended to accompany meals. Private functions can be accommodated both in the terrace, pavilion and the Orangery. The Roman Baths, Theatre Royal, Museum of Costume and a host of bijou shops offer plenty for visitors to see. The Garden Spa consists of a fitness suite, swimming pool, sauna, steam room and health and beauty spa.

Our inspector loved: *The inviting pool and beautiful gardens.*

       SPA

THE BATH SPA HOTEL

SYDNEY ROAD, BATH, SOMERSET BA2 6JF

Nestling in 7 acres of mature grounds dotted with ancient cedars, formal gardens, ponds and fountains, The Bath Spa Hotel's elegant Georgian façade can only hint at the warmth, style, comfort and attentive personal service. It is a handsome building in a handsome setting with antique furniture, richly coloured carpeting and well defined colour schemes lending an uplifting brightness throughout. The bedrooms are elegantly decorated; the bathrooms are luxuriously appointed in mahogany and marble. The Bath Spa offers all amenities that guests would expect of a 5-star hotel whilst retaining the character of a homely country house. Chef Andrew Hamer's imaginative, contemporary style is the primary inspiration for the award-winning cuisine served in the 2 restaurants. For relaxation there is a fully equipped health and leisure spa which includes an indoor swimming pool, gymnasium, sauna, Jacuzzi, 3 treatment rooms, hair salon, tennis court and croquet lawn. Apart from the delights of Bath, there is motor racing at Castle Combe and hot air ballooning nearby.

Our inspector loved: This grand hotel with its inviting indoor pool, latest gym equipment and easy walk into Bath.

Directions: Exit M4 at jct18 onto the A46, follow signs to Bath for 8 miles until the major roundabout. Turn right onto A4 follow City Centre signs for a mile, at the 1st major set of traffic lights turn left toward the A36. At mini roundabout turn right then next left after Holburne Museum into Sydney Place. The hotel is 200 yards up the hill on the right.

Web: www.johansens.com/bathspa
E-mail: sales.bathspa@macdonald-hotels.co.uk
Tel: 0870 381 8346
International: +44 (0)1225 444424
Fax: 01225 444006

Price Guide:
double/twin £210
4-poster £310

COMBE GROVE MANOR HOTEL & COUNTRY CLUB

BRASSKNOCKER HILL, MONKTON COMBE, BATH, SOMERSET BA2 7HS

This exclusive 18th-century Country House Hotel is conveniently located just 2 miles from the beautiful city of Bath. Built on the hillside site of an ancient Roman settlement, Combe Grove Manor is set in 69 acres of beautiful private gardens and woodlands, with awe-inspiring panoramic views over the magnificent Limpley Stoke Valley and surrounding areas. The Manor House features luxurious four-poster rooms and suites with Jacuzzi baths, whilst the rooms in the Garden Lodge have spectacular views, some with private balconies. All 40 bedrooms are lavishly appointed and individual in design with superb en-suite facilities. Within the hotel's grounds are some of the finest leisure facilities in the south west, including indoor and outdoor heated pools, hydrospa beds and steam room, 4 all-weather tennis courts, a 5-hole par 3 golf course and a 16-bay driving range. Guests may use the fully-equipped gym, aerobics studio, sauna and solaria or simply indulge in the full range of treatments offered by professionally trained staff in the Clarins beauty rooms. There is also a choice of 2 superb restaurants; the elegant main restaurant features delicious traditional style cuisine and fine wines, whereas the informal Eden Bistro offers an exciting contemporary international menu.

Directions: Set south-east of Bath, off the A36 near the University. A map can be supplied on request.

Web: www.johansens.com/combegrovemanor
E-mail: info@combegrovemanor.com
Tel: 0870 381 8438
International: +44 (0)1225 834644
Fax: 01225 834961

Price Guide:
single from £110
double/twin from £110;
suite from £225

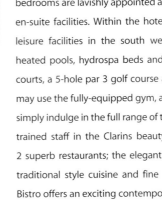

Bath

Taunton   Yeovil

Our inspector loved: The extensive spa facilities and wonderful views from the newly refurbished restaurant.

        SPA

THE FRANCIS HOTEL
QUEEN SQUARE, BATH, SOMERSET BA1 2HH

This classic Regency town house lies in the very centre of this striking and exciting city, and minutes away from the many attractions that it has to offer. The stunning Abbey, historical Roman Baths, Pump Room and Thermae Bath Spa are all within a stone's throw, making The Francis the ideal base from which to explore, not just the historical tourist trail, but also the many fine shops, cafés and restaurants. The hotel itself has some 95 en-suite bedrooms, each of which is decorated with careful flair – Regency stripes pay homage to the building's Georgian origins, but are brought up to date with exciting chenilles, damasks, stripes and checks. This modern approach is echoed by the style of food – simple and fresh Mediterranean recipes such as Goats Cheese and Sun Blushed Tomato Quiche or Pan Fried Black Bream with Provençale sauce, are served in The Square Restaurant, whilst more informal suppers are available in the Caffébar. There are 2 well-equipped meeting rooms available for conferences, product launches and meetings; and with London Paddington being less than 2 hours away, The Francis is a great location for the business traveller as well as weekenders. Weddings can also be organised and catered for.

Our inspector loved: The great location within walking distance of Bath's main attractions.

Directions: The Francis is located on Queen Square, a short distance from The Circus. Simply follow the A4 through route, which forms the north side of Queen Square.

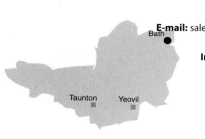

Web: www.johansens.com/francis
E-mail: sales.francis@macdonald-hotels.co.uk
Tel: 0870 381 8728
International: +44 (0)1225 424105
Fax: 01225 319715

Price Guide:
single £59-£69
double £118-£198
suite £178-£198

THE QUEENSBERRY

RUSSEL STREET, BATH, SOMERSET BA1 2QF

When the Marquis of Queensberry commissioned John Wood to build this house in Russel Street in 1772, little did he know that 200 years hence guests would still be entertained in these elegant surroundings. An intimate town house hotel, The Queensberry is in a quiet residential street just a few minutes' walk from Wood's other splendours – the Royal Crescent, Circus and Assembly Rooms. Bath is one of England's most beautiful cities. Regency stucco ceilings, ornate cornices and panelling combined with enchanting interior décor complement the strong architectural style. However, the standards of hotel-keeping have far outpaced the traditional surroundings, with high-quality en-suite bedrooms, room service and up-to-date office support for executives. The Olive Tree Restaurant is one of the leading restaurants in the Bath area. Proprietors Laurence and Helen Beere are thoroughly versed in offering hospitality and look forward to welcoming all their guests personally.

Directions: From junction 18 off the M4, enter Bath along A4 London Road. Turn sharp right up Lansdown Road, left into Bennett Street, then right into Russel Street opposite the Assembly Rooms.

Web: www.johansens.com/queensberry
E-mail: enquiries@bathqueensberry.com
Tel: 0870 381 8845
International: +44 (0)1225 447928
Fax: 01225 446065

Price Guide:
single £90–£160
double/twin £120–£210
four poster £225

Our inspector loved: The central location, courtyard garden and popular restaurant.

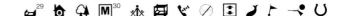

THE ROYAL CRESCENT HOTEL

16 ROYAL CRESCENT, BATH, SOMERSET BA1 2LS

The Royal Crescent Hotel is a Grade I listed building of the greatest historical and architectural importance and occupies the central 2 houses of one of Europe's finest masterpieces. The Royal Crescent is a sweep of 30 houses with identical façades stretching in a 500ft curve. Built by 1775, the hotel was completely refurbished in 1998 and the work undertaken has restored many of the classical Georgian features with all the additional modern comforts. Each of the 45 bedrooms is equipped with air conditioning, the Cliveden bed, video/compact disc player and personal facsimile machine. Pimpernel's restaurant offers a relaxed and informal dining atmosphere, presenting a contemporary menu. Comprehensively equipped, the secure private boardroom provides self-contained business meeting facilities. Exclusive use of the hotel can be arranged for a special occasion or corporate event. Magnificent views of Bath and the surrounding countryside may be enjoyed from the hotel's vintage river launch and hot air balloon. The Bath House is a unique spa, in which to enjoy both complementary therapies and holistic massage. Adjacent to this tranquil setting is the gym and studio comprising 17 pieces of cardio-vascular and resistance equipment.

Our inspector loved: The spacious elegant suites and prime location in Bath.

Directions: Detailed directions are available from the hotel on booking.

Web: www.johansens.com/royalcrescent
E-mail: reservations@royalcrescent.co.uk
Tel: 0870 381 8874
International: +44 (0)1225 823333
Fax: 01225 339401

Price Guide: (room only)
double/twin from £230
suites from £420

THE WINDSOR HOTEL

69 GREAT PULTENEY STREET, BATH BA2 4DL

Elegant wrought-iron railings front this attractive town house situated in the heart of the best preserved Georgian city in Britain. Grade I listed and refurbished to the highest standards, The Windsor Hotel stands on one of the finest boulevards in Europe just a short stroll from the Royal Crescent, Circus, Assembly Rooms and Roman Baths. The hotel's tall front windows look across Georgian façades inspired by Palladio, whilst rooms at the back have views of the rolling hills beyond. Enchanting interior décor complements the strong and pleasing architectural style and fine furniture and fabrics abound. Each individually designed en-suite bedroom and suite is the essence of high quality and comfort. Afternoon tea or after-dinner drinks can be enjoyed in an exquisite drawing room while memorable menus are served in a small Japanese restaurant which overlooks its own special garden. Great Pulteney Street leads onto Pulteney Bridge and the city's tempting boutiques, antique shops and award-winning restaurants. Within easy reach are Longleat Estate, Ilford Manor, the American Museum and Limpley Stoke Valley. Parking is available.

Directions: From junction18 off the M4, enter Bath along the A4 London Road. Turn left into Bathwick Street, then right into Sydney Place and right again into Great Pulteney Street.

Web: www.johansens.com/windsorhotel
E-mail: sales@bathwindsorhotel.com
Tel: 0870 381 9003
International: +44 (0)1225 422100
Fax: 01225 422550

Price Guide:
single £85-£115
double/twin £135-£195
suite £275

Our inspector loved: The wonderful location of this town house hotel in one of the most famous streets in Bath.

HOMEWOOD PARK

HINTON CHARTERHOUSE, BATH, SOMERSET BA2 7TB

Standing amid 10 acres of beautiful grounds and woodland on the edge of Limpley Stoke Valley, designated area of outstanding natural beauty is Homewood Park, one of Britain's finest privately-owned smaller country house hotels. This lovely 19th-century building has an elegant interior, adorned with beautiful fabrics, antiques, oriental rugs and original oil paintings. Lavishly furnished bedrooms offer the best in comfort, style and privacy. Each of them has a charm and character of its own and most have good views over the Victorian garden. The outstanding cuisine overseen by chef Jean de La Rouziere has won the hotel an excellent reputation. The à la carte menu uses wherever possible produce from local suppliers. A range of carefully selected wines, stored in the hotel's original medieval cellars, lies patiently waiting to augment lunch and dinner. Before or after a meal guests can enjoy a drink in the comfortable bar or drawing rooms, both of which have a log fire during the cooler months. The hotel is well placed for guests to enjoy the varied attractions of the wonderful city of Bath with its unique hot springs, Roman remains, superb Georgian architecture and American Museum. Further afield but within reach are Stonehenge and Cheddar caves.

Our inspector loved: Its quiet, relaxing atmosphere, a real home from home.

Directions: On the A36 6 miles from Bath towards Warminster.

Web: www.johansens.com/homewoodpark
E-mail: res@homewoodpark.com
Tel: 0870 381 8605
International: +44 (0)1225 723731
Fax: 01225 723820

Price Guide:
single from £115
double/twin from £145
suites from £265

HUNSTRETE HOUSE

HUNSTRETE, NR BATH, SOMERSET BS39 4NS

Directions: From Bath take the A4 towards Bristol and then the A368 to Wells.

Web: www.johansens.com/hunstretehouse
E-mail: reservations@hunstretehouse.co.uk
Tel: 0870 381 8630
International: +44 (0)1761 490490
Fax: 01761 490732

Price Guide:
single from £145
double/twin from £170
suite from £265

In a classical English landscape on the edge of the Mendip Hills stands Hunstrete House. This unique hotel, surrounded by lovely gardens, is largely 18th century, although the history of the estate goes back to 963AD. Each of the bedrooms is individually decorated and furnished to a high standard, combining the benefits of a hotel room with the atmosphere of a charming private country house. Many offer uninterrupted views over undulating fields and woodlands. The reception areas exhibit warmth and elegance and are liberally furnished with beautiful antiques. Log fires burn in the hall, library and drawing room through the winter and on cooler summer evenings. The Terrace dining room looks out on to an Italianate, flower-filled courtyard. A highly skilled head chef offers light, elegant dishes using produce from the extensive garden, including organic meat and vegetables. The menu changes regularly and the hotel has an excellent reputation for the quality and interest of its wine list. In a sheltered corner of the walled garden there is a heated swimming pool for guests to enjoy. For the energetic, the all-weather tennis court provides another diversion and there are riding stables in Hunstrete village, a 5-minute walk away.

Our inspector loved: *The cottage rooms leading directly out onto the lovely gardens.*

MOORE PLACE HOTEL

THE SQUARE, ASPLEY GUISE, MILTON KEYNES, BEDFORDSHIRE MK17 8DW

This elegant Georgian manor house was built by Francis Moore in the peaceful Bedfordshire village of Aspley Guise in 1786. The original house, which is set on the village square, has been sympathetically extended to create extra rooms. The additional wing has been built around an attractive courtyard with a rock garden, lily pool and waterfall. The pretty Victorian-style, award-winning conservatory restaurant, serves food that rates among the best in the area. Vegetarian and special diet options can always be found on the menus, which offer dishes prepared in the modern English style and balanced with a selection of fine wines. The 52 bedrooms are well-appointed with many amenities, including a trouser press, hairdryer, welcome drinks and large towelling bathrobes. Banquets, conferences and dinner parties can be accommodated in 5 private function rooms: all are decorated in traditional style and can be equipped with the latest audio-visual facilities. The hotel is close to Woburn Abbey, Safari Park, Bletchley Park, Silverstone, Whipsnade Zoo, Milton Keynes. The convenient location and accessibility to the motorway network makes Moore Place Hotel an attractive choice, whether travelling for business or pleasure.

Our inspector loved: *The newly available, spacious and attractive rooms in the cottage.*

Directions: Only 2 minutes drive from the M1, junction 13.

Web: www.johansens.com/mooreplace
E-mail: manager@mooreplace.com
Tel: 0870 381 8745
International: +44 (0)1908 282000
Fax: 01908 281888

Price Guide:
single £65–£110
double/twin £85–£150
suite £160–£220

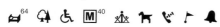

FLITWICK MANOR

CHURCH ROAD, FLITWICK, BEDFORDSHIRE MK45 1AE

Directions: Flitwick is on the A5120 just north of the M1, junction 12.

Web: www.johansens.com/flitwickmanor
E-mail: flitwick@menzies-hotels.co.uk
Tel: 0870 381 8525
International: +44 (0)1525 712242
Fax: 01525 718753

Price Guide: (room only)
single from £140
double/twin/suite £165-£315

Flitwick Manor is a Georgian gem, classical in style, elegant in décor, comfortable in appointment, a country house hotel that remains true to the traditions of country house hospitality. Nestling in acres of glorious rolling parkland complete with lake, grotto and church, the manor has the intimacy and warmth that make it the ideal retreat for both pleasure and business. The 17 bedrooms, with their distinctive characters and idiosyncrasies, add to the charm of the reception rooms: a soothing drawing room, a cosy library and pine-panelled morning room, the latter 2 doubling up as both meeting and private dining rooms. Fine antiques and period pieces, easy chairs and inviting sofas, winter fires and summer flowers, they all blend effortlessly together to make a perfect combination. The restaurant is highly acclaimed by all the major food guides and indeed the AA, with its bestowal of 2 Rosettes, rated Flitwick Manor as the county's best and one of the top 200 hotels in the UK and Ireland. Outside pleasures are afforded by the all-weather tennis court, croquet lawns and putting green as well as a range of local attractions such as Woburn Abbey and Safari Park. Special weekend rates available.

Our inspector loved: This elegant country house with its romantic appeal.

MONKEY ISLAND HOTEL

BRAY-ON-THAMES, MAIDENHEAD, BERKSHIRE SL6 2EE

The name Monkey Island derives from the medieval Monk's Eyot. Circa 1723 the island was purchased by Charles Spencer, the third Duke of Marlborough, who built the fishing lodge now known as the Pavilion and the fishing temple, both of which are Grade I listed buildings. The Pavilion's Candles Lounge, overlooking acres of riverside lawn, is an ideal spot for a relaxing cocktail and the award-winning Pavilion Restaurant, perched on the island's narrowest tip with fine views upstream, boasts fine English cuisine, an award-winning cellar and friendly service. The River Room is suitable for weddings or other large functions, whilst the Regency-style boardroom is perfect for smaller parties. It is even possible to arrange exclusive use of the whole island for a truly memorable occasion. The Temple houses 26 comfortable bedrooms and suites, the Wedgwood Room, with its splendid ceiling in high-relief plaster and the octagonal Temple Room. Monkey Island is 1 mile downstream from Maidenhead, within easy reach of Royal Windsor, Eton, Henley and London. The hotel offers weekend breaks from £105 per person and in the summer, boat hire and picnic days.

Our inspector loved: The walk across the private bridge onto this magical island.

Directions: Jct 8/9 M4 - Take A308 from Maidenhead towards Windsor; turn left following signposts to Bray. Entering Bray, go right along Old Mill Lane, which goes over M4; the entrance to the hotel is on the left after approx ¼ mile.

Web: www.johansens.com/monkeyisland
E-mail: monkeyisland@btconnect.com
Tel: 0870 381 8742
International: +44 (0)1628 623400
Fax: 01628 784732

Price Guide:
single from £130
double/twin £190–£235
suite £295

FREDRICK'S HOTEL & RESTAURANT

SHOPPENHANGERS ROAD, MAIDENHEAD, BERKSHIRE SL6 2PZ

"Putting people first" is the guiding philosophy behind the running of this sumptuously equipped hotel and indeed, is indicative of the uncompromising service guests can expect to receive. Set in 2 acres of grounds, Fredrick's overlooks the fairways and greens of Maidenhead Golf Club beyond. The immaculate reception rooms are distinctively styled to create something out of the ordinary. Minute attention to detail is evident in the 37 bedrooms, all immaculate with gleaming, marble-tiled bathrooms, whilst some of the suites have their own patio garden or balcony. A quiet drink can be enjoyed in the light, airy Wintergarden lounge, or in warmer weather on the patio, before entering the air-conditioned restaurant. Amid the elegant décor of crystal chandeliers and crisp white linen, fine gourmet cuisine is served which has received recognition from leading guides for many years. As well as being suitable for leisure stays and fine dining, Fredrick's is perfectly located for conferences and corporate hospitality with its 4 superbly appointed function rooms, which overlook the hotel's lawns and landscaped gardens. Helicopter landing can be arranged. Easily accessible from Windsor, Henley, Ascot, Heathrow and London. Closed 24 Dec to 3 Jan.

Directions: Leave M4 at junction 8/9, take A404(M) and leave at first exit 9A signed Cox Green/White Waltham. Turn left into Shoppenhangers Road towards Maidenhead. Fredrick's is on the right.

Web: www.johansens.com/fredricks
E-mail: reservations@fredricks–hotel.co.uk
Tel: 0870 381 8531
International: +44 (0)1628 581000
Fax: 01628 771054

Price Guide:
single from £195
double/twin from £260
suite from £390

Our inspector loved: *The sunny terrace overlooking the peaceful gardens.*

CLIVEDEN

TAPLOW, BERKSHIRE SL6 0JF

Cliveden, Britain's only 5 Red AA star hotel that is also a stately home, is set in 376 acres of gardens and parkland, overlooking the Thames. The former home of Frederick, Prince of Wales, 3 Dukes and the Astor family, Cliveden has been at the centre of Britain's social and political life for over 300 years. It is exquisitely furnished in a classical English style; oil paintings, antiques and objets d'art abound. The guest rooms and suites are spacious and luxurious and the choice of dining rooms and the scope of the menus are superb. The French Dining Room, with its original Madame de Pompadour Rococo decoration, is the finest 18th-century boiserie outside France. Relish the award-winning cuisine of Waldo's Restaurant. Spring Cottage, secluded in its own gardens on the edge of the River Thames, provides unrivalled peace and privacy. Guests can enjoy a range of treatments in the Pavilion Spa, roam the magnificent gardens or enjoy a river cruise. A choice of sports, including indoor and outdoor swimming, tennis, squash, gymnasium, golf, clay pigeon shooting, horse riding and polo lessons are also available. Well-equipped, the 2 secure private boardrooms provide self-contained business meeting facilities. Exclusive use of the house can be arranged. Cliveden's style may also be enjoyed at the Royal Crescent in Bath.

Our inspector loved: The grand approach along the crunchy gravelly drive, the welcome and "the perfection of the place".

Directions: Situated on the B476, Cliveden is 2 miles north of Taplow.

Web: www.johansens.com/cliveden
E-mail: Reservations@clivedenhouse.co.uk
Tel: 0870 381 8432
International: +44 (0)1628 668561
Fax: 01628 661837

Price Guide:
(full English breakfast incl. VAT)
double/twin from £250
suites from £465

DONNINGTON VALLEY HOTEL & GOLF CLUB

OLD OXFORD ROAD, DONNINGTON, NEWBURY, BERKSHIRE RG14 3AG

Directions: Leave the M4 at junction 13, go south towards Newbury on A34, then follow signs for Donnington Castle. The hotel is on the right before reaching the castle.

Web: www.johansens.com/donningtonvalley
E-mail: general@donningtonvalley.co.uk
Tel: 0870 381 8484
International: +44 (0)1635 551199
Fax: 01635 551123

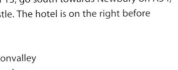

Price Guide:
single from £165
double/twin £165–£190
suite from £230

Uncompromising quality is the hallmark of this hotel built in contrasting styles in 1991 with its own golf course. The grandeur of the Edwardian era has been captured by the interior of the hotel's reception area with its splendid wood-panelled ceilings and impressive overhanging gallery. Each individually designed bedroom has been thoughtfully equipped to guarantee comfort and peace of mind. In addition to the standard guest rooms Donnington Valley offers a number of non-smoking rooms, family rooms, superior executive rooms and luxury suites. With its open log fire and elegant surroundings, the Piano Bar is an ideal place to meet friends or enjoy the relaxed ambience. Guests lunch and dine in The Winepress Restaurant, which offers fine international cuisine, awarded 2 Rosettes by the AA, and complemented by an extensive choice of wines and liqueurs. The 18-hole par 71 golf course is a stern test for golfers of all abilities, through a magnificent parkland setting. Special corporate golfing packages are offered and tournaments can be arranged. 11 purpose-built function suites provide the flexibility to meet the demands of corporate and special events. Donnington Castle, despite a siege during the Civil War, still survives for sight-seeing.

Our inspector loved: *This very comfortable hotel with its exceptional staff, glorious flowers and grounds.*

THE VINEYARD AT STOCKCROSS

NEWBURY, BERKSHIRE RG20 8JU

The Vineyard at Stockcross, Sir Peter Michael's "restaurant-with-suites" is a European showcase for the finest Californian wines including those from the Peter Michael Winery. Head Sommelier, Edoardo Amadi, has selected the best from the most highly-prized, family-owned Californian wineries, creating one of the widest, most innovative, international wine lists. Awarded 5 Stars and 4 Rosettes by the AA, the modern British cuisine matches the calibre of the wines. Pure flavours, fresh ingredients and subtle design blend harmoniously with the fine wines. A stimulating collection of paintings and sculpture includes the keynote piece, "Fire and Water" by William Pye FRBS and "Deconstructing the Grape", a sculpture commissioned for The Vineyard Spa. A vine-inspired steel balustrade elegantly dominates the restaurant and the luxurious interior is complemented by subtle attention to detail throughout with stunning china and glass designs. The 49 well-appointed bedrooms include 31 suites offering stylish comfort with distinctive character. The Vineyard Spa features an indoor pool, spa bath, sauna, steam room, gym and treatment rooms.

Our inspector loved: The space, the light, the sophistication and more than a "touch of the sublime."

Directions: From M4, exit Jct13, A34 towards Newbury, then Hungerford exit. 1st roundabout Hungerford exit, 2nd roundabout Stockcross exit. Hotel on right.

Web: www.johansens.com/vineyardstockcross
E-mail: general@the-vineyard.co.uk
Tel: 0870 381 8965
International: +44 (0)1635 528770
Fax: 01635 528398

Price Guide: (excluding VAT)
single/double/twin £169–£240
suite £310–£630

THE REGENCY PARK HOTEL

BOWLING GREEN ROAD, THATCHAM, BERKSHIRE RG18 3RP

Ideally situated for access to both London and the South West, the Regency Park is a modern hotel that takes great pride in providing not only the most sophisticated facilities but combining them with the most attentive service and care. The style is neat and crisp with an understated elegance throughout, from the airy and spacious bedrooms to the array of meeting venues housed in the Business Centre. The Parkland Suite is a beautiful setting for any occasion, and with its own entrance and facilities for up to 200 guests it is the ideal place for wedding receptions and parties, as well as conferences and launches. "Escape" is the name of the leisure complex, and true to its name it really is a place where state-of-the-art technology and sheer luxury meet to form a special retreat. The serenity of the 17m swimming pool and the large health and beauty salon create an instantly relaxing atmosphere where fully qualified staff offer holistic health and beauty treatments. The Watermark Restaurant again has a contemporary elegance and stunning views over the Waterfall gardens, reflected in its excellent menu of modern flavours and fusions. There is even a children's menu to ensure all guests are catered for.

Directions: Between Newbury and Reading. Leave M4 at Jct12 or 13; the hotel is signposted on A4, on the western outskirts of Thatcham.

Web: www.johansens.com/regencypark
E-mail: info@regencyparkhotel.co.uk
Tel: 0870 381 8852
International: +44 (0)1635 871555
Fax: 01635 871571

Price Guide:
single £93–£229
double/twin £101–£229
suite £233–£379

Our inspector loved: The superb range of spacious facilities, from the restaurant, to the leisure, to the function areas.

THE FRENCH HORN

SONNING-ON-THAMES, BERKSHIRE RG4 6TN

For over 150 years The French Horn has provided a charming riverside retreat from the busy outside world. Today, although busier on this stretch of the river, it continues that fine tradition of comfortable accommodation and outstanding cuisine in a beautiful setting. Ideal for an awaybreak or special corporate occasion. The hotel nestles beside the Thames near the historic village of Sonning. The bedrooms and suites are fully equipped with modern amenities and many have river views. The old panelled bar provides an intimate scene for pre-dinner drinks and the restaurant speciality, locally reared duck, is spit roasted here over an open fire. By day the sunny restaurant is a lovely setting for lunch, while by night diners can enjoy the floodlit view of the graceful weeping willows which fringe the river. Dinner is served by candlelight and the cuisine is a mixture of French and English cooking using the freshest ingredients. The French Horn's wine list is reputed to be amongst the finest in Europe. Places of interest in the area include Henley, Windsor Stratfield Saye, and Mapledurham. There are numerous golf courses, equestrian centres and a spa nearby.

Our inspector loved: *The glorious riverside setting and "Old World" charm.*

Directions: Leave the M4 at J8/9. Follow A404/M then at Thickets Roundabout turn left on A4 towards Reading for 8 miles. Turn right for Sonning. Cross Thames on B478. Hotel is on right.

Web: www.johansens.com/frenchhorn
E-mail: TheFrenchHorn@Compuserve.com
Tel: 0870 381 8532
International: +44 (0)1189 692204
Fax: 01189 442210

Price Guide:
single £100–£160
double/twin £120–£195

THE SWAN AT STREATLEY

STREATLEY-ON-THAMES, BERKSHIRE RG8 9HR

In a beautiful setting on the banks of the River Thames, this hotel offers visitors comfortable accommodation. All of the 46 bedrooms, many of which have balconies overlooking the river, are appointed with individual décor and furnishings. The hotel's innovative cooking ensures it maintains its 2 AA Rosettes. Guests can dine in the Cygnetures restaurant, which, with the Cygnet Bar and outdoor terrace, offers superb riverside views. Business guests are well catered for with 6 conference suites – all with natural daylight. Moored alongside the hotel is the Magdalen College Barge – a unique venue for small meetings and cocktail parties. Reflexions leisure club is equipped with a heated 'fitness' pool, sauna, sunbeds, spa bath, steam room and a wide range of exercise equipment. Cruising on the river may be arranged by the hotel and golf, horse riding, and clay pigeon shooting are available locally. Events in the locality include Henley Regatta, Ascot and Newbury Races, while Windsor Castle, Blenheim Palace, Oxford and London's airports are easily accessible. Special breaks such as "family weekends," "winter warmers," "summer sizzler," racing and romance are available.

Directions: M4 junction 12. A340 to Pangbourne. A329 to Streatley. Turn right at Streatley traffic lights. The hotel is on the left before the bridge. Only 20 minutes from the M4

Web: www.johansens.com/swanatstreatley
E-mail: sales@swan-at-streatley.co.uk
Tel: 0870 381 8928
International: +44 (0)1491 878800
Fax: 01491 872554

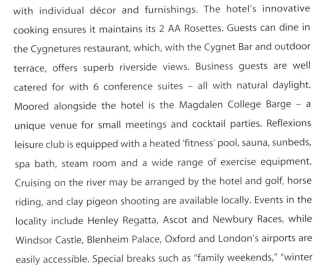

Price Guide:
single £89–£137.50
double/twin £119–£177
suites £179-£258

Our inspector loved: *The ideal "away from it all" riverside location - perfect for business and pleasure.*

SIR CHRISTOPHER WREN'S HOUSE HOTEL

THAMES STREET, WINDSOR, BERKSHIRE SL4 1PX

A friendly and homely atmosphere makes Sir Christopher Wren's House a perfect location for guests seeking a break from the hectic pace of modern life. Built by the famous architect in 1676, it nestles beneath the ramparts and towers of Windsor Castle, beside the River Thames and Eton Bridge. With a quiet charm and dignity of its own, the hotel combines fine furnishings from the past with every comfort and convenience associated with life today. Additions to the original house, include a beautiful pavillion overlooking the Thames and Riverside terrace. There are now 90 bedrooms available for guests, all richly furnished to the highest standards and, while some feature a balcony and river views, others overlook the famous castle. All offer a full range of amenities, including state-of-the-art technology. For longer stays guests may wish to use the hotels' apartments. Stroks Riverside Restaurant offers a good selection of beautifully cooked and well-presented meals by the master chef. The hotel also has a top class gym with outdoor spa pool and beauty treatments. The Windsor area has a great deal to offer, for those with time to explore. Among the many attractions within easy reach are Windsor Castle, Eton College, Royal Ascot, Thorpe Park, Henley, Savill Gardens and Legoland.

Our inspector loved: *Discovering the richly furnished rooms, the comfortable bar and the Riverside Restaurant and terrace.*

Directions: Windsor is just 2 miles from Jct 6 of the M4. Follow one-way system with River Thames on your left towards Datchet. Turn left into Thames Street. The hotel's car park (by arrangement) is on the left. (Thames Street is pedestrianised).

Web: www.johansens.com/sirchristopher
E-mail: reservations@wrensgroup.com
Tel: 0870 381 8896
International: +44 (0)1753 861354
Fax: 01753 860172

Price Guide:
single from £170
double/twin from £225
suite from £275

31

HOTEL DU VIN & BISTRO

CHURCH STREET, BIRMINGHAM B3 2NR

Hotel du Vin & Bistro, originally the Birmingham Eye Hospital, is a unique venue in the heart of cosmopolitan Birmingham. Its stunning early Victorian architecture enhances the luxury of the tasteful, modern interior design. 66 tranquil bedrooms emphasize simplicity and quality with superb beds, luxurious Egyptian linens and attention to detail. The hotel has 2 bars: The Bubble Lounge is based on a Venetian café and serves over 50 different types of champagne; The Cellar Bar features an eye-catching oil painting of a lobster, the colourful backdrop for its vast selection of wines; big, comfortable sofas, low-lighting and relaxation are essential to the Cigar Divan. The hotel's excellent chef chooses only the freshest of local ingredients to create a sumptuous feast, which is served in the elegant surrounds of the Bistro. Guests may unwind and pamper themselves in the hotel's private health and beauty spa, which features state-of-the-art equipment, sauna, steam room, massage, aromatherapy and a range of wonderful beauty treatments using natural ingredients. Only minutes away from Birmingham's old city centre, there is fantastic shopping, waterways, art galleries, theatres and the Symphony Hall nearby.

Directions: From the M6, jct 6 take the A38 to the city centre. Take the flyover and exit at St Chad's Circus signposted "Jewellery Quarter". Take the second left into Great Charles Street, then the first left into Livery Street. Take the third turning right into Barwick Street then right into Church Street.

Web: www.johansens.com/hoteduvinbirmingham
E-mail: info@birmingham.hotelduvin.com
Tel: 0870 381 8618
International: +44 (0)121 200 0600
Fax: 0121 236 0889

Price Guide:
double/twin from £110
studios from £185

Wolverhampton

Birmingham

Coventry

Our inspector loved: The internal courtyard, with its bronze statues and large terracotta pots. The ideal place to sip champagne from Bubbles lounge.

   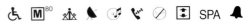   SPA

NEW HALL

WALMLEY ROAD, ROYAL SUTTON COLDFIELD, WEST MIDLANDS B76 1QX

Cocooned by a lily filled moat and surrounded by 26 acres of beautiful gardens and parkland, New Hall dates from the 12th century and is reputedly the oldest fully moated manor house in England. This prestigious hotel is full of warmth and luxury and exudes a friendly, welcoming atmosphere. New Hall proudly holds the coveted RAC Gold Ribbon Award, and AA Inspectors' Hotel of the Year for England 1994. The cocktail bar and adjoining drawing room overlook the terrace from which a bridge leads to the yew topiary, orchards and sunlit glades. The superbly appointed bedrooms and individually designed suites offer every modern comfort and amenity and have glorious views over the gardens and moat. A 9-hole par 3 golf course and floodlit tennis court are available for guests' use, as are a heated indoor pool, Jacuzzi, sauna, steam room and gymnasium. For those wishing to revitalise mind, body and soul, New Hall offers a superb range of beauty treatments. Surrounded by a rich cultural heritage, New Hall is convenient for Lichfield Cathedral, Warwick Castle, Stratford-upon-Avon, the NEC and the ICC in Birmingham. The Belfry Golf Centre is also nearby.

Our inspector loved: *Walking around the grounds, overlooking the moat and trout pool.*

Directions: From exit 9 of the M42, follow A4097 (ignoring signs to A38 Sutton Coldfield). At B4148 turn right at the traffic lights. New Hall is 1 mile on the left.

Web: www.johansens.com/newhall
E-mail: new-hall@thistle.co.uk
Tel: 0870 381 8756
International: +44 (0)121 378 2442
Fax: 0121 378 4637

Price Guide:
single from £166
double/twin from £200
suite from £230

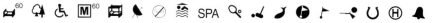

HOTEL DU VIN & BISTRO

THE SUGAR HOUSE, NARROW LEWINS MEAD, BRISTOL BS1 2NU

Set around a courtyard dating from the 1700s, this hotel comprises 6 listed warehouses that have been used for a number of industrial purposes over the centuries. The imposing 100-foot chimney is a lasting testimony to the buildings' impressive past and other distinctive vestiges relating to this period feature inside. The individually named bedrooms are decorated with fine fabrics such as Egyptian linen and offer a good range of facilities including oversized baths and power showers. Guests may relax in the convivial cocktail bar with its walk-in cigar humidor or enjoy a glass of wine from the well-stocked cellar before dining in the Bistro. The traditional menu has been created using the freshest local ingredients and is complemented by an excellent wine list. Throughout the property the cool, understated elegance is evident as is the owners attention to even the smallest detail. The hotel has a selection of specially designed rooms for private meetings or dinner parties. Do not expect stuffy formality at the Hotel du Vin!

Directions: Follow the M32 and then follow signs for the city centre. Go past Broadmead Shopping Centre on your left, and approx 500 yards further on the War Memorial in the centre. Turn right and get onto the opposite side of the carriageway. The hotel is located about 400 yards further down on the left, offset from the main road.

Web: www.johansens.com/hotelduvinbristol
E-mail: info@bristol.hotelduvin.com
Tel: 0870 381 8616
International: +44 (0)117 925 5577
Fax: 0117 925 1199

Bath

Taunton   Yeovil

Price Guide:
double/twin from £120
studio suite from £175

Our inspector loved: *The spacious airy bedrooms and great location for the city centre.*

HARTWELL HOUSE

OXFORD ROAD, NR AYLESBURY, BUCKINGHAMSHIRE HP17 8NL

Standing in 90 acres of gardens and parkland landscaped by a contemporary of Capability Brown, Hartwell House has both Jacobean and Georgian façades. This beautiful house, brilliantly restored by Historic House Hotels, was the residence in exile of King Louis XVIII of France from 1809 to 1814. The large ground floor reception rooms, with oak panelling and decorated ceilings, have antique furniture and fine paintings which evoke the elegance of the 18th century. There are 46 individually designed bedrooms and suites, some in the house and some in Hartwell Court, the restored 18th-century stables. The dining room at Hartwell is the setting for excellent food awarded 3 AA Rosettes (Gentlemen are requested to wear a jacket for dinner). The Old Rectory, Hartwell with its 2 acres of gardens, tennis court and swimming pool, provides beautiful accommodation and offers great comfort and privacy. The Hartwell Spa adjacent to the hotel includes an indoor pool, whirlpool spa bath, steam room, saunas, gymnasium and beauty salons. Situated in the Vale of Aylesbury, the hotel, which is a member of Relais & Châteaux, is only an hour from London and 20 miles from Oxford. Blenheim Palace, Waddesdon Manor and Woburn Abbey are nearby. Dogs are permitted only in Hartwell Court bedrooms.

Directions: On the A418 Oxford Road, 2 miles from Aylesbury.

Web: www.johansens.com/hartwellhouse
E-mail: info@hartwell–house.com
Tel: 0870 381 8585
International: +44 (0)1296 747444
Fax: 01296 747450

Price Guide: (room only)
single £145–£195
double/twin £240–£425
suites £355–£700

Our inspector loved: The peaceful sophistication of this splendid house.

STOKE PARK CLUB

PARK ROAD, STOKE POGES, BUCKINGHAMSHIRE SL2 4PG

Amidst 350 acres of sweeping parkland and gardens, Stoke Park Club is the epitome of elegance and style. For more than 900 years the estate has been at the heart of English heritage, playing host to lords, noblemen, kings and queens. History has left an indelible mark of prestige on the hotel and today it effortlessly combines peerless service with luxury. The magnificence of the Palladian mansion is echoed by the lavishly decorated interior where intricate attention to detail has been paid to the décor with antiques, exquisite fabrics and original paintings and prints ensuring that each room is a masterpiece of indulgence. All 21 individually furnished bedrooms and suites are complemented by marble en-suite bathrooms and some open onto terraces where an early evening drink can be enjoyed as the sun descends over the lakes and gardens. 8 beautiful function rooms, perfect for private dining and entertaining, also continue the theme of tasteful elegance. Since 1908 the hotel has been home to one of the finest 27-hole championship parkland golf courses in the world, Stoke Poges, and the addition of an all indulging spa, health and racquet pavilion re-affirms the hotel's position as one of the country's leading sporting venues. Luxury facilities include 11 beauty treatment rooms, indoor swimming pool, state-of-the-art gymnasium and studio and 13 tennis courts.

Directions: From the M4 take junction 6 or from the M40 take junction 2 then the A344. At the double roundabout at Farnham Royal take the B416. The entrance is just over 1 mile on the right.

Web: www.johansens.com/stokepark
E-mail: info@stokeparkclub.com
Tel: 0870 381 8915
International: +44 (0)1753 717171
Fax: 01753 717181

Price Guide:
single £270
suite £390

Milton Keynes

Aylesbury

High Wycombe

Our inspector loved: *The wonderful setting and stunning spa.*

TAPLOW HOUSE HOTEL

BERRY HILL, TAPLOW, NR MAIDENHEAD, BUCKINGHAMSHIRE SL6 0DA

Elegance and splendour are the hallmarks of this majestic hotel which stands in 6 acres of land adorned by a historic and protected landscape. Taplow House dates back to 1598 and was given by James I to the first Governor of Virginia in 1628. Most of the house was destroyed by fire in the early 1700s but was rebuilt and purchased by the Grenfell family, famed for their equestrian activities, who commissioned the renowned gardener, Springhall, to landscape the grounds. The results can be seen today in the great trees, one of which is reputed to have been planted by Queen Elizabeth I. When the Marquess of Thomond took over the house in 1838 he had architect George Basevi redesign it to introduce the magnificent Doric columns to the reception hall and the elaborate chiselled brass banisters to the staircase which greet today's guests. It was last a private residence in 1958. Taplow House is splendid inside and out. A £1.5-million refurbishment has further enhanced its traditional charm and luxurious comfort. All 32 en-suite bedrooms have every amenity. Chef Phillip Sturgeon produces creative cuisine to please every palate. His outstanding menus are complemented by an excellent and extensive wine list. Windsor, Henley, Ascot and Cliveden are close by as is Heathrow and easy access to London.

Our inspector loved: The comfortable, welcoming rooms and the views over the beautiful grounds.

Directions: Just outside Maidenhead off the A4. Junction 7 M4 or junction 4 M40.

Web: www.johansens.com/taplowhouse
E-mail: taplow@wrensgroup.com
Tel: 0870 381 8939
International: +44 (0)1628 670056
Fax: 01628 773625

Price Guide: (room only)
single £95–£130
double/twin £120–£200
suite £170–£260

DANESFIELD HOUSE HOTEL AND SPA

HENLEY ROAD, MARLOW-ON-THAMES, BUCKINGHAMSHIRE SL7 2EY

Directions: Danesfield is situated between Henley-on-Thames and Marlow and is easily accessed by the M4 junction 8/9 and the M40.

Web: www.johansens.com/danesfieldhouse
E-mail: sales@danesfieldhouse.co.uk
Tel: 0870 381 8474
International: +44 (0)1628 891010
Fax: 01628 890408

Price Guide:
£185
double/twin £225
suites £265

Danesfield House is set within 65 acres of gardens and parkland overlooking the River Thames and offering panoramic views across the Chiltern Hills. It is the third house since 1664 to occupy this lovely setting and it was designed and built in sumptuous style at the end of the 19th century. After years of neglect the house has been fully restored, combining its Victorian splendour with the very best modern hotel facilities. Among the many attractions of its luxury bedrooms, all beautifully decorated and furnished, are the extensive facilities they offer. These include 2 telephone lines (one may be used for personal fax), satellite TV, in-room movies, mini bar, trouser press, hair dryers, bath robes and toiletries. Guests can relax in the magnificent drawing room with its galleried library or in the sun-lit atrium. There is a choice of 2 restaurants, the Oak Room and Orangery Brasserie, both of which offer a choice of international cuisine. The hotel also has 6 private banqueting and conference rooms. Leisure facilities include the award-winning luxurious spa with 20-metre pool, sauna, steam room, gymnasium and superb treatment rooms. Windsor Castle, Marlow, Henley and Oxford are nearby.

Our inspector loved: *The grand sweep of the drive opening out to reveal this splendid hotel and its river views.*

HOTEL FELIX

WHITEHOUSE LANE, HUNTINGDON ROAD, CAMBRIDGE CB3 0LX

Hotel Felix combines Victorian and modern architecture and sits in 4 acres of landscaped gardens offering peaceful surroundings, yet is within minutes' reach of Cambridge with its famous contrast of high-tech science parks and beautiful medieval university buildings. The furniture in the hotel's public areas is handmade and the décor softly neutral with splashes of colour and carefully selected sculptures and artwork. All of the 52 en-suite bedrooms comprise king-sized beds and state-of-the-art communication facilities. Rooms have elegant proportions and are light and airy with high ceilings and views over the gardens. A restaurant and adjacent Café Bar act as a focal point and guests experience modern cuisine with a strong Mediterranean influence or continental coffees and pastries, fine teas, wine and champagne by the glass. Hotel Felix specialises in private corporate and celebration dining and its 4 meeting rooms with natural daylight and ISDN connections will accommodate 34 boardroom and 60 theatre style. Other activities to be enjoyed in Cambridge are visits to Kings College, the Botanical Gardens, Fitzwilliam Museum and punting on the River Cam. Nearby places of interest include Ely, Bury St Edmunds and the races at Newmarket.

Directions: 1 mile north of Cambridge city centre.

Web: www.johansens.com/felix
E-mail: help@hotelfelix.co.uk
Tel: 0870 381 9056
International: +44 (0)1223 277977
Fax: 01223 277973

Price Guide:
single £125
double/twin £155–£260

Peterborough

Ely

Huntingdon

Cambridge

Our inspector loved: The impressive Felix guarding the front entrance.

NEW

GREAT NORTHERN HOTEL

STATION APPROACH, PETERBOROUGH, PE1 1QL

Directions: From the A1 follow signs to the city centre.

Web: www.johansens.com/greatnorthern
E-mail: sales@greatnorthernhotel.co.uk
Tel: 0870 381 9145
International: +44 (0)1733 552331
Fax: 01733 566411

Price Guide:
Pullman rooms
single £90
double £110-£130

A delightful oasis within the city centre, the Great Northern Hotel is a truly classic "Railway Hotel" with all the elegance and charm of the Victorian period, during which time the main part of the original building was built. Extensive renovation has ensured that spacious and light rooms with characteristic Victorian high ceilings have been preserved and potted palms and timber floors pave the ground floor corridor. Original, and occasionally quirky artwork, is displayed throughout the hotel which retains a romantic ambience filled with tales from times aboard the Orient Express. Traditional and contemporary décor is combined in the Pullman rooms where modern bathrooms complement the comfortably styled bedrooms. The restaurant and the cosy, comfortable lounge open onto the attractive gardens, which surround the hotel providing a tranquil, relaxing environment. Peterborough is in an ideal position for a leisure break, within easy reach of Cambridge, Ely and horse racing at Huntingdon. Activities such as boating, bird-watching and walking expeditions at Rutland Water can all be arranged and diverse entertainment in the city together with its historic cathedral and Burghley House in Stamford provide places of interest to visit nearby. Weekend rates are available.

Our inspector loved: *The Old Soke bar with its dashing décor and picture decked walls.*

THE HAYCOCK

WANSFORD, PETERBOROUGH, CAMBRIDGESHIRE PE8 6JA

The Haycock is a handsome old coaching inn of great charm, character and historic interest. It was host to Mary Queen of Scots in 1586 and Princess Alexandra Victoria, later Queen Victoria, in 1835. Overlooking the historic bridge that spans the River Nene, the Hotel is set in a delightful village of unspoilt cottages. Recently restored to private ownership, The Haycock is enjoying a renewed attention to detail - the fragrance of fresh flowers, upgrading and refurbishment. All bedrooms are individually designed and equipped to the highest standards with beautiful soft furnishings. The restaurant is renowned for the quality of its contemporary-style menu complemented by a selection of interesting and outstanding wines with dishes utilising the freshest possible ingredients. A purpose-built ballroom, with lovely oak beams and its own private garden, is a popular venue for a wide range of events, including balls, wedding receptions and Christmas parties. The Business Centre has also made its mark; it is well-equipped with every facility required and offers the flexibility to cater for meetings, product launches, seminars and conferences. Places of interest nearby include Stamford, Burghley House, Nene Valley Railway, Elton Hall, Rutland Water, and Peterborough Cathedral.

Our inspector loved: Coming off the busy A1 straight into this quiet, historic and pretty riverside village.

Directions: Clearly signposted on the A1, a few miles south of Stamford, on the A1/A47 intersection west of Peterborough.

Web: www.johansens.com/haycock
E-mail: info@the haycock.co.uk
Tel: 0870 381 8587
International: +44 (0)1780 782223
Fax: 01780 783031

Price Guide:
single from £80
double/twin room from £95
Four posters from £120

THE ALDERLEY EDGE HOTEL

MACCLESFIELD ROAD, ALDERLEY EDGE, CHESHIRE SK9 7BJ

This privately owned award-winning hotel has 52 bedrooms including the Presidential and Bridal Suites, which are beautifully decorated to a high standard. Located in the sumptuous conservatory, the restaurant offers exceptional views and the highest standards of cooking; fresh produce, including fish delivered daily, is provided by local suppliers. Specialities include hot and cold seafood dishes, puddings served piping hot from the oven and a daily selection of unusual and delicious breads, baked each morning in the hotel bakery. The food is complemented by an extensive wine list, featuring 100 champagnes and 600 wines. Special wine and champagne dinners are held quarterly. In addition to the main conference room there is a suite of meeting and private dining rooms. The famous Edge walks are nearby, as are Tatton and Lyme Parks, Quarry Bank Mill and Dunham Massey. Manchester's thriving city centre is 15 miles away and the airport is a 20-minute drive.

Directions: Follow M6 to M56 Stockport. Exit Jct 6, take A538 to Wilmslow. Follow signs 1½ miles to Alderley Edge. Turn left at end of the main shopping area on to Macclesfield Rd (B5087). The hotel is 200 yards on the right. From M6 take Jct 18 and follow signs for Holmes Chapel and Alderley Edge.

Web: www.johansens.com/alderleyedge
E-mail: sales@alderleyedgehotel.com
Tel: 0870 381 8307
International: +44 (0)1625 583033
Fax: 01625 586343

Price Guide:
single £55–£168
double £99–£225
suite from £250

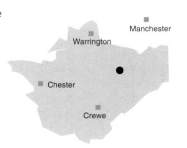

Our inspector loved: *The dining experience in the Alderley Restaurant with its extensive list of champagnes and wines.*

THE CHESTER CRABWALL MANOR

PARKGATE ROAD, MOLLINGTON, CHESTER, CHESHIRE CH1 6NE

Crabwall Manor can be traced back to Saxon England, prior to the Norman Conquest. Set in 11 acres of mature woodland on the outskirts of Chester, this Grade II listed manor house has a relaxed ambience, which is enhanced by staff who combine attentive service with friendliness and care. The interior boasts elegant drapes complemented by pastel shades which lend a freshness to the décor of the spacious lounge and reception areas, whilst the log fires in the inglenook fireplaces add warmth. The hotel has won several awards for their renowned cuisine, complemented by an excellent selection of fine wines and outstanding levels of accommodation. 7 meeting suites and a further 10 syndicate rooms are available. The Reflections leisure club features a 17-metre pool, gymnasium, dance studio, sauna, spa pool and juice bar. Those wishing to be pampered will enjoy the 3 beauty treatment rooms. 100 yards from the hotel guests have reduced green fees at Mollington Grange 18 hole championship golf course. The ancient city of Chester with its many attractions is only 1½ miles away. Weekend breaks available.

Our inspector loved: The excellent exclusive leisure club with its large swimming pool and beauty retreat.

Directions: Go to end of the M56, ignoring signs to Chester. Follow signs to Queensferry and North Wales, taking the A5117 to next roundabout. Turn left onto the A540, towards Chester for 2 miles. The hotel is on the right.

Web: www.johansens.com/crabwallmanor
E-mail: crabwallmanor@marstonhotels.com
Tel: 0870 381 8423
International: +44 (0)1244 851666
Fax: 01244 851400

Price Guide:
single from £146
double/twin from £175–£195
suite from £225–£350

43

Green Bough Hotel

60 HOOLE ROAD, CHESTER, CHESHIRE CH2 3NL

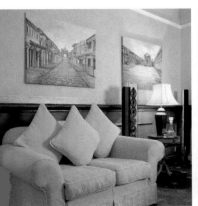

Directions: Leave M53 at Jct12. Take A56 into Chester for 1 mile. The Green Bough Hotel is on the right.

Web: www.johansens.com/greenbough
E-mail: luxury@greenbough.co.uk
Tel: 0870 381 8571
International: +44 (0)1244 326241
Fax: 01244 326265

Price Guide:
single from £80/€125
double/twin from £125/€175
suites from £195/€275

Proprietors Janice and Philip Martin have worked ceaselessly to create this friendly, relaxing haven, which is now Chester's premier small luxury hotel. The 16 sumptuous bedrooms and suites have been completely refurbished using Italian wall coverings and fabrics in keeping with the Roman theme which is evident throughout the hotel. Original oil paintings depicting scenes from a bygone era in Pompeii add to the exclusive ambience. Bedrooms feature original antique cast-iron beds and some have four-posters, plasma televisions, CD players and Jacuzzi baths. There are 7 deluxe bedrooms and 1 master suite in the Lodge. This totally non-smoking hotel enjoys an outstanding reputation reflected in the prestigious awards it has accumulated: Regional Small Hotel of the Year 2002, RAC Blue Ribbon, ETC Gold Award, Excellence in England Finalist 2003. The Olive Tree restaurant offers a fine dining experience bringing together an eclectic mix of aromas and flavours to produce imaginative and innovative dishes for the à la carte and table d'hôte menus, which are complemented by wines from the extensive cellar. The hotel is located within walking distance of the ancient and historic city of Chester and centrally placed for easy access to Snowdonia, Cumbria, Manchester and Liverpool. There is ample off-road parking.

Our inspector loved: *The Roman theme prevalent throughout the hotel.*

NUNSMERE HALL

TARPORLEY ROAD, OAKMERE, NORTHWICH, CHESHIRE CW8 2ES

Set in peaceful Cheshire countryside and surrounded on three sides by a lake, Nunsmere Hall epitomises the elegant country manor where superior standards of hospitality still exist. Wood panelling, antique furniture, exclusive fabrics, Chinese lamps and magnificent chandeliers evoke an air of luxury. The 29 bedrooms and 7 junior suites, most with spectacular views of the lake and gardens, are beautifully appointed with king-size beds, comfortable breakfast seating and marbled bathrooms containing soft bathrobes and toiletries. The Brocklebank, Delamere and Oakmere business suites are air-conditioned, soundproofed and offer excellent facilities for boardroom meetings, private dining and seminars. The restaurant has a reputation for fine food and uses only fresh seasonal produce. Twice County Restaurant of the Year in the Good Food Guide. A snooker room is available and there are several championship golf courses nearby. Oulton Park racing circuit and the Cheshire Polo Club are next door. Golf pitch and putt is available in the grounds. Archery and air rifle shooting by arrangement. Although secluded, Nunsmere is convenient for major towns and routes. AA 3 Red Star and 2 Rosettes.

Our inspector loved: *This elegant country house surrounded by its own lake.*

Directions: Leave M6 at junction 19, take A556 to Chester (approximately 12 miles). Turn left onto A49. Hotel is 1 mile on left.

Web: www.johansens.com/nunsmerehall
E-mail: reservations@nunsmere.co.uk
Tel: 0870 381 8772
International: +44 (0)1606 889100
Fax: 01606 889055

Price Guide:
single £140–£165
double/twin £195–£230
junior suites £260–£350

Rowton Hall Hotel

WHITCHURCH ROAD, ROWTON, CHESTER, CHESHIRE CH3 6AD

Directions: From the centre of Chester, take A41 towards Whitchurch. After 3 miles, turn right to Rowton village. The hotel is in the centre of the village.

Web: www.johansens.com/rowtonhall
E-mail: rowtonhall@rowtonhall.co.uk
Tel: 0870 381 8871
International: +44 (0)1244 335262
Fax: 01244 335464

Price Guide:
single £137–£170
double/twin £149–£185
suites £224

Set in over 8 acres of award-winning gardens, Rowton Hall is located at the end of a leafy lane, only 3 miles from Chester city centre. Built as a private residence in 1779, it retains many of its original features, including extensive oak panelling, a self-supporting hand-carved staircase, an original Inglenook fireplace and an elegant Robert Adam fireplace. Each luxury bedroom is individually and tastefully decorated with attention to detail, and is equipped with every modern amenity, including private bathroom, satellite television, direct dial telephone with modem points, personal safe, luxury bathrobes, trouser press and hostess tray. Dining in the oak-panelled Langdale Restaurant is a delight; every dish is carefully created by executive chef, Anthony O'Hare, who uses the finest ingredients from local markets and the Hall's gardens to produce exquisite cuisine. Guests can enjoy the indoor Health Club and relax in the Jacuzzi, steam room or sauna. For the more energetic, a workout in the well-equipped gymnasium and dance studio is available and 2 floodlit all-weather tennis courts are within the grounds. Four main conference and banqueting suites make the Hall an ideal venue for meetings, weddings, private dining or conferences and corporate events for up to 200 guests. Marquee events can be arranged in the gardens.

Our inspector loved: *The lovingly tended gardens.*

CREWE HALL

WESTON ROAD, CREWE, CHESHIRE CW1 6UZ

Set in vast, impressive grounds, the magnificent Crewe Hall is the jewel of Cheshire. Once the seat of the Earls of Crewe and owned by the Queen as part of the estate of the Duchy of Lancaster, this stately home transports guests back to an age of splendour and luxury where quality and service were imperative. An exquisite Jacobean carving, which adorns the lavish main entrance, is reflected over the whole exterior from the balustraded terraces to the tip of the tall West Wing Tower. Crewe Hall's beautiful interior boats a confident juxtaposition between the traditional and modern. The newly refurbished and air-conditioned west wing, with its stylish, contemporary décor, is contrasted with the traditional home rooms, which have magnificent panelling and marble, huge stone fireplaces, intricate carvings, stained glass and antique furniture. Regarded as one of the finest specimens of Elizabethan architecture, the staircase in the East Hall climbs majestically upwards. Guests can dine in the quiet, elegant dining room or the informal Brasserie, which has a unique revolving bar (whose smooth motion means you will not notice you are moving until the view has suddenly changed) and offers imaginative, delicious meals complemented by international beers and wines.

Directions: From the M6, exit at junction 16 and follow the A500 towards Crewe. At the first roundabout take the last exit. At the next roundabout take the first exit. After ¼ mile turn right into the drive.

Web: www.johansens.com/crewehall
E-mail: crewehall@marstonhotels.com
Tel: 0870 381 8458
International: +44 (0)1270 253333
Fax: 01270 253322

Price Guide:
single £135–£195
double/twin £160–£220
suite £260–£395

Our inspector loved: The eclectic mix of tradition and modern in this Jacobean mansion.

HILLBARK HOTEL

ROYDEN PARK, FRANKBY, WIRRAL CH48 1NP

Surrounded by 240 acres of parkland, Hillbark hotel is a magnificent Elizabethan style mansion with a fascinating history and views over the Dee estuary and hills of North Wales. It was originally built in Birkenhead for the soap manufacturer, Robert William Hudson. Germany's crown prince Wilhelm was so impressed by it that he built a replica of it for himself in Potsdam, Germany. It is there that the famous Potsdam Agreement was signed at the end of World War II. In 1931, the mansion was moved brick by brick to its present location in Frankby on the Wirral Peninsula. There are many extraordinary features in the hotel - a Jacobean fireplace dates from 1527 and was taken from Sir Walter Raleigh's home and there are beautiful stained glass windows by William Morris. The library was originally in a stately home in Gloucestershire whilst the dining room doors are from an old tea clipper. Delicious and imaginative haute cuisine is served in the stylish restaurant together with an excellent choice of fine wines from the cellar. Leisure activities include world-class golf and windsurfing.

Directions: M53 Jct 3 A552. Turn right onto the A551. After the hospital on the left, turn left onto Arrowe Brook Road, then left onto Arrowe Brooke Lane. Entrance to Royden Park is ½ mile along this road, continue straight up the drive.

Web: www.johansens.com/hillbark
E-mail: enquiries@hillbarkhotel.co.uk
Tel: 0870 381 9128
International: +44 (0)151 625 2400
Fax: 0151 625 4040

Price Guide:
single £110–£135
double/twin £110–£135
suite £195–£345

Our inspector loved: *The oak panelling in this magnificent Elizabethan style black and white timber house.*

MERE COURT HOTEL

WARRINGTON ROAD, MERE, KNUTSFORD, CHESHIRE WA16 0RW

This attractive Edwardian house stands in 7 acres of mature gardens and parkland in one of the loveliest parts of Cheshire. Maintained as a family home since being built in 1903, Mere Court has been skilfully restored into a fine country house hotel offering visitors a peaceful ambience in luxury surroundings. Comforts and conveniences of the present mix excellently with the ambience and many original features of the past. The bedrooms have views over the grounds or ornamental lake. All are individually designed and a number of them have a Jacuzzi spa bath and mini bar. Facilities include safes, personalised voice mail telephones and modem points. Heavy ceiling beams, polished oak panelling and restful waterside views are features of the elegant Aboreum Restaurant, which serves the best of traditional English and Mediterranean cuisines. Lighter meals can be enjoyed in the Lounge Bar. The original coach house has been converted into a designated conference centre with state-of-the-art conference suites and syndicate rooms accommodating up to 120 delegates. Warrington, Chester, Manchester Airport and many National Trust properties are within easy reach.

Our inspector loved: The oak-panelled restaurant overlooking the ornamental lake.

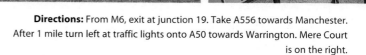

Directions: From M6, exit at junction 19. Take A556 towards Manchester. After 1 mile turn left at traffic lights onto A50 towards Warrington. Mere Court is on the right.

Web: www.johansens.com/merecourt
E-mail: sales@merecourt.co.uk
Tel: 0870 381 8727
International: +44 (0)1565 831000
Fax: 01565 831001

Price Guide:
single £80–£140
double/twin £98–£185

THE STANNEYLANDS HOTEL

STANNEYLANDS ROAD, WILMSLOW, CHESHIRE SK9 4EY

Owned and managed by a dedicated family, Stanneylands is a handsome country house set in several acres of impressive, tranquil gardens with a collection of unusual trees and shrubs. Guests experience a truly warm welcome in a unique and special atmosphere, where luxurious comfort provides the perfect setting for business or pleasure. Some of the bedrooms offer lovely views over the gardens whilst others overlook the undulating Cheshire countryside. A sense of quiet luxury prevails in the reception rooms, where classical décor and comfortable furnishings create a relaxing ambience. In the award-winning restaurant guests can choose from an enticing blend of innovative and traditional English and international cuisine. Stanneylands is an excellent venue for both private and business events. The Oak Room accommodates up to 60 people, whilst the Stanley Suite is available for conferences and larger celebrations. The hotel is conveniently located for tours of the Cheshire plain or the more rugged Peak District, as well as the bustling market towns and industrial heritage of the area. Special corporate and weekend rates are available.

Directions: 3 miles from Manchester International Airport. Come off at Junction 5 on the M56 (airport turn off). Follow signs to Cheadle/Wilmslow, turn left into station road, bear right onto Stanneylands Road.

Web: www.johansens.com/stanneylands
E-mail: sales@stanneylandshotel.co.uk
Tel: 0870 381 8909
International: +44 (0)1625 525225
Fax: 01625 537282

Price Guide:
single £70–£135
double/twin £102–£145
suite £145

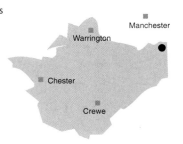

Manchester

Warrington

Chester

Crewe

Our inspector loved: Strolling through the landscaped gardens and water gardens.

THE NARE HOTEL

CARNE BEACH, VERYAN-IN-ROSELAND, TRURO, CORNWALL TR2 5PF

Peace, tranquillity and stunning sea views make The Nare a real find. Superbly positioned, the hotel overlooks the fine sandy beach of Gerrans Bay, facing south and sheltered by The Nare and St Mawes headlands. In recent years extensive refurbishments have ensured comfort and elegance without detracting from the country house charm of this friendly family-run hotel. All bedrooms are close to the sea, many with patios and balconies taking advantage of the spectacular outlook. In the main dining room guests can enjoy the sea views from 3 sides of the room where local seafood, such as lobster and delicious homemade puddings, are served with Cornish cream, complemented by an interesting range of wines. The Quarterdeck Restaurant is open all day serving morning coffee, light luncheons, cream teas and offers relaxed dining in the evening. The Nare remains the highest rated AA 4 star hotel in the south west with 2 Rosettes for its food. Surrounded by subtropical gardens and National Trust land the hotel's seclusion is ideal for exploring the coastline and villages of the glorious Roseland Peninsula. It is also central for many of Cornwall's beautiful houses and gardens including the famous Heligan. Guests arriving by train or air are met, without charge, by prior arrangement, at Truro Station or Newquay Airport. The hotel is open throughout the year, including Christmas and New Year.

Directions: Follow the road to St Mawes. 2 miles after Tregony Bridge turn left for Veryan. The hotel is 1 mile beyond Veryan.

Web: www.johansens.com/nare
E-mail: office@narehotel.co.uk
Tel: 0870 381 8755
International: +44 (0)1872 501111
Fax: 01872 501856

Price Guide:
single £96-£183
double/twin £182-£336
suite £324-£530

Newquay   Bodmin

Penzance

Isles of Scilly

Our inspector loved: The unique presentation of the Quarterdeck restaurant.

THE GREENBANK HOTEL

HARBOURSIDE, FALMOUTH, CORNWALL TR11 2SR

Surrounded by the vibrant atmosphere of Falmouth, the Greenbank is the only hotel on the banks of one of the world's largest and deepest natural harbours. Because of its position as a ferry point to Flushing, its history stretches back to the 17th century, and visitors have included Florence Nightingale and Kenneth Grahame, whose letters from the hotel to his son formed the basis for his book "The Wind in the Willows". Seaward views from the hotel are stunning, and reaching out from each side are lovely clifftop paths leading to secluded coves where walkers can relax while enjoying a paddle in clear blue waters and breathing in fresh, clean sea air. Most of the charming, delightfully furnished and well equipped en-suite bedrooms enjoy panoramic views across the harbour to Flushing and St Mawes. Keen appetites will be well satisfied by the variety of dishes offered in the Harbourside Restaurant with seafood and local lamb specialities on the menu. There are opportunities locally for golf, sailing, riding and fishing. Interesting places nearby include Cornwall's National Maritime Museum, several heritage sites and many National Trust properties and gardens.

Directions: Take the A39 from Truro and on approaching Falmouth join the Old Road going through Penryn. Turn left at the second roundabout where the hotel is signposted.

Web: www.johansens.com/greenbank
E-mail: sales@greenbank-hotel.com
Tel: 0870 381 8573
International: +44 (0)1326 312440
Fax: 01326 211362

Price Guide:
single £70–£85
double/twin £115–£165
suite £185–£225

Our inspector loved: *The magnificent location and breathtaking views across Falmouth harbour's ever changing scenery.*

BUDOCK VEAN - THE HOTEL ON THE RIVER

NEAR HELFORD PASSAGE, MAWNAN SMITH, FALMOUTH, CORNWALL TR11 5LG

This family-run, 4-star Cornwall Tourist Board Hotel of the Year 2002, is nestled in 65 acres of award-winning gardens and parkland with a private foreshore on the tranquil Helford River. Set in a designated area of breathtaking natural beauty, the hotel is a destination in itself with outstanding leisure facilities and space to relax and be pampered. The AA Rosette restaurant offers excellent cuisine using the finest local produce to create exciting and imaginative 5-course dinners, with fresh seafood being a speciality. On site are a golf course, large indoor swimming pool, tennis courts, a billiard room, boating, fishing, and the Natural Health Spa. The local ferry will take guests from the hotel's jetty to waterside pubs, to Frenchman's Creek or to hire a boat. The hotel also takes out guests on its own 32-foot "Sunseeker". A myriad of magnificent country and coastal walks from the wild grandeur of Kynance and the Lizard to the peace and tranquillity of the Helford itself, as well as several of the Great Gardens of Cornwall, are in the close vicinity.

Directions: From the A39, Truro to Falmouth road, follow the brown tourist signs for Trebah Garden. Budock Vean appears ½ mile after passing Trebah on the left-hand side.

Web: www.johansens.com/budockvean
E-mail: relax@budockvean.co.uk
Tel: 0870 381 8392
International: reservations+44 (0)1326 252100
Fax: 01326 250892

Price Guide: (including dinner)
single £66–£105
double/twin £132–£210
suites £217–£275

Our inspector loved: The total tranquillity set within 65 acres of beautiful grounds and secluded creek on the Helford River.

         SPA

MEUDON HOTEL

MAWNAN SMITH, NR FALMOUTH, CORNWALL TR11 5HT

Directions: From Truro A39 torwards Falmouth at Hillhead roundabout take 2nd exit. The hotel is 4 miles on the left.

Web: www.johansens.com/meudon
E-mail: wecare@meudon.co.uk
Tel: 0870 381 8730
International: +44 (0)1326 250541
Fax: 01326 250543

Price Guide: (including dinner)
single £110
double/twin £210
suite £280

Set against a delightfully romantic backdrop of densely wooded countryside between the Fal and Helford Rivers, Meudon Hotel is a unique, family-run, superior retreat with sub-tropical gardens leading to its own private sea beach. The French name originates from a nearby farmhouse built by Napoleonic prisoners of war and called after their eponymous home village in the environs of Paris. 9 acres of sub-tropical gardens are coaxed into early bloom by the Gulf Stream and mild Cornish climate; Meudon is safely surrounded by 200 acres of beautiful National Trust land and the sea. All bedrooms are in a modern wing, have en-suite bathrooms and each enjoys spectacular garden views. Many a guest is enticed by the cuisine to return; in the restaurant fresh seafood, caught by local fishermen, is served with wines from a judiciously compiled list. Rich in natural beauty with a myriad of watersports and country pursuits to indulge in, you can play golf free at nearby Falmouth Golf Club and 5 others in Cornwall, sail aboard the hotel's skiperd 34-foot yacht or just laze on the beach.

Our inspector loved: *Standing looking out of the mullioned windows over the beautiful grounds admiring the magnolias, camellias and other delightful species.*

FOWEY HALL HOTEL & RESTAURANT

HANSON DRIVE, FOWEY, CORNWALL PL23 1ET

Situated in five acres of beautiful grounds overlooking the Estuary, Fowey Hall Hotel is a magnificent Victorian mansion renowned for its excellent service and comfortable accommodation. The fine panelling and superb plasterwork ceilings add character to the spacious public rooms. Located in either the main house or the Court, the 24 bedrooms include suites and interconnecting rooms. All are well-proportioned with a full range of modern comforts. The panelled dining rooms provide an intimate atmosphere where guests may savour the local delicacies. Using the best of regional produce, the menu comprises tempting seafood and fish specialities. The hotel offers a full crèche service. Guests may swim in the indoor swimming pool or play croquet in the gardens. Older children have not been forgotten and "The Garage" in the courtyard is well-equipped with table tennis, table football and many other games. Outdoor pursuits include sea fishing, boat trips and a variety of water sports such as sailing, scuba-diving and windsurfing. There are several coastal walks for those who wish to explore Cornwall and its beautiful landscape.

Our inspector loved: The beautiful proportioned rooms, the grandeur yet wonderful warm welcome for families.

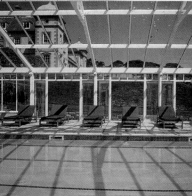

Directions: On reaching Fowey, go straight over the mini roundabout and follow the road all the way eventually taking a sharp right bend, take the next left turn and Fowey Hall drive is on the right.

Newquay
Bodmin
Penzance
Isles of Scilly

Web: www.johansens.com/foweyhall
E-mail: info@foweyhall.com
Tel: 0870 381 8529
International: +44 (0)1726 833866
Fax: 01726 834100

Price Guide:
double/twin from £145
superior double from £180
suite from £200

Trenython Manor Hotel & Spa

TYWARDREATH, NEAR FOWEY, CORNWALL PL24 2TS

Built between 1854 and 1872 by an Italian architect, Trenython Manor stands amidst 25 acres of wooded parkland. The manor boasts an interesting and varied history; originally home to Colonel Peard, a former Bishop's palace, a Great Western Railway Convalescent Home and host to the Daphne Du Maurier Festival of Arts. The Italian influence is evident throughout the hotel with its grand staircase and colonnades together with attractive oak panelling, Italian fabrics and fine marble. The 24 bedrooms and suites are beautifully decorated with no expense spared to ensure pure luxury! The panelled dining room, featuring carved wood obtained from Worcester Cathedral, York Minster and many churches, provides a magnificent setting for meals prepared from only the freshest of ingredients. More informal meals can be taken in the lounge bar. The manor's recently opened Health & Beauty Salon offers a great variety of treatments to guests wishing to relax and be pampered by the professional staff. Trenython is only 3 miles away from glorious Cornish beaches and in an ideal position to explore Bodmin Moor, the rugged north coast of Cornwall and the Eden Project. Many water sports as well as shark fishing trips can be arranged.

Directions: From Exeter join the A30 towards Cornwall then the B3269 signposted Lostwithiel. Take the A390 St Austell/Fowey B3269, follow Fowey signs for approximately 4 miles. The hotel is then signposted.

Web: www.johansens.com/trenython
E-mail: hotel@trenython.co.uk
Tel: 0870 381 9139
International: +44 (0)1726 814797
Fax: 01726 817030

Price Guide:
single from £75
double £95-£195

Newquay   Bodmin

Penzance

Isles of Scilly

Our inspector loved: *The beautiful staircase, oak panelling and stunning location.*

St Martin's On The Isle

ST MARTIN'S, ISLES OF SCILLY, CORNWALL TR25 0QW

This unique hotel offers guests the chance to "step back in time" and appreciate the serenity and unspoilt beauty of one of the most remote offshore islands in the UK. Upon arrival at St Martin's a warm and personal welcome is extended by the General Manager, Keith Bradford, whose staff are always on hand to advise, guide, or simply assist in the art of relaxation. Unwinding in the laidback atmosphere of the Round Island Bar or garden is easy, and many people choose to chat and share experiences with fellow visitors. Surrounded by clear blue seas, white sandy beaches and spectacular views, the island offers endless opportunities for walking, picnics, watersports and boat trips. On foot, it takes a leisurely 4 hours to explore the coastal paths' ever changing scenery, while launches leave the hotel quay regulary for visits to the Eastern Isles where colonies of Atlantic grey seals bask on the rocks. Nature lovers can also enjoy a dusk walk with local "bird man" Viv Jackson, and the more adventurous will be satisfied with snorkelling at the Dive Centre or a day out shark fishing with one of the island's boatmen. After a hard day, dinner of Scillonian crab or lobster in the hotel's excellent restaurant is a must.

Our inspector loved: The peace, seclusion, fresh air and overall feeling of welcome.

Directions: A 20 minute launch transfer from St Mary's.

Web: www.johansens.com/stmartins
E-mail: stay@stmartinshotel.co.uk
Tel: 0870 381 8905
International: +44 (0)1720 422090
Fax: 01720 422298

Price Guide: (including dinner)
single £110–£140
double/twin £220–£320
suite £320–£410

HELL BAY

BRYHER, ISLES OF SCILLY, CORNWALL TR23 0PR

Bryher is the smallest community of the Isles of Scilly, 28 miles west of Land's End, and Hell Bay its only hotel. It stands in a spectacular and dramatic setting in extensive lawned grounds on the rugged West Coast overlooking the unbroken Atlantic Ocean. Described as a "spectacularly located getaway-from-it-all destination that is a paradise for adults and children alike" .. and it is. Outdoor heated swimming pool, gym, sauna, spa bath, children's playground, games room and par 3 golf course ensure there is never a dull moment. Daily boat trips available so that you can discover the islands, the world famous tropical Abbey Garden is on the neighbouring island of Tresco. White sanded beaches abound with an array of water sports available. Dining is an integral part of staying at Hell Bay and the food will not disappoint; as you would expect, seafood is a speciality. Closed December to March

Directions: The Isles of Scilly are reached by helicopter or boat from Penzance or fixed-wing aircraft from Southampton, Bristol, Exeter, Newquay and Lands End. The hotel can make all necessary travel arrangements and will co-ordinate all transfers to Bryher on arrival.

Web: www.johansens.com/hellbay
E-mail: contactus@hellbay.co.uk
Tel: 0870 381 8591
International: +44 (0)1720 422947
Fax: 01720 423004

Price Guide: (including dinner)
suites £180–£400

Our inspector loved: From stepping off the boat on arrival - the peace, seclusion and time warp.

TALLAND BAY HOTEL

PORTHALLOW, CORNWALL PL13 2JB

Surrounded by 2 acres of beautiful sub-tropical gardens and with dramatic views over Talland Bay, this lovely old Cornish manor house is a real gem. Each of the 23 comfortable bedrooms has its own individual character and is traditionally furnished. Many offer stunning views of the sea and the garden's magnificent Monterey pines. In the bathrooms, fluffy bathrobes and Molton Brown toiletries are just some of the extra touches that are the hotel's hallmark. The award-winning restaurant under the guidance of 2 AA Rosetted chef, Mark Turton, provides a first-class menu of high-quality, local produce. Starters could include Stilton soufflé with spinach, or freshly picked local crab with quail's eggs. Typical main courses include seared Newlyn scallops and langoustine tagliatelle, or best end of Cornish lamb with boulangère potatoes with a rosemary jus. And to finish, poached pear with fresh raspberries glazed with citrus sabayon, or dark chocolate Marquise with orange tuille. The wine list has been specially selected by the owners to complement the menus. There are fabulous coastal walks all year round, whilst in summer, putting and croquet can be played on the beautiful lawns, and the heated outdoor swimming pool, with its south-facing terrace, is a constant temptation. In winter, there's the chance to read that favourite book by a roaring log fire.

Directions: The hotel is signposted from the A387 Looe–Polperro road.

Web: www.johansens.com/tallandbay
E-mail: info@tallandbayhotel.co.uk
Tel: 0870 381 8937
International: +44 (0)1503 272667
Fax: 01503 272940

Price Guide:
single £55–£90
double/twin £110–£180

Our inspector loved: The charming, friendly atmosphere.

THE ROSEVINE HOTEL

PORTHCURNICK BEACH, PORTSCATHO, ST MAWES, TRURO, CORNWALL TR2 5EW

Directions: From Exeter take A30 towards Truro. Take the St Mawes turn and the hotel is signed to the left.

Web: www.johansens.com/rosevinehotel
E-mail: info@rosevine.co.uk
Tel: 0870 381 8867
International: +44 (0)1872 580206
Fax: 01872 580230

Price Guide:
single £85–£185
double/twin £170–£245
suite £250–£350

At the heart of Cornwall's breathtaking Roseland Peninsula, the Rosevine is an elegant and gracious late Georgian hotel that offers visitors complete comfort and peace. The Rosevine stands in its own landscaped grounds overlooking Portscatho Harbour, a traditional Cornish fishing village. The superbly equipped bedrooms are delightfully designed, with some benefiting from direct access into the gardens and from their own private patio. This is the only hotel in Cornwall to hold the awards of 3 AA Red Stars and the RAC Blue Ribbon and Triple Dining Rosettes. The restaurant serves exceptional food, using the freshest seafood and locally grown produce. After dining, guests can relax in any of the 3 tastefully and comfortably presented lounges, bathe in the spacious heated swimming pool, or read in the hotel's well stocked library. Drinks are served in the convivial bar which offers a dizzy array of top quality wines and spirits. Visitors to the region do not forget the walks to the charming villages dotted along the Roseland Peninsula, and the golden sand of the National Trust maintained beach. Visitors can also take river trips on small ferries, once the only means of travel around the peninsula. The region is awash with National Trust gardens and the beautiful town of Truro is easily reached.

Our inspector loved: *This elegant and gracious hotel offering total peace, seclusion and first-class cuisine.*

THE LUGGER HOTEL

PORTLOE, NR TRURO, CORNWALL TR2 5RD

Set on the water's edge and sheltered on three sides by green rolling hills tumbling into the sea, this lovely little former inn is as picturesque as any you will come across. Reputedly the haunt of 17th-century smugglers The Lugger Hotel overlooks a tiny working harbour in the scenic village of Portloe on the unspoilt Roseland Peninsula. It is a conservation area of outstanding beauty and an idyllic location in which to escape the stresses of today's hectic world. Seaward views from the hotel are stunning and reaching out from each side are lovely coastal paths leading to secluded coves. Welcoming owners Sheryl and Richard Young have created an atmosphere of total comfort and relaxation whilst retaining an historic ambience. The 21 bedrooms have every amenity; each is en suite, tastefully decorated and furnished, whilst some are situated across an attractive courtyard. A great variety of dishes and innovative dinner menus are offered in the restaurant overlooking the harbour. Local seafood is a specialty with crab and lobster being particular favourites. For beach lovers, the sandy stretches of Pendower and Carne are within easy reach, as are many National Trust properties and gardens, including the Lost Gardens of Heligan and the Eden project.

Our inspector loved: The idyllic location and wonderful relaxing feel throughout.

Directions: Turn off A390 St Austell to Truro onto B3287 Tregony. Then take A3048 signed St Mawes, after 2 miles take left fork following signs for Portloe.

Web: www.johansens.com/lugger
E-mail: office@luggerhotel.com
Tel: 0870 381 8708
International: +44 (0)1872 501322
Fax: 01872 501691

Price Guide: (including dinner)
double/twin from £200

Newquay · Bodmin
Penzance
Isles of Scilly

ROSE-IN-VALE COUNTRY HOUSE HOTEL

MITHIAN, ST AGNES, CORNWALL TR5 0QD

Directions: From the major A30 roundabout just NW of Truro, take the B3277 signed for St Agnes, after 500 metres pick up the brown signs for Rose-in-Vale Hotel.

Web: www.johansens.com/roseinvalecountryhouse
E-mail: reception@rose-in-vale-hotel.co.uk
Tel: 0870 381 8866
International: +44 (0)1872 552202
Fax: 01872 552700

Price Guide:
single from £64
double/twin £112–£152
suite £152

This 18th-century Cornish manor house lies hidden away in 11 acres of glorious gardens, woodland and pasture in a wooded valley of great natural beauty. There is a sense of timelessness: a world apart from the bustle of modern living. Tasteful décor contrasts with dark mahogany throughout the elegant public rooms and pretty bedrooms, many of which have outstanding views across the valley gardens. 3 ground floor rooms have level access. The Rose Suite and Master Rooms feature four-poster/half-tester beds, other rooms have coronet king-sized beds. Chefs Phillip Sims and Brian Hatton serve imaginative international cuisine and speciality Cornish crab/lobster/fish dishes in the Valley Restaurant where sweeping, softly-draped bay windows overlook lawns and flowerbeds. The gardens feature ponds, a gliding stream, a secluded, heated swimming pool, croquet, badminton, dovecote and summer house. There is a solarium, sauna and games room. National Trust properties abound and special walks are available. 6 golf courses, The Eden Project, the new National Maritime Museum, The Glorious Gardens of Cornwall, riding, fishing, gliding, swimming and water sports are all close by.

Our inspector loved: This beautifully hidden away hotel offering total comfort.

THE GARRACK HOTEL & RESTAURANT

BURTHALLAN LANE, ST IVES, CORNWALL TR26 3AA

This family-run hotel, secluded and full of character, ideal for a family holiday, is set in 2 acres of gardens with fabulous sea views over Porthmeor Beach, the St Ives Tate Gallery and the old town of St Ives. The bedrooms in the original house are in keeping with the style of the building. The additional rooms are modern in design. All rooms have private bathrooms and baby-listening facilities. Superior rooms have either four-poster beds or whirlpool baths. A ground-floor room has been fitted for guests with disabilities. Visitors return year after year to enjoy informal yet professional service, good food and hospitality. The restaurant specialises in seafood especially fresh lobsters. The wine list includes over 70 labels from ten regions. The lounges have books, magazines and board games for all and open fires. The small attractive leisure centre contains a small swimming pool with integral spa, sauna, solarium and fitness area. The hotel has its own car park. Porthmeor Beach, just below the hotel, is renowned for surfing. Riding, golf, bowls, sea-fishing and other activities can be enjoyed locally. St Ives, with its harbour, is famous for artists and for the new St Ives Tate Gallery.

Our inspector loved: This family-run relaxed informal hotel overlooking Porthmeor Beach.

Directions: A30–A3074–B3311–B3306. Go ½ mile, turn left at mini-roundabout, hotel signs are on the left as the road starts down hill.

Web: www.johansens.com/garrack
E-mail: garrack@accuk.co.uk
Tel: 0870 381 8536
International: +44 (0)1736 796199
Fax: 01736 798955

Price Guide:
single £68–£70
double/twin £114–£170

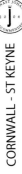

THE WELL HOUSE

ST KEYNE, LISKEARD, CORNWALL PL14 4RN

Directions: Leave A38 at Liskeard, take A390 to town centre, then take B3254 south to St Keyne Well and hotel.

Web: www.johansens.com/wellhouse
E-mail: enquiries@wellhouse.co.uk
Tel: 0870 381 8975
International: +44 (0)1579 342001
Fax: 01579 343891

Price Guide:
single from £75
double/twin £115–£170
family suite from £180

The West Country is one corner of England where hospitality and friendliness are at their most spontaneous and nowhere more so than at The Well House, just beyond the River Tamar. New arrivals are entranced by their first view of this lovely Victorian country manor. Its façade wrapped in rambling wisteria and jasmine trailers is just one of a continuous series of delights including top-quality service, modern luxury and impeccable standards of comfort and cooking. The hotel is professionally managed by proprietor Nick Wainford and General Manager Guy Down, whose attention to every smallest detail has earned his hotel numerous awards, among them the AA 2 Red Stars. From the tastefully appointed bedrooms there are fine rural views and each private bathroom offers luxurious bath linen, soaps and gels. Continental breakfast can be served in bed – or a traditional English breakfast may be taken in the dining room. Chef Matthew Corner selects fresh, seasonal produce to create his superbly balanced and presented cuisine. Tennis and swimming are on site and the Cornish coastline offers matchless scenery for walks. The Eden Project is a short drive away.

Our inspector loved: *The friendly, warm ambience and superb cuisine.*

ALVERTON MANOR

TREGOLLS ROAD, TRURO, CORNWALL TR1 1ZQ

Standing in the heart of the cathedral city of Truro and rising majestically over immaculate surrounds, Alverton Manor is the epitome of a mid-19th-century family home. With its handsome sandstone walls, mullioned windows and superb Cornish Delabole slate roof, this elegant and gracious hotel is reminiscent of the splendour of a bygone era and proudly defends its claim to a Grade II* listing. Built for the Tweedy family over 150 years ago, it was acquired by the Bishop of Truro in the 1880s and later occupied by the Sister of the Epiphany before being taken over and restored to its former glory. Owner Michael Sagin and his talented and dedicated staff take pride in not only providing a high standard of service and modern English cuisine but also in enthusiastically maintaining a welcoming and relaxing ambience that attracts guests time and again. A superb entrance hall with a huge, decorative York stone archway leads to rooms that are comfortable in a quiet, elegant way. Lounges are restful, finely furnished, tastefully decorated and warmed by open fires in winter. The dining room is exquisite, and each of the 33 bedrooms has been individually designed to provide a special character, from the intimate to the grand. Golf, sailing and fishing nearby. Special golf and garden breaks available.

Our inspector loved: The peace and tranquillity throughout this former beautiful nunnery.

Directions: Exit the M5, junction 30 and join the A30 through Devon into Cornwall at Fraddon and join the A39 to Truro.

Web: www.johansens.com/alverton
E-mail: reception@alvertonmanor.demon.co.uk
Tel: 0870 381 9152
International: +44 (0)1872 276633
Fax: 01872 222989

Price Guide:
single £75
double £115-£130
suite £165

65

LOVELADY SHIELD COUNTRY HOUSE HOTEL

NENTHEAD ROAD, ALSTON, CUMBRIA CA9 3LF

Directions: The hotel's driveway is by the junction of the B6294 and the A689, 2¼ miles east of Alston.

Web: www.johansens.com/loveladyshield
E-mail: enquiries@lovelady.co.uk
Tel: 0870 381 8705
International: +44 (0)1434 381203
Fax: 01434 381515

Price Guide:
single £60–£100
double/twin £120–£200

Reached by the A646, one of the worlds 10 best drives and 2½ miles from Alston, England's highest market town, Lovelady Shield, nestles in 3 acres of secluded riverside gardens. Bright log fires in the library and drawing room enhance the hotel's welcoming atmosphere. Owners Peter and Marie Haynes take great care to create a peaceful and tranquil haven where guests can relax and unwind. The 5-course dinners prepared by master chef Barrie Garton, rounded off by homemade puddings and a selection of English farmhouse cheeses, have consistently been awarded AA Rosettes for the past 10 years for food. Many guests first discover Lovelady Shield en route to Scotland. They then return to explore this beautiful and unspoilt part of England and experience the comforts of the hotel. Golf, fishing, shooting, pony-trekking and riding can be arranged locally. The Pennine Way, Hadrian's Wall and the Lake District are within easy reach. Facilities for small conferences and boardroom meetings are available. Open all year, Special Christmas, New Year, and short breaks are offered with special rates for 2 and 3-day stays.

Our inspector loved: *This informal relaxing hotel set in a picturesque valley.*

HOLBECK GHYLL COUNTRY HOUSE HOTEL

HOLBECK LANE, WINDERMERE, CUMBRIA LA23 1LU

The saying goes that all the best sites for building a house in England were taken long before the days of the motor car. Holbeck Ghyll has one such prime position. It was built in the early days of the 19th century and is superbly located overlooking Lake Windermere and the Langdale Fells. Today this luxury hotel has an outstanding reputation and is managed personally and expertly by its proprietors, David and Patricia Nicholson. As well as being awarded the RAC Gold Ribbon and 3 AA Red Stars they are among an élite who have won an AA Courtesy and Care Award, Holbeck Ghyll was 2002 Country Life Hotel of the Year. The majority of bedrooms are large and have spectacular and breathtaking views. All are recently refurbished to a very high standard and include decanters of sherry, fresh flowers, fluffy bathrobes and much more. There are 6 suites in the lodge. The oak-panelled restaurant, awarded a coveted Michelin star and 3 AA Rosettes, is a delightful setting for memorable dining and the meals are classically prepared, with the focus on flavours and presentation, while an extensive wine list reflects quality and variety. The hotel has an all-weather tennis court and a health spa with gym, sauna and treatment facilities.

Our inspector loved: The delicious dinner in the oak-panelled restaurant with extensive views over Lake Windermere.

Directions: From Windermere, pass Brockhole Visitors Centre, then after ½ mile turn right into Holbeck Lane. Hotel is ½ mile on left.

Web: www.johansens.com/holbeckghyll
E-mail: stay@holbeckghyll.com
Tel: 0870 381 8601
International: +44 (0)15394 32375
Fax: 015394 34743

Price Guide: (including 4 course dinner)
single from £125
double/twin £170–£360
suite £200–£360

ROTHAY MANOR

ROTHAY BRIDGE, AMBLESIDE, CUMBRIA LA22 0EH

Just a ¼ mile from Lake Windermere and a short walk from the centre of Ambleside, this Regency country house stands in its own landscaped gardens. Managed by the Nixon family for over 35 years the Manor is renowned for its relaxed, comfortable and friendly ambience. There are 14 individually designed bedrooms in the hotel, some with balconies overlooking the garden, and 3 suites in the grounds for those who require extra space and privacy. Family rooms/suites are available, and a ground floor bedroom and one suite has been designed with particular attention to the comfort of those with disabilities. The varied menu is prepared with flair and imagination from local produce, complemented by a comprehensive, personally compiled wine list. Residents have free use of the nearby Low Wood Leisure Club with swimming pool, sauna, steam room, gym, Jacuzzi, squash courts, sunbeds and a health and beauty salon. Walking, sightseeing, cycling, sailing, horse-riding and fishing (permits available) can all be arranged. Alternatively, a day's cruise along Lake Windermere stopping at various points along the lake can be organised. Special interest holidays are offered, such as gardening, antiques, painting, bridge, photography, music and Lake District heritage. Small functions and conferences can be catered for.

Directions: ¼ mile from Ambleside on the A593 to Coniston. Closed 3rd January to 6th February.

Web: www.johansens.com/rothaymanor
E-mail: hotel@rothaymanor.co.uk
Tel: 0870 381 8869
International: +44 (0)15394 33605
Fax: 015394 33607

Price Guide:
single £76–£95
double/twin £124–£155
suite £165–£180

Our inspector loved: The delicious homemade cakes and biscuits served with afternoon tea and morning coffee.

THE SAMLING

AMBLESIDE ROAD, WINDERMERE, CUMBRIA LA23 1LR

Tucked away in 67 acres of woodlands and gardens on the northeastern shore of Lake Windermere, the Samling is a real gem and wonderfully relaxing. Secluded and private, with stunning views of the lake, guests will enjoy a unique getaway where attention to detail and excellent service provide a luxurious home from home experience. Beautifully decorated bedrooms retain their authentic rustic features, which are combined with stylish modern comforts, Turkish rugs and huge baths. Breakfast is in bed! Irresistibly delicious cuisine and splendid wines are served in the gracious dining room, which is light and airy. The cosy drawing room has comfortable sofas and a warm ambience, the perfect place for a drink by the fireside. Guests can admire a magnificent sunset from the outdoor hot tub. Horse riding, water skiing, hiking, sailing, paragliding, diving and canoeing is available for the adventurous whilst picnics on the hillside or 10-course banquets can be provided. There are first-class business facilities available. The Dutch Barn is available for wedding celebrations or conferences for up to 60 delegates.

Our inspector loved: Relaxing in the outdoor spa bath, with its stunning views over Lake Windermere.

Directions: Leave M6 at Jct36 and take A590/A591 past Windermere towards Ambleside. The Samling is up a long drive, 100 yards past the Low Wood Hotel.

Web: www.johansens.com/samling
E-mail: info@thesamling.com
Tel: 0870 381 8884
International: +44 (0)15394 31922
Fax: 015394 30400

Price Guide:
single £175–£375
double/twin £245–£445

Carlisle

Penrith

Windermere

Kendal

APPLEBY MANOR COUNTRY HOUSE HOTEL

ROMAN ROAD, APPLEBY-IN-WESTMORLAND, CUMBRIA CA16 6JB

Directions: From the south take junction 38 of the M6 and then the B6260 to Appleby (13 miles). Drive through the town to a T-junction, turn left, first right and follow road for ⅔ of a mile.

Web: www.johansens.com/applebymanor
E-mail: reception@applebymanor.co.uk
Tel: 0870 381 8317
International: +44 (0)17683 51571
Fax: 017683 52888

Price Guide:
single £77–£94
double/twin £114–£148

Surrounded by half a million acres of some of the most beautiful landscapes in England, sheltered by the mountains and fells of the Lake District, by the North Pennine Hills and Yorkshire Dales, in an area aptly known as Eden, stands Appleby Manor, a friendly and relaxing hotel owned and run by the Dunbobbin family. The high-quality, spotlessly clean bedrooms induce peaceful, undisturbed sleep. (Dogs are welcome in The Coach House accommodation). The public areas are also restfully comfortable – the inviting lounges nicely warmed by log fires on cooler days, the cocktail bar and sunny conservatory luring guests with a choice of more than 70 malt whiskies and the restaurant offering an imaginative selection of tasty dishes and fine wines. The hotel pool, sauna, steam room, Jacuzzi, solarium and games room keep indoor athletes happy. Locally there are outdoor sports: fishing, golf, riding, squash and for the more venturesome, rambling on the fells. Appleby is an ideal base from which to visit the Lake District and an attractive stopover on journeys north-south.

Our inspector loved: Relaxing in the conservatory looking at the views of the Eden Valley and the award-winning gardens.

TUFTON ARMS HOTEL

MARKET SQUARE, APPLEBY-IN-WESTMORLAND, CUMBRIA CA16 6XA

This distinguished Victorian coaching inn, owned and run by the Milsom family, has been refurbished to provide a high standard of comfort. The bedrooms evoke the style of the 19th century, when the Tufton Arms became one of the premier hotels in Victorian England. The kitchen is run under the auspices of David Milsom and Shaun Atkinson, who spoil guests for choice with a gourmet dinner menu as well as a grill menu, the restaurant being renowned for its fish dishes. Complementing the cuisine is an extensive wine list. There are conference and meeting rooms including the air-conditioned Hothfield Suite which can accommodate up to 100 people. Appleby, the historic county town of Westmorland, stands in splendid countryside and is ideal for touring the Lakes, Yorkshire Dales and Pennines. It is also a convenient stop-over en route to Scotland. Members of the Milsom family also run The Royal Hotel in Comrie. Superb fishing for wild brown trout on a 24-mile stretch of the main River Eden, salmon fishing can be arranged on the lower reaches of the river. Shooting parties for grouse, duck and pheasant are a speciality. Appleby has an 18-hole moorland golf course.

Our inspector loved: Being taken fishing by Nigel Milsom on the River Eden.

Directions: In centre of Appleby (bypassed by the A66), 38 miles west of Scotch Corner, 13 miles east of Penrith (M6 junction 40), 12 miles from M6 junction 38.

Web: www.johansens.com/tuftonarms
E-mail: info@tuftonarmshotel.co.uk
Tel: 0870 381 8956
International: +44 (0)17683 51593
Fax: 017683 52761

Price Guide:
single £67.50–£105
double/twin £95–£140
suite £155

FARLAM HALL HOTEL

BRAMPTON, CUMBRIA CA8 2NG

Directions: Farlam Hall is 2½ miles east of Brampton on the A689, not in Farlam village.

Web: www.johansens.com/farlamhall
E-mail: farlamhall@dial.pipex.com
Tel: 0870 381 8514
International: +44 (0)16977 46234
Fax: 016977 46683

Price Guide: (including dinner)
single £130–£145
double/twin £240–£270

Farlam Hall was opened in 1975 by the Quinion and Stevenson families who over the years have managed to achieve and maintain consistently high standards of food, service and comfort. These standards have been recognised and rewarded by all the major guides and membership of Relais et Châteaux. This old border house, dating in parts from the 17th century, is set in mature gardens, which can be seen from the elegant lounges and dining room, creating a relaxing and pleasing environment. The fine silver and crystal in the dining room complement the quality of the English country house cooking produced by Barry Quinion and his team of chefs. There are 12 individually decorated bedrooms varying in size and shape, some having Jacuzzi baths, one an antique four-poster bed and there are 2 ground floor bedrooms. This area offers many different attractions: miles of unspoilt countryside for walking, 8 golf courses within 30 minutes of the hotel, Hadrian's Wall, Lanercost Priory and Carlisle with its castle, cathedral and museum. The Lake District, Scottish Borders and Yorkshire Dales each make an ideal day's touring. Winter and spring breaks are offered. Closed Christmas.

Our inspector loved: *The Luxurious elegance of this borders hotel.*

NETHERWOOD HOTEL

LINDALE ROAD, GRANGE-OVER-SANDS, CUMBRIA LA11 6ET

This dramatic and stately residence was built as a family house in the 19th century, and still retains its family ambience in the careful hands of its long - standing owners, the Fallowfields. Impressive oak panelling is a key feature of the property and provides a marvellous backdrop to the public areas – the lounge, lounge bar and ballroom, where log fires roar in the winter months. All of the bedrooms have en-suite facilities, and many have been furnished to extremely high modern standards; all have picturesque views of the sea, woodland or gardens. The light and airy restaurant is housed in the conservatory area on the first floor of the property, maximising the dramatic views over Morecambe Bay. Here, a daily changing menu of freshly prepared specialities caters for a wide variety of tastes and is complemented by an extensive selection of fine wines. A stunning indoor swimming pool and fitness centre is a delightful haven and a keen favourite with families – the pool even has a playpen and toys for younger guests - whilst an extensive range of beauty treatments, massage and complementary therapies is available at "Equilibrium", the hotel's health spa.

Our inspector loved: *The oak panelling in the hall and lounge and the stunning views over Morecambe Bay.*

Directions: Take the M6, exit 36 then the A590 towards Barrow-in-Burness. Then the B5277 into Grange-Over-Sands. The hotel is on the right before the town.

Web: www.johansens.com/netherwood
E-mail: Blawith@aol.com
Tel: 0870 381 8729
International: +44 (0)15395 32552
Fax: 015395 34121

Carlisle

Penrith

Windermere

Kendal

Price Guide:
single £80
double £120-£160

       SPA

THE DERWENTWATER HOTEL

PORTINSCALE, KESWICK, CUMBRIA CA12 5RE

Built as a doctor's summer residence in 1837, this handsome lakeside hotel lies amidst 16 acres of gardens and watermeadow, dedicated to the preservation of local wildlife. For a number of years the hotel's owners have worked alongside English Nature to create a safe and natural haven for hundreds of creatures. Guests can sit in the comfortable conservatory and watch red squirrels, mallards, hedgehogs and pheasants, while a wander down to the lake may reveal sightings of water fowl, frogs, and even a family of timid roe deer. The Derwentwater has a unique style, each bedroom is individually furnished, and most enjoy views over the lake or the mountains beyond. Local produce is used in the wide variety of dishes served in The Deer's Leap restaurant. The hotel is immensely proud of its excellent reputation for quality of staff and high standards of hospitality. The surrounding area lends itself to numerous activities, from walking and cycling, to fishing, trips on the lake and golf. Adult guests have complimentary use of nearby health spa.

Directions: Take the M6, exit at junction 40. Take the A66 westwards, bypass Keswick, after about a mile turn left into Portinscale, then follow signs to hotel.

Web: www.johansens.com/derwentwater
E-mail: info@derwentwater–hotel.co.uk
Tel: 0870 381 8479
International: +44 (0)17687 72538
Fax: 017687 71002

Price Guide:
single £80–£120
double/twin £130–£190
suite £160

Our inspector loved: The gardens and wildlife wetlands leading down to the lake.

ARMATHWAITE HALL HOTEL

BASSENTHWAITE LAKE, KESWICK, CUMBRIA CA12 4RE

With an awe-inspiring backdrop of Skiddaw Mountain and the surrounding Lakeland fells, on the shores of Bassenthwaite Lake, the romantic Armathwaite Hall is the perfect location for lovers of boating, walking and climbing. Amidst 400 acres of deer park and woodland, this 4-star country house is a tranquil hideaway for those wishing to relax and escape from modern day living, where comfort is intensified by an emphasis on quality and old-fashioned hospitality, as you would expect of a family-owned and run hotel. The timeless elegance of this stately home is complemented by original features such as wood panelling, magnificent stonework, artworks and antiques. Beautiful bedrooms are decorated in a warm, traditional style and guests can arrange to have champagne, chocolates and flowers on their arrival. The Rosette restaurant offers exceptional cuisine created by Masterchef Kevin Dowling, who uses the finest local seasonal produce. In the Spa there is a gym, indoor swimming pool and a holistic Beauty Salon. Clay pigeon shooting, quad bike safaris, falconry, mountain biking, tennis and croquet are all available, with sailing, fishing and golf nearby. Family friendly with a programme of activities for children and the attraction of Trotters World of Animals on the estate, home to many traditional favourites and endangered species.

Our inspector loved: The spectacular views over Bassenthwaite Lake.

Directions: Take the M6 to Penrith. At J40 take the A66 to Keswick roundabout then the A591 towards Carlisle. Go 8 miles to Castle Inn junction, turn left and Armanthwaite Hall is 300 yards ahead.

Carlisle

Penrith

Windermere

Kendal

Web: www.johansens.com/armathwaite
E-mail: reservations@armathwaite-hall.com
Tel: 0870 381 8478
International: +44 (0)17687 76551
Fax: 017687 76220

Price Guide:
single £70–£155
double/twin£140–£300

THE BORROWDALE GATES COUNTRY HOUSE HOTEL

GRANGE-IN-BORROWDALE, KESWICK, CUMBRIA CA12 5UQ

Directions: M6 junction 40 A66 into Keswick. B5289 to Borrowdale. After 4 miles right into Grange over double hump back bridge.

Web: www.johansens.com/borrowdalegates
E-mail: hotel@borrowdale-gates.com
Tel: 0870 381 8375
International: +44 (0)17687 77204
Fax: 017687 77254

Price Guide: (Including dinner)
single £70–£98
double/twin £120–£180

Built in 1860, Borrowdale Gates, owned and personally run by Carol and Colin Slaney, is surrounded on all sides by the rugged charm of the Lake District National Park. It affords a panoramic vista of the Borrowdale Valley and glorious fells and nestles in 2 acres of wooded gardens on the edge of the ancient hamlet of Grange, close to the shores of Derwentwater. Tastefully decorated bedrooms offer every modern comfort and most command picturesque views of the surrounding scenery. The comfortable lounges and bar, decorated with fine antiques and warmed by glowing log fires in cooler months, create the perfect setting in which to enjoy a drink and forget the bustle of everyday life. Fine food is served in the restaurant, with menus offering a wide and imaginative selection of dishes. The cuisine is complemented by a thoughtfully chosen wine list and excellent service. It is a haven of peace and tranquillity and is ideally located for walking, climbing and touring. There are also many places of literary and historic interest within easy reach, for example Wordsworth's birthplace in Cockermouth. The hotel is closed in January. Special breaks available.

Our inspector loved: The beautiful setting in the Borrowdale Valley.

SHARROW BAY COUNTRY HOUSE HOTEL

HOWTOWN, LAKE ULLSWATER, PENRITH, CUMBRIA CA10 2LZ

Now in its 56th year, Sharrow Bay is known to discerning travellers the world over, who return again and again to this magnificent lakeside hotel. It wasn't always so. The late Francis Coulson arrived in 1948, he was joined by the late Brian Sack in 1952 and the partnership flourished, to make Sharrow Bay what it is today. Nigel Lightburn and his staff are carrying on the tradition of Sharrow. All the bedrooms are elegantly furnished and guests are guaranteed the utmost comfort. In addition to the main hotel, there are 4 cottages nearby which offer similarly luxurious accommodation. All the reception rooms are delightfully decorated. Sharrow Bay is universally renowned for its wonderful cuisine. The team of chefs, led by Johnnie Martin and Colin Akrigg, ensure that each meal is a special occasion, a mouth-watering adventure! With its private jetty and 12-acres of lakeside gardens Sharrow Bay offers guests boating, swimming and fishing. Fell-walking is a challenge for the upwardly mobile. Sharrow Bay is the oldest British member of Relais et Châteaux. Closed in December, January and February.

Our inspector loved: The dining experience in the newly refurbished Lakeside restaurant.

Directions: Take the M6, junction 40, A592 to Lake Ullswater, into Pooley Bridge, then take Howtown road for 2 miles.

Web: www.johansens.com/sharrowbaycountryhouse
E-mail: enquiries@sharrow–bay.com
Tel: 0870 381 8891
International: +44 (0)17684 86301/86483
Fax: 017684 86349

Price Guide: (including 6-course dinner and full English breakfast)
single £145–£250
double/twin £300–£400
suites from £420

THE INN ON THE LAKE

LAKE ULLSWATER, GLENRIDDING, CUMBRIA CA11 0PE

With its 15 acres of grounds and lawns sweeping down to the shore of Lake Ullswater, The Inn on the Lake truly boasts one of the most spectacular settings in the Lake District. Recently bought and refurbished by the Graves family, it now offers a wide range of excellent facilities as well as stunning views of the surrounding scenery. Downstairs, comfortable lounges provide a calm environment in which to relax with a drink, whilst dinner can be enjoyed in the Lake View restaurant. Most of the 46 en-suite bedrooms look across to the Lake or the fells and 5 lake view four-poster rooms add an extra touch of luxury. The hotel welcomes wedding ceremonies and receptions and is happy to provide a full private function service as well as conference facilities for up to 120 business delegates. The list of nearby leisure activities for children and adults alike is endless; rock climbing, pony trekking, canoeing, windsurfing, sailing and fishing are all available. Trips around the Lake can be taken aboard the Ullswater steamers and many of the most stunning Lake District walks begin in this area.

Directions: Leave the M6 at junction 40, then take the A66 west. At the first roundabout, by Rheged Discovery Centre, head towards Pooley Bridge then follow the shoreline of Lake Ullswater to Glenridding.

Web: www.johansens.com/innonthelake
E-mail: info@innonthelakeullswater.co.uk
Tel: 0870 381 8640
International: +44 (0)17684 82444
Fax: 017684 82303

Price Guide:
single £59–£140
double/twin £96–£150

Carlisle

Penrith
Windermere

Kendal

Our inspector loved: Strolling across the lawned garden down to Lake Ullswater.

RAMPSBECK COUNTRY HOUSE HOTEL

WATERMILLOCK, LAKE ULLSWATER, NR PENRITH, CUMBRIA CA11 0LP

A beautifully situated hotel, Rampsbeck Country House stands in 18 acres of landscaped gardens and meadows leading to the shores of Lake Ullswater. Built in 1714, it first became a hotel in 1947, before the present owners acquired it in 1983. Thomas and Marion Gibb, with the help of Marion's mother, Marguerite MacDowall, completely refurbished Rampsbeck with the aim of maintaining its character and adding only to its comfort. Most of the well-appointed bedrooms have lake and garden views. Three have a private balcony and the suite overlooks the lake. In the elegant drawing room, a log fire burns and French windows lead to the garden. Guests and non-residents are welcome to dine in the intimate candle-lit restaurant. Imaginative menus offer a choice of delicious dishes, carefully prepared by Master Chef Andrew McGeorge and his team. A good bar lunch menu offers light snacks as well as hot food. Guests can stroll through the gardens, play croquet or fish from the lake shore, around which there are designated walks. Lake steamer trips, riding, golf, sailing, wind-surfing and fell-walking are available nearby. Closed January to mid-February. Dogs by arrangement only.

Our inspector loved: The wonderful views of Lake Ullswater and the beautiful landscaped gardens.

Directions: Leave M6 at junction 40, take A592 to Ullswater. At T-junction at lake turn right; hotel is 1½ miles on left.

Web: www.johansens.com/rampsbeckcountryhouse
E-mail: enquiries@rampsbeck.fsnet.co.uk
Tel: 0870 381 8848
International: +44 (0)17684 86442
Fax: 017684 86688

Carlisle

Penrith

Windermere

Kendal

Price Guide:
single £60–£120
double/twin £100–£215
suite £215

GILPIN LODGE

CROOK ROAD, NEAR WINDERMERE, CUMBRIA LA23 3NE

Directions: M6 exit 36. A591 Kendal bypass then B5284 to Crook.

Web: www.johansens.com/gilpinlodge
E-mail: hotel@gilpinlodge.com
Tel: 0870 381 8546
International: +44 (0)15394 88818
Fax: 015394 88058

Price Guide: (including 5 course dinner)
single £150
double/twin £200–£280

Carlisle

Penrith

Windermere

Kendal

Gilpin Lodge is a friendly, elegant, relaxing country house hotel set in 20 acres of woodlands, moors and country gardens 2 miles from Lake Windermere, yet just 12 miles from the M6. The original building, tastefully extended and modernised, dates from 1901. A profusion of flower arrangements, picture-lined walls, antique furniture and log fires in winter are all part of the Cunliffe families perception of hospitality. The 14 sumptuous bedrooms all have en-suite bathrooms and every comfort. Some have four-poster beds, split levels and whirlpool baths. The exquisite food, created by a team of 7 chefs, earns 3 rosettes from the AA. The award winning wine list contains 175 labels from 13 different countries. The beautiful gardens are the perfect place in which to muse while savouring the lovely lake-land scenery. Windermere golf course is $\frac{1}{2}$ a mile away. There is almost every kind of outdoor activity imaginable. Guests have free use of a nearby private leisure club. This is Wordsworth and Beatrix Potter country and nearby there are several stately homes, gardens and castles. English Tourist Board Gold award, AA 3 Red Stars, AA's Top 10 Small Hotels and Top 10 Country Retreats for 2003, RAC Gold Ribbon award and Johansens Most Excellent Service Award 1998. A Pride of Britain Hotel. Special breaks available.

Our inspector loved: The relaxing ambience, superb service and the new garden room.

LANGDALE CHASE

WINDERMERE, CUMBRIA LA23 1LW

Langdale Chase stands in 5 acres of landscaped gardens on the shores of Lake Windermere, with panoramic views over England's largest lake to the Langdale Pikes beyond. Visitors will receive warm-hearted hospitality in this Lakeside hotel, which is splendidly decorated with oak panelling, fine oil paintings and ornate, carved fireplaces. A magnificent staircase leads to the well-appointed bedrooms, many overlooking the lake. One unique bedroom is sited over the lakeside boathouse, where the traveller may be lulled to sleep by the gently lapping waters below. The facilities also include a private boat mooring which is available on request. For the energetic, there is a choice of water-skiing, swimming or sailing from the hotel jetty. Guests can stroll through the gardens along the lake shore; in May the gardens are spectacular when the rhododendrons and azaleas are in bloom. Being pampered by attentive staff will be one of the many highlights of your stay at Langdale Chase. The variety of food and wine is sure to delight the most discerning diner. Combine this with a panoramic tableau across England's largest and loveliest of lakes and you have a truly unforgettable dining experience.

Our inspector loved: The views over Lake Windermere.

Directions: Situated on the A591, 3 miles north of Windermere, 2 miles south of Ambleside.

Web: www.johansens.com/langdalechase
E-mail: sales@langdalechase.co.uk
Tel: 0870 381 8677
International: +44 (0)15394 32201
Fax: 015394 32604

Price Guide:
single £80–£150
double/twin £100–£175
suite £200

MILLER HOWE HOTEL & RESTAURANT

RAYRIGG ROAD, WINDERMERE, CUMBRIA LA23 1EY

Directions: From the M6 junction 36 follow the A591 through Windermere, then turn left onto the A592 towards Bowness. Miller Howe is ½ mile on the right.

Web: www.johansens.com/millerhowe
E-mail: lakeview@millerhowe.com
Tel: 0870 381 8738
International: +44 (0)15394 42536
Fax: 015394 45664

Price Guide: (including 5-course dinner)
single £95–£185
double/twin £140–£310
cottage suites £240–£360

One of the finest views in the entire Lake District can be enjoyed from the restaurant, conservatory and terrace of this lovely hotel, which stands high on the shores of Lake Windermere. Lawned gardens bedded with mature shrubs, trees and borders of colour sweep down to the water's edge. It is a spectacular scene. Visitors receive warm hospitality from this well-run and splendidly decorated hotel owned by Charles Garside, the former Editor-in-Chief of the international newspaper "The European". All the bedrooms are furnished in a luxurious style; the majority have views over the lake to the mountains beyond. There are 3 luxury cottage suites which feature every modern amenity amongst the antiques. Chef Paul Webster's imaginative menus will delight the most discerning guest, whilst the panoramic tableau across England's largest lake as the sun sets, presents an unforgettable dining experience. Guests can enjoy a range of water sports or boat trips on Lake Windermere and there are many interesting fell walks close by.

Our inspector loved: *The luxurious new suites in the cottage and the spectacular views over Lake Windermere.*

Storrs Hall

LAKE WINDERMERE, CUMBRIA LA23 3LG

From this magnificent listed Georgian manor house not another building can be seen, just a spectacular, seemingly endless view over beautiful Lake Windermere. Built in the 18th century for a Lancashire shipping magnate, Storrs Hall stands majestically in an unrivalled peninsular position surrounded by 17 acres of landscaped, wooded grounds which slope down to half a mile of lakeside frontage. Apart from Wordsworth, who first recited "Daffodils" in the Drawing Room at Storrs, the hotel was frequented by all the great Lakeland poets and Beatrix Potter. The manor house re-opened as a hotel in 1996, when it was rescued from decay and restored to its former glory. Furnished with antiques and objets d'art including a private collection of ship models, it reflects the maritime fortunes which built it. Now part of the English Lakes Hotels group the Hall has 30 beautifully furnished bedrooms, each en suite, spacious and with every comfort. Most of the rooms have views over the lake, and equally splendid views are enjoyed from an exquisite lounge, study and cosy bar. The Terrace Restaurant is renowned for the superb cuisine prepared by head chef Michael Dodd. Guests receive complimentary use of leisure club facilities at sister hotel, Lowwood, just 3 miles away. Special breaks available.

Directions: On A592 2 miles south of Bowness and 5 miles north of Newby Bridge.

Web: www.johansens.com/storrshall
E-mail: storrshall@elhmail.co.uk
Tel: 0870 381 8919
International: +44 (0)15394 47111
Fax: 015394 47555

Price Guide:
single £125
double/twin £150–£295

Our inspector loved: Strolling in the gardens on the shore of Lake Windermere.

LINTHWAITE HOUSE HOTEL

CROOK ROAD, BOWNESS-ON-WINDERMERE, CUMBRIA LA23 3JA

Directions: From the M6, junction 36 follow Kendal by-pass for 8 miles. Take the B5284, Crook Road, for 6 miles. 1 mile beyond Windermere Golf Club, Linthwaite House is signposted on the left.

Web: www.johansens.com/linthwaitehouse
E-mail: admin@linthwaite.com
Tel: 0870 381 8694
International: +44 (0)15394 88600
Fax: 015394 88601

Price Guide:
single £99–£140
double/twin £109–£240
suite £266–£315

Situated in 14 acres of gardens and woods in the heart of the Lake District, Linthwaite House overlooks Lake Windermere and Belle Isle, with Claife Heights and Coniston Old Man beyond. Here guests will find themselves amid spectacular scenery, yet only a short drive from the motorway network. The hotel combines stylish originality with the best of traditional English hospitality. Superbly decorated en-suite bedrooms, most of which have lake or garden views. The comfortable lounge is the perfect place to unwind and there is a fire on winter evenings. In the restaurant excellent cuisine features the best of fresh, local produce, accompanied by a fine selection of wines. Within the hotel grounds, there is a 9-hole putting green and a par-3 practice hole. Fly fishermen can fish for brown trout in the hotel tarn. Guests have complimentary use of a private swimming pool and leisure club nearby, while fell walks begin at the hotel's front door. The area around Linthwaite abounds with places of interest: this is Beatrix Potter and Wordsworth country, and there is much to interest the visitor.

Our inspector loved: *Walking through the landscaped gardens up to the tarn with its spectacular views of Lake Windermere.*

LAKESIDE HOTEL ON LAKE WINDERMERE

LAKESIDE, NEWBY BRIDGE, CUMBRIA LA12 8AT

Lakeside Hotel offers you a unique location on the water's edge of Lake Windermere. It is a classic, traditional Lakeland hotel offering 4-star facilities and service. All the bedrooms are en suite and enjoy individually designed fabrics and colours, many of the rooms offer breathtaking views of the lake. Guests may dine in either the award-winning Lakeview Restaurant or Ruskin's Brasserie, where extensive menus offer a wide selection of dishes including Cumbrian specialities. The Lakeside Conservatory serves drinks and light meals throughout the day – once there you are sure to fall under the spell of this peaceful location. Berthed next to the hotel there are cruisers which will enable you to explore the lake from the water. To enhance your stay, there is a leisure club including a 17m indoor pool, gymnasium, sauna, steam room and health and beauty suites. The hotel offers a fully equipped conference centre and many syndicate suites allowing plenty of scope and flexibility. Most of all you are assured of a stay in an unrivalled setting of genuine character. The original panelling and beams of the old coaching inn create an excellent ambience, whilst you are certain to enjoy the quality and friendly service. Special breaks available.

Our inspector loved: Enjoying a delicious afternoon tea in the Lakeside conservatory watching the boats sail by.

Directions: From M6 junction 36 join A590 to Newby Bridge, turn right over bridge towards Hawkshead; hotel is one mile on right.

Web: www.johansens.com/lakeside
E-mail: sales@lakesidehotel.co.uk
Tel: 0870 381 8672
International: +44 (0)1539 530001
Fax: 015395 31699

Price Guide:
single from £120
double/twin £160–£230
suites from £240

85

CALLOW HALL

MAPPLETON ROAD, ASHBOURNE, DERBYSHIRE DE6 2AA

Directions: Take the A515 through Ashbourne towards Buxton. At the Bowling Green Inn on the brow of a steep hill, turn left, then take the first right, signposted Mappleton and the hotel is over the bridge on the right.

Web: www.johansens.com/callowhall
E-mail: stay@callowhall.co.uk
Tel: 0870 381 8400
International: +44 (0)1335 300900
Fax: 01335 300512

Price Guide:
single £85–£110
double/twin £130–£165
suite £190

The approach to Callow Hall is up a tree-lined drive through the 44-acre grounds. On arrival visitors can take in the splendid views from the hotel's elevated position, overlooking the valleys of Bentley Brook and the River Dove. The majestic building and Victorian gardens have been restored by resident proprietors, David, Dorothy, son Anthony and daughter, Emma Spencer, who represent the fifth and sixth generations of hoteliers in the Spencer family. The famous local Ashbourne mineral water and homemade biscuits greet guests in the spacious period bedrooms. Fresh local produce is selected daily for use in the kitchen, where the term "homemade" comes into its own. Home-cured bacon, sausages, fresh bread, traditional English puddings and melt-in-the-mouth pastries are among the items prepared on the premises, which can be enjoyed by non-residents. Visiting anglers can enjoy a rare opportunity to fish for trout and grayling along a mile-long private stretch of the Bentley Brook, which is mentioned in Izaak Walton's "The Compleat Angle"r. Callow Hall is ideally located for some of England's finest stately homes. Closed at Christmas. East Midlands Airport is 35 minutes away.

Our inspector loved: The chocolate dessert, just exquisite - to die for.

THE IZAAK WALTON HOTEL

DOVEDALE, NEAR ASHBOURNE, DERBYSHIRE DE6 2AY

This converted 17th-century farmhouse hotel, named after the renowned author of "The Compleat Angler", enjoys glorious views of the surrounding Derbyshire Peaks. The River Dove runs in the valley below. The Izaak Walton is ideal for guests wishing to indulge in a warm welcome and a relaxing ambience. The 36 en-suite bedrooms are diverse in their designs; some have four-poster beds whilst others are located in the old farmhouse building and still retain their old oak beams and décor. The Haddon Restaurant, with an AA Rosette, has a diverse menu of creative yet traditional cuisine. Informal meals and light snacks can be enjoyed in the Dovedale Bar. The hotel is ideal for family parties, out of the way meetings and conferences. Leisure pursuits include rambling, fishing (the hotel has 4 rods on the River Dove and private tuition is available), mountain biking and hand-gliding. Places of interest nearby include the Peak District, Alton Towers, the Staffordshire Potteries and fine country properties such as Chatsworth House and Haddon Hall.

Our inspector loved: *Looking out of the windows and being mesmerised by the views.*

Directions: Dovedale is 2 miles north-west of Ashbourne between A515 and A52.

Web: www.johansens.com/izaakwalton
E-mail: reception@izaakwaltonhotel.com
Tel: 0870 381 8642
International: +44 (0)1335 350555
Fax: 01335 350539

Price Guide:
single £89-£105
double/twin £115–£176

87

RIVERSIDE HOUSE

ASHFORD-IN-THE-WATER, NR BAKEWELL, DERBYSHIRE DE45 1QF

This graceful Georgian mansion nestles peacefully on the banks of the river Wye in one of the Peak District's most picturesque villages. It is an intimate gem of a country hotel, a tranquil rural retreat in the finest traditions of classic hospitality and friendliness. Small and ivy-clad, Riverside House sits majestically in the heart of secluded grounds that feature exquisite landscaped gardens and lawns. Elegance, style, intimacy and informality abound within its interior. Individually designed en suite bedrooms have their own distinctive character and are comfortably and delightfully furnished with rich fabrics and antique pieces. An atmosphere of complete relaxation is the hallmark of the welcoming public rooms whose large windows offer superb views. Guests can enjoy a distinctive fusion of modern English, International and local cuisine in the excellent and charming 2 AA Rosette awarded restaurant where service is of the highest quality. As well as being conveniently situated to explore the glories of the Peak District, Chatsworth House and Haddon Hall, the hotel is also an ideal base for guests wishing to visit the Derbyshire Dales, Lathkill and Dovedale.

Directions: Exit M1 at junction 29. Take A617 to Chesterfield, then A619 to Bakewell, then take A6 to Ashford-in-the-Water. Riverside House is at the end of the villge main street next to the Sheepwash Bridge.

Web: www.johansens.com/riversidehouse
E-mail: riversidehouse@enta.net
Tel: 0870 381 8860
International: +44 (0)1629 814275
Fax: 01629 812873

Price Guide:
single £85–£125
double/twin £115–£150

Our inspector loved: The care and enthusiasm given to generate a relaxed and pampered stay.

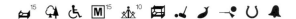

HASSOP HALL

HASSOP, NR BAKEWELL, DERBYSHIRE DE45 1NS

The recorded history of Hassop Hall reaches back 900 years to the Domesday Book, to a time when the political scene in England was still dominated by the power struggle between the barons and the King, when the only sure access to that power was through possession of land. By 1643, when the Civil War was raging, the Hall was under the ownership of Rowland Eyre, who turned it into a Royalist garrison. It was the scene of several skirmishes before it was recaptured after the Parliamentary victory. Since purchasing Hassop Hall in 1975, Thomas Chapman has determinedly pursued the preservation of its outstanding heritage. Guests can enjoy the beautifully maintained gardens as well as the splendid countryside of the surrounding area. The bedrooms, some of which are particularly spacious, are well furnished and comfortable. A four-poster bedroom is available for romantic occasions. A comprehensive dinner menu offers a wide and varied selection of dishes, with catering for most tastes. As well as the glories of the Peak District, places to visit include Chatsworth House, Haddon Hall and Buxton Opera House. Christmas opening – details on application. Inclusive rates available on request.

Our inspector loved: The historic garden now being developed and including 20,000 box cuttings!

Directions: From M1 exit 29 (Chesterfield), take A619 to Baslow, then A623 to Calver; left at lights to B6001 Hassop Hall is 2 miles on right.

Web: www.johansens.com/hassophall
E-mail: info@hassophallhotel.co.uk
Tel: 0870 381 8586
International: +44 (0)1629 640488
Fax: 01629 640577

Price Guide: (excluding breakfast)
double/twin £79–£149

EAST LODGE COUNTRY HOUSE HOTEL

ROWSLEY, NR MATLOCK, DERBYSHIRE DE4 2EF

Directions: Set back from the A6 in Rowsley village, 3 miles from Bakewell. The hotel entrance is adjacent to the B6012 junction to Sheffield/Chatsworth.

Web: www.johansens.com/eastlodgecountryhouse
E-mail: info@eastlodge.com
Tel: 0870 381 8496
International: +44 (0)1629 734474
Fax: 01629 733949

Price Guide:
single £80
double/twin from £100

This graceful 17th-century lodge on the edge of the Peak District was originally built as the East Lodge to Haddon Hall, the Derbyshire seat of the Duke of Rutland. Converted to a hotel in the 1980s, East Lodge is now owned and run by Joan and David Hardman and their attentive staff. The lodge has won many accolades including AA 3 star 77%. The attractive conservatory, charming restaurant and spacious hall offers high levels of comfort combined with a warm and relaxed atmosphere. The 14 en-suite bedrooms are tastefully furnished, each having its own distinctive character. Imaginative lunches and dinners are served daily in the excellent AA Rosetted restaurant with lighter meals available in the conservatory. A wide selection of fine wines is on offer. Set in 10 acres of attractive gardens and surrounded by rolling Derbyshire countryside, East Lodge provides a tranquil setting for relaxing breaks, conferences and corporate activity/team building events. The nearby Peak District National Park, boasts some of the country's most spectacular walks. The famous stately homes, Chatsworth House and Haddon Hall, are within 2 miles. Bakewell, Buxton, Matlock and Crich are a short drive away.

Our inspector loved: *The feeling of calm, its vibes generating such a feeling of wellbeing. A real retreat.*

CAVENDISH HOTEL

BASLOW, DERBYSHIRE DE45 1SP

This enchanting hotel offers travellers an opportunity to stay on the famous Chatsworth Estate, close to one of England's greatest stately houses, the home of the Duke and Duchess of Devonshire. The hotel has a long history of its own – once known as the Peacock Inn on the turnpike road to Buxton Spa. When it became The Cavendish in 1975, the Duchess personally supervised the transformation, providing some of the furnishings from Chatsworth, and her design talents are evident throughout. Guests receive a warm welcome before they are led to the luxurious bedrooms, all of which overlook the Estate. Harmonious colours, gorgeous fabrics and immense comfort prevail. Every imaginable extra is provided, from library books to bathrobes. Breakfast is served until lunchtime – no rising at cockcrow – and informal meals are served from morning until bed-time in The Garden Room. Sit at the kitchen table and watch super food being prepared as you dine. At dusk you can sample cocktails and fine wines in the bar before dining in the handsome restaurant with its imaginative menu and extensive list of carefully selected wines. Climbing The Peak, exploring The Dales, fishing, golf and Sheffield's Crucible Theatre are among the many leisure pursuits nearby.

Our inspector loved: The thrill of hearing a contented couple paying their bill after a pleasurable stay.

Directions: Take the M1, junction 29, A617 to Chesterfield then A619 west to Baslow.

Web: www.johansens.com/cavendish
E-mail: info@cavendish–hotel.net
Tel: 0870 381 8412
International: +44 (0)1246 582311
Fax: 01246 582312

Price Guide: (excluding breakfast)
single from £100
double/twin from £130

FISCHER'S

BASLOW HALL, CALVER ROAD, BASLOW, DERBYSHIRE DE45 1RR

Situated on the edge of the magnificent Chatsworth Estate, Baslow Hall enjoys an enviable location surrounded by some of the country's finest stately homes and within easy reach of the Peak District's many cultural and historical attractions. Standing at the end of a winding chestnut tree-lined driveway, this fine Derbyshire manor house was tastefully converted by Max and Susan Fischer into an award-winning country house hotel in 1989. Since opening, Fischer's has consistently maintained its position as one of the finest establishments in the Derbyshire/South Yorkshire regions earning the prestigious Johansens Most Excellent UK Restaurant award in 2001. Whether staying in the area for private or business reasons, it is a welcome change to find a place that feels less like a hotel and more like a home, combining comfort and character with an eating experience which is a delight to the palate. Max presides in the kitchen, which offers exciting Michelin-starred gourmet menus and prestigious "tasting" menus alongside superb value for money lunches and the less formal Max's table d'hôte menu. Baslow Hall has facilities to cater for small conferences or private functions.

Directions: Baslow is within 12 miles of the M1 motorway, Chesterfield and Sheffield. Fischer's is on the A623 in Baslow.

Web: www.johansens.com/fischers
E-mail: m.s@fischers–baslowhall.co.uk
Tel: 0870 381 8523
International: +44 (0)1246 583259
Fax: 01246 583818

Price Guide:
single £100-£120
double/twin £120–£180
suite £150

Our inspector loved: The wonderful range of menus; from the superbly simple to purely exciting. Quite special.

RINGWOOD HALL HOTEL

RINGWOOD ROAD, BRIMINGTON, CHESTERFIELD, DERBYSHIRE S43 1DQ

Since its purchase by Lyric Hotels in November 1999, the Ringwood Hall Hotel has undergone major refurbishment. Sensitive and tasteful, the transformation has created one of the finest country house hotels in North East Derbyshire. The charm and character of the Grade II exterior is continued inside with an impressive reception area featuring intricate plaster frieze work, a galleried landing and glazed dome ceiling. 29 acres of gardens and parkland provide a magnificent backdrop, and even the original Victorian gardens are being carefully restored and replanted to provide vegetables and herbs for the hotel kitchen. Finest local produce is used for the extensive menus in the Expressions Restaurant. The hotel offers numerous conference packages and provides a wonderful setting for wedding receptions and civil ceremonies. Staff are on hand to assist in planning events. Ringwood Hall sits on the brink of the Peak District, and offers plenty of opportunities to explore the surrounding area. Families can enjoy trips to theme parks such as Alton Towers and The Wind in the Willows Exhibition, whilst those with an interest in history can soak up the past at the Chesterfield Museum, Hardwick Hall and Bolsover Castle. An impressive array of local events such as the Chatsworth Country Fair take place through the year. An exclusive health and fitness club opened in 2003.

Our inspector loved: The variety of possibilities available at this hotel.

Directions: From Jct 30 M1 take the A619 towards Chesterfield, passing through Mastin Moor and Staveley. Continue on A619 and rising out of the valley the hotel is set back on the left.

Sheffield
Glossop
Chesterfield
Bakewell
Nottingham
Derby

Web: www.johansens.com/ringwood
E-mail: ringwood-hall-reception@lyrichotels.co.uk
Tel: 0870 381 8857
International: +44 (0)1246 280077
Fax: 01246 472241

Price Guide:
single from £70
double/twin from £80
suite from £108

RISLEY HALL

DERBY ROAD, RISLEY, DERBYSHIRE DE72 3SS

Directions: The nearest motorway is the M1. Exit at junction 25 towards Sandiacre.

Web: www.johansens.com/risleyhall
E-mail: johansens@risleyhallhotel.co.uk
Tel: 0870 381 8859
International: +44 (0)115 939 9000
Fax: 0115 939 7766

Price Guide:
single £105–£125
double/twin £125–£145
suites £150–£195

Situated equal distance between Derby and Nottingham in a quiet location and close to East Midlands airport, the former glory of Risley Hall is evident once more as this Country House Hotel has recently undergone a careful and extensive restoration. A Grade II listed building, Risley Hall is an ideal retreat for those seeking a peaceful atmosphere. The beautiful gardens were laid out in Elizabethan times and are quite spectacular with colourful floral arrangements and an old moat. Inside, the décor is rather charming with comfortable furnishings, oak beams and ornate fireplaces. The bedrooms, individually designed and all tastefully decorated in period style, offer every modern amenity including a television, hairdryer and tea/coffee making facilities. 20 new suites boast separate lounge areas with wide-screen televisions and DVD players, mini-bars and ISDN lines. Guests recline in the cosy Drawing Room with their afternoon tea or enjoy an after-dinner coffee, whilst the Cocktail Bar serves lunchtime drinks or pre-dinner apéritifs. Risley Hall has the perfect surroundings for corporate meetings or any special occasion. The area is surrounded by historic buildings such as Chatsworth House, Nottingham Castle and Kedleston Hall and is also known for its literary connections with Lord Byron and DH Lawrence.

Our inspector loved: *The quiet environment and attention to detail offered. So near to excellent air, rail and road links. "A little oasis."*

THE GEORGE AT HATHERSAGE

MAIN ROAD, HATHERSAGE, DERBYSHIRE S32 1BB

The George dates back to the end of the Middle Ages, when it was an alehouse serving the packhorse road; it later became well-known to Charlotte Brontë and features anonymously in Jane Eyre. Today, awarded 2 AA Rosettes, it has evolved into a modern 21st-century hotel whilst retaining the value of traditional hospitality. The team of professional, senior personnel, recently awarded the RAC Sponsored Housekeeping Award, guarantee guests a warm welcome and excellent personal service in a relaxed, comfortable environment. Great care has been taken to preserve the character of the old inn and the stone walls, oak beams, open fires and antique furniture all remain. The simple and pleasant bedrooms offer every modern amenity, including power showers and luxuriously enveloping bath sheets. Guests may enjoy an apéritif in the cosy bar before moving on to the brasserie-style restaurant. The regularly changing menu is created by head chef, Ben Handley, whose 2 RAC Dining Awarded restaurant also serves light snacks and lunches. Chatsworth and Haddon Halls, Buxton and Bakewell are nearby. The area provides some of the most picturesque countryside for walking, including Stanage Ridge (overlooking the Derwent Reservoirs) and Hope Valley. The Cavendish at Baslow is its sister hotel.

Our inspector loved: The fact that Charlotte Brontë could actually have placed one foot in The George and one foot in The Cavendish at Baslow.

Directions: From the M1, junction 29 take the A617 to Baslow, then the A623 and B6001 to Hathersage. The George is in the main street of the village.

Web: www.johansens.com/georgehathersage
E-mail: info@george-hotel.net
Tel: 0870 381 8538
International: +44 (0)1433 650436
Fax: 01433 650099

Price Guide:
single £75–£105
double/twin £100–£150

RIBER HALL

MATLOCK, DERBYSHIRE DE4 5JU

Directions: 20 minutes from junction 28 of the M1, off the A615 at Tansley; 1 mile further to Riber.

Web: www.johansens.com/riberhall
E-mail: info@riber-hall.co.uk
Tel: 0870 381 8854
International: +44 (0)1629 582795
Fax: 01629 580475

Price Guide:
single £95–£105
double/twin £123–£165

There could be few more picturesque settings than this stately Elizabethan manor house standing in its own walled garden at the foothills of the Pennine range. Views over the Peak National Park are outstanding and the atmosphere is one of total tranquillity. Privately owned and managed by the same family for 30 years the latest round of awards stands testament to their skill and high standards of service. The 14 spacious bedrooms are each furnished with period antiques and elegant beds, the majority of which are four-poster. The log fires and oak beams of the lounge convey an instant sense of intimacy and timelessness. The restaurant is renowned for its attentive service, game (when in season) and inspired French classical and modern English cuisine. The excellent wine list has also been rated AA Wine Award Finalist in the Top 25 in the UK for the third consecutive year. This is the perfect setting for both weddings and conferences and there is much to see in the surrounding area for conference delegate or wedding guest with time to spare. Chatsworth House, Haddon Hall and many world heritage sites are within easy reach. The beautiful Peak District scenery is breathtaking. East Midlands, Sheffield and Birmingham Airports are all nearby.

Our inspector loved: The wine list; do ask to read it in advance of dining.

NORTHCOTE MANOR COUNTRY HOUSE HOTEL

BURRINGTON, UMBERLEIGH, DEVON EX37 9LZ

This 18th-century manor with grounds high above the Taw River Valley offers an ambience of timeless tranquillity. Situated in 20 acres of peaceful Devonshire countryside, Northcote Manor provides complete relaxation and refreshment. Extensive refurbishment has created 11 luxury bedrooms and suites, resulting in a total redesign of the décor in the spacious sitting rooms, hall and restaurant. One of the south west's leading country houses, the Manor has received a series of accolades. In 2002: Condé Nast Johansens Country Hotel of the Year; and AA 3 Red Stars. In 2001: the RAC Gold Ribbon Award; The Which? Hotel Guide; Tourist Board Silver Award; Michelin 2 Red Turrets Award; RAC Cooking Award level 3; and AA 2 Rosettes. Exmoor and Dartmoor are within easy reach and guests may visit RHS Rosemoor and the many National Trust properties nearby. A challenging 18-hole golf course is next door whilst outstanding fishing from the Taw River, at the bottom of the drive, can be arranged with the Gillie. The area also hosts some of the best shoots in the country. A tennis court and croquet lawn are on site. Helicopters can land at Eaglescott Airfield, approximately 2 miles away. Special breaks are available.

Our inspector loved: The peaceful, calm location and atmosphere of warmth and welcome.

Directions: From Exeter stay on the A377 towards Barnstaple (do not enter Burrington village). The driveway to the Manor is opposite the Portsmouth Arms pub on the A377.

Web: www.johansens.com/northcotemanor
E-mail: rest@northcotemanor.co.uk
Tel: 0870 381 8767
International: +44 (0)01769 560501
Fax: 01769 560770

Price Guide:
single from £99
double/twin from £140
suite from £235

97

GIDLEIGH PARK

CHAGFORD, DEVON TQ13 8HH

Directions: Approach from Chagford: go along Mill Street from Chagford Square. Fork right after 150 yards, cross into Holy Street at factory crossroads and follow lane for 2 miles.

Web: www.johansens.com/gidleighpark
E-mail: gidleighpark@gidleigh.co.uk
Tel: 0870 381 8545
International: +44 (0)1647 432367
Fax: 01647 432574

Price Guide: (including dinner)
single £370–£470
double/twin £430–£550

Gidleigh Park enjoys an outstanding international reputation among connoisseurs for its comfort and gastronomy. It has collected a clutch of top culinary awards including 2 Michelin stars for its imaginative cuisine and the Gidleigh Park wine list is one of the best in Britain. Service throughout the hotel is faultless. The en-suite bedrooms – 2 of them in a converted chapel – are luxuriously furnished with antiques. The public rooms are elegantly appointed and during the cooler months, a fire burns merrily in the lounge's impressive fireplace. Set amid 45 secluded acres in the Teign Valley, Gidleigh Park is 1½ miles from the nearest public road. 2 croquet lawns, an all-weather tennis court, a bowling lawn and a splendid water garden can be found in the grounds. A 360 yard long, par 52 putting course designed by Peter Alliss was opened in 1995. Guests can swim in the river or explore Dartmoor on foot or in the saddle. There are 14 miles of trout, sea trout and salmon fishing, as well as golf facilities nearby. Gidleigh Park is a Relais et Châteaux member.

Our inspector loved: *The total peace and tranquillity surrounding this superb hotel.*

MILL END

DARTMOOR NATIONAL PARK, CHAGFORD, DEVON TQ13 8JN

Gleaming white under slate grey roof tiles and with windows and doors opening onto a beautiful English country garden, Mill End is an idyllic hideaway in Dartmoor's National Park. The lawned garden with its wide, deeply shrubbed and colourful borders runs down to the languid waters of the River Teign, a water wheel slowly turns in the courtyard to the enjoyment of guests and diners. Built in the mid 1700s the hotel was a former flour mill, and inside there are numerous little corner nooks, paintings and old photographs that imbue a feeling of seclusion, enhanced by the smell of wood smoke and polished wood. The delightful en-suite bedrooms have undergone major refurbishment incorporating excellent décor, lovely fabrics and attractive local hand-crafted furniture. Plus, of course, every facility one would expect. The elegance of the dining room is matched by the delicious award-winning cuisine of Master Chef of Great Britain– Wayne Pearson. His menus are full and varied; one shouldn't miss, for example, lobster ravioli with seared scallops and lemon grass broth followed by grilled turbot with aubergine caviar and a dark chocolate tort with burnt orange sauce and rosewater ice creme. An 18-hole golf course is nearby and pony trekking and shooting can be arranged.

Our inspector loved: The total feel of relaxation and tranquillity within Dartmoor National Park.

Directions: From the M5 exit at junction 31 towards Okehampton. Take the A382 at Merrymount roundabout towards Moretonhampstead. Mill End is on the right.

Web: www.johansens.com/millend
E-mail: millendhotel@talk21.com
Tel: 0870 381 8734
International: +44 (0)1647 432282
Fax: 01647 433106

Price Guide:
single £60–£94
double/twin £80–£125
suite £150–£180

COMBE HOUSE HOTEL & RESTAURANT

GITTISHAM, HONITON, NEAR EXETER, DEVON EX14 3AD

Directions: From the M5 take exit 28 to Honiton and Sidmouth or exit 29 to Honiton. Follow signs to Fenny Bridges and Gittisham.

Web: www.johansens.com/combehousegittisham
E-mail: stay@thishotel.com
Tel: 0870 381 8440
International: +44 (0)1404 540400
Fax: 01404 46004

Price Guide:
single £99–£165
double/twin £138–£265
suites £265–£285

Combe House is a wildly romantic Grade I Elizabethan manor hidden in 3,500 acres of Devon's finest estates where magnificent Arabian horses and pheasants roam freely. Total peace and tranquillity together with generous hospitality can be enjoyed here in this warm and welcoming atmosphere created by the comfy sofas, flamboyant flowers and roaring log-fires. 15 intimate bedrooms and suites, many with panoramic views, are decorated with style and individuality. The candle-lit restaurant serves innovative, contemporary British cuisine prepared by Master Chef of Great Britain, Philip Leach, perfectly complemented by a well-chosen wine list, including a specialist Chablis collection. The recently restored Georgian Kitchen is the ideal setting for a highly individual private lunch or dinner, dining by lamps and candlelight. Down Combe's mile-long drive is Gittisham, once described by H.R.H. Prince Charles as "the ideal English village," with its thatched cottages, Norman church and village green. The World Heritage Jurassic coast, from Lyme Regis to Sidmouth, Honiton antique shops, numerous historic houses and gardens, the cathedral of Exeter and the wide open spaces of Dartmoor can all be explored.

Our inspector loved: This unspoilt country house with delicious food, comfy beds and peaceful countryside.

FAIRWATER HEAD COUNTRY HOUSE HOTEL

HAWKCHURCH, AXMINSTER, DEVON EX13 5TX

In an idyllic setting on the Devon, Dorset and Somerset borders, Fairwater Head – also the name of the stream's source – not only has its own magnificent landscaped gardens but is situated at the highest point of the land and boasts the most spectacular views over the Axe valley. Built from local stone and with a rich local history, this is a perfect retreat for guests seeking peace and tranquillity from which to explore the Devon and Dorset environs. The bedrooms are charming, both in the main house and the "garden rooms", and most overlook the beautiful grounds and open countryside. The spacious dining room is light and airy, and again has wonderful views, and it is here that a superb menu of traditional and contemporary cuisine is served – recently awarded 1 AA Rosette and 2 RAC dining awards. This is an area rich in countryside walks and historic houses and gardens, and there is also Forde Abbey, picturesque Lyme Regis, and a donkey sanctuary nearby. Escorted tours and special breaks are available.

Our inspector loved: This idyllically tucked away country house offering total peace and relaxation.

Directions: Exit M5 at junction 25 onto A358. Then left onto A35 towards Bridport; left onto B3165 to Lyme Regis, Crewkerne road. Follow signs for Hawkchurch and hotel on left.

Web: www.johansens.com/fairwaterhead
E-mail: reception@fairwaterhead.demon.co.uk
Tel: 0870 381 8511
International: +44 (0)1297 678349
Fax: 01297 678459

Price Guide:
single £91–£95
double/twin £157–£167

ILSINGTON COUNTRY HOUSE HOTEL

ILSINGTON VILLAGE, NEAR NEWTON ABBOT, DEVON TQ13 9RR

The Ilsington Country House Hotel stands in 10 acres of beautiful private grounds within the Dartmoor National Park. Run by friendly proprietors, Tim and Maura Hassell, the delightful furnishings and ambience offer a most comfortable environment in which to relax. Stylish bedrooms all boast outstanding views across the rolling pastoral countryside and every comfort and convenience to make guests feel at home. The distinctive candle-lit dining room is perfect for savouring the superb cuisine, awarded an AA Rosette, created by talented chefs from fresh local produce. The library is ideal for an intimate dining party or celebration whilst the conservatory or lounge is the place for morning coffee or a Devon cream tea. There is a fully-equipped, purpose-built gymnasium, heated indoor pool, sauna, steam room and spa. Some of England's most idyllic and unspoilt scenery surrounds Ilsington, with the picturesque villages of Lustleigh and Widecombe-in-the-Moor close by. Guests have easy access to the moors from the hotel. Riding, fishing and many other country pursuits can be arranged. Special breaks are available.

Directions: From the M5 join the A38 at Exeter following Plymouth signs. After approximately 12 miles, exit for Moretonhampstead and Newton Abbot. At the roundabout follow signs for Ilsington.

Web: www.johansens.com/ilsington
E-mail: hotel@ilsington.co.uk
Tel: 0870 381 8635
International: +44 (0)1364 661452
Fax: 01364 661307

Price Guide:
single from £76
double/twin from £115

Our inspector loved: The newly refurbished bathrooms and, as always, the outstanding beautiful location.

LEWTRENCHARD MANOR
LEWDOWN, NEAR OKEHAMPTON, DEVON EX20 4PN

This beautiful Jacobean manor is tucked away within its own estate on rolling Devon hills, and with just 9 exquisite bedrooms is a delightful retreat from city life. Built in 1600 by the Monk family it was later embellished by the Victorian hymn writer Rev Sabine Baring Gould, and today is a stunning example of ornate ceilings, elegant carved oak staircases and leaded light windows. Carefully incorporated family antique pieces and elegant soft furnishings to create a sense of luxury combined with a warmth that is truly welcoming. Each of the bedrooms looks out over the valley, and the oak-panelled dining room with its coffered ceiling provides a stunning backdrop for some excellent cooking and superb wines. The restaurant has won 2 Rosettes for its exquisitely prepared and artistically presented cuisine, which is based on the freshest of local ingredients. The estate offers clay pigeon shooting and rough shooting and fishing, making this an ideal place for weekend parties, as well as an idyllic setting for weddings and functions. Exeter is on the doorstep with its cathedral and sophisticated shops, whilst Devon's numerous tourist attractions are all within easy reach.

Our inspector loved: This wonderful manor house, peacefully tucked away and so welcoming.

Directions: Located off the A386, 6 miles south of the A30. 30 miles from junction 31 on the M5 at Exeter.

Web: www.johansens.com/lewtrenchard
E-mail: info@lewtrenchard.co.uk
Tel: 0870 381 9177
International: +44 (0)1566 783222
Fax: 01566 783332

Barnstaple

Exeter
Sidmouth

Plymouth

Price Guide:
single £100–£120
double/twin £135–£185
suite £200

DEVON - LIFTON (NR LAUNCESTON)

THE ARUNDELL ARMS

LIFTON, DEVON PL16 0AA

In a lovely valley close to the uplands of Dartmoor, the Arundell Arms is a former coaching inn which dates back to Saxon times. Its flagstone floors, cosy fires, paintings and antiques combine to create a haven of warmth and comfort in an atmosphere of old world charm. One of England's best-known sporting hotels for more than half a century, it boasts 20 miles of exclusive salmon and trout fishing on the Tamar and five of its tributaries and a famous school of Fly Fishing. Guests also enjoy a host of other country activities, including hill walking, shooting, riding and golf. The hotel takes great pride in its elegant 3 AA Rosette restaurant, presided over by Master Chefs Philip Burgess and Nick Shopland. Their gourmet cuisine has won the restaurant an international reputation. A splendid base from which to enjoy the wonderful surfing beaches nearby, the Arundell Arms is also well placed for visits to Tintagel and the historic houses and gardens of Devon and Cornwall and the Eden Project. Only 45 minutes from Exeter and Plymouth, it is also ideal for the business executive, reached by fast roads from all directions. A spacious conference suite is available.

Directions: Lifton is approximately ¼ mile off A30 2 miles east of Launceston and the Cornish Border.

Web: www.johansens.com/arundellarms
E-mail: reservations@arundellarms.com
Tel: 0870 381 8323
International: +44 (0)1566 784666
Fax: 01566 784494

Price Guide:
single £70–£90
double/twin £140
suite £170

Our inspector loved: A haven for fishing, outdoor sports and the finest cuisine.

KITLEY HOUSE HOTEL & RESTAURANT

THE KITLEY ESTATE, YEALMPTON, NR PLYMOUTH, DEVON PL8 2NW

This imposing Grade I listed country house hotel, built of silver-grey Devonshire "marble", is situated in 300 acres of richly timbered parkland at the head of one of Yealm estuary's wooded creeks, only 10 minutes from the city of Plymouth. It is one of the earliest Tudor revival houses in England and has been splendidly restored to its former glory. Approached by a mile-long drive through a magnificent private estate, Kitley is an oasis of quiet luxury, providing the highest standards in comfort, cuisine and personal service. A sweeping staircase leads to 18 spacious bedrooms and suites. Each has panoramic views over the estate and is richly appointed with furnishings designed to reflect the traditional elegance of the house whilst incorporating all modern facilities. The lounge area, with its huge open fireplace and bar, are stylish and relaxing. The restaurant is sumptuously decorated in burgundy and gold and provides the perfect atmosphere in which to enjoy the finest of cuisine – whatever the occasion. Guests can enjoy fishing in the private lake and golf, shooting and riding are nearby. Murder mystery dinners and mid-week breaks are available.

Directions: Take the A38 towards Plymouth (A3121) then turn right onto the A379. The hotel entrance is on the left after Yealmpton village.

Web: www.johansens.com/kitleyhouse
E-mail: sales@kitleyhousehotel.com
Tel: 0870 381 8660
International: +44 (0)1752 881555
Fax: 01752 881667

Price Guide:
single £95–£115
double/twin £110–£130
suite from £120

Our inspector loved: The room proportions, welcoming log fires and magnificent location.

SOAR MILL COVE HOTEL

SOAR MILL COVE, SALCOMBE, SOUTH DEVON TQ7 3DS

Directions: A384 to Totnes, then A381 to Soar Mill Cove.

Web: www.johansens.com/soarmillcove
E-mail: info@makepeacehotels.co.uk
Tel: 0870 381 8897
International: +44 (0)1548 561566
Fax: 01548 561223

Price Guide:
single £94–£160
double/twin £164–£190
suite from £216

Owned and loved by the Makepeace family who, for over 25 years, have provided a special blend of friendly yet professional service, this hotel is spectacularly set in a flower-filled combe, facing its own sheltered sandy bay and entirely surrounded by 2000 acres of dramatic National Trust coastline. While it is perhaps one of the last truly unspoiled corners of South Devon, Soar Mill Cove is only 15 miles from the motorway system (A38). "Serendipity", the fine dining restaurant holds 3 RAC Dining Awards and this luxury 4-star hotel is the AA's highest rated in Devon. All the bedrooms are at ground level, each with a private patio opening onto the gardens, which in spring or summer provides wonderful alfresco opportunities. In winter, the efficient double glazing keeps cooler weather at bay. A strict "no conference policy" guarantees that the peace of guests shall not be compromised. Both the indoor and outdoor pools are spring-water fed, the former being maintained all year at a constant 88°F. Here is Keith Stephen Makepeace's award-winning cuisine, imaginative and innovative, reflecting the very best of the West of England; fresh crabs and lobster caught in the bay are a speciality. Soar Mill Cove is situated midway between the old ports of Plymouth and Dartmouth.

Our inspector loved: *The genuine warmth and welcome and the location - it just has to be seen.*

THE TIDES REACH HOTEL

SOUTH SANDS, SALCOMBE, DEVON TQ8 8LJ

This luxuriously appointed hotel is situated in an ideal position for those wishing to enjoy a relaxing or fun-filled break. Facing south in a tree-fringed sandy cove just inside the mouth of the Salcombe Estuary it has an extensive garden on one side, the sea and a safe bathing sandy beach a few steps opposite and, to the rear, a sheltering hill topped by the subtropical gardens of Overbecks. The Tides Reach has been under the supervision of owners, the Edwards family, for more than 35 years and they have built up a reputation for hospitality and courteous service. The atmosphere is warm and friendly, the décor and furnishings tasteful and comfortable. All 35 spacious bedrooms are en suite, well equipped and decorated with flair and originality. The lawned garden centres around an ornamental lake with waterfall and fountain which is surrounded by landscaped tiers of colourful plants, shrubs and palms. Overlooking it is the restaurant where chef Finn Ibsen's excellent gourmet cuisine has earned AA Rosettes. A superb indoor heated swimming pool is the nucleus of the hotel's leisure complex which includes a sauna, solarium, spa bath, gymnasium, squash court and snooker room. The hotel has facilities for windsurfing, sailing and canoeing.

Our inspector loved: *The warm welcome, superb location and relaxing ambience.*

Directions: From the M5, exit at junction 30 and join the A38 towards Plymouth. Exit for Totnes and then take the A381.

Web: www.johansens.com/tidesreach
E-mail: enquire@tidesreach.com
Tel: 0870 381 8947
International: +44 (0)1548 843466
Fax: 01548 843954

Price Guide: (incl dinner)
single £75–£130
double/twin £130–£280

107

BUCKLAND-TOUT-SAINTS

GOVETON, KINGSBRIDGE, DEVON TQ7 2DS

Directions: Signed from A381 between Totnes and Kingsbridge.

Web: www.johansens.com/bucklandtoutsaints
E-mail: buckland@tout–saints.co.uk
Tel: 0870 381 8391
International: +44 (0)1548 853055
Fax: 01548 856261

Price Guide:
single from £80
double/twin from £150
suite from £300

One of the top 200 hotels in Britain and Ireland, Buckland-Tout-Saints is an impressive Grade II* listed manor house, built in 1690 during the reign of William and Mary. Recently refurbished to a superb standard, the wonderful hospitality and cuisine that guests enjoy at this hotel today would certainly have impressed its royal visitors of the past. Idyllic amongst its own woodlands and beautiful gardens, it is invitingly close to the spectacular beaches and dramatic cliffs of the Devonshire coastline. A warm and welcoming atmosphere prevails throughout, from the leather-clad couches of the convivial bar to the family of bears – Teddy Tout-Saints – whose individual members welcome guests to their de luxe rooms and suites. Many of these delightful period style rooms enjoy stunning views across the beautiful South Hams countryside with its moorland and river estuaries. Gastronomic delights using fresh local fish, meat and game accompanied by an equally tantalising selection of fine wines and vintage ports are served in the award-winning Queen Anne Resturant. Conferences, weddings and seminars are effortlessly accommodated in the Kestrel Rooms, where helpful staff and elegant surroundings ensure a successful occasion. Several well-known golf courses and sailing centres such as Salcome and Dartmouth are nearby. Details of golf breaks are available via the hotels website.

Our inspector loved: The location and feel of tranquillity.

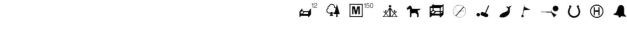

HOTEL RIVIERA

THE ESPLANADE, SIDMOUTH, DEVON EX10 8AY

A warm welcome awaits guests arriving at this prestigious award-winning hotel. With accolades such as the AA Courtesy and Care Award and more recently, the Which? Hotel Guide's Hotel of the Year 1999, it comes as no surprise that Peter Wharton's Hotel Riviera is arguably one of the most comfortable and most hospitable in the region. The exterior, with its fine Regency façade and bow fronted windows complements the elegance of the interior comprising handsome public rooms and beautifully appointed bedrooms, many with sea views. Perfectly located at the centre of Sidmouth's historic Georgian esplanade and awarded 4 stars by both the AA and the RAC, the Riviera is committed to providing the very highest standard of excellence which makes each stay at the property a totally pleasurable experience. Guests may dine in the attractive salon, which affords glorious views across Lyme Bay, and indulge in the superb cuisine, prepared by Swiss and French trained chefs. The exceptional cellar will please the most discerning wine connoisseur. Activities include coastal walks, golf, bowling, croquet, putting, tennis, fishing, sailing, riding and exploring the breathtaking surroundings with its gardens, lush countryside and stunning coastline.

Our inspector loved: The wonderful location overlooking Lyme bay and the feeling of warmth and welcome.

Directions: The hotel is situated at the centre of the esplanade.

Web: www.johansens.com/riviera
E-mail: enquiries@hotelriviera.co.uk
Tel: 0870 381 8624
International: +44 (0)1395 515201
Fax: 01395 577775

Price Guide: (including 7 course dinner):
single £100–£132
double/twin £180–£244
suite £260–£280

THE PALACE HOTEL

BABBACOMBE ROAD, TORQUAY, DEVON TQ1 3TG

Directions: From seafront follow signs for Babbacombe. Hotel entrance is on the right.

Web: www.johansens.com/palacetorquay
E-mail: info@palacetorquay.co.uk
Tel: 0870 381 8798
International: +44 (0)1803 200200
Fax: 01803 299899

Price Guide:
single £75–£85
double/twin £150–£170
executive £199
suite £240–£280

Once the residence of the Bishop of Exeter, the privately owned Palace Hotel is a gracious Victorian building set in 25 acres of beautifully landscaped gardens and woodlands. The comfortable bedrooms are equipped with every modern amenity and there are also elegant, spacious suites available. Most rooms overlook the hotel's magnificent grounds. The main restaurant provides a high standard of traditional English cooking, making full use of fresh, local produce, as well as offering a good variety of international dishes. The cuisine is complemented by a wide selection of popular and fine wines. Light meals are also available from the lounge and during the summer months, a mediterranean-style menu is served on the terrace. A host of sporting facilities has made this hotel famous. These include a short par 3 9-hole championship golf course, indoor and outdoor swimming pools, 2 indoor and 4 outdoor tennis courts, 2 squash courts, saunas, snooker room and a well-equipped fitness suite. Places of interest nearby include Dartmoor, South Hams and Exeter. Paignton Zoo, Bygone's Museum and Kent's Cavern are among the local attractions.

Our inspector loved: *This gracious hotel - beautiful grounds and the fact one can stay onsite and forget the car.*

ORESTONE MANOR HOTEL & RESTAURANT

ROCKHOUSE LANE, MAIDENCOMBE, TORQUAY, DEVON TQ1 4SX

Stylishly refurbished as a colonial manor house, Orestone Manor is a luxury country house hotel and restaurant located on the rural fringe of Torquay, with stunning views across the Torbay coastline and Lyme Bay. The house was built in 1809 and was once the home of painter John Calcott Horsley RA, whose celebrated portrait of his brother-in-law, Isambard Kindom Brunel, hangs in the National Gallery. He is also renowned for having painted the very first Christmas card. Each room has its own décor and character with full amenities and luxury en-suite bathrooms; some have their own terrace or balcony. Excellent service and superb food and wine can be enjoyed in the 2 AA Rosette restaurant. Using only the best seasonal local produce – some from Orestone's own gardens – light lunches, snacks and afternoon teas are served in the conservatory or on the terrace, whilst a full set lunch and à la carte dinner menu are available in the restaurant. Numerous places of interest are close by, including Dartmoor, Exmoor and many National Trust properties and gardens, as well as a wide range of activities and picturesque coastal walks. Whether for a relaxing break, afternoon tea, lunch with friends or a special dinner, Orestone Manor provides the perfect setting, and adds style and elegance to any occasion.

Our inspector loved: The beautiful location and overall ambience, quite superb.

Directions: About 3 miles north of Torquay on the A379 (Formerly B3199). Take the coast road towards Teignmouth.

Web: www.johansens.com/orestonemanor
E-mail: enquiries@orestone.co.uk
Tel: 0870 381 8794
International: +44 (0)1803 328098
Fax: 01803 328336

Price Guide:
single £69–£129
double/twin £109–£179

111

THE OSBORNE HOTEL & LANGTRY'S RESTAURANT

MEADFOOT BEACH, TORQUAY, DEVON TQ1 2LL

Directions: The hotel is in Meadfoot, to the east of Torquay.

Web: www.johansens.com/osborne
E-mail: enq@osborne-torquay.co.uk
Tel: 0870 381 8795
International: +44 (0)1803 213311
Fax: 01803 296788

Price Guide:
single £55–£90
double/twin £95–£170
suite £120–£220

The combination of Mediterranean chic and the much-loved Devon landscape has a special appeal, which is reflected at The Osborne. The hotel is the centrepiece of an elegant recently refurbished Regency crescent in Meadfoot, a quiet location within easy reach of the centre of Torquay. Known as a "country house by the sea", the hotel offers the friendly ambience of a country home complemented by the superior standards of service and comfort expected of a hotel on the English Riviera. Most of the 29 bedrooms have magnificent views and are decorated in pastel shades. Overlooking the sea, Langtry's acclaimed award-winning restaurant provides fine English cooking and tempting regional specialities, whilst the Brasserie has a menu available throughout the day. Guests may relax in the attractive 5-acre gardens and make use of indoor and outdoor swimming pools, gymnasium, sauna, solarium, tennis court and putting green – all without leaving the grounds. Sailing, archery, clay pigeon shooting and golf can be arranged. Devon is a county of infinite variety, with its fine coastline, bustling harbours, tranquil lanes, sleepy villages and the wilds of Dartmoor. The Osborne is ideally placed to enjoy all these attractions.

Our inspector loved: The magnificent location and the ambience of a country house by the sea.

 # PERCY'S COUNTRY HOTEL & RESTAURANT

COOMBESHEAD ESTATE, VIRGINSTOW, DEVON EX21 5EA

A soft, tranquil ambience filters through every part of this stylish, charming Devon hideaway. Set amongst 130 acres of unspoilt countryside positively alive with stunning wildlife, Percy's is ideal for those wishing to relax and unwind in a smoke and child-free environment. Against the backdrop of the breathtaking and striking wilds of both Dartmoor and Bodmin Moor, Percy's combines modern architectural intelligence and traditional country house comfort with eye-catching results. The highly accoladed and fully certified organic restaurant - another first in these parts – only serves ingredients that have the distinctive "zing" and potency of true freshness. The fish bought at auction is only a few hours old, vegetables and lamb are nurtured on the estate from infancy and the eggs that greet your breakfast order are so rich in dazzling shades of intense yellow that they will revitalise even the most jaded of urban guests. If a passion for organics characterises the food then it is understated luxury that best defines the accommodation. Soothing colours, king-size beds, Jacuzzis, DVD players and freshly baked lavender and walnut shortbread will all help to unwind and recharge. Outside your door lies a stunning estate to explore, any one of three black labs to accompany you and the anticipation of dining in the 2003 Johansens Restaurant of the Year.

Our inspector loved: The peaceful "away-from-it-all" location.

Directions: From Okehampton take the A3079 to Metherell Cross. After 8.3 miles turn left. The hotel is 6.5 miles on the left.

Web: www.johansens.com/percys
E-mail: info@percys.co.uk
Tel: 0870 381 8817
International: +44 (0)1409 211236
Fax: 01409 211460

Price Guide:
single from £115
double from £150

NEW

LANGDON COURT HOTEL & RESTAURANT

DOWN THOMAS, PLYMOUTH, DEVON PL9 0DY

Directions: From Exeter join the A38 towards Plymouth then take the exit signed Plymouth, Yelverton Plymstock into Brixton. Follow Brixton Tor/Otter Nurseries and carry on the Leyford Lane. Turn left into the hotel's drive.

Web: www.johansens.com/langdon
E-mail: enquiries@langdoncourt.co.uk
Tel: 0870 381 9157
International: +44 (0)1752 862358
Fax: 01752 863428

Price Guide:
single from £65
double £85-£150

Barnstaple

Exeter

Sidmouth

Plymouth

Originally built for Katherine Parr, the 6th wife of Henry VIII, this Grade II listed Tudor manor has even earlier origins, evidence of which can be found in its cellars. Rebuilt in 1648, the house is now surrounded by fields and woodland and has its own Jacobean walled gardens and well kept lawns. Behind its impressive grey façade lie tiled floors, warmly painted stone walls and classic, uncluttered furnishings. Some of the 17 bedrooms are simply stunning, and more than half are currently undergoing an upgrading programme to create the same, unparalleled standard. 3 function suites, Calmady, Cory and Courtney, are available for wedding receptions, shooting and house parties. An impressive menu is served in the modern brasserie, the bar or on the terrace, specialising in fish and seafood. Year round, the best produce and organically farmed meats are selected from local suppliers, and the cellar holds well-established favourites along with wines from the New World. The hotel has a direct path to the beach at Wembury, access to the coastal paths, and is ideally placed for exploring the South Hams countryside, numerous National Trust properties and the Eden project.

Our inspector loved: *The away-from-it-all relaxing, informal atmosphere offering total peace and mouth-watering cuisine.*

WOOLACOMBE BAY HOTEL

SOUTH STREET, WOOLACOMBE, DEVON EX34 7BN

Woolacombe Bay Hotel stands in 6 acres of grounds, leading to 3 miles of golden sand. Built by the Victorians, the hotel has an air of luxury, style and comfort. All rooms are en suite with satellite TV, baby listening, ironing centre, some with a balcony. Traditional English and French dishes are offered in the dining room. Superb recreational amenities on site include unlimited free access to tennis, squash, indoor and outdoor pools, billiards, bowls, croquet, dancing and films, a health suite with steam room, sauna, spa bath with high impulse shower. Power-boating, fishing, shooting and riding can be arranged and preferential rates are offered for golf at the Saunton Golf Club. There is a "Hot House" aerobics studio, beauty salon, cardio vascular weights room, solariums, masseur and beautician. However, being energetic is not a requirement for enjoying the qualities of Woolacombe Bay. Many of its regulars choose simply to relax in the grand public rooms and in the grounds, which extend to the rolling surf of the magnificent bay. A drive along the coastal route in either direction will guarantee splendid views. Exmoor's beautiful Doone Valley is an hour away by car. Closed January.

Our inspector loved: The total joy and oasis for families.

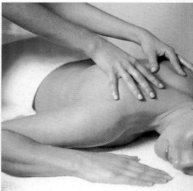

Directions: At the centre of the village, off main Barnstaple–Ilfracombe road.

Web: www.johansens.com/woolacombebay
E-mail: woolacombe.bayhotel@btinternet.com
Tel: 0870 381 9007
International: +44 (0)1271 870388
Fax: 01271 870613

Price Guide: (including dinner)
single £65–£120
double/twin £145–£240

WATERSMEET HOTEL

MORTEHOE, WOOLACOMBE, DEVON EX34 7EB

Directions: From the M5, junction 27, follow the A361 towards Ilfracombe. Turn left at the roundabout and follow signs to Mortehoe.

Web: www.johansens.com/watersmeet
E-mail: info @watersmeethotel.co.uk
Tel: 0870 381 8972
International: +44 (0)1271 870333
Fax: 01271 870890

Price Guide: (including dinner)
single £98–£150
double/twin £140–£285

Watersmeet personifies the comfortable luxury of a country house hotel. Majestically situated on the rugged North Atlantic coastline, the hotel commands dramatic views across the waters of Woolacombe Bay past Hartland Point to Lundy Island. The gardens reach down to the sea and private steps lead directly to the beach. A tasteful refurbishment to the lounge has ensured that the attractive décor, combined with striking coloured fabrics, creates a warm impression all year round. All bedrooms look out to sea and guests can drift off to sleep to the sound of lapping waves or rolling surf. Morning coffee, lunch and afternoon tea can be served in the relaxing comfort of the lounge, on the terrace or by the heated outdoor pool. The new indoor pool and spa is a favourite with everyone. English and international dishes are served in the award-winning, tiered Watersmeet Restaurant where each evening candles flicker as diners absorb a sea view from each table and watch the sun slipping below the horizon. The hotel has been awarded an AA Rosette for cuisine, the AA Courtesy and Care Award and a Silver Award by the English Tourism Council. There is a grass tennis court and local surfing, riding, clay pigeon shooting and bracing walks along coastal paths. Open February to January.

Our inspector loved: The recently refurbished lounge and restaurant.

BRIDGE HOUSE HOTEL

PROUT BRIDGE, BEAMINSTER, DORSET DT8 3AY

Country house relaxed informality, together with excellent wine and food, are the hallmarks of Peter Pinkster's lovely old mellow stone house. Dating back to the 13th century, this former priest's house is at the heart of the market town of Beaminster, and is set in a restful and beautiful walled garden. Staff and owner alike strive to create a welcome for guests and to provide them with the highest standards of home comforts. The warm stone, ancient beams and large fireplaces combine with a refreshingly uncomplicated approach to hotelkeeping, to provide a pleasing and unpretentious enviroment which guests will recall with pleasure. Attractively decorated and furnished bedrooms include a colour television and tea and coffee making facilities. Four of them are on the ground floor and offer easy access. The pride of the house is its food, where attention to detail is evident. In the candle-lit Georgian dining room an imaginative menu offers dishes that make use of fresh produce from the local farms and fishing ports. Beaminster is convenient for touring, walking and exploring the magnificent Dorset countryside. Places of interest nearby include many fine houses and gardens. Several golf courses, fresh and salt water fishing, riding, sailing and swimming in the sea are all within reach.

Our inspector loved: *An outstanding breakfast in the big new conservatory - garden views in all directions.*

Directions: From M3 take A303 Crewkerne exit then A356 through Crewkerne, then A3066 to Beaminster. Hotel is 100 yds from town centre car park, on the left.

Web: www.johansens.com/bridgehousebeam
E-mail: enquiries@bridge–house.co.uk
Tel: 0870 381 8379
International: +44 (0)1308 862200
Fax: 01308 863700

Price Guide:
single £54–£96
twin/double £102–£134

LANGTRY MANOR

DERBY ROAD, EAST CLIFF, BOURNEMOUTH, DORSET BH1 3QB

Known originally as The Red House, this fine house was built in 1877 by Edward VII (then Prince of Wales) as a love nest for his mistress. The concept of a themed small hotel was created by the present owners around the famous Lillie Langtry story exactly a hundred years later. The Edward VII suite is a fine spacious room which retains two original floral wall paintings and features a grand Jacobean four-poster bed. Other feature rooms have four-posters, corner spa baths and are all designed to engender a romantic ambience. This was the first hotel in Dorset to be licensed for civil marriages; it is a popular wedding venue – and a natural for honeymoons, anniversaries and birthdays. Saturday night guests are invited to take part in a delicious 6 course Edwardian Banquet – which features an interlude of words and music based on the life of the "Jersey Lily" – served in the quite splendid Dining Hall with its minstrels gallery and stained glass windows. Some of the bedrooms offered are close by in The Lodge – once the home of Lord Derby. Guests can enjoy complimentary use of a state-of-the-art leisure club just 2 minutes away. Sandy beaches, Hardy Country, the New Forest, art galleries, theatres and gardens are nearby.

Directions: Take A338 Wessex Way to the station. First exit at roundabout, over next roundabout, first left into Knyveton Road, second right into Derby Road.

Web: www.johansens.com/langtrymanor
E-mail: lillie@langtrymanor.com
Tel: 0870 381 8681
International: +44 (0)1202 553887
Fax: 01202 290115

Price Guide:
single from £95
double/twin £139.50–£219.50

Our inspector loved: The attention to every small detail to bring alive the Edward and Lillie romance.

NORFOLK ROYALE HOTEL

RICHMOND HILL, BOURNEMOUTH, DORSET BH2 6EN

Bournemouth has long been a popular seaside resort and has not lost its unique character – The Norfolk Royale is a fine example of the elegant buildings that grace the town. It is a splendid Edwardian house, once the holiday home of the Duke of Norfolk, after whom it is named. Extensive restoration work throughout the hotel, while enhancing its comfort, has not eliminated the echoes of the past and new arrivals are impressed by the elegant furnishings and courtesy of the staff. The designs of the spacious bedrooms reflect consideration for lady travellers, busy business executives, non-smokers and the disabled. The rich fabrics of the delightful colour schemes contribute to their luxurious ambience. Guests relax in the lounge or attractive club bar, in summer enjoying the gardens or patio – all with waiter service – and delicious breakfasts, lunches and candle-lit dinners are served in the Orangery Restaurant, which has an excellent wine list. The good life includes the pleasures of a pool and spa whilst Bournemouth offers golf courses, tennis, water sports, a casino and theatre. It has a large conference and exhibition centre. Poole Harbour, The New Forest, Thomas Hardy country and long sandy beaches are nearby.

Our inspector loved: *The refurbished bedrooms, now presented with simplicity and style.*

Directions: From the M27, A31 & A338 find the hotel on the right, halfway down Richmond Hill approaching the town centre.

Shaftesbury
Sherborne
Bridport
Dorchester
Bournemouth

Web: www.johansens.com/norfolkroyale
E-mail: norfolkroyale@englishrosehotels.co.uk
Tel: 0870 381 8765
International: +44 (0)1202 551521
Fax: 01202 299729

Price Guide:
single from £105
double/twin £145–£175
suite £185–£350

THE DORMY

NEW ROAD, FERNDOWN, NEAR BOURNEMOUTH, DORSET BH22 8ES

Directions: Nearest motorway is M27 to Ringwood, then A31 to Ferndown, then left at the traffic lights onto A347. The hotel is just a mile on the left hand side.

Web: www.johansens.com/dormybournemouth
E-mail: dormy@devere-hotels.com
Tel: 0870 381 8486
International: +44 (0)1202 872121
Fax: 01202 895388

Price Guide:
single £95–£115
double/twin £125–£200
suite £200–£300

Situated close to the picturesque New Forest, this country style hotel, with its log fires and oak-panelled lounges, is the essence of comfort. All bedrooms are furnished in either a traditional or a more modern fashion and include all the latest amenities such as satellite television, radio, telephone and hospitality tray. Guests can relax in the Dormy Bar and the golf themed Alliss Bar. Recently awarded 2 AA Rosettes, the elegant Hennessys Restaurant, situated in the hotel grounds, offers the finest contemporary cuisine. The Garden Restaurant continues to build upon its reputation and a third, more relaxed, option is the Pavillion Brasserie. The newly upgraded Leisure Club comprises of a large indoor pool and various other facilities such as sauna, spa bath and solaria. Fitness fanatics may exercise in the well-equipped gymnasium, toning suite and aerobics studio or make use of the squash and tennis courts. The Dormy lies centre to some of Dorset's finest golf courses. Activities nearby include quad biking, clay pigeon shooting and riding in the New Forest.

Our inspector loved: *Cormac O'Keefe's ability to provide for every need before you know you need it.*

SUMMER LODGE

SUMMER LANE, EVERSHOT, DORSET DT2 0JR

A charming Georgian building, idyllically located in Hardy country, Summer Lodge was formerly the dower house of the Earls of Ilchester. Now it is a luxurious hotel where owners Nigel and Margaret Corbett offer their guests a genuinely friendly welcome, encouraging them to relax as if in their own home. Summer Lodge was Johansens Country Hotel of the Year in 1999. The bedrooms have views over the 4-acre sheltered gardens or overlook the village rooftops across the meadowland. In the dining room, with its French windows that open on to the garden, the cuisine is highly regarded. Fresh local produce is combined with culinary expertise to create a distinctive brand of English cooking. The unspoilt Dorset countryside and its coastline, 12 miles south, make for limitless exploration and bring to life the setting of Tess of the d'Urbervilles, The Mayor of Casterbridge, Far from the Madding Crowd and the other Hardy novels. Many National Trust properties and gardens in the locality are open to the public. There are stables, golf courses and trout lakes nearby.

Our inspector loved: This garden takes some beating! Bring notebooks and pencils to take home wonderful ideas.

Directions: The turning to Evershot leaves the A37 halfway between Dorchester and Yeovil. Once in the village, turn left into Summer Lane and the hotel entrance is 150 yards on the right.

Web: www.johansens.com/summerlodge
E-mail: reception@summerlodgehotel.com
Tel: 0870 381 8926
International: +44 (0)1935 83424
Fax: 01935 83005

Price Guide:
single from £95
double/twin £145–£385
suite £225–£305

THE HAVEN

SANDBANKS, POOLE, DORSET BH13 7QL

Directions: M3/M27/A31/A338 to Poole. The hotel is at the tip of the Sandbanks Peninsula.

Web: www.johansens.com/havenhotel
E-mail: reservations@havenhotel.co.uk
Tel: 0870 381 8631
International: +44 (0)1202 707333
Fax: +44 (0)1202 708796

Price Guide:
single from £90
double/twin £180–£310
suite from £325

From its idyllic location on the tip of the exclusive Sandbanks Peninsula, overlooking the sweep of Poole Bay, this 4-star hotel, which has stood here for more than 100 years, offers first-class service in a friendly environment. The comfortable bedrooms are light and spacious, whilst the cosy lounges are the perfect place to unwind. Guests can choose from a variety of dining options: the 2 AA Rosette La Roche restaurant on the water's edge, which serves fresh fish and fine wines, the more informal Club Lounge, also on the water's edge, the Seaview restaurant and the Terrace for al fresco dining in summer. The hotel's 2,500sq ft Leisure Club includes an indoor swimming pool with split-level spa pools, fitness studio, gymnasium, hot tub, outdoor heated pool and poolside sauna as well as tennis court. The Spa has 6 state-of-the-art treatment rooms, a dry-float system and hydrotherapy unit to meet guests' every requirement. Renowned as an excellent conference and training centre, the Haven Hotel offers a purpose-built Business Centre. A ferry takes guests on trips across to Brownsea Island, owned by the National Trust, and Shell Bay with its miles of golden sand. The hotel's yacht, Haven Voyager II, is available for half or full day charter.

Our inspector loved: *The amazing position commanding the mouth of Poole Harbour – sailing boats, motor boats, yachts and ferries all cruise by.*

 SPA

PLUMBER MANOR

STURMINSTER NEWTON, DORSET DT10 2AF

An imposing Jacobean building of local stone, occupying extensive gardens in the heart of Hardy's Dorset, Plumber Manor has been the home of the Prideaux-Brune family since the early 17th century. Leading off a charming gallery, hung with family portraits, are 6 very comfortable bedrooms. The conversion of a natural stone barn lying within the grounds, as well as the courtyard building, has added a further 10 spacious bedrooms, some of which have window seats overlooking the garden and the Develish stream. 3 interconnecting dining rooms comprise the restaurant, where a good choice of imaginative, well-prepared dishes is presented, supported by a wide-ranging wine list. Chef Brian Prideaux-Brune's culinary prowess has been recognised by all the major food guides. Open for dinner every evening and Sunday lunch. The Dorset landscape, with its picture-postcard villages such as Milton Abbas and Cerne Abbas, is close at hand, while Corfe Castle, Lulworth Cove, Kingston Lacy and Poole Harbour are not far away. Riding can be arranged locally; however, if guests wish to bring their own horse to hack or hunt with local packs, the hotel provides free stabling on a do-it-yourself basis. Closed during February.

Our inspector loved: The epitome of a true country house in an exquisite setting.

Directions: Plumber Manor is 2 miles south-west of Sturminster Newton on the Hazelbury Bryan road, off the A357.

Web: www.johansens.com/plumbermanor
E-mail: book@plumbermanor.com
Tel: 0870 381 8829
International: +44 (0)01258 472507
Fax: 01258 473370

Price Guide:
single from £90
double/twin from £100

THE PRIORY HOTEL

CHURCH GREEN, WAREHAM, DORSET BH20 4ND

Directions: Wareham is on the A351 to the west of Bournemouth and Poole. The hotel is beside the River Frome at the southern end of the town near the parish church.

Web: www.johansens.com/priorywareham
E-mail: reservations@theprioryhotel.co.uk
Tel: 0870 381 8841
International: +44 (0)1929 551666
Fax: 01929 554519

Price Guide:
single £110
double/twin £140–£245
suite £285

Dating from the early 16th century, the one-time Lady St Mary Priory has, for hundreds of years, offered sanctuary to travellers. In Hardy's Dorset, "far from the madding crowd", it placidly stands on the bank of the River Frome in 4 acres of immaculate gardens. Steeped in history, The Priory has undergone a sympathetic conversion to a hotel which is charming yet unpretentious. Each bedroom is distinctively styled, with family antiques lending character and many rooms have views of the Purbeck Hills. A 16th century clay barn has been transformed into the Boathouse, consisting of 4 spacious luxury suites at the river's edge. Tastefully furnished, the drawing room, residents' lounge and intimate bar together create a convivial atmosphere. The Garden Room Restaurant is open for breakfast and lunch, while splendid dinners are served in the vaulted stone cellars. There are moorings for guests arriving by boat. Dating back to the 9th century, the market town of Wareham has more than 200 listed buildings. Corfe Castle, Lulworth Cove, Poole and Swanage are all close by with superb walks and beaches.

Our inspector loved: The true country house atmosphere and its delightful riverside setting at the heart of historic Wareham.

MOONFLEET MANOR

FLEET, WEYMOUTH, DORSET DT3 4ED

Overlooking Chesil Beach, a unique feature of the Dorset coast, Moonfleet Manor is both a luxury hotel and a family resort. The owners have applied the same flair for design evident in their other family friendly properties, Woolley Grange and Fowey Hall in Cornwall. The use of a variety of unusual antiques and objects from around the world lends a refreshing and individual style to this comfortable and attractive hotel. Bedrooms are beautifully decorated and furnished and a range of amenities ensures that guests enjoy standards of maximum comfort and convenience. An enthusiastic and attentive staff works hard to ensure that guests feel at home, whatever their age. Moonfleet's dining room, whose décor and style would do credit to a fashionable London restaurant, offers an excellent and varied menu based on fresh local produce but bringing culinary styles from around the world. Facilities at the hotel include an indoor swimming pool with squash and tennis courts for the more energetic. Key places of interest nearby include Abbotsbury, Dorchester, Corfe Castle and Lulworth Cove, whilst in Weymouth itself the Sea Life Park, The Deep Sea Adventure and The Titanic Story are worth a visit.

Our inspector loved: *Its unique, stylish provision for families with children.*

Directions: Take B3157 Weymouth to Bridport Road, then turn off towards the sea at sign for Fleet.

Web: www.johansens.com/moonfleetmanor
E-mail: info@moonfleetmanor.com
Tel: 0870 381 8744
International: +44 (0)1305 786948
Fax: 01305 774395

Price Guide:
single from £95
double/twin £125–£265
suite £275–£350

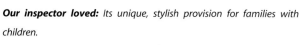

125

HEADLAM HALL

HEADLAM, NR GAINFORD, DARLINGTON, COUNTY DURHAM DL2 3HA

Directions: Headlam is 2 miles north of Gainford off A67 Darlington–Barnard Castle road.

Web: www.johansens.com/headlamhall
E-mail: admin@headlamhall.co.uk
Tel: 0870 381 8590
International: +44 (0)1325 730238
Fax: 01325 730790

Price Guide:
single £75–£95
double/twin £90–£115
suite from £120

This magnificent 17th-century Jacobean mansion stands in 4 acres of formal walled gardens. The grand main lawn, ancient beach hedges and flowing waters evoke an air of tranquillity. Located in the picturesque hamlet of Headlam and surrounded by over 200 acres of its own rolling farmland, Headlam Hall offers guests a special ambience of seclusion and opulence. The traditional bedrooms are all en suite and furnished to a high standard, many with period furniture. The restaurant offers the very best of classic English and Continental cuisine with the kitchen team enjoying a fine reputation for their dishes. An extensive well-chosen wine list highlights the dining experience. Guests may dine in the tasteful surroundings of either the Panelled room, the Victorian room, the Patio room or Conservatory. The main hall features huge stone pillars and the superb original carved oak fireplace, which has dominated the room for over 300 years. The elegant Georgian drawing room opens on to a stepped terrace overlooking the main lawn. The hotel also offers extensive conference facilities and a fine ballroom, the Edwardian Suite with its oak floor and glass ceiling, suitable for up to 150 people. The vast range of leisure facilities include an indoor pool, sauna, gym, tennis court, croquet lawn, course fishery, a snooker room and a new 9-hole golf course due to open in the spring 2004.

Our inspector loved: *The four-poster and antique beds in this friendly family hotel.*

SEAHAM HALL HOTEL & SERENITY SPA

LORD BYRON'S WALK, SEAHAM, CO DURHAM SR7 7AG

Standing near the cliffs of the north sea, Seaham Hall is an unforgettably charming hotel set amongst 30 acres of landscaped clifftop grounds. Lord Byron married here and regal court was held within its solid stone walls. Within the elegant interior, quality and attention to detail are immediately palpable and guests are welcomed by extremely hospitable staff. Spacious bedrooms have sea views and exude an air of opulent decadence with huge beds, a pillow menu, stunning limestone fireplaces and original works of art, all with CD, surround sound, intelligent lighting and internet access. Outstanding bathrooms have baths for 2 and ground floor suites have private gardens. Eclectic modern cuisine that is both imaginative and delicious is created using only the finest fresh ingredients. Guests may enjoy a wonderful breakfast in bed every morning. The Serenity spa is based on Feng Shui principles and promises to be the best of its kind in Europe. It offers a variety of holistic and exotic body treatments for complete relaxation. Guests can enjoy a taste of Siam in the Thai Brasserie & Juice Bar.

Our inspector loved: The life-size baby elephant surrounded by water at the entrance to the Serenity spa.

Directions: From A1 (north) take exit A19 for Tyne Tunnel. From A1 (south) take exit at Jct 62 for A690, then travel north through Houghton le Spring. Take exit for A19 southbound. Come off A19 at exit marked B1404 Seaham.

Web: www.johansens.com/seahamhall
E-mail: reservations@seaham-hall.com
Tel: 0870 381 8889
International: +44 (0)191 516 1400
Fax: 0191 516 1410

Price Guide:
single £185–£315
double/twin £195–£325
suites £385–£500

FIVE LAKES RESORT

COLCHESTER ROAD, TOLLESHUNT KNIGHTS, MALDON, ESSEX CM9 8HX

Set in 320 acres, Five Lakes is a superb hotel which combines the latest in sporting, leisure and health activities with a range of conference, meeting and banqueting facilities. The 194 bedrooms are furnished to a high standard and offer every comfort and convenience. With its 2 18-hole golf courses – one of them, the Lakes Course, designed by Neil Coles MBE and used annually by the PGA European Tour – the hotel is already recognised as one of East Anglia's leading golf venues. Guests are also invited to take advantage of the championship standard indoor tennis courts, outdoor tennis, squash, badminton, indoor pool with Jacuzzi, steam and sauna; gymnasium; jogging trail, snooker and Health & Beauty Spa. There is a choice of restaurants, where good food is complemented by excellent service. Lounges and 2 bars provide a comfortable environment in which to relax and enjoy a drink. Extensive facilities for conferences, meetings, exhibitions and functions include 18 meeting rooms, a 3,500 sqm exhibition hall suitable for over 2,000 people and a dedicated activity field.

Directions: From M25 jct 28 to A12, look for brown signs at Gt Braxted/Silver End exit or A12 from north, look for brown signs at Kelvedon all the way.

Web: www.johansens.com/fivelakes
E-mail: johansens@fivelakes.co.uk
Tel: 0870 381 8524
International: +44 (0)1621 868888
Fax: 01621 869696

Price Guide: (room only)
single £110
double/twin £155
suites £225

Our inspector loved: *The glass staircase and water features in the Atrium style lounge.*

        SPA

MAISON TALBOOTH

STRATFORD ROAD, DEDHAM, COLCHESTER, ESSEX CO7 6HN

In the north-east corner of Essex, where the River Stour borders with Suffolk, is the Vale of Dedham, an idyllic riverside setting immortalised in the early 19th century by the paintings of John Constable. One summer's day in 1952, the young Gerald Milsom enjoyed a "cuppa" in the Talbooth tearoom and soon afterwards took the helm at what would develop into Le Talbooth Restaurant. Business was soon booming and the restaurant built itself a reputation as one of the best in the country. In 1969 Maison Talbooth was created in a nearby Victorian rectory, to become, as it still is, a standard bearer for Britain's premier country house hotels. Indeed, in 1982 Gerald Milsom became the founder of the Pride of Britain group. With its atmosphere of opulence, Maison Talbooth has 10 spacious guest suites which all have an air of quiet luxury. Every comfort has been provided. Breakfast is served in the suites. The original Le Talbooth Restaurant is about half a mile upstream on a riverside terrace reached by leisurely foot or courtesy car. The hotel arranges special Constable tours. New for 2003 is the opportunity for a special exclusive use package; please call for details. Special short breaks also available.

Our inspector loved: The welcoming greeting on the front steps.

Directions: Dedham is about a mile from the A12 between Colchester and Ipswich.

Web: www.johansens.com/maisontalbooth
E-mail: maison@talbooth.co.uk
Tel: 0870 381 8712
International: +44 (0)1206 322367
Fax: 01206 322752

Price Guide:
single £120–£160
double/twin £160–£220

GREENWOODS ESTATE

STOCK ROAD, STOCK, ESSEX CM4 9BE

Directions: From the A12 take the B1007.

Web: www.johansens.com/greenwoods
E-mail: info@greenwoodsestate.com
Tel: 0870 381 8575
International: +44 (0)1277 829990
Fax: 01277 829899

Price Guide:
single from £100
double/twin from £120
suite from £180

For rest, relaxation and rebuilding energy few places can better this luxury health spa and peaceful retreat situated in the Essex countryside, just 40 minutes from London. Greenwoods stands on a high point at the edge of the village of Stock, famed for its church belfry whose beams originate from Spanish galleons. A beautifully restored and extended Grade II listed manor house, its architecture is a combination of Georgian and Victorian. Amidst the 42 acres of parkland there are 4 acres of formal gardens, a sunken herb garden supplying the kitchens with the freshest produce. The yoga-loving chef offers an imaginative and creative combination of fine dining and a naturally balanced "act of well-being" menu. The emphasis is on nutritional balance and the style contemporary with a twist! Guests are offered opulence without intimidation, character, charm and welcoming hospitality. Public areas are lavishly decorated with sumptuous panelling, superb original fireplaces and comfortable sofas. Bedrooms are individually designed and furnished and fitted to the highest standards. Some have antique beds, many have panoramic views. The spa facilities include a full range of health, beauty and holistic treatments, 25 qualified therapists, sauna, steam and ice rooms, gymnasium and a 20-metre swimming pool. There are excellent facilities available for business meetings and small conferences.

Our inspector loved: *The original hand-painted graphics in the new wing.*

          SPA

THE SWAN HOTEL AT BIBURY

BIBURY, GLOUCESTERSHIRE GL7 5NW

The Swan Hotel at Bibury in the South Cotswolds, a 17th-century coaching inn, is a perfect base for both leisurely and active holidays which will appeal especially to motorists, fishermen and walkers. The hotel has its own fishing rights and a moated ornamental garden encircled by its own crystalline stream. Bibury itself is a delightful village, with its honey-coloured stonework, picturesque ponds, the trout-filled River Coln and its utter lack of modern eyesores. The beautiful Arlington Row and its cottages are a vision of old England. When Cotswold Inns and Hotels recently acquired the Swan they gained a distinctive hotel in the English countryside which acknowledges the needs of the sophisticated modern-day traveller. The property has previously undergone a programme of refurbishment and upgrading of the hotel and its services with the accent on unpretentious comfort. Oak panelling, plush carpets and sumptuous fabrics create the background for the fine paintings and antiques that grace the interiors. The 18 bedrooms are superbly appointed with luxury bathrooms and comfortable furnishings. Guests may dine in the brassiere for lunch or the magnificent signet dining room for dinner. Midweek special rates available.

Our inspector loved: The pretty riverside location.

Directions: Bibury is signposted off A40 Oxford–Cheltenham road, on the left hand side. Secure free parking now available next to the hotel.

Web: www.johansens.com/swanhotelatbibury
E-mail: swanhotl@swanhotel-cotswold.co.uk
Tel: 0870 381 8931
International: +44 (0)1285 740695
Fax: 01285 740473

Price Guide:
single £99–£155
double/twin £130–£260

HOTEL ON THE PARK

EVESHAM ROAD, CHELTENHAM, GLOUCESTERSHIRE GL52 2AH

Directions: The hotel is opposite Pittville Park, a 5-minute walk from the town centre.

Web: www.johansens.com/hotelonthepark
E-mail: stay@hotelonthepark.co.uk
Tel: 0870 381 8623
International: +44 (0)1242 518898
Fax: 01242 511526

Price Guide:
single from £91.50
double/twin from £122

Set in the Regency town of Cheltenham, Hotel on the Park is an attractive town house hotel which combines the attentive service of bygone times with an excellent standard of accommodation. The impressive façade, dominated by the grand pillared doorway, hints at the splendour that lies inside. Each of the 12 bedrooms is individually styled and decorated with interesting antiques and exquisite fabrics. Every possible comfort has been provided. Throughout the property the theme of understated elegance prevails and this is truly evident in The Bacchanalian Restaurant with its high ceilings and beautiful hand-detailed cornice work. Guests may enjoy the glorious views of Pittville Park whilst sampling the inspired creations from the extensive menu along with a selection from the detailed wine list. The well-appointed Library is an ideal venue for board meetings or seminars. Special occasions including private banquets or wedding receptions can be arranged. Synonymous with National Hunt Racing, the spa town of Cheltenham is particularly popular during the racing season and hosts the Gold Cup. The town is also renowned for its Regency architecture, attractive promenade and exclusive boutiques. Historic properties, museums and theatres abound whilst other activities include golf, horse-riding, rambling and exploring the Cotswolds.

Our inspector loved: The stylish decoration throughout and the massaging beds!

THE GREENWAY

SHURDINGTON, CHELTENHAM, GLOUCESTERSHIRE GL51 4UG

Set amidst gentle parkland with the rolling Cotswold hills beyond, The Greenway is an Elizabethan country house with a style that is uniquely its own – very individual and very special. Renowned for the warmth of its welcome, its friendly atmosphere and its immaculate personal service, The Greenway is the ideal place for total relaxation. The public rooms with their antique furniture and fresh flowers are elegant and spacious yet comfortable, with roaring log fires in winter and access to the formal gardens in summer. The 21 bedrooms all have private bathrooms and are individually decorated with co-ordinated colour schemes. Eleven of the rooms are located in the main house with a further ten rooms in the converted Georgian coach house immediately adjacent to the main building. The award-winning conservatory dining room overlooks the sunken garden, providing the perfect backdrop to superb cuisine of international appeal complemented by an outstanding selection of wines. Situated in one of Britain's most charming areas, The Greenway is well placed for visiting the spa town of Cheltenham, the Cotswold villages and Shakespeare country.

Our inspector loved: The welcoming entrance hall with grand fire place and fresh flowers.

Directions: On the outskirts of Cheltenham off the A46 Cheltenham–Stroud road, 2½ miles from the town centre.

Web: www.johansens.com/greenway
E-mail: greenway@btconnect.com
Tel: 0870 381 8574
International: +44 (0)1242 862352
Fax: 01242 862780

Price Guide:
single from £99
double/twin £150–£240

CHARINGWORTH MANOR

NR CHIPPING CAMPDEN, GLOUCESTERSHIRE GL55 6NS

Directions: Charingworth Manor is on the B4035 between Chipping Campden and Shipston-on-Stour.

Web: www.johansens.com/charingworthmanor
E-mail: charingworthmanor@englishrosehotels.co.uk
Tel: 0870 381 8414
International: +44 (0)1386 593555
Fax: 01386 593353

Price Guide: (including full breakfast)
limited double sole occupancy from £125
double/twin from £180

The ancient manor of Charingworth lies amid the gently rolling Cotswold countryside, just a few miles from the historic towns of Chipping Campden and Broadway. Beautiful old stone buildings everywhere recall the flourishing wool trade that gave the area its wealth. The 14th-century manor house overlooks its own 50-acre grounds and offers peace and enthralling views. Inside, Charingworth is a historic patchwork of intimate public rooms with log fires burning during the colder months. There are 26 individually designed bedrooms, including a limited number of non smoking rooms, all furnished with antiques and fine fabrics. Outstanding cuisine is regarded as being of great importance and guests at Charingworth are assured of imaginative dishes. Great emphasis is placed on using only the finest produce and the AA has awarded the cuisine 2 Rosettes. There is an all-weather tennis court within the grounds, while inside, a beautiful swimming pool, sauna, steam room, solarium and gym are available, allowing guests to relax and unwind. Warwick Castle, Hidcote Manor Gardens, Batsford Arboretum, Stratford-upon-Avon, Oxford and Cheltenham are all within easy reach. Short break rates are available on request.

Our inspector loved: *The oak beamed bedrooms and inviting swimming pool.*

COTSWOLD HOUSE HOTEL

HIGH STREET, CHIPPING CAMPDEN, GLOUCESTERSHIRE GL55 6AN

Chipping Campden is a nostalgic Cotswold town, unspoilt by the 20th-century, and Cotswold House is a splendid 17th-century mansion facing the town square, impressive with colonnades flanking the front door and built in the lovely soft local stone. The interior has been sensitively decorated and modernised so there is no distraction from the graceful pillared archway and staircase. Lovely antiques, fine paintings and fabrics reminiscent of the Regency era blend easily with comfortable sofas in the elegant drawing room. The bedrooms are very individual, but all are peaceful, decorated in harmonious colours and have country house style furnishings. Cotswold House is deservedly proud of its kitchen, which has won many accolades. The attractive Garden Room Restaurant has a splendid menu and a cellar book of 150 wines. Informal meals are served in Hicks' Brasserie. Private functions and small conferences can be held in the secluded Courtyard Room and The Grammar School Suite. Guests enjoy exploring Chipping Campden's intriguing shops and alleyways. The hotel is a superb base for Stratford-on-Avon, Oxford. The hotel has parking facilities.

Our inspector loved: Everything - comfortable bedrooms with high-tech facilities, great food and beautiful gardens.

Directions: Chipping Campden is 2 miles north-east of A44, on the B4081.

Web: www.johansens.com/cotswoldhouse
E-mail: reception@cotswoldhouse.com
Tel: 0870 381 8449
International: +44 (0)1386 840330
Fax: 01386 840310

Price Guide:
single from £120
double/twin from £175
four poster from £275
cottage rooms from £295
grammar school 2-bed suite from £550

THE NOEL ARMS HOTEL

HIGH STREET, CHIPPING CAMPDEN, GLOUCESTERSHIRE GL55 6AT

Directions: The Noel Arms is in the centre of Chipping Campden, which is on the B4081, 2 miles east of the A44.

Web: www.johansens.com/noelarms
E-mail: bookings@cotswold–inns–hotels.co.uk
Tel: 0870 381 8763
International: +44 (0)1386 840317
Fax: 01386 841136

Price Guide:
single £85
double £120–£140

A long tradition of hospitality awaits you at the Noel Arms Hotel. In 1651 the future Charles II rested here after his Scottish army was defeated by Cromwell at the battle of Worcester, and for centuries the hotel has entertained visitors to the ancient and unspoilt, picturesque Cotswold Village of Chipping Campden. Many reminders of the past, fine antique furniture, swords, shields and other mementoes can be found around the hotel. There are 26 en-suite bedrooms in either the main house or in the tastefully constructed new wing, some of which boast luxurious antique four-poster beds and all offering the standards you expect from a country hotel. The impressive oak-panelled restaurant, awarded 1 AA Rosette, offers an excellent menu including a seasonal selection of fresh local produce. You may be tempted to choose from the extensive range of bar snacks available in the conservatory or Dovers Bar. The fine selection of wines from around the world are delicious accompaniments to any meal. Try some of the traditional cask ales and keg beers. Browse around the delightful array of shops in Chipping Campden or many of the enchanting honey-coloured Cotswold Villages, Hidcote Manor Gardens, Cheltenham Spa, Worcester, Oxford and Stratford-upon-Avon which are all close by.

Our inspector loved: *The stained glass window and armoury in reception.*

THE BEAR OF RODBOROUGH

RODBOROUGH COMMON, STROUD, NR CIRENCESTER, GLOUCESTERSHIRE GL5 5DE

This 17th-century former coaching inn offers comfortable accommodation in an area of outstanding beauty. Nestling on the top of a steep hill, The Bear of Rodborough is situated in the verdant landscape of the western Cotswolds, described by the author, Laurie Lee, as "vegetative virginity". The hotel has undergone a careful and precise restoration, yet many of its past features such as the original archway entrance have been retained. The refurbished bedrooms are exquisite, adorned with plush carpets and beautiful fabrics. All have en-suite facilities and several thoughtful extras. The superb bar, popular with the locals, is renowned for its large selection of traditional beers. Elegantly furnished, the restaurant is enhanced by the ceiling beams with a "running bear" design. Specialities include the full English breakfast, made with fresh local produce, whilst the light luncheons and sumptuous dinners must also be savoured.

Our inspector loved: The warm welcome - also from the big brown bear.

Directions: The nearest motorway is the M5, junction 13.

Web: www.johansens.com/bearofrodborough
E-mail: bookings@cotswold-inns-hotels.co.uk
Tel: 0870 381 8348
International: +44 (0)1453 878522
Fax: 01453 872523

Gloucester
Cheltenham
Cirencester

Price Guide:
single £75–£95
double/twin £120–£130
suite £160

LOWER SLAUGHTER MANOR

LOWER SLAUGHTER, GLOUCESTERSHIRE GL54 2HP

Directions: The Manor is on the right as you enter Lower Slaughter from A429.

Web: www.johansens.com/lowerslaughtermanor
E-mail: lowsmanor@aol.com
Tel: 0870 381 8706
International: +44 (0)1451 820456
Fax: 01451 822150

Price Guide:
single £175–£375
double/twin £200–£400
suite £350–£400

With a history that spans nearly a thousand years, this Grade II listed Manor stands in complete tranquillity within private grounds on the edge of one of the Cotswold's prettiest villages. Lower Slaughter Manor is now owned by Daphne and Roy Vaughan, who have lovingly overseen its transformation. Visitors are warmly welcomed by a team of dedicated staff, and enjoy elegant, spacious surroundings. All rooms are beautifully furnished, with carefully chosen antiques, fine china and original paintings. The Manor has a stunning indoor heated swimming pool, whilst outside the wonderful grounds reveal a croquet lawn and tennis court, and, within the delightful walled garden, a unique 2-storey dovecote dating back to the 15th century when the Manor was a convent. The award-winning cuisine is prepared using the best local and continental ingredients, and an outstanding wine list offers a range of 800 specially selected wines from the Old and New Worlds. An excellent setting for business meetings, The Sir George Whitmore Suite accommodates up to 16 people, and offers phone line, full secretarial services and audio-visual equipment. For more leisurely pursuits, visitors can explore the Cotswolds, Cheltenham, Stratford, and Warwick and Sudeley Castles. Lower Slaughter Manor is a member of The Leading Small Hotels of the World.

Our inspector loved: The beautifully manicured lawns and walled garden.

WASHBOURNE COURT HOTEL

LOWER SLAUGHTER, GLOUCESTERSHIRE GL54 2HS

Under the private ownership of Roy and Daphne Vaughan, Washbourne Court Hotel is in the heart of the tranquil and beautiful Cotswold village of Lower Slaughter, set on the bank of the River Eye. The 4 acres of private gardens have been lovingly re-landscaped with lawns and many delightful features. With just 28 bedrooms, it has parts dating back to the 17th century. The recent additions to the hotel, a spacious new dining room and a further 6 guest rooms with comfortable and elegant furnishings, blend in perfectly with the original building. Always full of freshly picked flowers and planted bowls, the hotel has the feel of a private house with its many personal touches. The modern English cuisine offers an abundance of fresh local produce, concentrating on good textures and intense flavours combined with outstanding presentation. Head chef Sean Ballington now oversees the running of the kitchen. Drinks, light lunches and traditional afternoon tea are also served on the garden terrace during the summer months.

Our inspector loved: *The beautiful setting by the river in this picturesque village.*

Directions: The hotel is situated ½ a mile from the main A429 Fosseway between Stow-on-the-Wold and Bourton-on-the-Water (signed To the Slaughters).

Web: www.johansens.com/washbournecourt
E-mail:
Tel: 0870 381 8970
International: +44 (0)1451 822143
Fax: 01451 821045

Price Guide: (including dinner)
single from £155
double/twin £210–£270

28 🛏 ⚓ **M**50 ⚔7 🎵 ⛳ 🏇 ↻ Ⓗ

BURLEIGH COURT

BURLEIGH, MINCHINHAMPTON, NEAR STROUD, GLOUCESTERSHIRE GL5 2PF

Directions: Leave Stroud on A419 towards Cirencester. After approximately 2½ miles turn right, signposted Burleigh and Minchinhampton. After a further 500 yards turn left and the hotel is signposted.

Web: www.johansens.com/burleighgloucestershire
E-mail: info@burleighcourthotel.co.uk
Tel: 0870 381 8664
International: +44 (0)1453 883804
Fax: 01453 886870

Gloucester
Cheltenham
Cirencester

Price Guide:
single £80-£100
double £105-£145
suite £145

Built in the 18th century, Burleigh Court Hotel is a former gentleman's manor house nestling on the edge of a steep hillside overlooking the Golden Valley in the heart of the Cotswolds. Comfortable surroundings, quality service, the ambience of a bygone era and a tranquil, relaxed atmosphere are combined with 3½ acres of beautifully tended gardens featuring terraces, ponds, pools, hidden pathways and Cotswold stone walls to create an idyllic setting. All the bedrooms are individually and delightfully furnished, with the highest standard of facilities and stunning scenic views. The coach house bedrooms, located by a Victorian plunge pool, and those within the courtyard gardens provide versatile accommodation for families. The elegant restaurant has a reputation for classical cuisine which utilises only the best local produce, whilst an extensive cellar produces a wine list to satisfy the most demanding palate. For special occasions a private dining room overlooking the rear terrace is available. Burleigh Court is perfectly situated to explore the famous honey-stoned villages of the Cotswolds, the market towns of Minchinhampton, Tedbury, Cirencester, Painwick and Bibury and attractions such as Berkely Castle and Chavenage House.

Our inspector loved: The Victorian outdoor pool amongst landscaped gardens.

THE MANOR HOUSE HOTEL

MORETON-IN-MARSH, GLOUCESTERSHIRE GL56 0LJ

This former 16th-century manor house is set in beautiful gardens in the Cotswold village of Moreton-in-Marsh. The Manor House Hotel has been tastefully extended and restored, yet retains many of its historic features, among them a priest's hole and secret passages. The 38 well-appointed bedrooms have been individually decorated and furnished. The 2 Red Rosettes restaurant offers imaginative and traditional English dishes using only the freshest ingredients, accompanied by an expertly selected wine list. For the guest seeking relaxation, leisure facilities include an indoor heated swimming pool and spa bath. Sports enthusiasts will also find that tennis, golf and riding can be arranged locally. Spacious modern business facilities, combined with the peaceful location, make this an excellent venue for executive meetings. It is also an ideal base for touring, with many attractions nearby, including Stratford-upon-Avon, Warwick and the fashionable centres of Cheltenham, Oxford and Bath.

Our inspector loved: The delicious homemade bread and superb sea bass for lunch.

Directions: The Hotel is on the A429 Fosse Way near the junction of the A44 and A429 north of Stow, on the Broadway side of the intersection.

Web: www.johansens.com/manorhousemoreton
E-mail: bookings@cotswold–inns–hotels.co.uk
Tel: 0870 381 8717
International: +44 (0)1608 650501
Fax: 01608 651481

Price Guide:
single £115
double/twin £135–£175
suite £210

THE PAINSWICK HOTEL

KEMPS LANE, PAINSWICK, GLOUCESTERSHIRE GL6 6YB

The village of Painswick stands high on a hill overlooking the beautiful rolling valleys of the Cotswolds. Dating back to the 14th century, the village was an old wool community; medieval cottages mingle gracefully with elegant Georgian merchants' houses. A feature of the village is the church, with its ancient churchyard graced by 99 Yew trees planted in 1792 and 17th-century table tombs in memory of the wealthy clothiers. Situated majestically within these architectural gems is the Palladian-style Painswick Hotel, built in 1790 and formerly the home of affluent village rectors. Each of the luxury en-suite bedrooms have modern amenities, beautiful fabrics, antique furniture and objets d'art, creating a restful atmosphere and the impression of staying in a comfortable private house. The stylish restaurant, with its pine panelling, offers delicious cuisine with an emphasis upon regional produce such as locally reared Cotswold meat, game, wild Severn salmon and Gloucestershire cheeses. The private Dining Room accommodates quiet dinner parties, wedding occasions and business meetings.

Directions: M5 Jct13. Painswick is on A46 between Stroud and Cheltenham, turn into road by the church and continue round the corner, taking the first right. The hotel is at the bottom of the road on the right hand side.

Web: www.johansens.com/painswick
E-mail: Reservations@Painswickhotel.com
Tel: 0870 381 8797
International: +44 (0)1452 812160
Fax: 01452 814059

Price Guide:
single from £90
double/twin from £120–£195

Our inspector loved: The homely atmosphere in a beautiful house with stunning views of the surrounding countryside.

THE GRAPEVINE HOTEL

SHEEP STREET, STOW-ON-THE-WOLD, GLOUCESTERSHIRE GL54 1AU

Set in the pretty town of Stow-on-the-Wold, regarded by many as the jewel of the Cotswolds, The Grapevine Hotel has an atmosphere which makes visitors feel welcome and at ease. The outstanding personal service provided by a loyal team of staff is perhaps the secret of the hotel's success. This, along with the exceptionally high standard of overall comfort and hospitality, earned The Grapevine the 1991 Johansens Hotel Award for Excellence – a well-deserved accolade. Beautifully furnished bedrooms, including 6 superb garden rooms across the courtyard, offer every facility. Visitors can linger over imaginative cuisine in the relaxed and informal atmosphere of the Conservatory Restaurant. Awarded 1 AA Rosette for food, the restaurant, like all of the bedrooms, is non-smoking. Whether travelling on business or pleasure, guests will wish to return to The Grapevine again and again. The local landscape offers unlimited scope for exploration, whether to the numerous picturesque villages in the Cotswolds or to the towns of Oxford, Cirencester and Stratford-upon-Avon. Nature enthusiasts must visit the beautiful gardens of Hidcote, Kifsgate and Barnsley House nearby. Open over Christmas.

Our inspector loved: *The comfortable rooms and relaxed atmosphere.*

Directions: Sheep Street is part of A436 in the centre of Stow-on-the-Wold.

Web: www.johansens.com/grapevine
E-mail: enquiries@vines.co.uk
Tel: 0870 381 8564
International: +44 (0)1451 830344
Fax: 01451 832278

Price Guide:
single from £80
double/twin from £130

THE UNICORN HOTEL

SHEEP STREET, STOW-ON-THE-WOLD, GLOUCESTERSHIRE GL54 1HQ

Low oak-beamed ceilings and large stone fireplaces pay tribute to The Unicorn's lengthy past. Over the last 300 years, the inn has changed its standards of accommodation, incorporating the latest modern facilities, yet many vestiges of the former centuries remain. The recently refurbished interior is decorated in a stylish manner featuring Jacobean furniture and antique artefacts whilst log fires abound. Enhanced by floral quilts and comfortable armchairs, the 20 en-suite bedrooms are simple yet charming. Fine paintings adorn the walls of the public rooms and the cosy bar offers hand-carved wooden chairs and rich carpets. Modern British cooking is served in the elegant surroundings of the Georgian restaurant from an imaginative à la carte menu. The hotel is well frequented on Sundays by guests wishing to indulge in the delicious lunchtime roast. Local leisure facilities include horse riding and the golf course. Shooting and fishing are popular outdoor pursuits. Many historic buildings and castles are within easy reach including the magnificent Blenheim Palace and Warwick Castle. Nature enthusiasts will be delighted with the splendid gardens at Sudeley Castle.

Directions: The nearest motorway is the M40 junction 10. Then take the A44 or the A436 in the direction of Stow-on-the-Wold. The hotel is located on the A429.

Web: www.johansens.com/unicorn
E-mail: reception@birchhotels.co.uk
Tel: 0870 381 8960
International: +44 (0)01451 830257
Fax: 01451 831090

Price Guide:
single £65–£75
double/twin £105–£125

Our inspector loved: The homely welcoming sitting room.

WYCK HILL HOUSE

WYCK HILL, STOW-ON-THE WOLD, GLOUCESTERSHIRE GL54 1HY

Wyck Hill House is a magnificent Cotswold mansion built in the early 1700s, reputedly on the site of an early Roman settlement. It is set in 100 acres of gardens and wooded grounds, overlooking the beautiful Windrush Valley. The hotel has been elegantly restored and the bedrooms, some of which are located in the Coach House and Orangery, are individually furnished to combine superb antiques with modern comforts. There is a suite with a large, antique four-poster bed, which is perfect for a honeymoon or for other special occasions. The cedar-panelled library is an ideal room in which to read, if you wish, and to relax with morning coffee or afternoon tea. The award-winning restaurant provides the highest standards of modern British cuisine from the freshest seasonally available local produce. The menus are complemented by a superb wine list. Wyck Hill House hosts several special events, including opera, travel talks, cultural weekends and a variety of theme activities. The hotel is an ideal base from which to tour the university city of Oxford and the Georgian city of Bath. Cheltenham, Blenheim Palace and Stratford-upon-Avon are just a short drive away. Special price 2-night breaks are available.

Our inspector loved: *The wonderful views of the Windrush Valley from the Conservatory Restaurant.*

Directions: 1½ miles south of Stow-on-the-Wold on A424 Stow–Burford road.

Web: www.johansens.com/wyckhillhouse
E-mail: wyckhill@wrensgroup.com
Tel: 0870 381 9014
International: +44 (0)1451 831936
Fax: 01451 832243

Price Guide:
single £115
double/twin £170
suite £270

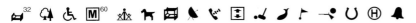

LORDS OF THE MANOR HOTEL

UPPER SLAUGHTER, NR BOURTON-ON-THE-WATER, GLOUCESTERSHIRE GL54 2JD

Directions: Upper Slaughter is 2 miles west of the A429 between Stow-on-the-Wold and Bourton-on-the-Water.

Web: www.johansens.com/lordsofthemanor
E-mail: lordsofthemanor@btinternet.com
Tel: 0870 381 8704
International: +44 (0)1451 820243
Fax: 01451 820696

Price Guide:
single from £99
double/twin £155–£305

Situated in the heart of the Cotswolds, on the outskirts of one of England's most unspoilt and picturesque villages, stands the Lords of the Manor Hotel. Built in the 17th century of honeyed Cotswold stone, the house enjoys splendid views over the surrounding meadows, stream and parkland. For generations the house was the home of the Witts family, who historically had been rectors of the parish. It is from these origins that the hotel derives its distinctive name. Charming, walled gardens provide a secluded retreat at the rear of the house. Each bedroom bears the maiden name of one of the ladies who married into the Witts family; each room is individually and imaginatively decorated with period furniture. The reception rooms are magnificently furnished with fine antiques, paintings, traditional fabrics and masses of fresh flowers. Log fires blaze in cold weather. The heart of this English country house is its dining room, where truly memorable dishes are created from the best local ingredients. Nearby are Blenheim Palace, Warwick Castle, the Roman antiquities at Bath and Shakespeare country.

Our inspector loved: *The wonderfully quiet location and beautiful countryside surroundings.*

CALCOT MANOR

NR TETBURY, GLOUCESTERSHIRE GL8 8YJ

This delightful hotel built of Cotswold stone offers guests tranquillity amidst acres of rolling countryside. Situated in the southern Cotswolds close to the historic town of Tetbury, the building dates back to the 15th century and was a farmhouse until 1983. Its beautiful stone barns and stables include one of the oldest tithe barns in England, built in 1300 by the Cistercian monks from Kingswood Abbey. These buildings form a quadrangle and the stone glistening in the dawn or glowing in the dusk is quite a spectacle. Professional service is complemented by cheerful hospitality without any hint of over-formality. Excellent facilities for families include a number of family suites complete with bunk beds and baby listening devices. A new play facility to keep older children entertained with Playstation, X boxes and a small cinema, and a full-day care crèche for younger children is now open 7 days a week. Parents can escape to the state-of-the-art spa with 16-metre pool, steam room and sauna, gym and outdoor hot tub. The spa also offers a full range of beauty treatments. In the elegant conservatory restaurant dinner is very much the focus of a memorable stay and the congenial Gumstool Bistro and Bar offers a range of simpler traditional food and local ales. A discreet conference facility is available.

Our inspector loved: *The fabulous new health and leisure spa.*

Directions: From Tetbury, take the A4135 signposted Dursley; Calcot is on the right after 3½ miles

Web: www.johansens.com/calcotmanor
E-mail: reception@calcotmanor.co.uk
Tel: 0870 381 8398
International: +44 (0)1666 890391
Fax: 01666 890394

Price Guide:
double/twin £165–£205
family rooms £205
family suites £240

THE CLOSE HOTEL

LONG STREET, TETBURY, GLOUCESTERSHIRE GL8 8AQ

Built in 1585, the Close Hotel and Restaurant is an idyllic Elizabethan manor house with 15 charming, individually styled bedrooms, set in the heart of the delightful market town of Tetbury. Since becoming a hotel in 1974, its reputation has developed, and today it holds the prestigious accolade of 3 AA Rosettes for food over 3 consecutive years. The dinner menu offers a delightful composition of modern and contemporary tastes, each enhanced by thoughtful companions such as star anise ice cream or balsamic jelly and pear chutney, whilst the Tastings menu offers guests a gastronomic journey through 7 courses of the chef's latest creations. An appetite for such a culinary experience can easily be worked up by scouring the many antique shops within walking distance of the hotel, as this area really is a collector's paradise. The historic towns of Cirencester, Cheltenham and Bath are all within easy access, as are the Royal Estates of Highgrove and Gatcombe. Horticulturalists will love the arboretum at Westonbirt, and sporting enthusiasts can enjoy Cheltenham races and motor racing at Castle Combe. The Close is an ideal venue for weddings and small conferences, offering a range of beautifully styled meeting rooms and private use. (N.B. min. age in the restaurant: 12 years).

Directions: The Close is on Long Street, the main street of Tetbury which can be found on the A433, minutes from the M4 and M5. Private parking is at the rear of the hotel in Close Gardens.

Web: www.johansens.com/closehotel
E-mail: reception@theclosehotel.co.uk
Tel: 0870 381 8434
International: +44 (0)1666 502272
Fax: 01666 504401

Price Guide:
single £90
double/twin £160

Our inspector loved: The rooms at the rear overlooking the lovely walled garden.

CORSE LAWN HOUSE HOTEL

CORSE LAWN, NR TEWKESBURY, GLOUCESTERSHIRE GL19 4LZ

Although only 6 miles from the M5 and M50, Corse Lawn is a completely unspoilt, typically English hamlet in a peaceful Gloucestershire backwater. The hotel, an elegant Queen Anne listed building set back from the village green, stands in 12 acres of gardens and grounds and still displays the charm of its historic pedigree. Visitors can be assured of the highest standards of service and cooking: Baba Hine is famous for the dishes she produces, while Denis Hine, of the Hine Cognac family, is in charge of the wine cellar. The service here, now in the hands of son Giles, is faultlessly efficient, friendly and personal. As well as the renowned restaurant, there are 3 comfortable drawing rooms, a large lounge bar, a private dining-cum-conference room for up to 45 persons and a similar, smaller room for up to 20. A tennis court, heated indoor swimming pool and croquet lawn adjoin the hotel and most sports and leisure activities can be arranged. Corse Lawn is ideal for exploring the Cotswolds, Malverns and Forest of Dean.

Our inspector loved: *The personal service in a traditional family-run hotel.*

Directions: Corse Lawn House is situated on the B4211 between the A417 (Gloucester–Ledbury road) and the A438 (Tewkesbury–Ledbury road).

Web: www.johansens.com/corselawn
E-mail: enquiries@corselawn.com
Tel: 0870 381 8448
International: +44 (0)1452 780479/771
Fax: 01452 780840

Price Guide:
single £85
double/twin £130
four-poster £150

HATTON COURT

UPTON HILL, UPTON ST LEONARDS, NR CHELTENHAM, GLOUCESTERSHIRE GL4 8DE

Directions: Leave M5 at Jct 12, A38 towards Gloucester, then B4073 towards Upton St Leonards and Painswick. Hatton Court is located on this road. From North leave M5 at Jct 11a, take A417 towards Cirencester, following signs for A46 Cheltenham/Stroud. At the roundabout take the third exit towards Stroud until you reach Painswick. Turn right onto B4073 towards Upton St Leonards.

Web: www.johansens.com/hattoncourt
E-mail: res@hatton-court.co.uk
Tel: 0870 381 8773
International: +44 (0)1452 617412
Fax: 01452 612945

Price Guide:
single £80–£100
double/twin £115–£196

Tucked away behind a bank of mature trees, Hatton Court sits on the edge of the Cotswold escarpment, between the cathedral city of Gloucester and the glorious village of Painswick. A former splendid private home, the hotel has its own extensive grounds encompassing magnificent gardens and terraced areas, ideal for summer parties. The pace is unhurried, relaxation and comfort are foremost. On arrival guests are welcomed into the reception area which is more of a lounge, with armchairs, magazines, and an open fireplace. The sumptuous ambience is extended in to the bedrooms, all of which are individually decorated and boast en-suite facilities. Executive rooms are available with four-poster bed, mini-bar and whirlpool. . The restaurant combines efficient, friendly service with an elegant, warm setting. Guests can enjoy breathtaking views over the Malvern Hills, Forest of Dean and the Severn Estuary whilst savouring delicious cuisine. The restaurant is complemented by an exceptional wine shop, a unique and unusual feature of this hotel. Visitors to Hatton Court have use of the Health Suite, complete with sauna, whirlpool, and mini gym, while in warmer weather a game of croquet on the lawn makes for relaxing afternoon. This is the perfect location to explore the glorious Cotswold countryside, the Rococo Gardens in Painswick and the "Regency" Cheltenham Spa.

Our inspector loved: *The panoramic view.*

THORNBURY CASTLE

THORNBURY, SOUTH GLOUCESTERSHIRE BS35 1HH

Built in 1511 by Edward Stafford, third Duke of Buckingham, Thornbury Castle was later owned by Henry VIII, who stayed here in 1535 with Anne Boleyn. Today it stands in 15 acres of regal splendour with its vineyard, high walls and the oldest Tudor garden in England. Rich furnishings are displayed against the handsome interior features, including ornate oriel windows, panelled walls and large open fireplaces. The 25 carefully restored bedchambers retain many period details. Thornbury Castle has received many accolades for its luxurious accommodation and excellent cuisine, which includes delights such as Brixham fish and shellfish, Goosnargh ducklings and chickens, Scotch beef, West Country game, pork and local vegetables. The Castle also provides peaceful and secluded meeting facilities. Thornbury is an ideal base from which to explore Bath, Wales and the Cotswolds. Personally guided tours are available to introduce guests to the little-known as well as the famous places which are unique to the area. In addition, clay pigeon shooting, archery and golf may be enjoyed locally.

Our inspector loved: The high ceilings with ornate plasterwork and huge open fireplaces.

Directions: The entrance to the Castle is left of the Parish Church at the lower end of Castle Street.

Web: www.johansens.com/thornburycastle
E-mail: info@thornburycastle.co.uk
Tel: 0870 381 8944
International: +44 (0)1454 281182
Fax: 01454 416188

Price Guide:
single from £110
double/twin from £140
suite from £280

ESSEBORNE MANOR

HURSTBOURNE TARRANT, ANDOVER, HAMPSHIRE SP11 0ER

Directions: Midway between Newbury and Andover on the A343, 1½ miles north of Hurstbourne Tarrant.

Web: www.johansens.com/essebornemanor
E-mail: esseborne@aol.com
Tel: 0870 381 8506
International: +44 (0)1264 736444
Fax: 01264 736725

Price Guide:
single £95–£130
double/twin £100–£180

Esseborne Manor is small and unpretentious, yet stylish. The present house was built at the end of the 19th century and carries the name used to record details of the local village in the Domesday Book. It is set in a pleasing garden amid the rich farmland of the North Wessex Downs in a designated area of outstanding natural beauty. Ian and Lucilla Hamilton, who own the house, have established the restful atmosphere of a private country home where guests can unwind and relax. There are just 15 comfortable bedrooms, some reached via a courtyard. Two doubles and a delightful suite are in converted cottages with their own patio overlooking the main gardens. The pretty sitting room and cosy library are comfortable areas in which to relax. Dave Morris's fine 2 Rosette cooking is set off to advantage in the new dining room and adjoining bar. There is now a spacious meeting and function facility. In the grounds there is a herb garden, an all-weather tennis court, a croquet lawn and plenty of good walking beyond. Nearby Newbury racecourse has a busy programme of steeple-chasing and flat racing. Places to visit include Highclere Castle, Stonehenge, Salisbury, Winchester and Oxford.

Our inspector loved: *This delightful country house where nothing is ever too much trouble. The Hamilton family love to please their guests.*

TYLNEY HALL

ROTHERWICK, HOOK, HAMPSHIRE RG27 9AZ

Arriving at this hotel in the evening with its floodlit exterior and forecourt fountain, you can imagine arriving for a party in a private stately home. Grade II listed and set in 66 acres of ornamental gardens and parkland, Tylney Hall typifies the great houses of the past. Apéritifs are taken in the wood-panelled library bar; haute cuisine is served in the glass-domed Oak Room restaurant. The hotel holds RAC and AA food awards and also AA 4 Red Stars and RAC Gold Ribbon. The Health and leisure facilities include a heated pool and whirlpool, solarium, fitness studio, beauty and hairdressing, sauna, tennis, croquet and snooker, whilst hot-air ballooning, archery, clay pigeon shooting, golf and riding can be arranged. Surrounding the hotel are wooded trails ideal for jogging. Functions for up to 100 people are catered for in the Tylney Suite or Chestnut Suite; more intimate gatherings are available in one of the other ten private banqueting rooms. Tylney Hall is licensed to hold wedding ceremonies on site. The cathedral city of Winchester and Stratfield Saye House are nearby. Legoland and Windsor Castle are a 40-minute drive away.

Our inspector loved: Coming up the winding drive, through the stately trees to 66 acres of garden and a wonderful welcome.

Directions: M4, Jct11, towards Hook and Rotherwick, follow signs to hotel. M3, Jct5, A287 towards Newnham, over A30 into Old School Road. Left for Newnham and right onto Ridge Lane. Hotel is on the left after 1 mile.

Web: www.johansens.com/tylneyhall
E-mail: reservations@tylneyhall.com
Tel: 0870 381 8958
International: +44 (0)1256 764881
Fax: 01256 768141

Price Guide:
single £135–£400
double/twin £165–£220
suite £285–£430

153

THE MONTAGU ARMS HOTEL

BEAULIEU, NEW FOREST, HAMPSHIRE SO42 7ZL

Situated at the head of the River Beaulieu in the heart of the New Forest, The Montagu Arms Hotel carries on a tradition of hospitality started 700 years ago. As well as being a good place for a holiday, the hotel is an ideal venue for small conferences. Each of the 24 bedrooms has been individually styled and many are furnished with four-poster beds. Dine in the oak-panelled restaurant overlooking the garden, where you can enjoy cuisine prepared by award-winning chef Haydn Laidlow. The menu is supported by an outstanding wine list. Alternatively dine less formally in Monty's Bar Brasserie now delightfully presented in keeping with the building. It offers homemade fare together with real ales and an extensive choice of wine. The hotel offers complimentary membership of an exclusive health club 6 miles away. Facilities there include a supervised gymnasium, large indoor ozone pool, Jacuzzi, steam room, sauna and beauty therapist. With much to see and do around Beaulieu why not hire a mountain bike? Visit the National Motor Museum, Exbury Gardens or Bucklers Hard, or walk for miles through the beautiful New Forest. Special tariffs are available throughout the year.

Directions: The village of Beaulieu is well signposted and the hotel commands an impressive position at the foot of the main street.

Web: www.johansens.com/montaguarms
E-mail: reservations@montaguarmshotel.co.uk
Tel: 0870 381 8743
International: +44 (0)1590 612324
Fax: 01590 612188

Price Guide: (inclusive terms available)
single £100–£145
double/twin £160–£190
suites £190–£210

Our inspector loved: The polished floors and resident donkeys.

CAREYS MANOR HOTEL

BROCKENHURST, NEW FOREST, HAMPSHIRE SO42 7RH

Careys Manor dates from 1888 and is built on the site of a royal hunting lodge used by Charles II. Situated close to the glorious New Forest countryside, the hotel is proud of the personal welcome and care it extends to its visitors. The bedrooms are comfortably appointed and furnished in a range of styles. In the modern Garden Wing some rooms have balconies and others open directly onto lawns and borders. The restaurant offers a hearty breakfast and an English and French influenced cuisine at dinner. The superb new leisure complex is an outstanding state of the art facility. A huge range of specialist sport, beauty therapies and massage are available to guests by skilled Thai staff in a wide selection of treatment rooms. Windsurfing, riding and sailing can all be enjoyed locally, whilst Stonehenge, Beaulieu, Broadlands, Salisbury and Winchester are a short distance away. Business interests can be catered for – there are comprehensive self-contained conference facilities.

Our inspector loved: This hotel's commitment to the continual enchantment of the guest experience.

Directions: From M27 junction 1, follow A337 signed to Lymington. Careys Manor is on the left after 30 mph sign at Brockenhurst.

Web: www.johansens.com/careysmanor
E-mail: info@careysmanor.com
Tel: 0870 381 8405
International: +44 (0)1590 623551
Fax: 01590 622799

Price Guide:
double/twin £129–£179
suite £199

NEW PARK MANOR

LYNDHURST ROAD, BROCKENHURST, NEW FOREST, HAMPSHIRE SO42 7QH

Escape from the pressures of a hectic lifestyle in this Grade II listed former hunting lodge of Charles II which dates from the 16th century. The house stands within its own clearing in the heart of the New Forest, yet is easily accessed from the main Lyndhurst/Lymington road. All bedrooms boast fine views of the surrounding parklands and forest and are individually decorated, in keeping with the historic nature of the house. The New Forest rooms are contemporary in style and even have LCD TV screens in the bathrooms! Wandering ponies and wild deer can be viewed from the hotel and on the many walks and paths that run through the forest. The hotel has its own Equestrian Centre, with BHS trained stable crew, heated outdoor pool and tennis courts. It affords a perfect starting point from which to explore the surrounding countryside and to visit the nearby coast and sailing of the Solent. The new lively Polo Bar offers a light menu throughout the day whilst the romantic restaurant provides a more extensive menu serving traditional British cuisine with a continental twist. The views from the New Forest room, with its picture windows, provides a wonderful setting for parties and functions, which are tailor-made to suit personal requirements.

Directions: New Park Manor is ½ mile off the A337 between Lyndhurst and Brockenhurst, easily reached from the M27 junction 1.

Web: www.johansens.com/newparkmanor
E-mail: enquiries@newparkmanorhotel.co.uk
Tel: 0870 381 8761
International: +44 (0)1590 623467
Fax: 01590 622268

Price Guide:
single from £85
double/twin £110–£190
four poster £190

Our inspector loved: *The new-look bedrooms and the restyled mezzanine.*

OLD THORNS HOTEL, GOLF & COUNTRY CLUB

LONGMOOR ROAD, GRIGGS GREEN, LIPHOOK, HAMPSHIRE GU30 7PE

Originally a 17th-century farmhouse, Old Thorns is situated within 400 acres of some of the finest Hampshire countryside. The 33 en-suite bedrooms are elegantly decorated and have generously oversized beds. Guests are able to enjoy one of Britain's best authentic Japanese restaurants, Nippon Kan, where Teppan Yaki is a speciality or alternatively they can dine in the informal Sands brasserie, which combines contemporary cuisine with traditional favourites. The hotel has a stunning 18-hole championship golf course designed by Peter Alliss and Dave Thomas – the elevated positions of many of the holes offer spectacular views and the rolling fairways bring the numerous natural springs, lakes and trees into play. The Country Club offers an indoor pool, sauna, steam room, solarium, fitness centre, outdoor tennis as well as luxurious facials, wraps and spa treatments. Easily accessible from London and the M25, Old Thorns is also a popular conference venue – from small meetings in the Boardroom to larger functions in the Hampshire Suite for up to 80. All around are pretty villages and historic towns and the maritime history of Portsmouth is just a short drive away. Places of interest include Jane Austen's home, Chawton House, the Gilbert White Museum and the Hollycombe Steam Collection.

Our inspector loved: *Golfers will love the marvellous facilities and the spacious green acres.*

Directions: From the M25 jct 10 turn south on the A3 and exit at Griggs Green. The hotel is signed after ½ mile.

Web: www.johansens.com/oldthorns
E-mail: info@oldthorns.com
Tel: 0870 381 8788
International: +44 (0)1428 724555
Fax: 01428 725036

Price Guide:
single from £140
double/twin from £160
suite from £195

PASSFORD HOUSE HOTEL

MOUNT PLEASANT LANE, LYMINGTON, HAMPSHIRE SO41 8LS

Directions: Exit 1/M27, A337 to Brockenhurst. After railway bridge and mini roundabout, right at Tollhouse Pub and bear right into Mount Pleasant Lane. Hotel is 1 mile past garden centre.

Web: www.johansens.com/passfordhouse
E-mail: sales@passfordhousehotel.co.uk
Tel: 0870 381 8804
International: +44 (0)1590 682398
Fax: 01590 683494

Price Guide:
single from £80
double/twin from £130

Set in 9 acres of picturesque gardens and rolling parkland, the Passford House Hotel lies midway between the charming New Forest village of Sway and the Georgian splendour of Lymington. Once the home of Lord Arthur Cecil, it is steeped in history and the traditions of leisurely country life. Pleasantly decorated bedrooms include a number of superior rooms, whilst comfort is the keynote in the 4 public lounges. The hotel prides itself on the standard and variety of cuisine served in its delightful restaurant and the extensive menu aims to give pleasure to the most discerning of palates. Meals are complemented by a speciality wine list. The hotel boasts a compact leisure centre, catering for all ages and activities. In addition to 2 heated swimming pools, there is a multi-gym, sauna, pool table, croquet lawn, pétanque and tennis court. Just a short drive away are Beaulieu, the cathedral cities of Winchester and Salisbury and ferry ports to the Isle of Wight and France. The New Forest has numerous golf courses, riding and trekking centres, cycling paths, beautiful walks, and of course sailing on the Solent. Milford-on-Sea, 4 miles away, is the nearest beach.

Our inspector loved: *The dedication to guests' comfort and the 2 swimming pools.*

LE POUSSIN AT PARKHILL

BEAULIEU ROAD, LYNDHURST, NEW FOREST, HAMPSHIRE SO43 7FZ

A winding drive through glorious parkland and lawned grounds leads to this gracious 18th-century country house which is now a renowned and popular restaurant with accommodation. Built on the site of a 13th-century hunting lodge, Le Poussin stands in an elevated position with superb views across its 13-acre surrounds and open forest. It offers remoteness and period comfort coupled with an outstanding excellence of standards, service and cuisine. Dining in the elegant restaurant is a delight to be sampled leisurely while viewing deer grazing just a few steps away. Internationally acclaimed chef patron Alex Aiken holds a Michelin Star and 3 AA Rosettes. His innovative, imaginative cuisine is a joy not to be missed. The bedrooms are being refurbished to high standards compatible with the delightful restaurant and public rooms. There is also a small cottage with its own walled garden for those wishing to bring a dog. It is ideal for visiting the many places of interest, all within easy driving distance. These include Exbury Gardens, home to one of the world's finest collections of rhododendrons and azaleas, Broadlands, the old home of Lord Mountbatten, and the cathedral cities of Salisbury and Winchester.

Our inspector loved: The tiles in the gentlemen's toilet; and the stunning food - be prepared to eat.

Directions: From Lyndhurst take B3056 towards Beaulieu. Parkhill is approximately a mile from Lyndhurst on the right.

Web: www.johansens.com/lepoussinatparkhill
E-mail: sales@lepoussinatparkhill.co.uk
Tel: 0870 381 8683
International: +44 (0)23 8028 2944
Fax: 023 8028 3268

Price Guide:
single from £70
double/twin from £80
suites from £140

CHEWTON GLEN

NEW MILTON, HAMPSHIRE BH25 6QS

Voted Best Country House Hotel in the World by Gourmet magazine, Chewton Glen is set in 130 acres of gardens, woodland and parkland on the edge of the New Forest, close to the sea. Owners Martin and Brigitte Skan have created a haven of tranquillity, luxury and comfort. The wonderful setting of the restaurant, which overlooks the landscaped gardens, adds to the sublime culinary experience created by head chef Alan Murchison, who uses fresh local produce to create surprising and delicious dishes, complemented by an impressive wine list. The 59 sumptuous bedrooms, all individually designed with carefully chosen fabrics, are the ultimate in luxury with fantastic marble bathrooms, cosy bathrobes and views over the surrounding parkland. The stunning new Spa opened in spring 2002. In addition to the magnificent 17.5m pool, there are now improved changing rooms with their own steam room and sauna, more treatment rooms, larger gym, hydrotherapy pool and a totally new lounge, buffet and bar with a conservatory and sun terrace. There are indoor and outdoor tennis courts, a 9-hole par 3 golf course and an outdoor swimming pool. Fishing, shooting and riding can be arranged locally.

Directions: Take A35 from Lyndhurst towards Bournemouth. Turn left at Walkford, then left before roundabout. The hotel is on the right.

Web: www.johansens.com/chewtonglen
E-mail: reservations@chewtonglen.com
Tel: 0870 381 8427
International: +44 (0)1425 275341
Fax: 01425 272310

Price Guide: (room only)
double £195–£425
suites £460–£745

Our inspector loved: The spacious, superbly styled ambience of the stunningly beautiful spa – here is your opportunity for total indulgence.

 SPA

GRAND HARBOUR

WEST QUAY ROAD, SOUTHAMPTON, HAMPSHIRE SO15 1AG

With its dramatic glazed Atrium and vast expanse of glass, the De Vere Grand Harbour is unique, a futuristically designed hotel occupying an attractive location alongside Southampton's medieval town wall. Planned and built in a "Y" shape to provide magnificent views for as many as possible of the 172 guest rooms, its focal point is the Atrium, which overlooks the historic site from where the Mayflower set sail in 1620. Each en-suite room is superbly decorated with every comfort and many have king-size beds. Most waterfront rooms have balconies so guests can fully appreciate the view. Facilities in the split-level pavilion include the Leisure Club, which offers hi-tech gymnasium equipment and a 15-metre heated indoor pool. Further relaxation can be found in the sauna and steam room and a complete range of pampering treatments are available in the Beauty Salon. Guests have a choice of dining experiences; from the award winning, informal Brewsters restaurant to the more intimate fine dining Allertons, the à la carte restaurant, which is possibly Southampton's best kept secret where the elegant seating and surrounds offer more privacy for special occasions. The hotel is an ideal setting from which to explore aspects of the south coast such as the New Forest, Winchester and even the Isle of Wight.

Our inspector loved: The proximity to the city's maritime heritage and today's great cruise liners.

Directions: The nearest motorways are the M3, junction 13 and the M27, junction 3. Follow waterfront signs to West Quay Road.

Web: www.johansens.com/grandharbour
E-mail: grandharbour@devere-hotels.com
Tel: 0870 381 9068
International: +44 (0)23 8063 3033
Fax: 023 8063 3066

Price Guide:
single from £165
double £185 - £215
suite £295 - £430

HOTEL DU VIN & BISTRO

SOUTHGATE STREET, WINCHESTER, HAMPSHIRE SO23 9EF

Relaxed, charming and unpretentious are words which aptly describe the stylish and intimate Hotel du Vin & Bistro. This elegant hotel is housed in one of Winchester's most important Georgian buildings, dating back to 1715. It was the first of this successful group's properties and established an entirely new approach to what hotels are all about. The 23 individually decorated bedrooms feature superb beds made up with crisp Egyptian cotton and offer every modern amenity, including trouser press, mini bar and CD players. Each bedroom is sponsored by a wine house whose vineyard features in its decorations. Bathrooms boasting power showers, oversized baths and fluffy towels and robes add to guests' sense of luxury and comfort. Quality food cooked simply with fresh ingredients is the philosophy behind the Bistro, where, as you would expect, an outstanding and reasonably priced wine list is available. There are also 2 function rooms for special occasions. The welcoming and enthusiastic staff cater for every need. The hotel is a perfect base for exploring England's ancient capital, famous for its cathedral, its school and antique shops. The New Forest is a short drive away.

Directions: Take the M3 to Winchester. Southgate Street leads from the city centre to St Cross.

Web: www.johansens.com/hotelduvinwinchester
E-mail: info@winchester.hotelduvin.com
Tel: 0870 381 8615
International: +44 (0)1962 841414
Fax: 01962 842458

Price Guide:
single/double/twin from £105
suite from £185

Our inspector loved: *The relaxed informality of service and rooms.*

ALLT-YR-YNYS HOTEL

WALTERSTONE, NR ABERGAVENNY, HEREFORDSHIRE HR2 0DU

Nestling in the foothills of the Black Mountains, on the fringes of the Brecon Beacons National park, Allt-yr-Ynys is an impressive Grade II 16th-century manor house hotel. The Manor was the home of the Cecil family whose ancestry dates back to Rhodri Mawr, King of Wales in the 8th century. A more recent Cecil was Lord Burleigh, Chief Minister to Queen Elizabeth I, portrayed by Sir Richard Attenborough in the recent film, "Elizabeth". Features of this interesting past still remain and include moulded ceilings, oak panelling and beams and a 16th-century four-poster bed in the Jacobean suite. However, whilst the charm and the character of the period remains, the house has been sympathetically adapted to provide all the comforts expected of a modern hotel. The former outbuildings have been transformed into spacious and well-appointed guest bedrooms. Fine dining is offered in the award-winning restaurant and the conference/function suite accommodates up to 200 guests. Facilities include a heated pool, Jacuzzi, clay pigeon shooting range and private river fishing. Pastimes include exploring the scenery, historic properties and plethora of tourist attractions.

Our inspector loved: *The spacious individually decorated bedrooms, all with glorious secluded views of the countryside.*

Directions: 5 miles north of Abergavenny on A465 Abergavenny/ Hereford trunk road, turn west at Old Pandy Inn in Pandy. After 400 metres turn right down lane at grey/green barn. The hotel is on the right after 400 metres.

Web: www.johansens.com/alltyrynys
E-mail: allthotel@compuserve.com
Tel: 0870 381 8309
International: +44 (0)1873 890307
Fax: 01873 890539

Price Guide: (per room)
single from £75
double/twin from £110
suite £150

THE CHASE HOTEL

GLOUCESTER ROAD, ROSS-ON-WYE, HEREFORDSHIRE HR9 5LH

The Chase Hotel, just a few minutes' walk from the historic market town of Ross-on-Wye, is a handsome Georgian country house hotel situated in 11 acres of beautiful grounds and landscape gardens. The 36 en-suite bedrooms contain all the latest amenities, including satellite television, whilst the bedrooms and lounge areas preserve the original Georgian style of the hotel. Guests wishing to relax will enjoy the convivial ambience and comfortable décor in the Chase Lounge and Bar. Overlooking Chase Hill, the tall elegant windows of the Lounge expose the splendour of the surrounding landscape. The delightful Chase Restaurant, with its delicate peach furnishings, is renowned for its superb traditional cuisine and excellent service and has won several accolades and awards including an AA Rosette. The hotel is an ideal venue for conferences, exhibitions, training activities, weddings including civil ceremonies and events for up to 300 guests. Activities within the locality include water sports, theatre, countryside rambles, fascinating antique centres or perusing the shops in either the historic city of Hereford or Regency Cheltenham.

Our inspector loved: The friendly welcome and relaxing atmosphere.

Directions: From the M50 (Jct4) turn left for Ross-on-Wye, take A40 Gloucester at the second roundabout and turn right for town centre at third roundabout. The Hotel is ½ mile on the left.

Web: www.johansens.com/chasehotel
E-mail: info@chasehotel.co.uk
Tel: 0870 381 8418
International: +44 (0)1989 763161
Fax: 01989 768330

Price Guide:
single £70–£110
double/twin £85–£130
suite £150

Leominster

Hereford

Ross-on-Wye

NEW

THE GROVE HOTEL

CHANDLER'S CROSS, HERTFORDSHIRE WD3 4TG

This magnificent 18th-century former home of the Earls of Clarendon stands in 300 acres of Hertfordshire countryside and has been painstakingly restored and transformed into an impressive cosmopolitan country estate just 45 minutes from the centre of London. The Grove brings together the best of 21st-century living with all that makes a memorable past era so beguiling and attractive: the peace of the countryside, a friendly, personal welcome, a sense of sanctuary and refuge. The attention to detail and quality is balanced with the ethos of pleasure and the wellbeing of guests. The Grove has character, feel and style. Its gardens, grounds and woodland walks are superb; its food, wine, and staff are excellent. The interior is gorgeous and grand with antiques set against contemporary elegance, fine pictures and quirky little effects. Guest rooms and suites are luxuriously appointed. Many have balconies or terraces, some boast working fireplaces, and all offer panoramic garden and parkland views. There are 3 bars, 3 restaurants and a spa with 13 treatment rooms, a saltwater vitality pool, fitness and exercise studios, plus an indoor and outdoor swimming pool, tennis courts and 18-hole golf course.

Our inspector loved: The way the natural beauty of the estate has been incorporated into all aspects of the hotel.

Directions: From M25 clockwise junction 19, anti-clockwise junction 20.

Stevenage
Stansted
Bishop's Stortford
Hertford
St Albans

Web: www.johansens.com/thegrove
E-mail: info@the grove.co.uk
Tel: 0870 381 8646
International: +44 (0)1923 807807
Fax: 01923 221008

Price Guide: (excluding VAT)
single £190–£320
double/twin £190–£320
suite £450–£900

DOWN HALL COUNTRY HOUSE HOTEL

HATFIELD HEATH, NR BISHOP'S STORTFORD, HERTFORDSHIRE CM22 7AS

Set in 110 acres of parkland, this Italianate mansion is the perfect choice for those wishing to escape the pressures of everyday life. A peaceful ambience pervades this tastefully restored country house hotel. The well-appointed bedrooms all feature period furnishings and in-room safes and afford picturesque views across the grounds. Gastronomes will be pleased with the excellent cuisine served in the Downham and the new Ibbetsons 2 Rosette restaurant. Here, English and French dishes are prepared with only the finest fresh ingredients. The superb on-site sporting facilities include 2 all-weather tennis courts, a putting green, croquet lawn, swimming pool, sauna and whirlpool. Clay pigeon shooting, horse-riding and golf can be arranged nearby. Day excursions include visits to Cambridge, horse racing at Newmarket, Constable Country and the old timbered village of Thaxted. This is an ideal venue for board meetings, conferences and corporate hospitality as it offers elegant, airy meeting rooms, a range of good facilities and a secluded environment. The rooms accommodate 10 delegates boardroom style and up to 180 theatre style. Weekend rates are available.

Directions: The hotel is 14 miles from the M25, 7 miles from the M11 and Bishop's Stortford Station. Heathrow Airport is 60 miles away; Stansted is 9 miles. There is ample free parking.

Web: www.johansens.com/downhall
E-mail: sales@downhall.co.uk
Tel: 0870 381 8489
International: +44 (0)1279 731441
Fax: 01279 730416

Price Guide:
single £130–£170
double/twin £150–£190
suite £260

Colchester
Stansted Airport
Harlow   Chelmsford
Southend-on-Sea

Our inspector loved: The chandeliers and beautiful flower arrangements in the elegant lounge with high ceiling.

THE MANOR OF GROVES

HIGH WYCH, SAWBRIDGEWORTH, HERTFORDSHIRE CM21 0JU

After undergoing a £7.5-million refurbishment, Manor of Groves, with its magnificent architecture and grounds is truly a sight to behold. Originally a Georgian manor house, it was transformed into an exquisite country hotel incorporating a state-of-the-art health, beauty and fitness centre, whilst retaining its former grandeur. The main house is linked to the new complex by an eye-catching glass hall that accommodates a brasserie, lounge and bar/coffee area overlooking the picturesque gardens. Guests can choose from the spacious, romantic bedrooms in the original manor, or the beautifully streamlined rooms in the new wing. All boast full facilities, including marble-tiled bathrooms. Extensive conference and banqueting services make this venue perfect for functions such as weddings, board meetings and private parties. Golf is a major feature, as the 18-hole championship course is built around the hotel in 150 acres of sweeping countryside and woodland. Manor of Groves has hosted the PGA East Anglian Open for 2 years and is an excellent location for society and corporate golf days. There is easy access to major motorways and Stansted Airport. London is within easy reach, as are Cambridge and the towns of Essex and East Anglia.

Our inspector loved: *The light, airy and spacious modern architecture of the new entrance lounge.*

Directions: Take the M11, junction 7 and follow the A414 to Harlow, then the A1184 for 2 miles, High Wych and Manor of Groves are signposted.

Web: www.johansens.com/manorofgroves
E-mail: info@manorofgroves
Tel: 0870 381 9163
International: +44 (0)1279 600777
Fax: 01279 600374

Price Guide:
single from £95
double/twin from £125
suite from £145

         SPA

SOPWELL HOUSE HOTEL, COUNTRY CLUB & SPA

COTTONMILL LANE, SOPWELL, ST ALBANS, HERTFORDSHIRE AL1 2HQ

Once the country home of Lord Mountbatten, surrounded by a peaceful and verdant 12-acre estate, Sopwell House is an oasis just minutes away from the motorways. The classic reception rooms reflect its illustrious past and the grand panelled ballroom opens out onto the terraces and gardens. The bedrooms, some with four-posters, are spacious and well-equipped. Beautifully designed Mews Suites are ideal for long-stay executives and bridal parties. Superb English and international cuisine and fine wines are served in the enchanting Magnolia Restaurant amidst the trees after which it is named, whilst Bejerano's Brasserie offers an informal ambience. The conference and banqueting suites, overlooking the splendid gardens and terrace, are popular venues for weddings and special events. A Business Centre provides guests with facilities such as photocopier, fax and e-mail. The Country Club & Spa, dedicated to health and relaxation, has a full range of fitness facilities and highly qualified beauty therapists.

Directions: Close to M25, M1, M10, A1(M). 28m from Heathrow Airport. From M25 or A414 take A1081 to St Albans. Turn left at Grillbar. Cross mini-roundabout. Hotel is ¼ mile on left.

Web: www.johansens.com/sopwellhouse
E-mail: enquiries@sopwellhouse.co.uk
Tel: 0870 381 8898
International: +44 (0)1727 864477
Fax: 01727 844741/845636

Price Guide: (room only)
single £99–£129
double/twin £158–£169
suites from £188

Our inspector loved: The huge entrance lobby with sofas and open fire set in a French Chateâu fireplace.

ST MICHAEL'S MANOR

ST MICHAEL'S VILLAGE, FISHPOOL STREET, ST ALBANS, HERTFORDSHIRE AL3 4RY

Owned and run by the Newling Ward family for the past 37 years, St Michael's Manor is a rare gem – peaceful, intimate, and set in delightful landscaped grounds. It is also within the historic village of St Michael's and a stone's throw from the magnificent St Albans Abbey. Each of the 22 bedrooms has been individually designed – some have four-poster beds and some are sitting-room suites – and all have an elegance and charm. Many of the bedrooms overlook the award-winning grounds, set in 5 acres, with wide sweeping lawns and a beautiful lake that hosts a variety of wildlife. The Georgian lounge and the award-winning conservatory dining room also overlook the gardens and make a wonderful setting for a tantalising dinner. There is also an excellent variety of vegetarian dishes. Coffee may be served in the Oak Lounge, which dates from 1586, with its fine panelled walls and original Elizabethan ceiling. Hatfield House and the Roman remains of Verulamium are within easy reach, as is London, which is only 20 minutes away by train. Weekend rates from £60 per person are available.

Directions: Easily access to the M1, junction 6/7, M25, junction 21a - 10 minutes; M4/M40 - 25 minutes; Luton Airport - 20 minutes.

Web: www.johansens.com/stmichaelsmanor
E-mail: reservations@stmichaelsmanor.com
Tel: 0870 381 8906
International: +44 (0)1727 864444
Fax: 01727 848909

Stevenage
Stansted
Bishop's
Stortford
Hertford
St Albans

Price Guide:
single £125–£195
double/twin £160–£260
suites £245–£320

Our inspector loved: *The gardens and the lake; they are wonderful.*

PENDLEY MANOR HOTEL & CONFERENCE CENTRE

COW LANE, TRING, HERTFORDSHIRE HP23 5QY

The Pendley Manor was commissioned by Joseph Grout Williams in 1872. His instructions, to architect John Lion, were to build it in the Tudor style, reflecting the owner's interest in flora and fauna on the carved woodwork and stained-glass panels. The bedrooms are attractively furnished and well equipped and the restaurant boasts AA and RAC awards. Pendley Manor offers flexible conference facilities for up to 250 people. 9 purpose-built conference suites and 8 syndicate rooms, all with natural daylight, are available. Team-building and multi-activity days within the grounds can be arranged as well as marquee events. On the estate, which lies at the foot of the Chiltern Hills, sporting facilities include tennis courts, gymnasium, a snooker room with full-size table, games rooms, buggy riding, laser shooting, archery and hot-air balloon rides. The hotel's new health and leisure facilities include an indoor heated swimming pool, Jacuzzi, sauna and solarium. Places of interest nearby include Woburn, Winslow Hall, Chenies Manor, Tring Zoological Museum and Dunstable Downs.

Our inspector loved: *The sophisticated swimming pool and in summer, the production of opera and Shakespeare in the gardens.*

Directions: Leave the M25 at junction 20 and take the new A41. Take the exit marked "Tring". At the roundabout take the A4251, then 1st right turn into Cow Lane.

Web: www.johansens.com/pendleymanor
E-mail: sales@pendley–manor.co.uk
Tel: 0870 381 8812
International: +44 (0)1442 891891
Fax: 01442 890687

Price Guide:
single £110
double/twin £130–£150
suites £160

THE PRIORY BAY HOTEL

PRIORY DRIVE, SEAVIEW, ISLE OF WIGHT PO34 5BU

From decades gone by this beautiful site has been built upon by Medieval monks, Tudor farmers and Georgian gentry. Now its medley of buildings has been sympathetically restored and brought to life as a splendid hotel. Situated in a gorgeous open coastal setting to the south of Seaview, the Priory Bay overlooks its own private beach. Everything about it is stylish and elegant, from the impressive arched stone entrance with magnificent carved figures to the delightful, flower-filled gardens with their shady corners and thatched roofed tithe barns. The public rooms are a delight, exquisitely and comfortably furnished, with tall windows framed by rich curtains and liberally filled with vases of flowers. Log fires blaze in open fireplaces during colder months. Each of the 18 comfortable bedrooms is individually decorated and has picturesque views over the gardens. The dining room is establishing a reputation for first-class gastronomy, complemented by a fine wine list. Guests can relax under shady umbrellas in the garden or on the surrounding terraces. For the more energetic guest, there is an outdoor pool and the hotel's adjoining 9-hole golf course. The islands' coastal paths for walking and riding passes the gate, Carisbrooke Castle and Osborne House are nearby.

Our inspector loved: *The combination of charming eccentricity and up to the minute provision for business and leisure.*

Directions: Ferry from Portsmouth, Lymington or Southampton to Fishbourne, Yarmouth. Ryde, East or West Cowes. The hotel is on the B3330.

Web: www.johansens.com/priorybayiow
E-mail: reception@priorybay.co.uk
Tel: 0870 381 8839
International: +44 (0)1983 613146
Fax: 01983 616539

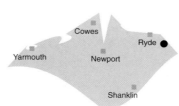

Price Guide:
single £70–£195
double/twin £140–£258

171

Eastwell Manor

BOUGHTON LEES, NR ASHFORD, KENT TN25 4HR

Directions: M20 Jct 9. Turn left into Trinity road over 4 roundabouts, turn left into A251. The Hotel is on the left 1 mile onwards.

Web: www.johansens.com/eastwellmanor
E-mail: eastwell@marstonhotels.com
Tel: 0870 381 8498
International: +44 (0)1233 213000
Fax: 01233 635530

Price Guide:
single From £170
double/twin £200–£245
suites £265–£400

Set in the "Garden of England", Eastwell Manor has a past steeped in history dating back to the 16th century when Richard Plantagenet, son of Richard III, lived on the estate. Surrounded by impressive grounds it encompasses a formal Italian garden, scented rose gardens and attractive lawns and parkland. The magnificent exterior is matched by the splendour of the interior. Exquisite plasterwork and carved oak panelling adorn the public rooms whilst throughout the Manor interesting antique pieces abound. The individually furnished bedrooms and suites, some with fine views across the gardens, feature every possible comfort. There are 19 courtyard apartments giving 39 more bedrooms, all with en-suite facilities. The new health and fitness spa features an indoor and outdoor heated 20m pool, hydrotherapy pool, sauna, steam room, Technogym gymnasium and 14 beauty treatment rooms. Guests can enjoy a choice of dining experiences, fine British cuisine in the Manor Restaurant, and a similar standard of food at the less formal Brasserie. Nearby attractions include the cathedral city of Canterbury, Leeds Castle and several charming market towns. Situated near Ashford Eurostar station, Eastwell is perfect for trips to Paris and Brussels.

Our inspector loved: *The flagstones, the open fires and the flowers everywhere.*

NEW

BRANDSHATCH PLACE HOTEL

BRANDS HATCH ROAD, FAWKHAM, KENT DA3 8NQ

Built in 1806 and set amidst 12 acres of private parkland and gardens, Brandshatch Place is a distinguished Georgian residence. Approached along an impressive tree-lined drive, it offers an attractive getaway from London, only 20 miles to the south-east. The hotel has been the subject of an extensive renovation programme to include every modern amenity, banqueting and conference rooms and fully-equipped leisure club. Bedrooms are exquisitely decorated and 12 rooms are located in the converted mews. The highly acclaimed Restaurant serves dishes of originality using only the finest and freshest ingredients and after a meal guests may enjoy a relaxing drink in the restful bar. The health and leisure club, Fredericks, features an indoor pool, solarium, sauna, steam room, dance studio, Jacuzzi, beauty salon, snooker room, tennis courts, 2 squash courts and a supervised gymnasium. Business and private functions are easily accommodated in the 5 meeting rooms. Eltham Palace, Brandshatch Grand Prix Circuit and Leeds Castle are all nearby.

Directions: From the M25, junction 3, follow the A20 south then signs to Fawkham Green. The hotel is on the right about ¹/₂ mile before Fawkham village.

Web: www.johansens.com/brandshatch
E-mail: brandshatch@handpicked.co.uk
Tel: 0870 381 9147
International: +44 (0)1474 875000
Fax: 01474 879652

Maidstone
Canterbury
Tunbridge Wells
Dover

Price Guide:
single £85
double £120
suite £220

Our inspector loved: *The bold refurbishment: the spacious state-of-the-art kitchens, the wonderful new restaurant, and bedrooms that radiate comfort and style.*

SPA

ROWHILL GRANGE HOTEL AND SPA

WILMINGTON, DARTFORD, KENT DA2 7QH

Directions: M20 junction 1/M25 junction 3. Take the B2173 into Swanley and B258 north at Superstore roundabout. After Hextable Green the entrance is almost immediately on the left.

Web: www.johansens.com/rowhillgrange
E-mail: admin@rowhillgrange.com
Tel: 0870 381 8870
International: +44 (0)1322 615136
Fax: +44 (0)1322 615137

Price Guide: (room only)
single £150–£265
double/twin £175–£225
suite £225–£325

Maidstone   Canterbury

Tunbridge Wells

Dover

An unexpected find on the outer edge of London bordering on the Kent countryside, Rowhill Grange nestles in 9 acres of woodlands and mature gardens descending to a picturesque lake. A combination of top service and friendliness makes Rowhill Grange the perfect venue for everything from weekend breaks to special occasions such as weddings and anniversaries. All the luxurious bedrooms boast individual character and decoration, with a full range of facilities available to ensure maximum comfort and convenience for guests. The à la carte Restaurant is supplemented with the delightful Brasserie. From late spring and through the summer months guests may take dinner on the terrace, sharing a scenic view with the swans and ducks. For special occasions, business meetings or dinners, private dining rooms are available. The Clockhouse Suite is a self-contained functions annexe with a dining/dancing area, comfortable lounge and a bar. The Utopia Health and Leisure Spa is outstanding with all the latest equipment for women and for men including the UK's first therapy pool of its kind.

Our inspector loved: *The modern European décor matched by some fine cooking which made the restaurant a joy.*

CHILSTON PARK

SANDWAY, LENHAM, NR MAIDSTONE, KENT ME17 2BE

This magnificent Grade I listed mansion, one of England's most richly decorated hotels, was built in the 13th century and remodelled in the 18th century. Now sensitively refurbished, the hotel's ambience is enhanced by the lighting, at dusk each day, of over 200 candles. The drawing room and reading room offer guests an opportunity to relax and to admire the outstanding collection of antiques. The entire hotel is a treasure trove full of many interesting objets d'art. The opulently furnished bedrooms are fitted to a high standard and many have four-poster beds. Good, fresh English cooking features on outstanding menus supported by an excellent wine list. Several intimate and delightful rooms afford wonderful opportunities for private dining parties. In keeping with the traditions of a country house, a wide variety of sporting activities are available, golf and riding nearby, fishing in the natural spring lake and punting.

Our inspector loved: The astonishing collections of object d,art.

Directions: Take junction 8 off the M20, then A20 towards Lenham. Turn left into Boughton Road. Go over the crossroads and M20; Chilston Park is on the left.

Web: www.johansens.com/chilstonpark
E-mail: chilstonpark@handpicked.co.uk
Tel: 0870 381 8428
International: +44 (0)1622 859803
Fax: 01622 858588

Price Guide:
single from £90
double/twin from £130
suite from £295

HOTEL DU VIN & BISTRO

CRESCENT ROAD, ROYAL TUNBRIDGE WELLS, KENT TN1 2LY

Set in the historic town of Tunbridge Wells, this Grade II* sandstone mansion dates back to 1762 and although in the centre, it enjoys spectacular views over Calverley Park. An inviting ambience is present throughout the property, from the convivial bar to the sunny terrace. The 36 en-suite bedrooms have been individually decorated and are enhanced by the superb Egyptian linen, CD players and satellite television. The spacious bathrooms feature power showers, large baths and fluffy robes and towels. The hotel takes great pride in its excellent bistro cuisine and the outstanding wine list. The imaginative dishes are prepared using the freshest local ingredients and are exceptionally good value. Fine wine dinners are often held at the hotel, whilst private tastings may be organised given prior notice. There are many castles, gardens and stately homes within the vicinity, such as Chartwell, Groombridge Place and Hever Castle. Guests can work up their appetites by rambling through the orchards and hop fields, perusing the shops and boutiques in the Pantiles or playing golf nearby.

Directions: From M25 take A21 south in the direction of Hastings. to Tunbridge Wells. The hotel has parking facilities.

Web: www.johansens.com/hotelduvintunbridge
E-mail: info@tunbridgewells.hotelduvin.com
Tel: 0870 381 8614
International: +44 (0)1892 526455
Fax: 01892 512044

Price Guide: (room only)
double/twin from £89
large double/twin from £140

Our inspector loved: The ambience - this is such a relaxed and comfortable hotel - entirely at ease with its place in the scheme of things.

THE SPA HOTEL

MOUNT EPHRAIM, ROYAL TUNBRIDGE WELLS, KENT TN4 8XJ

The Spa Hotel was originally built in 1766 as a country mansion with its own landscaped gardens and 3 beautiful lakes. A hotel for over a century now, it retains standards of service reminiscent of life in Georgian and Regency England. All the bedrooms are individually furnished and many offer spectacular views. Above all else, The Spa prides itself on the excellence of its cuisine. The grand, award-winning Chandelier restaurant features the freshest produce from Kentish farms and London markets, complemented by a carefully selected wine list. Within the hotel is Sparkling Health, a magnificent health and leisure centre which is equipped to the highest standards. Leisure facilities include an indoor heated swimming pool, a fully-equipped state-of-the-art gymnasium, cardio-vascular gymnasium, steam room, sauna, beauty and hairdressing salons, floodlit hard tennis court and ½ mile jogging track. The newly established stables include gentle trails and safe paddocks for children to enjoy pony-riding under expert guidance. Special half-board weekend breaks are offered, for a minimum 2 nights stay, with rates from £88 per person per night – full details available on request.

Directions: The hotel faces the common on the A264 in Tunbridge Wells.

Web: www.johansens.com/spahotel
E-mail: reservations@spahotel.co.uk
Tel: 0870 381 8901
International: +44 (0)1892 520331
Fax: 01892 510575

Price Guide: (room only)
single £91–£101
double/twin £115–£170

Our inspector loved: *The classic English dining room and the new spacious suites.*

ASTLEY BANK HOTEL & CONFERENCE CENTRE

BOLTON ROAD, DARWEN, LANCASHIRE BB3 2QB

Astley Bank stands high and impressive overlooking 6 acres of magnificent grounds and flower-filled gardens adjacent to the peaceful West Pennine Moors midway between Blackburn and Bolton. Built in the early 19th century it was, over the years, home to some of Lancashire's leading dignitaries. Today it is a stylish, comfortable country retreat with a character and ambience reflecting its mansion house era combined with all modern facilities demanded by today's discerning visitor. The public rooms are spacious and elegant and the en-suite bedrooms are decorated and furnished to the highest standard. Most of them enjoy superb views over the garden and the four-poster and executive bedrooms provide additional luxury. In the attractive garden restaurant chef James Andrew produces tasty à la carte and table d'hôte menus which are complemented by an extensive selection of wines. Being within easy reach of the motorway network and Manchester Airport, Astley Bank is a popular venue with meetings organisers. There are three conference rooms supported by 6 purpose-built syndicate rooms. All have natural daylight and are fitted with a variety of audio-visual equipment.

Directions: From Blackburn take the M65 east. Exit at junction 4 and take the A666 south towards Bolton. After approximately 2 miles pass through Darwen. The hotel is on the right.

Web: www.johansens.com/astleybank
E-mail: sales@astleybank.co.uk
Tel: 0870 381 8328
International: +44 (0)1254 777700
Fax: 01254 777707

Price Guide:
single £83–£115
double/twin £103–£130

Our inspector loved: The stained glass windows on the upstairs landing.

NORTHCOTE MANOR

NORTHCOTE ROAD, LANGHO, BLACKBURN, LANCASHIRE BB6 8BE

Large, redbrick and typically Victorian, this attractive and externally decorative hotel stands in the foothills of the Ribble Valley amidst some of Lancashire's most spectacular countryside. Excellently run by joint proprietors Craig Bancroft, a wine connoisseur, and Nigel Haworth, an award-winning chef, Northcote Manor has been an esteemed restaurant with rooms since 1983. Its high standards of hospitality, comfort, décor and food has earned it the prestigious award of "The Independent Hotel of the Year" by the Caterer and Hotelkeeper. Nigel, proud member of the Academy of Culinary Arts, trained in Switzerland and London and his gourmet cuisine has received innumerable accolades, including a Michelin Star and Egon Ronay's 1995 Chef of the Year distinction. His superb local and creative International dishes are presented with professionalism and aplomb in a delightful restaurant. Each meal is complemented by a superb wine list that is 400 bin strong. The hotel has 14 beautifully furnished, en-suite bedrooms that offer every comfort. Nearby are the Trough of Bowland and the Roman town of Ribchester, and 4 golf courses are within a 10 mile radius. The Yorkshire Dales and Lake District are within easy reach.

Our inspector loved: Nigel Haworth's herb and organic vegetable garden.

Directions: From M6 junction 31 take A59 towards Glitheroe. After 8 miles turn left into Northcote Road, immediately before the Langho roundabout.

Web: www.johansens.com/northcotelancs
E-mail: sales@northcotemanor.com
Tel: 0870 381 8766
International: +44 (0)1254 240555
Fax: 01254 246568

Price Guide:
single £100–£130
double/twin £130–£160

THE GIBBON BRIDGE HOTEL

NR CHIPPING, FOREST OF BOWLAND, LANCASHIRE PR3 2TQ

This award-winning hotel in the heart of Lancashire in the Forest of Bowland is a welcoming and peaceful retreat. The area, a favourite of the Queen, is now officially recognised as the Centre of the Kingdom! Created in 1982 by resident proprietor Janet Simpson and her late Mother Margaret, the buildings combine traditional architecture with interesting Gothic masonry. Individually designed and equipped to the highest standard, the 7 bedrooms and 22 suites include four-posters, half-testers, Gothic brass beds and whirlpool baths. The restaurant overlooks the garden and is renowned for traditional and imaginative dishes incorporating home-grown vegetables and herbs. The garden bandstand is perfect for musical repertoires or civil wedding ceremonies. Elegant rooms, lounges and a unique al fresco dining area are available for private dinner parties and wedding receptions. For executive meetings and conference facilities the hotel will offer that "something a bit different". Leisure facilities include beauty studio, gymnasium, solarium, steam room, all-weather tennis court and outdoor activities.

Our inspector loved: *The spectacular landscaped gardens surrounding the bandstand.*

Directions: From the south: M6 Exit 31A, follow signs for Longridge. From the north: M6 Exit 32, follow A6 to Broughton and B5269 to Longridge. At Longridge follow signs for Chipping for approx 3 miles, then follow Gibbon Bridge brown tourism signs.

Web: www.johansens.com/gibbonbridge
E-mail: reception@gibbon–bridge.co.uk
Tel: 0870 381 8544
International: +44 (0)1995 61456
Fax: 01995 61277

Price Guide:
single £80–£120
double/twin £120
suite £140–250

Lancaster
Blackpool
Preston · Blackburn

NEW

CHAMPNEYS SPRINGS

ASHBY DE LA ZOUCH, LEICESTERSHIRE LE65 1TG

A recent £8million-refurbishment has produced state-of-the-art leisure, business and accommodation facilities at this contemporary health resort. It is situated 5 minutes from the historic town of Ashby de la Zouch, famed for its High Street of half-timbered houses and bow-fronted Georgian shops, its 15th-century castle ruins, and as the setting for the tournament in Sir Walter Scott's "Ivanhoe". The improvements combine excellently with a fresh design and minimalist approach. Spacious en-suite bedrooms are tastefully furnished, extremely comfortable and offer a host of modern touches and thoughtful extras. Excellent cuisine is enjoyed in a relaxing restaurant with a talented team of chefs using the freshest ingredients to create a wide choice of dinner dishes, buffet lunches and healthy breakfasts. The business centre has 3 air-conditioned conference suites, accommodating up to 70 delegates theatre style. A full range of high-tech equipment is available and an experienced conference team can organise and run a package to suit the most discerning corporate client. In keeping with Champneys' Health Resort ambience, leisure, fitness and relaxation facilities are of the highest standard. There is a 25m indoor swimming pool, gymnasium, luxury steam and sauna rooms, various aerobic programmes, badminton and tennis courts, yoga and a wide range of spa, beauty and holistic treatments.

Directions: From the M42 exit at junction 12.

Web: www.johansens.com/champneyssprings
E-mail: cbeldon@champneys.co.uk
Tel: 0870 381 9095
International: +44 (0)1530 273873
Fax: 01530 270987

Price Guide:
(24hr corporate rate)
single from £165
twin from £140
suite price upon request

Burton-Upon-Trent

Melton Mowbray

Leicester

Hinckley

Our inspector loved: *The Lakeside Suite with its panoramic views.*

QUORN COUNTRY HOTEL

66 LEICESTER ROAD, QUORN, LEICESTERSHIRE LE12 8BB

Directions: Situated just off the A6 Leicester to Derby main road, in the bypassed village of Quorn (Quorndon), 5 miles from Jct 23 of the M1 from North, Jct 21A from South, East and West.

Web: www.johansens.com/quorncountry
E-mail: reservations@quorncountryhotel.co.uk
Tel: 0870 381 8847
International: +44 (0)1509 415050
Fax: 01509 415557

Price Guide: (room only)
single £105
double/twin £120–£145
suite £155

Originally Leicestershire's most exclusive private club, created around the original 17th-century listed building, this award-winning 4-star hotel is set in 4 acres of landscaped gardens. For the tenth consecutive year the hotel has received all 3 RAC merit awards for excellence in cuisine, hospitality and comfort and was also a recipient of a second AA Rosette Award in 1997. The bedrooms are equipped to the very highest standard with attention given to every detail. Suitable for both the business traveller or for weekend guests seeking those extra touches, which help create the ideal peaceful retreat. Ladies travelling alone can feel reassured that their special needs are met and indeed exceeded. Particular emphasis is given to the enjoyment of food with a declared policy of using, whenever possible, the freshest local produce. Guests' stay will be enhanced by the choice of two different dining experiences. They can choose between the Shires Restaurant with its classical cuisine with a modern style or the Orangery Brasserie with its changing selection of contemporary dishes.

Our inspector loved: *The new banqueting suite overlooking the gardens and river.*

STAPLEFORD PARK HOTEL, SPA, GOLF & SPORTING ESTATE

NR. MELTON MOWBRAY, LEICESTERSHIRE LE14 2EF

A stately home and sporting estate where casual luxury is the byword. This 16th-century house was once coveted by Edward, Prince of Wales, but his mother Queen Victoria forbade him to buy it for fear that his morals would be corrupted by the Leicestershire hunting society! Today, Stapleford Park offers guests and club members a "lifestyle experience" to transcend all others in supreme surroundings with views over 500 acres of parkland. Stapleford was voted Top UK Hotel for Leisure Facilities by Condé Nast Traveller, Johansens Most Excellent Business Meeting Venue 2000 and holds innumerable awards for its style and hospitality. Individually designed bedrooms and a 4-bedroom cottage have been created by famous names such as Mulberry, Wedgwood, Zoffany and Crabtree & Evelyn. British cuisine lightened up with Asian flavours is carefully prepared to the highest standards and complemented by an adventurous wine list. Sports include fishing, shooting, falconry, riding, tennis and an 18-hole championship golf course designed by Donald Steel. The luxurious Clarins Spa with indoor pool, Jacuzzi, sauna and fitness room offers an array of health therapies. 11 elegant function and dining rooms are suited to private dinners, special occasions and corporate hospitality.

Our inspector loved: The stunning views from the new clubhouse overlooking the golf course.

Directions: By train Kings Cross/Grantham in 1 hour. Take the A1 north to Colsterworth then the B676 via Saxby.

Web: www.johansens.com/staplefordpark
E-mail: reservations@stapleford.co.uk
Tel: 0870 381 8912
International: +44 (0)1572 787 522
Fax: 01572 787 651

Price Guide:
double/twin £205–£359
suites from £488

KILWORTH HOUSE HOTEL

LUTTERWORTH ROAD, NORTH KILWORTH, LEICESTERSHIRE LE17 6JE

Directions: 4 miles from junction 20 off the M1, Kilworth House Hotel is accessible from the M6, M42, M69 and A14.

Web: www.johansens.com/kilworth
E-mail: reservations@kilworthhouse.co.uk
Tel: 0870 381 9076
International: +44 (0)1858 880058
Fax: 01858 880349

Price Guide:
garden room £120
luxury room £160
four poster £220

At the end of a tree-lined approach stands this 19th-century country house within 38 acres, overlooking rural Leicestershire. A family home until 1999, this magnificent Grade II* listed property has been subject to a great restoration project. Meticulous care has been taken to ensure that the Victorian Orangery, the stained-glass windows, wrought-iron finials and black and white mosaic floor have all been preserved. The beautifully decorated bedrooms are individually and luxuriously styled and provide glorious havens. Meals can be taken in the Wordsworth Restaurant, where an interesting à la carte menu is served under the ornate ceiling and surrounding stained-glass windows with views over the courtyard. Alternatively, there is the more informal Orangery Restaurant, which boasts panoramic views across the estate. There are 3 golf courses within a 7-mile radius, Rockingham Speedway is nearby where many motor sport tours exhibit and Silverstone is a short drive away. Kilworth is an ideal venue to host conference or wedding parties, with its wide variety of state-of-the-art equipment and amazing parkland scenery for those memorable photographs. The hotel also offers a mini-gym and health and beauty treatment rooms.

Our inspector loved: The wonderful views of the countryside from the stunning Victorian Orangery with its mosaic floor.

THE ANGEL AND ROYAL HOTEL

HIGH STREET, GRANTHAM, LINCOLNSHIRE NG31 6PN

With a history spanning 800 years and a reputation as the oldest inn in England, the Angel and Royal is a fascinating and memorable place to stay. The "Angel" was a medieval sign illustrating the connection between religious houses and travellers' inns, but despite visitations by 7 kings over the centuries, it wasn't until a visit from Edward VII in 1866 that "Royal" was added to create the existing name. The main façade was built 600 years ago, although the site had already been an inn for 200 years, and the ancient cellars and tunnels date back to the 9th century. Since undergoing a recent £2-million refurbishment, the present owners have successfully combined the enthralling history of the Angel and Royal with every contemporary comfort and convenience. The centre-piece of the Angel Bar must be its impressive 9ft x 6ft medieval fireplace, whilst the Kings Restaurant features original carved stone panelling, oriel windows and a spiral staircase leading to the turret. Both make excellent venues for private functions. A perfect blend of luxury and elegance, the bedrooms feature sophisticated bathrooms and novel extras. Local attractions include Belvoir Castle, Rutland Water and the historic town of Stamford.

Our inspector loved: *The Angel bar - contrasting historic features with comfortable modern furnishings and a choice of 200 malt whiskies.*

Directions: From A1 take the town centre signs.

Web: www.johansens.com/angelandroyal
E-mail: enquiries@angelandroyalhotel.co.uk
Tel: 0870 381 9164
International: +44 (0)1476 565816
Fax: 01476 567149

Price Guide:
single £75–£115
double/twin £115–£165

THE GEORGE OF STAMFORD

ST MARTINS, STAMFORD, LINCOLNSHIRE PE9 2LB

Directions: Stamford is a mile from the A1 on the B1081. The George is in the town centre opposite the gallows sign. Car parking is behind the hotel.

Web: www.johansens.com/georgeofstamford
E-mail: reservations@georgehotelofstamford.com
Tel: 0870 381 8543
International: +44 (0)1780 750750
Fax: 01780 750701

Price Guide:
single from £78–£120
double/twin from £110–£225
suite £150–£155

The George, a beautiful, 16th-century coaching inn, retains the charm of its long history, as guests will sense on entering the reception hall with its oak travelling chests and famous oil portrait of Daniel Lambert. Over the years, The George has welcomed a diverse clientèle, ranging from highwaymen to kings – Charles I and William III were both visitors. At the heart of the hotel is the lounge, its natural stone walls, deep easy chairs and softly lit alcoves imparting a cosy, relaxed atmosphere, whilst the blazing log fire is sometimes used to toast muffins for tea! The flair of Julia Vannocci's interior design is evident in all the expertly styled, fully appointed bedrooms. Exotic plants, orchids, orange trees and coconut palms feature in the Garden Lounge, where a choice of hot dishes and an extensive cold buffet are offered. Guests may also dine al fresco in the courtyard garden. The more formal, oak-panelled restaurant serves imaginative but traditional English dishes and an award-winning list of wines. Superb facilities are incorporated in the Business Centre, converted from the former livery stables. Special weekend breaks available.

Our inspector loved: *The Stamford Room, which has been decorated with fabulous murals by Jenny Bell.*

THE HALKIN

5 HALKIN STREET, BELGRAVIA, LONDON SW1X 7DJ

Quality of service, luxury, opulence and style are the very essence of The Halkin, an elegant and tranquil haven in the very heart of fashionable Belgravia just minutes from Knightsbridge's exclusive shopping and dining. Room design, décor, furniture, furnishings and facilities are magnificently modernistic, clear and refreshing, giving the hotel a very special feel that has guests returning time and again. Each of 41 spacious and luxurious air-conditioned rooms and suites have individual harmonious colour themes and combine the comforts of home with personal, 24-hour service. Facilities include superb all-marble bathroom, direct number fax, dual line telephone with voice mail, cable and CNN television, VCR and CD player and a high-security key system. Valet and butler services are also available together with a concierge handling entertainment, travel and sightseeing. The Halkin is renowned for its innovative restaurant Nahm. Serving stunning Thai cuisine, the restaurant has 1 Michelin star and is open for both lunch and dinner - Pre and post-dinner drinks can be enjoyed in the comfortable lounge bar.

Our inspector loved: *The huge, luxurious marble bathrooms.*

Directions: The nearest tube station is Hyde Park Corner.

Web: www.johansens.com/halkin
E-mail: res@halkin.co.uk
Tel: 0870 381 8581
International: +44 (0)20 7333 1000
Fax: 020 7333 1100

Price Guide:
Room £305
suite from £460

THE ACADEMY, THE BLOOMSBURY TOWN HOUSE

21 GOWER STREET, LONDON WC1E 6HG

Directions: Nearest tube Goodge Street or Tottenham Court Road. Euston and King's Cross stations are within a mile.

Web: www.johansens.com/academytownhouse
E-mail: resacademy@theetongroup.com
Tel: 0870 381 8305
International: +44 (0)20 7631 4115
Fax: 020 7636 3442

Price Guide: (excluding VAT)
single £140
double/twin £163
suites £215–£225

Set in a superb location within London's leafy Bloomsbury district with its many garden squares, The Academy is just a few minutes' walk from the West End, Oxford Street and Covent Garden and very convenient for The British Museum. This charming collection of 5 Georgian Town Houses, which hides away 2 private patio gardens, offers an oasis of style and tranquillity that belies its prime location amongst the city hustle and bustle. Having undergone a complete refurbishment programme, the result is a unique blend of contemporary style and period charm creating a wonderfully comfortable ambience. Each of the 49 guest rooms is beautifully designed, retaining many of the original Georgian features, with elegant drapes, Regency striped wallpaper and free-standing baths. The Garden Suite even has its own private courtyard garden – a real luxury in the heart of London. The Boardroom leads directly to the Conservatory Lounge and Garden, and with facilities for up to 16 delegates makes it an ideal small meeting venue, and perfect for intimate cocktail or wedding parties. The Alchemy breakfast room and Bar also lend themselves to functions.

Our inspector loved: The pretty garden - perfect for summer drinks.

DRAYCOTT HOUSE APARTMENTS

10 DRAYCOTT AVENUE, CHELSEA, LONDON SW3 3AA

Draycott House is an attractive period town house, standing in a quiet, tree-lined avenue in the heart of Chelsea. Housed in an attractive period building, the apartments have been designed in traditional styles to provide the ideal surroundings and location for a leisure or business visit, combining comfort, privacy and security with a convenient location. All are spacious, luxury suites with a kitchen and a wonderful alternative to a hotel, with 1, 2 or 3 bedrooms. Some have private balconies, a roof terrace and overlook the private courtyard garden. Each apartment is fully equipped with all home comforts; cable television, video, DVD, CD/hi-fi, private direct lines for own telephone/fax/answer machine/data, provisions/continental breakfast on arrival. A complimentary membership to an exclusive nearby health club, maid service, covered garage parking and laundry service. Additional services include airport transfers, transport, catering, travel, theatre tickets, dry cleaning/laundry, childminding and secretarial services. The West End and the City are within easy reach. Knightsbridge within walking distance. Long term reservations may attract preferential terms. Contact Jane Renton, General Manager.

Our inspector loved: The light, comfortable spacious apartments decorated in a traditional English style in a fabulous location.

Directions: Draycott House is situated on the corner of Draycott Avenue and Draycott Place, close to Sloane Square.

Web: www.johansens.com/draycotthouseapartments
E-mail: sales@draycotthouse.co.uk
Tel: 0870 381 8490
International: +44 (0)20 7584 4659
Fax: 020 7225 3694

Price Guide: (excluding VAT)
£195–£490 per night
from £1215–£3095 per week

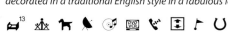

GREAT EASTERN HOTEL

LIVERPOOL STREET, LONDON EC2M 7QN

Directions: Adjacent to Liverpool Street rail and tube station on the corner of Bishopgate.

Web: www.johansens.com/greateastern
E-mail: sales@great-eastern-hotel.co.uk
Tel: 0870 381 8567
International: +44 (0)20 7618 5000
Fax: 020 7618 5001

Price Guide:
room from £225
suite from £325

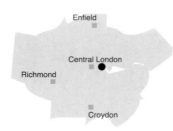

From the moment visitors enter the hotel lobby or the imposing, high-rise atrium they realise that this is an especially exciting hotel. It reopened with 246 bedrooms and 21 suites, 4 restaurants, 4 bars, gym, treatment rooms and 12 private dining rooms in 2000 after extensive refurbishment. Grade II listed and situated on the eastern edges of the City of London, the Great Eastern originally opened in 2 phases, in 1884 and 1901. The refurbishment beautifully revives the splendour of those eras, combined with 21st-century modernity and facilities. No 2 bedrooms are alike. Those on the 5th and 6th floors have a light and airy "loft" feel; those below have higher ceilings and period features. Rooms in the east wing are detailed with ornate late Victorian features; those in the west wing are more restrained. All have every home comfort and high-tech business facilities. Each of the hotel's restaurants and bars has its own distinctive identity. Terminus re-interprets the classic railway buffet-brasserie, Fishmarket is sea green beneath plaster cherubs, Aurora is grand and beautiful and George is Jacobean style oak-panelled. The food is equally distinctive, from classically inspired dishes to sushi and sashimi or fish and crustacea. London's major tourist attractions and theatre land are within easy reach.

Our inspector loved: *The great choice of bars and restaurants within the hotel.*

THREADNEEDLES
5 THREADNEEDLE STREET, LONDON EC2R 8AY

One of London's newest boutique hotels situated in the heart of the City, Threadneedles is within minutes of The Strand and Thames water taxis that link the capital's bustling business area with the bright lights of the West End. It is a sympathetically converted mid-19th-century banking hall with an interior of understated luxury that features solid oak doors, rich mahogany panelling, impressive marble columns and a beautiful hand-painted glass dome. Soft tones and innovative lighting create a relaxed environment in the guest rooms, complemented by luxurious en-suite bathrooms featuring stylish chrome and glass accessories. The ultimate indulgence for visitors is the Penthouse with its unique interior and private balcony. Discreet modern facilities and the latest technology ensure every comfort. Bonds Restaurant & Bar, with leather seating and plush fabrics, exudes style, whilst the restaurant, serving modern European cuisine, combines classic sophistication with City chic. Private rooms can be arranged for more intimate dining. Threadneedles has excellent corporate event facilities with 3 state-of-the-art meeting rooms seating up to 30 theatre style. City airport, Canary Wharf, Tate Modern, the Tower and St Paul's Cathedral are within close proximity.

Our inspector loved: The beautiful 19th-century handpainted glass dome.

Directions: Nearest underground stations are Bank and Liverpool Street.

Web: www.johansens.com/threadneedles
E-mail: res_threadneedles@theetoncollection.com
Tel: 0870 381 9178
International: +44 (0)20 7657 8080
Fax: 020 7289 4878

Enfield

Central London

Richmond

Croydon

Price Guide: (room only, excluding VAT)
single from £155
double/twin £265–£310
suite £395–£2370

THE MAYFLOWER HOTEL

24-28 TREBOVIR ROAD, LONDON SW5 9NJ

Directions: Between Earls Court Road and Warwick Road. The nearest underground station is Earls Court.

Web: www.johansens.com/mayflower
E-mail: mayfhotel@aol.com
Tel: 0870 381 9195
International: +44 (0)20 7370 0991
Fax: 020 7370 0994

Price Guide:
single £79
double £109
family room £130

This recently renovated hotel is located in 2 Edwardian town houses conveniently situated in central London. The interior has been designed in a unique style – a fusion of eastern influences with serene and spacious modern luxury. Pale stone and wood floors, rich, vibrant fabrics with Indian and oriental antiques abound in 48 individually decorated bedrooms, 4 of which have balconies. The elegant light rooms have high ceilings and fans, enhanced by beautiful hand-carved wardrobes and bedside tables with ornate beds covered in luxurious Andrew Martin fabrics. All rooms offer state-of-the-art technology with Internet access, wide-screen televisions, CD players, safes and tea and coffee making facilities. The en-suite bathrooms are stylish and sparkling in marble and chrome with superb walk-in showers. Guests can enjoy a complimentary continental buffet breakfast before venturing out to explore the nearby fashionable shopping areas of Knightsbridge and Chelsea or visit the V&A and The Natural History and Science Museum. The Mayflower's proximity to the famous Earl's Court Exhibition Centre makes it perfectly located to suit business travellers and corporate events. Earl's Court underground station is only a minute's walk away and provides direct access to Heathrow Airport, the City and the West End.

Our inspector loved: *The Eastern influence in all bedrooms.*

 48  M 25

WEST LODGE PARK COUNTRY HOUSE HOTEL

COCKFOSTERS ROAD, HADLEY WOOD, BARNET, HERTFORDSHIRE EN4 0PY

West Lodge Park is a country house hotel which stands in 34 acres of Green Belt parklands and gardens. These include a lake and an arboretum with hundreds of mature trees. Run by the Beale family for over 50 years, West Lodge Park was originally a gentleman's country seat, rebuilt in 1838 on the site of an earlier keeper's lodge. In the public rooms, antiques, original paintings and period furnishings create a restful atmosphere. All the bright and individually furnished bedrooms, many of which enjoy country views, have a full range of modern amenities. Well presented cuisine is available in the elegant restaurant. A private terrace with hot tub and sauna is available for guests in The Lodge, and in the main building beauty rooms featuring Elemis products are now open. Residents enjoy free membership and a free taxi to the nearby leisure centre, which has excellent facilities. Hatfield House and St Albans Abbey are a 15 minutes drive away. The hotel is credited with AA 4 stars and 1 Rosette, RAC 4 stars plus 3 merit awards.

Our inspector loved: The countryside views and fabulous arboretum, yet only 1 mile from either London underground or M25.

Directions: The hotel is on A111, 1 mile north of Cockfosters underground station and 1 mile south of junction 24 on the M25.

Web: www.johansens.com/westlodgepark
E-mail: westlodgepark@bealeshotels.co.uk
Tel: 0870 381 8978
International: +44 (0)20 8216 3900
Fax: 020 8216 3937

Price Guide:
single £90–£160
double/twin from £115–£180

KENSINGTON HOUSE HOTEL

15-16 PRINCE OF WALES TERRACE, KENSINGTON, LONDON W8 5PQ

Directions: The nearest underground station is High Street Kensington.

Web: www.johansens.com/kensingtonhouse
E-mail: reservations@kenhouse.com
Tel: 0870 381 8648
International: +44 (0)20 7937 2345
Fax: 020 7368 6700

Price Guide:
single £150
double/twin £175-£195
junior suites £215

This attractive hotel with its architecturally splendid tall, ornate windows and pillared entrance stands grandly on a 19th-century site long associated with style and elegance. Just off Kensington High Street, this charming town house is an ideal base from which to explore London's attractions. Views cover delightful mews houses, leafy streets and out across the City rooftops. The emphasis is on providing informal, professional service in an atmosphere of relaxation and comfort. Each of the 41 intimate bedrooms offers en-suite facilities. Rooms are bright and airy with modern furniture and fittings adding to the fresh, contemporary treatment of a classic design. Home-from-home comforts include crisp linen, duvets and bathrobes. Other features offered: courtesy tray, ceiling fan, voicemail, modem connection and in-room safe. The 2 junior suites can convert into a family room. The stylish Tiger Bar is a popular venue for coffee or cocktails prior to enjoying a delicious dinner, with a menu that draws on a range of influences offering both traditional and modern dishes. The serenity of Kensington Gardens is just a gentle stroll away and some of the capital's most fashionable shops, restaurants and cultural attractions are within walking distance. Weekend rates are available.

Our inspector loved: *The fresh contemporary feel to this hidden away town house hotel.*

TWENTY NEVERN SQUARE

LONDON SW5 9PD

A unique experience in hospitality awaits guests at this elegant 4-star town house hotel. Sumptuously restored, the emphasis is on natural materials and beautiful hand-carved beds and furniture. The hotel overlooks a tranquil garden square and has its own delightful restaurant, Café Twenty, which is also available for small dinner and cocktail parties. Each of the 20 intimate bedrooms provides white marble, compact en-suite facilities, and is individually designed echoing both Asian and European influences. You can choose the delicate silks of the Chinese Room or a touch of opulence in the Rococo Room. The grandeur of the Pasha Suite, complete with four-poster bed and balcony, makes an ideal setting for a special occasion. All rooms have full modern facilities including wide-screen digital TV, CD player, private safe and a separate telephone and Internet/fax connection. Gym facilities are available by arrangement. The location is ideal – close to Earl's Court and Olympia exhibition centres and the tube. The Picadilly Line brings guests arriving at Heathrow in just over 30 minutes. Guests are a mere 10 minutes from London's most fashionable shopping areas, restaurants, theatres and cultural attractions such as the V&A and Science Museums.

Our inspector loved: The fusion of Eastern and European influences in all the rooms.

Directions: 2 minutes from Earls Court station.

Web: www.johansens.com/twentynevernsquare
E-mail: hotel@twentynevernsquare.co.uk
Tel: 0870 381 8957
International: +44 (0)20 7565 9555
Fax: 020 7565 9444

Price Guide:
single £130
double/twin £165–£195
suite £275

WARREN HOUSE

WARREN ROAD, COOMBE, KINGSTON-UPON-THAMES, SURREY KT2 7HY

Directions: From M25 Jct 10 follow A3 north to Robin Hood roundabout. Turn left onto A308 to Kingston Hill. At the top turn left after 2nd zebra crossing into Warren Road.

Web: www.johansens.com/warren
E-mail: info@warrenhouse.com
Tel: 0870 381 8969
International: +44 (0)20 8547 1777
Fax: 020 8547 1175

Price Guide:
single from £188
double/twin from £240

This impressive 19th-century redbrick house with its York stone door surrounds, balustrades and tall chimneys stands in 4 acres of landscaped gardens. It is ideally situated for the business visitor, just 5 miles from central London, within easy reach of Heathrow and Gatwick airports and on the doorstep of Surrey's sweeping countryside and attractions. For some years Warren House has been an outstanding meeting venue with an unparalleled range of technology and equipment. Built in 1884, the house has been sensitively restored to its original style with the addition of 21st-century facilities. The en-suite bedrooms and suites are individually designed, tastefully decorated and furnished to the highest standard, including desk, television, direct dial telephone and modem connection. Chef Paul Bellingham prides himself on his international cuisine, attentively served in an elegant restaurant featuring an Oriental tiled fireplace. There is a spacious lounge, well-stocked library and excellent leisure facilities including a heated swimming pool and gymnasium. Richmond Park and 2 golf courses are close by with Hampton Court, Kew Gardens, Windsor, Sandown Park, Epsom and Kempton racecourses within easy reach.

Our inspector loved: This, the ultimate destination for the discerning business visitor.

THE BEAUFORT

33 BEAUFORT GARDENS, KNIGHTSBRIDGE, LONDON SW3 1PP

The Beaufort offers the sophisticated traveller all the style and comfort of home – combining warm contemporary colourings with the highest possible attention. The Beaufort is tucked away in a quiet tree-lined square only 100 yards from Harrods and the designer boutiques of Knightsbridge. On arrival guests are greeted at the front door and given their own door key to come and go as they please. The closed front door gives added security and completes the feeling of home. All bedrooms are individually decorated with air conditioning, state-of-the-art television offering free Internet, E-mail and movies, CD players, twice daily maid service and many extras such as chocolates, biscuits, fruit, water and flowers. A magnificent collection of English floral watercolours is displayed throughout the hotel. Breakfast in bed is recommended with warm croissants, crusty rolls, fresh fruit salad, cereal, fruit juice, preserves and tea and coffee delivered to your room each morning. Other complimentary offerings include champagne and all drinks from the bar in the sitting room and a traditional cream tea with homemade scones and clotted cream.

Our inspector loved: The relaxing atmosphere and cosy bright rooms.

Directions: From Harrods exit at Knightsbridge underground station take third left.

Web: www.johansens.com/beaufortknights
E-mail: enquiries@thebeaufort.co.uk
Tel: 0870 381 8349
International: +44 (0)20 7584 5252
Fax: 020 7589 2834

Price Guide: (excluding VAT)
single from £155
double/twin £195–£260
junior suite £310

BEAUFORT HOUSE

45 BEAUFORT GARDENS, KNIGHTSBRIDGE, LONDON SW3 1PN

Directions: Beaufort Gardens leads off Brompton Road near Knightsbridge underground station. There is a 24hr car park nearby.

Web: www.johansens.com/beauforthouseapartments
E-mail: info@beauforthouse.co.uk
Tel: 0870 381 8350
International: +44 (0)20 7584 2600
Fax: 020 7584 6532

Price Guide: (excluding VAT)
£230–£650

Situated in Beaufort Gardens, a quiet tree-lined Regency cul-de-sac in the heart of Knightsbridge, 250 yards from Harrods, Beaufort House is an exclusive establishment comprising 21 self-contained fully serviced luxury apartments. All the comforts of a first-class hotel are combined with the privacy, discretion and relaxed atmosphere of home. Accommodation ranges in size from an intimate 1- bedroom to a spacious 4-bedroom apartment. Each apartment has been individually and traditionally decorated to the highest standard. All apartments have direct dial telephones with voice mail, personal safes, satellite television, DVD players and high speed Internet access. Some apartments benefit from balconies or patios. The fully equipped kitchens include washer/dryers and many have dishwashers. A daily maid service is included at no additional charge. Full laundry/dry cleaning services are available. A dedicated Guests Services team provides 24 hours coverage and will be happy to organise tours, theatre tickets, restaurant bookings, taxis or chauffeur driven limousines and other services. Complimentary membership at Aquilla's Health Club is offered to all guests during their stay. Awarded 5 stars by the English Tourism Council.

Our inspector loved: *This well-equipped and comfortable establishment, as ideal for weekend breaks as it is for longer stays.*

THE DRAYCOTT HOTEL

26 CADOGAN GARDENS, LONDON SW3 2RP

The award-winning Draycott Hotel offers the perfect balance of luxury, service, privacy and location. Tucked away in a tranquil, tree-lined garden square between Harrods and the Kings Road, it is at the centre of fashionable London and epitomises style and elegance. It combines the grandeur of the past with the conveniences of today, offering guests the exclusive ambience of a grand private residence. All 35 rooms are individually decorated reflecting the Edwardian period and combine 24-hour room service with all that today's discerning traveller requires. 9 of the opulent suites can be arranged to create the atmosphere of a private home with a fully-equipped kitchen and/or separate sitting room. The beautifully panelled boardroom overlooking the private residents' garden provides the perfect venue for small meetings and private parties. Johansens Most Excellent Hotel Award Winner 2000. The shops and restaurants of Knightsbridge, Chelsea and Belgravia, West End theatres and the City are within easy reach, and a chauffeur is available for airport transfers and personalised tours. Enjoy complimentary afternoon tea or a glass of champagne in the Drawing Room.

Our inspector loved: The elegant sunny drawing room overlooking one of London's prettiest squares.

Directions: Nearest underground station is Sloane Square.

Web: www.johansens.com/draycotthotel
E-mail: reservations@draycotthotel.com
Tel: 0870 381 8433
International: +44 (0)20 7730 6466
Fax: 020 7730 0236

Price Guide: (excluding VAT)
single from £110
double from £160
deluxe double/twin from £220
suites £320

Enfield

Central London

Richmond

Croydon

NUMBER ELEVEN CADOGAN GARDENS

11 CADOGAN GARDENS, SLOANE SQUARE, KNIGHTSBRIDGE, LONDON SW3 2RJ

Directions: Off Sloane Street. Nearest underground is Sloane Square.

Web: www.johansens.com/numberelevencadogangardens
E-mail: reservations@number–eleven.co.uk
Tel: 0870 381 8770
International: +44 (0)20 7730 7000
Fax: 020 7730 5217

Price Guide: (excl VAT)
single from £145
double/twin from £185
suite from £275

In a quiet tree-lined square between Harrods and the Kings Road, Number Eleven Cadogan Gardens is an elegant town house hotel with a reputation for first-class service. The hotel remains traditional yet stylish; no reception desk, no endless signing of bills, total privacy and security. The 60 bedrooms are well-appointed and furnished with antiques and oriental rugs. The Garden Suite, with its large double bedroom, has a particularly spacious drawing room overlooking the attractive gardens. Pre-dinner drinks and canapés are served every evening in the Drawing Room, whilst a varied menu is available throughout the day in the very pretty, light and airy dining room; room service operates around the clock. The Library is one of 3 private rooms available where small parties and business meetings can be held. Sauna and massage facilities are available or for a more strenuous work out, a personal trainer is on call in the in-house gymnasium. The fashionable shops and restaurants of Knightsbridge and Chelsea are within easy walking distance whilst a chauffeured Mercedes is available for airport and Eurostar connections. Theatre tickets, restaurant bookings and travel arrangements are all part of the hotel's unique personal service.

Our inspector loved: *This very traditional town house hotel in a superb location.*

THE COLONNADE, THE LITTLE VENICE TOWN HOUSE

2 WARRINGTON CRESCENT, LONDON W9 1ER

This tall, elegant Victorian town house is delightfully situated in the smart and sophisticated residential area of Little Venice, which embodies the tranquil Regents Canal. It is a beautifully furnished residence offering all the comforts of a luxury hotel and is conveniently within reach of London's many sights, restaurants, theatres and business areas. The Colonnade was originally built as 2 private homes in 1865 and later converted into a girl's boarding school and a hospital for ladies until opening as a hotel in 1935. The House has recently been completely refurbished and has an innovative, boutique style interior. Sumptuous fabrics and lavish antiques have been carefully selected to create a unique style and ambience in each of the 43 guest rooms and suites, many of them with a terrace and four-poster bed. All are individually decorated and feature every modern facility. The relaxing drawing room is ideal for guests to have pre-dinner drinks or a night cap. The renowned Town House breakfast is served in the stylish breakfast room and is second to none. Car parking and airport transfers can be arranged.

Our inspector loved: Its wonderful beds with their copious cushions and luxury fabrics.

Directions: Warwick Avenue underground station and taxi rank are close by. Paddington station with its direct Heathrow link is one stop away or a quick taxi ride.

Enfield

Central London

Richmond

Croydon

Web: www.johansens.com/colonnadetownhouse
E-mail: res_colonnade@etontownhouse.com
Tel: 0870 381 8436
International: +44 (0)20 7286 1052
Fax: 020 7286 1057

Price Guide: (excluding VAT)
single £126
suites from £230

THE LEONARD

15 SEYMOUR STREET, LONDON W1H 7JW

Directions: The Leonard is north of Marble Arch off Portman Square and just around the corner from Oxford Street and Selfridges. Parking in Bryanston Street.

Web: www.johansens.com/leonard
E-mail: the.leonard@dial.pipex.com
Tel: 0870 381 8688
International: +44 (0)20 7935 2010
Fax: 020 7935 6700

Price Guide: (excl VAT)
double £170–£220
suites £280– £550

4 late 18th-century Georgian town houses set the character of this relaxing Johansens award-winning property. Superbly located off Portman Square, which celebrated its 7th anniversary in 2003, The Leonard has become popular very quickly with discerning travellers and celebrities alike. Imaginative reconstruction has created 11 rooms and 21 suites decorated individually to a very high standard, with a further 12 rooms and a small roof garden completed in 2002. All rooms are fully air-conditioned and include private safe, mini-bar, hi-fi system, provision for fax/modem and within the reception area complimentary access to the Internet. Bathrooms are finished in marble, and some of the larger suites have a butler's pantry or fully-fitted kitchen. The first-floor Grand suites are particularly impressive, and the Café Bar offers breakfast and light meals throughout the day. For physical fitness and stress reduction there is a compact exercise room. With professional, friendly "Can-do" staff, The Leonard is the epitome of casual luxury in the heart of London's West End. Available opposite, also part of the hotel, The Leonard Residence offers 5 serviced apartments which are available for longer stays.

Our inspector loved: *The pretty patio roof terrace and the warm, relaxed atmosphere of the reception.*

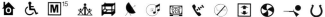

DORSET SQUARE HOTEL

39 DORSET SQUARE, MARYLEBONE, LONDON NW1 6QN

This little gem of a hotel is in a prime location for all that the west end of London has to offer. Set in a leafy square that was the original site for Thomas Lord's cricket ground, this Regency town house has been lovingly restored and designed to offer the ultimate in comfort and charm with a chic London edge. Each of the 38 bedrooms has been perfectly appointed to offer the latest amenities such as air conditioning, modem ports, and the marble bathrooms are equipped to an extremely high standard. The Potting Shed restaurant is a delight – light and airy and exuding character with an array of terracotta pots along one wall. The cuisine is a selection of modern British. For those who prefer to remain in the luxury of their bedrooms there is also the wonderful "bedroom picnic" – a basket laden with cold meats, fresh fruits, cheeses and pastries and chilled champagne. Madame Tussauds, the Planetarium and Regent's Park zoo are all within 2 minutes walk, and the shops of Oxford Street, Baker Street and even Bond Street are not far away. Theatreland is only a few minutes away, and the city is easily accessible by tube.

Our inspector loved: The pretty bedrooms and brilliant Potting Shed restaurant.

Directions: Left from Marylebone tube or right from Baker street tube – the hotel is just minutes from each.

Web: www.johansens.com/dorsetsquare
E-mail: info@dorsetsquare.co.uk
Tel: 0870 381 8488
International: +44 (0)20 7723 7874
Fax: 020 7724 3328

Price Guide: (excluding VAT)
double £160–£180
twin/king £195–£215
suite/four poster £240–£260

THE DORCHESTER

PARK LANE, MAYFAIR, LONDON W1A 2HJ

Directions: Towards Hyde Park Corner/Piccadilly end of Park Lane.

Web: www.johansens.com/thedorchester
E-mail: reservations@dorchesterhotel.com
Tel: 0870 381 8485
International: +44 (0)20 7629 8888
Fax: 020 7409 0114

Price Guide: (incl breakfast, VAT & service)
single £337–£390
double/twin £427–£491
suite £627–£2,535

Built in 1931, this grand hotel successfully combines ultra-modern convenience with traditional service and atmosphere. All 250 rooms, including 55 suites, have air conditioning, an entertainment and business system, video on demand (up to 60 films), direct Internet access and Microsoft Word, Excel and Powerpoint operated via an infrared keyboard on the TV. These individually decorated, cosy English country house style bedrooms also boast a fax, scanner, copier, DVD and CD player, with a music library of 5,000 tracks available in all the rooms, 90 of which have 42" plasma screens. All the rooms have recently undergone a multi million pound refurbishment programme. A variety of cuisine is on offer; from traditional British food in The Grill Room, Cantonese in The Oriental Restaurant, Italian cooking in The Dorchester Bar and an award-winning traditional afternoon tea in The Promenade. The fully air-conditioned banqueting rooms can be hired independently. There is a highly regarded day spa, offering a wide range of treatments. Personalised care is a pillar of The Dorchester's fine reputation. Year round packages are available.

Our inspector loved: *This sophisticated classical hotel with its outstanding service.*

 SPA

PEMBRIDGE COURT HOTEL

34 PEMBRIDGE GARDENS, LONDON W2 4DX

This gracious Victorian town house has been lovingly restored to its former glory whilst providing all the modern facilities demanded by today's discerning traveller. The 20 rooms, all of which have air conditioning, are individually decorated with pretty fabrics and the walls adorned with an unusual collection of framed fans and Victoriana. The charming and tranquil sitting room is as ideal for a quiet drink and light snacks as it is for a small informal meeting. There is also a small boardroom and sitting room on the lower ground floor. The Pembridge Court is renowned for the devotion and humour with which it is run. Its long serving staff and its famous cat "Churchill" assure you of a warm welcome and the very best in friendly, personal service. Over the years the hotel has built up a loyal following amongst its guests, many of whom regard it as their genuine "home from home" in London. The Pembridge is situated in quiet tree-lined gardens in Londons' trendy Notting Hill Gate. The area is colourful and full of life with lots of great pubs and restaurants and the biggest antiques market in the world at nearby Portobello Road.

Our inspector loved: *The wonderful friendly atmosphere of this very cosy hotel.*

Directions: Pembridge Gardens is a small turning off Notting Hill Gate/Bayswater Road, just 2 minutes from Portobello Road Antiques Market.

Web: www.johansens.com/pembridgecourt
E-mail: reservations@pemct.co.uk
Tel: 0870 381 8808
International: +44 (0)20 7229 9977
Fax: 020 7727 4982

Enfield

Central London

Richmond

Croydon

Price Guide: (inclusive of English breakfast & VAT)
single £130–£170
double/twin £190–£200

THE ATHENAEUM HOTEL & APARTMENTS

116 PICCADILLY, LONDON W1J 7BJ

Directions: The nearest underground station is Green Park.

Web: www.johansens.com/athenaeum
E-mail: info@athenaeumhotel.com
Tel: 0870 381 8329
International: +44 (0)20 7499 3464
Fax: 020 7493 1860

Price Guide: (excl VAT)
single from £265
double/twin from £295
suite/apartment from £415

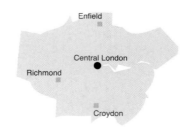

Set in a superb location, the stylish Athenaeum Hotel & Apartments is extremely welcoming with friendly staff and highly personalised service. Comfortable and luxurious décor adorns the cosy, secluded Windsor Lounge and the public areas. Lovely airy and bright bedrooms, some with views over Green Park, have fresh colour schemes, double, twin or king-size beds and all modern conveniences to create a contemporary yet traditional ambience. Housed in Edwardian town houses adjacent to the hotel, the spacious and elegantly furnished 1 and 2-bedroom apartments have a private entrance and kitchen facilities. Modern British cuisine using the finest seasonal ingredients is served in the highly acclaimed Bullochs restaurant, whose warm and intimate surroundings feature a floor of imported Jerusalem stone. For the energetic or those wishing to be pampered, the Spa offers a well-equipped gym, Jacuzzi, steam room, sauna, beauty therapy and massage. With its central location, the Athenaeum is ideal for business, leisure and shopping. Buckingham Palace, Hyde Park, Bond Street and the theatre district are a short walk away, whilst Harrods, Covent Garden, Westminster, Kensington Palace and Soho are only a few minutes by taxi or underground.

Our inspector loved: *The park views, dedicated staff and fabulous apartments.*

THE PETERSHAM

NIGHTINGALE LANE, RICHMOND-UPON-THAMES, SURREY TW10 6UZ

With its curves, columns and arches, tall slim windows, elaborate carvings, wrought-iron balcony railings and a majestic peaked tower this luxurious Victorian hotel impresses its visitors again and again. Beautifully situated in "the London countryside", it is just 8 miles from the capital's centre. It stands high on Richmond Hill with views over one of the most attractive stretches of the River Thames. Built in 1865, the hotel's character emanates from its architecture which, as well as the landmark tower, features the tallest unsupported Portland Stone staircase in England. Overhead are superb restored ceiling paintings. The classically styled en-suite bedrooms and suites combine every modern comfort with the elegance and grandeur of the past. The Petersham Penthouse is particularly sumptuous and extremely good value. Many of the guest rooms offer panoramic river views. Exceptional and imaginative cuisine, complemented by an extensive wine list, is prepared by talented chef Russell Williams and served with style in the sophisticated restaurant. Apart from large Richmond Park with its herds of deer there are many visitor attractions nearby, including Hampton Court Palace, Syon Park, Ham House and the Royal Botanic Gardens at Kew.

Our inspector loved: The up-to-the-minute new styling in the restaurant with its stunning views of the river and stunning cuisine to match.

Directions: From the M25, exit at junctions 8, 9, 12 or 15. From London via Cromwell Road and the A316.

Web: www.johansens.com/petersham
E-mail: enq@petershamhotel.co.uk
Tel: 0870 381 8819
International: +44 (0)20 8940 7471
Fax: 020 8939 1098

Price Guide:
single £135–£160
double/twin £170–£230
suite £295

THE RICHMOND GATE HOTEL AND RESTAURANT

RICHMOND HILL, RICHMOND-UPON-THAMES, SURREY TW10 6RP

Directions: Opposite the Star & Garter Home at the top of Richmond Hill.

Web: www.johansens.com/richmondgate
E-mail: richmondgate@corushotels.com
Tel: 0870 381 8855
International: +44 (0)20 8940 0061
Fax: 020 8332 0354

Price Guide:
single from £120
double/twin from £150
suite from £225

This former Georgian country house stands on the crest of Richmond Hill close to the Royal Park and Richmond Terrace with its commanding views over the River Thames. The 68 stylishly furnished en-suite bedrooms combine every comfort of the present with the elegance of the past and include several luxury four-poster rooms and suites. Exceptional and imaginative cuisine, complemented by an extensive wine list offering over 100 wines from around the world is served in the sophisticated surroundings of the Gates On The Parks Restaurant. Weddings, business meetings and private dining events can be arranged in a variety of rooms. The beautiful Victorian walled garden provides for summer relaxation. Cedars Health and Leisure Club is accessed through the hotel and includes a 20-metre pool, 6-metre spa, sauna, steam room, aerobics studio, cardiovascular and resistance gymnasia and a health and beauty suite. Richmond is close to London and the West End yet in a country setting. The Borough offers a wealth of visitor attractions, including Hampton Court Palace, Syon House and Park and the Royal Botanic Gardens at Kew.

Our inspector loved: Its unique location at the gates of Richmond Park - acres of open parkland where deer still graze beneath the trees.

NEW

HOTEL ST JAMES

6 WATERLOO PLACE, LONDON SW1Y 4AN

Located on the corner of Waterloo Place and Pall Mall, this imposing Grade II listed building is the former home of the Cox's and King's Bank and has been carefully renovated to create an elegant 5-star hotel. Sofitel acquired the majority of the original artwork from the bank, which is now proudly displayed and balanced out by contemporary design. Bedrooms and suites are sophisticated and equipped with ultra-modern technology, and in the bathrooms black and white marble harmonises with granite tops and chrome fittings. The elegant Rose Lounge is the ideal place for a traditional afternoon tea amidst an eclectic mix of colours and styles, whilst the St James Bar with its clubby atmosphere offers the largest selection of champagnes in London. French flair and refined cuisine are the hallmark of the buzzing Brasserie Roux. Guests can enjoy a pampering session in the hotel's fitness and massage centre complete with treatment rooms and steam room. The hotel's business centre includes a state-of-the-art boardroom with private dining room as well as a banqueting suite for up to 150 people. Numerous of London's major attractions, such as Trafalgar Square, Piccadilly Circus and the theatre district, are just around the corner.

Our inspector loved: *The grand marble entrace with its skilful mix of original and contemporary features.*

Directions: The nearest underground station is Piccadilly Circus.

Enfield

Central London

Richmond

Croydon

Web: www.johansens.com/stjames
E-mail: H3144@accor-hotels.com
Tel: 0870 381 9185
International: +44 (0)20 7747 2200
Fax: 020 7747 2210

Price Guide:
single from £275
double from £320
suite £430–£1,200

 186 150

THE CRANLEY

10 BINA GARDENS, SOUTH KENSINGTON, LONDON SW5 0LA

Standing in a quiet, tree-lined street in the heart of Kensington, this charming and sophisticated Victorian town house is an ideal city venue for the leisure and business visitor alike, blending traditional style and service with 21st-century technology. Furnished with beautiful antiques and hand-embroidered linen fabrics, The Cranley has an understated elegance. Striking colour combinations and stone used throughout the bedrooms and reception areas are derived from the original floor in the entrance hall. Recently completely refurbished, The Cranley's bedrooms are now among some of the most comfortable in the Capital. All are delightfully decorated and have king-sized, four-poster or half-tester canopied beds. Each room is light, air-conditioned and has facilities ranging from antique desk, 2 direct dial telephone lines and voicemail to interactive television with Internet access. The luxury bathrooms have traditional Victorian-style fittings combined with a lavish use of warm limestone. Guests can enjoy copious continental breakfasts, complimentary English afternoon tea and an evening help-yourself apéritif with canapés. Many of London's attractions are within easy walking distance, including the shops and restaurants of Knightsbridge and the Kings Road.

Directions: The nearest underground stations are Gloucester Road and South Kensington.

Web: www.johansens.com/cranley
E-mail: info@thecranley.com
Tel: 0870 381 8456
International: +44 (0)20 7373 0123
Fax: 020 7373 9497

Price Guide:
single £182.12
double/twin £211.50
suite £246.75

Our inspector loved: This charming hotel with an abundance of four-poster beds.

THE GALLERY

8-10, QUEENSBERRY PLACE, SOUTH KENSINGTON, LONDON SW7 2EA

A unique experience awaits guests at this elegant Victorian house where the highest standards of comfort and amenities can be enjoyed. The Gallery's atmosphere is one of quiet refinement and, true to its name, the hotel displays original art in every room. The welcoming mahogany panelled reception area and lounge features an imposing Jacobean Revival chimney piece, plump sofas and discrete bar. Old kilims adorn side tables, an Ottoman theme is repeated in the rich pile carpeting. Everything from Oriental porcelain in the lobby to the furniture and décor of the Morris Room has been expertly selected. The beautiful drawing room evokes the arts and crafts style popularised by the famed Victorian painter and designer – arbutus wallpaper, tulip and lily carpet, an oak-cased Manxman piano and an antique bar billiards table. The 34 individually decorated guest rooms offer every facility including 2 direct dial telephones with data port. 2 master suites, Rossetti and Leighton, are furnished with the refinement befitting their names; each has its own roof terrace, Jacuzzi, CD and DVD players. Light snacks are available. The Gallery's location is ideal – close to Harrods, fashionable Knightsbridge, bohemian Chelsea and numerous museums.

Our inspector loved: *The large welcoming reception with it's own private art gallery.*

Directions: Three minutes' walk from South Kensington underground station, just off Cromwell Road.

Web: www.johansens.com/thegallery
E-mail: reservations@eeh.co.uk
Tel: 0870 381 8535
International: +44 (0)20 7915 0000
Fax: 020 7915 4400

Price Guide: (excl. VAT)
single £120
double/twin £145
suites £220

NUMBER SIXTEEN

16 SUMNER PLACE, LONDON SW7 3EG

Directions: Sumner Place is off the old Brompton Road near Onslow Square.

Web: www.johansens.com/numbersixteen
E-mail: sixteen@firmdale.com
Tel: 0870 381 8771
International: +44 (0)20 7589 5232
Fax: 020 7584 8615

Price Guide: (excluding VAT)
single from £95
double/twin from £165

Freshly refurbished behind an immaculate pillared façade, Number Sixteen, situated in the heart of South Kensington, is surrounded by some of London's best restaurants, bars, shops and museums. Harrods, Knightsbridge shopping, Hyde Park and the Victoria & Albert Museum are all just a short walk away. Although the area has a buzzy, cosmopolitan character, the hotel is a haven of calm and seclusion. In winter an open fire and honesty bar in the drawing room entices with its warmth, whilst in summer the conservatory opens onto an award-winning private garden. The library is ideal for greeting friends or holding an informal business meeting. The 41 bedrooms are individually designed and decorated in a traditional English style complete with crisp Frette bedlinen and white, hand-embroidered bedspreads. Each is appointed with facilities expected by the modern traveller, including mini-bar, personal safe and direct dial telephone with voice mail and modem point. Staff are friendly and attentive ensuring that guests are looked after almost as if they were staying in a private home. South Kensington underground station is just a two-minute walk away, providing easy access to the West End and the City and a direct link to Heathrow airport.

Our inspector loved: *The calming elegant interior and pretty secret back garden.*

DOLPHIN SQUARE HOTEL

DOLPHIN SQUARE, CHICHESTER STREET, LONDON SW1V 3LX

Dolphin Square Hotel is centrally located in large, exquisite gardens bordered by the River Thames and Westminster. This quiet oasis, decorated in a contemporary style, offers discreet service and a friendly welcome. The 148 attractive suites offer a classical or modern décor with subtle colour co-ordinated design. Most suites have a compact, well-equipped kitchen, whilst 24-hour room service and full hotel facilities are available for those who prefer not to cater for themselves. Guests can enjoy delicious international cuisine in the informal Brasserie, and the Clipper Bar is a fun yet stylish venue for a drink and chat. The hotel's fine dining restaurant, Allium, is an exciting new venue under the direction of internationally renowned master chef Anton Edelmann. The menu features the best of French and British cuisine in a relaxed but sophisticated atmosphere. A variety of shops in Dolphin Square provides for your every need, including a newsagent, chemist, hair salon and travel agent. The hotel's heated swimming pool and health club include a fully-equipped gym, tennis courts, squash courts, croquet lawn, sauna, steam room and numerous beauty and health treatments offered by qualified professionals. There are superb facilities for celebrations of any size as well as excellent business and corporate services.

Our inspector loved: *The spacious light rooms, its fabulous health club and mini shopping mall.*

Directions: The closest underground station is Pimlico.

Web: www.johansens.com/dolphinsquare
E-mail: reservations@dolphinsquarehotel.co.uk
Tel: 0870 381 8483
International: +44 (0)20 7834 3800
Fax: 020 7798 8735

Price Guide:
studio suite single £155
studio suite double/twin £180–£190
1 bedroom suite £190–£400
2 bedroom suite £320
3 bedroom suite £450

51 BUCKINGHAM GATE

51 BUCKINGHAM GATE, WESTMINSTER, LONDON SW1E 6AF

Directions: Nearest underground stations are St James's Park and Victoria.

Web: www.johansens.com/buckinghamgate
E-mail: info@51-buckinghamgate.co.uk
Tel: 0870 381 8301
International: +44 (0)20 7769 7766
Fax: 020 7828 5909

Price Guide:
suites £405–£975

Close to Buckingham Palace, St James's Park and the Houses of Parliament, 51 Buckingham Gate is contemporary style and luxury on a grand scale. This attractive Victorian town house offers everything the discerning guest could wish for: privacy, relaxation and superb service delivered by multilingual staff which includes a team of Ivor Spencer trained butlers. Guests have a choice of dining options: Quilon, offering southern coastal Indian cuisine, Bank Westminster, Zander Bar and The Library. There are 82 suites and apartments, ranging from junior suites to the 5-bedroom Prime Minister's Suite, which combine contemporary interior design with luxury hotel facilities. De luxe suites offer award-winning bathrooms, whilst designated Ivor Spencer Suites have 16-hour personal butler service, limousine pick-up and an exclusive range of special amenities. Each suite provides sophisticated technology including 2-line speaker telephones, voicemail, dataport, fax/copier/printer, CD and DVD player. Fully equipped kitchens as well as 24-hour room service are available. A team of talented chefs is also at hand to prepare private dinners. Guests can enjoy treatments at the exclusive Shiseido Qi Salon Spa and a fully equipped gymnasium at the Club at St James Court.

Our inspector loved: *The beautifully designed contemporary bathrooms.*

       SPA

CANNIZARO HOUSE

WEST SIDE, WIMBLEDON COMMON, LONDON SW19 4UE

Cannizaro House, an elegant Georgian country house, occupies a tranquil position on the edge of Wimbledon Common, yet is only 18 minutes by train from London Waterloo and the Eurostar terminal. Cannizaro House restored as a superb hotel has, throughout its history, welcomed Royalty and celebrities such as George III, Oscar Wilde and William Pitt. The 18th century is reflected in the ornate fireplaces and mouldings, gilded mirrors and many antiques. All the hotel's 45 bedrooms are individually designed, with many overlooking beautiful Cannizaro Park. All of the 17 executive rooms have air conditioning. Several intimate rooms are available for meetings and private dining, including the elegant Queen Elizabeth Room – a popular venue for wedding ceremonies. The Viscount Melville Suite offers air-conditioned comfort for up to 100 guests. There is a spacious south-facing summer terrace as ideal for afternoon tea and receptions as it is for evening cocktails. The award-winning kitchen produces the finest modern and classical cuisine, complemented by an impressive list of wines.

Our inspector loved: The feeling you are in the country and the huge terrace overlooking the grounds.

Directions: The nearest tube and British Rail station is Wimbledon.

Web: www.johansens.com/cannizarohouse
E-mail: cannizarohouse@thistle.co.uk
Tel: 0870 381 8402
International: +44 (0)208 879 1464
Fax: 020 8970 2753

Price Guide: (room only):
double/twin from £156
feature room from £184

HOTEL ROSSETTI

107 PICCADILLY, MANCHESTER M1 2DB

Directions: The hotel is in the centre of Manchester, between Piccadilly Gardens and Piccadilly station.

Web: www.johansens.com/rossetti
E-mail: info@aliasrossetti.com
Tel: 0870 381 9148
International: +44 (0)161 247 7744
Fax: 0161 247 7747

Price Guide:
single £105-£150
double £105-£150
suite £330

This stunning and individual hotel lies in the heart of Manchester and is as lively and refreshing as the city itself. Formerly a cotton mill, the building dates back to the Victorian age and has been carefully, innovatively and stylishly designed without losing reference to its heritage. There are 61 bedrooms and 5 magnificent penthouse suites, where guests can experience the utmost luxury with cutting-edge design and modern pieces of art. The atmosphere, however, is placed on impeccable service mixed with informality; there is even a 24-hour "diner" on each floor, where guests can meet in the small hours to share a cappuccino or fruit juice. The Café Paradiso (Metro Newcomer of the Year 2003) boasts its own wood-fired pizza oven and some delicious Italian-inspired dishes, whilst the basement is the place to enjoy antipasti and seafood or just sip some exotic cocktails. Just 400 paces from Manchester Piccadilly station, the Rossetti is also a great venue for any business meeting, conference or party offering 2 creative, stimulating meeting spaces, with an abundance of natural light. There is capacity for 10 or 25 in each of these spaces, the basement can also cater for 125. The attractions of the city itself lie just outside the door for breakout sessions!

Our inspector loved: *The 24-hour "diner" on each floor where guests can help themselves to beverages, breakfast and snacks.*

DIDSBURY HOUSE

DIDSBURY PARK, DIDSBURY VILLAGE, MANCHESTER M20 5LJ

This stylish and contemporary small boutique hotel, in a leafy south Manchester suburb, is a careful refurbishment and extension of a Grade II listed, mid-19th-century Victorian villa and coach house. It is the second town house hotel concept to be opened in the city by Eamonn and Sally O'Loughlin, the first being the acclaimed Eleven Didsbury Park. Their new hotel, just 100 yards away, is double the size and twice as stunning. It seduces guests immediately as they enter its beautiful hallway. The superb original carved wooden staircase carries the eye up to a magnificent stained-glass window. Ornate ceilings and architraves, polished wooden floors and warm décor dominate the luxurious public rooms. The exquisite and romantic attic suite has separate his and hers cast-iron roll-top baths and his and hers seats in a huge shower and steam cubicle, whilst in every gorgeous en-suite bedroom the bath fits 2. A top floor footbridge spans a central atrium and a charming lounge with ostrich-egg sized lights and pewter bar leads onto a secluded courtyard furnished with a restful and imaginative combination of steel, bamboo and water features. Gym, steam room and face, body and holistic treatments are available in the SO Spa. Breakfast and a room service menu are available in the evenings, but complimentary transport is provided for dining out.

Our inspector loved: *The original 18th-century staircase set in front of the stained-glass window .*

Directions: Exit the M56 at junction 1 and take the A34 towards Manchester. At the traffic lights turn left onto the A5145 towards Didsbury. At the 2nd set of traffic lights turn right into Didsbury Park. The Hotel is on the left.

Web: www.johansens.com/didsburyhouse
E-mail: enquiries@didsburyhouse.co.uk
Tel: 0870 381 8481
International: +44 (0)161 448 2200
Fax: 0161 448 2525

Price Guide:
single £93–£170
double/twin £103–£183
suite £195–£350

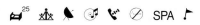

ETROP GRANGE

THORLEY LANE, MANCHESTER AIRPORT, GREATER MANCHESTER M90 4EG

Hidden away near Manchester Airport lies Etrop Grange, a beautiful country house hotel and restaurant. The original house was built in 1780 and more than 200 years on has been lovingly restored. Today, the hotel enjoys a fine reputation for its accommodation, where the luxury, character and sheer elegance of the Georgian era are evident in every feature. The magnificent award-winning restaurant offers a well balanced mix of traditional and modern English cuisine, complemented by an extensive selection of fine wines. Attention to detail ensures personal and individual service. In addition to the obvious advantage of having an airport within walking distance, the location of Etrop Grange is ideal in many other ways. With a comprehensive motorway network and InterCity stations minutes away, it is accessible from all parts of the UK. Entertainment for visitors ranges from the shopping, sport and excellent nightlife offered by the city of Manchester to golf, riding, clay pigeon shooting, water sports and outdoor pursuits in the immediate countryside. Cheshire also boasts an abundance of stately homes, museums and historical attractions.

Directions: Leave M56 at junction 5 towards Manchester Airport. Follow signs for Terminal 2. Go up the slip road. At roundabout take first exit, take immediate left and hotel is 400yds on the right.

Web: www.johansens.com/etropgrange
E-mail: etropgrange@corushotels.com
Tel: 0870 381 8507
International: +44 (0)161 499 0500
Fax: 0161 499 0790

Price Guide:
single £137–£145
double/twin £175–£205
suites £199

Our inspector loved: The complimentary chauffeured Jaguar to Manchester Airport.

CONGHAM HALL

GRIMSTON, KING'S LYNN, NORFOLK PE32 1AH

Dating from the mid-18th century, this stately manor house is set in acres of parkland, orchards and gardens. The conversion from country house to luxury hotel in 1982 was executed with care to enhance the elegance of the classic interiors. The hotel's renowned herb garden grows over 700 varieties of herb, many are used by the chef to create modern English dishes with the accent on fresh local produce and fish from the local Norfolk markets. The hotel's hives even produce the honey for your breakfast table. The beautiful flower displays, homemade pot pourri and roaring log fires blend together to create a welcoming and relaxing atmosphere. Congham Hall is the ideal base from which to tour the spectacular beaches of the north Norfolk coastline, Sandringham, Burnham Market and Holkham Hall.

Directions: Go to the A149/A148 interchange northeast of King's Lynn. Follow the A148 towards Sandringham/Fakenham/ Cromer for 100 yards. Turn right to Grimston. The hotel is then 2 miles on the left

Web: www.johansens.com/conghamhall
E-mail: info@conghamhallhotel.co.uk
Tel: 0870 381 8443
International: +44 (0)1485 600250
Fax: 01485 601191

Price Guide:
single from £105
double/twin from £165
suites from £250

Our inspector loved: The wonderful herb garden.

PARK FARM COUNTRY HOTEL & LEISURE

HETHERSETT, NORWICH, NORFOLK NR9 3DL

Directions: By road, just off A11 on B1172, Norwich Airport 8 miles, Norwich rail station 6 miles and Norwich bus station 5 miles.

Web: www.johansens.com/parkfarm
E-mail: enq@parkfarm–hotel.co.uk
Tel: 0870 381 8800
International: +44 (0)1603 810264
Fax: 01603 812104

King's Lynn
Cromer
Norwich
Great Yarmouth

Price Guide:
single £92-£120
double/twin £118-£155
suites £165

Park Farm Hotel occupies a secluded location in beautifully landscaped grounds south of Norwich, once the second greatest city in England. There are executive rooms for additional comfort, with four-poster beds and Jacuzzi baths. Additional bedrooms have been sympathetically converted from traditional and new buildings to reflect the style of the 5 rooms available in the main house. A superb leisure complex to suit all ages has been carefully incorporated alongside the original Georgian house to include heated swimming pool, sauna, steam room, solarium, spa bath, gymnasium, aerobics studio and a new beauty therapy area. The delightful restaurant is renowned for its high standards of cuisine and service, with a wide selection of dishes and fine choice of wines. Conference facilities cater for up to 120 candidates, (24-hour and daily delegate rates available). Ideal location for wedding receptions. The Norfolk broads, the coast, Norwich open market, Castle museum and Cathedral are nearby. A self-catering apartment is also available.

Our inspector loved: *The newly refurbished bedrooms and bathrooms.*

FAWSLEY HALL

FAWSLEY, NEAR DAVENTRY, NORTHAMPTONSHIRE NN11 3BA

Set in the beautiful Northamptonshire countryside and surrounded by acres of rolling parkland with lakes, landscaped by Capability Brown, Fawsley Hall combines the charm and character of a gracious manor with the facilities and comforts of a modern hotel. The original Tudor Manor House opened as a hotel in 1998 but many traces of its illustrious past have been retained, such as the vaulted hall and Queen Elizabeth I chamber. 43 wonderfully decorated rooms offer a range of Tudor, Georgian, Victorian and "classic modern"styles, many of which include four-poster beds. The Knightley Restaurant has established a reputation as being the finest in Northamptonshire and the Old Laundry Bar provides delicious light meals at lunchtime. The hotel's new spa in the Georgian cellar includes a beauty salon, fitness studio, steam, sauna and spa bath. 6 conference and syndicate rooms can accommodate up to 80 delegates and the attractive Salvin Suite can seat up to 140 for a private banquet or wedding reception. Places of historic interest include: Sulgrave Manor, ancestral home of George Washington; Althorp; Canons Ashby; Blenheim Palace; Silverstone; Towcester Racecourse; an Elizabethan manor house and Warwick Castle. Oxford and Stratford-upon-Avon are nearby.

Our inspector loved: The views of the rolling countryside from the bedroom windows.

Directions: Fawsley Hall can be reached by the M40, junction 11 or the M1, junction16. Both are 10 miles from the hotel.

Web: www.johansens.com/fawsleyhall
E-mail: reservations@fawsleyhall.com
Tel: 0870 381 8516
International: +44 (0)1327 892000
Fax: 01327 892001

Market Harborough

Northampton

Towcester

Price Guide:
single from £135
double/twin from £160
suite from £275

WHITTLEBURY HALL

WHITTLEBURY, NR TOWCESTER, NORTHAMPTONSHIRE NN12 8QH

Directions: 11 miles from M1 Junction 15A. 18 miles from M40 Junction 10.

Web: www.johansens.com/whittleburyhall
E-mail: sales@whittleburyhall.co.uk
Tel: 0870 381 8995
International: +44 (0)1327 857857
Fax: 01327 857867

Price Guide:
single £125
double/twin £155
suite £260

Whittlebury Hall is a modern building where the elegance of classic Georgian architecture has been complemented by contemporary furnishings and fabrics to create a truly fabulous hotel. The spacious bedrooms have all been elegantly decorated with a host of modern touches and thoughtful extras, whilst 3 superbly appointed, individually styled suites have a whirlpool spa bath and shower. The Silverstone Bar is aptly named with a host of motor racing memorabilia adorning the walls. Astons Restaurant offers a relaxed atmosphere with menus blending classic and contemporary cuisine with a dash of continental inspiration, whilst Murrays Restaurant boasts 2 AA Rosettes for fine food. The management training centre offers 12 suites and 24 dedicated syndicate rooms and a lecture room for up to 300 delegates. Guests can relax and unwind at the Spa, where over 60 treatments are available in the health and beauty treatment suite. There is a 19-metre swimming pool, whirlpool spa, Turkish steam room, sauna and a 42-station StairMaster® gym, whilst the adjacent Whittlebury Park golf course offers preferred rates for guests. Motor racing enthusiasts can enjoy racing action at nearby Silverstone. Warwick Castle, Towcester racecourse and Oxford are all within a easy drive.

Our inspector loved: Bentleys, the new wine and tapas bar overlooking the courtyard.

MARSHALL MEADOWS COUNTRY HOUSE HOTEL

BERWICK-UPON-TWEED, NORTHUMBERLAND TD15 1UT

Marshall Meadows can truly boast that it is England's most northerly hotel, just a quarter of a mile from the Scottish border, an ideal base for those exploring the rugged beauty of Northumberland. A magnificent Georgian mansion standing in 15 acres of woodland and formal gardens, Marshall Meadows today is a luxurious retreat, with a country house ambience – welcoming and elegant. It has a burn and small waterfall with attractive woodland walks. This is not a large hotel; there are just 19 bedrooms, each individually designed. Restful harmonious colour schemes, comfortable beds and the tranquillity of its surroundings ensure a good night's sleep! The lounge is delightful, with traditional easy chairs and sofas, overlooking the patio. Ideal for summer afternoon tea. The congenial Duck & Grouse Bar stocks a range of whiskies, beers and fine wines. Marshall Meadows has a galleried restaurant where diners enjoy local game, fresh seafood and good wine. Private dining facilities are also available. Excellent golf, fishing and historic Berwick-on-Tweed are nearby.

Our inspector loved: The peaceful country setting in close proximity to the sea and its coastal walks.

Directions: A1 heading North, take Berwick by-pass and at Meadow House roundabout, head towards Edinburgh. After 300 yards, turn right, indicated by white sign – hotel is at end of small side road.

Web: www.johansens.com/marshallmeadows
E-mail: stay@marshallmeadows.co.uk
Tel: 0870 381 8721
International: +44 (0)1289 331133
Fax: 01289 331438

Price Guide:
single £90–£95
double/twin £120–£130
suite £150–£160

TILLMOUTH PARK

CORNHILL-ON-TWEED, NEAR BERWICK-UPON-TWEED, NORTHUMBERLAND TD12 4UU

Directions: Tillmouth Park is on the A698 Coldstream to Berwick-upon-Tweed road.

Web: www.johansens.com/tillmouthpark
E-mail: reception@tillmouthpark.f9.co.uk
Tel: 0870 381 8948
International: +44 (0)1890 882255
Fax: 01890 882540

Price Guide:
single £70–£140
twin/double £135–£195

This magnificent mansion house, built in 1882 using stones from nearby Twizel Castle, offers the same warm welcome to visitors today as when it was an exclusive private house. Tillmouth Park is situated in 15 acres of mature parkland gardens above the river Till. The generously sized bedrooms are individually designed with period and antique furniture, and are fully appointed with bathrobes, toiletries, hairdryer and trouser press. Most bedrooms offer spectacular views of the surrounding countryside. The wood-panelled restaurant serves a fine table d'hôte menu offering contemporary British cuisine, whilst the Bistro is less formal. A well-chosen wine list and a vast selection of malt whiskies complement the cuisine. The elegant, galleried main hall offers country house comfort with open log fires. Tillmouth Park is ideally situated for country pursuits, with fishing on the Tweed and Till and clay shooting available on the grounds. The area also abounds in fine golf courses. Coldstream and Kelso are within easy reach; the Northumbrian coast and Berwick are 15 minutes away, and Flodden Field, Lindisfarne and Holy Island are nearby. There are many stately homes to visit in the area including Floors, Manderston, Paxton and the spectacular Alnwick Garden Project.

Our inspector loved: The magnificent galleried main hall.

MATFEN HALL

MATFEN, NEWCASTLE-UPON-TYNE, NORTHUMBERLAND NE20 0RH

Originally built in 1830 by Sir Edward Blackett, Matfen Hall has been carefully restored by Sir Hugh and Lady Blackett. This magnificent family seat lies in the heart of some of Northumberland's most beautiful countryside. Recently awarded Small Hotel of the Year in the Excellence in England awards, Matfen Hall offers splendid facilities for conferences, weddings and leisure breaks. The Great Hall is awe-inspiring with its stained glass windows, massive pillars and stone floors, whilst each of the 31 bedrooms has its own individual character, combining modern features with traditional opulence. A huge open fireplace adds charm to the elegantly furnished Drawing Room and the unique Library and Print Room restaurant serves contemporary English cuisine and has been awarded 2 AA rosettes for the highest standard of cuisine and service. Matfen Hall enjoys stunning views over its own championship golf course, laid out on a classic parkland landscape with manicured greens and fairways flanked by majestic trees. Rated as one of the finest in the North East, it provides a pleasurable test for players of all abilities. There is also a 9-hole par 3 golf course. A swimming pool, beauty and leisure facilities and additional bedrooms will be available from 2004. Scenic coastal, rural and ancient sites are within comfortable driving distance. Newcastle-upon-Tyne is only 20 minutes away. Special breaks available.

Directions: From A1 take A69 towards Hexham. At Heddon on the Wall take B6318 towards Chollerford, travel 7 miles and turn right to Matfen.

Web: www.johansens.com/matfenhall
E-mail: info@matfenhall.com
Tel: 0870 381 8724
International: +44 (0)1661 886500
Fax: 01661 886055

Berwick-upon-Tweed
Alnwick
Morpeth
Hexham

Price Guide:
single £102–£147
double £140–£235

Our inspector loved: The view of the golf course from the "Keeper's Lodge".

LINDEN HALL

LONGHORSLEY, MORPETH, NORTHUMBERLAND NE65 8XF

Directions: From Newcastle take A1 north for 15 miles, then A697 toward Coldstream and Wooler. The hotel is 1 mile north of Longhorsley.

Web: www.johansens.com/lindenhall
E-mail: stay@lindenhall.co.uk
Tel: 0870 381 8692
International: +44 (0)1670 50 00 00
Fax: 01670 50 00 01

Price Guide:
single £84.50–£155
double/twin £121–£161
luxury rooms: £161–£201

Berwick-upon-Tweed

Alnwick

● Morpeth

Hexham

Ivy-clad, hidden away among 450 acres of fine park and woodland in mid-Northumberland, Linden Hall is a superb Georgian country house within easy reach of Newcastle-upon-Tyne. An impressive mile-long drive sweeps up to its main door where, upon entering, the visitor will discover a relaxed, dignified atmosphere enhanced by gracious marble hearths, antiques and period pieces. Those wishing to escape the urban stress will be delighted to find every fitness and relaxation requirement catered for on the 18-hole golf course or at the health and beauty spa. Beauty therapy treatments, fitness and steam room, swimming pool, sun terrace and solarium are all available on the premises. The 50 bedrooms are individually and elegantly furnished. Some rooms have four-poster beds; each has its own private bathroom, supplied with thoughtful extras. The Linden Tree serves informal drinks and bar meals and the Dobson Restaurant, with panoramic views of the Northumberland coastline, serves delicious food, imaginatively prepared. Wedding ceremonies and receptions, banquets, dinner parties and business conferences can be held in comfort in any one of Linden Hall's conference and banqueting suites.

Our inspector loved: *Having a relaxing swim after a game of golf.*

LANGAR HALL

LANGAR, NOTTINGHAMSHIRE NG13 9HG

Set in the Vale of Belvoir, mid-way between Nottingham and Grantham, Langar Hall is the family home of Imogen Skirving. It was built in 1837 on the site of a great historic house, the home of Admiral Lord Howe. It stands in quiet seclusion overlooking gardens, where sheep graze among the ancient trees in the park. Below the croquet lawn lies a romantic network of medieval fishponds stocked with carp. Epitomising "excellence and diversity", Langar Hall combines the standards of good hotel-keeping with the hospitality and style of country house living. The popular neighbourhood restaurant serves English dishes of local meat, poultry, game, fish and shell fish with garden vegetables in season. The en-suite bedrooms are individually designed and comfortably appointed, whilst the public rooms feature fine furnishings and most rooms afford beautiful views of the garden, park and moat. Langar Hall is an ideal venue for small boardroom meetings. It is also an ideal base from which to visit Belvoir Castle, see cricket at Trent Bridge, visit students at Nottingham University and to see Robin Hood's Sherwood Forest. Dogs can be accommodated by arrangement.

Our inspector loved: The feeling of home comfort as you arrive through the door.

Directions: Langar is accessible via Bingham on the A52, or via Cropwell Bishop from the A46 (both signposted). The house adjoins the church and is hidden behind it.

Worksop

Mansfield

Nottingham

Web: www.johansens.com/langarhall
E-mail: langarhall–hotel@ndirect.co.uk
Tel: 0870 381 8676
International: +44 (0)1949 860559
Fax: 01949 861045

Price Guide:
single £65–£97.50
double/twin £130–£150
suite £175

BIGNELL PARK HOTEL & RESTAURANT

CHESTERTON, BICESTER, OXFORDSHIRE OX26 1UE

In the lovely setting of the pretty village Chesterton, this friendly and welcoming Cotswold stone hotel combines traditional old-world charm with the grace of a delightfully run country home. Originally an 18th-century farmhouse, Bignell Park stands in 2½ acres of secluded, lawned gardens and orchard. Close by is the distinguished Kirtlington Polo Club and the historic market town and important hunting centre of Bicester. It is an ideal location for those wishing to explore a succession of enchanting, honey-coloured Cotswold villages and enjoy the attractions of Stratford-Upon-Avon, Warwick Castle, Oxford and Blenheim Palace, ancestral home to the Dukes of Marlborough. The tastefully refurbished en-suite bedrooms, which include 3 four-posters, are spacious, attractively decorated and provide every facility to make visiting a pleasure. During winter months guests can relax before a roaring log fire in the comfortable and elegant drawing room which looks out over the garden. The candle-lit restaurant, with wood-beamed ceiling, minstrels' gallery and open fire, has gained a deserved reputation. Head Chef Stuart Turvey and his team carefully prepare imaginative and varied English/French menus to suit all tastes.

Directions: From M40, junction 9, follow A41 towards Bicester. After approximately 1½ miles turn left to Chesterton and then take A4095.

Web: www.johansens.com/bignellpark
E-mail: enq@bignellparkhotel.co.uk
Tel: 0870 381 8362
International: +44 (0)1869 326550
Fax: 01869 322729

Price Guide:
single £70–£90
double/twin £90–£110
four poster£135

Banbury

Oxford

Henley-on-Thames

Our inspector loved: *The contemporary yet classic style.*

THE BAY TREE HOTEL

SHEEP STREET, BURFORD, OXON OX18 4LW

The Bay Tree has been expertly refurbished so that it retains all its Tudor splendour whilst offering every modern facility. The oak-panelled rooms have huge stone fireplaces and a galleried staircase leads upstairs from the raftered hall. All the bedrooms are en suite, three of them furnished with four-poster beds and 2 of the 5 suites have half-tester beds. In the summer, guests can enjoy the delightful walled gardens, featuring landscaped terraces of lawn and flower beds. A relaxing atmosphere is enhanced by the staff's attentive service in the flagstoned dining room where the head chef's creative cuisine is complemented by a comprehensive selection of fine wines. Light meals are served in a country-style bar. Burford, often described as the gateway to the Cotswolds, is renowned for its assortment of antique shops and the Tolsey Museum of local history. The Bay Tree Hotel makes a convenient base for day trips to Stratford-upon-Avon, Stow-on-the-Wold and Blenheim Palace. Golf, clay pigeon shooting and riding can be arranged locally.

Our inspector loved: The cosiness of the library.

Directions: Burford is on the A40 between Oxford and Cheltenham. Proceed halfway down the hill into Burford, turn left into Sheep Street and The Bay Tree Hotel is 30 yards on your right.

Web: www.johansens.com/baytree
E-mail: bookings@cotswold–inns–hotels.co.uk
Tel: 0870 381 8347
International: +44 (0)1993 822791
Fax: 01993 823008

Price Guide:
single £119
double/twin £155–£185
suite £195–£230

PHYLLIS COURT CLUB

MARLOW ROAD, HENLEY-ON-THAMES, OXFORDSHIRE RG9 2HT

Directions: M40 junction 4 to Marlow or M4 junction 8/9 then follow signposts to Henley-on-Thames.

Web: www.johansens.com/phylliscourt
E-mail: enquiries@phylliscourt.co.uk
Tel: 0870 381 8822
International: +44 (0)1491 570500
Fax: 01491 570528

Price Guide:
single £110
twin/double £129

Founded in 1906 by the owner of the house and a group of friends and London businessmen, the Club has an intriguing history spanning 6 centuries and involving royal patronage. Phyllis Court occupies an unrivalled position on the banks of the Thames and overlooking the Henley Royal Regatta course. Phyllis Court prides itself on retaining the traditions of its illustrious past, whilst guests today who now stay in this fine historic residence can enjoy the highest standards of up-to-date hospitality. Oliver Cromwell slept here and he built the embankment wall; and it was here that William II held his first Royal Court. Years later, when the name Henley became synonymous with rowing, they came as patrons of the Royal Regatta: Prince Albert, King George V and Edward, Prince of Wales. The character of the place remains unaltered in its hallowed setting, but the comfortable bedrooms, the restaurant, the "cellar" and the entire complement of amenities are of the latest high quality. Residents become temporary members as the dining room and bar are open to members only. Likely to be fully booked far ahead during the season. Ideal for meetings, functions and wedding parties.

Our inspector loved: *The new bedrooms and watching competitive croquet.*

THE COTSWOLD LODGE HOTEL

66A BANBURY ROAD, OXFORD OX2 6JP

Situated in a quiet conservation area just ½ mile away from Oxford is this picturesque Victorian building, which has been restored in the style of a stately manor house. An ideal location for tourists and those on business, the hotel offers a comfortable and relaxed environment. The Scholars bar is ideal for a light lunch or pre-dinner drink, and during winter, log fires enhance the cosy ambience. The elegant Fellows restaurant serves outstanding seasonal menus, with high-quality ingredients a priority. Fresh fish and lobster come from Cornwall, sausages are made specially for the hotel, wild salmon is delivered from Scotland, and local lamb and game are used extensively. An impressive wine list ensures that there is something to suit all tastes and complement every meal. The tastefully furnished en-suite bedrooms differ in size and style. The Cotswold Lodge happily caters for conferences on a daily or residential basis, and over the years has become renowned for its superb reputation in hosting wedding receptions. Staff are on hand to provide their expertise and tailor arrangements to suit individual requirements. The Banquet room accommodates up to 100 people and has access to a patio with fountain and walled garden.

Our inspector loved: The warmth of welcome and attention to detail.

Directions: From M40 junction 8, take A40 for Oxford; or junction 9, take A34; or from M4, junction 13, take A34 for Oxford.

Web: www.johansens.com/cotswoldlodge
E-mail: info@cotswoldlodgehotel.co.uk
Tel: 0870 381 8450
International: +44 (0)1865 512121
Fax: 01865 512490

Price Guide:
single £125
double/twin £175
suite from £295

HAWKWELL HOUSE

CHURCH WAY, IFLEY VILLAGE, OXFORD OX4 4D2

Directions: From Oxford, take the A34 south, then A4142 east. Iffley is signed on your left.

Web: www.johansens.com/hawkwell
E-mail: info@hawkwellhouse.co.uk
Tel: 0870 381 8326
International: +44 (0)1865 749988
Fax: 01865 748525

Price Guide:
single from £90
double from £130
suite from £150

A secluded, quintessentially English country garden with 3 acres of lush lawns, shady trees, deep beds of mature shrubs and colourful flowers surround this imposing, white-fronted hotel in the leafy village of Iffley, just 2 miles from the centre of Oxford. Next door is the 12th-century Norman Church of St Mary, noted for its carvings, rich decorations and splendid west front. Hawkwell House is a homely environment providing total tranquillity in a sleepy Thamesside setting. It offers comfort, charm and style with 51 individually designed, en-suite bedrooms and suites that provide luxurious solace and an abundance of modern facilities. The elegant, award-winning Arezzo restaurant overlooks an attractive fountain patio and serves seasonal menus of highly individual dishes, with quality ingredients a high priority. An impressive wine list ensures that there is something to suit all tastes. More informal dining can be enjoyed in Barezzo, a conservatory-style bar with distinctive décor, where talented kitchen staff provide everything from a tasty tiffin to an exotic 3-course meal. The hotel happily caters for conferences for up to 200 delegates and banquets for 180. Blenheim Palace, Woodstock and the Cotswolds are within easy reach and the attractions of Oxford are to hand.

Our inspector loved: *The secluded garden.*

LE MANOIR AUX QUAT' SAISONS

GREAT MILTON, OXFORDSHIRE OX44 7PD

Situated in secluded grounds a few miles south of the historic city of Oxford, the restaurant and the contemporary classic hotel of Le Manoir aux Quat' Saisons are among the finest in Europe. Le Manoir is the inspired creation of Raymond Blanc whose extraordinary cooking has received the highest tributes from all international guides to culinary excellence. The Times uniquely gives Blanc's cooking 10 out of 10 and rates it "the best in Britain". The atmosphere throughout is one of understated elegance whilst all 32 bedrooms and suites offer guests the highest standards of comfort and luxury. Every need is anticipated, for service is a way of life here, never intrusive but always present. For dedicated 'foodies', Raymond Blanc's highly successful cookery school is a must. 4-day courses are run from August to April and participation is restricted to 10 guests to ensure the highest level of personal tuition. Participants stay at Le Manoir and their partners are welcome to stay free of charge although their meals and drinks are charged separately.

Our inspector loved: The tranquillity that prevails and the new marble bathrooms.

Directions: From London, M40 and turn off at junction 7 (A329 to Wallingford). From the North, leave M40 at junction 8A and follow signs to Wallingford (A329). After 1½ miles, turn right, follow the brown signs for Le Manoir aux Quat' Saisons.

Banbury

Oxford

Henley-on-Thames

Web: www.johansens.com/lemanoirauxquatsaisons
E-mail: lemanoir@blanc.co.uk
Tel: 0870 381 8682
International: +44 (0)1844 278881
Fax: 01844 278847

Price Guide:
double/twin £265–£525
suites £525–£1200

STUDLEY PRIORY

HORTON HILL, HORTON-CUM-STUDLEY, OXFORD, OXFORDSHIRE OX33 1AZ

Directions: From London leave M40 at Jct8. Follow A40 towards Oxford. At 1st roundabout take 4th exit signed Horton-cum-Studley. Follow road into Horton-cum-Studley and the hotel is at the top of the hill on the right.

Web: www.johansens.com/studleypriory
E-mail: res@studley-priory.co.uk
Tel: 0870 381 8924
International: +44 (0)1865 351203
Fax: 01865 351613

Price Guide:
single from £125
double/twin from £175
suite £275–£300

Set within minutes of the famous University City of Oxford, yet amidst the beautiful countryside of Otmoor and close to the Cotswolds, Studley Priory is ideally suited for business and pleasure. A former Benedictine nunnery dating from the 12th century, this historic building exudes a sense of timelessness, its exterior little altered since Elizabethan times. The interior has been sympathetically updated yet retains numerous evocative architectural features such as oak panelling and mullioned windows. The 18 highly individual en-suite bedrooms are complemented by fine furnishings and luxurious bathrooms, most with Jacuzzi baths. The Elizabethan Suite offers a half-tester bed dating from 1700. Fine wines and seasonally changing menus based on fresh local produce are served in the restaurant, which has received 3 AA Rosettes for its creative cuisine. Conference facilities are available for up to 50 people, and larger events, can be accommodated in an attached marquee. Guests can wander in the woodlands and mature grounds or play croquet, whilst for the more energetic, there is a grass tennis court and the outstanding Studley Wood golf course. Nearby attractions include Blenheim Palace, the Manors of Waddesdon and Milton, the Cotswolds and Oxford, horse racing at Cheltenham and Ascot, motor racing at Silverstone. Member of Small Luxury Hotels of the World.

Our inspector loved: *The ceilings and coats of arms in the drawing room.*

FALLOWFIELDS

KINGSTON BAGPUIZE WITH SOUTHMOOR, OXON OX13 5BH

Fallowfields, once the home of Begum Aga Khan, dates back more than 300 years. It has been updated and extended over past decades and today boasts a lovely early Victorian Gothic southern aspect. The house is set in 2 acres of gardens, surrounded by 10 acres of grassland. The guests' bedrooms, which offer a choice of four-poster or coroneted beds, are large and well appointed and offer every modern amenity to ensure maximum comfort and convenience. During the winter months, there are welcoming log fires in the elegant main reception rooms. The cuisine is mainly British, awarded 3 RAC dining awards, imaginative in style and presentation and there is a good choice of menus available. The walled kitchen garden provides most of the vegetables and salads for the table and locally grown and organic produce is otherwise used wherever possible. Fallowfields is close to Stratford, the Cotswolds, Stonehenge, Bath and Bristol to the west, Oxford, Henley on Thames, the Chilterns and Windsor to the east. Heathrow airport is under an hour away.

Our inspector loved: The conservatory restaurant with views out to the garden.

Directions: Take the Kingston Bagpuize exit on the A420 Oxford to Swindon. Fallowfields is at the west end of Southmoor, just after the Longworth sign.

Banbury

Oxford

Henley-on-Thames

Web: www.johansens.com/fallowfields
E-mail: stay@fallowfields.com
Tel: 0870 381 8513
International: +44 (0)1865 820416
Fax: 01865 821275

Price Guide:
single £115–£145
double £122–£170

WESTON MANOR

WESTON-ON-THE-GREEN, OXFORDSHIRE OX25 3QL

Directions: From the M40, exit at junction 9 onto the A34 towards Oxford. Leave the A34 at the first junction, towards Middleton Stoney. At the mini roundabout turn right onto the B430. The hotel is approx 500m on the left.

Web: www.johansens.com/westonmanor
E-mail: reception@westonmanor.co.uk
Tel: 0870 381 8981
International: +44 (0)1869 350621
Fax: 01869 350901

Price Guide:
single £115
double/twin £154
suite £225

Banbury
Oxford
Henley-on-Thames

Imposing wrought-iron gates flanked by sculptured busts surmounting tall grey stone pillars lead into the impressive entrance to this delightful old manor house, the showpiece of the lovely village of Weston-on-the Green since the 11th century. The ancestral home of the Earls of Abingdon and Berkshire, and once the property of Henry VIII, Weston Manor stands regally in 12 acres of colourful gardens restored as a unique country house hotel of character. A peaceful retreat for visitors wishing to discover the delights of the surrounding Cotswold countryside and of Oxford, Woodstock, Blenheim Palace and Broughton Castle. Many of the manor's 35 charming bedrooms, including 4 in a cottage and 16 in the old coach-house, retain antique furniture and all have garden views, private bathrooms and elegant surroundings. There is a croquet lawn and a secluded, heated outdoor swimming pool. Golf and riding are nearby. At the heart of the Manor is the restaurant, a magnificent vaulted and oak-panelled Baronial Hall where delectable cuisine is served. Dining in such historic splendour is very much the focus of a memorable stay. Weston Manor is ideal for exclusive-use house parties.

Our inspector loved: *The Baronial Hall restaurant and Minstrel Gallery.*

THE SPREAD EAGLE HOTEL

CORNMARKET, THAME, OXFORDSHIRE OX9 2BW

The historic market town of Thame with its mile-long main street is a delightful town just 6 miles from the M40 and surrounded by beautiful countryside speckled with tiny, charming villages, many of them with cosy thatched cottages. The Spread Eagle has stood tall, square and imposingly in the heart of Thame since the 16th century and over the years has played host to Charles II, French prisoners from the Napoleonic wars, famous politicians and writers such as Evelyn Waugh. The former proprietor John Fothergill introduced haute cuisine to the provinces and chronicled his experiences in the best seller, "An Innkeeper's Diary". The book is still available at The Spread Eagle and the restaurant is named after him. It serves excellent English and French cuisine made with the freshest local produce. Seasonal changing menus are complemented by a well-balanced wine list which includes some superb half-bottles of unusual vintages. Guests have 33 bedrooms to choose from, comprising 2 suites, 23 doubles, 3 twins and 5 singles. All are en suite, well equipped and tastefully decorated. Good conference facilities are available. The Spread Eagle is ideally situated for visits to many fascinating historic places such as Blenheim Palace and Waddesdon Manor.

Our inspector loved: *The easy access into town.*

Directions: Exit M40 at junction 6. Take B4009 to Chinnor and then B4445 to Thame. The hotel is on the left after the roundabout at the west end of Upper High Street.

Banbury

Oxford

Henley-on-Thames

Web: www.johansens.com/spreadeaglethame
E-mail: enquiries@spreadeaglethame.co.uk
Tel: 0870 381 8902
International: +44 (0)1844 213661
Fax: 01844 261380

Price Guide:
single from £98
double/twin from £115

THE SPRINGS HOTEL & GOLF CLUB

NORTH STOKE, WALLINGFORD, OXFORDSHIRE OX10 6BE

The Springs is a grand old country house which dates from 1874 and is set deep in the heart of the beautiful Thames Valley. One of the first houses in England to be built in the Mock Tudor style, it stands in 6 acres of grounds. The hotel's large south-facing windows overlook a spring-fed lake, from which it takes its name. Many of the luxurious bedrooms and suites offer beautiful views over the lake and lawns, whilst others overlook the quiet woodland that surrounds the hotel. Private balconies provide patios for summer relaxation. The Lakeside restaurant has an intimate atmosphere inspired by its gentle décor and the lovely view of the lake. The award-winning restaurant's menu takes advantage of fresh local produce and a well-stocked cellar of international wines provides the perfect accompaniment to a splendid meal. Leisure facilities include a 18-hole par 72 golf course, clubhouse and putting green, a swimming pool, sauna and touring bicycles. Oxford, Blenheim Palace and Windsor are nearby and the hotel is conveniently located for racing at Newbury and Ascot and the Royal Henley Regatta.

Directions: From the M40 take exit 6 onto B4009, through Watlington to Benson; turn left onto A4074 towards Reading. After 2 miles go right onto B4009. The hotel is ½ mile further on the right.

Web: www.johansens.com/springshotel
E-mail: info@thespringshotel.com
Tel: 0870 381 8904
International: +44 (0)1491 836687
Fax: 01491 836877

Price Guide:
single from £95
double/twin from £110
suite from £155

Banbury

Oxford

Henley-on-Thames

Our inspector loved: *The panelled bar and views of the lake.*

THE FEATHERS HOTEL

MARKET STREET, WOODSTOCK, OXFORDSHIRE OX20 1SX

The Feathers is a privately owned and run town house hotel, situated in the centre of Woodstock, a few miles from Oxford. Woodstock is one of England's most attractive country towns, constructed mostly from Cotswold stone and with some buildings dating from the 12th century. The hotel, built in the 17th century, was originally four separate houses. Antiques, log fires and traditional English furnishings lend character and charm. There are 20 bedrooms, all of which have private bathrooms and showers. Public rooms, including the drawing room and study, are intimate and comfortable. The small garden is a delightful setting for a light lunch or afternoon tea and guests can enjoy a drink in the cosy courtyard bar, which has an open fire in winter. The antique-panelled restaurant is internationally renowned for its fine cuisine, complemented by a high standard of service and 3 AA Rosettes. The menu changes frequently and offers a wide variety of dishes, using the finest local ingredients. Blenheim Palace, seat of the Duke of Marlborough and birthplace of Sir Winston Churchill, is just around the corner. The Cotswolds and the dreaming spires of Oxford are a short distance away.

Our inspector loved: The newly decorated bar and secluded courtyard gardens.

Directions: From London leave the M40 at junction 8; from Birmingham leave at junction 9. Take A44 and follow the signs to Woodstock. The hotel is on the left.

Banbury

Oxford

Henley-on-Thames

Web: www.johansens.com/feathers
E-mail: enquiries@feathers.co.uk
Tel: 0870 381 8519
International: +44 (0)1993 812291
Fax: 01993 813158

Price Guide:
single £115
double/twin £130–£185
suite £235–£290

239

HAMBLETON HALL

HAMBLETON, OAKHAM, RUTLAND LE15 8TH

Directions: In the village of Hambleton, signposted from the A606, 1 mile east of Oakham.

Web: www.johansens.com/hambletonhall
E-mail: hotel@hambletonhall.com
Tel: 0870 381 8582
International: +44 (0)1572 756991
Fax: 01572 724721

Price Guide:
single £155
double/twin £180–£345
suite £600

Winner of Johansens Most Excellent Country Hotel Award 1996, Hambleton Hall, originally a Victorian mansion, became a hotel in 1980. Since then its renown has continually grown. It enjoys a spectacular lakeside setting in a charming and unspoilt area of Rutland. The hotel's tasteful interiors have been designed to create elegance and comfort, retaining individuality by avoiding a catalogue approach to furnishing. Delightful displays of flowers, an artful blend of ingredients from local hedgerows and the London flower markets colour the bedrooms. In the restaurant, chef Aaron Patterson and his enthusiastic team offer a menu which is strongly seasonal. Grouse, Scottish ceps and chanterelles, partridge and woodcock are all available at just the right time of year, accompanied by the best vegetables, herbs and salads from the Hall's garden. The Croquet Pavilion, a 2-bedroom suite with living room and breakfast room is a luxurious addition to the accommodation options. For the energetic there are lovely walks around the lake and opportunities for tennis and swimming, golf, riding, bicycling, trout fishing, and sailing. Burghley House and Belton are nearby, as are the antique shops of Oakham, Uppingham and Stamford. Hambleton Hall is a Relais & Châteaux member.

Our inspector loved: Standing on the terrace overlooking the beautiful gardens and magnificent views of Rutland water.

BARNSDALE LODGE

THE AVENUE, RUTLAND WATER, NR OAKHAM, RUTLAND LE15 8AH

Situated in the ancient county of Rutland, amid unspoilt countryside, Barnsdale Lodge overlooks the rippling expanse of Rutland Water. After 13 years, the expansion is finally complete and guests are invited to enjoy the hospitality offered by hosts The Hon. Thomas Noel and Robert Reid. A restored 17th-century farmhouse, the atmosphere and style are distinctively Edwardian. This theme pervades throughout, from the courteous service to the furnishings, including chaises-longues and plush, upholstered chairs. The 45 en-suite bedrooms, mostly on the ground floor, including 2 superb rooms specifically designed for disabled guests, evoke a mood of relaxing comfort. Traditional English cooking and fine wines are served. The chef makes all the pastries and cakes as well as preserves. Elevenses, buttery lunches, afternoon teas and suppers are enjoyed in the garden, conservatory, courtyard and à la carte dining rooms. There are 5 conference rooms and facilities for wedding receptions and parties. Interconnecting bedrooms, a baby-listening service and safe play area are provided for children. Robert Reid has strived to maintain the friendly intimacy of the lodge and is often on hand, offering advice and suggestions. Belvoir and Rockingham Castles are nearby. Rutland Water, a haven for nature lovers, offers several water sports. A health spa is planned for 2004.

Our inspector loved: This popular country hotel has affected many a waistline with its homemade pastries and preserves, and that includes the inspector!

Directions: The Lodge is on A606 Oakham–Stamford road.

Web: www.johansens.com/barnsdalelodge
E-mail: barnsdale.lodge@btconnect.com
Tel: 0870 381 8342
International: +44 (0)1572 724678
Fax: 01572 724961

Price Guide:
single £75
double/twin £99.50
lake view/family room £120

THE LAKE ISLE

16 HIGH STREET EAST, UPPINGHAM, RUTLAND LE15 9PZ

Directions: Uppingham is near the intersection of A47 and A6003. The hotel is on the High Street and is reached on foot via Reeves Yard and by car via Queen Street.

Web: www.johansens.com/lakeisle
E-mail: Info@LakeIsleHotel.com
Tel: 0870 381 8670
International: +44 (0)1572 822951
Fax: 01572 824400

Price Guide:
single £55–£70
double/twin £70–£80
suite £80–£90

This small personally run restaurant and town house hotel is situated in the pretty market town of Uppingham, dominated by the famous Uppingham School and close to Rutland Water. The entrance to the building, which dates back to the 18th century, is via a quiet courtyard where a wonderful display of flowering tubs and hanging baskets greets you. In winter, sit in the bar where a log fire burns or relax in the upstairs lounge which overlooks the High Street. In the bedrooms, each named after a wine growing region in France and all of which are en suite, guests will find fresh fruit, homemade biscuits and a decanter of sherry. Those in the courtyard are cottage-style suites. Under the personal direction of chef Gary Thomas, the restaurant offers regular weekly changing menus using fresh ingredients from far afield. There is an extensive wine list of more than 200 wines ranging from regional labels to old clarets. Special "Wine Dinners" are held throughout the year, enabling guests to appreciate this unique cellar. Burghley House, Rockingham speedway and Belvoir Castle are within a short drive.

Our inspector loved: *This super cosy little town house hotel with a lovely cottage courtyard garden.*

DINHAM HALL

LUDLOW, SHROPSHIRE SY8 1EJ

Tall, square, solid and stylish Dinham Hall is the epitome of a grand, late 18th-century family home. Now an elegant hotel, it stands prestigiously in the centre of the historic market town of Ludlow, just a short stroll from the ruins of a great sandstone castle built by Roger Montgomery, Earl of Shrewsbury, in 1085. An enviable location that provides guests with ready access to the town's broad streets, narrow lanes, graceful buildings and mellow beauty. Dinham offers a comfortable and relaxing atmosphere. Lounges are restful and warmed by open fires in winter and each of the 14 bedrooms offers modern facilities with period design. Some have four-posters and 2 of the bedrooms are within a cottage in the garden grounds. Dinham has gained the deserved reputation as Ludlow's latest gastronomic delight. The restaurant serves innovative, modern British cuisine with an Italian influence prepared by talented new chef, P. J. McGregor; only the highest quality of local and seasonal produce is used. While dining, guests can enjoy superb views over the walled garden and open countryside towards the Whitcliffe hills and Mortimer forests or when taking tea on the hotel terrace during summer months. As well as browsing in the town's famed antique shops guests can delight in visiting Ludlow races and take lovely river walks.

Our inspector loved: The charm of this charismatic hotel situated in the heart of Ludlow offering fine views over the town.

Directions: Ludlow is approached via A49. Dinham Hall is in the centre of town overlooking the castle.

Web: www.johansens.com/dinhamhall
E-mail: info@dinhamhall.co.uk
Tel: 0870 381 8482
International: +44 (0)1584 876464
Fax: 01584 876019

Price Guide:
single £70–£99
double/twin £130–£180

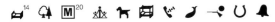

243

SHROPSHIRE - TELFORD (IRONBRIDGE)

MADELEY COURT

TELFORD, SHROPSHIRE TF7 5DW

Directions: 4 miles from Jct 4 off M54; follow A442 then B4373. Signposted Dawley then Madeley.

Web: www.johansens.com/madeleycourt
E-mail: admin@g6068.u−net.com
Tel: 0870 381 8711
International: +44 (0)1952 680068
Fax: 01952 684275

Price Guide: (room only)
single from £105
double/twin £120–£145
historic £140

This veritable gem of a residence has remained virtually unaltered since the 16th century, when it was mainly built, whilst the interior has been expertly restored and recently refurbished to provide a unique style and elegance tuned to the requirements of private and business guests. Furnishings have been judiciously selected to enrich Madeley's period appeal; scatterings of fine fabrics, handsome antique pieces and elaborate fittings all accentuate the historic atmosphere and ensure that every guest leaves with an indelible impression. The bedrooms, recently refurbished, are quiet and full of character; all are en suite and offer interactive television; some have whirlpool baths and views over the lake. At the heart of this company-owned Grade I listed manor house is the original 13th-century hall where the restaurant is now located, serving inventive food, awarded 2 RAC Ribbons, with a wine list to match. Another dining option is the Cellar Vaults, which offers a more informal setting and the Lakeside Bar is open all day for refreshments and light snacks. Business meetings and private functions are happily catered for in the 3 rooms available. Places of interest nearby include Ironbridge Gorge, Shrewsbury, Powys Castle and Weston Park.

Our inspector loved: *The rooms situated in the oldest part of the building and the wonderful wide landings in this area.*

STON EASTON PARK

STON EASTON, BATH, SOMERSET BA3 4DF

The internationally renowned hotel at Ston Easton Park is a Grade I Palladian mansion of notable distinction. A showpiece for some exceptional architectural and decorative features of its period, it dates from 1739 and has recently undergone extensive restoration, offering a unique opportunity to enjoy the opulent splendour of the 18th century. A high priority is given to the provision of friendly and unobtrusive service. The hotel has won innumerable awards for its décor, service and food. Jean Monro, an acknowledged expert on 18th-century decoration, supervised the design and furnishing of the interiors, complementing the original features with choice antiques, paintings and objets d'art. Fresh, quality produce, delivered from all parts of Britain, is combined with herbs and vegetables from the Victorian kitchen garden to create English and French dishes. To accompany your meal, a wide selection of rare wines and old vintages is stocked in the house cellars. The grounds, landscaped by Humphry Repton in 1793, consist of romantic gardens and parkland. The 17th-century Gardener's Cottage, close to the main house on the wooded banks of the River Norr, provides private suite accommodation.

Our inspector loved: The feeling of a bygone era and the peace and seclusion at this magnificent location.

Directions: 11 miles south of Bath on the A37 between Bath and Wells.

Web: www.johansens.com/stoneastonpark
E-mail: stoneastonpark@stoneaston.co.uk
Tel: 0870 381 8916
International: +44 (0)1761 241631
Fax: 01761 241377

Price Guide:
single from £99
double/twin £185–£345
four-poster £245–£345

DANESWOOD HOUSE HOTEL

CUCK HILL, SHIPHAM, NR WINSCOMBE, SOMERSET BS25 1RD

This tall, pebble-dashed Edwardian house nestles on the slopes of the Mendip Hills commanding spectacular views over the Somerset countryside towards the Bristol Channel and South Wales. Originally a homeopathic health hydro, it is now a hotel of distinction which has been in the enthusiastic ownership of David and Elise Hodges for almost 25 years. They have created a homely, welcoming and relaxing atmosphere and their continual pursuit of excellence has earned the hotel a reputation for comfort, culinary delights and service. The generous en-suite bedrooms are individually designed, delightfully furnished and have every facility from colour TV to direct dial telephone. The Honeymoon Suite boasts a 7ft king-size bed whilst the Victorian Room has a Queen Anne four-poster. Some bedrooms open out onto the 5 acres of grounds and have private patios. Great emphasis is placed on using fresh produce and local meat and poultry for the superb dishes served in the period dining room, which has been awarded 2 AA Rosettes. Breakfast is in the sunny conservatory. Conference facilities. The hotel grounds offer direct access to the Mendip Walkway. Nearby are 5 18-hole golf courses, trout fishing, riding and several National Trust houses.

Directions: Shipham is signposted from the A38 Bristol-Bridgwater road. Go through the village towards Cheddar and the hotel is on the left.

Web: www.johansens.com/daneswoodhouse
E-mail: info@daneswoodhotel.co.uk
Tel: 0870 381 8475
International: +44 (0)1934 843145
Fax: 01934 843824

Price Guide:
single £89.50–£99.50
double/twin £105–£150
suites £150

Our inspector loved: The rooms with garden views and the Somerset countryside beyond.

MOUNT SOMERSET COUNTRY HOUSE HOTEL

HENLADE, TAUNTON, SOMERSET TA3 5NB

This elegant Regency residence, awarded 2 Rosettes and 3 stars, stands high on the slopes of the Blackdown Hills, overlooking miles of lovely countryside. The Hotel is rich in intricate craftsmanship and displays fine original features. Its owners have committed themselves to creating an atmosphere in which guests can relax, confident that all needs will be catered for. The bedrooms are sumptuously furnished and many offer views over the Quantock Hills. All of the bedrooms have luxurious bathrooms and some have spa baths. Light lunches, teas, coffees and home-made cakes can be enjoyed in the beautifully furnished drawing room, whilst in the restaurant the finest food and wines are served. A team of chefs work together to create dishes which exceed the expectations of the most discerning gourmet. Places of interest nearby include Glastonbury Abbey, Wells Cathedral and the vibrant city of Exeter.

Our inspector loved: Driving along the winding approach and finding total comfort within this gracious residence.

Directions: At the M5 exit at junction 25, join the A358 towards Ilminster. Just past Henlade turn right at the sign for Stoke St. Mary. At the T-junction turn left, the Hotel drive is 150 yards on the right.

Web: www.johansens.com/mountsomerset
E-mail: info@mountsomersethotel.co.uk
Tel: 0870 381 8750
International: +44 (0)1823 442500
Fax: 01823 442900

Price Guide:
single from £95–£105
double/twin from £135–£160
suites £185–£200

THE SWAN HOTEL

SADLER STREET, WELLS, SOMERSET BA5 2RX

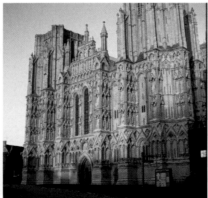

Directions: Exit the M5 at junction 23. On reaching Wells, follow the signs for hotels and deliveries. Once in Sadler Street the Hotel is on the right.

Web: www.johansens.com/swanwells
E-mail: swan@bhere.co.uk
Tel: 0870 381 8930
International: +44 (0)1749 836300
Fax: 01749 836301

Price Guide:
single from £89
double/twin from £125-£155

This truly historic hotel with charm and an ambience all of its own combines English tradition and architectural splendour. Dating back to the 15th century, The Swan nestles in the shadow of the 12th-century west front of the magnificent Wells Cathedral, a short walk from Vicars Close, the oldest complete medieval street in Western Europe. Formerly a major Posting House, it has been sympathetically restored and extended with an ongoing refurbishment plan to ensure every comfort and facility whilst retaining the beauty, ambience, elegance and attentive personal service of the past. Reflecting its background and character, The Swan offers superb accommodation in a relaxing environment. There are open log fires with York stone surrounds, heavy beamed ceilings, highly polished panelling, fine paintings and antiques galore. Individually styled, en-suite bedrooms have every 21st-century amenity. Most are lavishly adorned with exquisite period furniture and many boast original four-poster beds. Downstairs, guests can enjoy an uninterrupted read or chat over tea in the spacious lounge and sip cocktails in a cosy bar overlooking the Cathedral prior to sampling acclaimed traditional and modern cuisine in the dining room. Cheddar Gorge, Wookey Hole Caves and many historic houses and gardens are within easy reach.

Our inspector loved: *All the superb upgrading and the location overlooking the cathedral.*

HOLBROOK HOUSE HOTEL & SPA

WINCANTON, SOMERSET BA9 8BS

Holbrook House is a quiet and easily accessible hotel surrounded by 17 acres of gardens, lush meadows, unspoilt woodland, abundant wildlife and deep, clear rivers on the borders of Somerset and Dorset. Comfortable, exquisitely furnished rooms exude warmth and cosiness with open fires, beautiful antique furniture and warm, attractive décor. En-suite bedrooms are extremely spacious and overlook the gorgeous grounds. Dining at the hotel is a pleasure with exceptionally imaginative and delicious seasonal dishes to tempt any discerning palate together with an extensive cellar and first-class service. An indoor heated pool, sauna, steam rooms, gymnasium, solarium and beauty studio are available for guests' complete relaxation, and outdoor enthusiasts will appreciate the beautifully calm river (perfect for fishing). There is also hiking, horse riding, cycling, shooting and a wealth of excellent golf courses nearby. For the more energetic there is a specially dedicated lawn on which guests can play tennis, croquet, badminton or volleyball. Leisure and spa breaks are available. Nearby tourist attractions include Longleat, Stourhead, Salisbury and Glastonbury as well as the beautiful cities of Wells and Bath. The beautiful Exmoor countryside with wild ponies and idyllic villages is within easy reach.

Our inspector loved: The so many first-class facilities to enjoy.

Directions: Leave the A303 at Wincanton slip road and join the A371 towards Castle Cary at the first roundabout. Continue over 3 more roundabouts and the hotel driveway is immediately on the right.

Web: www.johansens.com/holbrookhouse
E-mail: reservations@holbrookhouse.co.uk
Tel: 0870 381 9174
International: +44 (0)1963 32377
Fax: 01963 32681

Bath
Taunton   Yeovil

Price Guide:
single £107
double/twin £135-£175
suite £245

Swinfen Hall Hotel

SWINFEN, NR LICHFIELD, STAFFORDSHIRE WS14 9RE

Swinfen Hall was built with immense extravagance in 1757 under the direction of local architect Benjamin Wyatt, and the same extravagance has been faithfully lavished on the building recently in a magnificent restoration programme. Awarded 4 stars by the AA and RAC, the Hotel is the epitome of luxury and elegance and is totally complementary to the building's beautiful architecture. The grand entrance hall with stuccoed ceiling and balustraded minstrel's gallery provide an impressive welcome to the Hotel and the elegant atmosphere continues throughout with each room being gracefully and sensitively appointed to its period origins. The 2 RAC Ribbons and 2 AA Rosettes awarded Four Seasons restaurant is panelled in oak from floor to ceiling and is a dramatic backdrop to some wonderfully prepared dishes using seasonal and locally grown ingredients. The hotel provides an idyllic setting for wedding ceremonies and the ballroom can accommodate up to 120 for a spectacular wedding breakfast whilst the private dining room (the original dining room of the house) can be hired for private parties between 10 and 20 guests. Strikingly, this oasis of luxury is also only 20 minutes from Birmingham City centre and airport.

Directions: Exit the M42 at junctions 9 or 10. Swinfen Hall is set back from the A38, 2 miles south of Lichfield.

Web: www.johansens.com/swinfenhall
E-mail: info@swinfenhallhotel.co.uk
Tel: 0870 381 8932
International: +44 (0)1543 481494
Fax: 01543 480341

Price Guide: (including continental breakfast)
single from £110
double/twin from £125
suite from £170

Our inspector loved: Its unspoilt style creating excellent hospitality.

HOAR CROSS HALL HEALTH SPA RESORT

HOAR CROSS, NR YOXALL, STAFFORDSHIRE DE13 8QS

Surrounded by 80 acres of beautiful countryside, lakes and exquisite formal gardens with water features, exotic plants and beautiful flowers, Hoar Cross Hall is a secluded haven and the perfect venue for those who want a peaceful environment in which to be pampered. Oak panelling, tapestries, rich furnishings and paintings adorn the interior and an impressive library, with 3,000 books to browse through, has Spanish leather walls. A stunning Jacobean staircase leads to luxurious bedrooms, all with crown tester or four-poster beds and elegant design. Penthouses have private saunas and balconies overlooking the treetops. Breathtaking gilded ceilings and William Morris wallpaper in the original ballroom set the scene for the dining room, where a superb à la carte menu is offered. A tasty breakfast and buffet lunch is served in the Plantation Restaurants overlooking the pools. There are unlimited ways in which visitors can de-stress at Hoar Cross Hall; yoga, meditation, tai chi, aqua-aerobics and dance classes are all available and outdoor pursuits include tennis, croquet, archery and a fantastic golf academy. Trained professionals are ready to assist and the spa consists of hydrotherapy baths, flotation therapy, saunas, a gymnasium, steam rooms, water grotto, saunarium, aromatherapy room and aerobics.

Our inspector loved: The balance of excellent meals and welcoming restaurant combined with serious facilities. Relaxed but so professional. Something for everyone.

Directions: From Lichfield turn off the A51 onto the A515 towards Ashbourne. Go through Yoxall and turn left to Hoar Cross.

Web: www.johansens.com/hoarcrosshall
E-mail: info@hoarcross.co.uk
Tel: 0870 381 8598
International: +44 (0)1283 575671
Fax: 01283 575652

Price Guide: (fully inclusive price including some treatments per person)
single £150-£170
double/twin £150-£170

        SPA

BRUDENELL HOTEL

THE PARADE, ALDEBURGH, SUFFOLK IP15 5BU

Directions: Take the M25, junction 28 onto the A12, then take the A1094 to Aldeburgh. The hotel is on the seafront at the south end of town.

Web: www.johansens.com/brudenell
E-mail: info@brudenellhotel.co.uk
Tel: 0870 381 9182
International: +44 (0)1728 452071
Fax: 01728 454082

Price Guide:
single £61-£91
double £96-£186

Following a total refurbishment, this delightful hotel is now the epitome of a charming contemporary seaside hideaway with a light, airy and relaxed ambience. Informal décor and comfortable furnishings complement the occasional piece of driftwood, and welcoming staff attend to your every need. The newly AA Rosette awarded restaurant is situated immediately on the seafront and has the feel of an ocean liner. Fresh fish and grills is the speciality. The interior has been cleverly arranged so that the majority of guests can enjoy a stunning panoramic sea view. Decorated in a fresh modern style the spacious bedrooms are well-equipped and many offer either a sea, marsh or river view. Aldeburgh has something for everybody - scenic walks past pastel-coloured houses and fisherman's huts, superb boutique shopping, highly acclaimed restaurants and the annual Aldeburgh Festival. Thorpeness is an unusual and interesting village to explore and also has a splendid golf course. For those interested in history, there are many historic buildings, castles and an abbey in the area. The marshes are a haven for wading birds and birdwatchers or for the more adventurous there is horse riding, archery and rally karting. Access to the hotel is very easy for the less mobile and there is a lift.

Our inspector loved: *Watching the sun glistening on the waves from so many windows.*

ANGEL HOTEL

BURY ST EDMUNDS, SUFFOLK IP33 1LT

Being the most historic coaching inn in East Anglia, the hotel was immortalised by Charles Dickens, and has welcomed King Louis Phillippe of France and more recently Pierce Brosnan. On one of the prettiest squares in England, visitors will have the immediate impression of a hotel that is loved and nurtured by its owners. In the public rooms, guests will appreciate the carefully chosen ornaments and pictures, fresh flowers and log fires. The hotel has numerous suites and four-poster bedrooms, some with air conditioning. All bedrooms are individually furnished and decorated and all have en-suite bathrooms. The elegant dining room has been awarded 2 Rosettes by the AA for excellent food and service. Overlooking the ancient abbey, the restaurant serves classic English cuisine, including local speciality dishes and succulent roasts. The Angel can offer a wide range of quality conference and banqueting facilities catering for private dinners, meetings and weddings from 10–60 persons. The hotel is within an hour of the east coast ferry ports and 45 minutes from Stansted Airport. Nearby there is racing at Newmarket and several golf courses within easy reach. Bury St Edmunds is an interesting and historic market town and an excellent centre for touring the surrounding area.

Our inspector loved: *The dining room, dramatic yet elegant, which complements this historic building.*

Directions: Follow the signs to Historic Centre.

Web: www.johansens.com/angelburysted
E-mail: sales@angel.co.uk
Tel: 0870 381 8315
International: +44 (0)1284 714000
Fax: 01284 714001

Price Guide:
single from £85
double/twin from £119
suite from £165

RAVENWOOD HALL COUNTRY HOTEL & RESTAURANT

ROUGHAM, BURY ST EDMUNDS, SUFFOLK IP30 9JA

Directions: 2 miles east of Bury St Edmunds off the A14

Web: www.johansens.com/ravenwoodhall
E-mail: enquiries@ravenwoodhall.co.uk
Tel: 0870 381 8849
International: +44 (0)1359 270345
Fax: 01359 270788

Price Guide:
single £80.50–£109
double/twin £105.50–£149

Nestling within 7 acres of lovely lawns and woodlands deep in the heart of Suffolk lies Ravenwood Hall. Now an excellent country house hotel, this fine Tudor building dates back to 1530 and retains many of its original features. The restaurant, still boasting the carved timbers and huge inglenook from Tudor times, creates a delightfully intimate atmosphere in which to enjoy imaginative cuisine. The menu is a combination of adventurous and classical dishes, featuring some long forgotten English recipes. The Hall's extensive cellars are stocked with some of the finest vintages, along with a selection of rare ports and brandies. A cosy bar offers a less formal setting in which to enjoy some unusual meals. Comfortable bedrooms are furnished with antiques, reflecting the historic tradition of the Hall, although each is equipped with every modern facility. A wide range of leisure facilities is available for guests, including a croquet lawn and heated swimming pool. There are golf courses and woodland walks to enjoy locally; hunting and shooting can be arranged. Places of interest nearby include the famous medieval wool towns of Lavenham and Long Melford; the historic cities of Norwich and Cambridge are within easy reach, as is Newmarket, the home of horseracing.

Our inspector loved: The huge inglenook fireplaces and the informal reminders of a private country estate.

THE ICKWORTH HOTEL

HORRINGER, BURY ST EDMUNDS, SUFFOLK IP29 5QE

This stylish and contemporary Hotel is the newly opened East Wing of the Ickworth House and estate, formerly home of the Marquess of Bristol and left in legacy to the National Trust in 1956. It is surrounded by some 1,800 acres of glorious parkland with views from the hotel overlooking the beautifully manicured lawns and the Italian garden. The hotel prides itself on its winning combination of contemporary style and elegance whilst ensuring guests' every comfort. The traditional and the modern sit side-by-side in stunning effect, the overall atmosphere is one of peace and tranquillity without pomposity. An ideal venue for business as well as pleasure, there are a number of syndicate and private dining rooms available, including the stunning Chinese Room with its hand-painted wallpaper. The Aquae Sulis Spa offers a range of natural treatments, facials and massages to aid relaxation, and with excellent children's clubs and babysitting facilities this is also an excellent retreat for parents and children alike. 3 tempting restaurants offer a winning selection of relevant dishes; choose either the elegant dining room for formal evening dinner, the buzzy Italian Café Inferno for pizza and light lunches with the children or the Grand Conservatory for cucumber sandwiches and a relaxed afternoon tea.

Our inspector loved: *The selection of artwork, particularly the imaginative contemporary slant on traditional portraiture.*

Directions: From the A14 at Bury St Edmunds take the A143 in the direction of Haverhill.

Web: www.johansens.com/ickworth
E-mail: info@ickworthhotel.com
Tel: 0870 381 8634
International: +44 (0)1284 735350
Fax: 01284 736300

Price Guide:
double/twin £150-£270
suite from £350

SALTHOUSE HARBOUR HOTEL

1 NEPTUNE QUAY, IPSWICH, SUFFOLK IP4 1AS

Directions: From the A14 take A137 and head for Ipswich town centre. Keep to the outside lane in the one-way system and follow tourist signs to hotel.

Web: www.johansens.com/salthouse
E-mail: staying@salthouseharbour.co.uk
Tel: 0870 381 9196
International: +44 (0)1473 226789
Fax: 01473 226927

Price Guide:
single £90–£115
double/twin £100–£125
suite £155–£180

This newly opened hotel is situated in a unique and historic waterfront location on the bustling and sophisticated Ipswich marina, stylishly transformed from the town's wet dock. The hotel owes its name to the building's former function as a 19th-century store for salt. Salt was kept here before being shipped to Yarmouth for the herring trade, once one of the largest in Europe. Throughout the hotel, Victorian architecture, natural materials, subdued colours and contemporary design combine to form an intriguing and elegant blend, and the hotel's own collection of contemporary artwork is displayed to complement the original style of the industrial structure. All 41 bedrooms, some of which with balconies, are cleverly arranged to offer beautiful views, above all the 2 spectacular penthouse suites with their large panoramic windows. Details such as the original carved bed heads reflect earlier trade with distant places. Guests can enjoy culinary delights in the hotel's bustling brasserie and bar, or explore this exciting new part of the town. Conferences can be arranged in the nearby Custom House. A Thames sailing barge and boat trips down the Orwell River and beyond are available from the quay, whilst the more active guest can enjoy the facilities of a nearby ski centre as well as sailing and windsurfing.

Our inspector loved: The dramatic "Red Lady" in the restaurant – the inspiration for the staff uniforms.

HINTLESHAM HALL

HINTLESHAM, IPSWICH, SUFFOLK IP8 3NS

The epitome of grandeur, Hintlesham Hall is a house of evolving styles: its splendid Georgian façade belies its 16th-century origins, to which the red-brick Tudor rear of the hall is a testament. The Stuart period also left its mark, in the form of a magnificent carved oak staircase leading to the north wing of the hall. The combination of styles works extremely well, with the lofty proportions of the Georgian reception rooms contrasting with the timbered Tudor rooms. The décor throughout is superb – all rooms are individually appointed in a discriminating fashion. Iced mineral water, toiletries and towelling robes are to be found in each of the comfortable bedrooms. The herb garden supplies many of the flavours for the well-balanced menu which will appeal to the gourmet and the health-conscious alike, complemented by a 300-bin wine list. Bounded by 175 acres of rolling countryside, leisure facilities include the Hall's own 18-hole championship golf course, new state-of-the-art gymnasium, sauna, steam room, spa bath, tennis, croquet, snooker and a health and beauty suite with a full range of E'Spa products available at weekends and by arrangement during the week. Guests can also explore Suffolk's 16th-century wool merchants' villages, its pretty coast, Constable country and Newmarket.

Our inspector loved: The great cookery days and wine dinners.

Directions: Hintlesham Hall is 4 miles west of Ipswich on the A1071 Sudbury road.

Web: www.johansens.com/hintleshamhall
E-mail: reservations@hintleshamhall.com
Tel: 0870 381 8595
International: +44 (0)1473 652334
Fax: 01473 652463

Price Guide:
single £98–£120
double/twin £110–£235
suite £225–£375

257

BLACK LION HOTEL & RESTAURANT

CHURCH WALK, THE GREEN, LONG MELFORD, SUFFOLK CO10 9DN

Directions: From A14 take A134 in direction of Sudbury. Hotel overlooks Long Melford village green.

Web: www.johansens.com/blacklion
E-mail: enquiries@blacklionhotel.net
Tel: 0870 381 8366
International: +44 (0)1787 312356
Fax: 01787 374557

Price Guide:
single £85–£106
double/twin £109–£120
suite from £146

One of Long Melford's oldest Inns The Black Lion glories in its superb position overlooking the green, and the village with its elegant broad street and imposing church. Having been in existence for over 300 years, the hotel recently entered a fresh era in its illustrious history. Under owner Craig Jarvis a transformation has taken place, with rich colours, comfortable antique furniture and welcoming open fires all creating a charming country house ambience. Flanked by the stately homes of Kentwell and Melford Hall, good sized bedrooms are furnished with antiques and offer individual design plus modern facilities; some have picturesque views. The menu, based on traditional dishes with a modern approach, may be sampled casually in the Lounge Bar or more formally in the Rosette-awarded Restaurant, each providing superb presentation and excellent food. The Victorian walled garden is an ideal setting to enjoy summer barbecues. A prolifery of antique emporiums, interesting shops, picturesque country walks and stately homes are within walking distance of the hotel, and many other places of interest are just a short drive away. Racegoers will find The Black Lion a perfect base from which to attend Newmarket, whilst those simply longing to get away from it all could not wish for a more peaceful and inviting country retreat.

Our inspector loved: The understated elegance and luxury of the newly refurbished Sancere suite.

THE RUTLAND ARMS HOTEL

HIGH STREET, NEWMARKET, SUFFOLK CB8 8NB

Formerly a coaching inn, the Rutland Arms is one of Newmarket's most attractive and distinctive buildings, conveniently located in the heart of the town, yet sufficiently tucked away to avoid the hustle and bustle. The ambience is one of warmth and comfort from the moment one arrives, made possible by several cosy lounges, snug and bar, as well as enthusiastic and friendly staff. Recently renovated, great care has been taken to preserve the features of the inn, with its barrel vaulted ceiling, and original flooring still being in use. Each of the 46 bedrooms has been individually designed, with modern well-lit bathrooms, and courtyard or town views. The attractive Saddle Room Restaurant serves a combination of contemporary English and European dishes, taking great pride in its use of locally-grown produce, and has a daily changing table d'hôte menu. Conferences and functions are also ideally catered for here, with the elegant Wolverton Room providing a stunning backdrop for weddings or presentations, as well as a range of smaller meeting rooms. Newmarket is famous for its horse racing and sales, and the Horse Racing Museum is in the High Street, although the University city of Cambridge, Ely Cathedral and pretty Bury St Edmunds are all just a short drive away.

Directions: Take the M11, junction 9 then the A11.

Web: www.johansens.com/rutland
E-mail: gapleisure@rutlandarmshotel.com
Tel: 0870 381 8720
International: +44 (0)1638 664251
Fax: 01638 666298

Price Guide: (room only)
single from £74.50
double from £86.50

Our inspector loved: The breathtaking "tented" bed.

SWYNFORD PADDOCKS HOTEL AND RESTAURANT

SIX MILE BOTTOM, NR NEWMARKET, SUFFOLK CB8 0UE

Directions: From M11, exit at jct 9 and take A11 towards Newmarket. After 10 miles join A1304 signed Newmarket. Hotel is on left after ¾ of a mile.

Web: www.johansens.com/swynfordpaddocks
E-mail: info@swynfordpaddocks.com
Tel: 0870 381 8935
International: +44 (0)1638 570234
Fax: 01638 570283

Price Guide:
single £110
double/twin £135–£155
suite £175

This classical white mansion standing in glorious gardens and idyllic countryside with racehorses grazing its pastures has a romantic history. In 1813 it was the scene of a passionate love affair between Lord Byron and the wife of the owner, Colonel George Leigh. Swynford was converted into a hotel 20 years ago. It has a country house atmosphere with antique furniture, open fires and attention to detail of times gone by. Each individually decorated, en-suite bedroom has colour television, clock radio alarm, telephone and many other amenities. Silks conservatory overlooks the gardens whilst the elegantly refurbished dining room offers an imaginative menu, changed regularly to incorporate the season's fresh produce. The award-winning restaurant has been awarded two RAC Dining Awards and an AA Rosette. Conference facilities are available and a luxury marquee for private and special functions. Tennis, croquet and a few games for children are within the grounds and guided tours of Newmarket with a look at the horseracing world can be arranged. Heliquisine: For a special occasion guests are chauffeur driven in a limousine to Cambridge airport for a helicopter ariel view of the surrounding towns, then land for a superb lunch at the hotel.

Our inspector loved: *The new Silks conservatory – just the place for morning coffee, informal lunch or afternoon tea.*

THE SWAN HOTEL

MARKET PLACE, SOUTHWOLD, SUFFOLK IP18 6EG

Rebuilt in 1659, following the disastrous fire which destroyed most of the town, The Swan Hotel was remodelled in the 1820s, with further additions made in 1938. The hotel provides all modern amenities required by today's discerning traveller and an extensive refurbishment programme has ensured that a modern, stylish sophistication exudes throughout the hotel. This refined yet relaxed environment together with the friendly staff onhand guarantees a most comfortable stay. Many of the bedrooms in the main hotel offer a glimpse of the sea, whilst the contemporary designed garden rooms are clustered around the old bowling green. The elegant Drawing Room and the Reading Room upstairs are perfect for quiet relaxation; the Reading Room is also ideal for private parties. The daily menu offers dishes ranging from simple, delicious fare through the English classics to the chef's personal specialities as well as a full à la carte menu. An exciting selection of wines is offered. Southwold is bounded on 3 sides by creeks, marshes and the River Blyth, making it a paradise for birdwatchers and nature lovers. Little has changed in the town for a century, built around a series of greens; there is a fine church, lighthouse and golf course close by. Music lovers flock to nearby Snape Maltings for the Aldeburgh Festival.

Our inspector loved: *The quirky chicken pictures in one of the newly decorated bedrooms.*

Directions: Southwold is off the A12 Ipswich–Lowestoft road. The Swan Hotel is in the town centre.

Web: www.johansens.com/swansouthwold
E-mail: swan.hotel@adnams.co.uk
Tel: 0870 381 8929
International: +44 (0)1502 722186
Fax: 01502 724800

Price Guide:
single £70
double/twin £120
suite £185

SECKFORD HALL

WOODBRIDGE, SUFFOLK IP13 6NU

Directions: Remain on the A12 Woodbridge bypass until the blue and white hotel sign.

Web: www.johansens.com/seckfordhall
E-mail: reception@seckford.co.uk
Tel: 0870 381 8890
International: +44 (0)1394 385678
Fax: 01394 380610

Price Guide:
single £79–£130
double/twin £120–£190
suite £150–£190

Seckford Hall dates from 1530 and it is said that Elizabeth I once held court here. Furnished as a private house with many fine period pieces, the panelled rooms, beamed ceilings, carved doors and great stone fireplaces are set against the splendour of English oak. Local delicacies such as the house speciality, lobster, feature on the à la carte menu. The original minstrels gallery can be viewed in the banqueting hall, which is now a conference and function suite designed inkeeping with the general style. The Courtyard area was converted from a giant Tudor tithe barn, dairy and coach house; it now incorporates 10 charming cottage-style suites and a modern leisure complex, which includes a heated swimming pool, exercise machines, spa bath and beauty salon. Alternatively, guests may use the Internet Café where Internet access and office equipment is available. Set in 34 acres of tranquil parkland with sweeping lawns and a willow-fringed lake, guests may stroll about the grounds or simply relax in the attractive terrace garden. Equipment can be hired for the 18-hole golf course or a gentle walk along the riverside to picturesque Woodbridge, with its tide mill, antique shops and yacht harbours can be enjoyed. Visit the Sutton Hoo burial ship site and new museum and the Constable country and Suffolk coast nearby.

Our inspector loved: *Being inspired at the first sight of this beautiful Tudor building.*

GREAT FOSTERS

STROUDE ROAD, EGHAM, SURREY TW20 9UR

Probably built as a Royal hunting lodge in Windsor Forest, very much a stately home since the 16th century, today Great Fosters is a prestigious hotel within half an hour of both Heathrow Airport and central London. Its past is evident in the mullioned windows, tall chimneys and brick finials, whilst the Saxon moat – crossed by a Japanese bridge – surrounds 3 sides of the formal gardens, complete with topiary, statuary and a charming rose garden. Inside are fine oak beams and panelling, Jacobean chimney pieces, superb tapestries and a rare oakwell staircase leading to the Tower. Some of the guest rooms are particularly magnificent – one Italian styled with gilt furnishings and damask walls, others with moulded ceilings, beautiful antiques and Persian rugs. Guests relax in the bar before enjoying good English and French cooking and carefully selected wines in The Oak Room. Celebrations, meetings and weddings take place in the elegant Orangery and impressive Tithe Barn. Great Fosters is close to polo in Windsor Great Park, racing at Ascot, golf at Wentworth, boating in Henley and pageantry at Windsor Castle, Runneymede and Hampton Court.

Our inspector loved: Summer lunching beneath umbrellas on the long terrace overlooking immaculate gardens.

Directions: M25/J13, head for Egham and watch for brown Historic Buildings signs.

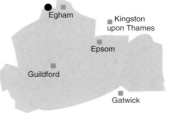

Web: www.johansens.com/greatfosters
E-mail: enquiries@greatfosters.co.uk
Tel: 0870 381 8569
International: +44 (0)1784 433822
Fax: 01784 472455

Price Guide:
single from £120
double/twin from £155
suite from £280

LANGSHOTT MANOR

LANGSHOTT, HORLEY, SURREY RH6 9LN

The peace and seclusion of this beautiful Manor House, tucked away down a quiet country lane amidst 3 acres of lovely garden, belies its proximity to London's Gatwick Airport, only 10 minutes away by car. Retaining the essential feel of a fine Elizabethan house, Langshott has recently been sympathetically expanded to encompass an attractive new dining room with views over ponds and gardens. Additional to the main house, superb bedrooms have been created in both the Coach House Mews and the Moat Mews. The Manor prides itself on outstanding levels of hospitality, service, cuisine and comfort acknowledged by 3 AA Red Stars and an RAC Gold Ribbon. Each of the bedrooms is decorated in individual style and offers exceptional standards of provision exemplified by luxurious towelling robes and comfy slippers. There are Egyptian cotton sheets on the beds, hot water bottles to go in the beds and homemade cookies beside the beds. There are romantic and honeymoon breaks, and if you are flying from Gatwick special arrangements include 2 weeks car parking and a chauffeured car to the airport.

Directions: From the A23 at Horley take Ladbroke Road immediately north of the Chequers Hotel roundabout. The Manor is ¾ of a mile (1 kilometre) on the right.

Web: www.johansens.com/langshottmanor
E-mail: admin@langshottmanor.com
Tel: 0870 381 8680
International: +44 (0)1293 786680
Fax: 01293 783905

Price Guide:
single from £165
double/twin from £185
suite £290

Our inspector loved: The richness of fabrics and furnishings - every room is a delight.

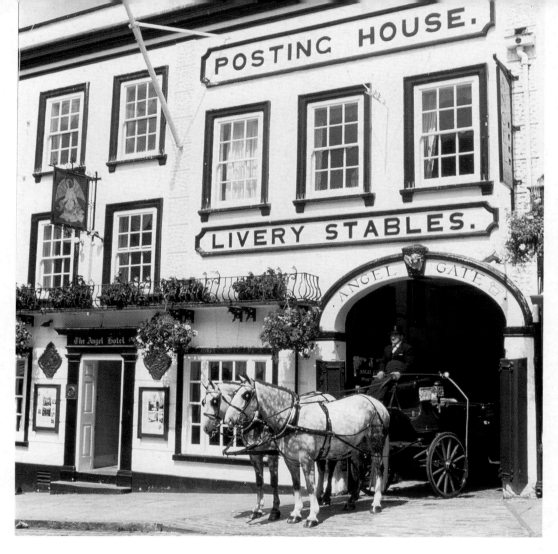

THE ANGEL POSTING HOUSE AND LIVERY

91 THE HIGH STREET, GUILDFORD, SURREY GU1 3DP

The Angel, a delightful historic coaching inn on the old Portsmouth road, now a luxurious small hotel, has stood on the cobbled High Street in the centre of Guildford since the 16th century. This timber-framed building has welcomed many famous visitors, including Lord Nelson, Sir Francis Drake, Jane Austen and Charles Dickens. Today, with easy access to Gatwick, Heathrow, the M4, M3 and M25, it is ideally placed for both business and leisure weekends. Relax with afternoon tea in the galleried lounge with its oak-beamed Jacobean fireplace and 17th-century parliament clock; a welcome retreat from the bustle of the nearby shops. Following the trend of town houses, only room and breakfast are offered but guests have an extensive choice of restaurants within a few minutes stroll from the hotel. The charming bedrooms and suites are all unique and named after a famous visitor. Excellent communications and presentation facilities and 24-hour service make this a good choice for business meetings. Guests can enjoy complimentary use of modern leisure club facilities just a short drive away.

Our inspector loved: The most convenient town centre setting with excellent shopping right on the doorstep.

Directions: From M3 jct3 take A322; or from M25 jct10 take A3. The Angel is in the centre of Guildford, within the pedestrian priority area – guests should enquire about vehicle access and parking when booking.

Egham
Kingston upon Thames
Epsom
Guildford
Gatwick

Web: www.johansens.com/angelpostinghouse
E-mail: the.angel@btconnect.com
Tel: 0870 381 8316
International: +44 (0)1483 564555
Fax: 01483 533770

Price Guide: (room only)
double/twin £150–£175
suite £195–£215

²¹ ⁷⁵

LYTHE HILL HOTEL & SPA

PETWORTH ROAD, HASLEMERE, SURREY GU27 3BQ

Directions: Lythe Hill lies about 1½ miles from the centre of Haslemere, east on the B2131.

Web: www.johansens.com/lythehill
E-mail: lythe@lythehill.co.uk
Tel: 0870 381 8709
International: +44 (0)1428 651251
Fax: 01428 644131

Price Guide: (room only)
single from £98
double/twin from £125
suite from £150

Cradled by the Surrey foothills in a tranquil setting is the enchanting Lythe Hill Hotel & Spa. It is an unusual cluster of ancient buildings – parts of which date from the 14th century. While most of the beautifully appointed accommodation is in the more recently converted part of the hotel, there are 5 charming bedrooms in the Tudor House, including the Henry VIII room with a four-poster bed dated 1614. There are 2 delightful restaurants: the Auberge de France offers classic French cuisine in the oak-panelled room which overlooks the lake and parklands, and the 'Dining Room' has the choice of imaginative English fare. An exceptional wine list offers over 200 wines from more than a dozen countries. The hotel boasts a splendid leisure facility called Amarna (which was voted hotel spa of the year) within the grounds of the hotel. It has a 16 x 8 metre swimming pool, steam room and sauna, gym, hairdressing, treatment rooms and a nail bar. National Trust hillside adjoining the hotel grounds provides interesting walks and views over the surrounding countryside. The area is steeped in history, with the country houses of Petworth, Clandon and Uppark to visit as well as racing at Goodwood and polo at Cowdray Park. Brighton and the south coast are only a short drive away.

Our inspector loved: *Dining in the Auberge de France restaurant in its ancient timbered setting.*

FOXHILLS

STONEHILL ROAD, OTTERSHAW, SURREY KT16 0EL

This magnificent 400-acre estate is a delightful environment for any discerning traveller, whatever their interests may be. Named after the 18th-century foreign secretary, Charles James Fox, Foxhills comprises a large Manor House, elegant suites, 3 golf courses, numerous tennis courts, indoor and outdoor swimming pools, 3 restaurants and a host of health and fitness facilities including a gymnasium and beauty salon. The 38 bedrooms, located in a superb courtyard setting, are the essence of comfort; elegantly furnished and offering all the latest amenities, they are designed in a number of styles; some have gardens whilst others are on 2 floors. The 2 restaurants pride themselves on their culinary excellence. Inside the Manor itself, the award-winning restaurant serves fine cuisine and is renowned for the Sunday buffet – a gourmet's delight! The sport and health facilities at Foxhills are particularly impressive and with 20 qualified instructors on hand, guests may wish to acquire a new skill such as racquetball or T'ai Chi. Those wishing to be pampered will enjoy the sauna, steam room and the fine beauty salon. Awarded 4-stars by the AA.

Our inspector loved: Finding all the unusual and tempting delights on the extensive wine list - don't hurry over your choice.

Directions: From M25 Jct 11, follow signs to Woking. After a dual carriageway, turn left into Guildford Road. 3rd exit at roundabout and immediately right into Foxhills Road. Turn left at the end of the road, Foxhills is on the right.

Web: www.johansens.com/foxhills
E-mail: reservations@foxhills.co.uk
Tel: 0870 381 8530
International: +44 (0)1932 704500
Fax: 01932 874762

Price Guide: (room only)
double/twin from £170
suite from £225

NUTFIELD PRIORY

NUTFIELD, NEAR REDHILL, SURREY RH1 4EN

Built in 1872 by the millionaire MP, Joshua Fielden, Nutfield Priory is an extravagant folly embellished with towers, elaborate carvings, intricate stonework, cloisters and stained glass, all superbly restored to create an unusual country house hotel. Set high on Nutfield Ridge, the priory has far-reaching views over the Surrey and Sussex countryside, while being within easy reach of London and also Gatwick Airport. The elegant lounges and library have ornately carved ceilings and antique furnishings. Unusually spacious bedrooms – some with beams – enjoy views over the surrounding countryside. Fresh fruit is a thoughtful extra. The Cloisters Restaurant provides a unique environment in which to enjoy the high standard of cuisine, complemented by an extensive wine list. Conferences and private functions can be accommodated in the splendid setting of one of the hotel's 10 conference rooms. The Priory Health and Leisure Club, adjacent to the hotel, provides all the facilities for exercise and relaxation that one could wish for, including a swimming pool, sauna, spa, solarium, gym, steam room and extensive beauty treatments.

Directions: Nutfield is on the A25 between Redhill and Godstone and can be reached easily from junctions 6 and 8 of the M25. From Godstone, the Priory is on the left just after the village.

Web: www.johansens.com/nutfieldpriory
E-mail: nutbooking@arcadianhotels.uk
Tel: 0870 381 8775
International: +44 (0)1737 824400
Fax: 01737 823321

Price Guide:
single from £110
double/twin from £140
suite from £185

Our inspector loved: The quite delightful Cloisters Restaurant - with its spectacular views and intimate corners for private dining.

       SPA

OATLANDS PARK HOTEL

146 OATLANDS DRIVE, WEYBRIDGE, SURREY KT13 9HB

Records of the Oatlands estate show that Elizabeth I and the Stuart kings spent time in residence in the original buildings. The present mansion dates from the late 18th century and became a hotel in 1856: famous guests included Émile Zola, Anthony Trollope and Edward Lear. The hotel stands in acres of parkland overlooking Broadwater Lake, with easy access to Heathrow, Gatwick and central London. Although it caters for the modern traveller, the hotel's historic character is evident throughout. The accommodation ranges from superior rooms to large de luxe rooms and suites. The elegant, high-ceilinged Broadwater Restaurant is the setting for creative à la carte menus with dishes to suit all tastes. A traditional roast is served every Sunday lunchtime. The 6 air-conditioned meeting rooms and 6 syndicate rooms offer up-to-date facilities and are complemented by the professional conference team. Many sporting and leisure activities are offered including a 9 hole, par 27 golf course and tennis court.

Our inspector loved: *The size and scale appropriate to a former royal residence - all set in lovely wooded grounds.*

Directions: From M25 junction 11, follow signs to Weybridge. Follow A317 through High Street into Monument Hill to mini-roundabout. Turn left into Oatlands Drive; hotel is 50 yards on left.

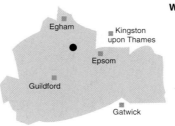

Web: www.johansens.com/oatlandspark
E-mail: info@oatlandsparkhotel.com
Tel: 0870 381 8779
International: +44 (0)1932 847242
Fax: 01932 842252

Price Guide: (room only)
single £75–£195
double/twin £108–£216
suite from £145–£222

WHITE LODGE COUNTRY HOUSE HOTEL

SLOE LANE, ALFRISTON, EAST SUSSEX BN26 5UR

Nestled in 5 acres of landscaped grounds in the heart of the Cuckmere Valley, the White Lodge Country House Hotel offers a friendly welcome in relaxed and peaceful surroundings. All bedrooms have private facilities, colour television and a hospitality tray, many have views over Alfriston and the South Downs. The elegant Orchid Restaurant offers guests a diverse menu of traditional dishes, served in a relaxing atmosphere and is complemented by a well-stocked cellar. Guests can relax in the cosy lounges or the drawing room, which have real log fires in the winter. Murder Mystery evenings, gourmet weekends and a full programme of special events are held at the Hotel. Outdoor activities might include lazing in the hotel gardens, enjoying a game of croquet or putting, or taking a pleasant stroll into the village of Alfriston with its Olde Worlde shops and The National Trust property The Clergy House. Glynebourne, Lewes, Eastbourne and Brighton are only a short drive away.

Our inspector loved: *The views over Alfriston and the Downs.*

Directions: Alfriston is on the B2108 between the A27/A259. The hotel is well signed from the village centre.

Web: www.johansens.com/whitelodgecountryhouse
E-mail: sales@whitelodge–hotel.com
Tel: 0870 381 8990
International: +44 (0)1323 870265
Fax: 01323 870284

Price Guide:
single from £50
double/twin from £100
suite from £130

THE POWDERMILLS

POWDERMILL LANE, BATTLE, EAST SUSSEX TN33 0SP

The PowderMills is an 18th-century listed country house skilfully converted into an elegant hotel. Originally the site of a famous gunpowder works, reputed to make the finest gunpowder in Europe during the Napoleonic wars, the beautiful and tranquil grounds are set amidst 150 acres of parks, lakes and woodlands, and feature a 7-acre specimen fishing lake. Wild geese, swans, ducks, kingfishers and herons abound. Situated close to the historic town of Battle, the hotel adjoins the famous battlefield of 1066, and guests can enjoy a leisurely walk through woodlands and fields to the Abbey. The hotel has been carefully furnished with locally acquired antiques and paintings, and on cooler days log fires burn in the entrance hall and drawing room. There is a range of 40 individually decorated en-suite bedrooms and junior suites in keeping with the style of the house, many with four-poster beds. Fine classical cooking by chef James Penn is served in the Orangery Restaurant, whilst light meals and snacks are available in the library and conservatory. The location is an ideal base from which to explore the beautiful Sussex and Kent countryside.

Our inspector loved: Always something new here - this year there's an antique barge on the upper lake.

Directions: From centre of Battle take the Hastings road south. After ¼ mile turn right into Powdermill Lane. After a sharp bend, the entrance is on the right; cross over the bridge and lakes to reach the hotel.

Web: www.johansens.com/powdermills
E-mail: powdc@aol.com
Tel: 0870 381 8835
International: +44 (0)1424 775511
Fax: 01424 774540

Price Guide:
single from £85
double/twin £110–£175

HOTEL DU VIN & BISTRO

SHIP STREET, BRIGHTON BN1 1AD

Since 1994, the Hotel du Vin group has successively excited visitors and residents of Winchester, Tunbridge Wells, Bristol and Birmingham with its alternative hotel style; it arrived in Brighton during the autumn of 2002. A well-located but neglected area has been completely transformed to introduce the south coast to their very individual formula of relaxed eating, fine wines and supremely comfortable bedrooms in a stunning building. Immediately off the sea front and adjacent to the famous Lanes, with its myriad of inviting little shops, this is a real treat. Inside, the various public areas provide several choices for relaxing; the fine wine bar offers 16 wines by the glass and bourbon as the featured drink, the main bistro opens onto the pavement and on sunny days, lunch in the inner courtyard is available. The cellar dining room is one of 2 private dining areas and the original wine cellar can be visited; tastings are on offer as well as tours of the walk-in cigar humidor. Brighton positively explodes with exhilarating, sophisticated, quirky, colourful and vibrant things to see and do; enjoy the exotic beauty of The Royal Pavilion, visit the Regency Town House or experience how the Edwardians lived at Preston Manor. The Brighton Festival each May is the biggest Arts Fiesta in England.

Directions: Take the A23 to Brighton city centre. Follow signposts to the sea front, at the roundabout turn right and pass Ship Street. Turn right into Middle Street and right again into Ship Street. The hotel is at the end of the road.

Web: www.johansens.com/hotelduvinbrighton
E-mail: info@brighton.hotelduvin.com
Tel: 0870 381 8617
International: +44 (0)1273 718588
Fax: 01273 718599

Price Guide: (room only)
double/twin from £115
suite from £185

Our inspector loved: The free-standing twin baths and enormous party shower in the suite. The hotel is a key social focus in Brighton's vibrant scene.

HOTEL SEATTLE

BRIGHTON MARINA, BRIGHTON BN2 5WA

Set within a stunning new waterfront development in Brighton Marina, this tranquil new hotel is a welcome escape from the hustle and bustle of the town. Perfectly complementing the hotel's vibrant yet relaxed feel, the 71 bedrooms are calm and dreamy and offer natural light, views of the sea and large beds covered with crisp, cool linen. Bathrooms are stylish, with monsoon-like showers and fine Aquae Sulis toiletries. For breakfast, guests can enjoy a "Bento in Bed" experience, which comes either as a light or luxury version. The Saloon is the perfect place to soak up the sun, read the paper and enjoy a drink or some freshly baked pastries, which are served each afternoon. Imaginative Mediterranean cuisine, fresh fish and seafood straight from the boat can be savoured at the hotel's waterside restaurant, Café Paradiso, whilst the Black and White bar invites guests to enjoy classic cocktails with a twist. Spacious meeting facilities are available for up to 100 guests for a conference or dinner, or 200 for a party. Guests can use the fitness facilities of the David Lloyd centre in the marina, whilst sailing and windsurfing lessons as well as horse riding expeditions on the South Downs can be arranged.

Our inspector loved: The exciting use of space, the Edwardian pond yachts and the pictures of the Mediterranean ladies.

Directions: At the heart of Brighton Marina, 1 mile to the east of the town centre.

Web: www.johansens.com/aliasseattle
E-mail: info@aliasseattle
Tel: 0870 381 8503
International: +44 (0)1273 679799
Fax: 01273 679899

Price Guide:
double/twin £95–£135

THE GRAND HOTEL

KING EDWARD'S PARADE, EASTBOURNE, EAST SUSSEX BN21 4EQ

The Grand Hotel is a fine property, steeped in history, which evokes the charm and splendour of the Victorian era. The majestic façade complements the elegant interior whilst the reception rooms are beautifully appointed with rich fabrics and ornaments. Many of the 152 bedrooms are of vast proportions: all being refurbished to include every comfort with attractive bathrooms. The hotel has numerous areas in which to relax and a good choice of restaurants and bars. The Mirabelle in particular achieves exceptional standards of fine dining. The array of new leisure facilities includes both indoor and outdoor pools, gymnasium, sauna, solarium, spa bath, steam room, snooker tables and a hair salon and 8 beauty rooms. Guests may choose to try the nearby racquet and golf clubs. For the meeting organiser, the hotel offers an impressive range of rooms which can cater for a number of business purposes from a board meeting for 12 to a larger conference for up to 300 delegates. Those seeking a peaceful retreat will be pleased with the tranquil atmosphere of Eastbourne. Pastimes include walks along the Downs, sea fishing and trips to the 2 nearby theatres.

Directions: A22 from London. A259 from East or West. Hotel is at the western end of the seafront.

Web: www.johansens.com/grandeastbourne
E-mail: reservations@grandeastbourne.com
Tel: 0870 381 8560
International: +44 (0)1323 412345
Fax: 01323 412233

Price Guide:
single £135–£400
double/twin £165–£220
suite £220–£430

Our inspector loved: This traditional coastal Grand Hotel with quite exceptional standards and service to match.

       SPA

ASHDOWN PARK HOTEL AND COUNTRY CLUB

WYCH CROSS, FOREST ROW, EAST SUSSEX RH18 5JR

Ashdown Park is a grand, rambling 19th-century mansion overlooking almost 200 acres of landscaped gardens to the forest beyond. Built in 1867, the hotel is situated within easy reach of Gatwick Airport, London and the South Coast and provides the perfect backdrop for every occasion, from a weekend getaway to a honeymoon or business convention. The hotel is subtly furnished throughout to satisfy the needs of escapees from urban stress. The 107 en-suite bedrooms are beautifully decorated – several with elegant four-poster beds, all with up-to-date amenities. The Anderida restaurant offers a thoughtfully compiled menu and wine list, complemented by discreetly attentive service in soigné surroundings. Guests seeking relaxation can retire to the indoor pool and sauna, pamper themselves with a massage, before using the solarium, or visiting the beauty salon. Alternatively, guests may prefer to amble through the gardens and nearby woodland paths; the more energetic can indulge in tennis, croquet or use the Fitness Studio and Beauty Therapy. There is also an indoor driving range, a lounge/bar and an 18-hole par 3 golf course with an outdoor driving range.

Our inspector loved: The quite exceptional welcome and standards of service.

Directions: East of A22 at Wych Cross traffic lights on road signposted to Hartfield.

Web: www.johansens.com/ashdownpark
E-mail: reservations@ashdownpark.com
Tel: 0870 381 8325
International: +44 (0)1342 824988
Fax: 01342 826206

Price Guide:
single £135–£325
double/twin £165–£220
suite £285–£355

HORSTED PLACE COUNTRY HOUSE HOTEL

LITTLE HORSTED, EAST SUSSEX TN22 5TS

Directions: The hotel entrance is on the A26 just short of the junction with the A22, 2 miles south of Uckfield and signposted towards Lewes.

Web: www.johansens.com/horstedplace
E-mail: hotel@horstedplace.co.uk
Tel: 0870 381 8609
International: +44 (0)1825 750581
Fax: 01825 750459

Price Guide:
double/twin from £130
suite from £220

Horsted Place enjoys a splendid location amid the peace of the Sussex Downs. This magnificent Victorian Gothic Mansion, which was built in 1851, overlooks the East Sussex National golf course and boasts an interior predominantly styled by the celebrated Victorian architect, Augustus Pugin. In former years the Queen and Prince Philip were frequent visitors. Guests today are invited to enjoy the excellent service offered by a committed staff. Since the turn of 2001, and under new management, the bedrooms have been refurbished to provide luxurious décor and every modern comfort, whilst all public areas have been refurbished and upholstered. Dining at Horsted is guaranteed to be a memorable experience. Chef Allan Garth offers a daily fixed price menu as well as the seasonal à la carte menu. The Terrace Room is an elegant and airy private function room, licensed for weddings for up to 100 guests. The smaller Morning Room and Library are ideal for boardroom style meetings and intimate dinner parties. Places of interest nearby include Royal Tunbridge Wells, Lewes and Glyndebourne. For golfing enthusiasts there is the added attraction of the East Sussex National Golf Club, one of the finest golf complexes in the world.

Our inspector loved: *This gem of a country house with wonderful Pugin features.*

NEWICK PARK

NEWICK, NEAR LEWES, EAST SUSSEX BN8 4SB

This magnificent Grade II listed Georgian country house, set in over 200 acres of breathtaking parkland and landscaped gardens, overlooks the Longford River and lake and the South Downs. Whilst situated in a convenient location near to the main road and rail routes and only 30 minutes away from Gatwick Airport, Newick Park maintains an atmosphere of complete tranquillity and privacy. The en-suite bedrooms are decorated in a classic style and contain elegant antique furnishings. The exquisite dining room offers a wide choice of culinary delights, carefully devised by the Head Chef, Mark Taylor. The convivial bar complements the restaurant with its delicate style and understated elegance. The friendly staff ensure that guests receive a warm welcome and an outstanding level of comfort. The house and grounds are ideal for weddings or conferences and may be hired for exclusive use by larger groups. The Dell gardens, planted primarily in Victorian times, include a rare collection of Royal Ferns. Vibrant and diverse colours saturate the lawns during the changing seasons, courtesy of the various flowers and shrubs encompassing the gardens. The activities on the estate itself include fishing, shooting and tennis, whilst nearby distractions include the East Sussex Golf Club and racing at Goodwood.

Our inspector loved: The sheer peace and tranquillity of this most relaxing country house.

Directions: The nearest motorway is the M23, jct 11.

Web: www.johansens.com/newickpark
E-mail: bookings@newickpark.co.uk
Tel: 0870 381 8762
International: +44 (0)1825 723633
Fax: 01825 723969

Price Guide:
single from £95
double/twin from £165

DALE HILL

TICEHURST, NR WADHURST, EAST SUSSEX TN5 7DQ

Directions: From the M25, junction 5, follow the A21 to Flimwell. Then turn right onto the B2087. Dale Hill is on the left.

Web: www.johansens.com/dalehill
E-mail: info@dalehill.co.uk
Tel: 0870 381 8471
International: +44 (0)1580 200112
Fax: 01580 201249

Price Guide:
single £90–£110
double/twin £110–£180
suites: £170-£210

Situated in over 350 acres of fine grounds, high on the Kentish Weald, The newly refurbished Dale Hill Hotel combines the best in golfing facilities with the style and refinement desired by discerning guests. The décor is enhanced by soft coloured fabrics and carpets, creating a summery impression throughout the year. Golfers have the choice of 2 18-hole courses, a gently undulating, 6,093 yards par 70 and a new, challenging championship-standard course designed by former U.S. Masters champion Ian Woosnam. Just 20 minutes' drive away, under the same ownership as the hotel, is the Nick Faldo designed Chart Hills course hailed as "the best new course in England". Packages allow guests to play both championship courses. Diners enjoy glorious views in a choice of restaurants where traditional award-winning cuisine is complemented by a fine wine list and service. The fully equipped health club features a heated swimming pool and a range of health, beauty and fitness facilities. Dale Hill is only a short drive from Tunbridge Wells and its renowned Pantiles shopping walk. Also nearby are medieval Scotney Castle, which dates back to 1380, Sissinghurst, a moated Tudor castle with gardens and Bewl Water, renowned for fly-fishing and water sports.

Our inspector loved: *The refurbishment. The new owners have totally transformed the hotel and lifted it to the front rank of our recommendations.*

AMBERLEY CASTLE

AMBERLEY, NEAR ARUNDEL, WEST SUSSEX BN18 9ND

Winner of the Johansens Award for Outstanding Excellence and Innovation, Amberley Castle boasts an amazing history spanning over 900 years. Set between the rolling South Downs and the peaceful expanses of the Amberley Wildbrooks, its towering battlements give breathtaking views and massive 14th-century curtain walls and the mighty portcullis bear silent testimony to a fascinating past. Proprietors, Joy and Martin Cummings, have transformed this medieval fortress into a unique country castle hotel. They offer a warm, personal welcome and their hotel provides the ultimate in contemporary luxury, whilst retaining an atmosphere of timelessness. 5 distinctive suites were added recently in the Bishopric by the main gateway. Each room is individually designed and has its own Jacuzzi bath. The exquisite 12th-century Queen's Room is the perfect setting for the creative cuisine of head chef James Peyton and his team. Amberley Castle is a natural first choice for romantic or cultural weekends, sporting breaks or confidential executive meetings. Roman ruins, antiques, stately homes, castle gardens, horse-racing and history "everywhere" you look, all within a short distance. It is easily accessible from London and the major air and channel ports.

Our inspector loved: *The castle walls, the black swans, the white peacocks - a dream-like experience.*

Directions: Amberley Castle is on the B2139, off the A29 between Bury and Storrington. Look out for the Union flag, which clearly marks the driveway.

Web: www.johansens.com/amberleycastle
E-mail: info@amberleycastle.co.uk
Tel: 0870 381 8312
International: +44 (0)1798 831992
Fax: 01798 831998

Price Guide:
(room only)
double/twin £145–£340
suite £275–£340

BAILIFFSCOURT

CLIMPING, WEST SUSSEX BN17 5RW

Directions: 3 miles south of Arundel, off the A259.

Web: www.johansens.com/bailiffscourt
E-mail: bailiffscourt@hshotels.co.uk
Tel: 0870 381 8333
International: +44 (0)1903 723511
Fax: 01903 723107

Price Guide:
single from £165
double £185–£295
suite £345–£450

Bailiffscourt is a perfectly preserved "medieval" house, built in the 1930s using authentic material salvaged from historic old buildings. Gnarled 15th-century beams and gothic mullioned windows combine to recreate a home from the Middle Ages. Set in 30 acres of beautiful pastures and walled gardens, it provides guests with a wonderful sanctuary in which to relax or work. The bedrooms are all individually decorated and luxuriously furnished, with many offering four-poster beds, open log fires and beautiful views over the surrounding countryside. The restaurant offers a varied menu and summer lunches can be taken alfresco in a rose-clad courtyard or the walled garden. A good list of well-priced wines accompanies meals. Private dining rooms are available for weddings, conferences and meetings and companies can hire the hotel as their "country house" for 2 or 3 days. Bailiffscourt, is surrounded by tranquil parkland with a golf practice area, heated outdoor pool and tennis courts. Climping Beach, 100 yards away, is ideal for windsurfing. Nearby are Arundel with its castle, Chichester and Goodwood.

Our inspector loved: *The remarkable new timber framed spa with 2 pools and a sea view.*

THE MILLSTREAM HOTEL

BOSHAM, NR CHICHESTER, WEST SUSSEX PO18 8HL

A village rich in heritage, Bosham is depicted in the Bayeux Tapestry and is associated with King Canute, whose daughter is buried in the local Saxon church. Moreover, sailors from the world over navigate their way to Bosham, which is a yachtsman's idyll on the banks of Chichester Harbour. The Millstream, just 300 yards from the harbour, consists of a restored 18th-century malthouse and adjoining cottages linked to The Grange, a small English manor house. Individually furnished bedrooms are complemented by chintz fabrics and pastel décor. Period furniture, a grand piano and bowls of freshly cut flowers feature in the drawing room. A stream meanders past the front of the beautiful gardens. Cross the bridge to the 2 delightful new suites in "Waterside" the thatched cottage. Whatever the season, care is taken to ensure that the composition and presentation of the dishes reflect high standards. An appetising luncheon menu is offered and includes local seafood specialities such as: dressed Selsey crab, the Millstream's own home-smoked salmon and grilled fresh fillets of sea bass. During the winter, good-value "Hibernation Breaks" are available.

Our inspector loved: The welcome achieved and the remarkably consistent standards maintained for so many years by manager Antony Walllace, chef Bev Boakes and their team.

Directions: South of the A259 between Chichester and Havant.

Web: www.johansens.com/millstream
E-mail: info@millstream–hotel.co.uk
Tel: 0870 381 8739
International: +44 (0)1243 573234
Fax: 01243 573459

Price Guide:
single £79–£109
double/twin £125–£159
suite £165–£189

OCKENDEN MANOR

OCKENDEN LANE, CUCKFIELD, WEST SUSSEX RH17 5LD

Set in 9 acres of grounds in the centre of the Tudor village of Cuckfield on the Southern Forest Ridge, this hotel is an ideal base from which to discover Sussex and Kent, the Garden of England. First recorded in 1520, Ockenden Manor has become a hotel of great charm and character. The bedrooms all have their own individual identity: climb your private staircase to Thomas or Elizabeth, look out across the glorious Sussex countryside from Victoria's bay window or choose Charles, with its handsome four-poster bed. The elegant wood-panelled restaurant with its beautiful handpainted ceiling is the perfect setting in which to enjoy the chef's innovative cooking. An outstanding, extensive wine list offers, for example, a splendid choice of first-growth clarets. Spacious and elegantly furnished, the Ockenden Suite welcomes private lunch and dinner parties. A superb conservatory is part of the Ockenden Suite, this opens on to the lawns, where marquees can be set up for summer celebrations. The gardens of Nymans, Wakehurst Place and Leonardslee are nearby, as is the opera at Glyndebourne.

Directions: In the centre of Cuckfield on the A272. Less than 3 miles east of the A23.

Web: www.johansens.com/ockendenmanor
E-mail: ockenden@hshotels.co.uk
Tel: 0870 381 8780
International: +44 (0)1444 416111
Fax: 01444 415549

Price Guide:
single from £105
double/twin from £160
suite from £290

Our inspector loved: Their 14th visit - just as good as their 1st.

GRAVETYE MANOR

NEAR EAST GRINSTEAD, WEST SUSSEX RH19 4LJ

This fine Elizabethan stone mansion is situated on a sheltered hill top site above a trout lake and encircled by 1,000 acres of forest just 30 miles away from Hyde Park Corner. William Robinson, the great English gardener bought the Manor and its extensive grounds in 1884, and it was here at Gravetye that he developed his pioneering ideas for the creation of the English natural garden. Peter Herbert has owned Gravetye since 1958 and with meticulous care has restored and extended the house with stone from the original quarry and oak from the surrounding forests. Guests enjoy an exceptional level of comfort, service and gastronomic pleasure in this traditional English manor house set in gardens of outstanding beauty whose designer had few peers. The bedrooms are well furnished, comfortable and individually designed and decorated to capture the spirit of this great house and to secure the best views of the gardens, meadows and forest beyond. The oak panelled restaurant offers both table d'hote and á la carte menus complemented by wines from the cellar that contains a formidable 500 bins. Places of interest nearby include Glyndebourne Opera, Chartwell and Royal Ashdown Golf Club.

Our inspector loved: The timeless perfection - the perfect marriage of house and garden.

Directions: From the M23 junction 10 onto A264 towards East Grinstead, at the Duke's Head roundabout take 3rd exit signposted Haywards Heath B2028. Go straight through Turner's Hill and after 1 mile Gravetye Manor is signposted on the left.

E-mail: info@gravetyemanor.co.uk
Tel: 0870 381 8565
International: +44 (0)1342 810567
Fax: 01342 810080

Price Guide: (room only)
single £155–£235
double/twin £195–£360

ALEXANDER HOUSE HOTEL

EAST STREET, TURNER'S HILL, WEST SUSSEX RH10 4QD

Directions: Alexander House lies on the B2110 road between Turner's Hill and East Grinstead, 6 miles from junction 10 of the M23 motorway.

Web: www.johansens.com/alexanderhouse
E-mail: info@alexanderhouse.co.uk
Tel: 0870 381 8308
International: +44 (0)1342 714914
Fax: 01342 717328

Price Guide:
single from £120
double/twin from £140
junior suite from £260

A previous winner of Johansens Most Excellent Service Award, Alexander House is a magnificent mansion with its own secluded 175 acres of parkland, including a gently sloping valley which forms the head of the River Medway. Records trace the estate from 1332 when a certain John Atte Fen made it his home. Alexander House is now a modern paragon of good taste and excellence. Spacious rooms throughout this luxurious hotel are splendidly decorated to emphasise their many original features and the bedrooms are lavishly furnished to the highest standards of comfort. The House is renowned for its delicious classic English and French cuisine, rare wines and vintage liqueurs. Music recitals and garden parties feature among a full programme of special summer events and the open fires and cosy atmosphere make this the ideal place to pamper yourself in winter. The many facilities include a resident beautician. Transport can take guests to Gatwick Airport in under 15 minutes. Antique shops, National Trust properties, museums and the Royal Pavilion in Brighton are nearby. Gardens close by include Wakehurst Place, Nymans and Leonardslee.

Our inspector loved: The splendid new look that has transformed the bedrooms and bathrooms.

THE SPREAD EAGLE HOTEL & HEALTH SPA

SOUTH STREET, MIDHURST, WEST SUSSEX GU29 9NH

Dating from 1430, when guests were first welcomed here, The Spread Eagle Hotel is one of England's oldest hotels and is steeped in history. Following a recent refurbishment, the hotel is the essence of opulence and those wishing to be pampered will enjoy the superb fitness facilities and excellent standard of service. Located in either the main building or the market house, the 39 en-suite bedrooms, some with four-poster beds, are well-appointed with soft furnishings and fine ornaments. A roaring log fire attracts guests into the historic lounge bar, ideal for relaxing in the afternoons or enjoying an apéritif. Sumptuous modern British cuisine may be savoured in the candle-lit restaurant, complemented by an extensive wine list. Weddings, banquets and meetings are held in the Jacobean Hall and Polo Room. The Aquila Health Spa is an outstanding facility featuring a blue tiled swimming pool as its centrepiece. A Scandinavian sauna, Turkish steam room, hot tub, fitness centre and a range of beauty treatments, aromatherapy and massage are also offered. The stately homes at Petworth, Uppark and Goodwood are all within a short drive, with Chichester Cathedral, the Downland Museum and Fishbourne Roman Palace among the many local attractions. Cowdray Park Polo Club is only 1 mile away.

Directions: Midhurst is on the A286 between Chichester and Milford.

Web: www.johansens.com/spreadeaglemidhurst
E-mail: spreadeagle@hshotels.co.uk
Tel: 0870 381 8903
International: +44 (0)1730 816911
Fax: 01730 815668

Price Guide:
single £85–£195
double/twin £99–£235

Our inspector loved: The ancient buildings and the up-to-date spa.

THE VERMONT HOTEL

CASTLE GARTH, NEWCASTLE-UPON-TYNE, TYNE & WEAR NE1 1RQ

Directions: Close to the A1(M), and 7 miles from Newcastle International Airport.

Web: www.johansens.com/vermont
E-mail: info@vermont-hotel.co.uk
Tel: 0870 381 8962
International: +44 (0)191 233 1010
Fax: 0191 233 1234

Price Guide:
single from £95
double from £115
suites from £220

Whitley Bay
Newcastle upon Tyne
Sunderland

Situated next to the historic Castle and overlooking the famous Tyne Bridge, The Vermont boasts an unrivalled position and impressive façade. Winner of the RAC Blue Ribbon and the AA Courtesy & Care Award, it was converted from the County Hall into a 12-storey hotel in 1993, and today its charm lies in an attentive service which makes guests feel welcome and pampered. With classic décor and stylish design throughout, all bedrooms offer maximum comfort, whilst pleasant public areas provide ample space for further relaxation. Morning coffee or afternoon tea is served in the Lounge, and the traditional Redwood Bar with its fireplace and sofas is the ideal venue to meet for a drink. For food, The Bridge Restaurant is informal with great views, whilst the Blue Room has won awards for its service and modern classical cuisine. All menus are complemented by a carefully chosen wine list. For those wishing to sample the atmosphere of the Quayside, Martha's Bar and Courtyard on the ground floor is the entrance to the bars, restaurants and bustling nightlife. The first floor of Martha's is also available for private hire. Located in the heart of the city, The Vermont is the ideal base from which to explore Newcastle's excellent shops as well as the surrounding areas of Northumberland, Durham and The Borders.

Our inspector loved: *Peaceful luxury next to the castle in the centre of Newcastle.*

NAILCOTE HALL

NAILCOTE LANE, BERKSWELL, NR SOLIHULL, WARWICKSHIRE CV7 7DE

Nailcote Hall is a charming Elizabethan country house hotel set in 15 acres of gardens and surrounded by Warwickshire countryside. Built in 1640, the house was used by Cromwell during the Civil War and was damaged by his troops prior to the assault on Kenilworth Castle. Ideally located in the heart of England, Nailcote Hall is within 15 minutes' drive of the castle towns of Kenilworth and Warwick, Coventry Cathedral, Birmingham International Airport/Station and the NEC. Situated at the centre of the Midlands motorway network, Birmingham city centre, the ICC and Stratford-upon-Avon are less than 30 minutes away. Leisure facilities include indoor swimming pool, gymnasium, solarium and sauna. Outside there are all-weather tennis courts, pétanque, croquet, a challenging 9-hole par-3 golf course and putting green (host to the British Championship Professional Short Course Championship). In the intimate Tudor surroundings of the Oak Room restaurant, the chef will delight you with superb cuisine, whilst the cellar boasts an extensive choice of international wines. En-suite bedrooms offer luxury accommodation and elegant facilities are available for conferences, private dining and corporate hospitality.

Our inspector loved: The lovely oak dining room.

Directions: Situated 6 miles south of Birmingham International Airport/ NEC on the B4101 Balsall Common–Coventry road.

Web: www.johansens.com/nailcotehall
E-mail: info@nailcotehall.co.uk
Tel: 0870 381 8752
International: +44 (0)2476 466174
Fax: 02476 470720

Price Guide:
single £165
double/twin £175
suite £195–£275

NUTHURST GRANGE

HOCKLEY HEATH, WARWICKSHIRE B94 5NL

Directions: From M42 exit 4 take A3400 signposted Hockley Heath (2 miles, south). Entrance to Nuthurst Grange Lane is ¼ mile south of village. Also, M40 (exit 16 – southbound only), take first left, entrance 300 yards.

Web: www.johansens.com/nuthurstgrange
E-mail: info@nuthurst-grange.com
Tel: 0870 381 8776
International: +44 (0)1564 783972
Fax: 01564 783919

Nuneaton

Leamington Spa

Stratford upon Avon

Price Guide:
single £139
double/twin £159–£179
suite £189

The most memorable feature of this friendly country house hotel is its outstanding restaurant. David Randolph and his head chef Ben Davies have won many accolades for their imaginative menus, described as "English, cooked in the light French style". Diners can enjoy their superb cuisine in one of the 3 adjoining rooms which comprise the restaurant and form the heart of Nuthurst Grange. The rest of the house is no less charming – the spacious bedrooms have a country house atmosphere and are appointed with extra luxuries such as an exhilarating air-spa bath, a trouser press, hairdryer and a safe for valuables. For special occasions there is a room furnished with a four-poster bed and a marble bathroom. There are fine views across the 7½ acres of landscaped gardens. Executive meetings can be accommodated at Nuthurst Grange – within a 12 mile radius of the hotel lie central Birmingham, the NEC, Stratford-upon-Avon, Coventry and Birmingham International Airport. Sporting activities available nearby include golf, canal boating and tennis.

Our inspector loved: *Relaxing in the Jacuzzi bath.*

MALLORY COURT

HARBURY LANE, BISHOPS TACHBROOK, LEAMINGTON SPA, WARWICKSHIRE CV33 9QB

Surrounded by 10 acres of attractive gardens, Mallory Court boasts a truly stunning backdrop across the beautiful Warwickshire countryside and is just a stone's throw away from Stratford-upon-Avon and Warwick Castle. Offering every home comfort, arriving guests are enveloped by the welcoming and tranquil ambience. Guests may begin their evening sipping champagne on the terrace before setting off to visit the Royal Shakespeare Theatre. During the winter season, afternoon tea may be enjoyed in the comfortable lounges beside the burning log fires. The 18 luxurious suites are enhanced by thoughtful finishing touches and stunning views across the grounds. Modern, English-style dishes are served in the elegant restaurant where chef is happy to create tailor-made menus. Diners may begin with roasted Skye scallops chicken with Avruga caviar with marinated cucumber and oyster jus followed by braised shoulder and roasted fillet of Lighthorne lamb with Provençal vegetables ending with a hot passion fruit soufflé. This is an ideal venue for weddings and executive meetings for up to 27 delegates can be accommodated. A proposed extension for 2004 includes conference facilities for up to 120 delegates and additional accommodation. Luxury leisure breaks and exclusive use of the hotel is available.

Our inspector loved: *The views from the bedrooms overlooking the traditional rose garden.*

Directions: 2 miles south of Leamington Spa on Harbury Lane, just off the B4087 Bishops Tachbrook-Leamington Spa Road. Harbury Lane runs from the B4087 towards Fosse Way. M40, Jct13 from London/Jct14 from Birmingham.

Web: www.johansens.com/mallorycourt
E-mail: reception@mallory.co.uk
Tel: 0870 381 8713
International: +44 (0)1926 330214
Fax: 01926 451714

Price Guide:
double (single occupancy) from £175
double from £195
suite from £295

WARWICKSHIRE - STRATFORD-UPON-AVON

ALVESTON MANOR

CLOPTON BRIDGE, STRATFORD-UPON-AVON, WARWICKSHIRE CV37 7HP

Legend has it that the first performance of Shakespeare's A Midsummer's Night Dream was given under the ancient cedar tree standing in the grounds of this historic and charming hotel. Alveston Manor is conveniently situated on the south side of the River Avon a short walk from the town centre. With its wood-framed façade, leaded windows, pointed roof peaks and tall, ornate chimneys it is an imposing sight to visitors and passing travellers. The interior is enhanced by tasteful décor, rich furnishings, antiques, fine pictures and striking floral displays. There is also a delightful, delicate aroma created by years of polish on original oak panelling and an Elizabethan staircase. Guests can relax in total peace and enjoy an appealing period charm that sympathetically encompasses every modern day comfort. The en-suite bedrooms are fitted to a high standard, with many of the bedrooms being situated in the adjoining modern Warwick and Charlecote Wings. A selection of suites and feature rooms are located in the original Manor House. Pre-dinner apéritifs can be sipped in an intimate cocktail bar before the enjoyment of a superbly prepared dinner.

Directions: Exit the M40, junction 15 and take the A46 and A439 towards Stratford. Join the one-way system towards Banbury and Oxford. Alveston Manor is at the junction of A422/A3400

Web: www.johansens.com/alvestonmanor
E-mail: alvestonmanor@macdonald–hotels.co.uk
Tel: 0870 381 8310
International: +44 (0)1789 205478
Fax: 01789 414095

Nuneaton

Leamington Spa

Stratford upon Avon

Price Guide:
single from £65
double/twin from £130
suite from £180

Our inspector loved: The oak-panelled bar with its tapestry walls and gold leaf ceiling.

       SPA

BILLESLEY MANOR

BILLESLEY, ALCESTER, NR STRATFORD-UPON-AVON, WARWICKSHIRE B49 6NF

This magnificent 4-star 16th-century Manor House is set in 11 acres of its own private parkland and has a unique topiary garden and sun terrace. Centuries of history and tradition with Shakespearian connection welcome guests to this beautiful hotel. Billesley Manor has 71 beautiful bedrooms, including four-poster rooms and suites, all of which are en suite and many with stunning gardens views. Cuisine of the highest standard is served in the Stuart restaurant, awarded 2 AA Rosettes. A selection of rooms for private dining are available for family, friends or business guests. The Cedar Barns offer a new dimension in conference facilities incorporating state-of-the-art equipment in unique and impressive surroundings. An impressive indoor heated swimming pool, new spa, gym, beauty treatment rooms, tennis courts, croquet lawn and activity field are available. The organisation of corporate events such as clay pigeon shooting, archery and quad biking are also on offer. Weekend breaks are available – ideal for visiting the Royal Shakespeare Theatre, Warwick Castle, Ragley Hall and the Cotswolds. Situated in the heart of England, minutes away from Shakespeare's Stratford-upon-Avon and only 23 miles from Birmingham International Airport, the hotel can be easily accessed by air, rail and road.

Directions: Leave M40 at exit 15, follow A46 towards Evesham and Alcester. 4 miles beyond Stratford-upon-Avon turn right to Billesley.

Web: www.johansens.com/billesley
E-mail: bookings@billesleymanor.co.uk
Tel: 0870 381 8363
International: +44 (0)1789 279955
Fax: 01789 764145

Price Guide:
single £115
double/twin £170
suite £220

Our inspector loved: The wonderful topiary garden.

ETTINGTON PARK

ALDERMINSTER, STRATFORD-UPON-AVON, WARWICKSHIRE CV37 8BU

Directions: From M40 junction 15 (Warwick) take A46, A439 signposted Stratford, then left-hand turn onto A3400. Ettington Park is 5 miles south of Stratford-upon-Avon off the A3400.

Web: www.johansens.com/ettingtonpark
E-mail: ettington@arcadianhotels.co.uk
Tel: 0870 381 8508
International: +44 (0)1789 450123
Fax: 01789 450472

Price Guide:
single from £125
double/twin from £185
suites from £265

Nuneaton

Leamington Spa

Stratford upon Avon

The foundations of Ettington Park date back at least 1000 years. Mentioned in the Domesday Book, Ettington Park rises majestically over 40 acres of Warwickshire parkland, surrounded by terraced gardens and carefully tended lawns, where guests can wander at their leisure to admire the pastoral views. The interiors are beautiful, their striking opulence enhanced by flowers, beautiful antiques and original paintings. Amid these elegant surroundings guests can relax totally, pampered with every luxury. On an appropriately grand scale, the 48 bedrooms and superb leisure complex, comprising an indoor heated swimming pool, spa bath, and sauna, make this a perfect choice for the sybarite. The menu reflects the best of English and French cuisine, served with panache in the dining room, with its elegant 18th-century rococo ceiling and 19th-century carved family crests. The bon viveur will relish the fine wine list. Splendid conference facilities are available: the panelled Long Gallery and 14th-century chapel are both unique venues. Clay pigeon shooting, archery and fishing can be arranged on the premises.

Our inspector loved: *The view of the Norman church from the restaurant.*

THE WELCOMBE HOTEL AND GOLF COURSE

WARWICK ROAD, STRATFORD-UPON-AVON, WARWICKSHIRE CV37 0NR

Only minutes from the motorway network, yet peacefully set amid its own 157-acre parkland estate, The Welcombe Hotel and Golf Course is the leading hotel in the heart of England. Continuous refurbishment of the 1869 mansion has resulted in a stunning hotel and championship 18-hole golf course. The magnificent public areas include an oak-panelled lounge, immaculate cocktail bar and light and airy 2 AA Rosette restaurant, where finest contemporary cuisine is matched by a well-balanced wine list. The setting is extremely elegant, with breathtaking views over the gardens to the parkland beyond. Accommodation includes suites, gallery rooms and bedrooms, all appointed to the highest standards and beautifully decorated. Superb private rooms are available for conferences, board meetings and product launches. All enjoy natural daylight and 3 feature French doors onto a terrace overlooking the gardens. Corporate golf events can be arranged on the hotel's own course, with brand new clubhouse facilities including private function rooms, bistro-style restaurant, changing rooms and professional golf shop. Floodlit tennis courts are on site with superb country walks in the Welcombe Hills. Stratford-upon-Avon, Royal Shakespeare Theatres, The Cotswolds and Warwick Castle are nearby.

Our inspector loved: The magnificent views from the clubhouse onto the golf course.

Directions: 5 miles from exit 15 of the M40, on the A439. 1mile from Stratford-upon-Avon.

Nuneaton

Leamington Spa

Stratford upon Avon

Web: www.johansens.com/welcombe
E-mail: sales@welcombe.co.uk
Tel: 0870 381 8974
International: +44 (0)1789 295252
Fax: 01789 414666

Price Guide:
single £120–£160
double/twin £160–£310
suite £275–£750

THE GLEBE AT BARFORD

CHURCH STREET, BARFORD, WARWICKSHIRE CV35 8BS

Directions: M40 exit Junction 15 A429 signed Barford & Wellesbourne. Turning left at mini-roundabout, the hotel is on the right just past the church.

Web: www.johansens.com/glebeatbarford
E-mail: sales@glebehotel.co.uk
Tel: 0870 381 8548
International: +44 (0)01926 624218
Fax: 01926 624625

Price Guide:
single £98
double/twin £118
suite £150

Nuneaton

Leamington Spa

Stratford upon Avon

"Glebe" means belonging to the Church, which explains why this beautiful Georgian country house is in a unique and quiet position next to the church in Barford, an attractive village in Warwickshire. It is a Grade II listed building, dating back to 1820, with an unusual central atrium and surrounded by gardens. The bedrooms are spacious, comfortable and peaceful. They have all the accessories expected by today's travellers. The restaurant is in an elegant, conservatory, green plants adding cool colour. There are excellent table d'hôte and à la carte menus and the wine list has been carefully selected to complement the dishes. The Glebe is an ideal venue for private celebrations and corporate events as it has several well-equipped conference rooms – the Bentley Suite seats 120 people for a banquet and the Directors Suite, with leather armchairs, is ideal for a discreet strategy meeting. Those wishing to be pampered will be pleased with the new beauty and sunbed room. Guests appreciate the Glebe Leisure Club with a pool, gymnasium, sauna, steam room and spa facilities. They can play tennis and golf nearby. Ideally situated for Warwick and Stratford races.

Our inspector loved: *The light, airy atmosphere of the Orangery Restaurant overlooking the garden.*

ARDENCOTE MANOR HOTEL, COUNTRY CLUB & SPA

LYE GREEN ROAD, CLAVERDON, NR WARWICK, WARWICKSHIRE CV35 8LS

Under private ownership, this former Gentlemen's residence, which was built around 1860, has been sympathetically refurbished and substantially extended to provide a luxury hotel with all modern amenities and comforts, whilst retaining its traditional elegance and appealing intimacy. Set in 42 acres of landscaped grounds in the heart of Shakespeare country, it offers beautifully appointed en-suite accommodation – many rooms have glorious views of the lake and gardens – fine cuisine and extensive sports and leisure facilities, including indoor pool and spa bath, outdoor whirlpool, sauna and steamrooms, squash and tennis courts, fully equipped gymnasia and a 9-hole golf course. The Ardencote Spa is also at the disposal of guests, offering an extensive range of relaxing and holistic treatments. Ardencote Manor's award-winning restaurant, the Lakeside Lodge, offers an exciting and innovative menu. Places of interest nearby include the NEC, Warwick Castle (discounted tickets available through hotel), Stratford-upon-Avon and the Cotswolds. Weekend breaks available.

Our inspector loved: The Lodge Restaurant where you can dine overlooking the water and the golf course.

Directions: From M40 follow signs to Henley-in-Arden. Lye Green Road is off A4189 Henley-in-Arden/Warwick Road at Claverdon Village Green.

Web: www.johansens.com/ardencote
E-mail: hotel@ardencote.com
Tel: 0870 381 8320
International: +44 (0)1926 843111
Fax: 01926 842646

Nuneaton

Leamington Spa
Stratford upon Avon

Price Guide:
single £105
double £145

WROXALL ABBEY ESTATE

BIRMINGHAM ROAD, WROXALL, NR.WARWICK, WARWICKSHIRE CV35 7NB

Directions: From the M42, exit at jct 5 onto the A4141 to Knowle. Continue towards Warwick for about 10 miles. Drive through Chadwick End and the entrance to Wroxall Abbey Estate is approx 2 miles further on, on the right.

Web: www.johansens.com/wroxallcourt
E-mail: info@wroxallestate.com
Tel: 0870 381 9013
International: +44 (0)1926 484470
Fax: 01926 485206

Price Guide:
single £75–£109
double/twin £99–£399

Nuneaton

Leamington Spa

Stratford upon Avon

Wroxall Abbey Estate, once the home of Sir Christopher Wren, is a collection of listed buildings including Wroxall Court and Wroxall Mansion and nestles in 27 acres of beautiful landscaped gardens. The hotel offers unrivalled service and quality for both business and pleasure amidst the peace and tranquillity of glorious Warwickshire countryside. Wroxall Court's 22 individually designed bedrooms are furnished with stylish fabrics and boast every modern comfort one would expect from such a unique venue. Delicious, imaginative cuisine is served in the Bistro which has an inviting, informal atmosphere, whilst Tapestries is ideal for receptions and Christmas parties. A fabulous historic clock tower tops the Court. Within the gardens are the ruins of the Abbey and Wren's Chapel which date back to c.1141; the latter displays breathtaking stained glass and a brick tower. Services are held in the Chapel every Sunday and it is a romantic place to exchange wedding vows. Sonnets is Wroxall Mansion's fine dining restaurant and seats up to 80 guests. A further 48 spacious bedrooms and suites, function rooms, panelled snooker room and bar, spa and indoor pool have undergone a complete refurbishment and are now open. Guests can enjoy the delights of nearby Warwick and its castle, with Stratford-upon-Avon and the Cotswolds only a short distance away.

Our inspector loved: *The stunning façade of this wonderful mansion appearing as you drive down the tree-lined avenue.*

LUCKNAM PARK, BATH

COLERNE, CHIPPENHAM, WILTSHIRE SN14 8AZ

For over 250 years Lucknam Park has been a focus of fine society and aristocratic living, something guests will sense immediately upon their approach along the mile-long avenue lined with beech trees. Built in 1720, this magnificent Palladian mansion is situated just 6 miles from Bath on the southern edge of the Cotswolds. The delicate aura of historical context is reflected in fine art and antiques dating from the late Georgian and early Victorian periods. Award winning food can be savoured in the elegant restaurant, at tables laid with exquisite porcelain, silver and glassware, accompanied with wines from an extensive cellar. Set within the walled gardens of the hotel is the spa, comprising an indoor pool, sauna, solarium, steam room, whirlpool spa, gymnasium, beauty salon and snooker room. Numerous activities can be arranged on request, including hot-air ballooning, golf and archery. The Lucknam Park Equestrian Centre, which is situated on the estate, welcomes complete beginners and experienced riders and takes liveries. Bowood House, Corsham Court and Castle Combe are all nearby. Lucknam Park is now a member of Relais et Châteaux.

Our inspector loved: *The mile long driveway, the grand suites and the inviting swimming pool and spa.*

Directions: 15 minutes from M4, junctions 17 and 18, located between A420 and A4 near the village of Colerne.

Web: www.johansens.com/lucknampark
E-mail: reservations@lucknampark.co.uk
Tel: 0870 381 8707
International: +44 (0)1225 742777
Fax: 01225 743536

Price Guide: (room only)
single from £175
double/twin from £215
suite from £465

297

WOOLLEY GRANGE

WOOLLEY GREEN, BRADFORD-ON-AVON, WILTSHIRE BA15 1TX

Woolley Grange is a 17th-century Jacobean stone manor house set in 14 acres of formal gardens and paddocks. Standing on high ground, it affords southerly views of The White Horse at Westbury and beyond. Furnished with flair and an air of eccentricity, a homely atmosphere pervades the hotel alongside pure luxury and well-being. Woolley Grange has gained a reputation for outstanding cuisine; using local farm produce and organically grown fruit and vegetables from the Victorian kitchen gardens, the chef has created a sophisticated style of country house food which aims to revive the focus on flavours. The Orangery provides lighter meals and snacks. Children are particularly welcome, the owners have 4 of their own, and they do not expect their young visitors to be "seen but not heard." In the Victorian coach house there is a huge games room and a well-equipped nursery with a full-time nanny available to look after guests' children 10–6pm every day. A children's lunch and tea are provided daily. Nearby attractions include medieval Bradford-on-Avon, Georgian Bath, Longleat and prehistoric Stonehenge. Riding can be arranged.

Directions: From Bath on the A363, fork left at Frankleigh House after the town sign. From Chippenham take the A4 to Bath, fork left on the B3109 then turn left after the town sign.

Web: www.johansens.com/woolleygrange
E-mail: info@woolleygrange.com
Tel: 0870 381 9008
International: +44 (0)1225 864705
Fax: 01225 864059

Price Guide:
single £95
double/twin £105–£200
suite from £175–£270

Swindon
Bath
Warminster
Salisbury

Our inspector loved: *Luxury and relaxation for the parents; heaven for the children.*

THE OLD BELL

ABBEY ROW, MALMESBURY, WILTSHIRE SN16 0AG

The Old Bell was established by the Abbot of Malmesbury during the reign of King John as a place to refresh guests who came to consult the Abbey's library. Situated at the edge of the Cotswolds, this Grade I listed building may well be England's most ancient hotel, including features such as a medieval stone fireplace in the Great Hall. A classic and imaginative, 2 Rosettes awarded, menu exemplifies the best in English cooking, with meals ranging from 4-course dinners complemented by fine wines served in the Edwardian dining room, to innovative snacks in the Great Hall. In the main house rooms are decorated and furnished with an individual style and character. The Coach House features bedrooms styled on an oriental theme and many of these are suitable for families as interconnecting pairs of suites. Families are particularly welcomed at The Old Bell; there is no charge for children sharing parents' rooms and children's portions are available. The "Den" is equipped with a multitude of toys and is managed by staff on Fridays and weekends. Malmesbury is only 30 minutes from Bath and is close to a number of other beautiful villages such as Castle Combe, Bourton-on-the-Water and Lacock. Other places of interest include the mysterious stone circle at Avebury and the Westonbirt Arboretum.

Our inspector loved: *The interesting history of this listed building dating back to 1220.*

Directions: Near the market cross in the centre of Malmesbury.

Web: www.johansens.com/oldbell
E-mail: info@oldbellhotel.com
Tel: 0870 381 9209
International: +44 (0)1666 822344
Fax: 01666 825145

Price Guide:
single from £85
double/twin £110–£170

WHATLEY MANOR

EASTON GREY, MALMESBURY, WILTSHIRE SN16 0RB

Directions: The hotel is situated off the B4040, 8 miles from junction 17 of the M4 motorway. 2 hours from London.

Web: www.johansens.com/whatley
E-mail: reservations@whatleymanor.com
Tel: 0870 381 9197
International: +44 (0)1666 822888
Fax: 01666 826120

Price Guide:
single/double/twin from £275
suite from £650

After 2½ years of ceaseless and meticulous restoration and building, Whatley Manor first opened its doors in July 2003. Guests staying at this breathtakingly stylish and sophisticated retreat, set amidst 12 acres of superb landscaped gardens, will find a relaxing yet luxurious atmosphere of understated elegance, reminiscent of a friendly, welcoming private home. Every detail has been thought of in the 15 bedrooms and 8 suites, which are all individually designed with Italian furniture and handmade French wallpaper, and equipped with state-of-the-art sound and vision systems. Renowned head chef Martin Burge creates innovative cuisine, which guests can enjoy in 2 restaurants: the elegant and luxuriously decorated Dining Room, which echoes the sumptuous décor of the hotel, and the less formal, brasserie-style Le Mazot, which evokes the ambience of a Swiss chalet with its roaring central fire. Designed to restore both the body and mind, the hotel's Aquarias Spa offers a wide range of luxurious facilities including one of the largest hydrotherapy pools in the country as well as a 5-star La Prairie beauty centre. The hotel also boasts a private cinema. The Georgian city of Bath, Cheltenham, Stonehenge and the beautiful Cotswold countryside are only a few of the attractions on the doorstep.

Our inspector loved: *This unique hotel and spa with a style all of its own – pure indulgence.*

HOWARD'S HOUSE

TEFFONT EVIAS, SALISBURY, WILTSHIRE SP3 5RJ

Tucked away in the depths of rural Wiltshire and surrounded by 2 acres of beautiful gardens the fragrance of jasmine exudes through the open windows of the House and the tinkling of the fountain in the lily pond can be gently heard. This charming small country house hotel, run by Noële Thompson, is located in the quintessential English hamlet of Teffon Evias, just 9 miles from Stonehenge. Howard's House is a haven of tranquillity for those seeking to escape the noise and stress of the modern world. The bedrooms are delightfully appointed, with additional touches of fresh fruit, homemade biscuits, plants and up-to-date magazines. The 3 Rosettes awarded restaurant is the height of elegance and serves modern British cuisine providing dishes of national acclaim. Cooked with flair and imagination and using home-grown and the best local produce, alfresco dining can be enjoyed during the summer. During winter guests may curl up by the genuine log fire with a good book and a glass of vintage port. Whatever the time of year you are guaranteed the ultimate in country house hospitality. Howard's House is ideally situated for visiting Stonehenge, Old Sarum, Salisbury Cathedral, Wilton House and Stourhead Gardens.

Our inspector loved: *The beautiful tranquil garden - the perfect place to relax and unwind.*

Directions: From London, turn left off A303. 2 miles after the Wylye intersection follow signs to Teffont and on entering the village join the B3089. Howard's House is signposted.

Web: www.johansens.com/howardshouse
E-mail: enq@howardshousehotel.com
Tel: 0870 381 8627
International: +44 (0)1722 716392
Fax: 01722 716820

Price Guide:
single £105
double/twin £165–£185

THE PEAR TREE AT PURTON

CHURCH END, PURTON, SWINDON, WILTSHIRE SN5 4ED

Directions: From M4 exit 16 follow signs to Purton and go through the village until reaching a triangle with Spar Grocers opposite. Turn right up the hill and the Pear Tree is on the left after the Tithe Barn.

Web: www.johansens.com/peartree
E-mail: relax@peartreepurton.co.uk
Tel: 0870 381 8806
International: +44 (0)1793 772100
Fax: 01793 772369

Price Guide:
single £110
double/twin £110–£130
suites £130

Dedication to service is the hallmark of this excellent honey-coloured stone hotel nestling in the Vale of the White Horse between the Cotswolds and Marlborough Downs. Owners Francis and Anne Young are justly proud of its recognition by the award of the RAC's Blue Ribbon for excellence. Surrounded by rolling Wiltshire farmland, The Pear Tree sits majestically in 7½ acres of tranquil grounds on the fringe of the Saxon village of Purton, famed for its unique twin towered Parish Church and the ancient hill fort of Ringsbury Camp. Each of the 17 individually and tastefully decorated bedrooms and suites is named after a character associated with the village, such as Anne Hyde, mother of Queen Mary II and Queen Anne. All are fitted to a high standard and have digital television, hairdryer, trouser press, a safe and a host of other luxuries. The award-winning conservatory restaurant overlooks colourful gardens and is the perfect setting in which to enjoy good English cuisine prepared with style and flair. Cirencester, Bath, Oxford, Avebury, Blenheim Palace, Sudeley Castle and the Cotswolds are all within easy reach.

Our inspector loved: The sitting room with its huge stone fireplace and lovely outlook over the garden.

BISHOPSTROW HOUSE

WARMINSTER, WILTSHIRE BA12 9HH

Bishopstrow House is the quintessential Georgian mansion. It combines the intimacy of a grand country hotel retreat with all the benefits of modern facilities and the luxury of the Ragdale Spa, which offers a superb range of beauty, fitness and relaxation therapies in addition to Michaeljohn's world famous hair styling. A Grade II listed building, Bishopstrow House was built in 1817 and has been sympathetically extended to include indoor and outdoor heated swimming pools, a gymnasium and a sauna. The attention to detail is uppermost in the library, drawing room and conservatory with their beautiful antiques and Victorian oil paintings. The bedrooms are grandly furnished; some have opulent marble bathrooms and whirlpool baths. Skilfully prepared modern British food is served in the Mulberry Restaurant, with lighter meals available in the Mulberry Bar and the conservatory which overlooks 27 acres of gardens. There is fly fishing on the hotel's private stretch of the River Wylye, golf at 5 nearby courses, riding, game and clay pigeon shooting. Longleat House, Wilton House, Stourhead, Stonehenge, Bath, Salisbury and Warminster are within easy reach.

Our inspector loved: The Wilton room, an ideal setting for private dining.

Directions: Bishopstrow House is south east of Warminster on the B3414 from London via the M3.

Web: www.johansens.com/bishopstrowhouse
E-mail: enquiries@bishopstrow.co.uk
Tel: 0870 381 8365
International: +44 (0)1985 212312
Fax: 01985 216769

Price Guide:
single £99
double/twin £160–£245
suite from £330

THE ELMS

ABBERLEY, WORCESTERSHIRE WR6 6AT

Directions: From M5, exit at jct 5 (Droitwich) or jct 6 (Worcester) then A443 towards Tenbury Wells. The Elms is 2 miles after Great Witley. Do not take Abberley village turning.

Web: www.johansens.com/elmsworcester
E-mail: management@theelmshotel.com
Tel: 0870 381 9153
International: +44 (0)1299 896666
Fax: 01299 896804

Price Guide:
single £100–£120
double/twin £140–£250
suite £350
coach house £130

Built in 1710 by a pupil of Sir Christopher Wren, and converted into a country house hotel in 1946, The Elms has achieved an international reputation for excellence spanning the past half century. Standing impressively between Worcester and Tenbury Wells, this fine Queen Anne mansion is surrounded by beautiful meadows, woodland, hop fields and orchards of cider apples and cherries of the Teme Valley, whose river runs crimson when in flood from bank-side soil tinged with red sandstone. Each of the hotel's 21 rooms and 2 suites has its own character, is furnished with period antiques and has splendid views across the landscaped gardens and beyond to the valley. There is a panelled bar and elegant restaurant offering fine and imaginative cuisine to award-winning standards. The surrounding countryside is ideal for walking, fishing, shooting, golf and horse racing. Within easy reach are the attractions of the market town of Tenbury Wells, Hereford with meppa murdi (oldest map in the world), Witley Court, Bewdley and the ancient city of Worcester with its cathedral, county cricket ground and porcelain factory. A member of Small Luxury Hotels.

Our inspector loved: *The cosy wood-panelled bar with open log fire and the abundance of fresh flowers throughout the hotel.*

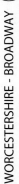

THE BROADWAY HOTEL

THE GREEN, BROADWAY, WORCESTERSHIRE WR12 7AA

The Broadway Hotel stands proudly in the centre of the picturesque Cotswold village of Broadway where every stone evokes memories of Elizabethan England. Once used by the Abbots of Pershore, the hotel was formerly a 16th-century house, as can be seen by its architecture which combines the half timbers of the Vale of Evesham with the distinctive honey-coloured and grey stone of the Cotswolds. It epitomises a true combination of Old World charm and modern day amenities with friendly, efficient service. All bedrooms provide television, telephone and tea and coffee making facilities. Traditional English dishes and a peaceful ambience are offered in the beamed Courtyard Restaurant. There is an impressive variety of à la carte dishes complemented by good wines. The congenial Jockey Club bar is a pleasant place to enjoy a drink. The hotel overlooks the village green at the bottom of the main street where guests can browse through shops offering an array of fine antiques. On a clear day, 13 counties of England and Wales can be viewed from Broadway Tower. Snowhill, Burford, Chipping Campden, Bourton-on-the-Water, Stow-on-the-Wold and Winchcombe as well as larger Cheltenham, Worcester and Stratford are within easy reach.

Our inspector loved: *The minstrels gallery above the atmospheric dining room.*

Directions: From London M40 to Oxford, A40 to Burford, A429 through Stow-on-the-Wold, then A44 to Broadway.

Web: www.johansens.com/broadwayworcestershire
E-mail: bookings@cotswold–inns–hotels.co.uk
Tel: 0870 381 8381
International: +44 (0)1386 852401
Fax: 01386 853879

Price Guide:
single £75–£85
double £125–£145

305

DORMY HOUSE

WILLERSEY HILL, BROADWAY, WORCESTERSHIRE WR12 7LF

This former 17th-century farmhouse has been beautifully converted into a delightful hotel which retains much of its original character. With its oak beams, stone-flagged floors and honey-coloured local stone walls it imparts warmth and tranquillity. Dormy House provides a wealth of comforts for the most discerning guest. Each bedroom is individually decorated – some are furnished with four-poster beds – and suites are available. Head chef, Alan Cutler, prepares a superb choice of menus and the dining room offers an extensive wine list with a diverse range of half bottles. The versatile Dormy Suite is an ideal venue for conferences, meetings or private functions – professionally arranged to individual requirements. The hotel has its own leisure facilities, which include a games room, gym, sauna/steam room, croquet lawn and putting green. Mountain bikes are available for hire. Broadway Golf Club is adjacent. The locality is idyllic for walkers. Stratford-upon-Avon, Cheltenham Spa, Hidcote Manor Garden and Sudeley Castle are all within easy reach. Closed 2 days at Christmas.

Directions: The hotel is ½ mile off the A44 between Moreton-in-Marsh and Broadway. Take the turning signposted Saintbury, the hotel is the first building on the left passed the picnic area.

Web: www.johansens.com/dormyhouse
E-mail: reservations@dormyhouse.co.uk
Tel: 0870 381 8487
International: +44 (0)1386 852711
Fax: 01386 858636

Kidderminster

Worcester

Evesham

Price Guide:
single £115
double/twin £155–£165
suite £200

Our inspector loved: *The character of the building and tastefully designed bedrooms in a tranquil location.*

THE LYGON ARMS

BROADWAY, WORCESTERSHIRE WR12 7DU

The Lygon Arms, a magnificent 16th-century building with numerous historical associations, stands in Broadway, acclaimed by many as the prettiest village in England, in the heart of the North Cotswolds. Over the years much restoration has been carried out, emphasising the outstanding period features, such as original 17th-century oak panelling and an ancient hidden stairway. All the bedrooms are individually and tastefully furnished and offer guests every modern luxury, combined with the elegance of an earlier age. The Great Hall, complete with a 17th-century minstrels' gallery and the smaller private dining rooms provide a fine setting for a well-chosen and imaginative menu. Conference facilities including the state-of-the-art Torrington Room are available for up to 80 participants. Guests can enjoy a superb range of leisure amenities in The Lygon Arms Spa, including all-weather tennis, indoor pool, spa bath, gymnasium, billiard room, beauty salons, steam room and saunas. Golf can be arranged locally. The many Cotswold villages, Stratford-upon-Avon, Oxford and Cheltenham are nearby, whilst Broadway itself is a paradise for the antique collector.

Directions: Set in the heart of Broadway.

Web: www.johansens.com/lygonarms
E-mail: info@the-lygon-arms.co.uk
Tel: 0870 381 9190
International: +44 (0)1386 852255
Fax: 01386 858611

Kidderminster

Worcester

Evesham

Price Guide:
single from £119
double/twin from £179
suite from £279

Our inspector loved: *The extensive spa and leisure facilities.*

BUCKLAND MANOR

NEAR BROADWAY, WORCESTERSHIRE WR12 7LY

Directions: From the M40, exit at junction 8. Take the A40 to Burford, the A424 to Broadway and then the B4632 signposted Winchcombe to Buckland.

Web: www.johansens.com/bucklandmanor
E-mail: enquire@bucklandmanor.com
Tel: 0870 381 9175
International: +44 (0)1386 852626
Fax: 01386 853557

Price Guide:
single £225-£360
double £235-£370

The warm glow of Buckland Manor's golden Cotswold stone exterior blends beautifully with the colourful flowers and green shades of the glorious grounds, serving as an appetiser to visitors of the tranquil luxury and history inside those weather-beaten walls. A manor house on the site was first mentioned in the records of Gloucester Abbey in 600AD when the Abbot received it as a gift from Kynred, ruler of Mercier and chief king of the 7 kingdoms of England. Managed by Nigel Power, Buckland retains gracious living and tradition, with the addition of all modern comforts and best service. Guests can relax before log fires in 2 delightfully decorated lounges, one with lovely panelling and a beamed ceiling. The 13 excellently decorated en-suite bedrooms are furnished with luxury fittings and accessories. Some have four-poster beds and fireplaces and all bathrooms use water drawn from the Manor's own spring. Views over the grounds with their small waterfalls, outdoor pool, tennis courts, putting green and croquet lawns are spectacular. The dining room is an oasis of calm, and chef Adrian Jarrad prepares delicious, award-winning cuisine. Broadway Golf Club, Cheltenham race course, Stratford, Stow-on-the-Wold, Warwick and Blenheim are nearby. Buckland Manor is a member of Relais & Châteaux hotels.

Our inspector loved: *The magnificent gardens and attention to detail throughout the hotel.*

BROCKENCOTE HALL

CHADDESLEY CORBETT, NR KIDDERMINSTER, WORCESTERSHIRE DY10 4PY

The Brockencote estate consists of 70 acres of landscaped grounds surrounding a magnificent hall. There is a gatehouse, half-timbered dovecote, lake, some fine European and North American trees and an elegant conservatory. The estate dates back over three centuries and the style of the building reflects the changes which have taken place in fashion and taste. The hotel has been awarded 3 AA Red Stars, 4 RAC dining awards and is Heart of England Tourist Board Midlands Hotel of the Year silver award 2002. At present, the interior combines classical architectural features with contemporary creature comforts. As in most country houses, each of the bedrooms is different: all have their own character, complemented by tasteful furnishings and décor. The friendly staff provide a splendid service under the supervision of owners Alison and Joseph Petitjean. The Hall specialises in traditional French cuisine with occasional regional and seasonal specialities. Brockencote Hall is an ideal setting for those seeking peace and quiet in an unspoilt corner of the English countryside. Located a few miles south of Birmingham, it is convenient for business people and sightseers alike and makes a fine base for touring historic Worcestershire. Special rates available Sunday to Saturday.

Our inspector loved: *The spacious and tastefully decorated bedrooms and the breathtaking setting in the heart of the English countryside .*

Directions: Exit 4 from M5 or exit 1 from M42 (southbound). Brockencote Hall is set back from A448 at Chaddesley Corbett between Bromsgrove and Kidderminster.

Web: www.johansens.com/brockencotehall
E-mail: info@brockencotehall.com
Tel: 0870 381 8382
International: +44 (0)1562 777876
Fax: 01562 777872

Price Guide:
single £120–£140
double/twin £145–£180

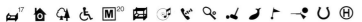

THE EVESHAM HOTEL

COOPER'S LANE, OFF WATERSIDE, EVESHAM, WORCESTERSHIRE WR11 1DA

It is the somewhat unconventional atmosphere at the Evesham Hotel that stays in the memory. Originally a Tudor farmhouse, the hotel was extended and converted into a Georgian mansion house in 1809. Unusually, it combines an award-winning welcome for families with the relaxed but efficient style required by business users. For the past quarter of a century it has been successfully run by the Jenkinson family. Each of the 40 en-suite bedrooms is furnished complete with a teddy bear and a toy duck for the bath. The restaurant offers delicious cuisine from a very imaginative and versatile menu, accompanied by a somewhat unique "Euro-sceptic" wine list (everything but French and German!). The drinks selection is an amazing myriad. The indoor swimming pool has a seaside theme. The peace of the 2½ acre garden belies the hotel's proximity to the town – a 5-minute walk away. In the gardens are 6 300-year-old mulberry trees and a magnificent cedar of Lebanon, planted in 1809. The hotel is a good base from which to explore the Cotswolds, Stratford-upon-Avon and the Severn Valley. Closed at Christmas.

Directions: Cooper's Lane lies just off Waterside (the River Avon).

Web: www.johansens.com/evesham
E-mail: reception@eveshamhotel.com
Tel: 0870 381 8510
International: +44 (0)1386 765566
Fax: 01386 765443

Price Guide:
single £75–£87
double/twin £118
family £176

Our inspector loved: This family orientated hotel with its quirky features.

NEW

WOOD NORTON HALL

WOOD NORTON, EVESHAM, WORCESTERSHIRE WR11 4YB

Wood Norton Hall is a glorious Grade II listed Victorian country house standing in 170 acres of beautiful Worcestershire countryside. A short drive from the historic market town of Evesham, 8 miles from Broadway and the Cotswolds with Stratford-upon-Avon only 15 miles away. French connections date back to 1872 and culminated in the wedding of Princess Louise of Orléans and Prince Charles of Bourbon in 1907. Original fleur-de-lys carved oak panelling lines the walls; grand fireplaces, elegant furniture and beautiful tapestries add comfort and colour. The en-suite rooms are furnished to the highest standards. The ground floor public rooms reflect the grandeur of the Victorian era with voluptuous window drapes framing views to the Vale of Evesham and the River Avon. The award-winning Le Duc's Restaurant provides the perfect ambience to savour a fine culinary tradition, whilst the new Brasserie offers delicious food in a more relaxed and informal setting. The hall has 8 rooms suitable for conferences and private banquets and is an ideal venue for incentive programmes. Extensive leisure facilities include a billiard room, fitness suite and golf at a nearby international course.

Our inspector loved: The original Victorian carved oak panelling throughout the main building and the glorious views from the house set in 170 acres of beautiful countryside.

Directions: The hotel stands on the A44 Worcester Road, 3 miles north of the town centre.

Kidderminster

Worcester

Evesham

Web: www.johansens.com/woodnortonhall
E-mail: info@wnhall.co.uk
Tel: 0870 381 9154
International: +44 (0)1386 425780
Fax: 01386 425781

Price Guide:
single £85-135
double/twin £130-£200
suite £145-£220

THE COTTAGE IN THE WOOD

HOLYWELL ROAD, MALVERN WELLS, WORCESTERSHIRE WR14 4LG

Directions: 3 miles south of Great Malvern on A449, turn into Holywell Road by post box and hotel sign. Hotel is 250 yards on right.

Web: www.johansens.com/cottageinthewood
E-mail: proprietor@cottageinthewood.co.uk
Tel: 0870 381 8452
International: +44 (0)1684 575859
Fax: 01684 560662

Price Guide:
single £79–£99
double/twin £99–£170

The Malvern Hills, once the home and inspiration for England's most celebrated composer, Sir Edward Elgar, are the setting for The Cottage in the Wood. With its spectacular outlook across the Severn Valley plain, this unique hotel won acclaim from the Daily Mail for the best view in England. The main house was originally the Dower House to the Blackmore Park estate and accommodation is offered here and in Beech Cottage, an old scrumpy house – and the magnificent new building, "the Pinnacles", named after the hill that rises above, which houses 19 of the traditional-styled bedrooms, many with patio's or balcomies and giving the best view of all. Owned and run by the Pattin family for over 16 years, the atmosphere is genuinely warm and relaxing. A regularly changing modern English menu is complemented by an almost obsessional wine list of 600 bins. If this causes any over-indulgence, guests can walk to the tops of the Malvern Hills direct from the hotel grounds. Nearby are the Victorian spa town of Great Malvern, the Three Counties Showground and the Cathedral cities of Worcester, Gloucester and Hereford.

Our inspector loved: *Its wonderful location with breathtaking views.*

WILLERBY MANOR HOTEL

WELL LANE, WILLERBY, HULL, EAST YORKSHIRE HU10 6ER

Originally the home of the Edwardian shipping merchant, Sir Henry Salmon, Willerby Manor was bought in the early 1970s by John Townend, a Wine Merchant from Hull. The elegance of the hotel, as it, stands today, is testament to the careful work of the Townend family over the years. Furnished in a stylish manner, the public rooms are the essence of comfort. The 51 bedrooms are beautifully decorated with colour co-ordinated fabrics and soft furnishings. Every modern amenity is provided as well as an array of thoughtful extras such as fresh floral arrangements. Restaurant Icon serves modern English food, which is complemented by an extensive well-chosen wine list from the House of Townend. A more informal ambience pervades the Everglades Brasserie where guests may savour bistro-style meals and beverages. Fitness enthusiasts will be delighted with the well-equipped Health Club which includes a spacious gymnasium, whirlpool spa bath, an exercise studio with daily classes and a beauty treatment room. The hotel is in a convenient location for those wishing to explore the cities of Hull and York.

Our inspector loved: The family wine shop "Hot Wines" next door to reception.

Directions: Take the M62 towards Hull, which runs into the A63, turn off onto the A164 in the direction of Beverley. Follow the signs to Willerby and then Willerby Manor.

Web: www.johansens.com/willerbymanor
E-mail: info@willerbymanor.co.uk
Tel: 0870 381 8998
International: +44 (0)1482 652616
Fax: 01482 653901

Price Guide:
single £47–£89
double/twin £74–£150

Bridlington
York
Beverley
Hull

THE DEVONSHIRE ARMS COUNTRY HOUSE HOTEL

BOLTON ABBEY, SKIPTON, NORTH YORKSHIRE BD23 6AJ

Directions: Off the A59 Skipton–Harrogate road at junction with the B6160

Web: www.johansens.com/devonshirearms
E-mail: reservations@thedevonshirearms.co.uk
Tel: 0870 381 8480
International: +44 (0)1756 718111
Fax: 01756 710564

Price Guide:
single £150–£330
double/twin £210–£330
suite £350

The Devonshire reflects its charming setting in the Yorkshire Dales: a welcome escape from a busy and crowded world, peace and quiet, beautiful countryside – the perfect place in which to relax. The hotel is owned by the Duke and Duchess of Devonshire and is set in rolling parkland on their 30,000-acre Bolton Abbey Estate in the Yorkshire Dales National Park. The Duchess of Devonshire personally supervises the decoration of the interiors which include antiques and paintings from their family home at Chatsworth. Fine dining led by Head Chef Michael Wignall in the elegant Burlington Restaurant is complemented by an outstanding award-winning wine list. Alternatively there is the less informal atmosphere of the Devonshire Brasserie and Bar with its lively décor and contemporary art. The Devonshire Club housed in a converted 17th-century barn offers a full range of leisure, health and beauty therapy facilities. There is plenty to do and see on the hotel's doorstep from exploring the ruins of the 12th-century Augustinian Bolton Priory to fly fishing on the river Wharfe. Managing Director, Jeremy Rata, together with General Manager Eamonn Elliott, lead an enthusiastic team committed to providing a high standard of service and hospitality.

Our inspector loved: *The unique glass-fronted wine rooms offering a choice of over 1400 bins of fine and rare wines.*

THE BALMORAL HOTEL

FRANKLIN MOUNT, HARROGATE, NORTH YORKSHIRE HG1 5EJ

The Balmoral is a delightful, privately owned individual hotel near the heart of the elegant spa town of Harrogate. All bedrooms are individually decorated and furnished offering the highest standard of comfort. 10 rooms have four-posters, each in a different style. The Windsor Suite even boasts its own whirlpool bath. Guests can marvel at the fascinating memorabilia on various themes throughout the hotel and they can relax in the exquisite Harry's Bar or enjoy a quiet drink in the cosy Snug before taking dinner in Villu Toots. The extensive modern Mediterranean menu embraces both the traditional and the unexpected, also popular with non-residents. The wine list is equally diverse with fine vintages rubbing shoulders with more youthful newcomers. Guests can enjoy the use of the Academy – one of the finest health and fitness centres in the North, 5 minutes from the hotel. Special spa breaks available throughout the year. Harrogate is famed for its antique and fashion shops, art galleries and Herriot country and the many historic homes and castles in the area.

Directions: From Harrogate Conference Centre, follow the Kings Road up and the hotel is 200 yards on the right.

Web: www.johansens.com/balmoral
E-mail: info@balmoralhotel.co.uk
Tel: 0870 381 8338
International: +44 (0)1423 508208
Fax: 01423 530652

Price Guide:
single £80–£105
double/twin £98–£120
suites £140– £220

Our inspector loved: The ceramic cats on all the beds and Trudie, the owner's dog.

GRANTS HOTEL

SWAN ROAD, HARROGATE, NORTH YORKSHIRE HG1 2SS

Directions: Swan Road is in the centre of Harrogate, off the A61 to Ripon.

Web: www.johansens.com/grants
E-mail: enquiries@grantshotel−harrogate.com
Tel: 0870 381 8562
International: +44 (0)1423 560666
Fax: 01423 502550

Price Guide:
single £99–£115
double/twin £110–£160
suites £168

Towards the end of the last century, Harrogate became fashionable among the gentry, who came to "take the waters" of the famous spa. Today's visitors have one advantage over their Victorian counterparts – they can enjoy the hospitality of Grants Hotel, the creation of Pam and Peter Grant. Their friendly welcome, coupled with high standards of service, ensures a pleasurable stay. All bedrooms are attractively decorated and have en-suite bathrooms. Downstairs, guests can relax in the comfortable lounge or take refreshments out to the terrace gardens. Drinks and light meals are available at all times from Harry Grant's Bar and dinner is served in the French café-style Chimney Pots Bistro, complete with brightly coloured check blinds and cloths and lots of humorous Beryl Cook pictures. Cuisine is basically traditional rustic with a smattering of Oriental influence complemented by the mouth-watering home-made puddings. Located less than 5 minutes' walk from Harrogate's Conference and Exhibition Centre, Grants offers its own luxury meeting and syndicate rooms, the Herriot Suite. The Royal Pump Room Museum and the Royal Baths Assembly Rooms are nearby. Guests have free use of The Academy Health and Leisure Club. Super value breaks available.

Our inspector loved: *The Beryl Cook pictures in the Bistro.*

HOTEL DU VIN & BISTRO

PROSPECT PLACE, HARROGATE HG1 1LB

After a £3 million renovation programme, this new hotel, which was built from an existing hotel property, the Harrogate Spa Hotel, will delight visitors and residents of this famous Yorkshire spa town alike. It is the 6th venture of the Hotel du Vin group, which since 1994 has opened successful venues in Winchester, Tunbridge Wells, Bristol, Brighton and Birmingham. The 43 classically decorated bedrooms, 4 of which are large "loft suites", offer all the Hotel du Vin trademarks such as superb beds, fine linens, fantastic showers and oversized baths. The Bistro with its leather banquettes and antique tables serves high-quality food, which can be enjoyed al fresco in the private courtyard during the warmer months. The wine cellar boasts over 600 bins, whilst the Champagne & Claret bar is a popular venue to mingle, and a walk-in cigar humidor, billiard room and cellar "snug" create a cosy ambience. 2 private dining rooms are available accommodating up to 60. The hotel also has a small but superbly equipped gym. Guests can enjoy Harrogate's fantastic shopping, whilst the Pump Room, the famous Betty's Tea Room and the Harrogate International Centre are all just a few minutes' walk away.

Our inspector loved: The wonderful location overlooking the "Stray" in the centre of Harrogate.

Directions: Close to town centre, overlooking the Stray.

Web: www.johansens.com/duvinharrogate
E-mail: reception@harrogate.hotelduvin.com
Tel: 0870 381 8493
International: +44 (0)1423 856800
Fax: 01423 856801

Price Guide:
double/twin £95–£145
suite from £185

RUDDING PARK HOTEL & GOLF

RUDDING PARK, FOLLIFOOT, HARROGATE, NORTH YORKSHIRE HG3 1JH

Rudding Park's award-winning hotel is just 2 miles from Harrogate town centre. Its setting is superb, surrounded by 230 acres of parkland. The hotel has an elegant façade and entrance, approached by a sweeping driveway. The Regency period house offers fine conference and banqueting rooms, whilst the adjoining hotel has been brilliantly designed and built to harmonise with the original mansion. A warm welcome awaits guests in the pleasant foyer, with its big fireplace and easy chairs. The bedrooms are spacious, with contemporary cherry wood furniture, relaxing colour schemes, many modern accessories and lovely views over the estate. Guests can relax in the Mackaness Drawing Room. The stylish 2 AA Rosette Clocktower Restaurant and Bar are inviting and on sunny days they extend onto the terrace. The food is delicious and the wine list extensive. Leisure facilities are excellent – there is an 18-hole par 72 parkland golf course which has played host to the PGA Mastercard tour series. The golf academy and driving range are ideal for lessons and practice. Hotel guests are welcome to use a local award-winning gym and health club.

Directions: Rudding Park is accessible from the A1 north or south, via the A661, just off the A658.

Web: www.johansens.com/ruddingpark
E-mail: sales@ruddingpark.com
Tel: 0870 381 8879
International: +44 (0)1423 871350
Fax: 01423 872286

Price Guide:
single £128–£150
double/twin £155–£190
suite from £290

Our inspector loved: The mature parkland golf course surrounding the hotel.

HOB GREEN HOTEL AND RESTAURANT

MARKINGTON, HARROGATE, NORTH YORKSHIRE HG3 3PJ

Set in 870 acres of farm and woodland this charming "country house" hotel is only a short drive from the spa town of Harrogate and the ancient city of Ripon. The restaurant has an excellent reputation locally with only the finest fresh local produce being used, much of which is grown in the hotel's own garden. The interesting menus are complemented by an excellent choice of sensibly priced wines. All 12 bedrooms have been individually furnished and tastefully equipped to suit the most discerning guest. The drawing room and hall, warmed by log fires in cool weather, are comfortably furnished with the added attraction of fine antique furniture, porcelain and pictures. Situated in the heart of some of Yorkshire's most dramatic scenery, the hotel offers magnificent views of the valley beyond from all the main rooms. York is only 23 miles away. There is a wealth of cultural and historical interest nearby with Fountains Abbey and Studley Royal water garden and deer park a few minutes' drive. The Yorkshire Riding Centre is in Markington Village. Simply relax in this tranquil place where your every comfort is catered for. Special breaks available.

Our inspector loved: Strolling around the large lovingly tended Victorian walled herb, vegetable and cutting flower garden.

Directions: Turn left signposted Markington off the A61 Harrogate to Ripon road, the hotel is 1 mile after the village on the left.

Web: www.johansens.com/hobgreen
E-mail: info@hobgreen.com
Tel: 0870 381 8600
International: +44 (0)1423 770031
Fax: 01423 771589

Price Guide:
single £85–£98
double/twin £100–£135
suite £135–£145

THE BOAR'S HEAD HOTEL

THE RIPLEY CASTLE ESTATE, HARROGATE, NORTH YORKSHIRE HG3 3AY

Imagine relaxing in a luxury hotel at the centre of a historic, private country estate in England's incredibly beautiful North Country. The Ingilby family who have lived in Ripley Castle for 28 generations invite you to enjoy their hospitality at The Boar's Head Hotel. There are 25 luxury bedrooms, individually decorated and furnished, most with king-sized beds. The restaurant's menu is outstanding, presented by a creative and imaginative kitchen brigade and complemented by a wide selection of reasonably priced, good quality wines. There is a welcoming bar serving traditional ales straight from the wood and popular bar meal selections. When staying at The Boar's Head, guests can enjoy complimentary access to the delightful walled gardens and grounds of Ripley Castle, which include the lakes and a deer park. A conference at Ripley is a different experience – using the idyllic meeting facilities available in the Castle, organisers and delegates alike will appreciate the peace and tranquillity of the location, which also offers opportunities for all types of leisure activity in the Deer Park.

Directions: Ripley is very accessible, just 10 minutes from the conference town of Harrogate, 20 minutes from the motorway network and Leeds/Bradford Airport, and 40 minutes from the City of York.

Web: www.johansens.com/boarsheadharrogate
E-mail: reservations@boarsheadripley.co.uk
Tel: 0870 381 8370
International: +44 (0)1423 771888
Fax: 01423 771509

Price Guide:
single £99–£120
double £120–£140

Our inspector loved: The historic Ripley Castle and the pretty village of Ripley.

SIMONSTONE HALL

HAWES, NORTH YORKSHIRE DL8 3LY

Fine cuisine, comfort, peace and tranquillity combine with breathtaking scenery to make any stay at Simonstone Hall totally memorable. This former 18th-century hunting lodge has been lovingly restored and furnished with antiques to create an idyllic retreat for its guests.The hall stands in 5 acres of beautiful landscaped gardens with an adjacent 14,000 acres of grouse moors and upland grazing. Many period features have been retained such as the panelled dining room, mahogany staircase with ancestral stained glass windows and a lounge with ornamental fireplace and ceilings. The bedrooms are of the highest standards and offer every modern comfort including four-poster and sleigh beds. In the restaurant, guests savour the freshest local produce presented with flair and imagination, whilst enjoying stunning views across Upper Wensleydale. An excellent wine list is available to complement any dish. Informal meals are served in the Game Tavern which provides a particularly warm and local atmosphere. Simonstone Hall, with its fine views, is the perfect base for enjoying and exploring the hidden Yorkshire Dales. The area abounds with ancient castles, churches and museums. Hardraw Force, England's highest single drop waterfall, which can be heard from the gardens, is only a walk away.

Our inspector loved: *The wonderful setting with stunning views across Upper Wensleydale.*

Directions: Hawes is on A684. Turn north on Buttertubs Pass towards Muker. Simonstone Hall is ½ mile on the left.

Ripon
Scarborough
Harrogate
York

Web: www.johansens.com/simonstonehall
E-mail: email@simonstonehall.demon.co.uk
Tel: 0870 381 8895
International: +44 (0)1969 667255
Fax: 01969 667741

Price Guide:
single £60–£90
double/twin £120–£180

THE PHEASANT

HAROME, HELMSLEY, NORTH YORKSHIRE YO62 5JG

The Pheasant, rich in oak beams and open log fires, offers two types of accommodation, some in the hotel and some in a charming, 16th-century thatched cottage. The Binks family, who built the hotel and now own and manage it, have created a friendly atmosphere which is part of the warm Yorkshire welcome that awaits all guests. The bedrooms and suites are brightly decorated in an attractive cottage style, and are all complete with en-suite facilities. Traditional English cooking is the speciality of the restaurant; many of the dishes are prepared using fresh fruit and vegetables from the hotel's garden. During summer, guests may relax on the terrace overlooking the pond. A new indoor heated swimming pool is an added attraction. Other sporting activities available locally include swimming, riding, golf and fishing. York is a short drive away, as are a host of historic landmarks including Byland and Rievaulx Abbeys and Castle Howard of Brideshead Revisited fame. Also nearby is the magnificent North York Moors National Park. Dogs by arrangement. Closed Christmas, January and February.

Directions: From Helmsley, take the A170 towards Scarborough; after ¼ mile turn right for Harome. The hotel is near the church in the village.

Web: www.johansens.com/pheasanthelmsley
Tel: 0870 381 8821
International: +44 (0)1439 771241
Fax: 01439 771744

Price Guide: (including five-course dinner)
single £68–£75
double/twin £136–£150

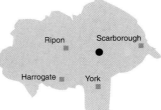

Our inspector loved: The friendly and relaxed ambience in this family-run hotel.

HAZLEWOOD CASTLE HOTEL

PARADISE LANE, HAZLEWOOD, TADCASTER, NR LEEDS & YORK, NORTH YORKSHIRE LS24 9NJ

Behind the restored 13th-century façade of this fascinating castle lies a vibrant and professional hotel, where outstanding cuisine and flawless hospitality are offered in magnificent surroundings. Famed for its gourmet food, the hotel houses its own cookery school, where John Benson-Smith, formerly a Masterchef Judge, gives lively demonstrations. The hotel has 2 excellent restaurants, the informal Prickly Pear and the chic Restaurant 1086, as well as a range of facilities for private dining. A distinct panache is lent to the atmosphere of a banquet set in the Old Dining Room and State Drawing Rooms, and Restaurant 1086, the signature restaurant of John Benson-Smith, can be hired to add charismatic zest to a dinner party. Hazlewood Castle is well designed to accommodate corporate or private events, whilst providing a sense of privilege and individuality for its guests. Its fortified buildings include the impressive Great Hall and the Chapel of St Leonards, ideal for musical occasions, amongst its many convivial reception rooms. The beautifully decorated bedrooms reflect the perfect balance of tradition and design that is evident throughout the hotel. Numerous activities include golf and clay pigeon shooting. Special weekend breaks available.

Our inspector loved: *The Victoria room, which has gold wallpaper from Queen Victoria's private bathroom at the Great Exhibition in 1851.*

Directions: Off the A64 east of the A1 Leeds/York intersection.

Web: www.johansens.com/hazlewoodcastle
E-mail: info@hazlewood-castle.co.uk
Tel: 0870 381 8589
International: +44 (0)1937 535353
Fax: 01937 530630

Price Guide:
single from £110
double/twin £175–£275
suites £195–£300

SWINTON PARK

MASHAM, NR RIPON, NORTH YORKSHIRE HG4 4JH

Directions: Masham is off the A6108 between Leyburn and Ripon.

Web: www.johansens.com/swintonpark
E-mail: enquiries@swintonpark.com
Tel: 0870 381 8934
International: +44 (0)1765 680900
Fax: 01765 680901

Price Guide:
single £100–£250
double/twin £100–£250
suites £250–£350

Swinton Park, with its battlement-topped turrets and a round tower coloured green with climbing ivy, is a Grade II* listed castle dating from the late 1600s. The heart of the building is essentially Regency style but heavily disguised by the Victorians with the addition of turrets and castellations. Sold by the Earl of Swinton in 1980 but recently bought back by the family and extensively refurbished, it is a luxurious hotel with every comfort and up-to-date facility. Rising picturesquely against the skyline, it is set in 200 acres of deer-stocked parkland and formal gardens surrounded by a 20,000-acre family estate ½ mile from the market town of Masham. The ground floor rooms enjoy sweeping views over the parkland, lake and gatehouse and are all furnished with antiques and family portraits. The guest rooms, sharing the first and second floors, are individually designed on the theme of a Yorkshire town, dale, castle, abbey or garden. 4 are suites and the turret room is on 2 floors with a wonderful free-standing rain bath. Superb British cuisine is served in an elegant dining room which features a gold leaf ceiling and sumptuous décor. Guests can enjoy country pursuits and golf, mountain biking, off-roading and model boat racing. There is a spa in the hotel's conservatory.

Our inspector loved: *The warm welcome and attentive service in this family ancestral home.*

HACKNESS GRANGE

NORTH YORK MOORS NATIONAL PARK, SCARBOROUGH, NORTH YORKSHIRE YO13 0JW

The attractive Georgian Hackness Grange country house lies at the heart of the dramatic North York Moors National Park – miles of glorious countryside with rolling moorland and forests. Set in acres of private grounds, overlooking a tranquil lake, home to many species of wildlife, Hackness Grange is a haven of peace and quiet for guests. There are charming bedrooms in the gardens and courtyard together with de luxe rooms in the main house. For leisure activities, guests can enjoy 9-hole pitch 'n' putt golf, tennis and an indoor heated swimming pool. Hackness Grange is an ideal meeting location for companies wishing to have exclusive use of the hotel for VIP gatherings. The attractive Derwent Restaurant with its quality décor, paintings and Rosette, is the setting for lunch and dinner. Here you will enjoy creatively prepared delicious cuisine, which is partnered by a wide choice of international wines. When you choose to stay at Hackness Grange you will find you have chosen well – a peaceful and relaxing location with so much to see and do: for example, visit Great Ayton, birthplace of Captain Cook.

Our inspector loved: *The ducks and wildlife around the lake.*

Directions: Take A64 York road until left turn to Seamer on to B1261, through to East Ayton and Hackness.

Web: www.johansens.com/hacknessgrange
E-mail: hacknessgrange@englishrosehotels.co.uk
Tel: 0870 381 8578
International: +44 (0)1723 882345
Fax: 01723 882391

Price Guide:
single £65–£95
double/twin £96–£170
suite £198

WREA HEAD COUNTRY HOTEL

SCALBY, NR SCARBOROUGH, NORTH YORKSHIRE YO13 0PB

Directions: Follow the A171 north from Scarborough, past the Scalby Village, until the hotel is signposted. Follow the road past the duck pond and then turn left up the drive.

Web: www.johansens.com/wreaheadcountry
E-mail: wreahead@englishrosehotels.co.uk
Tel: 0870 381 9012
International: +44 (0)1723 378211
Fax: 01723 355936

Price Guide:
single from £75
double/twin £120–£190
suite £190

Wrea Head Country Hotel is an elegant, beautifully refurbished Victorian country house built in 1881 and situated in 14 acres of wooded and landscaped grounds on the edge of the North York Moors National Park, just 3 miles from Scarborough. The house is furnished with antiques and paintings, and the oak-panelled front hall with its inglenook fireplace with blazing log fires in the winter, is very welcoming. All the bedrooms are individually decorated to the highest standards, with most having delightful views of the gardens. The elegant Four Seasons Restaurant is renowned for serving the best traditional English fare using fresh local produce and has a reputation for outstanding cuisine. There are attractive meeting rooms, each with natural daylight, ideal for private board meetings and training courses requiring privacy and seclusion. Scarborough is renowned for its cricket, music and theatre. Wrea Head is a perfect location from which to explore the glorious North Yorkshire coast and country, and special English Rose breaks are offered throughout the year.

Our inspector loved: *The large collection of Pietro Annigoni paintings in the main hall.*

JUDGES COUNTRY HOUSE HOTEL

KIRKLEVINGTON HALL, KIRKLEVINGTON, YARM, NORTH YORKSHIRE TS15 9LW

Stunningly located within 21 acres of idyllic landscaped gardens and woodlands, this gracious country house hotel is a haven of peace. Its charm and welcoming atmosphere create a sense of intimacy, whilst the warmth of the hotel's opulent interior design makes it perfect for relaxing and unwinding from the stresses of daily life. Beautiful public rooms are elegantly decorated with opulent fabrics, and guests are surrounded by books, stunning paintings and antiques. Sumptuous bedrooms are the ultimate in comfort with Jacuzzi baths, evening turndowns, foot spas and slippers. Attention to detail and expertly chosen décor enhance the feeling of luxury. A mouth-watering 6-course meal is served in the Conservatory Restaurant, accompanied by the finest of wines. Private dining is available, perfect for parties or the family. The hotel's location makes it ideal for exploring the North East, whilst local attractions include the historic city of Durham, various castles and museums, the races at York and Sedgefield and walking in the Cleveland Hills. Various adventure activities can also be organised including horse riding, canoeing, cycling, go karting, off roading, quad biking as well as many others.

Our inspector loved: *The friendly, attentive staff and goldfish in every bedroom.*

Directions: From A19 - Take the A67 Yarm exit, Judges is 1½ miles along A67 on the left after Kirklevington village.

Ripon

Scarborough

Harrogate

York

Web: www.johansens.com/judges
E-mail: enquiries@judgeshotel.co.uk
Tel: 0870 381 9165
International: +44 (0)1642 789000
Fax: 01642 782878

Price Guide:
single £120–£154
double/twin £140–£190

THE GRANGE HOTEL

1 CLIFTON, YORK, NORTH YORKSHIRE YO30 6AA

Directions: The Grange Hotel is on the A19 York–Thirsk road, 400 yards from the city centre.

Web: www.johansens.com/grangeyork
E-mail: info@grangehotel.co.uk
Tel: 0870 381 8561
International: +44 (0)1904 644744
Fax: 01904 612453

Price Guide:
single £110–£180
double/twin £140–£200
suite £240

Set near the ancient city walls, just a short walk from the world-famous Minster, this sophisticated Regency town house has been carefully restored and its spacious rooms richly decorated. Beautiful stone-flagged floors lead to the classically styled reception rooms. The flower-filled Morning Room is welcoming, with its deep sofas and blazing fire in the winter months. Double doors between the panelled library and drawing room can be opened up to create a dignified venue for parties, wedding receptions or business entertaining. Prints, antiques and English chintz in the bedrooms reflect the proprietor's careful attention to detail. The Ivy Restaurant has an established reputation for first-class gastronomy, incorporating the best in modern British and French cuisine. The Seafood Bar has two murals depicting racing scenes. The Brasserie is open for lunch Monday to Saturday and dinner every night until after the theatre closes most evenings. For conferences, a computer and fax are available as well as secretarial services. Brimming with history, York's list of attractions includes the National Railway Museum, the Jorvik Viking Centre and the medieval Shambles.

Our inspector loved: *The stunning orchid arrangement in the York stone-paved front hall.*

MIDDLETHORPE HALL

BISHOPTHORPE ROAD, YORK, NORTH YORKSHIRE YO23 2GB

Middlethorpe Hall is a delightful William III house, built in 1699 for Thomas Barlow, a wealthy merchant and was for a time the home of Lady Mary Wortley Montagu, the 18th-century diarist. The house has been immaculately restored by Historic House Hotels, who have decorated and furnished it in its original style and elegance. There are beautifully designed bedrooms and suites in the main house and the adjacent 18th-century courtyard and a health and fitness spa with pool and treatment rooms. The restaurant, which has been awarded 3 Rosettes from the AA, offers the best in contemporary English cooking. Middlethorpe Hall, which is a member of Relais & Chateaux Hotels, stands in 20 acres of parkland and overlooks York Racecourse yet is only 1½ miles from the medieval city of York with its fascinating museums, restored streets and world-famous Minster. From Middlethorpe you can visit Yorkshire's famous country houses, like Castle Howard, Beningbrough and Harewood, the ruined Abbeys of Fountains and Rievaulx and explore the magnificent Yorkshire Moors. Helmsley, Whitby and Scarborough are nearby. Special breaks available.

Our inspector loved: The Spa which is situated in the adjacent cottages and the organic walled garden.

Directions: Take A64 (T) off A1 (T) near Tadcaster, follow signs to York West, then smaller signs to Bishopthorpe.

Web: www.johansens.com/middlethorpehall
E-mail: info@middlethorpe.com
Tel: 0870 381 8731
International: +44 (0)1904 641241
Fax: 01904 620176

Price Guide:
single £124–£165
double/twin £190–£300
suite from £260–£370

ALDWARK MANOR

ALDWARK, NR ALNE, YORK, NORTH YORKSHIRE YO61 1UF

Aldwark Manor is set in 120 acres of natural parkland in the Vale of York with the River Ure meandering through its grounds. Originally commissioned in 1865 by Lord Walsingham as a gift to his daughter, it has since undergone extensive refurbishment and upgrading to create an eclectic and harmonious blend of a bygone age and contemporary-style architecture. Ornate traditional bedrooms, antiques and artworks in the original manor provide a stunning visual contrast to the crisp minimalism of the restaurant and leisure areas with their striking colour schemes and light, spacious feel. Delicious and imaginative meals are created in the hotel's fine restaurant, which has been awarded 2 AA Rosettes and the golfers bistro-style bar restaurant for a more informal meal. On warm summer days guest can relax on the terrace patio whilst admiring the picturesque and challenging 18-hole golf course that surrounds the hotel. For leisure visitors may test their golfing skills or use the luxurious leisure centre, which has an indoor heated pool, spa, steam room, solarium, gymnasium, beauty salon and treatment rooms. The hotel is close to York with its many shops and interesting historic buildings.

Directions: A1 Jct 47 - A59 towards York. After 3 miles, left onto theB6265. Cont. until signpost to Aldwark Manor. Left at T-junction over the bridge and right into Boat Lane. Continue over the toll bridge and take next turn right.

Web: www.johansens.com/aldwark
E-mail: aldwark@marstonhotels.com
Tel: 0870 381 8491
International: +44 (0)1347 838146
Fax: 01347 838867

Price Guide:
single £99
double/twin £158
suite £258

Our inspector loved: The views across the golf course on either side of the River Ure.

THE WORSLEY ARMS HOTEL

HOVINGHAM, NEAR YORK, NORTH YORKSHIRE YO62 4LA

The Worsley Arms is an attractive stone-built Georgian spa hotel in the heart of Hovingham, a pleasant and unspoilt Yorkshire village with a history stretching back to Roman times. The hotel, which overlooks the village green and is set amid delightful gardens, was built in 1841 by the baronet Sir William Worsley and is now owned and personally run by Anthony and Sally Finn. Hovingham Hall, home of the Worsley family and birthplace of the Duchess of Kent, is nearby. Elegant furnishings and open fires create a welcoming atmosphere. The spacious sitting rooms are an ideal place to relax over morning coffee or afternoon tea. The award-winning restaurant offers creatively prepared dishes, including game from the estate, cooked and presented with flair. Guests can visit the wine cellar to browse or choose their wine for dinner. The Cricketers bar provides a more informal setting to enjoy modern cooking at its best. The en-suite bedrooms range in size and have recently all been redecorated. There is plenty to do nearby, including tennis, squash, jogging, golf and scenic walks along nature trails. Guests can explore the beautiful Dales, the North Yorkshire Moors and the spectacular coastline or discover the abbeys, stately homes and castles nearby. Special breaks available.

Our inspector loved: Walking around the wine cellar choosing the wine for dinner.

Directions: Hovingham is on the B1257, 8 miles from Malton and Helmsley. 20 minutes north of York.

Web: www.johansens.com/worsleyarms
E-mail: worsleyarms@aol.com
Tel: 0870 381 9011
International: +44 (0)1653 628234
Fax: 01653 628130

Price Guide:
single £70–£90
double/twin £95–£170

MONK FRYSTON HALL HOTEL

MONK FRYSTON, NORTH YORKSHIRE LS25 5DU

A short distance from the A1 and almost equal distance from Leeds and York, this mellow old manor house hotel, built in 1740, is ideal for tourists, business people and those looking for an invitingly secluded spot for a weekend break. The mullioned and transom windows and the family coat of arms above the doorway are reminiscent of Monk Fryston's fascinating past. In 1954 the Hall was acquired by the late Duke of Rutland, who has created an elegant contemporary hotel, whilst successfully preserving the strong sense of heritage and tradition. The bedrooms, ranging from cosy to spacious, have private en-suite bathrooms and are appointed to a high standard. A generous menu offers a wide choice of traditional English dishes with something to suit all tastes. From the Hall, the terrace leads down to an ornamental Italian garden which overlooks a lake and is a delight to see at any time of year. Wedding receptions are held in the oak-panelled Haddon Room with its splendid Inglenook fireplace. The Rutland Room provides a convenient venue for meetings and private parties. York is 17 miles, Leeds 13 miles and Harrogate 18 miles away.

Directions: The Hall is 3 miles off the A1, on the A63 towards Selby in the centre of Monk Fryston.

Web: www.johansens.com/monkfrystonhall
E-mail: reception@monkfryston-hotel.com
Tel: 0870 381 8741
International: +44 (0)1977 682369
Fax: 01977 683544

Price Guide:
single £88–£148
double/twin £110–£158

Our inspector loved: The oak-panelled front hall with open fire.

HELLABY HALL HOTEL

OLD HELLABY LANE, NR ROTHERHAM, SOUTH YORKSHIRE S66 8SN

The impressive 17th-century façade of Hellaby Hall has been an unmistakable feature of the South Yorkshire skyline since 1692, when it was built by Ralph Fretwell on his return from Barbados. Today this award-winning hotel continues to nurture its excellent reputation, combining historic charm with luxurious and modern facilities. All 90 bedrooms are tastefully furnished in a variety of styles, including the romantic four-poster suite with its magnificent bed, private lounge and dining area. Elsewhere, guests can relax in the oak-panelled lounge where friendly staff are on hand to ensure that any stay is as comfortable as possible. The light and spacious Attic Restaurant is perfect for intimate celebrations or business lunches and an informal restaurant Rizzios, with south-west facing courtyard provides a popular alternative and alfresco dining. A selection of rooms can host corporate meetings or dining events and some are now licensed to hold civil wedding ceremonies. The Hotel also comprises of Bodyscene, a £2 million state-of-the-art health and leisure club with swimming pool and steam room, a large fitness suite and dedicated gym instructor and beauty team.

Our inspector loved: The large health and leisure club and swimming pool.

Directions: From the M18, exit at junction 1 and take the A631 towards Bawtry. The Hotel is ½ mile on the left.

Web: www.johansens.com/hellabyhall
E-mail: sales@hellabyhallhotel.co.uk
Tel: 0870 381 8592
International: +44 (0)1709 702701
Fax: 01709 700979

Price Guide:
single £45–£130
double/twin £79–£160
suite £165–£190

Charnwood Hotel

10 SHARROW LANE, SHEFFIELD, SOUTH YORKSHIRE S11 8AA

The Charnwood Hotel is a listed Georgian mansion dating from 1780. Originally owned by John Henfrey, a Sheffield Master Cutler, it was later acquired by William Wilson of the Sharrow Snuff Mill. Restored in 1985, this elegant "country house in town" is tastefully furnished, with colourful flower arrangements set against attractive décor. The non-smoking bedrooms are all individually decorated and the Woodford suite is designed specifically to meet the requirements of a family. Brasserie Leo has a relaxed atmosphere serving traditional English and French cuisine. The Library and Henfrey's are ideal for private dining or small meetings and larger functions are catered for in the Georgian Room and Coach House. Also there are 19 self-catering apartments nearby. While approximately a mile from Sheffield city centre, with its concert hall, theatre and hectic night-life, Charnwood Hotel is also convenient for the Peak District National Park. Meadowhall shopping centre and Sheffield Arena are a short ride away.

Directions: Sharrow Lane is near the junction of London Road and Abbeydale Road, 11/2 miles from city centre. Junction 33 from the M1.

Web: www.johansens.com/charnwood
E-mail: reception@charnwoodhotel.co.uk
Tel: 0870 381 8417
International: +44 (0)114 258 9411
Fax: 0114 255 5107

Price Guide:
single £68–£93
double/twin £83–£110

Our inspector loved: The lively atmosphere in Brasserie Leo.

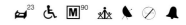

WHITLEY HALL HOTEL

ELLIOTT LANE, GRENOSIDE, SHEFFIELD, SOUTH YORKSHIRE S35 8NR

Carved into the keystone above one of the doors is the date 1584, denoting the start of Whitley Hall's lengthy country house tradition. In the bar is a priest hole, which may explain the local belief that a tunnel links the house with the nearby 11th-century church. In the 18th century, the house was a prestigious boarding school, with Gothic pointed arches and ornamentation added later by the Victorians. Attractively refurbished, Whitley Hall is now a fine hotel with all the amenities required by today's visitors. Stone walls and oak panelling combine with richly carpeted floors and handsome decoration. A sweeping split staircase leads to the bedrooms, all of which have en-suite bathrooms. Varied yet unpretentious cooking is served in generous portions and complemented by a wide choice from the wine cellar, including many clarets and ports. Peacocks strut around the 30 acre grounds, which encompass rolling lawns, mature woodland and 2 ornamental lakes. Banquets and private functions can be held in the conference suite.

Our inspector loved: *The peacocks fanning their tails in the garden.*

Directions: Leave M1 at junction 35, following signs for Chapeltown (A629), go down hill and turn left into Nether Lane. Go right at traffic lights, then left opposite Arundel pub, then immediately right into Whitley Lane. At fork turn right into Elliott Lane; hotel is on left.

Web: www.johansens.com/whitleyhall
E-mail: reservations@whitleyhall.com
Tel: 0870 381 8993
International: +44 (0)114 245 4444
Fax: 0114 245 5414

Price Guide:
single £65–£95
double/twin £80–£120

HOLDSWORTH HOUSE HOTEL & RESTAURANT

HOLDSWORTH, HALIFAX, WEST YORKSHIRE HX2 9TG

Directions: From M1 Jct42 take M62 west to Jct26. Follow A58 to Halifax (ignore signs to town centre). At Burdock Way roundabout take A629 to Keighley; after 1½ miles go right into Shay Lane; hotel is a mile on right.

Web: www.johansens.com/holdsworthhouse
E-mail: info@holdsworthhouse.co.uk
Tel: 0870 381 8603
International: +44 (0)1422 240024
Fax: 01422 245174

Price Guide:
single £93–£130
double/twin £114 –£160
suite £135–£170

Holdsworth House is a retreat of quality and charm standing 3 miles north of Halifax in the heart of Yorkshire's West Riding. Built in 1633, it was acquired by the Pearson family 40 years ago. With care, skill and professionalism they have created a hotel and restaurant of considerable repute. The interior, with its polished panelling and open fireplaces, has been carefully preserved and embellished with fine antique furniture and ornaments. The comfortable lounge opens onto a pretty courtyard and overlooks the herb garden and gazebo. The restaurant, which has 2 AA Rosettes comprises 2 beautifully furnished rooms, ideal for private dinner parties. Exciting modern English and continental cuisine is meticulously prepared and presented, complemented by a thoughtfully compiled wine list. The Stone Room has lighter and informal dining. Each cosy bedroom has its own style, from the 4 split-level suites to the 2 interconnecting rooms for families. This is the perfect base from which to explore the Pennines, the Yorkshire Dales and Haworth, home of the Brontë family. Weekend breaks available.

Our inspector loved: *The cosy, oak-panelled, award-winning restaurant.*

HALEY'S HOTEL & RESTAURANT

SHIRE OAK ROAD, HEADINGLEY, LEEDS, WEST YORKSHIRE LS6 2DE

Just 2 miles from Leeds City Centre, yet set in a quiet leafy lane in the Headingley conservation area close to the cricket ground and the university, Haley's is truly the country house hotel in the city. Each of the 28 guest rooms offers the highest levels of comfort and is as individual as the fine antiques and rich furnishings which grace the hotel. A new addition to the existing accommodation is Bedford House, the elegant Victorian Grade II listed building next door which contains 7 outstandingly furnished and beautifully equipped modern bedrooms, including 2 suites, one with its own private entrance. The Bramley Room and Library are popular venues for private meetings, lunch or dinner parties. Haley's Restaurant has an enviable reputation, holding 2 AA Rosettes. An imaginative menu of modern English cuisine is accompanied by a fine wine list. Leeds offers superb shopping (including Harvey Nichols) and the Victorian Arcades. Opera North and the theatres combine with Haley's superb accommodation and food to provide entertaining weekends.

Directions: 2 miles north of Leeds city centre off the main A660 Otley Road – the main route to Leeds/Bradford Airport, Ilkley and Wharfedale.

Web: www.johansens.com/haleys
E-mail: info@haleys.co.uk
Tel: 0870 381 8579
International: +44 (0)113 278 4446
Fax: 0113 275 3342

Price Guide:
single from £110
double/twin from £145
suite from £230

Our inspector loved: This elegant and peaceful retreat in the leafy suburbs of Leeds.

QUEBECS, THE LEEDS TOWN HOUSE

9 QUEBEC STREET, LEEDS, WEST YORKSHIRE LS1 2HA

Newly opened in February 2002, excellently located right in the centre of the city of Leeds, near City Square, this chic Victorian hotel has been beautifully restored with stunning original Victorian features. Classic tones and sumptuous surroundings reflect the grandeur of the breathtaking architecture of the building and 5 awe-inspiring stained glass windows, depicting the coats of arms of the principal towns of Yorkshire, light a magnificent winding oak staircase. Guests will admire the delicately carved panels of the circular Oak Room and the elegant style of the Hotel's public rooms. Opulent air-conditioned bedrooms are exquisitely furnished and have sleek granite and chrome bathrooms. Attention to detail with fresh fruit, crisp Egyptian cotton linen and luxury toiletries make a truly comfortable stay. Leeds is steeped in history and culture and there are numerous museums and galleries to visit. There is excellent shopping, with many designer shops a few minutes' walk away and a number of fine restaurants to choose from. The hotel is an ideal base for exploring the beautiful Yorkshire Dales, Moors and Brontë country. Superb business facilities make this venue perfect for any small corporate occasion.

Directions: From the M1 follow signs for Leeds and exit the M621 at jct 3. following signs for Leeds city centre, under the railway bridge and pass the lights. Beyond the right hand side of Majestic night club, Quebecs is on the left.

Web: www.johansens.com/quebecs
E-mail: res_quebecs@etontownhouse.com
Tel: 0870 381 8843
International: +44 (0)113 244 8989
Fax: 0113 244 9090

Price Guide:
single from £138
double/twin £162–£197
suite £110–£280

Our inspector loved: *The panelled Oak Room with carved faces in the panelling.*

42 THE CALLS

42 THE CALLS, LEEDS, WEST YORKSHIRE LS2 7EW

42 the Calls is a remarkable, award-winning hotel situated in the heart of Leeds, yet peacefully set in a quiet location alongside the river. Originally a corn mill, this unique hotel takes advantage of many of the original features of the mill, incorporating impressive beams, girders and old machinery into the décor. Each of the 41 bedrooms is imaginatively decorated in an individual style using beautiful fabrics and expert interior design to create a wonderful sense of harmony. Handmade beds and armchairs, a plethora of eastern rugs and extremely lavish bathrooms enhance the feeling of comfort and luxury. There is an excellent choice of restaurants in the vicinity, including the world renowned Michelin starred Pool Court at 42 next door and the stylish Brasserie 44. The hotel does offer round the clock room service or guests may dine in 6 of the city's restaurants and simply sign their lunch or dinner to their hotel bill. Shops, offices, galleries and theatres are all within a few minutes' walk from the hotel.

Our inspector loved: *The innovative design of the hotel and the privacy hatches for room service.*

Directions: M621 Jct 3. Follow City Centre and West Yorkshire Playhouse signs, turn left after Tetley's Brewery then turn left onto the City Centre Loop, following City signs. Take Jct 15 and The Calls is immediately in front of you.

Web: www.johansens.com/42thecalls
E-mail: hotel@42thecalls.co.uk
Tel: 0870 381 8737
International: +44 (0)113 244 0099
Fax: 0113 234 4100

Price Guide:
single £144–£230
double/twin £158–£245
suite from £300

339

CHEVIN COUNTRY PARK HOTEL

YORKGATE, OTLEY, WEST YORKSHIRE LS21 3NU

Directions: From A658 between Bradford and Harrogate, take the Chevin Forest Park road, then left into Yorkgate for Chevin Park.

Web: www.johansens.com/chevinlodge
E-mail: reception@chevinlodge.co.uk
Tel: 0870 381 8426
International: +44 (0)1943 467818
Fax: 01943 850335

Price Guide:
single £65–£135
double/twin £110–£155

A quite unique hotel – you would probably need to travel to Scandinavia to discover a similar hotel to Chevin Park. Built entirely of Finnish logs and surrounded by birch trees, it is set in 50 acres of lake and woodland in the beauty spot of Chevin Forest Park. The spacious, carefully designed bedrooms are tastefully furnished with pine and some have patio doors leading to the lakeside gardens. In addition, there are several luxury lodges tucked away in the woods, providing alternative accommodation to the hotel bedrooms. Imaginative and appetising meals are served in the beautiful balconied restaurant, which overlooks the lake. Chevin Lodge offers conference facilities in the Woodlands Suite which is fully equipped for all business requirements. The Leisure Club has a 11 x 7 metres swimming pool, spa bath, sauna, solarium and gym. There is also a games room, all-weather tennis court and jogging trails that wind through the woods. Leeds, Bradford and Harrogate are within 20 minutes' drive. Special weekend breaks are available.

Our inspector loved: *This small piece of Finland set in Yorkshire.*

For further information on the Channel Islands, please contact:

Guernsey Tourist Board
PO Box 23, St Peter Port, Guernsey GY1 3AN
Tel: +44 (0)1481 723552
Internet: www.guernseytouristboard.com

Jersey Tourism
Liberation Square, St Helier, Jersey JE1 1BB
Tel: +44 (0)1534 500777
Internet: www.jtourism.com

Sark Tourism
Harbour Hill, Sark, Channel Islands GY9 0SB
Tel: +44 (0)1481 832345
Internet: www.sark-tourism.com

Herm Tourist Office
The White House Hotel, Herm Island via Guernsey GY1 3HR
Tel: +44 (0)1481 722377
Internet: www.herm-island.com

or see **pages 437-440** for details of
local attractions to visit during your stay.

Images from www.britainonview.com

LA FRÉGATE HOTEL AND RESTAURANT

LES COTILS, ST PETER PORT, GUERNSEY GY1 1UT

Directions: From the harbour, continue along St Julian's Avenue which turns into College Street. Turn right into Grane and right again into Upland Road. Turn left into Monument Road then left into Candie Road and right into Cambridge Park Road; finally, turn right into Vauxlaurens.

Web: www.johansens.com/lafregate
E-mail: enquiries@lafregatehotel.com
Tel: 0870 381 9172
International: +44 (0)1481 724624
Fax: 01481 720443

Grandes Rocques

Herm

St Peter Port

Sark

Airport

Price Guide:
single £50-£82
double £135-£175

With its spectacular elevated position over St Peter Port, La Frégate has sweeping views over the town, the harbour and neighbouring islands of Herm, Jethou and Sark. Conveniently situated only a few minutes' walk from the busy town centre, the hotel has a surprising air of peace and tranquillity created by beautiful private gardens. En-suite bedrooms are luxurious and comfortable; some have a patio and balcony - ideal for enjoying a sumptuous breakfast. Outstanding French cuisine has been awarded the coveted 2 AA Rosettes and is popular both internationally and by locals alike. Seafood from nearby waters and fresh vegetables (some grown in the hotel's garden) are accompanied by delicious wines from an extensive cellar. Personal service is the norm and attention to detail such as fresh flowers enhances a sense of care and comfort. Outdoor activities include island hopping, cycling through the quiet country lanes or walking the scenic south coast cliffs with their small coves and secluded bays. Guernsey is a haven to more than 100 species of migrating birds, which stop off to feed before continuing their long passage north or south in autumn and spring.

Our inspector loved: Its minimalist style in the restaurant and rooms, and magnificent harbour views.

CHÂTEAU LA CHAIRE

ROZEL BAY, JERSEY JE3 6AJ

When the Victorians sought a stunning location to build a gracious château home on the island of Jersey they discovered the wonderful wooded valley of Rozel. Today, nestling on its sunny slopes and surrounded by beautiful gardens, is Château La Chaire, recognised by both the AA and RAC as one of the finest small hotels in the British Isles. The AA include it in their Top 200 Hotels whilst the RAC has awarded the hotel their coveted Gold Ribbon. Built in 1843, the château has been enhanced and transformed into a luxurious hotel offering a superb blend of comfort, service and cuisine. Each of the spacious, beautifully proportioned bedrooms has been furnished to the highest standards and offers an impressive array of personal comforts; many en-suite bathrooms feature Jacuzzis. Both adventurous and traditional dishes and, above all, seafood, can be enjoyed in the oak-panelled La Chaire restaurant. 2 AA Rosettes and 3 RAC dining awards acknowledge the excellence of the food and service. A few minutes away is the picturesque Rozel Bay, a bustling fishing harbour with safe beaches close by. St Helier is just 6 miles away. Spectacular cliff top walks, golf, fishing and riding are among the many leisure activities guests can enjoy during their stay.

Our inspector loved: The unique historic garden setting in the north of the island and excellent food in the conservatory.

Directions: The hotel is signposted off the main coastal road to Rozel Bay, 6 miles north-east of St Helier.

Web: www.johansens.com/chateaulachaire
E-mail: res@chateau-la-chaire.co.uk
Tel: 0870 381 8420
International: +44 (0)1534 863354
Fax: 01534 865137

Price Guide:
single from £100
double/twin from £132
suites from £231

THE ATLANTIC HOTEL

LE MONT DE LA PULENTE, ST BRELADE, JERSEY JE3 8HE

This is a stunning luxury hotel that offers elegance, grace, comfort, exquisite cuisine and impeccable service. It is excellent in every way, from majestic interior pillars and magnificent wood panelling to sumptuous furnishings, warm décor and perfect location. The Atlantic stands regally in 3 acres of private grounds alongside the La Moye Golf Course overlooking the 5-mile sweep of St Ouen's Bay. A multi-million pound refurbishment of the hotel including the enlargement of bedrooms and remodelling of the building's exterior to give a marine flavour, has resulted in even more venue quality and the hotel's elevation to 5-Sun status by Jersey Tourism. No expense has been spared in refurnishing the bedrooms, suites and garden studios. Tastefully decorated, they offer occupants the highest standard of facilities and comfort together with splendid views of the sea or the golf course. Most prestigious and stylish is the spacious Atlantic Suite with its own entrance hall, living room, guest cloakroom and service pantry in addition to the en suite master bedroom. The delightful, award-winning restaurant overlooks the open-air swimming pool and sun terrace. Head Chef Ken Healy specialises in modern British cooking and produces excellent and imaginative menus.

Directions: Off a private drive off the A13 at La Pulente, 2 miles from the airport.

Web: www.johansens.com/atlantic
E-mail: info@theatlantichotel.com
Tel: 0870 381 8330
International: +44 (0)1534 744101
Fax: 01534 744102

Price Guide:
single £140–£170
double/twin £185–£270
suite £260–£445

Our inspector loved: The green and tranquil views from the restaurant and the always impeccable service.

LONGUEVILLE MANOR

ST SAVIOUR, JERSEY JE2 7WF

Three generations of the Lewis family have welcomed guests to this 13th-century Manor, which is today a very fine and prestigious hotel. Ever attentive staff, superb public rooms, exquisite bedrooms and sumptuous cuisine, which in 2003 earned the Manor's restaurant its 10th consecutive Michelin star, suggest the standards you may expect. Guests dine in either the elegant oak-panelled room or the spacious garden room. Many of the fruits, vegetables and herbs for the kitchen are grown in the hotel's walled garden or the traditional greenhouse which provides fresh produce throughout the seasons - it even has a banana tree! The wine list offers a selection by Longueville's Master Sommelier, and includes gems from the New World, great vintages from the best of the French châteaux and superb Champagnes. Continued upgrading has seen the introduction of delightful new suites, both in the main house and in the restored garden cottage, along with a small meeting and private dining facility. The large heated pool has an adjoining bar, where guests may enjoy a light alfresco meal during the summer. Tennis can be played on the synthetic grass court whilst the lawn is ideal for croquet. Guests may stroll through the magnificent garden with its picturesque lake, home to black swans and mandarin ducks.

Our inspector loved: The delightful panelled dining room - a stylish setting for food, wine and service of the very highest standard.

Directions: On A3, 1 mile from St Helier.

Web: www.johansens.com/longuevillemanor
E-mail: info@longuevillemanor.com
Tel: 0870 381 8702
International: +44 (0)1534 725501
Fax: 01534 731613

Price Guide:
single from £175
double/twin £200–£380
suite £400–£670

a matter of taste.

Fresh ground coffee and equipment solutions

Contact: Local Call 0845 600 8244   **Fax:** 01372 748196   **email:** sales@tchibo.co.uk
Tchibo Coffee International, Tchibo House, Blenheim Road, Epsom, Surrey KT19 9AP
www.tchibocoffee.co.uk

For further information on Ireland, please contact:

The Irish Tourist Board
(Bord Fáilte Eíreann)
Baggot Street
Dublin 2
Tel: +353 (0)1 602 4000
Internet: www.ireland.travel.ie

Northern Ireland Tourist Information
Belfast Welcome Centre
47 Donegall Place
Belfast, BT1 5AD
Tel: +44 (0)28 9024 6609
Internet: www.discovernorthernireland.com

or see **pages 437-440** for details of
local attractions to visit during your stay.

Images from Fáilte Ireland

DROMOLAND CASTLE

NEWMARKET-ON-FERGUS, SHANNON AREA, CO CLARE

Dating from the 16th century, Dromoland Castle is one of the most famous baronial castles in Ireland. Dromoland was the ancestral seat of the O'Briens, direct descendants of Irish King Brian Boru. Reminders of its past are everywhere: in the splendid wood and stone carvings, magnificent panelling, oil paintings and romantic gardens. The 100 en-suite guest rooms and suites are all beautifully furnished. Stately halls and an elegant dining room are all part of the Dromoland experience. The Dromoland International Centre is one of Europe's most comprehensive conference venues, hosting groups of up to 450. Classical cuisine is prepared by award-winning chef David McCann. Following recent investment, Dromoland's 18-hole golf course has been newly designed and constructed to provide Ireland with a golf resort like no other. Designed by Ron Kirby & JB Carr, this over 6850-yard championship course roams through woodland and around lakes with subtlety and sensitivity (opening April 2004). Fishing, clay pigeon shooting and full Health and Beauty Centre are all available on the estate, whilst activities nearby include horse riding and golf on some of Ireland's other foremost courses. The castle is an ideal base from which to explore this breathtakingly beautiful area. Member of Preferred Hotels & Resorts World Wide.

Directions: Take the N18 to Newmarket-on-Fergus, go 2 miles beyond the village and the hotel entrance is on the right-hand side. 8 miles from Shannon Airport

Web: www.johansens.com/dromolandcastle
E-mail: sales@dromoland.ie
Tel: 00 353 61 368144
Fax: 00 353 61 363355

Price Guide: (room only)
double/twin €215–€546
suite €455–€923

Our inspector loved: The unique Dromoland experience in a stunning setting.

THE FITZWILLIAM HOTEL

ST STEPHEN'S GREEN, DUBLIN 2, IRELAND

Overlooking the elegant, tranquil gardens of St Stephen's Green in the centre of historic Dublin the Fitzwilliam is the ultimate in hotel chic, a "designer hotel" representing both a cosmopolitan landmark for the city and a stylish retreat from the bustle of everyday life. Style is at the heart of the Fitzwilliam, which was designed by Sir Terence Conran's group. Traditional hotel trappings of chintz and four-poster beds have given way to modernistic architecture entitled "Baronial Modern". The interior of the hotel features many themes often found in country houses but updated and given a contemporary feel. Solid yet contemporary furnishings, well-made in walnut or oak and complemented by carefully chosen accessories, offer elegance with comfort. Each bedroom has every modern amenity and luxury from stereo CD player and satellite television to a minibar, multi-line telephone facility, modem line and voice mail. In addition to the Mediterranean-style, all day brasserie Citron, superb cuisine is served in the 2 Michelin-star restaurant, Thornton's. The Fitzwilliam also has a popular cocktail bar, Inn on the Green, Ireland's largest roof garden and secure indoor car parking. Condé Nast's Traveller Magazine voted the Fitzwilliam in the top 21 of the World's Hottest Hotels.

Our inspector loved: The Thornton's restaurant and friendliness of the staff.

Directions: In the centre of the city adjacent to the top of Grafton Street, overlooking St Stephen's Green.

Balbriggan

Dublin

Dun Laoghaire

Web: www.johansens.com/fitzwilliam
E-mail: enq@fitzwilliamhotel.com
Tel: 00 353 1 478 7000
Fax: 00 353 1 478 7878

Price Guide:
single €320–€420
double/twin €360–€460
suite €525–€675

MERRION HALL

54-56 MERRION ROAD, BALLSBRIDGE, DUBLIN 4

Directions: From the city centre take Merrion Road; the Hotel is on the left hand side overlooking the RDS Convention Centre.

Web: www.johansens.com/merrionhall
E-mail: merrionhall@iol.ie
Tel: 00 353 1 668 1426
Fax: 00 353 1 668 4280

Price Guide:
single €99–€130
double/twin €124–€190
suite: €159–€240

Balbriggan

Dublin

Dun Laoghaire

This exclusive Edwardian property is located close to the RDS Convention centre just minutes from downtown Dublin. Merrion Hall shares its neighbourhood with the world's embassies in the fashionable Ballsbridge area of Dublin City. Executive bedrooms, some with four-poster suites, offer air conditioning, whirlpool spas and all the modern comforts expected by the discerning traveller. The hotel's library stocks a fine selection of Irish and international literature, whilst afternoon teas and fine wines are served in the main drawing room. A feature of this Edwardian town house is a very special breakfast, which can be enjoyed overlooking mature secluded gardens. There are also numerous restaurants within a short stroll of the hotel, leaving guests utterly spoilt for choice. Near to Lansdowne Road, it is linked to major tourist sites and the business district by the DART electric train. There is a direct luxury coach link to and from Dublin airport. Residents have complimentary parking on the grounds. The hotel can arrange golfing packages and scenic tours.

Our inspector loved: *The convenient location of this Edwardian house.*

THE MERRION HOTEL

UPPER MERRION STREET, DUBLIN 2, IRELAND

The Merrion is Dublin's most luxurious hotel and a historic landmark. It has been imaginatively and brilliantly conceived, 4 superb Grade I Georgian terrace houses meticulously restored. There is also an elegant Garden Wing. The interior decorations are impressive, authentically reflecting the Georgian era by the choice of wall colours, specially commissioned fabrics and well-researched antiques. By contrast, a private collection of 20th-century art is displayed throughout the hotel, and the neo-classic stairwell has a series of contemporary murals. Every guest room is luxurious, some situated in the Garden Wing, with views over the 2 gardens – delightful with box hedges, statuary and fountains, approached from the drawing rooms in summer. The Merrion offers a choice of 2 handsome bars, the larger a fascinating 18th-century cellar, the other more intimate, and 2 restaurants, the legendary Restaurant Patrick Guilbaud in a dramatic setting and The Cellar Restaurant, offering simple Irish cuisine, expertly prepared and executed. The Merrion has a state-of-the-art meeting and private dining facility, perfect for hosting banquets. Guests relax in The Tethra Spa, which has an 18m pool, gymnasium and salons for pampering.

Our inspector loved: The friendly and efficient service.

Directions: City centre. The hotel has valet parking.

Web: www.johansens.com/merrion
E-mail: info@merrionhotel.com
Tel: 00 353 1 603 0600
Fax: 00 353 1 603 0700

Price Guide: (room only)
single €320–€400
double/twin €345–€435
suite €630–€2400

Balbriggan

Dublin

Dun Laoghaire

RENVYLE HOUSE HOTEL

CONNEMARA, CO GALWAY, IRELAND

Directions: On the N59 from Galway turn right at Recess, take the Letterfrack turning to Tully Cross and Renvyle is signposted.

Web: www.johansens.com/renvylehouse
E-mail: renvyle@iol.ie
Tel: 00 353 95 43511
Fax: 00 353 95 43515

Price Guide:
single from €50
double/twin from €50

Renvyle House Hotel has occupied its rugged, romantic position on Ireland's west coast for over 4 centuries. Set between mountains and sea on the unspoilt coast of Connemara, this hardy, beautiful building with its superlative views over the surrounding countryside is just an hour's drive from Galway or Sligo. Originally constructed in 1541, Renvyle has been an established hotel for over 100 years, witnessing in that time a procession of luminaries through its doors – Augustus John, Lady Gregory, Yeats and Churchill, drawn no doubt by an atmosphere as warm and convivial then as it is today. Renvyle now welcomes visitors with turf fires glowing in public areas, wood-beamed interiors and comfortable, relaxed furnishings in the easy rooms. The bedrooms are comfortably appointed and all have been refurbished in the past 3 years. In the dining room, meals from a constantly-changing menu are served with emphasis on local fish and Renvyle lamb. In the grounds activities include tennis, croquet, riding, bowls and golf. Beyond the hotel, there are walks in the heather-clad hills, or swimming and sunbathing on empty beaches.

Our inspector loved: *The new rooms and additions to this Connemara hotel.*

SHEEN FALLS LODGE
KENMARE, CO. KERRY, IRELAND

AA Hotel of the Year and one of Ireland's most romantic and luxurious hotels, Sheen Falls Lodge is a haven set within 300 acres of magical woodlands and crystal cascading waterfalls. This gracious mansion evokes the atmosphere of a restful country house. The spacious bedrooms with their magnificent views are luxuriously appointed with fine linens and are decorated in soft, restful shades. The differing panoramas of Kenmare Bay and the Sheen waterfalls can be enjoyed from the Sun Lounge, the Billiard Room and the Library, which offers over 1200 books for our guests to peruse. Log fires, sumptuous seating, fresh flowers and warm, attentive service complete the ambience of utter relaxation. Choose between the dining experiences of Oscar's bistro with its Mediterranean influenced menu or the elegance of La Cascade, the hotel's signature restaurant. Complete your evening with a tour of our extensive wine cellar and sample a fine port or whiskey with the sommelier. Activities available on the estate include horse riding, salmon and trout fishing, clay pigeon shooting, walking, cycling and hiking. The health spa provides the opportunity to indulge in a variety of body and beauty treatments or soak in the Jacuzzi after a swim in the pool. Nearby are several excellent golf courses, the Beara peninsula and the Ring of Kerry.

Our inspector loved: *The very special wine cellar and sitting on the terrace watching the waterfalls.*

Directions: From Kenmare follow N71 in the direction of Glengarrif and turn left after the Suspension Bridge. Dublin airport is about 5 hours drive away, Shannon airport is 2½ hours travelling time, Cork airport is approx 1½ hours and Kerry airport is 50 minutes away.

Ballybunion

Dingle

Killarney

Web: www.johansens.com/sheenfallslodge
E-mail: info@sheenfallslodge.ie
Tel: 00 353 64 41600
Fax: 00 353 64 41386

Price Guide:
Deluxe Room €275–€415

KILLASHEE HOUSE HOTEL

KILLASHEE, NAAS, CO KILDARE, IRELAND

Originally a Victorian hunting lodge, Killashee House still bears the coats of arms of its founders, the Moore family. Guests are treated to tantalising views of its Jacobean-style facade and eye-catching bell tower as they approach on an elegant curving driveway, although the house actually dates from Victorian times when it was built for the influential Moore Family in the early 1860s. Today it is a glorious hotel situated within 80 acres of gardens and woodland, just 30 minutes from Dublin. There are 84 luxurious and comfortable guest rooms including 12 suites and 6 Presidential rooms, many with four-poster beds and stunning views of the gardens and, sometimes, the Wicklow Mountains. Every bedroom has multi-line telephone, data port and voicemail. Traditional Irish and Mediterranean cuisine can be enjoyed in the award-winning Turners Restaurant. State-of-the-art conference facilities include sophisticated audio-visual equipment as well as video conferencing and fibre optic data ports. Killashee House Country Club, which includes a 25m pool is the ultimate in luxury and sheer relaxation. The National Stud and the racecourses of Curragh, Punchestown and Naas are all within easy reach, as are several championship golf courses, including the K Club and the Curragh. There is car racing at Mondello Park, and the Japanese and St Fiachra's Gardens provide a tranquil setting for horticultural enthusiasts.

Directions: 30 minutes from Dublin on N7/M7 to Naas, then 1 mile along R448 Kilcullen Road.

Web: www.johansens.com/killashee
E-mail: reservations@killasheehouse.com
Tel: 00 353 45 879277
Fax: 00 353 45 879266

Price Guide: (per person sharing)
single from €144
double/twin from €99
suite €110–€210

Our inspector loved: The warm welcome at reception.

MOUNT JULIET CONRAD

THOMASTOWN, CO KILKENNY, IRELAND

Mount Juliet Conrad is an architectural gem, a magnificent 18th-century Georgian mansion standing proudly on the banks of the River Nore in the heart of a lush 1,500-acre estate. The entrance doorway leads into an impressive hall featuring elaborate stucco work with bas-reliefs on walls and ceilings. A feeling of opulence pervades all reception rooms, the bars recall a glorious equestrian past whilst the homeliness of the library and drawing rooms provide comfortable venues for relaxation. Afternoon tea or a pre-dinner glass of champagne can be enjoyed in the elegant Majors Room. Jewel in the crown, however, is the exquisite Lady Helen Dining Room, famed for its original stucco plasterwork, pastoral views and superb cuisine. The 32 en-suite guest rooms are individually designed and are full of the character and charm that reflects the quiet good taste and refinement of the Georgian period. Centre of activity for guests is Hunters Yard, which is situated on the edge of a championship golf course, which hosted the American Express World Golf Championships in 2002. The Hunters Yard is the epicentre of the estate's sporting and leisure life and offers stylish dining in Kendals Restaurant and 16 "Club" style rooms which offer direct access to the hotels sybaritic spa. For guests who require a greater degree of space and privacy, there are 10 lodges located beside the magnificent Rose Gardens.

Our inspector loved: The Trompe-L'œil in the entrance hall.

Directions: 16 miles from Kilkenny on the N9 via N10.

Web: www.johansens.com/mountjuliet
E-mail: mountjulietinfo@ConradHotels.com
Tel: 00 353 56 777 3000
Fax: 00 353 56 777 3019

Castlecomer

Kilkenny

Thomastown

Price Guide:
single from €175
double/twin from €230
suite €560

GLIN CASTLE

GLIN, CO LIMERICK, IRELAND

Directions: Take the ferry from Kilimer via the M68 from Ennis. Alternatively take the N69 from Limerick.

Web: www.johansens.com/glincastle
E-mail: knight@iol.ie
Tel: 00 353 68 34173
Fax: 00 353 68 34364

Price Guide:
standard €280
superior €360
de luxe €440

Home to the 29th Knight of Glin and Madam FitzGerald, Glin Castle has received accolades from all over the world, and maintains a reputation as one of the most unique places to stay in Ireland. The present castle was built with entertaining in mind in the late 18th century and has been sympathetically restored for modern day guests. Its famous collections of Irish furniture and paintings, built up over the centuries, fill reception rooms, whilst family portraits and photographs adorn the walls and mahogany side tables. Beautiful features are endless; the Corinthian pillars and rare flying staircase of the entrance hall, the Sittingroom's crackling fire, the Drawingroom with its 6 long windows overlooking the croquet lawn, the library with its secret bookcase doorway. Each of the sumptuous bedrooms is furnished with period pieces including rugs, chaise longues, and chintz covered beds. Those at the back look across the garden and those at the front have views of the River Shannon. The castle stands within 500 acres of grounds which comprise formal gardens, a series of follies, a parade of yew trees and a walled garden that supplies the hotel kitchen with fresh fruit and vegetables for its good Irish country house cooking, as well as fresh flowers for the rooms.

Our inspector loved: The aristocratic opulence of this wonderful castle home.

ASHFORD CASTLE

CONG, CO MAYO

Ashford Castle is set on the northern shores of Lough Corrib amidst acres of beautiful gardens and forests. Once the country estate of Lord Ardilaun and the Guinness family, it was transformed into a luxury hotel in 1939. The castle's Great Hall is lavishly decorated with rich panelling, fine period pieces, objets d'art and masterpiece paintings. Guest rooms are of the highest standards and many feature high ceilings, enormous bathrooms and delightful lake views. The main dining room offers superb continental and traditional menus, while the gourmet restaurant, The Connaught Room, specialises in excellent French cuisine. Before and after dinner in the Dungeon Bar guests are entertained by a harpist or pianist. Ashford Castle offers a full range of country sports, including fishing on Lough Corrib, clay pigeon shooting, riding, an exclusive 9-hole golf course and Ireland's only school of falconry. The hotel has a modern health centre comprising a whirlpool, sauna, steam room, fully equipped gymnasium and conservatory. Ashford is an ideal base for touring the historic West of Ireland, places like Kylemore Abbey, Westport House and the mediaeval town of Galway. A member of Leading Hotels of the World.

Our inspector loved: The stunning views across Lough Corrib.

Directions: 30 minutes from Galway on the shore of Lough Corrib, on the left when entering the village of Cong.

Web: www.johansens.com/ashfordcastle
E-mail: ashford@ashford.ie
Tel: 00 353 94 95 46003
Fax: 00 353 94 95 46260

Ballina

Castlebar

Westport

Ballyhaunis

Price Guide:
single/twin/double €215–€515
stateroom/suite €570–€995

KNOCKRANNY HOUSE HOTEL

KNOCKRANNY, WESTPORT, CO MAYO, IRELAND

Directions: Left off the N60 before entering Westport town.

Web: www.johansens.com/knockranny
E-mail: info@khh.ie
Tel: 00 353 98 28600
Fax: 00 353 98 28611

Price Guide:
single €120–€170
double/twin €190–€240
suite €255–€305

Situated on secluded grounds overlooking the picturesque Heritage town of Westport, Knockranny House Hotel enjoys unrivalled views of Croagh Patrick, Clew Bay and the Atlantic Ocean. This Victorian style hotel is privately owned and managed by Adrian and Geraldine Noonan, who guarantee the best in Irish hospitality. The 54 charming bedrooms and suites are tastefully furnished and offer luxury, comfort and every up-to-date convenience. The Executive Suites have four-poster beds, spa baths, dvd and cd players, a sunken lounge area with panoramic views and all the trimmings of pure luxury. Fresh flowers in spring to roaring open log fires in winter create a relaxing ambience with every possible comfort. La Fougère Restaurant offers imaginative modern Irish cuisine with International influences, complimented by a selection of fine wines. Activities such as golf, fishing, sailing, horse riding and much more can be enjoyed in the dramatic surrounding countryside, whilst a climb to the top of Croagh Patrick makes an exhilarating day's journey. The ideal location to combine business with pleasure, Knockranny offers extensive conference facilities for up to 500. The Conference Suites are fully air-conditioned with state-of-the-art communication and audiovisual equipment.

Our inspector loved: *The stunning view of the mountain Croagh Patrick and the Atlantic Ocean from the circular dining room windows.*

NUREMORE HOTEL AND COUNTRY CLUB

CARRICKMACROSS, CO MONAGHAN, IRELAND

Nestling on the outskirts of Carrickmacross, Nuremore Hotel and Country Club is set in 200 acres of rolling countryside with beautifully landscaped gardens. Its wide range of facilities include a swimming pool, tennis courts, treatment rooms and a health club featuring a gymnasium, spa bath, sauna and steam room. The hotel's renowned 18-hole championship golf course makes superb use of the surrounding lakes and landscape and has been described as one of the most picturesque parkland courses in the country. Resident professional, Maurice Cassidy, is on hand to offer advice and tuition. All 72 bedrooms and suites are beautifully appointed to ensure a generous feeling of personal space and guests can sample the classic European cuisine with Irish and French influences, prepared by award-winning chef Raymond McArdle. The restaurant has been listed in Food & Wine magazine and it also features in the Bridgestone Guide to Ireland's best 100 restaurants. Nuremore's impressive conference centre constantly evolves to ensure it remains at the cutting edge for business events. Conference and syndicate rooms boast natural lighting, AV equipment, air conditioning, fax and ISDN lines. A dedicated conference team ensures that all functions run smoothly.

Our inspector loved: The extensive sporting and health facilities, newly refurbished swimming pool and gym.

Directions: The hotel is ideally located on main N2 road between Dublin and Monaghan, only 1½ hours from both Dublin and Belfast.

Web: www.johansens.com/nuremore
E-mail: nuremore@eircom.net
Tel: 00 353 42 9661438
Fax: 00 353 42 9661853

Price Guide:
single €150–€200
double/twin €220–€260
suite €250–€300

DUNBRODY COUNTRY HOUSE & RESTAURANT

ARTHURSTOWN, NEW ROSS, CO WEXFORD, IRELAND

Directions: From Wexford take R733 to Duncannon and Arthurstown. Dunbrody is on the left coming into Arthurstown village.

Web: www.johansens.com/dunbrody
E-mail: dunbrody@indigo.ie
Tel: 00 353 51 389 600
Fax: 00 353 51 389 601

Price Guide:
single €120–€150
double/twin €195–€300
suite €300–€390

Once home to the Marquess of Donegal, this beautiful Georgian country house hotel stands in the heart of 20 acres of woodland and gardens on the dramatic hook peninsula of Ireland's sunny south-east coast. The charming interior is adorned with comfortable furniture, furnishings and paintings, fresh flowers, potted plants and crackling log fires in period fireplaces during cooler months. Owners Kevin and Catherine Dundon have perfected the art of relaxed elegance. Public rooms are large and comfortable with views over to distant parkland. Bedrooms and suites are understated opulence: spacious, delightfully decorated, superbly appointed and with a high standard of facilities including luxurious bathrooms. Kevin acquired star status as Master Chef in Canada and creates gastronomic delights for a discerning clientele in an elegant dining room overlooking the lawned garden. The Dunbrody Cookery school also offers residential cookery courses and demonstrations. Also highly acclaimed is the late breakfast which is served daily until noon. Waterford and Wexford are close, as are Tintern Abbey, Dunbody Abbey and a multitude of sandy coves. Croquet and clay pigeon shooting is on site, golf, riding and fishing nearby.

Our inspector loved: The newly converted rooms with a sea view!

MARLFIELD HOUSE

GOREY, CO WEXFORD

Staying at Johansens award-winning Marlfield House is a memorable experience. Set in 34 acres of woodland and gardens, this former residence of the Earl of Courtown preserves the Regency lifestyle in all its graciousness. Built in 1820 and situated just 55 miles south of Dublin, it is recognised as one of the finest country houses in Ireland and is supervised by its welcoming hosts and proprietors, Raymond and Mary Bowe and their daughter Margaret. The State Rooms have been built in a very grand style and have period fireplaces where open fires burn even in cooler weather. All of the furniture is antique and the roomy beds are draped with sumptuous fabrics. The bathrooms are made of highly polished marble and some have large freestanding bathtubs. There is an imposing entrance hall, luxurious drawing room and an impressive curved Richard Turner conservatory. The kitchen's gastronomic delights have earned it numerous awards. Located 2 miles from fine beaches and within easy reach of many golf courses, the house is central to many touring high points: Glendalough, Waterford Crystal and Powerscourt Gardens and the medieval city of Kilkenny. Closed mid-December to the end of January.

Our inspector loved: The instant calming influence caused by the Bowe family's devotion to quality.

Directions: On the Gorey–Courtown road, just over a mile east of Gorey.

Web: www.johansens.com/marlfieldhouse
E-mail: info@marlfieldhouse.ie
Tel: 00 353 55 21124
Fax: 00 353 55 21572

Price Guide:
single from €130
double/twin €235–€255
state rooms from €425–€730

Kelly's Resort Hotel

ROSSLARE, CO WEXFORD, IRELAND

Situated beside the long, sandy beach at Rosslare, Kelly's is very much a family hotel, now managed by the fourth generation of Kellys. With a firm reputation as one of Ireland's finest hotels, based on a consistently high standard of service, Kelly's extends a warm welcome to its guests, many of whom return year after year. The public rooms are tastefully decorated and feature a collection of carefully selected paintings. All bedrooms are en suite and have been refurbished in the last 4 years. The hotel restaurant is highly regarded for its superb cuisine and great attention to detail. An extensive wine list includes individual estate wines imported from France. To complement Chef Aherne's fine cuisine, Kelly's have a French bar/bistro, "La Marine", which is an inspired assemblage of design and offers the ideal venue for pre-dinner drinks. Ireland's numerous endeavour awards for tourism. For exercise and relaxation, guests have the use of the hotel's Aqua Club, with 2 swimming pools and a range of water and health facilities with extensive range of treatments, "swimming lounge", plunge pool and canadian hot tub, also a beauty salon. Golfers have courses at Rosslare, St Helens' Bay and Wexford, which has an excellent shopping centre. Places of interest nearby include the Irish National Heritage Park at Ferrycarrig.

Directions: Follow signs to Rosslare.

Web: www.johansens.com/kellysresort
E-mail: kellyhot@iol.ie
Tel: 00 353 53 32114
Fax: 00 353 53 32222

Price Guide:
single €84–€90
double/twin €148–€187

Our inspector loved: The complete family resort with something for every age.

NEW

THE BROOKLODGE HOTEL

MACREDDIN VILLAGE, CO WICKLOW, IRELAND

Set amidst stunning Wicklow countryside, the thriving village of Macreddin is home to this friendly 4-star hotel. Attention to detail, flagged floors, open fires and fresh flowers create a serene, relaxing country house setting. Bedrooms are sumptuously appointed and offer wonderful views. Guests can enjoy a cocktail in the Waterside Lounge, before sampling exquisite cuisine in the candle-lit Strawberry Tree Restaurant, one of Ireland's most romantic dining venues. Everything here is organic or wild, and beautifully prepared by a team of talented chefs. Brooklodge is perfect for celebrations and conferences, and the White Room caters for 150 guests for an unforgettable wedding. Activities include walking, clay pigeon shooting, off-road driving, quad biking and golf on several first-class golf courses nearby. Guests can enjoy the brand new spa centre, The Wells, a joint operation with Ireland's leading beauty and health company; its extravagant treatments and water features are taken from around the globe. A gym, juice bar and indoor-to-outdoor swimming pool complete the experience. Attached to the hotel is Macreddin Stables, a modern equestrian centre with a variety of horses and ponies for all levels. Guests' own horses are welcome. What better way to explore the beautiful Wicklow countryside than on horseback!

Our inspector loved: *The relaxing atmosphere, cosy log fires and the Strawberry Tree Restaurant.*

Directions: From Dublin, south on N11 to Rathnew (47km), then R752 to Rathdrum (13km), then R753 to Aughrim (12km). Follow signs to Macreddin Village (3km).

Web: www.johansens.com/brooklodge
E-mail: brooklodge@macreddin.ie
Tel: 00 353 402 36444
Fax: 00 353 402 36580

Price Guide:
single €125–€160
double/twin €170–€240
suite €270–€340

363

Hildon Ltd., Broughton, Hampshire SO20 8DQ, ☎ 01794 - 301 747, Fax 01794 - 301 718
e-mail: hildon@hildon.com – www.hildon.com

SCOTLAND

Recommendations in Scotland appear on pages 365-412

For further information on Scotland, please contact:

Visit Scotland
23 Ravelston Terrace, Edinburgh EH4 3TP
Tel: +44 (0)131 332 2433
Internet: www.visitscotland.com

or see **pages 437-440** for details of
local atractions to visit during your stay.

Images from www.britainonview.com

DARROCH LEARG HOTEL

BRAEMAR ROAD, BALLATER, ABERDEENSHIRE AB35 5UX

Directions: At the western edge of Ballater on the A93.

Web: www.johansens.com/darrochlearg
E-mail: nigel@darrochlearg.co.uk
Tel: 0870 381 8477
International: +44 (0)13397 55443
Fax: 013397 55252

Price Guide:
single £77–£102
double/twin £134–£164

4 acres of leafy grounds surround Darroch Learg, situated on the side of the rocky hill which dominates Ballater. The hotel, which was built in 1888 as a fashionable country residence, offers panoramic views over the golf course, River Dee and Balmoral Estate to the fine peaks of the Grampian Mountains. All bedrooms are individually furnished and decorated, providing modern amenities. The reception rooms in Darroch Learg are similarly elegant and welcoming, a comfortable venue in which to enjoy a relaxing drink. Log fires create a particularly cosy atmosphere on chilly nights. The beautifully presented food has been awarded 3 AA Rosettes. A wide choice of wines, AA "Wine List of the Year for Scotland", complements the cuisine, which is best described as modern and Scottish in style. To perfect the setting, there is a wonderful outlook south towards the hills of Glen Muick. The wealth of outdoor activities on offer include walking, riding, mountain-biking, loch and river fishing, gliding and skiing. The surrounding areas are interesting with an old ruined Kirk and ancient Celtic stones. A few miles away stands Balmoral Castle, the Highland residence of the British sovereign.

Our inspector loved: *The personal attention of the charming owners and staff, wonderful understated food, wine and décor.*

LOCH MELFORT HOTEL & RESTAURANT

ARDUAINE, BY OBAN, ARGYLL PA34 4XG

Spectacularly located on the west coast of Scotland, the Loch Melfort Hotel is a quiet hideaway on Asknish Bay, with the awe-inspiring backdrop of woodlands and the magnificent mountains of Argyll. Friendly staff attend to every need and there is a warm, welcoming atmosphere. Spacious bedrooms are lavishly appointed with bold bright fabrics, comfortable furnishings and have large patio windows overlooking the islands of Jura, Shuna and Scarba. The award-winning restaurant, which has breathtaking views stretching as far as the eye can see, is perfect for a romantic meal. Guests may feast on the sumptuous fresh local fish, shellfish and meat complemented by an extensive selection of fine wines. There is also a mouth-watering array of home-made desserts, delicious ice creams and Scottish cheeses. Skerry Bistro serves informal meals, lunches, suppers and afternoon teas. Outdoor activities include fishing, sailing, riding, windsurfing, walking and mountain biking. Visitors can explore the nearby islands and local places of interest include Mull, Kilchoan Castle, Castle Stalker and the stunning Dunstaffnage Castle (home of Clan Campbell). The Arduaine Gardens, situated adjacent to the hotel, are extremely beautiful and home to a diversity of plants and trees from all over the world. The Marine Sanctuary and Landmark Forest Heritage Park are well worth a visit.

Directions: From Oban take the A816 south for 19 miles. From Loch Lomond area follow A82 then A83, finally A816 north to Arduaine.

Oban

Dunoon

Campbelltown

Web: www.johansens.com/lochmelfort
E-mail: reception@lochmelfort.co.uk
Tel: 0870 381 8699
International: +44 (0)1852 200233
Fax: 01852 200214

Price Guide: (including dinner)
double/twin £118-£178
superior £138–£22

Our inspector loved: The super views.

ARDANAISEIG

KILCHRENAN BY TAYNUILT, ARGYLL PA35 1HE

Directions: Reaching Taynuilt on the A85, take the B845 to Kilchrenan.

Web: www.johansens.com/ardanaiseig
E-mail: ardanaiseig@clara.net
Tel: 0870 381 8319
International: +44 (0)1866 833333
Fax: 01866 833222

Price Guide:
single £80–£125
double/twin £108–£262

This romantic small luxury hotel, built in 1834, stands alone in a setting of almost surreal natural beauty at the foot of Ben Cruachan. Directly overlooking Loch Awe and surrounded by wild wooded gardens, Ardanaiseig is evocative of the romance and history of the Highlands. Skilful restoration has ensured that this lovely old mansion has changed little since it was built. The elegant drawing room has log fires, bowls of fresh flowers, superb antiques, handsome paintings and marvellous views of the islands in the Loch and of faraway mountains. The traditional library, sharing this outlook, is ideal for postprandial digestifs. The charming bedrooms are peaceful, appropriate to the era of the house, yet equipped thoughtfully with all comforts. True Scottish hospitality is the philosophy of the Ardanaiseig Restaurant, renowned for its inspired use of fresh produce from the Western Highlands. The wine list is magnificent. Artistic guests enjoy the famous 100-acre Ardanaiseig gardens and nature reserve, filled with exotic shrubs and trees brought back from the Himalayas over the years. Brilliant rhododendrons and azaleas add a riot of colour. The estate also offers fishing, boating, tennis and croquet (snooker in the evenings) and exhilarating hill or lochside walks.

Our inspector loved: *The feeling of complete escape.*

CAMERON HOUSE

LOCH LOMOND G83 8QZ

Set amidst 108 acres of beautiful countryside on the southern shores of Loch Lomond with views of Ben Lomond and beyond, this 5-star resort is the perfect destination for business and leisure travellers. Once the home of the illustrious Smollett family, Cameron House has been sympathetically restored to provide an elegant, timeless ambience. The bedrooms are luxuriously appointed, and the suites have four-poster beds and panoramic views over the loch. There are various dining options, including the elegant 3 AA Rosette Georgian Room Restaurant and the more informal Smolletts Restaurant, whilst traditional afternoon tea is served in the Drawing Room. Casual dining can be enjoyed in the stylish new Marina Restaurant and Bar, a contemporary restaurant centred around an open kitchen. Leisure facilities include a large lagoon-style swimming pool, sauna, steam room, Turkish bath and spa bath as well as gym, tennis, children's club, and a wide range of treatments offered at the Éspa health and beauty salon. There is golf on the "Wee Demon" 9-hole golf course, quad biking, clay pigeon shooting, and numerous water sports on the loch. The hotel's 46-foot luxury motor cruiser, the Celtic Warrior, can be hired for private cruises, weddings and other celebrations as well as small business meetings.

Our inspector loved: The great location in the heart of the Trossachs on the shore of Loch Lomond.

Directions: From Glasgow Airport, follow M8 towards Greenock, leave at jct 30, go over Erskine Toll Bridge. Join A82 towards Loch Lomond and Crianlarich. Approx 14 miles on, at Balloch roundabout, follow signs for Luss. Hotel is 1 mile on the right.

Isle of Mull
Oban
Dunoon
Campbelltown

Web: www.johansens.com/cameronhouse
E-mail: reservations@cameronhouse.co.uk
Tel: 0870 381 8588
International: +44 (0)1389 755565
Fax: 01389 759522

Price Guide:
single £175–£215
double/twin £242–£282
suite £380–£480

MV HEBRIDEAN PRINCESS

HEBRIDEAN ISLAND CRUISES, GRIFFIN HOUSE, BROUGHTON HALL, SKIPTON, NORTH YORKSHIRE BD23 3AN

Hebridean Princess offers its guests a truly relaxing experience with discreet and personal service, many returning time and again to enjoy the luxury of self-indulgence encouraged during a cruise. There are 20 differently themed cruises; most explore the Scottish Isles, some reach to the westernmost island of St Kilda and north to the Orkney and Shetland Islands. For 2004, Princess will also visit Troon for the Open golf championship. With no more than 49 guests on board, the atmosphere is one of a convivial house party. No formal events and entertainment programmes detract from the exclusivity of the cruise; on some evenings however, guests may dress formally for a gala dinner. Delicious cuisine and fine wines are enjoyed in the Columba Restaurant, where guests can marvel at the view gliding by. Every cruise offers 2 carefully planned shore visits most days from cultural to historical, energetic walks and bicycle rides to leisurely strolls along the beach. All food and drink including the wines from the Sommelier's house wine list, house spirits and beers are included in the price, as are the entrance fees to all castles, gardens and other attractions, also coach tours, bicycles and gym equipment.

Directions: Cruises mainly embark and disembark in Oban with a private coach from Glasgow airport and railway station.

Web: www.johansens.com/hebridean
E-mail: reservations@hebridean.co.uk
Tel: 0870 381 8746
International: +44 (0)1756 704704
Fax: 01756 704794

Price Guide: (7 nights, all inclusive per person)
single from £1,700
double/twin from £1,570
suite from £3,610

Our inspector loved: *The relaxed atmosphere of this immaculate "floating country house".*

AIRDS HOTEL

PORT APPIN, APPIN, ARGYLL PA38 4DF

Originally built as an 18th-century ferry inn for "those in passage" to Lismore Island, the Airds Hotel is situated in Port Appin with its loch-side walks and views across Loch Linnhe. The stunning scenery can be easily appreciated from the hotel as guests may request rooms with a view or relax and gaze at the loch and mountains beyond from the flower-filled conservatory. Each of the 12 bedrooms is individually decorated in a sophisticated country house style and comes complete with television, radio and private bathroom. Elsewhere, 2 comfortable lounges beckon with open log fires and large cosy sofas, the ideal setting for a pre-dinner drink, coffee, or a book or board game. Dinner is served in the light, airy non-smoking restaurant whose renowned reputation and 3 AA Rosettes precede it. With fresh ingredients being the key element, menus change daily and often feature wild salmon, seafood and Angus beef. Service in the dining room is impeccable yet friendly and informal, affording visitors breathtaking views whilst enjoying their meal. The Airds is well located for nearby places of interest such as Oban with its ferries to the Hebridean islands, Fort William and Ben Nevis and the awe-inspiring Glen Coe.

Our inspector loved: *The restaurant, which is so welcoming.*

Directions: The hotel is midway between Oban and Fort William on the A828. Follow signs for Port Appin and Lismore Ferry.

Isle of Mull
Oban
Dunoon
Campbelltown

Web: www.johansens.com/airds
E-mail: airds@airds-hotel.com
Tel: 0870 381 9168
International: +44 (0)1631 730236
Fax: 01631 730535

Price Guide:
(including dinner)
double/twin £224–£276
superior double £230–£300
suite £240–£336

STONEFIELD CASTLE

TARBERT, LOCH FYNE, ARGYLL PA29 6YJ

Directions: Take the A83, Stonefield Castle is less than 2 miles from Tarbert.

Web: www.johansens.com/stonefield
E-mail: enquiries@stonefieldcastle.co.uk
Tel: 0870 381 8918
International: +44 (0)1880 820836
Fax: 01880 820929

Price Guide:
single £85–£115
double/twin £170–£190
suite £230

Isle of Mull   Oban

Dunoon

Campbelltown

Nestled within 60 acres of its own woodland garden, Stonefield Castle stands high on the Kintyre peninsula overlooking the craggy Argyll coastline and Loch Fyne. Famed for their fisheries and smoke-houses this area has much to be proud of and guests sitting in the restaurant will have a heady combination of exemplary Scottish cuisine and the most spectacular scenery on the West Coast. The Castle was built in 1837 for a member of the famous Campbell clan and it stands today as a fine example of Scottish Baronial architecture, with long elegant windows, gothic turrets and imposing castellations. Each of its 33 bedrooms has been carefully designed to ensure that this period elegance is retained and indeed some of the original pieces of furniture remain in the hotel. The woodland gardens at Stonefield lure horticulturalists from far and wide to see its rare examples of exotic rhododendrons and shrubs. In fact Stonefield has the United Kingdom's second largest collection of Himalayan rhododendrons. The spectacular scenery of the local countryside makes this a stunning backdrop for summer walks or cosy autumn retreats.

Our inspector loved: *Some of the finest views and gardens in Scotland.*

WESTERN ISLES HOTEL

TOBERMORY, ISLE OF MULL, ARGYLLSHIRE PA75 6PR

With its warming, welcoming whiskies and log fire, delightful décor, elegant furnishings, superb scenic views and the cleanest of air to inhale this is a haven of relaxation, well-being and friendliness that welcomes guests time and time again. Built in 1883 for the proprietor of the Mish-Nish estate in Mull, Western Isles Hotel rises majestically against the skyline overlooking the beautiful Sound of Mull and Tobermory with its picturesque moorings. The view is considered one of the best in the Hebridean Islands and can be enjoyed from the hotel's sun-trap patio whilst taking afternoon tea or sipping an evening apéritif before delighting in superb cuisine served in the serenity of a classical dining room. The hotel has been host to the rich and famous and to many events in history. These range from use as a second world war allied H.Q. to the setting for films such as 'I Know Where I'm Going'. Western Isles Hotel has such charm, good taste, style, service and atmosphere that upon first entering its reception hall guests immediately feel as if they have stepped back to the elegance of a previous era. Guest rooms and the conservatory are particularly attractive and comfortable. This is an excellent base for exploring Mull and and a paradise for wildlife and birdlife enthusiasts. The island of Iona can be reached from Mull.

Our inspector loved: The views over Tobermory and the Sound of Mull: must be amongst the best in Scotland.

Directions: By ferry from Oban to Craignure, Lochaline to Fishnish or Kilchoan to Tobermory.

Web: www.johansens.com/westernisles
E-mail: wihotel@aol.com
Tel: 0870 381 8980
International: +44 (0)1688 302012
Fax: 01688 302297

Price Guide:
double £99–£134
master double £105–£147
suite £149–£216

BALCARY BAY HOTEL

AUCHENCAIRN, NR CASTLE DOUGLAS, DUMFRIES & GALLOWAY DG7 1QZ

Directions: Located off the A711 Dumfries–Kirkcudbright road, 2 miles out of Auchencairn on the Shore Road.

Web: www.johansens.com/balcarybay
E-mail: reservations@balcary-bay-hotel.co.uk
Tel: 0870 381 8334
International: +44 (0)1556 640217/640311
Fax: 01556 640272

Price Guide:
single £65
double/twin £115–£135

Enjoying a very warm climate due to its proximity to the Gulf Stream, Balcary Bay is one of Scotland's more romantic and secluded hideaways, yet only ½ hour from the bustling market town of Dumfries. As you sit in the lounge overlooking Balcary Bay, the calling of birds and the gently lapping waves compete for your attention. Guests will be greeted by genuine Scottish hospitality, which includes the provision of modern facilities with a traditional atmosphere, imaginatively prepared local delicacies such as lobsters, prawns and salmon, plus the reassuring intimacy of a family-run hotel. This hotel is a true haven for those wishing to get away from their hectic lives and an ideal break for a romantic weekend. This exciting corner of Scotland offers numerous great coastal and woodland walks, whilst nearby are several 9 and 18-hole golf courses at Colvend, Kirkcudbright, Castle Douglas, Southerness and Dumfries. There are also salmon rivers and trout lochs, sailing, shooting, riding and bird-watching facilities. The area abounds with National Trust historic properties and gardens. Seasonal short breaks and reduced inclusive rates are available for 3 and 7 night stays.

Our inspector loved: *The views from this hotel, which complete the feeling of total escape.*

374

CALLY PALACE HOTEL

GATEHOUSE OF FLEET, DUMFRIES & GALLOWAY DG7 2DL

Set in over 150 acres of forest and parkland, on the edge of Robert Burns country, this 18th-century country house has been restored to its former glory by the McMillan family, the proprietors since 1981. On entering the hotel, guests will initially be impressed by the grand scale of the interior. 2 huge marble pillars support the original moulded ceiling of the entrance hall. All the public rooms have ornate ceilings, original marble fireplaces and fine reproduction furniture. Combine these with grand, traditional Scottish cooking and you have a hotel par excellence. Awarded 1 Rosette for cuisine, Cally Palace offers a delightful dining experience enhanced by the atmospheric piano playing every evening. The 55 en-suite bedrooms have been individually decorated. Some are suites with a separate sitting room; others are large enough to accommodate a sitting area. An indoor leisure complex, completed in the style of the marble entrance hall, includes heated swimming pool, Jacuzzi, saunas and solarium. The hotel has an all-weather tennis court, a putting green, croquet and a lake. Also, for hotel guests' use only, is an 18-hole golf course, par 71, length 6,062 yards set around the lake in the grounds. Special weekend breaks are available out of season. Closed January and mid week in February.

Our inspector loved: The style and comfort of the hotel in a beautiful part of Scotland with golf on the doorstep.

Directions: 60 miles west of Carlisle, turn right off A75 from Gatehouse of Fleet. Hotel entrance on the left after approx 1 mile.

Web: www.johansens.com/callypalace
E-mail: info@callypalace.co.uk
Tel: 0870 381 8401
International: +44 (0)1557 814341
Fax: 01557 814522

Price Guide: (including dinner)
single £88–£134
double/twin £166–£190
(minimum stay 2 nights)

KIRROUGHTREE HOUSE

NEWTON STEWART, WIGTOWNSHIRE DG8 6AN

Directions: The hotel entrance is situated on the A712 Newton Stewart - New Galloway road approx 250 metres on the left from the junction with the A75 Dumfries/Stranrear road.

Web: www.johansens.com/kirroughtreehouse
E-mail: info@kirroughtreehouse.co.uk
Tel: 0870 381 8659
International: +44 (0)1671 402141
Fax: 01671 402425

Price Guide:
single £80–£113
double/twin £140–£160
suite £180–£200

A previous winner of the Johansens Most Excellent Service Award and the Good Hotel Guide's Scottish Hotel of the Year, Kirroughtree House is situated in the foothills of the Cairnsmore of Fleet, on the edge of Galloway Forest Park. Standing in 8 acres of landscaped gardens, guests can relax and linger over the spectacular views. Built by the Heron family in 1719, the oak-panelled lounge, with open fireplace, reflects the style of that period. From the lounge rises the original staircase, where Robert Burns often recited his poems. Each bedroom is well furnished; guests may choose to spend the night in one of the hotel's spacious de luxe bedrooms with spectacular views over the surrounding countryside. Many guests are attracted by Kirroughtree's culinary reputation, awarded 2 AA rosettes – only the finest produce is used to create meals of originality and finesse. An ideal venue for small meetings, family parties and weddings; exclusive use of the hotel can be arranged. Pitch and putt and croquet can be enjoyed in the grounds and the hotel's position makes it an ideal base for great walking expeditions. Residents can play golf on the many local courses and also have use of the exclusive 18-hole course at Cally Palace. Trout and salmon fishing, shooting and deer stalking during the season can all be organised. Short breaks available. Closed 3 January to mid February.

Our inspector loved: *The classic elegance of this beautiful hotel.*

KNOCKINAAM LODGE

PORTPATRICK, WIGTOWNSHIRE DG9 9AD

With an unsurpassed tradition of quality and excellence, Knockinaam Lodge has the reputation of being one of Scotland's finest hotels. Surrounded by woods, hills and magnificent unspoilt countryside, this beautiful country house displays traditional elegance and charm. Inside there is a wonderful welcoming atmosphere, enhanced by stunning arrangements of fresh flowers, soft lighting and extremely friendly staff. The large secluded grounds include immaculate lawns and gardens that stretch all the way down to the hotel's own private beach. Guests can relax and enjoy the soothing sound of rolling waves or the tuneful accompaniment of birds creating a sense of harmonious serenity. The hotel's 3-Rosetted restaurant uses fresh and local ingredients for its delicious contemporary French cuisine with an eclectic twist. There is an extensive international wine list, which boasts some outstanding top vintages. After dinner, the perfect place for a nightcap is the cosy wood-panelled bar with roaring log fire, where guests will have difficulty in choosing from the impressive collection of 160 whiskies. The bedrooms are sunny, warm and comfortable with emphasis on stylish décor and luxury.

Our inspector loved: The great views and feeling of privacy within the hotel.

Directions: From the A77 follow signs to Portpatrick. Turn left at the Knockinaam sign, 2 miles west of Lochans and continue past Smokehouse. The lodge is approximately 3 miles along this road.

Web: www.johansens.com/knockinaam
E-mail: reservations@knockinaamlodge.com
Tel: 0870 381 9166
International: +44 (0)1776 810471
Fax: 01776 810435

Moffat

Stranraer

Dumfries

Price Guide:
single £125–£145
double/twin £190–£270
master £260–£340

THE BONHAM

35 DRUMSHEUGH GARDENS, EDINBURGH EH3 7RN

Directions: The Hotel is situated in the city's West End.

Web: www.johansens.com/bonham
E-mail: reserve@thebonham.com
Tel: 0870 381 8373
International: +44 (0)131 623 6060
Fax: 0131 226 6080

Price Guide:
single: £105–£165
double/twin £127–£195
suprior double/twin £168–£245
suites £247–£335

This award-winning, boutique-style hotel is situated just a few minutes walk from the West End of Edinburgh and is equally suitable for a restful weekend or a high-intensity business trip. Many of the original Victorian features of the 3 converted town houses have been maintained. The interior has been designed to create a contemporary ambience within the classic timelessness of a Victorian town house. Each room has been elegantly and dramatically created with modern furniture and art, using rich, bold colours to produce tasteful oversized abundance throughout. The Bonham promises to offer a traditional feel with a modern twist, coupled with impeccable standards and individuality. Purely for pleasure, each of the 48 bedrooms offers 55 channel cable TV, a mini-bar and e-TV, which provides a complete PC capability, Internet and E-mail access as well as DVD video and CD player. The Events Room is a perfect setting for a range of select meetings and private dining. Restaurant at The Bonham, the most timeless contemporary restaurant in Edinburgh, serves distinct European inspired cuisine which is complemented by provocative wines. Along with its famous castle and numerous shops, Edinburgh houses Scotland's national galleries and some splendid museums.

Our inspector loved: *The design and décor which have blended the new with the old so well.*

BRUNTSFIELD HOTEL

69 BRUNTSFIELD PLACE, EDINBURGH EH10 4HH

This elegant Victorian town house first became a hotel in the 1920s and has maintained a reputation for its special charm and character ever since. Located just a few minutes from the hustle and bustle of the city centre, guests arriving here will relish the peace and tranquillity of its setting overlooking the leafy Bruntsfield Links, one of Edinburgh's oldest golfing areas and now an elegant park. The traditional Victorian architecture is mirrored inside the building with carefully decorated bedrooms and lounges to ensure that a welcoming ambience of warmth and comfort is maintained throughout the hotel. Many of the 73 carefully appointed bedrooms have delightful views, either of the Links or Edinburgh Castle and beyond towards the Old Town; there are also a number of larger rooms with four-poster beds. The hotel offers 2 dining settings: the restaurant with its brasserie-style atmosphere and conservatory, which serves an award-winning selection of freshly prepared dishes using local produce, and the less formal Kings Bar, a popular meeting place which is open all day for drinks, light meals, snacks and coffees. Bruntsfield Hotel is the ideal base from which to explore the vibrant and cosmopolitan Scottish capital with its excellent shopping, wonderful historic sites and many festivals.

Directions: Join the A702 city bypass, exit at Lothianburn to Bruntsfield Place. The hotel overlooks Bruntsfield Links Park.

Web: www.johansens.com/bruntsfield
E-mail: sales@thebruntsfield.co.uk
Tel: 0870 381 8388
International: +44 (0)131 229 1393
Fax: 0131 229 5634

Price Guide:
single £79-£120
double/twin £120-£250

Our inspector loved: The relaxed and comfortable dining options.

CHANNINGS

15 SOUTH LEARMONTH GARDENS, EDINBURGH EH4 1EZ

Directions: Go north-west from Queensferry Street, over Dean Bridge on to Queensferry Road. Take the 3rd turning on the right down South Learmonth Avenue, then turn right at the end into South Learmonth Gardens.

Web: www.johansens.com/channings
E-mail: reserve@channings.co.uk
Tel: 0870 381 8413
International: +44 (0)131 332 3232
Fax: 0131 332 9631

Price Guide:
single £100–£155
double/twin £131–£225
four poster/suite £157–£260

Channings is located on a quiet cobbled street only 10 minutes' walk from the centre of Edinburgh, with easy access to the shops on Princes Street and the timeless grandeur of Edinburgh Castle. The hotel, Formerly 5 Edwardian town houses, retains its original features, which have been restored with flair and consideration, and the atmosphere is like that of an exclusive country club. With an ambience of country-style tranquillity, guests can relax in one of the lounges with coffee or afternoon tea served by the friendliest of staff. For those who like to browse, the hotel has an interesting collection of antique prints, furniture, objets d'art, periodicals and books. The atmosphere is perfect for discreet company meetings, small conferences and private or corporate events, which may be held. These may be held in the oak-panelled Library or Kingsleigh. Fine dining at Channings can be experienced in the exclusive Channings Restaurant which boasts distinctive food in a warm and welcoming ambience. Alternatively, Ochre Vita is a delight with its vibrant and flavoursome Mediterranean food and wines.

Our inspector loved: *The location; as close to the centre as you can get yet still overlooking green grass.*

THE EDINBURGH RESIDENCE

7 ROTHESAY TERRACE, EDINBURGH EH3 7RY, SCOTLAND

Space, luxury, privacy and convenience can be enjoyed at this stylish, grey-stone venue situated in Edinburgh's West End, just a short stroll from the city's main shopping area and attractions. With its central yet peaceful location, The Edinburgh Residence consists of 29 superbly equipped suites in a row of 3 terraced town houses. These comprise classic suites, 3 with their own private entrance, grand suites and 8 apartments whose average floor area is approximately the size of a tennis court. Each is tastefully and comfortably furnished, beautifully appointed and has every modern facility, including crockery and discreetly stored microwave oven. The spacious bathrooms are particularly delightful; some have a traditional roll-top bath, others offer a Jacuzzi big enough for 2. There is wood panelling and sweeping staircases throughout, a splendid Georgian morning room and an elegant drawing room where visitors can relax with a drink from the honesty bar and take in the stunning views over Edinburgh and beyond. There is no dining room, but 24-hour room service is available, and just a short walk away is the Residence's sister restaurant, The Bonham, whose European-inspired cuisine has earned it a high reputation. Small private or corporate events can be accommodated.

Our inspector loved: This stylish and relaxed alternative to a traditional hotel; great service with great style.

Directions: From the West End of Princes Street continue towards Shandwich Place and turn right into Palmerston Place then take the first left into Rothesay Terrace.

Web: www.johansens.com/edinburghres
E-mail: reserve@theedinburghresidence.com
Tel: 0870 381 8913
International: +44 (0)131 622 5080
Fax: 0131 2263381

Price Guide:
Classic suite single £112–£150
classic suite £120–£200
grand suite £195–£265
town house apartment £260–£395

THE GLASSHOUSE

2 GREENSIDE PLACE, EDINBURGH EH1 3AA

With the façade of the 150-year-old Lady Glenorchy Church set against the modern glass architecture of this stunning contemporary and original hotel, The Glasshouse is a harmonious combination of tradition and imagination. In the bedrooms, warm colours combine with striking interior design and innovative use of space. Floor-to-ceiling windows create a feeling of light and tranquillity, which is complemented by the luxurious de luxe bathrooms with their contemporary glass fittings. Many of the rooms have a large patio terrace overlooking the private rooftop garden, which has unusual garden furniture and panoramic views over the City or Calton Hill folly. Attention to detail such as complimentary shoe shine, fresh fruit, Frette Egyptian cotton sheets, wonderfully opulent toiletries and state-of-the art facilities contribute to a most comfortable stay. The hotel is next door to the Playhouse and is only a few steps from Edinburgh Castle and Princes Street. Guests can view the latest artwork by local Edinburgh artists on display in the hotel's gallery.

Directions: The Glasshouse Hotel is located on Greenside Place, just off Princes Street. The nearest station is Waverley station.

Web: www.johansens.com/glasshouse
E-mail: resglasshouse@theetoncollection.com
Tel: 0870 381 8559
International: +44 (0)131 525 8200
Fax: 0131 525 8205

Price Guide:
double/twin £170–£225
suite £295–£375

Our inspector loved: *The amazing blend of contemporary style in a classic setting.*

THE HOWARD

34 GREAT KING STREET, EDINBURGH EH3 6QH

Situated in the heart of Edinburgh this 5-star Hotel, originally built as a private house, ensures that each guest is made to feel special and experiences traditional Georgian pampering as if a guest in a private home. Visitors take a step back in time when staying at The Howard where attention to detail and the "personal touch" is of paramount importance. A dedicated butler is on hand to tend to guests' every needs from unpacking bags to serving afternoon tea, and will even arrange a social itinerary for exploring nearby Edinburgh where chic designer boutiques are just 7 minutes' walk away in George Street and connections by train and Edinburgh airport are close by. Some of the 18 individually decorated bedrooms boast freestanding roll-top baths, Jacuzzi and power and double showers and 3 exclusive suites have their very own terraced gardens and private entrances. 24-hour room service is available and dinner may be served in the comfort of guests' own rooms, by their personal butler, from the à la carte menu. Alternatively, "Dining at The Atholl" is an unforgettable experience where the dedicated team of chefs serve meticulously prepared cuisine. The Howard offers an elegant Georgian setting ideal for personal entertaining and private corporate gatherings.

Our inspector loved: *The timeless elegance, peace and quiet in one of Edinburgh's smartest streets.*

Directions: From Queen Street turn north into Dundas Street, then take the third right into Great King Street. The Hotel is on the left.

Web: www.johansens.com/howardedinburgh
E-mail: reserve@thehoward.com
Tel: 0870 381 8626
International: +44 (0)131 315 2220
Fax: 0131 557 6515

Price Guide:
single £108–£210
double/twin £180–£275
suite £243–£395
grand suite £356–£475

THE ROXBURGHE

38 CHARLOTTE SQUARE, EDINBURGH EH2 4HG

Directions: The hotel is 5 minutes from Waverley Station and 20 minutes from Edinburgh Airport.

Web: www.johansens.com/roxburgheedinburgh
E-mail: roxburghe@csmm.co.uk
Tel: 0870 381 8872
International: +44 (0)131 240 5500
Fax: 0131 240 5555

Price Guide:
single £145
double/twin £170
suite £270

Offering some of the finest Georgian architecture in Scotland, this hotel provides an ideal base from which to explore the city of Edinburgh. Having undergone an extensive period of renovation in 1999, The Roxburghe has added a distinctly modern wing, carefully designed to complement the Georgian architecture of Adam's original terraced houses. Overlooking Charlotte Square, the classic rooms retain fine period detailing. The rooms in the modern wing are held in contemporary design, with an open aspect across the handsome George Street. The south-facing rooms on the top floor have stunning views across the rooftops to Edinburgh Castle. The Roxburghe's Rosette awarded restaurant is situated in a beautiful Georgian drawing room overlooking Charlotte Square. The cuisine is a blend of classical British style with the best flavours of the world beyond, complemented by a selection of wines from both the Old and New Worlds. The fitness facilities include a pool, fitness centre, sauna, steam room and solarium. Many rooms are suitable for conference and meeting purposes. Special packages include 2 to 5 day beauty breaks with massages and facial treatments. George Street, Prince's Street and Edinburgh Castle are all within easy walking distance.

Our inspector loved: *The relaxing lounges overlooking Edinburgh's Charlotte Square.*

ONE DEVONSHIRE GARDENS

1 DEVONSHIRE GARDENS, GLASGOW, G12 0UX

Within the heart of Glasgow's West End, One Devonshire Gardens is proud to maintain its reputation as the ultimate in comfort and individuality. The grandeur of a bygone era is created as guests are welcomed into the entrance hall with its impressive staircase. A tranquil ambience pervades the hotel where large cosy sofas, dim lighting and roaring fires are regular features. All the en-suite bedrooms are individually and tastefully furnished and 24-hour room service is available. One Devonshire Gardens boasts Scotland's only 3 Michelin-starred chef, Gordon Ramsay, whose amazing cuisine can be sampled in the Amaryllis Restaurant. Alternatively, the House Five Restaurant provides fine dining where the chef is willing to create requested dishes complemented by the extensive wine list, which includes the best modern traditions of Europe, the New World and Southern Hemisphere. The hotel's professional conference team is on hand to help organise any event and ensure its success. Glasgow offers many cultural and interesting attractions and there is an abundance of theatres, concert halls, golf courses and numerous museums to visit. The hotel is happy to plan an itinerary of the local sites.

Directions: From the M8 take junction 17 and follow signs for the A82 Dumbarton/Kelvinside (Great Western Road).

Web: www.johansens.com/onedevonshire
E-mail: info@onedevonshiregardens.com
Tel: 0870 381 9146
International: +44 (0)141 3392001
Fax: 0141 3371663

Dumbarton
Greenock
Johnstone
Glasgow

Price Guide:
continental breakfast £11
full Scottish breakfast £15
single/double £125-£275
town house suite £345-£475

Our inspector loved: *The classic style of this beautiful town house hotel.*

ROYAL MARINE HOTEL

GOLF ROAD, BRORA, SUTHERLAND KW9 6QS

Directions: One hour's drive from Inverness. Travel north on the A9, signposted Wick. In Brora cross bridge turn right and the hotel is 100 yards on the left.

Web: www.johansens.com/royalmarine
E-mail: info@highlandescape.com
Tel: 0870 381 9133
International: +44 (0)1408 621252
Fax: 01408 621181

Price Guide:
single £75
double £110-£150

Overlooking the mouth of River Brora, the Royal Marine, designed by Sir Robert Lorimer in 1913, has undergone great restoration to its original antique furniture, woodwork and panelling. Passing under the wooden arches of the entrance hall and ascending the grand staircase, guests step back in time to refined living of a bygone era. All 22 en suite bedrooms offer modern comfort whilst retaining the ambience of early 20th century elegance. Scottish cuisine is served in the Sir Robert Lorimer Dining Room where fresh seafood, local salmon, meat and game, are all on the menu, complemented by a varied wine list. Less formal meals are taken in the Hunter's Lounge where a fine selection of malt whiskies can be sampled and the Garden Room Café Bar in The Dolphin Leisure Centre also serves lighter snacks all day. The Leisure Centre features an indoor swimming pool, gymnasium, sauna, steam room and Jacuzzi. There are several golf courses nearby, including the Royal Dunoch and the Brora Championship course is just a 1 minute walk from the hotel. Sea angling, walking and hawking expeditions can all be arranged. The hotel maintains 2 fishing boats on Loch Brora, which are available for hire. A unique facility to the hotel is its four lane curling rink, which is open from October-March.

Our inspector loved: *This very traditional hotel with excellent facilities and great golf on the doorstep.*

NEW

THE ROYAL GOLF HOTEL

THE 1ST TEE, DORNOCH, HIGHLAND IV25 3LG

This handsome sandstone building has recently seen an altogether tasteful renovation, however the focus ultimately remains on golf and its location on the 1st tee of the Royal Dornoch Golf Club lends itself perfectly. Indeed many famous names including Nick Faldo, Tom Watson and Ben Crenshaw have raved about the world's second oldest Links course, established in the 16th century. 20 Highlands courses are within an hour's drive of Dornoch, and include other championship courses such as Nairn, or more hidden gems such as Brora, Golspie or Nairn Dunbar. The hotel is happy to take care of golfing arrangements, from tuition to personalised itineraries. Bedrooms – no two of which are identical – are comfortable, and furnished in a blend of the traditional and contemporary. Dining is available in the informal Conservatory with its views across the golf course and the Dornoch Firth, or the fine main restaurant, which serves the freshest local game, seafood, beef and lamb. The Tom Morris Bar features real log fires and the Malt Whisky Wall with an array of over 100 unusual malts. Nearby activities include birdwatching, fishing and hillwalking. Places of interest include Dunrobin Castle, Skibo Castle, Glenmorangie Distillery and "Harrods" of the north at the falls of Shin.

Our inspector loved: The majestic location of this stylish, revamped hotel.

Directions: Enter the town from the A4 and travel up the hill, across the cross roads and past the police station. The hotel is 200 yards on the right.

Web: www.johansens.com/royalgolf
E-mail: rooms@morton-hotels.com
Tel: 0870 381 9199
International: +44 (0)1667 458800
Fax: 01667 458818

Price Guide:
(dinner £26)
single £92-£113
double £114-£216
suite £209-£266

John O'Groats

Portree

Inverness

Fort William

MUCKRACH LODGE HOTEL & RESTAURANT

DULNAIN BRIDGE, BY GRANTOWN-ON-SPEY, INVERNESS-SHIRE PH26 3LY

Directions: Muckrach Lodge is 3 miles South West of Grantown-on-Spey on the B9102 and A95, through Dulnain Bridge Village on the A938.

Web: www.johansens.com/muckrachlodge
E-mail: stay@muckrach.co.uk
Tel: 0870 381 8751
International: +44 (0)1479 851257
Fax: 01479 851325

Price Guide:
single £60–£90
double/twin £120–£150

Set in 10 acres of landscaped grounds and surrounded by woods and estate, this former sporting lodge, Muckrach, has a relaxed and informal ambience with an awe-inspiring backdrop of the surrounding Cairngorm Mountains, the River Spey and a 16th-century castle. Quality of service is paramount in this relaxing hotel, where a comfortable atmosphere has been lovingly created with plump sofas, log fires and fresh flowers. The finest quality ingredients are served in the hotel's excellent restaurant, which offers fresh fish and superb Scottish beef, complemented by a distinguished wine cellar and rare malts. There is a large selection of books, magazines and games to enjoy by the fireside or for the more energetic, the beautiful National Park offers stunning heather moors, ancient forests and sparkling rivers and lochs. Muckrach Lodge is the ideal base for touring the Highlands, Loch Ness, Inverness and the picturesque Morayshire coastal villages. The Malt Whisky and Castle Trails are extremely interesting and Strathspey's turbulent history can be discovered by visiting the area's cathedrals, forts and museums. Nearby there are galleries, antiques, bird watching and superb golf with Royal Dornoch, Nairn, Boat of Garten and others. Alternatively climbing and watersport activities are available.

Our inspector loved: *The relaxed style and the abscence of pretentiousness.*

BUNCHREW HOUSE HOTEL

INVERNESS, SCOTLAND IV3 8TA

This splendid 17th-century Scottish mansion, "Hotel on the Shore", is set amidst 20 acres of landscaped gardens and woodlands on the shores of the Beauly Firth. Guests can enjoy breathtaking views of Ben Wyvis and the Black Isle, while just yards from the house the sea laps at the garden walls. Bunchrew has been carefully restored to preserve its heritage, whilst still giving its guests the highest standards of comfort and convenience. A continual schedule of refurbishment is on-going. The bedrooms are beautifully furnished and decorated to enhance their natural features. The elegant panelled drawing room is the ideal place to relax at any time, and during winter log fires lend it an added appeal which has given the hotel 4-star status. In the candle-lit restaurant the traditional cuisine includes prime Scottish beef, fresh lobster and langoustines, locally caught game and venison and freshly grown vegetables which has been rewarded with 2 AA Rosettes. A carefully chosen wine list complements the menu. Local places of interest include Cawdor Castle, Loch Ness, Castle Urquhart and a number of beautiful glens. For those who enjoy sport there is skiing at nearby Aviemore, sailing, cruising, golf, shooting and fishing.

Our inspector loved: The cosy charm and splendid shore location.

Directions: From Inverness follow signs to Beauly, Dingwall on the A862. One mile from the outskirts of Inverness the entrance to Bunchrew House is on the right

John O'Groats

Portree

Inverness

Fort William

Web: www.johansens.com/bunchrewhouse
E-mail: welcome@bunchrew–inverness.co.uk
Tel: 0870 381 8393
International: +44 (0)1463 234917
Fax: 01463 710620

Price Guide:
single £85–£145
double/twin £150–£199

NEW

GLEN MHOR HOTEL

9-12 NESS BANK, INVERNESS IV2 4SG

Directions: Opposite the Eden Court Theatre, the hotel is best approached from Bank Street, straight across the crossroads on north side of the bridge.

Web: www.johansens.com/glenmhor
E-mail: glenmhorhotel@btconnect.com
Tel: 0870 381 8407
International: +44 (0)1463 234308
Fax: 01463 713170

Price Guide:
single £59-£85
double £88-£120
junior suite £120-£150
suite £140-£160

John O'Groats

Portree

Inverness

Fort William

This well-established family business is situated in a quiet location on the River Ness. Dapper owner, Nico Manson, runs the hotel along with his wife and son, while his son-in-law is the chef. The traditional and modern cuisine of the classic Nico's by the River restaurant is long renowned, where specialities include local seafood, salmon, lamb, beef and game in season. The less formal Bistro & Wine Bar, a genuine Victorian Oak Room, serves local and international dishes in a relaxed, tavern style, and offers an extensive wine list. Al fresco dining on the terrace is available, weather permitting. Finally, Nicky Tams, a former baker's stables complete with log fire, provides a wide range of pure malt whiskies along with a cheery lounge bar atmosphere. All of the en-suite bedrooms are tidy and well furnished with individual heating, direct dial telephones and televisions, and some have river views. A number of the guest rooms are housed in the adjacent cottage-annexe, a charming riverside building. The hotel is a short walk from the town centre, and Inverness itself is ideally located for golf and fishing, which the Glen Mhor is happy to arrange on guests' behalf.

Our inspector loved: *This traditional hotel offering informal or more formal dining at great value.*

THE GLENMORISTON TOWN HOUSE HOTEL & LA RIVIERA RESTAURANT

NESS BANK, INVERNESS IV2 4SF

In the heart of the magnificent Scottish Highlands and a short walk from the town centre, the delightful award-winning Glenmoriston Hotel, with its breathtaking views, is superbly located on the banks of the River Ness. Totally refurbished, this hotel has been designed with a strong Italian influence and exudes a wonderful sense of warmth and serenity. Sumptuous fabrics and luxurious comfort create an atmosphere of quiet elegance in the cosy public areas and in contrast, the light infused conservatory is an oasis of peace, perfect for relaxing whilst enjoying a coffee or a delicious light lunch. Individually designed bedrooms are stylishly decorated with spacious bathrooms and offer all modern facilities. The mouth-watering cuisine, which consists of quality local produce, twinned with a Tuscan flair, is served in the traditional La Riviera Restaurant or the more contemporary surroundings of La Terrazza. The menu is complemented by a wide selection of excellent wines. Fully-equipped business and group facilities are available. Glenmoriston is an ideal base for exploring the Scottish Highlands and Inverness's shopping and theatre districts.

Our inspector loved: This stylish refurbishment – how fitting for the new city of Inverness to be home to this tasteful hotel.

Directions: On the opposite side of the river to the Eden Court Theatre, the Hotel is best approached from Bank St, straight across the crossroads on the north side of the bridge.

Web: www.johansens.com/glenmoriston
E-mail: glenmoriston@cali.co.uk
Tel: 0870 381 8555
International: +44 (0)1463 223777
Fax: 01463 712378

Price Guide:
single £85–£105
double/twin £95–£135

CULLODEN HOUSE

CULLODEN, INVERNESS, INVERNESS-SHIRE IV2 7BZ

Directions: Leave Inverness on the A96 towards Aberdeen and take the turn off to Culloden.

Web: www.johansens.com/cullodenhouseinverness
E-mail: info@cullodenhouse.co.uk
Tel: 0870 381 9137
International: +44 (0)1463 790461
Fax: 01463 792181

Price Guide:
single £155–£189
double £199–£249
suite £249–£279

A majestic circular drive leads to the splendour of this handsome Georgian mansion, battle headquarters of Bonnie Prince Charlie 253 years ago. 3 miles from Inverness, this handsome Palladian country house stands in 40 acres of beautiful gardens and peaceful parkland roamed by roe deer. Princes past and present and guests from throughout the world have enjoyed the hotel's ambience and hospitality. Rich furnishings, sparkling chandeliers, impressive Adam fireplaces and ornate plaster reliefs add to the grandness of the hotel's luxurious, high-ceilinged rooms. The bedrooms are appointed to the highest standard, many having four-poster beds and Jacuzzis. 4 non-smoking suites are in the Pavilion Annex, which overlooks a three acre walled garden and 2 in the West Pavilion. In the Dining Room guests can savour superb cuisine prepared by chef Michael Simpson, who trained at Gleneagles Hotel and the Hamburg Conference Centre. There is an outdoor tennis court and indoor sauna. Shooting, fishing and pony-trekking can be arranged, while nearby are Cawdor Castle, the Clava Cairns Bronze Age burial ground and Culloden battlefield. AA 4 stars and 2 Rosettes, Scottish Tourist Board 4 stars. From the USA Toll Free Fax/Phone 0800 980 4561.

John O'Groats
Portree
Inverness
Fort William

Our inspector loved: The elegant exterior and great comfort and service once inside.

CUILLIN HILLS HOTEL

PORTREE, ISLE OF SKYE IV51 9QU

Spectacular views of the majestic Cuillin Mountains and Portree Bay on the beautiful Isle of Skye make this hotel the perfect choice for any discerning visitor. Originally built in the 1870s as a hunting lodge, Cuillin Hills Hotel benefits from 15 acres of private mature grounds, which create a secluded setting and tranquil atmosphere. Quality and comfort is a priority, reflected in the beautiful furniture and décor of the lounge, where guests can relax in front of the log fire and sample the extensive choice of malt whiskys. Spacious bedrooms are elegantly furnished and decorated to the highest standard with all modern conveniences. Imaginative and traditional cuisine combine to create award-winning delights, which are served in the stylish restaurant overlooking the bay. Guests may feast on highland game, lobster, scallops and other deliciously fresh local produce as well as tasty homemade desserts. An interesting selection of informal meals is served in the bar. The island's rich history can be discovered through its castles, museums and visitor centres. There is an abundance of beautiful unspoilt coastal paths and woodland walks nearby. The town of Portree is a mere 10 minutes' walk away.

Our inspector loved: The considerable investment recently has lifted the rooms to a higher level and bathrooms are state of the art.

Directions: Skye can be reached by bridge from Kyle of Localsh or by ferry from Mallaig or Glenelg. From Portree take the A855 to Staffin. After ½ mile take the road to Budhmor.

Web: www.johansens.com/cuillinhills
E-mail: office@cuillinhills.demon.co.uk
Tel: 0870 381 8467
International: +44 (0)1478 612003
Fax: 01478 613092

Price Guide:
single £50–£105
double/twin £100–£210

NEW

THE GOLF VIEW HOTEL & LEISURE CLUB

THE SEAFRONT, NAIRN, BY INVERNESS IV12 4HD

This well kept and appointed 4-star hotel has seen much re-investment recently, and its tasteful, individually designed bedrooms offer great comfort and modern facilities such as DVD players and satellite television. Many overlook the Moray Firth, some have romantic four-poster beds and spa baths, and family units come equipped with integral bunk rooms and games consoles. A selection of menus is served in the informal conservatory and the restaurant, both of which take full advantage of the excellent local produce such as lamb, venison and salmon. Guests can swim in the pool, work out in the gymnasium or enjoy a pampering beauty treatment. There are also outdoor tennis courts, and the hotel has mountain bikes available for hire. Excellent nearby beaches offer perfect spots for bathing, relaxing, and leisurely walks along the seafront. Golfers are spoilt for choice, with 2 championship courses in town and 20 courses within easy driving distance. The closest is Nairn Golf Course, established in 1897 and host to the Walker Cup in 1999. Elsewhere, places of interest include the historic Cawdor Castle, Culloden Battlefield and Fort George, Urquhart Castle and the infamous Loch Ness. Many festivals such as the Nairn Highland Games are held throughout the year.

Directions: Driving through the town on the A96, the hotel is signposted off the main road, down Seabank Road.

Web: www.johansens.com/golfview
E-mail: rooms@morton-hotels.com
Tel: 0870 381 8404
International: +44 (0)1667 458800
Fax: 01667 458818

Price Guide: (dinner £26)
single £92-£113
double £114-£216
suite £209-£266

John O'Groats

Portree

Inverness

Fort William

Our inspector loved: This compact, tasteful hotel with its splendid leisure facilities and wonderful views over the Moray Firth.

      SPA

LOCH TORRIDON COUNTRY HOUSE HOTEL

TORRIDON, BY ACHNASHEEN, WESTER-ROSS IV22 2EY

Loch Torridon is gloriously situated at the foot of wooded mountains on the shores of the loch from which it derives its name. Built as a shooting lodge for the first Earl of Lovelace in 1887, in a 58-acre estate containing formal gardens, mature trees and resident Highland cattle. Today, Daniel and Rohaise Rose-Bristow welcome guests into their home offering the best in Highland hospitality. Awarded Top 200 status in the AA and 3 Red Stars, the hotel has 19 bedrooms which are luxuriously decorated. The Victorian kitchen garden provides chef, Kevin Broome, with fresh herbs, salad and a variety of fruits and vegetables. Dinner is served from 7pm - 8.45pm where an extensive fine dining table d'hôte menu is offered. Guests may begin with white bean and barley slice, wrapped in home cured wild sea salmon with garden beetroot and Marjoram fondue followed by roast fillet and braised aromatic belly free-range Highland pork, chickpea and olive casserole, shallot mash, jus of pork. Providing a seasonal alternative, dinner is also served in the more informal Ben Damph Bar and Restaurant with rooms where alternative accommodation is available. Outdoor pursuits: archery; mountain biking; clay pigeon shooting; a huge choice of low and high level walks; boating; fishing; and the opportunity to watch otters, seals and whales.

Our inspector loved: *The highly appropriate hotel legend, "where spirits soar and eagles fly."*

Directions: The hotel is 10 miles from Kinlochewe on the A896. Do not turn off to Torridon village.

Web: www.johansens.com/lochtorridon
E-mail: enquiries@lochtorridonhotel.com
Tel: 0870 381 9136
International: +44 (0)1445 791242
Fax: 01445 791296

Price Guide:
single £60–£104
double/twin £97–£242
master suite £192-£315

DALHOUSIE CASTLE AND SPA

NR EDINBURGH, BONNYRIGG EH19 3JB

For over 700 years Dalhousie Castle has nestled in beautiful parkland, providing warm Scottish hospitality. There are fascinating reminders of a rich and turbulent history, such as the 2 AA Rosette Vaulted Dungeon Restaurant; a delightful setting in which to enjoy classical French and traditional Scottish "Castle Cuisine". 14 of the 27 Castle bedrooms are historically themed and include the James VI, Mary Queen of Scots, Robert the Bruce and William Wallace. The "de Ramseia" suite houses the 500-year-old "Well". There are also 6 en-suite bedrooms in the 100-year-old Lodge. 5 carefully renovated function rooms provide a unique setting for conferences for up to 120 delegates, banquets and weddings for up to 100 guests. Extensive parking and a helipad are on site. Dalhousie Castle is only 7 miles from Edinburgh city centre and just 14 miles from the International Airport. The Castle has a Scottish Tourist Board 4 Star classification and is Taste of Scotland approved. The new Aqueous Spa includes a hydro pool, Laconium, Ottoman and treatment rooms. The Orangery Restaurant offers contemporary Scottish/European dining. Activities including falconry and clay pigeon shooting can be arranged given prior notice as well as golf at nearby courses.

Directions: From Edinburgh A7 south, through Newtongrange. Turn right at the junction onto B704, hotel is ¾ mile.

Web: www.johansens.com/dalhousiecastle
E-mail: info@dalhousiecastle.co.uk
Tel: 0870 381 8472
International: +44 (0)1875 820153
Fax: 01875 821936

Price Guide:
single £95–£140
double £125–£305

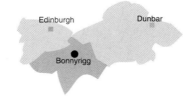

Our inspector loved: The contrast between lunch in the bright, modern conservatory and dinner in the dungeon restaurant.

    SPA

BORTHWICK CASTLE

BORTHWICK, NORTH MIDDLETON, MIDLOTHIAN EH23 4QY

To the south of Edinburgh, off the A7, stands historic Borthwick Castle Hotel, a 20-minute drive from Scotland's capital. Built in 1430 by the Borthwick family, this ancient stronghold has witnessed many of the great events of Scotland's history at first hand. Notably, the safe keeping of Mary Queen of Scots following her wedding to the Earl of Bothwell and a forceful visitation by Oliver Cromwell in 1650. At Borthwick Castle there are 10 bedchambers, each with en-suite facilities and 6 with four-poster beds. In the evening, guests dine in the magnificent setting of the candle-lit Great Hall where a 4-course set menu is prepared by the chef. The cooking is traditional Scottish, serving fresh local produce. A comprehensive wine list is complemented by a fine selection of malt whiskies. While the castle caters for banquets of up to 65 guests, it especially welcomes those in search of that intimate dinner for 2. In either case, the experience is unforgettable. Open from March to January 3rd.

Our inspector loved: *The magical high ceilings in the Great Hall with its roaring fire.*

Directions: 12 miles south of Edinburgh on the A7. At North Middleton, follow signs for Borthwick. A private road then leads to the castle.

Web: www.johansens.com/borthwickcastle
E-mail: borthwickcastle@hotmail.com
Tel: 0870 381 8376
International: +44 (0)1875 820514
Fax: 01875 821702

Price Guide:
single £80–£100
double/twin £135–£195

KNOCKOMIE HOTEL

GRANTOWN ROAD, FORRES, MORAYSHIRE IV36 2SG

Directions: Knockomie Hotel is located 1 mile south of Forres on the A940 to Grantown on Spey.

Web: www.johansens.com/knockomiehotel
E-mail: stay@knockomie.co.uk
Tel: 0870 381 8663
International: +44 (0)1309 673146
Fax: 01309 673290

Elgin

Keith

Auchnarrow

Price Guide:
single £87–£105
double/twin £99–£172

Dating back some 150 years, this elegant house owes much of its defining style to the Arts and Crafts movement, which in 1914 transformed the house into what it is today. Paying guests are recorded as early as the 1840s, although its metamorphosis into a stylish hotel is somewhat more recent! With just 15 bedrooms, the hotel has a winning combination of personal service and intimate atmosphere combined with an extremely stylish and elegant interior that ensures guests can relax from the moment they arrive and enjoy the local hospitality. This is Malt Whisky country and Knockomie has a fine collection for guests to savour, although a trip to one of the local distilleries is a must. It is a beautiful region with Loch Ness on the west and Speyside to the east. Country pursuits are plentiful including shooting, fishing and golf which can all be arranged by the hotel, whilst the less sporting can enjoy trips to nearby Brodie and Cawdor castles. At the end of such a day, guests can look forward to a relaxing drink in the comfortable surroundings of the bar, followed by a carefully prepared dinner from a menu that boasts a successful balance of traditional Scottish ingredients and lighter recipes.

Our inspector loved: *The unexpected pleasure of coming across this stylish hotel nicely positioned outside the town.*

GLENEAGLES

AUCHTERARDER, PERTHSHIRE PH3 1NF

Known as the "great palace in the glen" this luxurious hotel nestles in the heart of the Ochil Hills on the edge of the Highlands in the White Muir of Auchterarder. From its Georgian-style windows and lush green grounds guests can marvel at views of Ben Lomond and the Grampians. Gleneagles is enveloped by clean, crisp air and an artistic landscape capped by an ever-changing sky of blue, violet and autumnal gold. It is a haven of comfort and impeccable service. The interior has been redesigned and refurbished with 21st-century amenities, whilst offering the charm and atmosphere of a Scottish country house. The elegant public rooms are enhanced by superb antique furniture. The 257 bedrooms and 13 suites have every home-from-home comfort and stunning views across Gleneagles' lawns, estate and golf courses; some have hand-woven carpets, crystal chandeliers, tasseled silk hangings and four-poster beds. Guests may dine in the sophisticated Strathearn and Michelin-starred Andrew Fairlie restaurants, whilst a cosy bar serves light lunches and afternoon teas. Championship golf facilities and a variety of country sports and pursuits can be enjoyed. Superb leisure facilities. Less than 50 miles from Edinburgh and Glasgow airports.

Our inspector loved: This ever-improving star of Scottish hotels, great food options, polished service and everything to do , golf especially.

Directions: From the north, leave A9 at the exit for A823 and follow the sign for Gleneagles Hotel. From the south, turn off M9/A9 at junction with A823 signed Crieff and Gleneagles.

Web: www.johansens.com/gleneagles
E-mail: resort.sales@gleneagles.com
Tel: 0870 381 8553
International: +44 (0)1764 662231
Fax: 01764 662134

Pitlochry

Perth

Kinross

Price Guide:
single £185
double/twin £260–£445
suite £595–£1,500

THE ROYAL HOTEL

MELVILLE SQUARE, COMRIE, PERTHSHIRE PH6 2DN

Directions: Located in the centre of the village, on the A85.

Web: www.johansens.com/royalcomrie
E-mail: reception@royalhotel.co.uk
Tel: 0870 381 8875
International: +44 (0)1764 679200
Fax: 01764 679219

Price Guide:
single £70
double £110
suite £150

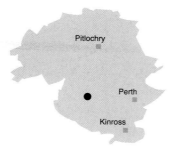

Set in an area of outstanding natural beauty, this former inn was once frequented by personalities such as Rob Roy McGregor and Queen Victoria, whose stay bestowed the name of The Royal Hotel on Comrie's major inn. Its homely yet luxurious and elegant atmosphere is enhanced by open log fires, period furnishings and genuine Highland hospitality provided by the cheerful staff and the Milsom family, who also own the Tufton Arms Hotel, Appleby. Each of the 11 bedrooms has been individually designed and shows exceptional attention to detail. An ideal place to unwind, the comfortable Lounge Bar is popular for pre-dinner drinks which include a choice of over 130 whiskies. Guests may enjoy Scottish cuisine and fine wines in the conservatory-style Brasserie or the more intimate Royal Restaurant, where chef David Milsom and his team, awarded an AA Rosette, create delicious dishes based on fresh local produce. The hotel is located amidst superb walking country; guests can go for gentle walks in the nearby Glens and across the hills and moorlands. The hotel has its own stretch of the river Earn for fishing, and horse riding and fowl or clay pigeon shooting can be arranged. Comrie is surrounded by excellent golf courses, which range from scenic Highland layouts to idyllic parkland settings, such as the famous Gleneagles.

Our inspector loved: *The blend of informality, correctness and style.*

KINNAIRD

KINNAIRD ESTATE, BY DUNKELD, PERTHSHIRE PH8 0LB

Offering a panoramic vista across the Tay valley, Kinnaird is surrounded by a beautiful estate of 9,000 acres and is ideally located for those seeking a relaxing break or enthusiasts of outdoor pursuits. Built in 1770, the Edwardian house now features 8 individually decorated bedrooms with exquisite fabrics, gas log fires and opulent bathrooms. There are also 8, 2 to 4 bedroomed self-catering holiday cottages on the estate. These delightfully decorated cottages offer ultimate seclusion and feature unique touches with amazing views. Throughout the house, rare pieces of antique furniture, china and fine paintings abound. The panelled Cedar Room is the essence of comfort where guests may relax before enjoying gourmet cuisine in the restaurants, enhanced by hand-painted Italian frescoes. The hotel's 2 dining rooms serve imaginative seasonal cuisine whilst magnificent views of the surrounding Perthshire countryside can be enjoyed. The original wine cellars are stocked with an extensive range of wines, liqueurs and malt whiskies. Sporting facilities include salmon and trout fishing, bird-watching, shooting of pheasant, grouse, duck and partridge and deer stalking can be arranged. The estate also features an all-weather tennis court and croquet and bowling lawns.

Our inspector loved: The spacious luxury of the rooms and overall grand elegance with food and wine to match.

Directions: 2 miles north of Dunkeld on the A9, take B898 for 4½ miles.

Web: www.johansens.com/kinnaird
E-mail: enquiry@kinnairdestate.com
Tel: 0870 381 9124
International: +44 (0)1796 482440
Fax: 01796 482289

Pitlochry

Perth

Kinross

Price Guide:
double/twin £375–£525
Winter rates £325 or £275 for 2 or more nights

DALMUNZIE HOUSE

SPITTAL O'GLENSHEE, BLAIRGOWRIE, PERTHSHIRE PH10 7QG

Directions: Dalmunzie is on the A93 at the Spittal O'Glenshee, south of Braemar.

Web: www.johansens.com/dalmunziehouse
E-mail: dalmunzie@aol.com
Tel: 0870 381 8473
International: +44 (0)1250 885224
Fax: 01250 885225

Price Guide:
single £43–£65
double/twin £66–£120

Dalmunzie House is beautifully tucked away high in the Scottish Highlands, 18 miles north of Blairgowrie and 15 miles south of Braemar. Standing in its own mountainous 6,000-acre sporting estate, it is run by Simon and Alexandra Winton. Guests come to enjoy the relaxed family atmosphere which, together with unobtrusive service and attention, ensures a comfortable stay. The bedrooms are individual in character, some with antiques, others romantically set in the turrets of the house, all tastefully decorated. Delicately cooked traditional Scottish fare is created from local ingredients fresh from the hills and lochs. The menu changes daily and meals are served in the dining room, accompanied by wines from the well-stocked cellar. Among the sporting activities available on site are golf (the 9-hole course is one of the highest in Britain) and shooting for grouse, ptarmigan and black game. Other country pursuits include river and loch fishing, clay pigeon shooting, mountain biking, stalking for red deer and pony-trekking. Glenshee Ski Centre is 6 miles away: it offers cross-country and downhill skiing. Closer to home, the hotel games room provides more sedate pastimes for all the family. 6 self-catering cottages are also available. Closed late November to 28 December. Special winter/skiing rates.

Our inspector loved: *This stunningly located traditional hotel with a plethora of leisure opportunities on site or close by.*

CROMLIX HOUSE

KINBUCK, BY DUNBLANE, NR STIRLING FK15 9JT

Set in a 2,000-acre estate in the heart of Perthshire, just off the A9, the STB 5 Star Cromlix House is a rare and relaxing retreat. Built as a family home in 1874, much of the house remains unchanged including many fine antiques acquired over the generations. Proprietors, David and Ailsa Assenti, are proud of their tradition of country house hospitality. The individually designed bedrooms and spacious suites have been redecorated with period fabrics to enhance the character and fine furniture whilst retaining the essential feeling of a much loved home. Unpretentious, restful and most welcoming, the large public rooms have open fires. In the restaurant, the finest local produce is used. Cromlix is an ideal venue for small exclusive conferences and business meetings. The private Chapel is a unique feature and perfect for weddings. Cromlix House was one of the AA top 10 hotels in Scotland 2003. Extensive sporting and leisure facilities include trout and salmon fishing and game shooting in season. There are several challenging golf courses within easy reach including Gleneagles, Rosemount, Carnoustie and St Andrews. The location is ideal for touring the Southern Highlands, with Edinburgh and Glasgow only an hour away.

Our inspector loved: The peaceful atmosphere where it's easy to believe you are in your own luxury house.

Directions: Cromlix House lies 4 miles north of Dunblane, north of Kinbuck on the B8033 and 4 miles south of Braco.

Web: www.johansens.com/cromlixhouse
E-mail: reservations@cromlixhouse.com
Tel: 0870 381 8460
International: +44 (0)1786 822125
Fax: 01786 825450

Price Guide:
single £125–£195
double/twin £215–£255
suite with private sitting room £245–£360

KINFAUNS CASTLE

NR PERTH, PERTHSHIRE PH2 7JZ

Directions: The hotel is 2 miles from Perth on the A90 Dundee Road.

Web: www.johansens.com/kinfaunscastle
E-mail: email@kinfaunscastle.co.uk
Tel: 0870 381 8653
International: +44 (0)1738 620777
Fax: 01738 620778

Price Guide:
single £130–£190
double £200–£230
suite £280–£320

Set within 26 acres of parkland and landscaped gardens, Kinfauns Castle stands on a promontory overlooking the River Tay. The Castle, built by Lord Gray in the 1820s, is located immediately off the A90 Dundee Road, just 2 miles from Perth. The new directors, Mr and Mrs James A Smith, made a commitment to the restoration of the wonderful building, the historical seat of Lord Gray. James Smith was until recently vice-president of Central Asia for Hilton International. The 16 suites and rooms are individually decorated and reflect the quality, comfort and ambience one expects of a luxury country house. The public rooms feature the rich Victorian décor which has survived the Castle's 70 years as a hikers' hotel. One particular lounge sports a William Morris hunting scene paper whilst another contains a Dragon Boat Bar, brought back from Taipai by the present owner. Chef Jeremy Brazelle leads an award-winning brigade serving an exquisite fusion of modern Scottish and classical French cuisine produced from the finest locally-sourced ingredients. The area abounds with castles and sites of historic interest: Scone Palace and Glamis Castle are only a few miles away. Salmon fishing on the River Tay, golf, shooting and riding are easily available.

Our inspector loved: The mixture of history and splendid grandeur interestingly intermingled with Oriental artefacts.

BALLATHIE HOUSE HOTEL

KINCLAVEN, STANLEY, PERTHSHIRE PH1 4QN

Set in an estate overlooking the River Tay near Perth, Ballathie House Hotel offers Scottish hospitality in a house of character and distinction. Dating from 1850, this mansion has a French baronial façade and handsome interiors. Overlooking lawns which slope down to the riverside, the drawing room is an ideal place to relax with coffee and the papers or to enjoy a malt whisky after dinner. The premier bedrooms are large and elegant, whilst the standard rooms are designed in a cosy, cottage style. On the ground floor there are several bedrooms suitable for guests with disabilities. Local ingredients such as Tay salmon, Scottish beef, seafood and piquant soft fruits are used by chef, Kevin MacGillivray, winner of the title Scottish Chef of the Year 1999–2000, to create menus catering for all tastes. The hotel has 2 Rosettes for fine Scottish cuisine. Activities available on the estate include salmon fishing, river walks, croquet and putting. The new Riverside Rooms are ideal for both house guests or sportsmen. The area has many good golf courses. Perth, Blairgowrie and Edinburgh are within an hour's drive. STB 4 star and AA 3 Red Stars (Top 200). Dogs are permitted in certain rooms only. 2 day breaks from £95, including dinner.

Our inspector loved: *Something of the grand hotel in rural Perthshire, with polished service and classic comforts.*

Directions: From the A93 at Beech Hedges, follow the signs for Kinclaven and Ballathie or take the A9 and turn off 2 miles north of Perth, then take Stanley Road. The hotel is 10 miles north of Perth.

Web: www.johansens.com/ballathiehouse
E-mail: email@ballathiehousehotel.com
Tel: 0870 381 8337
International: +44 (0)1250 883268
Fax: 01250 883396

Price Guide:
single £80–£120
double/twin £160–£220
suite £230–£260

GLEDDOCH HOUSE HOTEL & COUNTRY ESTATE

LANGBANK, RENFREWSHIRE PA14 6YE

Directions: M8 towards Greenock; take B789 Langbank/Houston exit. Follow signs to left and then right after ½ mile; hotel is on left

Web: www.johansens.com/gleddochhouse
E-mail: reservations@gleddochhouse.com
Tel: 0870 381 8550
International: +44 (0)1475 540711
Fax: 01475 540201

Price Guide:
single £99
double/twin £150
suite £185

Set amidst 360 acres with panoramic views across the River Clyde to Ben Lomond and the breathtaking countryside, Gleddoch House is regarded by many as the heart of the awe-inspiring land that surrounds it. The feeling of peace and tranquillity is evident the moment you approach the escalating driveway leading to this 4-star hotel, the former home of Glasgow Shipping Barron, Sir James Lithgow. Each of the executive rooms, four-poster suites, or family rooms is traditionally furnished and exudes an extremely personal welcome, with most offering picturesque views of the golf course, gardens and surrounding estate. In-room facilities include complimentary tea and coffee, satellite television, trouser press and hairdryer. For sports and leisure, there is a newly opened Leisure Centre with indoor pool, sauna, steam room, gymnasium and spa. And, with the added benefit of an 18-hole golf course, equestrian centre and a range of outdoor pursuits available for small to large groups, Gleddoch House is the perfect place to spend your time, be it business or pleasure. Glasgow city centre is a short 20-minute drive away and Glasgow International Airport just 10 minutes, making Gleddoch the ideal base for those who wish to explore the beautiful Highlands and Island whilst enjoying a taste of city life.

Our inspector loved: The spectacular views across the River Clyde from the hotel's elevated position.

EDNAM HOUSE HOTEL

BRIDGE STREET, KELSO, ROXBURGHSHIRE TD5 7HT

Overlooking the River Tweed, in 3 acres of gardens, Ednam House is one of the region's finest examples of Georgian architecture. This undulating, pastoral countryside was immortalised by Sir Walter Scott. Ednam House has been owned and managed by the Brooks family for over 70 years, spanning 4 generations. Although the grandiose splendour may seem formal, the warm, easy-going atmosphere is all-pervasive. The lounges and bars are comfortably furnished and command scenic views of the river and grounds. All 32 bedrooms are en suite, individually decorated and well-equipped. In the elegant dining room which overlooks the river, a blend of traditional and creative Scottish cuisine, using fresh local produce, is served. The wine list is very interesting and reasonably priced. Ednam House is extremely popular with fishermen, the Borders being renowned for its salmon and trout. Other field sports such as stalking, hunting and shooting can be arranged as can riding, golfing and cycling. Local landmarks include the abbeys of Kelso, Melrose, Jedburgh and Dryburgh. The hotel is closed Christmas and New Year.

Directions: From the south, reach Kelso via A698; from the north, via A68. The hotel is just off the market square by the river.

Web: www.johansens.com/ednamhouse
E-mail: contact@ednamhouse.com
Tel: 0870 381 8500
International: +44 (0)1573 224168
Fax: 01573 226319

Price Guide:
single from £67
double/twin £89–£124

Our inspector loved: The beautiful views from the hotel out to the River Tweed on one side and the short walk into the bustling market town.

THE ROXBURGHE HOTEL & GOLF COURSE

KELSO, ROXBURGHSHIRE TD5 8JZ

Directions: The hotel is at Heiton, just off the A698 Kelso–Jedburgh road.

Web: www.johansens.com/roxburghekelso
E-mail: hotel@roxburghe.net
Tel: 0870 381 8873
International: +44 (0)1573 450331
Fax: 01573 450611

Price Guide:
single £120
double/twin £175
4-poster £215
suite £265

Converted by its owners, the Duke and Duchess of Roxburghe, into a luxury hotel of character and charm, The Roxburghe is situated in over 200 acres of rolling grounds on the bank of the River Teviot. There are 22 bedrooms, including four-poster rooms and suites, and like the spacious reception rooms, they are furnished with care and elegance. The menu, which is changed daily, reflects the hotel's position at the source of some of Britain's finest fish, meat and game – salmon and trout from the waters of the Tweed, or grouse, pheasant and venison from the Roxburghe estate – complemented with wines from the Duke's own cellar. Fine whiskies are served in the Library Bar, with its log fire and leather-bound tomes. The Beauty Clinic brings to guests the régimes of Decleor, Paris. Surrounding the hotel is the magnificent Roxburghe Golf Course, designed by Dave Thomas. This parkland course, host to Charles Church Scottish seniors Open is the only championship golf course in the Scottish Borders. A full sporting programme can be arranged, including fly and coarse fishing, and falconry. The shooting school offers tuition in game and clay shooting. 7 great country houses are within easy reach including Floors Castle, the home of the Duke and Duchess of Roxburghe.

Our inspector loved: *A championship golf course on the doorstep.*

CASTLE VENLAW

EDINBURGH ROAD, PEEBLES EH45 8QG

Just 40 minutes from the city of Edinburgh, yet within the peaceful Borders countryside, the Castle sits majestically on the slopes of Venlaw Hill overlooking the royal and ancient town of Peebles. Originally built as a private house in 1782, it was bought by John and Shirley Sloggie in 1997. Now recognised as one of the leading 4-star hotels in the area, Castle Venlaw keeps the country house tradition alive and offers an air of elegance and relaxed informality. From the welcoming Library with its oak panelling and log fire to the 12 bedrooms – all named after Scotland's finest malt whiskies – great care has been taken to preserve the castle's charm and character. Guests can choose from a range of suites and, at the top of the tower, a family suite comes complete with children's den. The spacious and airy 2 AA Rosette restaurant provides the perfect ambience in which to enjoy menus where delicious local produce such as Borders salmon, lamb and game are given an international flavour. Outside, acres of beautiful woodland grounds can be explored, golf or fishing enjoyed and the history in the ruined Abbeys and historic houses can be appreciated. Edinburgh, Glasgow and Stirling are within easy reach. Short breaks, including dinner, are available throughout the year starting from £65.

Our inspector loved: *The exceptionally large rooms, the peace and quiet and the proximity to Edinburgh.*

Directions: From Edinburgh, follow the A703 to Peebles. After 30mph sign, the hotel drive is signposted on the left. From Peebles follow the A703 to Edinburgh the Hotel is on the right after .75 mile.

Web: www.johansens.com/venlaw
E-mail: enquiries@venlaw.co.uk
Tel: 0870 381 8410
International: +44 (0)1721 720384
Fax: 01721 724066

Price Guide:
single £60–£85
double/twin £120–£180

ENTERKINE COUNTRY HOUSE

ANNBANK, BY AYR, AYRSHIRE KA6 5AL

A winding tree-lined avenue leads to this elegant 1930s country house, which is an ideal base for leisure and sporting holidaymakers, and has won numerous awards including a Scottish Tourist Board 5 Star Rating, 3 RAC Dining Awards and 2 AA Rosettes. Built originally as a private residence, Enterkine is situated near the village of Annbank, 5 miles east of Ayr, and surrounded by 310 acres of woodland and meadows that are a mecca for those who like walking and countryside peace and quiet. Delightful soft furnishings and tasteful colour coordination grace the hotel's interior and create a warm and welcoming ambience. Privacy is a priority and the staff place emphasis on individual service and comfort. The 6 bedroom suites have luxurious bathrooms, are spacious, light and stunningly decorated. An oval-shaped library with open fire offers the perfect venue for relaxation whilst the restaurant provides first-class cuisine incorporating the best Scottish ingredients. There are 7 championship golf courses within a 30-minute drive, ranging from the famous links of Turnberry and Royal Troon to Western Gailes and Prestwick, and arrangements can be made for guests to play them. Also within easy reach is some of the finest fishing and game shooting in Scotland, which visitors can enjoy on inclusive outings.

Directions: From the A77 take A70 to Edinburgh, turn left onto B744 through Annbank turn right after Annbank towards Coylton. The Hotel is on the left.

Web: www.johansens.com/enterkine
E-mail: mail@enterkine.com
Tel: 0870 381 8505
International: +44 (0)1292 520580
Fax: 01292 521582

Price Guide: (including dinner)
single £110
double/twin £220

Our inspector loved: The lovely setting and absolute attention to detail.

GLENAPP CASTLE

BALLANTRAE, SCOTLAND KA26 0NZ

Glenapp is more of an experience rather than "just another hotel". As you turn through the castle gates, Glenapp stands proudly in front of you; imposing, exciting and inviting. The owners, Fay and Graham Cowan, offer a truly Scottish welcome to their glorious Ayrshire home. They bought Glenapp in a state of neglect and spent six years refurbishing it to combine the requirements of the discerning guest with the classic style of the house. No expense has been spared, from the stone fireplaces carved with the family crest to the Castle's own monogrammed china. Head Chef Tristan Welch will prepare exciting, innovative 6-course dinners, complemented by specially selected fine wines. The castle retains many original features as well as personally selected oil paintings and antique furnishings throughout bedrooms, lounges and oak panelled hallways. The 17 en-suite bedrooms are spacious, individually decorated, and furnished to the highest standard, all offering either views of the garden or coastline. The 30-acre gardens contain many rare trees and shrubs and an impressive Victorian glasshouse and walled garden. Tennis and croquet are available in the grounds. Guests may play golf on the many local courses including championship courses, and shoot or fish on local estates.

Our inspector loved: Everything about it - now in its 4th year yet it gets better and better.

Directions: Glenapp Castle is approximately 15 miles north of Stranraer or 35 miles south of Ayr on A77.

Troon

Ayr

Girvan

Web: www.johansens.com/glenappcastle
E-mail: enquiries@glenappcastle.com
Tel: 0870 381 8551
International: +44 (0)1465 831212
Fax: 01465 831000

Price Guide: (including all meals, unlimited wines & spirits)
luxury double/twin £440
suite £480
master room £550

CRUTHERLAND HOUSE HOTEL

STRATHAVEN ROAD, EAST KILBRIDE G75 0QZ

Upon arriving at Crutherland House Hotel, guests could be forgiven for thinking themselves in the depths of the Scottish countryside, as the hotel stands in some 37 acres of woodland. Peace and tranquillity abound at this pretty 18th-century house, which is actually only a short drive from Glasgow and hugely accessible for the host of attractions that lie within the region. In fact it makes the ideal destination for a leisurely weekend break, taking in the superb shopping now available in Glasgow city centre, followed by a 40-minute drive to get right away from it all at the shores of Loch Lomond. Weddings and other functions are also very popular at Crutherland House for its accessibility combined with its air of quiet and understated luxury. The opulent dining room and immaculately manicured grounds form the perfect backdrop for photographs, and for guests' personal comfort there is a wonderful health and beauty spa with an 18m indoor swimming pool. Each of the 75 elegantly styled bedrooms overlooks the grounds and park. The best of Scottish and international cuisine is served in the award-winning restaurant, with an excellent choice of accompanying wines; and some 13 private rooms are available for meetings, seminars or parties, with first-class audio-visual facilities and the utmost privacy.

Directions: From M74, exit at Jct5. Take A726 to East Kilbride and follow signs for Strathaven.

Web: www.johansens.com/crutherlandhouse
E-mail: crutherland@macdonald–hotels.co.uk
Tel: 0870 381 8710
International: +44 (0)1355 577000
Fax: 01355 220855

Price Guide:
single £95–£128
double/twin £105–£150
suites £160–£210

Our inspector loved: The great country location yet so close to Glasgow.

For further information on Wales, please contact:

Wales Tourist Board
Brunel House, 2 Fitzalan Road, Cardiff CF24 0UY
Tel: +44 (0)29 2049 9909
Web: www.visitwales.com

North Wales Tourism
Tel: +44 (0)1492 531731
Web: www.nwt.co.uk

Mid Wales Tourism
Tel: (Freephone) 0800 273747
Web: www.visitmidwales.co.uk

South West Wales Tourism Partnership
Tel: +44 (0)1558 669091
Web: www.swwtp.co.uk

or see **pages 437-440** for details of
local atractions to visit during your stay.

Images from www.britainonview.com

LLECHWEN HALL

ABERCYNON, NR LLANFABON, CARDIFF, MID GLAMORGAN CF37 4HP

Visitors step back in time when they enter this lovely 17th-century Welsh Long-House with its Victorian frontage standing in 6 acres of mature gardens on the hillside overlooking the Aberdare and Merthyr valleys. There are 4-foot thick walls with narrow embrasures, low ceilings, stout-blackened oak beams, huge fireplaces and stone-roofed outbuildings. Careful restoration and sympathetic refurbishment over the years, since being purchased as a near derelict building in 1988, has created a 3-star country house hotel with an award-winning restaurant. The 20 superbly appointed bedrooms are individually decorated and furnished to provide a truly comfortable environment. Guests have a choice of restaurants for memorable dining. Outstanding, freshly prepared cusine, with seasonal changes to the menu, is served either in the intimate atmosphere of the oak-beamed restaurant in part of the original Welsh Long-House or in the light and airy Victorian dining room with its stunning views across the valleys. Pre and after-dinner drinks can be enjoyed in an elegant cocktail lounge. The hotel is just a 20 minute drive from Cardiff and 15 minutes from the foothills of the Brecon Beacons.

Directions: Exit the M4 at junction 32 and follow the A470 towards Merthyr Tydfil for approximately 11 miles. Join the A472 towards Nelson and then the A4054 towards Cilfynydd. The hotel is on the left after ¹/₂ mile.

Web: www.johansens.com/Llechwenhall
E-mail: llechwen@aol.com
Tel: 0870 381 8698
International: +44 (0)1443 742050
Fax: 01443 742189

Price Guide:
single £54.50–£65.50
double/twin £75–£106

Our inspector loved: The sympathetic restoration of this 17th-century Welsh Long-House providing an oasis of comfort in spectacular surroundings.

YNYSHIR HALL

EGLWYSFACH, MACHYNLLETH, CEREDIGION SY20 8TA

Once owned by Queen Victoria, Ynyshir Hall is a captivating Georgian manor house that perfectly blends modern comfort and Old World elegance. Its 12 acres of landscaped gardens are set alongside the Dovey Estuary, one of Wales's most outstanding areas of natural beauty. The hotel is surrounded by the Ynyshir Bird Reserve. Hosts Rob and Joan Reen offer guests a warm welcome and ensure a personal service, the hallmark of a good family-run hotel. Period furniture and opulent fabrics enhance the 9 charming bedrooms. The suites, including a four-poster room and ground floor room, are particularly luxurious. The interiors are exquisitely furnished throughout with sofas, antiques, contemporary colour schemes, oriental rugs and original paintings. These works of art are the creation of Rob, an acclaimed artist. The artistry continues in the kitchen where local seafood, game and vegetables from the garden are used to create superb modern interpretations of classic French cuisine. The imaginative Michelin starred dishes prepared by Les Rennie, comprise a wonderful balance of colours, textures and flavours. Awarded The Catey's Independent Hotel of the Year 2002, Welsh Hotel of the Year 2001 by the AA. Winner of Johansens Most Excellent Restaurant Award 1999. Landmarks include Cader Idris, Wales's 2nd highest mountain. Closed in January.

Our inspector loved: *You just have to experience Ynyshir Hall to really see and feel what I loved.*

Directions: Off main road between Aberystwyth and Machynlleth.

Web: www.johansens.com/ynyshirhall
E-mail: info@ynyshir–hall.co.uk
Tel: 0870 381 9020
International: +44 (0)1654 781209
Fax: 01654 781366

Aberystwyth

Tregaron

Cardigan

Price Guide:
single £110–£180
double/twin £125–£180
suite £210–£275

St Tudno Hotel & Restauarant

NORTH PROMENADE, LLANDUDNO LL30 2LP

Directions: On the promenade opposite the pier entrance and gardens. Car parking and garaging is available for up to 12 cars.

Web: www.johansens.com/sttudno
E-mail: sttudnohotel@btinternet.com
Tel: 0870 381 8907
International: +44 (0)1492 874411
Fax: 01492 860407

Price Guide:
single from £70
double/twin £90–£200
suite from £230

Without doubt one of the most delightful small hotels to be found on the coast of Britain, St. Tudno Hotel, a former winner of the Johansens Hotel of the Year Award for Excellence, certainly offers a very special experience. The hotel has been elegantly and lovingly furnished with meticulous attention to detail, and offers a particularly warm welcome from owners, Janette and Martin Bland now in their 32nd year. Each beautifully co-ordinated bedroom has been individually designed with many thoughtful extras, half are equipped with spa baths. The bar lounge and sitting room, which overlook the sea, have an air of Victorian charm. Regarded as one of Wales' leading restaurants, the air-conditioned Garden Room has won 3 AA Rosettes for its excellent cuisine for the 10th consecutive year. This AA Red Star Hotel has won a host of other prestigious awards: Best Seaside Resort Hotel in Great Britain (Good Hotel guide); Welsh Hotel of the Year; Nominated for Johansens Most Excellent Coastal Hotel 2003; the AA's Wine Award for Wales and even an accolade for having the Best Hotel Loos in Britain! St Tudno is ideally situated for visits to Snowdonia, Conwy and Caernarfon Castles, delightful walks on the Great Orme, Bodnant Gardens and Anglesey. Golf, riding, swimming, dry-slope skiing and tobogganing can all be enjoyed locally.

Our inspector loved: Its wonderful, caring way with all its guests.

WILD PHEASANT HOTEL

BERWYN ROAD, LLANGOLLEN, DENBIGHSHIRE LL20 8AD

Set within beautiful countryside overlooking the Vale of Llangollen, the Berwyn Mountains and Castell Dinas Bran, this new hotel is a haven of tranquillity, yet easily accessible from the A5. The original building, dating back to the 19th century, has been sympathetically renovated and extended to provide a luxurious hotel, which retains its former country house charm whilst offering all modern amenities and an eclectic blend of contemporary and traditional design. The new bedrooms and suites in the extension are spacious and tastefully furnished, and the more traditional bedrooms in the old part have been updated and are small but extremely comfortable. The lavish Penthouse Suite is simply superb and boasts a hot tub on the balcony. Excellent dining options include the newly decorated Cinnamon Restaurant, which has been awarded 1 Rosette for its daily changing menus based on fresh local produce. The more informal Bistro Bar is ideal for light meals and drinks. Guests can completely unwind and relax in the hotel's Spa of Tranquillity, which offers a wide range of pampering health and beauty treatments. The Wild Pheasant is the ideal location for weddings, with the Glanafon Suite accommodating 120 guests in comfort and style. Comprehensive meeting and conference facilities are also available.

Our inspector loved: *Having a massage, then wallowing in the spa bath for 1 hour before enjoying a delicious dinner in the restaurant.*

Directions: From the north: M6, then take M56 to Chester, then follow A483 past Wrexham and take A5 to Langollen. From south: M6, then take M54 past Shrewsbury, onto A5 to Langollen.

Web: www.johansens.com/wildpheasant
E-mail: wildpheasant@talk21.com
Tel: 0870 381 8633
International: +44 (0)1978 860629
Fax: 01978 861837

Price Guide:
single £70–£221
double/twin £104–£130
suite £130–£230

PALÉ HALL

PALÉ ESTATE, LLANDDERFEL, BALA, GWYNEDD LL23 7PS

Directions: Situated off the B4401 Corwen to Bala Road, Palé Hall is 4 miles from Llandrillo.

Web: www.johansens.com/palehall
E-mail: enquiries@palehall.co.uk
Tel: 0870 381 8799
International: +44 (0)1678 530285
Fax: 01678 530220

Price Guide:
single £80–£140
double/twin £100–£200

Set in acres of peaceful, tranquil woodland on the edge of Snowdonia National Park, Palé Hall is a magnificent building, beautifully preserved by its current owners, and gives guests the opportunity to sample true country house lifestyle. Shooting parties are a regular occurrence on the surrounding estates, whilst clay shooting and fishing on the Dee are available on site. A new venture with Land Rover Experience also enables guests to experience off road driving in their preferred choice of 4-wheel drive, whilst the less adventurous can walk for miles on the beautiful Palé estate. The staff at Palé Hall carefully maintain the beautiful period interior of the building including the galleried staircase and painted ceilings, which have survived largely due to the hotel's unusual electricity system. Supplied by a turbine powered by water, the hotel's 18 electric fires were left burning during 22 years of unoccupancy! Queen Victoria and Winston Churchill have stayed at the Hall. The 17 individually designed suites with luxurious bathrooms have breathtaking views of the surrounding scenery. The restaurant has 2 AA Rosettes and serves seasonal table d'hôte menus complemented by a fine wine selection. Exclusive use is available for conferences, product launches and weddings.

Our inspector loved: *This delightful home offering comfort and standards equal to the quality of this wonderful building - a real oasis.*

PENMAENUCHAF HALL

PENMAENPOOL, DOLGELLAU, GWYNEDD LL40 1YB

Climbing the long tree lined driveway you arrive at Penmaenuchaf Hall to behold its idyllic setting. With stunning panoramic views across the spectacular Mawddach Estuary and wooded mountain slopes in the distance, this handsome Victorian mansion is truly an exceptional retreat. Set within the Snowdonia National Park, the 21-acre grounds encompass lawns, a formal sunken rose garden, a water garden and woodland. The beautiful interiors feature oak and mahogany panelling, stained-glass windows, log fires in winter, polished Welsh slate floors and freshly cut flowers. There are 12 luxurious bedrooms, some with four-poster and half-tester beds and all with interesting views. In the restaurant guests can choose from an imaginative menu prepared with the best seasonal produce and complemented by an extensive list of wines. An elegant panelled dining room can be used for private dinners or meetings. Penmaenuchaf Hall is perfect for a totally relaxed holiday. For recreation, guests can fish for trout and salmon along 10miles of the Mawddach River or take part in a range of water sports. They can also enjoy scenic walks, visit sandy beaches and historic castles and take trips on narrow-gauge railways.

Our inspector loved: *The tranquillity and loving care given to this delightful hotel.*

Directions: The hotel is off the A493 Dolgellau–Tywyn road, about 2 miles from Dolgellau.

Bangor

Pwllheli

Dolgellau

Web: www.johansens.com/penmaenuchafhall
E-mail: relax@penhall.co.uk
Tel: 0870 381 8813
International: +44 (0)1341 422129
Fax: 01341 422787

Price Guide:
single £75–£115
double/twin £116–£176

THE TREARDDUR BAY HOTEL

LON ISALLT, TREARDDUR BAY, ANGLESEY LL65 2UN

For both business traveller and holidaymaker, here is one of the most delightful retreats to be found on the Anglesey coast. The comfortable and welcoming Trearddur Bay Hotel, the 1st independent hotel in Wales to be awarded Hospitality Assured, is situated opposite a "Blue Flag Beach" and enjoys panoramic views across the sandy bay. This prime location is conveniently just 1¾ miles from the fully completed A55 North Wales Expressway, which makes the hotel a comfortable drive from the Midlands, Yorkshire and the North West. Guests have the choice of a variety of sporting and leisure facilities from kayaking, diving and sailing to bird watching, walking and golf. Close by are places of historical interest such as a medieval chapel, Beaumaris Castle and a Celtic burial mound. For a day out with a difference, take the 99-minute fast ferry service to Ireland from the nearby port of Holyhead. Inside the hotel's sparkling white exterior are spacious en-suite bedrooms, with first-class furnishings and facilities. All of the 16 charming studio suites have sea views and many boast their own private balconies. Morning coffee and afternoon tea are served in a relaxing lounge, whilst aperitifs can be enjoyed in an elegant cocktail bar as a prelude to sampling culinary delights from the restaurant's extensive table d'hôte menu. A heated indoor swimming pool is a popular alternative to the Irish Sea.

Directions: From Bangor, when the A55 Expressway terminates at Holyhead, at the 1st roundabout turn left onto the B4545, signposted Trearddur. Continue for 1.7 miles. Turn right at the Power Garage onto Lon Isallt. The hotel is 350 yards on the right.

Web: www.johansens.com/trearddurbay
E-mail: enquiries@trearddurbayhotel.co.uk
Tel: 0870 381 8949
International: +44 (0)1407 860301
Fax: 01407 861181

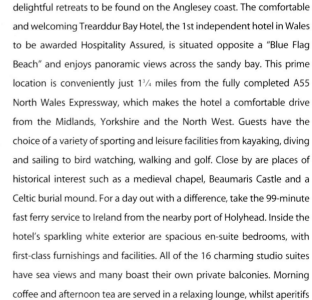

Price Guide:
single £85–£105
double/twin £124–£150

Our inspector loved: The informality, offering relaxed comfort.

LLANSANTFFRAED COURT HOTEL

LLANVIHANGEL GOBION, ABERGAVENNY, MONMOUTHSHIRE NP7 9BA

Llansantffraed Court is a perfect retreat from the fast pace of modern life. This elegant Georgian-style country house hotel, part of which dates back to the 14th century, is set in spacious grounds on the edge of the Brecon Beacons and the Wye Valley. Guests are provided with the highest level of personal, yet unobtrusive service. Most of the tastefully decorated and luxuriously furnished bedrooms offer views over the hotel's gardens and ornamental trout lake. While one has a four-poster bed, others feature oak beams and dormer windows. An excellent reputation is enjoyed by the 2 AA Rosette restaurant; the menus reflect the changing seasons and the availability of fresh local produce. Exquisite cuisine is complemented by fine wines. Afternoon tea can be taken in the lounge, where guests enjoy a blazing log fire during the cooler months and savour the views of the South Wales countryside. A range of excellent facilities is available for functions, celebrations and meetings. Llansantffraed Court is an ideal base for exploring the diverse history and beauty of this area and there are plenty of opportunities to take advantage of energetic or relaxing pursuits, including golf, trekking, walking, and salmon and trout fishing.

Our inspector loved: This elegant Georgian hotel surrounded by rolling parkland as far as the eye can see.

Directions: From M4 J24 (Via A449) off B4598 (formerly A40 old road) Leave A40 D/C at Abergavenny or Raglan. Follow signs to Clytha and the hotel is approx 4½ miles away.

Web: www.johansens.com/llansantffraedcourt
E-mail: reception@llch.co.uk
Tel: 0870 381 8697
International: +44 (0)1873 840678
Fax: 01873 840674

Price Guide:
single from £86
double/twin from £106
suites £140

PEMBROKESHIRE - PEMBROKE (LAMPHEY)

LAMPHEY COURT HOTEL

LAMPHEY, NR TENBY, PEMBROKESHIRE SA71 5NT

Directions: From M4, exit at Junction 49 onto the A48 to Carmarthen. Then follow the A477 and turn left at Milton Village for Lamphey.

Web: www.johansens.com/courtpembroke
E-mail: info@lampheycourt.co.uk
Tel: 0870 381 8675
International: +44 (0)1646 672273
Fax: 01646 672480

Price Guide:
single £75–£85
double/twin £100–£140

This magnificent Georgian mansion is idyllically situated in acres of grounds bordered by the beautiful Pembrokeshire National Park and just one mile from some of Britain's finest coastal scenery and beaches. Warm, friendly and efficient service is enriched by comfortable furnishings and decor. There are de luxe and superior bedrooms within the hotel and purpose-built Coach House studios provide the extra space required by families. The restaurant serves traditional flavours and local produce including such pleasures as Teifi salmon and Freshwater Bay lobster. Lighter meals and snacks can be taken in the elegant Conservatory. The wide range of facilities in the superb leisure centre include an indoor heated swimming pool, Jacuzzi, sauna and a gymnasium. There are aerobics classes, yoga, fitness programmes and beauty therapy and massage by appointment. Golf, sailing, fishing and yacht charter are all nearby. Well worth a visit is picturesque Tenby, the cliffside chapel of St Govan's, the Bishops Palace at Lamphey and Pembroke's impressive castle.

Our inspector loved: The extensive leisure centre offering an indoor swimming pool, well equipped gymnasium, hairdresser, sauna and solarium.

WARPOOL COURT HOTEL

ST DAVID'S, PEMBROKESHIRE SA62 6BN

Originally built as St David's Cathedral Choir School in the 1860s, Warpool Court enjoys spectacular scenery at the heart of the Pembrokeshire National Park, with views over the coast and St Bride's Bay to the islands beyond. First converted to a hotel over 40 years ago, continuous refurbishment has ensured all its up-to-date comforts are fit for the new century. All 25 bedrooms have immaculate en-suite bathrooms and most enjoy sea views. The 2 AA Rosette restaurant enjoys a splendid reputation. Imaginative menus, including vegetarian, offer a wide selection of modern and traditional dishes. Local produce, including Welsh lamb and beef, is used whenever possible, with crab, lobster, sewin and sea bass caught just off the coast. Salmon and mackerel are smoked on the premises. The hotel gardens are ideal for a peaceful stroll or an after-dinner drink in the summer. There is a covered heated swimming pool (open April to the end of October) and an all-weather tennis court in the grounds. A path from the hotel leads straight on to the Pembrokeshire Coastal Path, with its rich variety of wildlife and spectacular scenery. Boating and water sports are available locally. St David's Peninsula offers a wealth of history and natural beauty and has inspired many famous artists. Closed in January.

Our inspector loved: The spectacular views of the coast from the dining room complementing the superb 2 Rosette cuisine.

Directions: The hotel is signposted from St David's town centre.

Web: www.johansens.com/warpoolcourt
E-mail: warpool@enterprise.net
Tel: 0870 381 8968
International: +44 (0)1437 720300
Fax: 01437 720676

Price Guide:
single £80–£110
double/twin £135–£200

PENALLY ABBEY

PENALLY, TENBY, PEMBROKESHIRE SA70 7PY

Directions: Penally Abbey is situated adjacent to the church on Penally village green.

Web: www.johansens.com/penallyabbey
E-mail: penally.abbey@btinternet.com
Tel: 0870 381 8810
International: +44 (0)1834 843033
Fax: 01834 844714

Price Guide:
single £134
double/twin £126–£150
suite £150

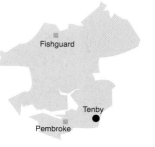

Penally Abbey, a beautiful listed Pembrokeshire country house, offers comfort and hospitality in a secluded setting by the sea. Standing in 5 acres of gardens and woodland on the edge of Pembrokeshire National Park, the hotel overlooks Carmarthen Bay and Caldey Island. The bedrooms in the main building and in the adjoining coach house are well furnished, many with four-poster beds. The emphasis is on relaxation – enjoy a late breakfast and dine at leisure. Fresh seasonal delicacies are offered in the candlelit restaurant, with its chandeliers and colonnades. Guests can enjoy a game in the snooker room or relax in the elegant sunlit lounge, overlooking the terrace and gardens. In the grounds there is a wishing well and a ruined chapel – the last surviving link with the hotel's monastic past. Water skiing, surfing, sailing, riding and parascending are available nearby. Sandy bays and rugged cliffs are features of the Pembrokeshire coastal park.

Our inspector loved: The romantic location and ambience of the hotel full of personal touches.

LLANGOED HALL

LLYSWEN, BRECON, POWYS, WALES LD3 0YP

The history of Llangoed Hall dates back to 560AD when it is thought to have been the site of the first Welsh Parliament. Inspired by this legend, the architect Sir Clough Williams-Ellis transformed the Jacobean mansion he found here in 1914 into an Edwardian country house. Situated deep in a valley of the River Wye, surrounded by a walled garden, the hotel commands magnificent views of the Black Mountains and Brecon Beacons beyond. The rooms are warm and welcoming, furnished with antiques and oriental rugs and on the walls, an outstanding collection of paintings acquired by the owner, Sir Bernard Ashley. The luxurious and spacious bedrooms enjoy fine views of the Wye Valley. Llangoed's restaurant is one of the principal reasons for staying here. Classic but light, the Michelin-starred menus represent the very best of modern cuisine, complemented by a cellar of more than 300 wines. Exclusive use of the entire hotel can be made available for weddings or meetings. Outdoor pursuits include golf, riding, shooting and some of the best mountain walking and gliding in Britain. For expeditions, there is Hay-on-Wye and its bookshops, the border castles, Hereford and Leominster. There are 3 heated kennels for dogs. The hotel is a member of Welsh Rarebits.

Our inspector loved: The classic Edwardian feel, one really does imagine being back in time - faded elegance and quite delightful.

Directions: 9 miles west of Hay, 11 miles north of Brecon on A470. Bristol and Cardiff Airports just under an hour away.

Web: www.johansens.com/llangoedhall
E-mail: Llangoed_Hall_Co_Wales_UK@compuserve.com
Tel: 0870 381 8696
International: +44 (0)1874 754525
Fax: 01874 754545

Welshpool

Llandrindod Wells

Brecon
Abergavenny

Price Guide:
single from £120
double/twin from £160
suite from £320

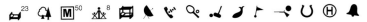

NANT DDU LODGE HOTEL

CWM TAF, BRECON BEACONS NR BRECON, POWYS, WALES CF48 2HY

Directions: On the A470, 12 miles south of Brecon, 6 miles north of Merthyr Tydfil.

Web: www.johansens.com/nantddulodge
E-mail: enquiries@nant−ddu−lodge.co.uk
Tel: 0870 381 8754
International: +44 (0)1685 379111
Fax: 01685 377088

Price Guide:
single £65–£75
double/twin £80–£100

This award-winning country hotel and inn offers excellent value for money in the lovely, unspoilt heart of the Brecon Beacons National Park. Impeccably run by the welcoming Ronson family, Nant Ddu has been renowned for its exceptional contemporary décor and superb cuisine since opening in 1992. Views from the hotel are spectacular, and it boasts its own well-kept lawns, which broaden out into the green hills of the surrounding National Park area. The individually designed bedrooms display inventiveness and style, and the very best are the river rooms, complete with queen-size or four-poster beds, sofas, wide-screen televisions and video players. The bar provides a cosy environment for drinking and eating, as food can be served here or in the Bistro-style restaurant. The extensive menu offers a surprising array of traditional and creative dishes and changes daily according to the availability of top-quality ingredients. A superb luxury health spa has recently opened, offering a 18-metre indoor swimming pool, 15-seat saunarium, large hydro-spa, air-conditioned gym and 3 treatment rooms. External membership is tightly controlled so that the spa never gets too crowded. Guests can explore the region's many castles and cathedrals and visit Cardiff, just 35 minutes away.

Our inspector loved: *The newly opened spa - so relaxing, an excellent addition to this vibrant hotel.*

GLIFFAES COUNTRY HOUSE HOTEL

CRICKHOWELL, POWYS NP8 1RH

Visitors may be surprised to discover a hotel featuring distinctive Italianate architecture midway between the Brecon Beacons and the Black Mountains. Gliffaes Country House Hotel is poised 150 feet above the River Usk and commands glorious views of the surrounding hills and valley. The elegantly furnished, Regency-style drawing room is an ideal place to relax and leads to a large conservatory and on to the terrace, from which guests may enjoy the magnificent scenery. In addition to a panelled sitting room, there is a billiard room with a full-size table. In the dining room modern British style cuisine combines with local produce to create an imaginative menu. The bedrooms have been refreshingly decorated by Susie Suter, one of the owners, in her own style to reflect the timeless ambience of Gliffaes generated by her parents. The Gliffaes fishery includes every type of water, from slow-flowing flats to fast-running rapids, on 3½ miles of the River Usk renowned for its wild brown trout and salmon fishing. The 33-acre hotel grounds have rare trees and shrubs as well as lawns for putting and croquet. There are 2 Golf courses within easy reach. Riding can be arranged nearby. Open throughout the year. There are now conference facilities available in the grounds. Cardiff and Bristol airports are within a 50-mile radius.

Our inspector loved: *This is a true country hotel - the river situation is a delight. Comfortable, welcoming and totaly unspoilt.*

Directions: Gliffaes is signposted from the A40, 2½ miles west of Crickhowell.

Web: www.johansens.com/gliffaescountryhouse
E-mail: calls@gliffaeshotel.com
Tel: 0870 381 8557
International: +44 (0)1874 730371
Fax: 01874 730463

Price Guide:
single from £57–£77.50
double/twin £119–£170

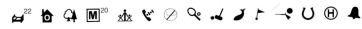

LAKE VYRNWY HOTEL

LAKE VYRNWY, LLANWDDYN, MONTGOMERYSHIRE SY10 0LY

Directions: From Shrewsbury take the A458 to Welshpool, then turn right onto the B4393 just after Ford (signposted to Lake Vyrnwy 28 miles).

Web: www.johansens.com/lakevyrnwy
E-mail: res@lakevyrnwy.com
Tel: 0870 381 8671
International: +44 (0)1691 870 692
Fax: 01691 870 259

Price Guide:
single £90–£155
double/twin £120–£190
suite £190–£220

A stunning location and relaxing environment are the hallmark of this impressive Victorian country house hotel, which has been maintained since 1890 as a peaceful retreat for lovers of nature and fine dining. Standing majestically on the hillside of the Berwyn Mountain range, Lake Vyrnwy Hotel offers breathtaking views over gardens, lake waters, a 24,000-acre estate teaming with wildlife and a background landscape of mountains, moor land and forest. As well as being an RSPB sanctuary the estate also provides 56 miles of forest tracks, excellent driven and rough shooting for pheasant and duck and some of the best fly-fishing in Wales. Other pursuits include sailing, quad trekking, clay shooting, archery, cycling and tennis. Horses can be accommodated in the livery. All 35 spacious bedrooms are individually decorated and furnished, some have four-posters beds, Jacuzzis, suites and balconies and most afford panoramic views. Dining is a delight in the 2 Rosettes awarded candle-lit restaurant where courteous staff provide the most attentive service. Mouth-watering menus change seasonally with even the breakfast marmalade and afternoon tea jams made by the talented kitchen team. Dedicated meeting and private dining facilities are available.

Our inspector loved: *The fact that a guest flew in by helicopter to buy a jar of hotel marmalade. It is delicious!*

THE LAKE COUNTRY HOUSE

LLANGAMMARCH WELLS, POWYS LD4 4BS

A welcoming Welsh Country house set in its own 50 acres with rhododendron lined pathways, riverside walks and a large well-stocked trout lake. Within the hotel, airy rooms filled with fine antiques, paintings and fresh flowers make this the perfect place to relax. Delicious homemade teas are served everyday beside log fires. From the windows, ducks and geese can be glimpsed wandering in the gardens which cascade down to the river. In the award-winning restaurant, fresh produce and herbs from the gardens are used for seasonal country house menus, complemented by one of the finest wine lists in Wales. Each of the supremely comfortable bedrooms or suites with beautifully appointed sitting rooms are furnished with the thoughtful attention to detail seen throughout the hotel. Guests can fish for trout or salmon on the four miles of river which runs through the grounds and the 3-acre lake regularly yields trout of 5 pounds and over. The grounds are a haven for wildlife: herons, dippers and kingfishers skim over the river, there are badgers in the woods and swans and waterfowl abound. There is a large billiard room in the hotel and a 9-hole par 3 golf course, tennis court, croquet lawn and putting green. Awarded an AA 3 Red star and RAC Gold Ribbon.

Our inspector loved: The superb service and delicious food in the restaurant - a lovely atmosphere.

Directions: From the A483, follow signs to Llangammarch Wells and then to the hotel.

Web: www.johansens.com/lakecountryhouse
E-mail: info@lakecountryhouse.co.uk
Tel: 0870 381 8668
International: +44 (0)1591 620202
Fax: 01591 620457

Price Guide:
single £120
double/twin £160–£200
suite £200–£250

419   ᗏᗏ   ⌂   ♿   [M]⁴⁰   ⅗⅖   🐕   ▭   ⚲   ⌣   ♪   ⌐   ↝   ♲   Ⓗ   🔔

NEW

MORGANS

SOMERSET PLACE, SWANSEA SA1 1RR

Directions: From the M4 take junction 42 and follow signs to the city centre. After the 6th set of traffic lights take a left turn to Dylan Thomas Centre and the hotel and car park are on the right.

Web: www.johansens.com/morgans
E-mail: info@morganshotels.co.uk
Tel: 0870 381 9158
International: +44 (0)1792 484848
Fax: 01792 484848

Price Guide:
double £100-£250

When it opened to great acclaim in 2002, Morgans not only made a dream come true for local entrepreneur Martin Morgan and his wife Louisa, it also brought a touch of 21st-century style to Wales's "City by the Sea". Swansea's Grade II listed Victorian Port Authority building has been transformed, yet behind the red brick exterior it retains many of its classic features, from mouldings to staircases, wooden floors and intricate windows. Each of the 20 individually named bedrooms is bursting with personality, the coolly elegant Zeta, the vibrant Digby Grande and the plush Henry Belle representing just a small selection. Sumptuous furnishings of suede, satin and fine Egyptian cotton combine with more fun interior design elements that include double showers, plasma screens and DVD players. Sophistication and attention to detail abound throughout the non-smoking hotel's public spaces, and no more so than in the chocolate and cream Morgans Bar with its one red chair, or the gently neon-lit Champagne Bar. Visitors can enjoy dinner in Morgans restaurant or the buzzing Plimsoll Line bistro, relax on the decked courtyard, or gaze at the exquisite stained glass of the cuppola.

Our inspector loved: The contemporary elegance and attention to detail throughout; simply stunning.

CONDÉ NAST JOHANSENS GUIDES

Recommending only the finest hotels in the world

As well as this Guide Condé Nast Johansens also publishes the following titles:

RECOMMENDED COUNTRY HOUSES, SMALL HOTELS & INNS, GREAT BRITAIN & IRELAND

255 smaller more rural properties, ideal for short breaks or more intimate stays

RECOMMENDED HOTELS, EUROPE & THE MEDITERRANEAN

351 continental gems featuring châteaux, resorts and

charming countryside hotels

RECOMMENDED HOTELS, INNS & RESORTS, NORTH AMERICA, BERMUDA, CARIBBEAN, MEXICO, PACIFIC

200 properties including many hidden properties from across the region

RECOMMENDED VENUES FOR BUSINESS MEETINGS, CONFERENCES AND EVENTS, GREAT BRITAIN & EUROPE

230 venues that cater specifically for a business audience

When you purchase two Guides or more we will be pleased to offer you a reduction in the cost.

The complete set of Condé Nast Johansens Guides may be purchased as 'The Chairman's Collection'.

**To order any Guides please complete the order form on page 487
or call FREEPHONE 0800 269 397**

MINI LISTINGS COUNTRY HOUSES

Condé Nast Johansens are delighted to recommend over 250 country houses, small hotels and inns across Great Britain & Ireland. Call 0800 269 397 or see the order forms on page 487 to order Guides.

England

Bath & North East Somerset

The County Hotel – 18/19 Pulteney Road, Bath, Somerset BA2 4EZ. Tel: 0870 381 8455

Dorian House – One Upper Oldfield Park, Bath BA2 3JX. Tel: 0870 381 8650

Oldfields – 102 Wells Road, Bath, Somerset BA2 3AL. Tel: 0870 381 8792

The Ring O' Roses – Stratton Road, Holcombe, Near Bath BA3 5EB. Tel: 0870 381 9181

Bedfordshire

Mill House Hotel & Restaurant – Mill House, Mill Road, Sharnbrook, Bedfordshire MK44 1NP. Tel: 0870 381 9189

Berkshire

Cantley House – Milton Road, Wokingham, Berkshire RG40 5GQ. Tel: 0870 381 9233

The Cottage Inn – Maidens Green, Winkfield, Berkshire SL4 4SW. Tel: 0870 381 9234

The Inn on the Green – The Old Cricket Common, Cookham Dean, Berkshire SL6 9NZ. Tel: 0870 381 8639

▼
The Leatherne Bottel Riverside Restaurant – The Bridleway, Goring-on-Thames, Berkshire RG8 0HS. Tel: 0870 381 8685

Stirrups – Maidens Green, Bracknell, Berkshire RG42 6LD. Tel: 0870 381 9238

Buckinghamshire

The Greyhound – High Street, Chalfont-St-Peter, Buckinghamshire SL9 9RA. Tel: 0870 381 9216

The Ivy House – London Road, Chalfont St Giles, Buckinghamshire HP8 4RS. Tel: 0870 381 9236

The Nags Head – London Road, Great Missenden, Buckinghamshire HP16 0DG. Tel: 0870 381 9237

Cambridgeshire

Crown Lodge Hotel – Downham Road, Outwell, Wisbech, Cambridgeshire PE14 8SE. Tel: 0870 381 8466

The Meadowcroft Hotel – Trumpington Road, Cambridge CB2 2EX. Tel: 0870 381 8651

Melbourn Bury – Melbourn, Cambridgeshire, Nr Royston SG8 6DE. Tel: 0870 381 8726

Cheshire

Broxton Hall Country House Hotel – Whitchurch Road, Broxton, Chester, Cheshire CH3 9JS. Tel: 0870 381 8387

Willington Hall Hotel – Willington, Nr Tarporley, Cheshire CW6 0NB. Tel: 0870 381 8999

Cornwall

Cormorant On The River, Hotel & Riverside Restaurant – Golant By Fowey, Cornwall PL23 1LL. Tel: 0870 381 8446

Mount Haven Hotel & Restaurant – Turnpike Road, Marazion, Nr Penzance, Cornwall TR17 0DQ. Tel: 0870 381 9228

The Old Quay House Hotel – 28 Fore Street, Fowey, Cornwall PL23 1AQ. Tel: 0870 381 8783

St. Georges Country Hotel – St. Georges Hill, Perranporth, Cornwall TR6 0ED. Tel: 0870 381 9140

Stenhill House – Stenhill Farm, North Petherwin, Cornwall PL15 8NN. Tel: 0870 381 9217

Tredethy House – Helland Bridge, Bodmin, Cornwall PL30 4QS. Tel: 0870 381 9142

Trehaven Manor Hotel – Station Road, Looe, Cornwall PL13 1HN. Tel: 0870 381 8952

Trehellas House Hotel & Restaurant – Washaway, Bodmin, Cornwall PL30 3AD. Tel: 0870 381 8953

Trelawne Hotel – The Hutches Restaurant – Mawnan Smith, Nr Falmouth, Cornwall TR11 5HS. Tel: 0870 381 8954

Trevalsa Court Hotel – School Hill, Mevagissey, St Austell, Cornwall PL26 6TH. Tel: 0870 381 8955

Wisteria Lodge – Boscundle, Tregrehan, St Austell, Cornwall PL25 3RJ. Tel: 0870 381 9183

Cumbria

Broadoaks Country House – Bridge Lane, Troutbeck, Windermere, Cumbria LA23 1LA. Tel: 0870 381 8380

Crosby Lodge Country House Hotel – High Crosby, Crosby-on-Eden, Carlisle, Cumbria CA6 4QZ. Tel: 0870 381 8461

Dale Head Hall Lakeside Hotel – Thirlmere, Keswick, Cumbria CA12 4TN. Tel: 0870 381 8470

Fayrer Garden House Hotel – Lyth Valley Road, Bowness-on-Windermere, Cumbria LA23 3JP. Tel: 0870 381 8517

Grey Friar Lodge – Clappersgate, Ambleside, Cumbria LA22 9NE. Tel: 0870 381 8576

The Leathes Head – Borrowdale, Keswick, Cumbria CA12 5UY. Tel: 0870 381 8686

Linthwaite House Hotel – Crook Road, Bowness-on-Windermere, Cumbria LA23 3JA. Tel: 0870 381 8694

The Pheasant – Bassenthwaite Lake, Nr Cockermouth, Cumbria CA13 9YE. Tel: 0870 381 9227

The Queen's Head Hotel – Main Street, Hawkshead, Cumbria LA22 0NS. Tel: 0870 381 8844

Sawrey House Country Hotel & Restaurant – Near Sawrey, Hawkshead, Ambleside, Cumbria LA22 0LF. Tel: 0870 381 8886

Temple Sowerby House Hotel – Temple Sowerby, Penrith, Cumbria CA10 1RZ. Tel: 0870 381 8942

Underwood – The Hill, Millom, Cumbria LA18 5EZ. Tel: 0870 381 8959

Derbyshire

Blenheim House – Main Street, Etwall, Derbyshire DE65 6LP. Tel: 0870 381 9160

▼
Boar's Head Hotel – Lichfield Road, Sudbury, Derbyshire DE6 5GX. Tel: 0870 381 8371

Buckingham's Hotel & Restaurant With One Table – 85 Newbold Road, Chesterfield, Derbyshire S41 7PU. Tel: 0870 381 8390

The Chequers Inn – Froggatt Edge, Hope Valley, Derbyshire S32 3ZJ. Tel: 0870 381 8422

Dannah Farm Country House – Bowman's Lane, Shottle, Nr Belper, Derbyshire DE56 2DR. Tel: 0870 381 8476

Donington Manor Hotel – Castle Donington, Derbyshire DE74 2PP. Tel: 0870 381 9225

Kegworth House – 42 High Street, Kegworth, Derbyshire DE74 2DA. Tel: 0870 381 9102

Littleover Lodge Hotel – 222 Rykneld Road, Littleover, Derby, Derbyshire DE23 7AN. Tel: 0870 381 8695

The Maynard Arms – Main Road, Grindleford, Derbyshire S32 2HE. Tel: 0870 381 8725

The Peacock At Rowsley – Rowsley, Nr Matlock, Derbyshire DE4 2EB. Tel: 0870 381 8805

The Plough Inn – Leadmill Bridge, Hathersage, Derbyshire S30 1BA. Tel: 0870 381 8827

The Wind In The Willows – Derbyshire Level, Glossop, Derbyshire SK13 7PT. Tel: 0870 381 9001

Devon

Browns Hotel, Wine Bar & Brasserie – 80 West Street, Tavistock, Devon PL19 8AQ. Tel: 0870 381 8386

Combe House Hotel & Restaurant – Gittisham, Honiton, Nr Exeter, Devon EX14 3AD. Tel: 0870 381 8440

The Edgemoor – Haytor Road, Bovey Tracey, South Devon TQ13 9LE. Tel: 0870 381 8499

Hewitt's - Villa Spaldi – North Walk, Lynton, Devon EX35 6HJ. Tel: 0870 381 8593

Home Farm Hotel – Wilmington, Nr Honiton, Devon EX14 9JR. Tel: 0870 381 8604

Ilsington Country House Hotel – Ilsington Village, Near Newton Abbot, Devon TQ13 9RR. Tel: 0870 381 8635

Kingston House – Staverton, Totnes, Devon TQ9 6AR. Tel: 0870 381 8655

MINI LISTINGS COUNTRY HOUSES

Condé Nast Johansens are delighted to recommend over 250 country houses, small hotels and inns across Great Britain & Ireland.
Call 0800 269 397 or see the order forms on page 487 to order Guides.

The Lord Haldon Country Hotel – Dunchideock, Nr Exeter, Devon EX6 7YF. Tel: 0870 381 8703

The New Inn – Coleford, Crediton, Devon EX17 5BZ. Tel: 0870 381 8757

Percy's Country Hotel & Restaurant – Coombeshead Estate, Virginstow, Devon EX21 5EA. Tel: 0870 381 8817

The Sea Trout Inn – Staverton, Nr Totnes, Devon TQ9 6PA. Tel: 0870 381 8888

Yeoldon House Hotel – Durrant Lane, Northam, Nr Bideford EX39 2RL. Tel: 0870 381 9019

Dorset

The Eastbury Hotel – Long Street, Sherborne, Dorset DT9 3BY. Tel: 0870 381 8497

The Grange At Oborne – Oborne, Nr Sherborne, Dorset DT9 4LA. Tel: 0870 381 9239

▼
Kemps Country Hotel & Restaurant – East Stoke, Wareham, Dorset BH20 6AL. **Tel: 0870 381 8647**

The Manor Hotel – West Bexington, Dorchester, Dorset DT2 9DF. Tel: 0870 381 8715

Mortons House Hotel – East Street, Corfe Castle, Dorset BH20 5EE. Tel: 0870 381 9180

Yalbury Cottage Hotel – Lower Bockhampton, Dorchester, Dorset DT2 8PZ. Tel: 0870 381 9015

Durham

Grove House – Hamsterley Forest, Nr Bishop Auckland, Co Durham DL13 3NL. Tel: 0870 381 8577

Horsley Hall – Eastgate, Nr Stanhope, Bishop Auckland, Co Durham DL13 2LJ. Tel: 0870 381 8608

Essex

The Crown House – Great Chesterford, Saffron Walden, Essex CB10 1NY. Tel: 0870 381 8465

De Vere Arms – High Street, Earls Colne, Colchester, Essex CO6 2PB. Tel: 0870 381 9150

Prested Hall – Feering, Colchester, Essex CO5 9EE. Tel: 0870 381 9220

The Pump House Apartment – 132 Church Street, Great Burstead, Essex CM11 2TR. Tel: 0870 381 8842

Gloucestershire

Bibury Court – Bibury Court, Bibury, Gloucestershire GL7 5NT. Tel: 0870 381 8360

Charlton Kings Hotel – Charlton Kings, Cheltenham, Gloucestershire GL52 6UU. Tel: 0870 381 8416

The Malt House – Broad Campden, Gloucestershire GL55 6UU. Tel: 0870 381 8714

New Inn At Coln – Coln St-Aldwyns, Nr Cirencester, Gloucestershire GL7 5AN. Tel: 0870 381 8758

Three Choirs Vineyards Estate – Newent, Gloucestershire GL18 1LS. Tel: 0870 381 8946

Tudor Farmhouse Hotel & Restaurant – High Street, Clearwell, Nr Coleford, Gloucestershire GL16 8JS. Tel: 0870 381 9223

The White Hart Inn – High Street, Winchcombe, Nr Cheltenham, Gloucestershire GL54 5LJ. Tel: 0870 381 8984

The Wild Duck Inn – Drakes Island, Ewen, Cirencester, Gloucestershire GL7 6BY. Tel: 0870 381 8997

Hampshire

Langrish House – Langrish, Nr Petersfield, Hampshire GU32 1RN. Tel: 0870 381 8679

The Mill At Gordleton – Silver Street, Hordle, Nr Lymington, New Forest, Hampshire SO41 6DJ. Tel: 0870 381 8558

The Nurse's Cottage – Station Road, Sway, Lymington, Hampshire SO41 6BA. Tel: 0870 381 8774

Thatched Cottage Hotel & Restaurant – 16 Brookley Road, Brockenhurst, New Forest, Hampshire SO42 7RR. Tel: 0870 381 8943

Westover Hall – Park Lane, Milford-on-Sea, Hampshire SO41 0PT. Tel: 0870 381 8982

Whitley Ridge Country House Hotel – Beaulieu Road, Brockenhurst, New Forest, Hampshire SO42 7QL. Tel: 0870 381 8994

Herefordshire

The Feathers Hotel – High Street, Ledbury, Herefordshire HR8 1DS. Tel: 0870 381 8518

Ford Abbey – Pudleston, Nr Leominster, Herefordshire HR6 0RZ. Tel: 0870 381 9144

Glewstone Court – Nr Ross-on-Wye, Herefordshire HR9 6AW. Tel: 0870 381 8556

Rhydspence Inn – Whitney-on-Wye, Near Hay-on-Wye, Herefordshire HR3 6EU. Tel: 0870 381 9156

The Steppes – Ullingswick, Nr Hereford, Herefordshire HR1 3JG. Tel: 0870 381 8914

Wilton Court Hotel – Wilton, Ross-on-Wye, Herefordshire HR9 6AQ. Tel: 0870 381 9000

Hertfordshire

Redcoats Farmhouse Hotel And Restaurant – Redcoats Green, Near Hitchin, Herts SG4 7JR. Tel: 0870 381 8851

Isle Of Wight

Rylstone Manor – Rylstone Gardens, Shanklin, Isle Of Wight PO37 6RE. Tel: 0870 381 8882

Kent

The George Hotel – Stone Street, Cranbrook, Kent TN17 3HE. Tel: 0870 381 8540

Hempstead House – London Road, Bapchild, Sittingbourne, Kent ME9 9PP. Tel: 0870 381 8649

Ringlestone Inn and Farmhouse Hotel – Twixt Harrietsham And Wormshill, Nr Maidstone, Kent ME17 1NX. Tel: 0870 381 8856

Romney Bay House – Coast Road, Littlestone, New Romney, Kent TN28 8QY. Tel: 0870 381 8863

Wallett's Court Hotel & Spa – West Cliffe, St Margaret's-at-Cliffe, Dover, Kent CT15 6EW. Tel: 0870 381 8966

Lancashire

▼
The Inn At Whitewell – Forest Of Bowland, Clitheroe, Lancashire BB7 3AT. **Tel: 0870 381 8638**

Tree Tops Country House Restaurant & Hotel – Southport Old Road, Formby, Nr Southport, Lancashire L37 0AB. Tel: 0870 381 8950

Leicestershire

Abbots Oak Country House – Abbots Oak, Warren Hills Road, Near Coalville, Leicestershire LE67 4UY. Tel: 0870 381 8303

Quenby Hall – Hungarton, Leicestershire LE7 9JF. Tel: 0870 381 9131

Lincolnshire

The Crown Hotel – All Saints Place, Stamford, Lincolnshire PE9 2AG. Tel: 0870 381 8464

The Lea Gate Inn – Leagate Road, Coningsby, Lincolnshire LN4 4RS. Tel: 0870 381 8684

Washingborough Hall – Church Hill, Washingborough, Lincoln LN4 1BE. Tel: 0870 381 8971

London

Oak Lodge Hotel – 80 Village Road, Bush Hill Park, Enfield, Middlesex EN1 2EU. Tel: 0870 381 8777

Greater Manchester

The White Hart Inn – 51 Stockport Road, Lydgate, Saddleworth, Greater Manchester OL4 4JJ. Tel: 0870 381 8985

MINI LISTINGS COUNTRY HOUSES

Condé Nast Johansens are delighted to recommend over 250 country houses, small hotels and inns across Great Britain & Ireland.
Call 0800 269 397 or see the order forms on page 487 to order Guides.

Norfolk

The Abbey Hotel – 10 Church Street, Wymondham, Norfolk NR18 0PH. Tel: 0870 381 9151

The Beeches Hotel And Victorian Gardens – 2–6 Earlham Road, Norwich, Norfolk NR2 3DB. Tel: 0870 381 8352

Beechwood Hotel – Cromer Road, North Walsham, Norfolk NR28 0HD. Tel: 0870 381 8353

Broom Hall Country Hotel – Richmond Road, Saham Toney, Thetford, Norfolk IP25 7EX. Tel: 0870 381 8384

Brovey Lair – Carbrooke Road, Ovington, Thetford, Norfolk IP25 6SD. Tel: 0870 381 8385

Elderton Lodge Hotel & Langtry Restaurant – Gunton Park, Thorpe Market, Nr North Walsham, Norfolk NR11 8TZ. Tel: 0870 381 8502

Felbrigg Lodge – Aylmerton, North Norfolk NR11 8RA. Tel: 0870 381 8520

The Great Escape Holiday Company – Docking, Kings Lynn, Norfolk PE31 8LY. Tel: 0870 381 8568

Idyllic Cottages At Vere Lodge – South Raynham, Fakenham, Norfolk NR21 7HE. Tel: 0870 381 8961

The Manor House – Barsham Road, Great Snoring, Norfolk NR21 0HP. Tel: 0870 381 8716

The Norfolk Mead Hotel – Coltishall, Norwich, Norfolk NR12 7DN. Tel: 0870 381 8764

The Old Rectory – 103 Yarmouth Road, Norwich, Norfolk NR7 0HF, uk. Tel: 0870 381 8784

Petersfield House Hotel – Lower Street, Horning, Nr Norwich, Norfolk NR12 8PF. Tel: 0870 381 8818

The Stower Grange – School Road, Drayton, Norfolk NR8 6EF. Tel: 0870 381 8921

The White Horse – Brancaster Staithe, Norfolk PE31 8BY. Tel: 0870 381 8986

Northamptonshire

The Falcon Hotel – Castle Ashby, Northamptonshire NN7 1LF. Tel: 0870 381 8512

Northumberland

The Otterburn Tower – Otterburn, Northumberland NE19 1NS. Tel: 0870 381 8796

Waren House Hotel – Waren Mill, Bamburgh, Northumberland NE70 7EE. Tel: 0870 381 8967

Nottinghamshire

Cockliffe Country House Hotel – Burnt Stump Country Park, Burnt Stump Hill, Nottinghamshire NG5 8PQ. Tel: 0870 381 8435

Langar Hall – Langar, Nottinghamshire NG13 9HG. Tel: 0870 381 8676

Oxfordshire

Duke Of Marlborough Country Inn – Woodleys, Woodstock, Oxford OX20 1HT. Tel: 0870 381 9219

Fallowfields – Kingston Bagpuize With Southmoor, Oxon OX13 5BH. Tel: 0870 381 8513

The Flying Pig At The Stonor Hotel – Stonor, Nr Henley-on-Thames, Oxfordshire RG9 6HE. Tel: 0870 381 9226

The George Hotel – High Street, Dorchester-on-Thames, Oxford OX10 7HH. Tel: 0870 381 8539

▼
The Kings Head Inn & Restaurant – The Green, Bledington, Nr Kingham, Oxfordshire OX7 6XQ. Tel: 0870 381 8654

The Lamb Inn – Sheep Street, Burford, Oxfordshire OX18 4LR. Tel: 0870 381 8674

The Plough At Clanfield – Bourton Road, Clanfield, Oxfordshire OX18 2RB. Tel: 0870 381 8826

The Shaven Crown Hotel – High Street, Shipton Under Wychwood, Oxfordshire OX7 6BA. Tel: 0870 381 8892

Rutland

Barnsdale Lodge – The Avenue, Rutland Water, Nr Oakham, Rutland, Leicestershire LE15 8AH. Tel: 0870 381 8342

Shropshire

The Hundred House Hotel – Bridgnorth Road, Norton, Nr Shifnal, Telford, Shropshire TF11 9EE. Tel: 0870 381 8629

Mynd House Hotel – Ludlow Road, Little Stretton, Church Stretton, Shropshire SY6 6RB. Tel: 0870 381 9159

The Old Vicarage Hotel – Worfield, Bridgnorth, Shropshire WV15 5JZ. Tel: 0870 381 8790

Overton Grange Hotel – Overton, Nr Ludlow, Shropshire SY8 4AD. Tel: 0870 381 9135

Pen-Y-Dyffryn Hall Hotel – Rhydycroesau, Nr Oswestry, Shropshire SY10 7JD. Tel: 0870 381 8809

Soulton Hall – Nr Wem, Shropshire SY4 5RS. Tel: 0870 381 8899

Somerset

Ashwick Country House Hotel – Dulverton, Somerset TA22 9QD. Tel: 0870 381 8327

Beryl – Wells, Somerset BA5 3JP. Tel: 0870 381 8358

Chestnut House – Hectors Stone, Lower Road, Woolavington, Bridgwater, Somerset TA7 8EQ. Tel: 0870 381 8425

Farthings Hotel & Restaurant – Hatch Beauchamp, Somerset TA3 6SG. Tel: 0870 381 8515

Glencot House – Glencot Lane, Wookey Hole, Nr Wells, Somerset BA5 1BH. Tel: 0870 381 8552

Karslake House Hotel & Restaurant – Halse Lane, Winsford, Exmoor National Park, Somerset TA24 7JE. Tel: 0870 381 9134

Porlock Vale House – Porlock Weir, Somerset TA24 8NY. Tel: 0870 381 8830

Three Acres Country House – Three Acres, Brushford, Dulverton, Somerset TA22 9AR. Tel: 0870 381 9229

Staffordshire

Oak Tree Farm – Hints Road, Hopwas, Nr Tamworth, Staffordshire B78 3AA. Tel: 0870 381 8778

Somerford Hall – Brewood, Staffordshire ST19 9DQ. Tel: 0870 381 9120

Suffolk

Clarice House – Horringer Court, Horringer Road, Bury St Edmunds Suffolk IP29 5PH. Tel: 0870 381 8431

The George – The Green, Cavendish, Sudbury, Suffolk CO10 8BA. Tel: 0870 381 8537

Thornham Hall & Restaurant – Thornham Magna, Nr Eye, Suffolk IP23 8HA. Tel: 0870 381 8945

Worlington Hall Country House Hotel – Worlington, Suffolk IP28 8RX. Tel: 0870 381 9161

Surrey

Chase Lodge – 10 Park Road, Hampton Wick, Kingston-upon-Thames, Surrey KT1 4AS. Tel: 0870 381 8419

▼
Stanhill Court Hotel – Stan Hill Road, Charlwood, Nr Horley, Surrey RH6 0EP. Tel: 0870 381 8908

East Sussex

Hooke Hall – High Street, Uckfield, East Sussex TN22 1EN. Tel: 0870 381 8606

The Hope Anchor Hotel – Watchbell Street, Rye, East Sussex TN31 7HA. Tel: 0870 381 8607

West Sussex

The Chequers At Slaugham – Slaugham, Nr Handcross, West Sussex RH17 6AQ. Tel: 0870 381 8421

Chequers Hotel – Old Rectory Lane, Pulborough, West Sussex RH20 1AD. Tel: 0870 381 9222

MINI LISTINGS COUNTRY HOUSES

Condé Nast Johansens are delighted to recommend over 250 country houses, small hotels and inns across Great Britain & Ireland.
Call 0800 269 397 or see the order forms on page 487 to order Guides.

Crouchers Country Hotel & Restaurant – Birdham Road, Apuldram, Near Chichester, West Sussex PO20 7EH. Tel: 0870 381 8462

Forge Hotel – Chilgrove, Chichester, West Sussex PO18 9HX. Tel: 0870 381 8527

The Mill House Hotel – Mill Lane, Ashington, West Sussex RH20 3BX. Tel: 0870 381 8735

The Old Tollgate Restaurant And Hotel – The Street, Bramber, Steyning, West Sussex BN44 3WE. Tel: 0870 381 8789

The Royal Oak Inn – Pook Lane, East Lavant, Nr Goodwood, Chichester, West Sussex PO18 0AX. Tel: 0870 381 9218

Warwickshire

Clarendon House – Old High Street, Kenilworth, Warwickshire CV8 1LZ. Tel: 0870 381 8430

Wiltshire

The George Inn – Longbridge Deverill, Warminster, Wiltshire BA12 7DG. Tel: 0870 381 8542

Hinton Grange – Nr Hinton, Dryham, Wiltshire SN14 8HG. Tel: 0870 381 8596

The Old Manor Hotel – Trowle, Nr Bradford-on-Avon, Wiltshire BA14 9BL. Tel: 0870 381 8782

Rudloe Hall – Leafly Lane, Near Box, Wiltshire SN13 0PA. Tel: 0870 381 8880

Stanton Manor – Stanton Saint Quintin, Nr Chippenham, Wiltshire SN14 6DQ. Tel: 0870 381 8910

Widbrook Grange – Widbrook, Bradford-on-Avon, Nr Bath, Wiltshire BA15 1UH. Tel: 0870 381 8996

Worcestershire

Colwall Park – Colwall, Near Malvern, Worcestershire WR13 6QG. Tel: 0870 381 8437

The Old Rectory – Ipsley Lane, Ipsley, Near Redditch, Worcestershire B98 0AP. Tel: 0870 381 9169

The Old Windmill – Withybed Lane, Inkberrow, Worcester WR7 4JL. Tel: 0870 381 9167

The White Lion Hotel – High Street, Upton-upon-Severn, Nr Malvern, Worcestershire WR8 0HJ. Tel: 0870 381 8989

North Yorkshire

The Austwick Traddock – Austwick, Via Lancaster, North Yorkshire LA2 8BY. Tel: 0870 381 8331

The Blue Lion – East Witton, Nr Leyburn, North Yorkshire DL8 4SN. Tel: 0870 381 8368

The Boar's Head Hotel – The Ripley Castle Estate, Harrogate, North Yorkshire HG3 3AY. Tel: 0870 381 8370

Dunsley Hall – Dunsley, Whitby, North Yorkshire YO21 3TL. Tel: 0870 381 8494

Hob Green Hotel And Restaurant – Markington, Harrogate, North Yorkshire HG3 3PJ. Tel: 0870 381 8600

The Kings Head Hotel – Market Place, Richmond, North Yorkshire DL10 4HS. Tel: 0870 381 9224

The Red Lion – By The Bridge At Burnsall, Near Skipton, North Yorkshire BD23 6BU. Tel: 0870 381 8850

Rookhurst Country House Hotel – West End, Gayle, Hawes, North Yorkshire DL8 3RT. Tel: 0870 381 8865

Stow House Hotel – Aysgarth, Leyburn, North Yorkshire DL8 3SR. Tel: 0870 381 8920

West Yorkshire

Hey Green Country House Hotel – Waters Road, Marsden, West Yorkshire HD7 6NG. Tel: 0870 381 8652

The Rock Inn Hotel – Holywell Green, Halifax, West Yorkshire HX4 9BS. Tel: 0870 381 8861

Channel Islands

Guernsey

La Favorita Hotel – Fermain Bay, Guernsey, Channel Islands GY4 6SD. Tel: 0870 381 8665

Herm Island

The White House – Herm Island, Guernsey, Channel Islands GY1 3HR. Tel: 0870 381 8988

Jersey

▼
Eulah Country House – Mont Cochon, St Helier, Jersey, Channel Islands JE2 3JA. Tel: 0870 381 8509

Sark

Aval du Creux Hotel – Harbour Hill, Sark, Guernsey, Channel Islands GY9 0SB. Tel: 0870 381 9173

La Sablonnerie – Little Sark, Sark, Channel Islands GY9 0SD. Tel: 0870 381 8666

Ireland

Clare

Gregans Castle – Ballyvaughan, Co Clare, Ireland. Tel: 00 353 6 57077 005

Galway

Ross Lake House Hotel – Rosscahill, Oughterard, Co Galway, Ireland. Tel: 00 353 91 550109

Zetland Country House Hotel – Cashel Bay, Connemara, Co Galway, Ireland. Tel: 00 353 9 531111

Kerry

Caragh Lodge – Caragh Lake, Co Kerry, Ireland. Tel: 00 353 66 9769115

Carrig House – Caragh Lake, Killorgin, Co Kerry, Ireland. Tel: 00 353 66 9769100

Emlagh House – Dingle, Co Kerry, Ireland. Tel: 00 353 66 915 2345

Gorman's Clifftop House & Restaurant – Glaise Bheag, Ballydavid, Dingle Peninsula – Tralee, Co Kerry, Ireland. Tel: 00 353 66 9155162

Killarney Royal Hotel – College Street, Killarney, Co Kerry, Ireland. Tel: 00 353 64 31853

Sligo

Coopershill House – Riverstown, Co Sligo, Ireland. Tel: 00 353 71 9165108

Wexford

Kilmokea Country Manor & Gardens – Kilmokea – Gt. Island, Campile, Co Wexford, Ireland. Tel: 00 353 51 388109

Scotland

Abderdeenshire

Maryculter House Hotel – South Deeside Road, Maryculter, Aberdeen AB12 5GB. Tel: 0870 381 8722

Balgonie Country House – Braemar Place, Ballater, Royal Deeside, Aberdeenshire AB35 5NQ. Tel: 0870 381 8335

Angus

Castleton House Hotel – Glamis, By Forfar, Angus DD8 1SJ. Tel: 0870 381 8411

Argyll & Bute

Ballachulish House – Ballachulish, Argyll PH49 4JX. Tel: 0870 381 8336

Enmore Hotel – Marine Parade, Kirn, Dunoon, Argyll PA23 8HH. Tel: 0870 381 8504

MINI LISTINGS COUNTRY HOUSES

Condé Nast Johansens are delighted to recommend over 250 country houses, small hotels and inns across Great Britain & Ireland.
Call 0800 269 397 or see the order forms on page 487 to order Guides.

The Frog At Port Dunstaffnage – Dunstaffnage Marina, Connel, By Oban, Argyll PA37 1PX.
Tel: 0870 381 8533

Highland Cottage – Breadabane Street, Tobermory, Isle of Mull PA75 6PD. Tel: 0870 381 9184

The Royal At Tighnabruaich – Tighnabruaich, Argyll, Scotland PA21 2BE. Tel: 0870 381 8876

Clackmannanshire

Castle Campbell Hotel – 11 Bridge Street, Dollar, Clackmannanshire FK14 7DE.
Tel: 0870 381 9232

Dumfries & Galloway

Fernhill Hotel – Heugh Road, Portpatrick DG9 8TD.
Tel: 0870 381 8521

Trigony House Hotel – Closeburn, Thornhill, Dumfriesshire DG3 5EZ. Tel: 0870 381 9121

Highland

Culduthel Lodge – 14 Culduthel Road, Inverness, Inverness-shire IV2 4AG.
Tel: 0870 381 8468

Hotel Eilean Iarmain – Sleat, Isle Of Skye IV43 8QR.
Tel: 0870 381 8619

The Lodge On The Loch – Onich, Near Fort William, Highlands PH33 6RY.
Tel: 0870 381 8700

The Steadings Hotel – Flichity, Farr, South Loch Ness, Inverness IV2 6XD.
Tel: 0870 381 9138

Perth & Kinross

The Four Seasons Hotel – St Fillans, Perthshire PH6 2NF.
Tel: 0870 381 8528

Knockendarroch House – Higher Oakfield, Pitlochry, Perthshire PH16 5HT. Tel: 0870 381 8662

The Lake Hotel – Port Of Menteith, Perthshire FK8 3RA.
Tel: 0870 381 8669

Monachyle Mhor – Balquidder, By Lochearnhead, Perthshire FK19 8PQ. Tel: 0870 381 9231

Renfrewshire

Bowfield Hotel & Country Club – Howwood, Renfrewshire PA9 1LA. Tel: 0870 381 8378

Scottish Borders

Ettrickshaws Country House Hotel – Ettrickbridge, Selkirkshire TD7 5HW. Tel: 0870 381 9230

Traquair House – Innerleithen, Peebleshire EH44 6PW.
Tel: 0870 381 9104

South Ayrshire

▼
Culzean Castle – The Eisenhower Apartment – Maybole, Ayrshire KA19 8LE. Tel: 0870 381 8469

Wales

Bridgend

The Great House – High Street, Laleston, Bridgend, Wales CF32 0HP. Tel: 0870 381 8570

Cardiff

The Inn At The Elm Tree – St Brides Wentlooge, Nr Newport NP10 8SQ. Tel: 0870 381 8637

Ceredigion

Conrah Country House Hotel – Rhydgaled, Chancery, Aberystwyth, Ceredigion SY23 4DF. Tel: 0870 381 8444

Falcondale Mansion – Lampeter, Dyfed SA48 7RX.
Tel: 0870 381 9235

Conwy

Castle Hotel – High Street, Conwy LL32 8DB.
Tel: 0870 381 8409

The Old Rectory Country House – Llanrwst Road, Llansanffraid Glan Conwy, Conwy LL28 5LF.
Tel: 0870 381 8787

Sychnant Pass House – Sychnant Pass Road, Conwy LL32 8BJ. Tel: 0870 381 8936

Tan-Y-Foel – Capel Garmon, Nr Betws-y-coed, Conwy LL26 0RE. Tel: 0870 381 8938

Gwynedd

Bae Abermaw – Panorama Hill, Barmouth, Gwynedd LL42 1DQ. Tel: 0870 381 8332

Llwyndu Farmhouse – Llanaber, Nr Barmouth, Gwynedd LL42 1RR. Tel: 0870 381 9143

Plas Dolmelynllyn – Ganllwyd, Dolgellau, Gwynedd LL40 2HP. Tel: 0870 381 8825

Porth Tocyn Country House Hotel – Abersoch, Pwllheli, Gwynedd LL53 7BU. Tel: 0870 381 8832

Isle Of Anglesey

Ye Olde Bull's Head – Castle Street, Beaumaris, Isle Of Anglesey LL58 8AP. Tel: 0870 381 9017

Monmouthshire

The Bell At Skenfrith – Skenfrith, Monmouthshire NP7 8UH.
Tel: 0870 381 8354

The Newbridge On Usk – Tredunnock Near Usk, Monmouthshire NP15 1LY. Tel: 0870 381 9194

Parva Farmhouse And Restaurant – Tintern, Chepstow, Monmouthshire NP16 6SQ. Tel: 0870 381 8803

Pembrokeshire

The Gower Hotel & Orangery Restaurant – Milford Terrace, Saundersfoot, Pembrokeshire SA69 9EL.
Tel: 0870 381 9149

Stone Hall Hotel & Restaurant – Welsh Hook, Haverfordwest, Pembrokeshire SA62 5NS.
Tel: 0870 381 8917

Wolfscastle Country House & Restaurant – Wolfscastle, Nr Haverfordwest, Pembrokeshire SA62 5LZ.
Tel: 0870 381 9162

Powys

▼
Glangrwyney Court – Glangrwyney, Nr Crickhowell, Powys NP8 1ES. Tel: 0870 381 8547

Swansea

Norton House Hotel And Restaurant – Norton Road, Mumbles, Swansea SA3 5TQ. Tel: 0870 381 8769

Vale Of Glamorgan

Egerton Grey – Porthkerry, Nr Cardiff, Vale Of Glamorgan CF62 3BZ. Tel: 0870 381 8501

HISTORIC HOUSES, CASTLES & GARDENS

Incorporating Museums & Galleries

We are pleased to feature over 200 places to visit during your stay at a Condé Nast Johansens recommended hotel.

England

Bedfordshire

John Bunyan Museum - Mill Street, Bedford, Bedfordshire MK40 3EU. Tel: 01234 213722

▼
Woburn Abbey - Woburn, Bedfordshire MK17 9WA. **Tel: 01525 290666**

Berkshire

Savill Garden - Windsor Great Park, Wick Lane, Nr Windsor, Berkshire SL4 2HT. Tel: 01753 847518

Taplow Court - Berry Hill, Taplow, Nr Maidenhead, Berkshire SL6 0ER. Tel: 01628 591209

Buckinghamshire

Hughenden Manor - High Wycombe, Buckinghamshire HP14 4LA. Tel: 01494 755573

Stowe Landscape Gardens - Stowe, Buckingham, Buckinghamshire MK18 5EH. Tel: 01280 822850

Waddesdon Manor - Nr Aylesbury, Buckinghamshire HP18 0JH. Tel: 01296 653226

Cambridgeshire

The Manor of Green Knowe - The Manor, Hemingford Grey, Cambridgeshire PE28 9BN. Tel: 01480 463134

Cheshire

Adlington Hall - Adlington, Macclesfield, Cheshire SK10 4LF. Tel: 01625 820201

Dorfold Hall - Nantwich, Cheshire CW5 8LD. Tel: 01270 625245

Dunham Massey: Hall, Park & Garden - Dunham, Altrincham, Cheshire WA14 4SJ. Tel: 0161 9411025

Norton Priory Museum & Gardens - Tudor Road, Manor Park, Runcorn, Cheshire WA7 1SX. Tel: 01928 569895

Tabley House Stately Home - Knutsford, Cheshire WA16 0HB. Tel: 01565 750151

Co Durham

Raby Castle - Staindrop, Darlington, Co Durham DL2 3AH. Tel: 01833 660202

Cornwall

Mount Edgcumbe House & Country Park - Cremyll Torpoint, Cornwall PL10 1HZ. Tel: 01752 822236

Royal Cornwall Museum - River Street, Truro, Cornwall TR1 2SJ. Tel: 01872 272205

Trebah Garden Trust - Mawnan Smith, Nr Falmouth, Cornwall TR11 5JZ. Tel: 01326 250448

Truro Cathedral - 14 St Mary's Street, Truro, Cornwall TR1 2AF.

Cumbria

Dove Cottage & The Wordsworth Museum - Grasmere, Cumbria LA22 9SH. Tel: 015394 35544

Isel Hall - Cockermouth, Cumbria CA13 0QG. Tel: 01900 821778

Levens Hall & Gardens - Kendal, Cumbria LA8 0PD. Tel: 01539 560321

Mirehouse Historic House & Gardens - Mirehouse, Keswick, Cumbria CA12 4QE. Tel: 01768 772287

Wordsworth House - Main Street, Cockermouth, Cumbria CA13 9RX. Tel: 01900 824805

Derbyshire

Chatsworth - Bakewell, Derbyshire DE45 1PP. Tel: 01246 565300

▼
Haddon Hall - Bakewell, Derbyshire DE45 1LA. **Tel: 01629 812855**

Melbourne Hall & Gardens - Melbourne, Derbyshire DE73 1EN. Tel: 01332 862502

Devon

Downes - Downes, Crediton, Devon EX17 3PL. Tel: 01392 680059

Ugbrooke Park - Ugbrooke, Chudleigh, Devon TQ13 0AD. Tel: 01626 852179

Dorset

Abbotsbury Sub Tropical Gardens - Bullers Way, Abbotsbury, Nr Weymouth, Dorset DT3 4LA. Tel: 01305 871387

Chiffchaffs - Chaffeymoor, Bourton, Gillingham, Dorset SP8 5BY. Tel: 01747 840841

Cranborne Manor Garden - Cranborne, Wimborne, Dorset BH21 5PP. Tel: 01725 517248

Deans Court Garden - Deans Court, Wimborne, Dorset BH21 1EE. Tel: 01202 886116

Mapperton - Mapperton, Beaminster, Dorset DT8 3Nr Tel: 01308 862645

Russell-Cotes Art Gallery & Museum - East Cliff, Bournemouth, Dorset BH1 3AA. Tel: 01202 451800

Essex

The Gardens of Easton Lodge - Warwick House, Easton Lodge, Great Dunmow, Essex CM6 2BB. Tel: 01371 876979

Ingatestone Hall - Hall Lane, Ingatestone, Essex CM4 9Nr Tel: 01277 353010

Gloucestershire

Cheltenham Art Gallery & Museum - Clarence Street, Cheltenham, Gloucestershire GL50 3JT. Tel: 01242 237431

Frampton Court - Frampton-on-Severn, Gloucestershire GL2 7EP. Tel: 01452 740267

Hardwicke Court - Nr Gloucester, Gloucestershire GL2 4RS. Tel: 01452 720212

Kelmscott Manor - Kelmscott, Nr Lechlade, Gloucestershire GL7 3HJ. Tel: 01367 253348

Old Campden House - Chipping Campden, Gloucestershire GL55 . Tel: 01628 825920

Rodmarton Manor Garden - Cirencester, Gloucestershire GL7 6PF. Tel: 01285 841253

Sezincote - Moreton-in-Marsh, Gloucestershire GL56 9AW. Tel: 01386 700444

Hampshire

Avington Park - Winchester, Hampshire SO21 1DB. Tel: 01962 779260

Beaulieu - Montagu Ventures Ltd., John Montagu Building, Beaulieu, Hampshire SO42 7ZN. Tel: 01590 612345

Beaulieu Vineyard and Gardens - Montagu Ventures Ltd., John Montagu Building, Beaulieu, Hampshire SO42 7ZN. Tel: 01590 612345

Breamore House & Museum - Breamore, Nr Fordingbridge, Hampshire SP6 2DF. Tel: 01725 512468

Broadlands - Romsey, Hampshire SO51 9ZE. Tel: 01794 505055

Gilbert White's House and The Oates Museum - Selborne, Hampshire GU34 3JH. Tel: 01420 511275

Greywell Hill House - Greywell, Hook, Hampshire RG29 1DG.

Hall Farm - Bentworth, Alton, Hampshire GU34 5JU. Tel: 01420 564010

Mottisfont Abbey and Garden - Mottisfont, Nr Romsey, Hampshire SO51 0LP. Tel: 01794 340757

Pylewell House - Pylewell Park Estate, Lymington, Hampshire SO41 5SJ. Tel: 01590 673010

Uppark - The National Trust, Uppark, South Harting, Petersfield, Hampshire GU31 5QR. Tel: 01730 825415

Herefordshire

Eastnor Castle - Eastnor, Ledbury, Herefordshire HR8 1RL. Tel: 01531 633160

Moccas Court - Moccas, Herefordshire HR2 9LH. Tel: 01981 500019

HISTORIC HOUSES, CASTLES & GARDENS
Incorporating Museums & Galleries
www.historichouses.co.uk

Hertfordshire

Ashridge - Berkhamsted, Hertfordshire HP4 1NS.
Tel: 01442 843491

Gorhambury - St Albans, Hertfordshire AL3 6AH.
Tel: 01727 855000

Hatfield House, Park & Gardens - Hatfield,
Hertfordshire AL9 5NQ. Tel: 01707 287010

Isle of Wight

Deacons Nursery - Moor View, Godshill,
Isle of Wight PO38 3HW. Tel: 01983 840750

Kent

Cobham Hall - Cobham, Kent DA12 3BL.
Tel: 01474 823371

Dickens House Museum - 2 Victoria Parade, Broadstairs,
Kent CT10 1JT. Tel: 01843 861232

Finchcocks, Living Museum of Music - Goudhurst,
Kent TN17 1HH. Tel: 01580 211702

Graham Clarke Up the Garden Studio - Green Lane,
Boughton Monchelsea, Maidstone, Kent ME17 4LF.
Tel: 01622 743938

Groombridge Place Gardens & Enchanted Forest -
Groombridge, Nr Tunbridge Wells, Kent TN3 9QG.
Tel: 01892 863999

▼
Hever Castle & Gardens - Edenbridge, Kent TN8 7NG.
Tel: 01732 861701

Leeds Castle - Maidstone, Kent ME17 1PL.
Tel: 01622 765400

Mount Ephraim Gardens - Hernhill, Nr Faversham, Kent
ME13 9TX. Tel: 01227 751496

The New College of Cobham - Cobhambury Road,
Cobham, Nr Gravesend, Kent DA12 3BG.
Tel: 01474 812503

Penshurst Place & Gardens - Penshurst, Nr Tonbridge, Kent
TN11 8DG. Tel: 01892 870307

Scotney Castle, Garden & Estate - Lamberhurst,
Kent TN3 8JN. Tel: 01892 891081

Smallhythe Place - Smallhythe, Tenterden, Kent TN30 7NG.
Tel: 01580 762334

Lancashire

Astley Hall Museum & Art Gallery - Astley Park, off Hallgate,
Chorley, Lancashire PR7 1NP. Tel: 01257 515555

Stonyhurst College - Stonyhurst, Clitheroe,
Lancashire BB7 9PZ. Tel: 01254 826345

Townhead House - Slaidburn, Via Clitheroe,
Lancashire BBY 3AG.

London

Dulwich Picture Gallery - Gallery Road, London SE21 7AD.
Tel: 0208 6935254

Handel House Museum - 25 Brook Street,
London W1K 4HB. Tel: 0207 4951685

Kensington Palace State Apartments - Kensington,
London W8 4PX. Tel: 0870 7515170

Leighton House Museum - 12 Holland Park Road,
London W14 8LZ. Tel: 020 7602 3316

National Portrait Gallery - St Martin's Place,
London WC2H 0HE. Tel: 0207 3060055

Pitzhanger Manor House - Walpole Park, Ealing,
London W5 5EQ. Tel: 020 85671227

Royal Institution Michael Faraday Museum - 21 Albemarle
Street, London W1S 4BS. Tel: 020 74092992

Sir John Soane's Museum - 13 Lincoln's Inn Fields,
London WC2A 3BP. Tel: 0207 4052107

Somerset House - Strand, London WC2R 1LA.
Tel: 0207 8454600

Strawberry Hill House - St Mary's University College,
Strawberry Hill, Waldegrave Road, Twickenham,
London TW1 4SX. Tel: 020 8270 4114

Syon Park - Brentford, Middlesex TW8 8JF.
Tel: 0208 5600882

Tower of London - Tower Hill, London EC3N 4AB.
Tel: 0870 7566060

Greater Manchester

Heaton Hall - Heaton Park, Prestwich, Manchester,
Greater Manchester M25 5SW. Tel: 0161 7731231

Salford Museums & Art Gallery - Peel Park, The Crescent,
Salford, Greater Manchester M5 4WU. Tel: 0161 7362649

Norfolk

Hoveton Hall Gardens - Hoveton, Wroxham,
Norfolk NR12 8RJ. Tel: 01603 782798

Sandringham - The Estate Office, Sandringham,
Norfolk PE35 6EN. Tel: 01553 772675

Walsingham Abbey Grounds - c/o The Estate Office,
Little Walsingham, Norfolk NR22 6BP.
Tel: 01328 820259

Wolterton and Mannington Estate - Mannington Hall,
Norwich, Norfolk NR11 7BB. Tel: 01263 584175

Northamptonshire

Althorp - Northampton, Northamptonshire NN7 4HQ.
Tel: 01604 770107

Cottesbrooke Hall and Gardens - Cottesbrooke,
Northampton, Northamptonshire NN6 8PF.
Tel: 01604 505808

Haddonstone Show Garden - The Forge House, Church
Lane, East Haddon, Northamptonshire NN6 8DB.
Tel: 01604 770711

Holdenby House Gardens & Falconry Centre - Holdenby,
Northampton, Northamptonshire NN6 8DJ.
Tel: 01604 770074

Kelmarsh Hall & Gardens - Kelmarsh, Northampton,
Northamptonshire NN6 9LT. Tel: 01604 686543

Northumberland

Alnwick Castle - Alnwick, Northumberland NE66 1NQ.
Tel: 01665 510777

Chillingham Castle - Chillingham,
Northumberland NE66 5NJ. Tel: 01668 215390

Chipchase Castle - Chipchase, Wark on Tyne, Hexham,
Northumberland NE48 3NT. Tel: 01434 230203

Paxton House & Country Park - Paxton,
Berwick-upon-Tweed, Northumberland TD15 1SZ.
Tel: 01289 386291

Seaton Delaval Hall - Seaton Sluice, Whitley Bay,
Northumberland NE26 4QR. Tel: 0191 2371493

Oxfordshire

Blenheim Palace - Woodstock, Oxfordshire OX20 1PX.
Tel: 01993 811325

Ditchley Park - Enstone, Chipping Norton,
Oxfordshire OX7 4ER. Tel: 01608 677346

Kingston Bagpuize House - Kingston Bagpuize,
Abingdon, Oxfordshire OX13 5AX.
Tel: 01865 820259

Mapledurham House - Mapledurham, Nr Reading,
Oxfordshire RG4 7TR. Tel: 01189 723350

▼
River & Rowing Museum - Mill Meadows,
Henley-on-Thames, Oxfordshire RG9 1BF.
Tel: 01491 415600

Wallingford Castle Gardens - Castle Street, Wallingford,
Oxfordshire. Tel: 01491 835373

Shropshire

Burford House Gardens - Tenbury Wells,
Shropshire WR15 8HQ. Tel: 01584 810777

The Dorothy Clive Garden - Willoughbridge, Market
Drayton, Shropshire, (Staffordshire Border) TF9 4EU.
Tel: 01630 647237

Hawkstone Park & Follies - Weston-under-Redcastle,
Shrewsbury, Shropshire SY4 5UY. Tel: 01939 200611

Hodnet Hall Gardens - Hodnet, Market Drayton,
Shropshire TF9 3NN. Tel: 01630 685786

Royal Air force Museum - Cosford, Shifnal,
Shropshire TF11 8UP. Tel: 01902 376200

Weston Park - Weston-under-Lizard, Nr Shifnal,
Shropshire TF11 8LE. Tel: 01952 852100

Somerset

The Bishop's Palace - Wells, Somerset BA5 2PD.
Tel: 01749 678691

Cothay Manor & Gardens - Greenham, Wellington, Somerset TA21 OJR. Tel: 01823 672283

Great House Farm - Wells Road, Theale, Wedmore, Somerset BS28 4SJ. Tel: 01934 713133

Hunstrete House Hotel - Hunstrete, Pensford, Bath, Somerset BS39 4NS. Tel: 01761 490490

Museum of Costume & Assembly Rooms - Bennett Street, Bath, Somerset BA1 2QH. Tel: 01225 477785

Orchard Wyndham - Williton, Taunton, Somerset TA4 4HH. Tel: 01984 632309

Roman Baths & Pump Room - Pump Room, Stall Street, Bath, Somerset BA1 1LZ. Tel: 01225 477785

Staffordshire

Ford Green Hall - Ford Green Road, Smallthorne, Stoke-on-Trent, Staffordshire ST6 1NG. Tel: 01782 233195

Sandon Hall - Sandon, Staffordshire ST18 0BZ. Tel: 01889 508004

Whitmore Hall - Whitmore, Newcastle-under-Lyme, Staffordshire ST5 5HW. Tel: 01782 680478

Suffolk

Ancient House - Clare, Suffolk CO10 8NY. Tel: 01628 825920

Hengrave Hall - Bury St Edmunds, Suffolk IP28 6LZ. Tel: 01284 701561

Newbourne Hall - Newbourne, Woodbridge, Suffolk IP12 4NP. Tel: 01473 736764

Shrubland Park Gardens - Shrubland Park, Coddenham, Ipswich, Suffolk IP6 9QQ. Tel: 01473 830221

Surrey

Claremont House - Claremont Drive, Esher, Surrey KT10 9LY. Tel: 01372 467841

Farnham Castle - Farnham, Surrey GU4 0AG. Tel: 01252 721194

Goddards - Abinger Common, Dorking, Surrey RH5 6JH. Tel: 01628 825920

Great Fosters - Stroude Road, Egham, Surrey TW20 9UR. Tel: 01784 433822

Hampton Court Palace - East Molesey, Surrey KT8 9AU. Tel: Info: 0870 752777 Sales: 0870 7537777

Loseley Park - Guildford, Surrey GU3 1HS. Tel: 01483 304440

▼
Painshill Park - Portsmouth Road, Cobham, Surrey KT11 1JE. **Tel: 01932 868113**

East Sussex

Bentley Wildfowl & Motor Museum - Halland, Nr Lewes, East Sussex BN8 5AF. Tel: 01825 840573

Firle Place - Firle, Lewes, East Sussex BN8 6LP. Tel: 01273 858307

Garden and Grounds of Herstmonceux Castle - Hailsham, East Sussex BN27 1RN. Tel: 01323 833816

Merriments Gardens - Hawkhurst Road, Hurst Green, East Sussex TN19 7RA. Tel: 01580 860666

Pashley Manor Gardens - Ticehurst, East Sussex TN5 7HE. Tel: 01580 200888

Wilmington Priory - Wilmington, Nr Eastbourne, East Sussex BN26 5SW. Tel: 01628 825920

West Sussex

Arundel Castle - Arundel, West Sussex BN18 9AB. Tel: 01903 883136

Denmans Garden - Clock House, Denmans, Fontwell, West Sussex BN18 0SU. Tel: 01243 542808

Goodwood House - Goodwood, Chichester, West Sussex PO18 0PX. Tel: 01243 755000

High Beeches Woodland & Water Gardens - High Beeches, Handcross, West Sussex RH17 6HQ. Tel: 01444 400589

Leonardslee - Lakes & Gardens - Lower Beeding, Horsham, West Sussex RH13 6PP. Tel: 01403 891212

Weald and Downland Open Air Museum - Singleton, Chichester, West Sussex PO18 0EU. Tel: 01243 811348

West Dean Gardens - West Dean, Chichester, West Sussex PO18 0QZ. Tel: 01243 818210

Worthing Museum & Art Gallery - Chapel Road, Worthing, West Sussex BN11 1HP. Tel: 01903 221150

Warwickshire

Arbury Hall - Nuneaton, Warwickshire CV10 7PT. Tel: 024 7638 2804

Coughton Court - Alcester, Warwickshire B49 5JA. Tel: 01789 400702

Ragley Hall - Alcester, Warwickshire B49 5NJ. Tel: 01789 762090

Shakespeare Houses - The Shakespeare Centre, Henley Street, Stratford-upon-Avon, Warwickshire CV37 6QW. Tel: 01789 204016

Stoneleigh Abbey - Kenilworth, Warwickshire CV8 2LF. Tel: 01926 858585

West Midlands

The Birmingham Botanical Gardens and Glasshouses - Westbourne Road, Edgbaston, Birmingham, West Midlands B15 3TR. Tel: 0121 4541860

Barber Institute of Fine Arts - University of Birmingham, Edgbaston, Birmingham, West Midlands B15 2TS. Tel: 0121 4147333

Castle Bromwich Hall Gardens - Chester Road, Castle Bromwich, Birmingham, West Midlands B36 9BT. Tel: 01217 494100

Coventry Cathedral - Priory Street, Coventry, West Midlands CV1 5ES. Tel: 024 76521200

Wiltshire

Charlton Park House - Charlton, Malmesbury, Wiltshire SN16 9DG.

Hamptworth Lodge - Hamptworth, Salisbury, Wiltshire SP5 2EA. Tel: 01794 390215

▼
Longleat - Warminster, Wiltshire BA12 7NW. Tel: 01985 844400

Sheldon Manor - Chippenham, Wiltshire SN14 0RG. Tel: 01249 653120

Stourhead - Stourton, Warminster, Wiltshire BA12 6QD. Tel: 01747 841152

Worcestershire

Hagley Hall - Hagley, Worcestershire DY9 9LG. Tel: 01562 882408

Hartlebury Castle - Nr Kidderminster, Worcestershire DY11 7XX. Tel: 01299 250410 (state rooms sec) Tel: 01299 250416 (museum)

Harvington Hall - Harvington, Kidderminster, Worcester DY10 4LR. Tel: 01562 777846

Little Malvern Court - Nr Malvern, Worcestershire WR14 4JN. Tel: 01684 892988

Spetchley Park Gardens - Spetchley Park, Worcester, Worcestershire WR5 1RS. Tel: 01453 810303

East Riding of Yorkshire

Burton Agnes Hall & Gardens - Burton Agnes, Driffield, East Yorkshire YO25 4NB. Tel: 01262 490324

North Yorkshire

Castle Howard - York, North Yorkshire YO6 7DA. Tel: 01653 648333

Duncombe Park - Helmsley, York, North Yorkshire YO62 5EB. Tel: 01439 770213

The Forbidden Corner - Tupgill Park Estate, Coverham, Nr Middleham, North Yorkshire DL8 4TJ. Tel: 01969 640638

Kiplin Hall - Nr Scorton, Richmond, North Yorkshire DL10 6AT. Tel: 01748 818178

Newby Hall & Gardens - Ripon, North Yorkshire HG4 5AE. Tel: 0845 4504068

Ripley Castle - Ripley Castle Estate, Harrogate, North Yorkshire HG3 3AY. Tel: 01423 770152

Skipton Castle - Skipton, North Yorkshire BD23 1AQ. Tel: 01756 792442

Thorp Perrow Arboretum & The Falcons of Thorp Perrow - Bedale, North Yorkshire DL8 2PR. Tel: 01677 425323

HISTORIC HOUSES, CASTLES & GARDENS
Incorporating Museums & Galleries
www.historichouses.co.uk

West Yorkshire

Bronte Parsonage Museum - Church Street, Haworth, Keighley, West Yorkshire BD22 8DR. Tel: 01535 642323

Harewood House - The Harewood House Trust, Moorhouse, Harewood, Leeds, West Yorkshire LS17 9LQ. Tel: 0113 2181010

Ledston Hall - Hall Lane, Ledstone, Castleford, West Yorkshire WF10 2BB. Tel: 01423 523423

Northern Ireland

Co Down

Seaforde Gardens - Seaforde, Downpatrick, Co Down BT30 8PG. Tel: 028 44811225

Ireland

Co Cork

Bantry House & Gardens - Bantry, Co Cork. Tel: + 353 2 750 047

Co Galway

Kylemore Abbey & Garden - Kylemore, Connemara, Co Galway. Tel: +353 95 41146

Co Kildare

Japanese Gardens & St Fiachra's Garden - Tully, Kildare Town, Co Kildare. Tel: +353 45 521617

Co Offaly

Birr Castle Demesne - Birr, Co Offaly. Tel: +353 509 20336

Co Wicklow

Mount Usher Gardens - Ashford, Co Wicklow. Tel: +353 404 40205

Scotland

Aberdeenshire

Craigston Castle - Turriff, Aberdeenshire AB53 5PX. Tel: 01888 551228

Argyll

Inveraray Castle - Cherry Park, Inveraray, Argyll PA32 8XE. Tel: 01499 302203

Ayrshire

Auchinleck House - Ochiltree, Ayrshire KA18 2LR. Tel: 01628 825920

Blairquhan - Straiton, Maybole, Ayrshire KA19 7LZ. Tel: 01655 770239

Kelburn Castle and Country Centre - Fairlie, Ayrshire KA29 0BE. Tel: 01475 568685

Maybole Castle - High Street, Maybole, Ayrshire KA19 7BX. Tel: 01655 883765

Sorn Castle - Sorn, Mauchline, Ayrshire KA5 6HR. Tel: 0141 9426460

Dumfriesshire

▼
Drumlanrig Castle, Gardens and Country Park - Nr Thornhill, Dumfriesshire DG3 4AQ. Tel: 01848 330248

Fife

Culross Palace, Town House & Study - Royal Burch of Culross, Fife KY12 8JH. Tel: 01383 880359

Isle of Skye

Armadale Castle, Gardens & Museum of the Isles - Armadale, Sleat, Isle of Skye IV45 8RS. Tel: 01471 844305

Orkney Islands

Balfour Castle - Shapinsay, Orkney Islands KW17 2DY. Tel: 01856 711282

Scottish Borders

Bowhill House & Country Park - Bowhill, Selkirk, Scottish Borders TD7 5ET. Tel: 01750 22204

Traquair House - Innerleithen, Peebles EH44 6PW. Tel: 01896 830323

South Lanarkshire

New Lanark World Heritage Site - New Lanark, South Lanarkshire ML11 9DB. Tel: 01555 661345

West Lothian

Hopetoun House - South Queensferry, Nr Edinburgh, West Lothian EH30 9SL. Tel: 0131 3312451

Wigtownshire

Ardwell Gardens - Ardwell House, Stranraer, Wigtownshire DG9 9LY. Tel: 01776 860227

Wales

Flintshire

Golden Grove - Llanasa, Nr Holywell, Flintshire CH8 9NA. Tel: 01745 854452

Newport

Fourteen Locks Canal Centre - High Cross, Newport NP10 9GN. Tel: 01633 894802

Newport Museum and Art Gallery - John Frost Square, Newport NP20 1PA. Tel: 01633 840064

Newport Transporter Bridge - Usk Way, Newport, South Wales NP20 2JT. Tel: 01633 250322

Tredegar House & Park - Newport NP10 8YW. Tel: 01633 815880

Pembrokeshire

Carew Castle & Tidal Mill - Carew, Tenby, Pembrokeshire SA70 8SL. Tel: 01646 651782

St Davids Cathedral - The Close, St David's, Pembrokeshire SA62 6RH. Tel: 01437 720199

Powys

The Judge's Lodging - Broad Street, Presteigne, Powys LD8 2AD. Tel: 01544 260650

Continental Europe

France

Château de Chenonceau - 37150 Chenonceaux, France. Tel: +33 2 47 23 90 07

Château Royal d'Amboise - B.P. 371, 37403 Amboise, France. Tel: +33 2 47 57 00 98

Fondation Claude Monet - 27620 Giverny, France. Tel: +33 2 32 51 28 21

Château de Thoiry - 78770 Thoiry, Yvelines, France. Tel: +33 1 34 87 53 65

The Netherlands

Paleis Het Loo National Museum - Koninklijk Park 1, 7315 JA Apeldoorn, Holland. Tel: +31 55 577 24 00

Now, all your guests
can have the room with the best view.

 TV

Introducing Philips new extended iTV range.
The addition of the **LCD and Mirror TV range**, confirms iTV's commitment and
pre-eminent position in the hospitality sector. With over 4 million hotel sets
already installed worldwide, Philips offers the most diverse and stylish range of
TVs designed for all interactive and non-interactive hotel rooms.

Smart TVs for Smart Hotels
www.philips.com/itv

PHILIPS

Let's make things better.

Mini Listings Europe

Condé Nast Johansens are delighted to recommend over 350 properties across Europe and The Mediterranean.
Call 0800 269 397 or see the order forms on page 487 to order guides.

Andorra

PAS DE LA CASA
Font d'Argent Hotel Ski & Resort - C/ Bearn 20, 22, 24, Pas de La Casa, Andorra. Tel: +376 739 739

Austria

KÄRNTEN (VELDEN)
Seeschlössl Velden - Klagenfurter Strasse 34, 9220 Velden, Austria. Tel: +43 4274 2824

▼
NIEDERÖSTERREICH (DÜRNSTEIN)
Hotel Schloss Dürnstein - 3601 Dürnstein, Austria. Tel: +43 2711 212

SALZBURG (BAD GASTEIN)
Alpine Spa Hotel & Spa Haus Hirt -
An der Kaiserpromenade 14, 5640 Bad Gastein, Austria. Tel: +43 64 34 27 97

VORARLBERG (LECH AM ARLBERG)
Sporthotel Kristiania - Omesberg 331, 6764 Lech am Arlberg, Austria. Tel: +43 5583 25 610

VORARLBERG (ZÜRS)
Thurnhers Alpenhof - 6763 Zürs - Arlberg, Austria. Tel: +43 5583 2191

WIEN (VIENNA)
Grand Hotel Wien - Kärntner Ring 9, 1010 Vienna, Austria. Tel: +43 1 515 80 0

Belgium

ANTWERP
Firean Hotel - Karel Oomsstraat 6, 2018 Antwerp, Belgium. Tel: +32 3 237 02 60

BORGLOON
Kasteel Van Rullingen - Rullingen 1, 3840 Kuttekoven-Borgloon, Belgium. Tel: +32 12 74 31 46

BRUGES
Die Swaene - 1 Steenhouwersdijk, 8000 Bruges, Belgium. Tel: +32 50 34 27 98

BRUGES
Hotel de Tuilerieën - Dyver 7, 8000 Bruges, Belgium. Tel: +32 50 34 36 91

BRUGES
Hotel Montanus - Nieuwe Gentweg 78, 8000 Bruges, Belgium. Tel: +32 50 33 11 76

BRUGES
Hotel Prinsenhof - Ontvangersstraat 9, 8000 Bruges, Belgium. Tel: +32 50 34 26 90

BRUGES
Walburg Hotel - Boomgaardstraat 13-15, 8000 Bruges, Belgium. Tel: +32 50 34 94 14

KNOKKE~HEIST
Romantik Hotel Manoir du Dragon - Albertlaan 73, 8300 Knokke~Heist, Belgium. Tel: +32 50 63 05 80

KORTRIJK
Hotel Damier - Grote Markt 41, 8500 Kortrijk, Belgium. Tel: +32 56 22 15 47

MALMÉDY
Hostellerie Trôs Marets - Route des Trôs Marets, 4960 Malmédy, Belgium. Tel: +32 80 33 79 17

MARCHE~EN~FAMENNE
Château d'Hassonville - Route d'Hassonville 105, 6900 Marche~en~Famenne, Belgium. Tel: +32 84 31 10 25

POPERINGE
Hotel Recour - Guido Gezellestraat 7, 8970 Poperinge, Belgium . Tel: +32 57 33 57 25

Croatia

DUBROVNIK
The Pucic Palace - Ulica OD Puca 1, 20000 Dubrovnik, Croatia. Tel: +385 20 324 111

Czech Republic

PRAGUE
Art Hotel Praha - Nad Královskou Oborou 53, 170 00 Prague 7, Czech Republic. Tel: +420 2 331 01 331

PRAGUE
Hotel Hoffmeister - Pod Bruskou 7, Klárov, 11800 Prague 1, Czech Republic. Tel: +420 251 017 111

PRAGUE
Romantik Hotel U Raka - Cernínská 10/93, 11800 Prague 1, Czech Republic. Tel: +420 2205 111 00

Denmark

HORNBÆK
Havreholm Slot - Klosterrisvej 4, Havreholm, 3100 Hornbæk, Denmark. Tel: +45 49 75 86 00

NYBORG
Hotel Hesselet - Christianslundsvej 119, 5800 Nyborg, Denmark. Tel: +45 65 31 30 29

RUDS-VEDBY
Kragerup Gods - Kragerupgårdsvej 33, 4291 Ruds-Vedby, Denmark. Tel: +45 58 26 12 50

Estonia

PÄRNU
Villa Ammende - Mere Pst. 7, 80010 Pärnu, Estonia. Tel: +372 44 73888

France

ALSACE~LORRAINE (COLMAR)
Hostellerie Le Maréchal - 4 Place Six Montagnes Noires, Petite Venise, 68000 Colmar, France. Tel: +33 3 89 41 60 32

ALSACE~LORRAINE (COLMAR)
Hôtel Les Têtes - 19 Rue de Têtes, 68000 Colmar, France. Tel: +33 3 89 24 43 43

ALSACE~LORRAINE (COLMAR - ROUFFACH)
Château d'Isenbourg - 68250 Rouffach, France. Tel: +33 3 89 78 58 50

ALSACE~LORRAINE (GÉRARDMER - VOSGES)
Hostellerie Les Bas Rupts - 88400 Gérardmer, Vosges, France. Tel: +33 3 29 63 09 25

ALSACE~LORRAINE (MURBACH - BUHL)
Hostellerie St Barnabé - 68530 Murbach - Buhl, France. Tel: +33 3 89 62 14 14

ALSACE~LORRAINE (OBERNAI - OTTROTT)
A L'Ami Fritz - 8 Rue des Châteaux, 67530 Ottrott, France. Tel: +33 3 88 95 80 81

ALSACE~LORRAINE (STRASBOURG)
Romantik Hotel Beaucour Baumann - 5 Rue des Bouchers, 67000 Strasbourg, France. Tel: +33 3 88 76 72 00

ALSACE~LORRAINE (STRASBOURG - OSTWALD)
Château de L'Ile - 4 Quai Heydt, 67540 Ostwald, France. Tel: +33 3 88 66 85 00

ALSACE~LORRAINE (THIONVILLE)
Romantik Hotel L'Horizon - 50 Route du Crève~Cœur, 57100 Thionville, France. Tel: +33 3 82 88 53 65

AUVERGNE - LIMOUSIN (SAINT~FLOUR)
Hostellerie Château de Varillettes - 15100 Saint~Georges par Saint~Flour, France. Tel: +33 4 71 60 45 05

BRITTANY (BILLIERS)
Domaine de Rochevilaine - Pointe de Pen Lan, 56190 Billiers, France. Tel: +33 2 97 41 61 61

BRITTANY (LA GOUESNIÈRE - SAINT~MALO)
Château de Bonaban - 35350 La Gouesnière, France. Tel: +33 2 99 58 24 50

BRITTANY (MISSILLAC)
Domaine de La Bretesche - 44780 Missillac, France. Tel: +33 2 51 76 86 96

BRITTANY (MOËLAN~SUR~MER)
Manoir de Kertalg - Route de Riec-Sur-Belon, 29350 Moëlan~sur~Mer, France. Tel: +33 2 98 39 77 77

BRITTANY (PLOERDÜT)
Château du Launay - 56160 Ploerdüt, France. Tel: +33 2 97 39 46 32

BRITTANY (RENNES)
LeCoq~Gadby - 156 Rue d'Antrain, 35700 Rennes, France. Tel: +33 2 99 38 05 55

BRITTANY (SAINT MALO - PLEVEN)
Manoir du Vaumadeuc - 22130 Pleven, France. Tel: +33 2 96 84 46 17

BRITTANY (TREBEURDEN)
Ti Al Lannec - 14 Allée de Mézo~Guen, BP 3, 22560 Trebeurden, France. Tel: +33 296 15 01 01

BURGUNDY - FRANCHE~COMTÉ (AUXERRE - VILLEFARGEAU)
Le Petit Manoir des Bruyères - 5 Allée de Charbuy, Les~Bruyères, 89240 Auxerre - Villefargeau, France. Tel: +33 3 86 41 32 82

MINI LISTINGS EUROPE

Condé Nast Johansens are delighted to recommend over 350 properties across Europe and The Mediterranean.
Call 0800 269 397 or see the order forms on page 487 to order guides.

BURGUNDY - FRANCHE~COMTÉ (AVALLON)
Château de Vault de Lugny - 11 Rue du Château, 89200 Avallon, France. Tel: +33 3 86 34 07 86

BURGUNDY - FRANCHE~COMTÉ (BEAUNE)
Ermitage de Corton - R.N. 74, 21200 Chorey~les~Beaune, France. Tel: +33 3 80 22 05 28

BURGUNDY - FRANCHE~COMTÉ (POLIGNY - JURA)
Hostellerie des Monts de Vaux - Les Monts de Vaux, 39800 Poligny, France. Tel: +33 3 84 37 12 50

BURGUNDY - FRANCHE~COMTÉ (VOUGEOT)
Château de Gilly - Gilly~les~Cîteaux, 21640 Vougeot, France. Tel: +33 3 80 62 89 98

CHAMPAGNE ~ ARDENNES (ÉPERNAY)
Hostellerie La Briqueterie - 4 Route de Sézanne, 51530 Vinay - Épernay, France. Tel: +33 3 26 59 99 99

CHAMPAGNE ARDENNES (ETOGES)
Château d'Etoges - 51270 Etoges en Champagne, France. Tel: +33 3 26 59 30 08

CHAMPAGNE ~ ARDENNES (TINQUEUX - REIMS)
L'Assiette Champenoise - 40 Avenue Paul Vaillant Couturier, 51430 Tinqueux, France. Tel: +33 3 26 84 64 64

CÔTE D'AZUR (AUPS)
Bastide du Calalou - Moissac-Bellevue, 83630 Aups, France. Tel: +33 4 94 70 17 91

CÔTE D'AZUR (CAGNES~SUR~MER)
Domaine Cocagne - Colline de La Route de Vence, 30, Chemin du Pain de Sucre, 08600 Cagnes~sur~Mer, France. Tel: +33 4 92 13 57 77

CÔTE D'AZUR (ÈZE VILLAGE)
Château Eza - Rue De La Pise, 06360 Èze Village, France. Tel: +33 4 93 41 12 24

CÔTE D'AZUR (GRASSE)
Bastide Saint Mathieu - 35 Chemin de Blumenthal, 06130 St. Mathieu, Grasse, France. Tel: +33 4 97 01 10 00

CÔTE D'AZUR (LE RAYOL - CANADEL)
Le Bailli de Suffren - Avenue des Américains, Golfe de Saint~Tropez, 83820 Le Rayol - Canadel, France. Tel: +33 4 98 04 47 00

CÔTE D'AZUR (NICE)
Hôtel La Pérouse - 11, Quai Rauba~Capeu, 06300 Nice, France. Tel: +33 4 93 62 34 63

CÔTE D'AZUR (SAINT~PAUL~DE~VENCE)
Le Mas d'Artigny - Route de la Colle, 06570 Saint~Paul~de~Vence, France. Tel: +33 4 93 32 84 54

CÔTE D'AZUR (SAINT~TROPEZ - RAMATUELLE)
La Ferme d'Augustin - Plage de Tahiti, 83350 Ramatuelle, Nr Saint-Tropez, France. Tel: +33 4 94 55 97 00

CÔTE D'AZUR (SERRE~CHEVALIER)
L'Auberge du Choucas - 05220 Monetier~les~Bains, Serre~Chevalier, Hautes~Alpes, France. Tel: +33 4 92 24 42 73

CÔTE D'AZUR (VENCE)
Hôtel Cantemerle - 258 Chemin Cantemerle, 06140 Vence, France. Tel: +33 4 93 58 08 18

CÔTE D'AZURE (JUAN~LES~PINS)
Hôtel Juana - La Pinède, Avenue Gallice, 06160 Juan~les~Pins, France. Tel: +33 4 93 61 08 70

LOIRE VALLEY (AMBOISE)
Château de Pray - Route de Chargé, 37400 Amboise, France. Tel: +33 2 47 57 23 67

LOIRE VALLEY (AMBOISE)
Le Choiseul - 36 Quai Charles Guinot, 37400 Amboise, France. Tel: +33 2 47 30 45 45

LOIRE VALLEY (AMBOISE)
Le Manoir Les Minimes - 34 Quai Charles Guinot, 37400 Amboise, France. Tel: +33 2 47 30 40 40

LOIRE VALLEY (CHISSAY~EN~TOURRAINE)
Hostellerie Château de Chissay - 41400 Chissay~en~Touraine, France. Tel: +33 2 54 32 32 01

LOIRE VALLEY (LANGEAIS)
Château de Rochecotte - Saint~Patrice, 37130 Langeais, France. Tel: +33 2 47 96 16 16

LOIRE VALLEY (SAUMUR-CHÊNEHUTTE~LES~TUFFEAUX)
Le Prieuré - 49350 Chênehutte~Les~Tuffeaux, France. Tel: +33 2 41 67 90 14

LOIRE VALLEY (THOIRÉ~SUR~DINAN)
La Hunauderie - 72500 Thoiré~sur~Dinan, Loire Valley, France. Tel: +33 2 43 79 32 20

LOIRE VALLEY (TOURS - LUYNES)
Domaine de Beauvois - Le Pont Clouet, Route de Clere~les~Pins, 37230 Luynes, France. Tel: +33 2 47 55 50 11

LOIRE VALLEY (TOURS - MONTBAZON)
Château d'Artigny - 37250 Montbazon, France. Tel: +33 2 47 34 30 30

▼
LOIRE VALLEY (TOURS - MONTBAZON)
Domaine de La Tortinière - Route de Ballan~Miré, 37250 Montbazon, France. Tel: +33 2 47 34 35 00

MIDI~PYRÉNÉES (CORDES~SUR~CIEL)
Le Grand Ecuyer - Haut de la Cité, 81170 Cordes~sur~Ciel, France. Tel: +33 5 63 53 79 50

MIDI~PYRÉNÉES (FLOURE)
Château de Floure - 1, Allée Gaston Bonheur, 11800 Floure, France. Tel: +33 4 68 79 11 29

NORMANDY (BAGNOLES DE L'ORNE)
Le Bois Joli - 12, Avenue Philippe du Rozier, 61140 Bagnoles de L'Orne, France. Tel: +33 2 33 37 92 77

NORMANDY (BREUIL~EN~BESSIN)
Château de Goville - 14330 Breuil~en~Bessin, France. Tel: +33 2 31 22 19 28

NORMANDY (DEAUVILLE)
Hostellerie de Tourgéville - Chemin de l'Orgueil, Tourgéville, 14800 Deauville, France. Tel: +33 231 14 48 68

NORMANDY (ETRETAT)
Domaine Saint Clair, Le Donjon - Chemin de Saint Clair, 76790 Etretat, France. Tel: +33 2 35 27 08 23

NORMANDY (HONFLEUR - CRICQUEBOEUF)
Manoir de la Poterie - Chemin Paul Ruel, 14113 Cricqueboeuf, France. Tel: +33 2 31 88 10 40

NORMANDY (PACY~SUR~EURE)
Hostellerie Château de Brécourt - Douains, 27120 Pacy~sur~Eure, France. Tel: +33 2 32 52 40 50

NORTH - PICARDY (ALBERT)
Hôtel Royal Picardie - Avenue du Général Leclerc, 80300 Albert, France. Tel: +33 3 22 75 37 00

NORTH - PICARDY (BETHUNE - GOSNAY)
La Chartreuse du Val St Esprit - 62199 Gosnay, France. Tel: +33 3 21 62 80 00

NORTH - PICARDY (CALAIS - RECQUES~SUR~HEM)
Château de Cocove - 62890 Recques~sur~Hem, France. Tel: +33 3 21 82 68 29

NORTH - PICARDY (ERMENONVILLE)
Hostellerie Château d'Ermenonville - 60950 Ermenonville, France. Tel: +33 3 44 54 00 26

NORTH - PICARDY (FÈRE~EN~TARDENOIS)
Château de Fère - 02130 Fère~en~Tardenois, France. Tel: + 33 3 23 82 21 13

NORTH - PICARDY (LILLE)
Carlton Hotel - Rue de Paris, 59000 Lille, France. Tel: +33 3 20 13 33 13

NORTH - PICARDY (VERVINS)
La Tour du Roy - 02140 Vervins, France. Tel: +33 3 23 98 00 11

PARIS (CHAMPS~ELYSÉES)
Hôtel Monna Lisa - 97 Rue de la Boétie, 75008 Paris, France. Tel: +33 1 56 43 38 38

PARIS (CHAMPS~ELYSÉES)
Hôtel Plaza Athénée - 25 Avenue Montaigne, 75008 Paris, France. Tel: +33 1 53 67 66 65

PARIS (CHAMPS~ELYSÉES)
Hôtel San Régis - 12 Rue Jean Goujon, 75008 Paris, France. Tel: +33 1 44 95 16 16

PARIS (CHAMPS~ELYSÉES)
La Trémoille - 14 Rue de La Trémoille, 75008 Paris, France. Tel: +33 1 56 52 14 00

PARIS (ÉTOILE - PORTE MAILLOT)
L'Hôtel Pergolèse - 3 Rue Pergolèse, 75116 Paris, France. Tel: +33 1 53 64 04 04

PARIS (ÉTOILE - PORTE MAILLOT)
La Villa Maillot - 143 Avenue de Malakoff, 75116 Paris, France. Tel: +33 1 53 64 52 52

PARIS (INVALIDES)
Hôtel Le Tourville - 16 Avenue de Tourville, 75007 Paris, France. Tel: +33 1 47 05 62 62

PARIS (INVALIDES)
Hôtel Mayet - 3 Rue Mayet, 75006 Paris, France. Tel: +33 1 47 83 21 35

PARIS (JARDIN DU LUXEMBOURG)
Le Sainte~Beuve - 9 Rue Sainte~Beuve, 75006 Paris, France. Tel: +33 1 45 48 20 07

PARIS (JARDIN DU LUXEMBOURG)
Relais Médicis*Luxe** - 23 Rue Racine, 75006 Paris, France. Tel: +33 1 43 26 00 60

PARIS (MADELEINE)
Hôtel de L'Arcade - 9 Rue de L'Arcade, 75008 Paris, France. Tel: +33 1 53 30 60 00

PARIS (MADELEINE)
Hôtel Le Lavoisier - 21 Rue Lavoisier, 75008 Paris, France. Tel: +33 1 53 30 06 06

PARIS (MADELEINE)
Hôtel Opéra Richepanse - 14 Rue du Chevalier de Saint-George, 75001 Paris, France. Tel: +33 (0) 1 42 60 36 00

PARIS (MONTPARNASSE)
Victoria Palace Hôtel - 6, Rue Blaise Desgoffe, 75006 Paris, France. Tel: +33 1 45 49 70 00

MINI LISTINGS EUROPE

Condé Nast Johansens are delighted to recommend over 350 properties across Europe and The Mediterranean.
Call 0800 269 397 or see the order forms on page 487 to order guides.

PARIS (PANTHÉON)
Hôtel des Grands Hommes - 17 Place du Panthéon, 75005 Paris, France. Tel: +33 1 46 34 19 60

PARIS (PANTHÉON)
Hôtel du Panthéon - 19 Place du Panthéon, 75005 Paris, France. Tel: +33 1 43 54 32 95

PARIS (SAINT~GERMAIN)
ArtusHôtel - 34 Rue de Buci, 75006 Paris, France. Tel: +33 1 43 29 07 20

PARIS (SAINT~GERMAIN)
Hôtel Le Saint~Grégoire - 43 Rue de L'Abbé Grégoire, 75006 Paris, France. Tel: 33 1 45 48 23 23

PARIS (SAINT~GERMAIN)
Hôtel Pont Royal - 5-7 Rue de Montalembert, 75007 Paris, France. Tel: +33 1 42 84 70 00

PARIS (SAINT~GERMAIN)
L' Hôtel - 13, Rue des Beaux Arts, 75006 Paris, France. Tel: +33 1 44 41 99 00

PARIS REGION (CERNAY~LA~VILLE)
Hostellerie Abbaye des Vaux de Cernay - 78720 Cernay~La~Ville, France. Tel: +33 1 34 85 23 00

PARIS REGION (GRESSY~EN~FRANCE - CHANTILLY)
Le Manoir de Gressy - 77410 Gressy~en~France, Roissy Cdg, Nr Paris, France. Tel: +33 1 60 26 68 00

PARIS REGION (SAINT SYMPHORIEN~LE~CHÂTEAU)
Château d'Esclimont - 28700 St. Symphorien~Le~Château, France. Tel: +33 2 37 31 15 15

PARIS REGION (YERRES - ORLY)
Hostellerie Château du Maréchal de Saxe - Domaine de La Grange, 91330 Yerres, France. Tel: +33 1 69 48 78 53

POITOU~CHARENTES (COGNAC - CHÂTEAUBERNARD)
Château de L'Yeuse - 65 Rue de Bellevue, Quartier de Echassier, 16100 Châteaubernard, France. Tel: +33 5 45 36 82 60

POITOU~CHARENTES (POITIERS - SAINT~MAIXENT~L'ECOLE)
Logis St. Martin - Chemin de Pissot, 79400 Saint~Maixent~L'Ecole, France. Tel: +33 549 0558 68

POITOU-CHARENTES (MASSIGNAC)
Domaine des Etangs - 16310 Massignac, France. Tel: +33 5 45 61 85 00

PROVENCE (AIX~EN~PROVENCE)
Le Pigonnet - 5 Avenue du Pigonnet, 13090 Aix~en~Provence, France. Tel: +33 4 42 59 02 90

PROVENCE (BONNIEUX~EN~PROVENCE)
La Bastide de Capelongue - 84480 Bonnieux~en~Provence, France. Tel: +33 4 90 75 89 78

PROVENCE (GRIGNAN)
Le Clair de la Plume - Place du Mail, 26230 Grignan, France. Tel: +33 4 75 91 81 30

PROVENCE (GRIGNAN)
Manoir de la Roseraie - Route de Valréas, 26230 Grignan, France. Tel: +33 4 75 46 58 15

PROVENCE (LES~BAUX~DE~PROVENCE)
Mas de l'Oulivie - 13520 Les~Baux~de~Provence, France. Tel: +33 4 90 54 35 78

PROVENCE (LORIOL~DU~COMTAT)
Château Talaud - 84870 Loriol du Comtat, France. Tel: +33 4 90 65 71 00

PROVENCE (LOURMARIN)
Le Moulin de Lourmarin - 84160 Lourmarin, Provence, France. Tel: +33 4 90 68 06 69

PROVENCE (MAZAN)
Château de Mazan - Place Napoléon, 84380 Mazan, France. Tel: +33 4 90 69 62 61

PROVENCE (SAINT~RÉMY~DE~PROVENCE)
Château des Alpilles - Route Départementale 31, Ancienne Route du Grès, 13210 Saint~Rémy~de~Provence, France. Tel: +33 4 90 92 03 33

PROVENCE (SAUVETERRE)
Château de Varenne - 30150 Sauveterre, France. Tel: +33 4 66 82 59 45

▼
PROVENCE (UZÈS)
Château d'Arpaillargues - Hôtel Marie d'Agoult, 30700 Uzès, France. Tel: +33 4 66 22 14 48

RHÔNE~ALPES (DIVONNE~LES~BAINS)
Château de Divonne - 01220 Divonne~les~Bains, France. Tel: +33 4 50 20 00 32

RHÔNE~ALPES (DIVONNE~LES~BAINS)
Le Domaine de Divonne Casino, Golf & Spa Resort - Avenue des Thermes, 01220 Divonne-les-Bains, France. Tel: +33 4 50 40 34 34

RHÔNE~ALPES (LES GETS)
Chalet Hôtel La Marmotte - 61 Rue du Chéne, 74260 Les Gets, France. Tel: + 33 4 50 75 80 33

RHÔNE~ALPES (LYON)
La Tour Rose - 22 Rue du Boeuf, 69005 Lyon, France. Tel: +33 4 78 92 69 10

RHÔNE ALPES (MANIGOD)
Chalet Hôtel de la Croix-Fry - 74230 Manigod, France. Tel: +33 4 50 44 90 16

RHÔNE~ALPES (SCIEZ~SUR~LÉMAN)
Château de Coudrée - Domaine de Coudrée, Bonnatrait, 74140 Sciez~sur~Léman, France. Tel: +33 4 50 72 62 33

SOUTH WEST (BIARRITZ)
Hôtel du Palais - 1 Avenue de L'Impératrice, 64200 Biarritz, France. Tel: +33 5 59 41 64 00

SOUTH WEST (SAINT~JEAN~DE~LUZ)
Hotel Lehen Tokia - Chemin Achotarreta, 64500 Ciboure, Saint~Jean~De~Luz, France. Tel: +33 5 59 47 18 16

SOUTH WEST (SAINTE~RADEGONDE - SAINT~EMILION)
Château de Sanse - 33350 Sainte~Radegonde, France. Tel: +33 5 57 56 41 10

WESTERN LOIRE (CHAMPIGNÉ)
Château des Briottières - 49330 Champigné, France. Tel: +33 2 41 42 00 02

WESTERN LOIRE (NANTES - LES SORINIÈRES)
Hostellerie Abbaye de Villeneuve - 44480 Nantes - Les Sorinières, France. Tel: +33 2 40 04 40 25

WESTERN LOIRE (NOIRMOUTIER)
Hostellerie du Général d'Elbée - Place du Château, 85330 Noirmoutier~en~L'Isle, France. Tel: +33 2 51 39 10 29

Germany

ROTHENBURG OB DER TAUBER
Hotel Eisenhut - Herrngasse 3-7, 91541 Rothenburg ob der Tauber, Germany. Tel: +49 9861 7050

Great Britain & Ireland

ENGLAND (AMBERLEY)
Amberley Castle - Amberley, Near Arundel, West Sussex BN18 9ND, England. Tel: +44 1798 831 992

ENGLAND (BAMBURGH)
Waren House Hotel - Waren Mill, Bamburgh, Northumberland NE70 7EE, England. Tel: +44 1668 214581

ENGLAND (CHALFONT ST PETER)
The Greyhound Inn - High Street, Chalfont St Peter SL9 9RA, England. Tel: +44 1753 883404

ENGLAND (DERBY - NOTTINGHAM)
Risley Hall - Derby Road, Risley, Derbyshire DE72 3SS, England. Tel: +44 115 939 9000

ENGLAND (FAWSLEY)
Fawsley Hall - Fawsley, Near Daventry, Northamptonshire NN11 3BA, England. Tel: +44 1327 892000

ENGLAND (HEATHROW)
Stoke Park Club - Park Road, Stoke Poges, Buckinghamshire SL2 4PG, England. Tel: +44 1753 717171

ENGLAND (LONDON)
Beaufort House Apartments - 45 Beaufort Gardens, Knightsbridge, London SW3 1PN, England. Tel: +44 20 7584 2600

ENGLAND (LONDON)
The Berkeley - Wilton Place, London SW1 7RL. Tel: +44 (0) 20 7235 6000

ENGLAND (LONDON)
The Colonnade, The Little Venice Town House - 2 Warrington Crescent, London W9 1ER, England. Tel: +44 20 7286 1052

ENGLAND (LONDON)
The Cranley - 10-12 Bina Gardens, South Kensington, London SW5 0LA, England. Tel: +44 20 7373 0123

ENGLAND (LONDON)
The Dorchester - Park Lane, Mayfair, London W1A 2HJ, England. Tel: +44 (0)20 7629 8888

ENGLAND (LONDON)
Draycott House Apartments - 10 Draycott Avenue, Chelsea, London SW3 3AA, England. Tel: +44 20 7584 4659

ENGLAND (LONDON)
Kensington House Hotel - 15-16 Prince of Wales Terrace, Kensington, London W8 5PQ, England. Tel: +44 20 7937 2345

MINI LISTINGS EUROPE

Condé Nast Johansens are delighted to recommend over 350 properties across Europe and The Mediterranean.
Call 0800 269 397 or see the order forms on page 487 to order guides.

ENGLAND (LONDON)
The Leonard - 15 Seymour Street, London W1H 7JW, England. Tel: +44 20 7935 2010

ENGLAND (LONDON)
Mayflower Hotel - 24-28 Trebovir Road, London SW5 9NJ, England. Tel: +44 20 7370 0991

ENGLAND (LONDON)
Number Eleven Cadogan Gardens - 11 Cadogan Gardens, Sloane Square, Knightsbridge, London SW3 2RJ, England. Tel: +44 20 7730 7000

ENGLAND (LONDON)
Number Sixteen - 16 Sumner Place, South Kensington, London SW7 3EG, England. Tel: +44 20 7589 5232

ENGLAND (LONDON)
Pembridge Court Hotel - 34 Pembridge Gardens, London W2 4DX, England. Tel: +44 20 7229 9977

ENGLAND (LONDON)
Twenty Nevern Square - 20 Nevern Square, London SW5 9PD, England. Tel: +44 20 7565 9555

ENGLAND (MELTON MOWBRAY)
Stapleford Park Hotel, Spa, Golf & Sporting Estate - Nr. Melton Mowbray, Leicestershire LE14 2EF, England. Tel: +44 1572 787 522

ENGLAND (ROWSLEY - DERBYSHIRE)
The Peacock at Rowsley - Rowsley, Near Matlock, Derbyshire DE4 2EB, England. Tel: +44 1629 733518

ENGLAND (SONNING ON THAMES)
The French Horn - Sonning on Thames, Berkshire, RG4 0TN England. Tel: +44 1189 692204

IRELAND (DUBLIN)
Aberdeen Lodge - 53-55 Park Avenue, Ballsbridge, Dublin 4, Ireland. Tel: +353 1 283 8155

SCOTLAND (BRORA)
Royal Marine Hotel - Golf Road, Brora, Sutherland KW9 6QS, Scotland. Tel: +44 1408 621252

SCOTLAND (GRANTOWN-ON-SPEY)
Muckrach Lodge Hotel & Restaurant - Dulnain Bridge, By Grantown-on-Spey, Inverness-shire PH26 3LY, Scotland. Tel: +44 1479 851257

SCOTLAND (HUNTERS QUAY, NR DUNOON)
Enmore Hotel - Marine Parade, Kirn, Dunoon, Argyll PA23 8HH, Scotland. Tel: +44 1369 702230

SCOTLAND (SCOTTISH BORDERS)
Castle Venlaw Hotel - Edinburgh Road, Peebles, Scotland EH45 8QG. Tel: +44 1721 720384

Greece

ATHENS
Hotel Pentelikon - 66 Diligianni Street, 14562 Athens, Greece. Tel: +30 10 62 30 650-6

CRETE
The Peninsula at Porto Elounda de luxe Resort - 72053 Elounda, Crete, Greece. Tel: +30 28410 68000

CRETE
Pleiades Luxurious Villas - Plakes-72, 100 Aghios Nikolaos, Crete, Greece. Tel: +30 28410 90450

CRETE
St Nicolas Bay Hotel - PO Box 47, 72100 Aghios Nikolaos, Crete, Greece. Tel: +30 2841 025041

MYKONOS
Apanema - Tagoo, Mykonos, Greece. Tel: +30 22890 28590

MYKONOS
Tharroe of Mykonos - Angelika, 84600 Mykonos, Greece. Tel: +30 22890 27370

PAROS
Acquamarina Resort - New Golden Beach, 84400 Paros, Greece. Tel: +30 228404 3281

PAROS
Astir of Paros - Kolymbithres, Naoussa, 84401 Paros, Greece. Tel: +30 2840 51976

Hungary

BUDAPEST
Uhu Villa - 1025 Budapest, Keselyü u. 1/a, Hungary. Tel: +36 1 275 1002

Italy

CAMPANIA (POSITANO)
Hotel Poseidon - Via Pasitea 148, 84017 Positano (Salerno), Italy. Tel: +39 089 811111

CAMPANIA (POSITANO)
Hotel Villa Franca - Viale Pasitea 318, 84017 Positano (SA), Italy. Tel: +39 089 875655

CAMPANIA (RAVELLO)
Hotel Villa Maria - Via S.Chiara 2, 84010 Ravello (SA), Italy. Tel: +39 089 857255

CAMPANIA (SORRENTO)
Grand Hotel Cocumella - Via Cocumella 7, 80065 Sant'Agnello, Sorrento, Italy. Tel: +39 081 878 2933

CAMPANIA (SORRENTO)
Grand Hotel Excelsior Vittoria - Piazza Tasso 34, 80067 Sorrento (Naples), Italy. Tel: +39 081 807 1044

EMILIA ROMAGNA (BAGNO DI ROMAGNA TERME)
Hotel Tosco Romagnolo - Piazza Dante Alighieri 2, 47021 Bagno di Romagna Terme, Italy. Tel: +39 0543 911260

EMILIA ROMAGNA (BRISIGHELLA)
Relais Torre Pratesi - Via Cavina 11, 48013 Brisighella (RA), Italy. Tel: +39 0546 84545

EMILIA ROMAGNA (DOZZA - IMOLA)
Monte del Re - 40050 Dozza (Bologna), Italy. Tel: +39 0542 678400

EMILIA ROMAGNA (FERRARA)
Ripagrande Hotel - Via Ripagrande 21, 44100 Ferrara, Italy. Tel: +39 0532 765250

EMILIA ROMAGNA (REGGIO EMILIA)
Hotel Posta - Piazza del Monte, 2, 42100 Reggio Emilia, Italy. Tel: +39 05 22 43 29 44

EMILIA ROMAGNA (RICCIONE)
Hotel des Nations - Lungomare Costituzione 2, 47838 Riccione (RN), Italy. Tel: +39 0541 647878

LAZIO (PALO LAZIALE - ROME)
La Posta Vecchia - Palo Laziale, 00055 Ladispoli, Rome, Italy. Tel: +39 0699 49501

LAZIO (ROME)
The Duke Hotel - Via Archimede 69, 00197 Rome, Italy. Tel: +39 06 367221

LAZIO (ROME)
Hotel Aventino - Via San. Domenico 10, 00153 Rome, Italy. Tel: +39 06 5745 174 / 5783 214

LAZIO (ROME)
Hotel dei Borgognoni - Via del Bufalo 126 (Piazza di Spagna), 00187 Rome, Italy. Tel: +39 06 6994 1505

LAZIO (ROME)
Hotel dei Consoli - 00193 Roma, Via Varrone 2/d, Italy. Tel: +39 0668 892972

LAZIO (ROME)
Hotel Giulio Cesare - Via degli Scipioni 287, 00192 Rome, Italy. Tel: +39 06 321 0751

LIGURIA (ALASSIO - RIVIERA DEI FIORI)
Diana Grand Hotel - Via Garibaldi 110, 17021 Alassio (SV), Riviera dei Fiori, Italy. Tel: +39 0182 642 701

LIGURIA (DIANO MARINA)
Grand Hotel Diana Majestic - Via Oleandri 15, 18013 Diano Marina (IM), Italy. Tel: +39 0183 402 727

LIGURIA (FINALE LIGURE)
Hotel Punta Est - Via Aurelia 1, 17024 Finale Ligure (SV) Italy. Tel: +39 019 600611

LIGURIA (PORTOFINO)
Hotel San Giorgio - Portofino House - Via del Fondaco, 11, 16034 Portofino (Genova), Italy. Tel: +39 0185 26991

LIGURIA (SESTRI LEVANTE)
Hotel Vis à Vis & Ristorante Olimpo - Via della Chiusa 28, 16039 Sestri Levante (GE), Italy. Tel: +39 0185 42661/480801

LOMBARDY (BELLAGIO - LAKE COMO)
Grand Hotel Villa Serbelloni - Via Roma 1, 22021 Bellagio, Lake Como, Italy. Tel: +39 031 950 216

▼
LOMBARDY (BRESCIA-LAKE GARDA)
Grand Hotel Gardone Riviera - Via Zanardelli 84, 25083 Gardone Riviera (BS), Lago di Garda, Italy. Tel: +39 0365 20261

LOMBARDY (CREMONA)
Dellearti Design Hotel - Via Bonomelli 8, 26100 Cremona, Italy. Tel: +39 0372 23131

PIEMONTE (STRESA - LAKE MAGGIORE)
Hotel Villa Aminta - Via Sempione Nord 123, 28838 Stresa (VB), Italy. Tel: +39 0323 933 818

PUGLIA (SAVELLETRI DI FASANO)
Masseria San Domenico - Litoranea 379, 72010 Savelletri di Fasano (Brindisi) Italy. Tel: +39 080 482 7769

SICILY (CATANIA)
Katane Palace Hotel - Via Finocchiaro Aprile 110, 95129 Catania, Italy. Tel: +39 095 747 0702

MINI LISTINGS EUROPE

Condé Nast Johansens are delighted to recommend over 350 properties across Europe and The Mediterranean.
Call 0800 269 397 or see the order forms on page 487 to order guides.

SICILY (SIRACUSA)
Hotel des Etrangers et Miramare - Passeggio Adorno 10/12, 96100 Siracusa, Italy. Tel: +39 0931 62671

SICILY (TAORMINA MARE)
Grand Hotel Atlantis Bay - Via Nazioale 161, Taormina Mare, Italy. Tel: +39 0942 612111

SICILY (TAORMINA MARE)
Grand Hotel Mazzarò Sea Palace - Via Nazionale 147, 98030 Taormina (ME), Italy. Tel: +39 0942 618011

SICILY (TAORMINA RIVIERA - MARINA D'AGRO)
Hotel Baia Taormina - Statale dello Ionio 39, 98030 Marina d'Agro (ME), Italy. Tel: +39 0942 756292

TRENTINO - ALTO ADIGE / DOLOMITES (COLFOSCO - CORVARA)
Art Hotel Cappella - Str. Pecei 17, Alta Badia - Dolomites, 39030 Colfosco/Corvara (BZ), Italy. Tel: +39 0471 836183

TRENTINO - ALTO ADIGE / DOLOMITES (MADONNA DI CAMPIGLIO)
Hotel Lorenzetti - Via Dolomiti di Brenta 119, 38084 Madonna Di Campiglio (Tn) Italy. Tel: +39 0465 44 14 04

TRENTINO - ALTO ADIGE / DOLOMITES (MARLING - MERAN)
Romantik Hotel Oberwirt - St Felixweg 2, 39020 Marling - Meran, Italy. Tel: +39 0473 44 71 11

TRENTINO - ALTO ADIGE / DOLOMITES (MERAN)
Park Hotel Mignon - Via Grabmayr 5, 39012 Merano, Italy. Tel: +39 0473 230353

TRENTINO - ALTO ADIGE / DOLOMITES (NOVA LEVANTE)
Posthotel Cavallino Bianco - Via Carezza 30, 39056 Nova Levante (Bz), Dolomites, Italy. Tel: +39 0471 613113

▼
TRENTINO - ALTO ADIGE / DOLOMITES (SAN CASSIANO)
Hotel & Spa Rosa Alpina - Strada Micura de Rue 20, 39030 San Cassiano, Dolomites (BZ) Italy.
Tel: +39 0471 849500

TRENTINO - ALTO ADIGE / DOLOMITES (VÖLS AM SCHLERN)
Romantik Hotel Turm - Piazza Della Chiesa 9, 39050 Völs Am Schlern, Süd Tirol (Bz), Italy. Tel: +39 0471 725014

TUSCANY (ASCIANO)
Castello di Leonina Relais - Strada S. Bartolomeo, Località Leonina, 53041 Asciano (Siena), Italy.
Tel: +39 0577 716088

TUSCANY (ASCIANO - SIENA)
CasaBianca - Loc. Casabianca, 53041 Asciano (SI), Italy.
Tel: +39 0577 704362

TUSCANY (CAMPIGLIA MARITTIMA - BOLGHERI)
Castello di Magona - Via di Venturina 27, 57021 Campiglia Marittima (Livorno), Italy.
Tel: +39 0565 851235

TUSCANY (CASTIGLION FIORENTINO)
Relais San Pietro in Polvano - Località Polvano, 52043 Castiglion Fiorentino (AR), Italy. Tel: +39 0575 650100

TUSCANY (COLLE VAL D'ELSA - SIENA)
Relais della Rovere - Via Piemonte 10, Loc. Badia, 53034 Colle Val d'Elsa (SI), Italy. Tel: +39 0577 924696

TUSCANY (FLORENCE)
J and J Historic House Hotel - Via di Mezzo 20, 50121 Florence, Italy. Tel: +39 055 26312

TUSCANY (FLORENCE)
Hotel Lorenzo Il Magnifico - Via Lorenzo Il Magnifico 25, 50129 Florence, Italy. Tel: +39 055 4630878

TUSCANY (FLORENCE)
Villa Montartino - Via Gherardo Silvani 151, 50125 Florence, Italy. Tel: +39 055 223520

TUSCANY (LIDO DI CAMAIORE)
Hotel Villa Ariston - Viale C. Colombo 355, 55043 Lido Di Camaioré (Lu), Italy. Tel: +39 0584 610633

TUSCANY (LUCCA)
Villa Michaela - Via di Valle 6/8, 55060 Vorno - Capannori (LU), Italy. Tel: +39 058 397 1371

TUSCANY (MONTEBENICHI)
Country House Casa Cornacchi - Loc. Montebenichi, 52021 Arezzo, Tuscany, Italy. Tel: +39 055 998229

TUSCANY (MONTERIGGIONI - SIENA)
Hotel Monteriggioni - Via 1 Maggio 4, 53035 Monteriggioni (SI), Italy. Tel: +39 0577 305009

TUSCANY (MONTERIGGIONI - STROVE)
Castel Pietraio - Strada di Strove 33, 53035 Monteriggioni, Italy. Tel: +39 0577 300020

TUSCANY (PIETRASANTA)
Albergo Pietrasanta - Palazzo Barsanti Bonetti - Via Garibaldi 35, 55045 Pietrasanta (Lucca), Italy.
Tel: +39 0584 793 727

TUSCANY (PIEVESCOLA)
Hotel Relais La Suvera - 53030 Pievescola - Siena, Italy.
Tel: +39 0577 960300

TUSCANY (PORTO ERCOLE)
Il Pellicano Hotel & Spa - Loc. Sbarcatello, 58018 Porto Ercole (Gr), Tuscany, Italy. Tel: +39 0564 858111

TUSCANY (RADDA IN CHIANTI)
Palazzo Leopoldo - Via Roma 33, 53017 Radda in Chianti, Italy. Tel: +39 0577 735605

TUSCANY (RADDA IN CHIANTI - SIENA)
Relais Fattoria Vignale - Via Pianigiani 8, 53017 Radda in Chianti (Siena), Italy. Tel: +39 0577 738300

TUSCANY (SIENA)
Hotel Certosa di Maggiano - Strada di Certosa 82, 53100 Siena, Italy. Tel: +39 0577 288180

UMBRIA (ASSISI)
Romantik Hotel Le Silve di Armenzano - 06081 Loc. Armenzano, Assisi (PG), Italy. Tel: +39 075 801 9000

UMBRIA (COLLE SAN PAOLO - PERUGIA)
Romantik Hotel Villa di Monte Solare - Via Montali 7, 06070 Colle San Paolo - Panicale (PG), Italy.
Tel: +39 075 832376

UMBRIA (GUBBIO)
Castello di Petroia - Località Petroia, 06020 Gubbio (Pg), Italy. Tel: +39 075 92 02 87/92 01 09

UMBRIA (MORRA - CITTÀ DI CASTELLO)
Palazzo Terranova - Loc. Ronti Morra, 06010 Morra (PG), Italy. Tel: +39 075 857 0083

UMBRIA (ORVIETO)
Villa Ciconia - Via dei Tigli 69, Loc. Ciconia, 05019 Orvieto (TR), Italy. Tel: +39 0763 305582/3

UMBRIA (PETRIGNANO)
Alla Corte del Sole Relais - Loc. I Giorgi, 06061 Petrignano (PG), Italy. Tel: +39 075 9689008/014

UMBRIA (SPOLETO)
Convento di Agghielli - Frazione Pompagnano, Località Agghielli, 06049 Spoleto (PG), Italy.
Tel: +39 0743 225 010

VENETIA (BASSANO DEL GRAPPA)
Hotel Ca' Sette - Via Cunizza da Romano 4, 36061 Bassano del Grappa, Italy. Tel: +39 0424 383350

VENETIA (CISON-TREVISO)
Castelbrando - Via Brandolini 29, 31030 Cison di Valmarino (TV), Italy. Tel: +39 0438 976093

VENETIA (LAKE GARDA)
Hotel Madrigale - Via Ghiandare 1, 37016 Marciaga, By Garda (VR), Italy. Tel: +39 045 627 9001

VENETIA (LIDO DI JESELO)
Park Hotel Brasilia - Via Levantina, 30017 Lido di Jesolo, Italy. Tel: +39 0421 380851

VENETIA (NEGRAR - VERONA)
Relais La Magioca - Via Moron 3, 37024 Negrar (Verona), Italy. Tel: +39 045 600 0167

VENETIA (SARCEDO - VICENZA)
Casa Belmonte Relais - Via Belmonte 2, 36030 Sarcedo (VI), Italy. Tel: +39 0445 884833

VENETIA (VENICE)
Hotel Giorgione - SS. Apostoli 4587, 30131 Venice, Italy.
Tel: +39 041 522 5810

VENETIA (VENICE)
Hotel Londra Palace - Riva degli Schiavoni, 4171, 30122 Venice, Italy. Tel: +39 041 5200533

VENETIA (VENICE - LIDO)
Albergo Quattro Fontane - Residenza d'Epoca - 30126 Lido di Venezia, Venice, Italy. Tel: +39 041 526 0227

VENETIA (VERONA)
Hotel Gabbia d'Oro - Corso Porta Borsari 4A, 37121 Verona, Italy. Tel: +39 045 8003060

VENETIA (VERONA)
Palazzo San Fermo - Strada San Fermo 8, 37121 Verona, Italy. Tel: +39 045 800 3060

Luxembourg

REMICH
Hotel Saint~Nicolas - 31 Esplanade, 5533 Remich, Luxembourg. Tel: +352 2666 3

Monaco

MONTE~CARLO
Monte~Carlo Beach Hotel - Avenue Princesse Grace, 06190 Roquebrune - Cap~Martin, France.
Tel: +377 92 16 25 25

The Netherlands

AMSTERDAM
Ambassade Hotel - Herengracht 341, 1016 Az Amsterdam, The Netherlands. Tel: +31 20 5550222

MINI LISTINGS EUROPE

Condé Nast Johansens are delighted to recommend over 350 properties across Europe and The Mediterranean.
Call 0800 269 397 or see the order forms on page 487 to order guides.

MAASTRICHT
Château St Gerlach - Joseph Corneli Allée 1, 6301 KK
Valkenburg A/D Geul, Maastricht, The Netherlands.
Tel: +31 43 608 88 88

Norway

OPPDAL - DOVREFJELL
Kongsvold Fjeldstue - Dovrefjell, 7340 Oppdal, Norway.
Tel: +47 72 40 43 40

OSLO
Hotel Bastion - Skippergaten 7, 0152 Oslo, Norway.
Tel: +47 22 47 77 00

VOSS
Fleischers Hotel - 5700 Voss, Norway.
Tel: +47 56 52 05 00

Portugal

ALENTEJO (REDONDO)
Convento de São Paulo - Aldeia da Serra, 7170 -120
Redondo, Portugal. Tel: +351 266 989160

ALGARVE (LAGOS)
Romantik Hotel Vivenda Miranda - Porto de Mós, 8600
Lagos, Portugal. Tel: +351 282 763222

LISBON & TAGUS VALLEY (LISBON)
Albatroz Palace, Luxury Suites - Rua Frederico Arouca,
100, 27570-353 Cascais, Lisbon, Portugal.
Tel: +351 21 484 73 80

LISBON & TAGUS VALLEY (LISBON)
Solar do Castelo - Rua das Cozinhas 2, 1100-181 Lisbon,
Portugal. Tel: +351 218 870 909

MADEIRA (FUNCHAL)
Quinta da Bela Vista - Caminho do Avista Navios 4, 9000
Funchal, Madeira, Portugal. Tel: +351 291 706400

MADEIRA (FUNCHAL)
Quinta das Vistas Palacio Gardens - Caminho de Santo
Antonio 52, 9000-187 Funchal, Madeira, Portugal.
Tel: +351 291 750 007

MADEIRA (FUNCHAL)
Quinta do Estreito - Rua José Joaquim da Costa, Estreito
de Câmara de Lobos, Funchal, 9325-034 Madeira,
Portugal. Tel: +351 291 910530

MADEIRA (FUNCHAL)
Quinta do Monte - Caminho do Monte 192, 9050-288
Funchal, Madeira, Portugal. Tel: +351 291 780 100

OPORTO & NORTHERN PORTUGAL (PINHÃO)
Vintage House Hotel - Lugar da Ponte, 5085-034 Pinhão,
Portugal. Tel: +351 254 730 230

Spain

ANDALUCÍA (ARCOS DE LA FRONTERA)
Hacienda El Santiscal - Avda. El Santiscal 129 (Lago de
Arcos), 11630 Arcos de La Frontera, Spain.
Tel: +34 956 70 83 13

ANDALUCÍA (BENHAVIS - MARBELLA)
Hotel Villa Padierna & Flamingos Golf Club - Ctra. de
Cádiz Km 166, 29679 Marbella, Spain.
Tel: +34 952 88 91 50

ANDALUCÍA (DOÑANA NATIONAL PARK)
El Cortijo de Los Mimbrales - Ctra del Rocio -
Matalascañas, Km 30, 21750 Almonte (Huelva), Spain.
Tel: +34 959 44 22 37

ANDALUCÍA (GRANADA)
Hotel Casa Morisca - Cuesta de la Victoria 9, 18010
Granada, Spain. Tel: +34 958 221 100

ANDALUCÍA (GRANADA)
Hotel La Bobadilla - Finca La Bobadilla, Apto. 144, 18300
Loja, Granada, Spain. Tel: +34 958 32 18 61

ANDALUCÍA (IZNÁJAR - CÓRDOBA)
Cortijo de Iznájar - Valdearenas, 14970 Iznájar (Córdoba),
Spain. Tel: +34 957 534 884

ANDALUCÍA (JEREZ DE LA FRONTERA)
Hotel Villa Jerez - Avda. de La Cruz Roja 7, 11407 Jerez
de La Frontera, Spain. Tel: +34 956 15 31 00

ANDALUCÍA (MÁLAGA)
El Molino de Santillán - Ctra. de Macharaviaya, Km 3,
29730 Rincón de La Victoria, Málaga, Spain.
Tel: +34 952 40 09 49

ANDALUCÍA (MÁLAGA)
Hotel La Fuente de La Higuera - Partido de Los
Frontones, 29400 Ronda, Málaga, Spain.
Tel: +34 95 2 11 43 55

ANDALUCÍA (MÁLAGA)
La Posada del Torcal - 29230 Villanueva de La
Concepción, Málaga, Spain. Tel: +34 952 03 11 77

ANDALUCÍA (MIJAS~COSTA)
Hotel Byblos Andaluz - Mijas Golf, 29650 Mijas~Costa,
Málaga, Spain. Tel: +34 952 47 30 50

ANDALUCÍA (OSUNA - SEVILLE)
Palacio Marqués de la Gomera - C/ San Pedro 20, 41640
Osuna, Seville, Spain. Tel: +34 95 4 81 22 23

ANDALUCÍA (SAN JOSÉ)
Hotel Cortijo el Sotillo - Carretera entrada a San José s/n,
04118 San José-Níjar, Spain. Tel: +34 950 61 11 00

ANDALUCÍA (SEVILLE)
Hotel Casa Palacio Casa de Carmona - Plaza de Lasso 1,
41410 Carmona, Spain. Tel: +34 5 419 1000

ANDALUCÍA (SEVILLE)
Hotel Cortijo Águila Real - Ctra. Guillena-Burguillos Km 4,
41210 Guillena, Sevilla, Spain. Tel: +34 955 78 50 06

ANDALUCÍA (SEVILLE)
Hotel Hacienda La Boticaria - Ctra. Alcalá - Utrera Km.2,
41500 Alcalá de Guadaira (Seville), Spain.
Tel: +34 955 69 88 20

ANDALUCÍA (SEVILLE)
Palacio de San Benito - c/San Benito S/N, 41370 Cazalla
de La Sierra, Sevilla, Spain. Tel: +34 954 88 33 36

ANDALUCÍA (SOTOGRANDE)
Almenara Golf Hotel & Spa - Avenida Almenara, 11310
Sotogrande, Spain. Tel: + 34 956 58 20 00

ARAGÓN (TORRE DEL COMPTE)
La Parada del Compte - Finca La Antigua Estación del
Ferrocarril, 44597 Torre del Compte, Teruel, Spain.
Tel: +34 978 76 90 72

ARAGON (VALDERROBRES)
La Torre del Visco - 44587 Fuentespalda, Teruel, Spain.
Tel: +34 978 76 90 15

ASTURIAS (VILLAMAYOR)
Palacio de Cutre - La Goleta S/N Villamayor, 33583
Infiesto, Asturias, Spain. Tel: +34 985 70 80 72

BALEARIC ISLANDS (IBIZA)
Cas Gasi - Apdo. Correos 117, 07814 Santa Gertrudis,
Ibiza, Balearic Islands. Tel: +34 971 197 700

BALEARIC ISLANDS (MALLORCA)
Agroturismo Es Puig Moltó - Ctra. Pina-Montuiri, 07230
Montuiri, Mallorca, Balearic Islands. Tel: +34 971 18 17 58

▼
BALEARIC ISLANDS (MALLORCA)
Ca's Xorc - Carretera de Deía, Km 56.1, 07100 Soller,
Mallorca, Balearic Islands. Tel: +34 971 63 82 80

BALEARIC ISLANDS (MALLORCA)
Can Furiós Petit Hotel - Cami Vell Binibona 11, Binibona,
07314 Caimari, Mallorca, Balearic Islands.
Tel: +34 971 51 57 51

BALEARIC ISLANDS (MALLORCA)
La Moraleja Hotel - Urbanizacion Los Encinares S/N,
07469 Cala San Vicente, Mallorca, Balearic islands.
Tel: +34 971 534 010

BALEARIC ISLANDS (MALLORCA)
Palacio Ca Sa Galesa - Carrer de Miramar 8, 07001 Palma,
Mallorca, Balearic Islands. Tel: +34 971 715 400

BALEARIC ISLANDS (MALLORCA)
Read's - Ca'N Moragues, 07320 Santa María, Mallorca,
Balearic Islands. Tel: +34 971 14 02 62

BALEARIC ISLANDS (MALLORCA)
Sa Posada d'Aumallia - Camino Son Prohens 1027, 07200
Felanitx, Mallorca, Balearic Islands. Tel: +34 971 58 26 57

BALEARIC ISLANDS (MALLORCA)
Sos Ferres d'en Morey - Ctra. Manacor - Colonia de Sant
Pere, km 10.7, 07500 Manacor, Balearic Islands.
Tel: +34 971 55 75 75

BALEARIC ISLANDS (MALLORCA)
Valldemossa Hotel - Ctra. Vieja de Valldemossa S/N,
07170 Valldemossa, Mallorca, Balearic Islands.
Tel: +34 971 61 26 26

CANARY ISLANDS (FUERTEVENTURA)
Elba Palace Golf Hotel - Urb. Fuerteventura Golf Club,
Cta. de Jandia, km11, 35610 Antigua, Fuerteventura,
Canary Islands. Tel: +34 928 16 39 22

CANARY ISLANDS (FUERTEVENTURA)
Gran Hotel Atlantis Bahia Real - Avenida Grandes Playa
s/n, 38660 Corratejo - La Oliva, Fuerteventura, Canary
Islands . Tel: +34 928 535 733

Mini Listings Europe

Condé Nast Johansens are delighted to recommend over 350 properties across Europe and The Mediterranean. Call 0800 269 397 or see the order forms on page 487 to order guides.

CANARY ISLANDS (GRAN CANARIA)
Gran Hotel Costa Meloneras **** - C/Mar Mediterráneo 1, 35100 Maspalomas, Gran Canaria, Canary Islands, Spain. Tel: +34 928 12 81 00

CANARY ISLANDS (LANZAROTE)
Hesperia Lanzarote Hotel - Urb. Cortijo Viejo, Puerto Calero, 35570 Yaiza, Lanzarote, Canary Islands. Tel: +34 828 0808 00

CANARY ISLANDS (TENERIFE)
Gran Hotel Bahía del Duque Resort - 38660 Adeje, Costa Adeje, Tenerife South, Canary Islands. Tel: +34 922 74 69 00

CANARY ISLANDS (TENERIFE)
Hotel Botánico - Avda. Richard J. Yeoward 1, Urb. Botánico, 38400 Puerto de La Cruz, Tenerife, Canary Islands. Tel: +34 922 38 14 00

CANARY ISLANDS (TENERIFE)
Hotel Jardín Tropical - Calle Gran Bretaña, 38670 Costa Adeje, Tenerife, Canary Islands. Tel: +34 922 74 60 11/2/3

CANARY ISLANDS (TENERIFE)
Hotel La Quinta Roja - Glorieta de San Francisco, 38450 Garachico, Tenerife, Canary Islands. Tel: +34 922 13 33 77

CANARY ISLANDS (TENERIFE)
Hotel San Roque - C/ Esteban de Ponte 32, 38450 Garachico, Tenerife, Canary Islands, Spain. Tel: +34 922 13 34 35

CASTILLA Y LEÓN (ÁVILA)
El Milano Real - C/Toleo S/N, Hoyos del Espino, 05634 Ávila, Spain. Tel: +34 920 349 108

CASTILLA Y LEÓN (SALAMANCA)
Hotel Rector - Rector Esperabé 10-Apartado 399, 37008 Salamanca, Spain. Tel: +34 923 21 84 82

CATALUÑA (BARCELONA)
Apartments at Hotel Arts - Carrer de la Marina 19-21, 08005 Barcelona, Spain. Tel: +34 93 22 11 000

CATALUÑA (BARCELONA)
Claris Hotel - Pau Claris 150, 08009 Barcelona, Spain. Tel: +34 934 87 62 62

CATALUÑA (BARCELONA)
Gallery Hotel - Rosselló 249, 08008 Barcelona, Spain. Tel: +34 934 15 99 11

CATALUÑA (BARCELONA)
Hotel Colón - Avenida de La Catedral 7, 08002 Barcelona, Spain. Tel: +34 933 01 14 04

CATALUÑA (COSTA BRAVA)
Hotel Rigat Park - Av. America 1, Playa de Fenals, 17310 Lloret de Mar, Costa Brava, Gerona, Spain. Tel: +34 972 36 52 00

CATALUÑA (GERONA)
Mas Falgarona - Avinyonet de Puigventos, 17742 Gerona, Spain. Tel: +34 972 54 66 28

CATALUÑA (ROSES)
Romantic Villa - Hotel Vistabella - Cala Canyelles Petites, PO Box 3, 17480 Roses (Gerona), SPAIN. Tel: +34 972 25 62 00

CATALUÑA (SITGES)
Hotel Estela Barcelona - Avda. Port d'Aiguadolç S/N, 08870 Sitges (Barcelona), Spain. Tel: +34 938 11 45 45

CATALUÑA (SITGES)
San Sebastian Playa Hotel - Calle Port Alegre 53, 08870 Sitges (Barcelona), Spain. Tel: +34 93 894 86 76

CATALUNYA (GUALBA)
Hotel Masferrer - 08474 Gualba, Spain. Tel: +34 93 848 77 05

GALICIA (PANXÓN)
Duende Rincones Encantados - C/Tomás Mirambell 77, Playa de Patos, Panxón, 36340 Nigrán, Spain. Tel: +34 986 36 53 38

MADRID (MADRID)
Antiguo Convento - C/ de Las Monjas, S/N Boadilla del Monte, 28660 Madrid, Spain. Tel: + 34 91 632 22 20

MADRID (MADRID)
Hotel Orfila - C/Orfila, No. 6, 28010 Madrid, Spain. Tel: +34 91 702 77 70

MADRID (MADRID)
Hotel Quinta de los Cedros - C/Allendesalazar 4, 28043 Madrid, Spain. Tel: +34 91 515 2200

MADRID (MADRID)
Hotel Villa Real - Plaza de Las Cortes 10, 28014 Madrid, Spain. Tel: +34 914 20 37 67

VALENCIA (ALICANTE)
Hesperia Alicante Golf, Spa, Hotel - Avda. de las Naciones, s/n Playa de San Juan, 03540 Alicante, Spain. Tel: +34 965 23 50 00

VALENCIA (ALICANTE)
Hotel Sidi San Juan & Spa - Playa de San Juan, 03540 Alicante, Spain. Tel: +34 96 516 13 00

VALENCIA (ALQUERIAS - CASTELLÓN)
Torre La Mina - C/ La Regenta 1, 12539 Alquerias-Castellón, Spain. Tel: +34 964 571 746

VALENCIA (DÉNIA)
Hotel Restaurante Buenavista - Partida Tossalet 82, La Xara, 03709 Dénia, Alicante, Spain. Tel: +34 965 78 79 95

VALENCIA (DÉNIA)
La Posada del Mar - Plaça de les Drassanes, s/n 03700 Dénia, Spain. Tel: +34 96 643 29 66

VALENCIA (VALENCIA)
Hotel Sidi Saler & Spa - Playa el Saler, 46012 Valencia, Spain. Tel: +34 961 61 04 11

VALENCIA (XÀTIVA)
Hotel Mont Sant - Subida Al Castillo, s/n Xàtiva, 46800 Valencia, Spain. Tel: +34 962 27 50 81

Sweden

BORGHOLM
Halltorps Gästgiveri - 38792 Borgholm, Sweden. Tel: +46 485 85000

HESTRA - SMÅLAND
Hestravikens Wärdshus - Vik, 33027, Hestra, Småland, Sweden. Tel: +46 370 33 68 00

TÄLLBERG
Romantik Hotel Åkerblads - 793/70 Tällberg, Sweden. Tel: +46 247 50800

Switzerland

CHÂTEAU D'OEX
Hostellerie Bon Accueil - 1837 Château d'Oex, Switzerland. Tel: +41 26 924 6320

GSTAAD
Le Grand Chalet - Neueretstrasse, 3780 Gstaad, Switzerland. Tel: +41 33 748 7676

WEGGIS - LAKE LUCERNE
Park Hotel Weggis - Hertensteinstrasse 34, CH - 6353, Weggis, Switzerland. Tel: +41 41 392 05 05

Turkey

ANTALYA
Divan Antalya Talya - Fevzi Çakmak Caddesi No. 30, 07100 Antalya, Turkey. Tel: +90 242 248 6800

ANTALYA
Renaissance Antalya Beach Resort & Spa - PO Box 654, 07004 Beldibi - Kemer, Antalya, Turkey. Tel: +90 242 824 84 31

ANTALYA
Tekeli Konaklari - Dizdar Hasan Sokak, Kaleici, Antalya, Turkey. Tel: +90 242 244 54 65

ANTALYA
Tuvana Residence - Tuzcular Mahallesi, Karanlik Sokak 7, 07100 Kaleiçi - Antalya, Turkey. Tel: +90 242 247 60 15

BODRUM
Ada Hotel - Bagarasi Mahallesi, Tepecik Caddesi, No. 128, PO Box 350, Göl - Türkbükü, Bodrum - Mugla, Turkey. Tel: +90 252 377 5915

BODRUM
Divan Bodrum Palmira - Kelesharim Caddesi 6, 48483 Türkbükü - Bodrum, Turkey. Tel: +90 252 377 5601

CAPPADOCIA - UÇHISAR
Les Maisons de Cappadoce - Belediye Meydani, PO Box 28, Uçhisar, Nevsehir, Turkey. Tel: +90 384 219 28 13

▼
CAPPADOCIA - UÇHISAR
Museum Hotel - Tekelli Mahalesi 1, Uçhisar - Nevsehir, Turkey. Tel: +90 384 219 22 20

CAPPADOCIA - ÜRGÜP
Ürgüp Evi - Esbelli Mahallesi 54, 5400 Ürgüp-Nevsehir, Turkey. Tel: +90 384 341 3173

FETHIYE
Ece Saray Marina & Resort - 1 Karagözler Mevkii, 48300 Fethiye, Mugla, Turkey. Tel: +90 252 612 5005

GÖCEK
Monte Negro - Gökgeovacik Köyü, Zeytinlik Mahallesi, Göcek, Fethiye, Turkey. Tel: +90 252 644 0181

ISTANBUL
Conrad - Istanbul - Yildez Caddesi, Besiktas, 80700 Istanbul, Turkey. Tel: +90 212 227 3000

KALKAN
Hotel Villa Mahal - P.K. 4 Kalkan, 07960 Antalya, Turkey. Tel: +90 242 844 32 68

MINI LISTINGS NORTH AMERICA

Condé Nast Johansens are delighted to recommend over 190 properties across North America, Bermuda, The Caribbean, Mexico, The Pacific. Call 0800 269 397 or see the order forms on page 487 to order guides.

ARIZONA - SEDONA

Canyon Villa Bed & Breakfast Inn
125 Canyon Circle Drive, Sedona, Arizona 86351
Tel: 1 928 284 1226
Fax: 1 928 284 2114

ARIZONA - SEDONA

Casa Sedona
55 Hozoni Drive, Sedona, Arizona 86336
Tel: 1 928 282 2938

ARIZONA - SEDONA

**The Lodge at Sedona
- A Luxury Bed & Breakfast Inn**
125 Kallof Place, Sedona, Arizona 86336
Tel: 1 928 204 1942
Fax: 1 928 204 2128

ARIZONA - TUCSON

Arizona Inn
2200 East Elm Street, Tucson, Arizona 85719
Tel: 1 520 325 1541
Fax: 1 520 881 5830

ARIZONA - TUCSON

Tanque Verde Ranch
14301 East Speedway, Tucson, Arizona 85748
Tel: 1 520 296 6275
Fax: 1 520 721 9426

ARIZONA - TUCSON

White Stallion Ranch
9251 West Twin Peaks Road, Tucson, Arizona 85743
Tel: 1 520 297 0252
Fax: 1 520 744 2786

CALIFORNIA - BORREGO SPRINGS

La Casa del Zorro Desert Resort
3845 Yaqui Pass Road, Borrego Springs,
California 92004
Tel: 1 760 767 5323
Fax: 1 760 767 5963

CALIFORNIA - FERNDALE

Gingerbread Mansion Inn
P.O. Box 40, 400 Berding Street, Ferndale,
California 95536
Tel: 1 707 786 4000
Fax: 1 707 786 4381

CALIFORNIA - LA JOLLA

The Bed & Breakfast Inn At La Jolla
7753 Draper Avenue, La Jolla, California 92037
Tel: 1 858 456 2066
Fax: 1 858 456 1510

CALIFORNIA - LODI

Wine & Roses Hotel
2505 Turner Road, Lodi, California 95242
Tel: 1 209 334 6988
Fax: 1 209 371 6049

CALIFORNIA - MILL VALLEY

Mill Valley Inn
165 Throckmorton Avenue, Mill Valley, California 94941
Tel: 1 415 389 6608
Fax: 1 415 389 5051

CALIFORNIA - PALM SPRINGS

Caliente Tropics Resort
411 East Palm Canyon Drive, Palm Springs,
California 92264
Tel: 1 760 327 1391
Fax: 1 760 318 1883

CALIFORNIA - PALM SPRINGS

The Willows
412 West Tahquitz Canyon Way, Palm Springs,
California 92262
Tel: 1 760 320 0771
Fax: 1 760 320 0780

CALIFORNIA - RANCHO SANTA FE

The Inn at Rancho Santa Fe
5951 Linea del Cielo, Rancho Santa Fe, California 92067
Tel: 1 858 756 1131
Fax: 1 858 759 1604

CALIFORNIA - SAN FRANCISCO

Hotel Drisco
2901 Pacific Avenue, San Francisco, California 94115
Tel: 1 415 346 2880
Fax: 1 415 567 5537

CALIFORNIA - SAN FRANCISCO

Nob Hill Lambourne
725 Pine Street, San Francisco, California 94108
Tel: 1 415 433 2287
Fax: 1 415 433 0975

CALIFORNIA - SAN FRANCISCO

The Union Street Inn
2229 Union Street, San Francisco, California 94123
Tel: 1 415 346 0424
Fax: 1 415 922 8046

CALIFORNIA - SAN FRANCISCO BAY AREA

Gerstle Park Inn
34 Grove Street, San Rafael, California 94901
Tel: 1 415 721 7611
Fax: 1 415 721 7600

MINI LISTINGS NORTH AMERICA

Condé Nast Johansens are delighted to recommend over 190 properties across North America, Bermuda, The Caribbean, Mexico, The Pacific. Call 0800 269 397 or see the order forms on page 487 to order guides.

CALIFORNIA - SANTA MONICA

Georgian Hotel
1415 Ocean Avenue, Santa Monica, California 90405
Tel: 1 310 395 9945
Fax: 1 310 451 3374

COLORADO - VAIL

Hotel Gasthof Gramshammer
231 East Gore Creek Drive, Vail, Colorado 81657
Tel: 1 970 476 5626
Fax: 1 970 476 8816

CALIFORNIA - TIBURON

Waters Edge Hotel
25 Main Street, Tiburon, California 94920
Tel: 1 415 789 5999
Fax: 1 415 789 5888

COLORADO - VAIL

Savory Inn & Cooking School of Vail
2405 Elliott Road, Vail, Colorado 81657
Tel: 1 970 476 1304
Fax: 1 970 476 0433

COLORADO - BEAVER CREEK

The Inn at Beaver Creek
10 Elk Track Lane, Beaver Creek Resort, Colorado, 81620
Tel: 1 970 845 5990
Fax: 1 970 845 6204

DELAWARE - REHOBOTH BEACH

Boardwalk Plaza Hotel
Olive Avenue & The Boardwalk, Rehoboth Beach, Delaware 19971
Tel: 1 302 227 7169
Fax: 1 302 227 0561

COLORADO - DENVER

Castle Marne
1572 Race Street, Denver, Colorado 80206
Tel: 1 303 331 0621
Fax: 1 303 331 0623

FLORIDA - KEY WEST

Simonton Court Historic Inn & Cottages
320 Simonton Street, Key West, Florida 33040
Tel: 1 305 294 6386
Fax: 1 305 293 8446

COLORADO - ESTES PARK

Taharaa Lodge
3110 So. Street Urain, PO Box 2586, Estes Park, Colorado 80517
Tel: 1 970 577 0098
Fax: 1 970 577 0819

FLORIDA - MIAMI BEACH

The Inn At Fisher Island
One Fisher Island Drive, Miami Beach, Florida 33109
Tel: 1 305 535 6080
Fax: 1 305 535 6003

COLORADO - MANITOU SPRINGS

The Cliff House at Pikes Peak
306 Cañon Avenue, Manitou Springs, Colorado 80829
Tel: 1 719 685 3000
Fax: 1 719 685 3913

FLORIDA - MIAMI BEACH

The Tides
1220 Ocean Drive, South Beach, Miami, Florida 33139
Tel: 1 305 604 5070
Fax: 1 305 604 5180

COLORADO - STEAMBOAT SPRINGS

The Antlers at Christie Base
2085 Ski Time Square Drive, Steamboat Springs, Colorado 80487
Tel: 1 970 879 8000
Fax: 1 970 879 8060

FLORIDA - NAPLES

Hotel Escalante
290 Fifth Avenue South, Naples, Florida 34102
Tel: 1 239 659 3466
Fax: 1 239 262 8748

COLORADO - STEAMBOAT SPRINGS

Canyon Creek at Eagle Ridge
2720 Eagle Ridge Circle, Steamboat Springs, Colorado 80487
Tel: 1 970 879 8000
Fax: 1 970 879 8060

FLORIDA - PALM BEACH

The Brazilian Court
301 Australian Avenue, Palm Beach, Florida 33480
Tel: 1 561 655 7740
Fax: 1 561 655 0801

COLORADO - STEAMBOAT SPRINGS

Vista Verde Guest Ranch
PO Box 770465, Steamboat Springs, Colorado 80477
Tel: 1 970 879 3858
Fax: 1 970 879 1413

GEORGIA - LITTLE ST SIMONS ISLAND

The Lodge on Little St Simons Island
PO Box 21078, Little St Simons Island, Georgia 31522 – 0578
Tel: 1 912 638 7472
Fax: 1 912 634 1811

Condé Nast Johansens are delighted to recommend over 190 properties across North America, Bermuda, The Caribbean, Mexico, The Pacific.
Call 0800 269 397 or see the order forms on page 487 to order guides.

GEORGIA - PERRY

Henderson Village
125 South Langston Circle, Perry, Georgia 31069
Tel: 1 478 988 8696
Fax: 1 478 988 9009

MARYLAND - FROSTBURG

Savage River Lodge
1600 Mt. Aetna Road, Frostburg, Maryland 21536
Tel: 1 301 689 3200
Fax: 1 301 689 2746

GEORGIA - SAVANNAH

The Eliza Thompson House
5 West Jones Street, Savannah, Georgia 31401
Tel: 1 912 236 3620
Fax: 1 912 238 1920

MARYLAND - TANEYTOWN

Antrim 1844
30 Trevanion Rd, Taneytown, Maryland 21787
Tel: 1 410 756 6812
Fax: 1 410 756 2744

GEORGIA - SAVANNAH

Granite Steps
126 East Gaston Street, Savannah, Georgia 31401

MISSISSIPPI - JACKSON

Fairview Inn
734 Fairview Street, Jackson, Mississippi 39202
Tel: 1 601 948 3429
Fax: 1 601 948 1203

GEORGIA - SAVANNAH

The President's Quarters
225 East President Street, Savannah, Georgia 31401
Tel: 1 912 233 1600
Fax: 1 912 238 0849

MISSISSIPPI - NATCHEZ

Dunleith Plantation
84 Homochitto Street, Natchez, Mississippi 39120
Tel: 1 601 446 8500
Fax: 1 601 446 8554

ILLINOIS - CHICAGO

Fitzpatrick - Chicago - Hotel
166 East Superior Street, Chicago, Illinois 60611
Tel: 1 312 787 6000
Fax: 1 312 787 6133

MISSISSIPPI - NATCHEZ

Monmouth Plantation
36 Melrose Avenue At John A. Quitman Parkway,
Natchez, Mississippi 39120
Tel: 1 601 442 5852
Fax: 1 601 446 7762

ILLINOIS - CHICAGO

The Sutton Place Hotel
21 East Bellevue Place, Chicago, Illinois 60611
Tel: 1 312 266 2100
Fax: 1 312 266 2103

MISSISSIPPI - VICKSBURG

Anchuca Historic Mansion & Inn
1010 First East Street, Vicksburg, Mississippi 39183
Tel: 1 601 661 0111
Fax: 1 601 661 0111

LOUISIANA - NAPOLEANVILLE

Madewood Plantation House
4250 Highway 308, Napoleanville, Louisiana 70390
Tel: 1 985 369 7151
Fax: 1 985 369 9848

MISSISSIPPI - VICKSBURG

The Duff Green Mansion
1114 First East Street, Vicksburg, Mississippi 39180
Tel: 1 601 636 6968
Fax: 1 601 661 0069

LOUISIANA - NEW ORLEANS

Hotel Maison De Ville
727 Rue Toulouse, New Orleans, Louisiana 70130
Tel: 1 504 561 5858
Fax: 1 504 528 9939

MISSOURI - ST LOUIS

The Chase Park Plaza
212-232 North Kingshighway Boulevard, St Louis,
Missouri 63108
Tel: 1 314 633 3000
Fax: 1 314 633 1144

MARYLAND - ANNAPOLIS

The Annapolis Inn
144 Prince George Street, Annapolis,
Maryland 21401-1723
Tel: 1 410 295 5200
Fax: 1 410 295 5201

NEW ENGLAND / CONNECTICUT - ESSEX

Copper Beech Inn
46 Main Street, Ivoryton, Connecticut 06442
Tel: 1 860 767 0330
Fax: 1 860 767 7840

MINI LISTINGS NORTH AMERICA

Condé Nast Johansens are delighted to recommend over 190 properties across North America, Bermuda, The Caribbean, Mexico, The Pacific. Call 0800 269 397 or see the order forms on page 487 to order guides.

NEW ENGLAND / CONNECTICUT - GREENWICH

Delamar

500 Steamboat Road, Greenwich, Connecticut 06830
Tel: 1 203 661 9800
Fax: 1 203 661 2513

NEW ENGLAND / MAINE - NEWCASTLE

The Newcastle Inn

60 River Road, Newcastle, Maine 04553
Tel: 1 207 563 5685
Fax: 1 207 563 6877

NEW ENGLAND / CONNECTICUT - NEW PRESTON

The Boulders Inn

East Shore Road, Route 45, New Preston,
Connecticut 06777
Tel: 1 860 868 0541
Fax: 1 860 868 1925

NEW ENGLAND / MASSACHUSETTS - BOSTON

The Charles Street Inn

94 Charles Street, Boston, Massachusetts 02114–4643
Tel: 1 617 314 8900
Fax: 1 617 371 0009

NEW ENGLAND / CONNECTICUT - RIDGEFIELD

West Lane Inn

22 West Lane, Ridgefield, Connecticut 06877
Tel: 1 203 438 7323
Fax: 1 203 438 7325

NEW ENGLAND / MASSACHUSETTS - BOSTON

The Lenox Hotel

710 Boylston Street, Boston, Massachusetts 02116-2699
Tel: 1 617 536 5300
Fax: 1 617 267 1237

NEW ENGLAND / MAINE - BOOTHBAY HARBOR

Spruce Point Inn

PO Box 237, Boothbay Harbor, Maine 04538
Tel: 1 207 633 4152
Fax: 1 207 633 7138

NEW ENGLAND / MASSACHUSETTS - CAMBRIDGE

A Cambridge House

2218 Massachusetts Avenue, Cambridge,
Massachusetts 02140–1836
Tel: 1 617 491 6300
Fax: 1 617 868 2848

NEW ENGLAND / MAINE - CAMDEN

Camden Maine Stay

22 High Street, Camden, Maine 04843
Tel: 1 207 236 9636
Fax: 1 207 236 0621

NEW ENGLAND / MASSACHUSETTS - CAPE COD

The Captain's House Inn

369–377 Old Harbor Road, Chatham, Cape Cod,
Massachusetts 02633
Tel: 1 508 945 0127
Fax: 1 508 945 0866

NEW ENGLAND / MAINE - CAMDEN

The Inns at Blackberry Common

82 Elm Street, Camden, Maine 04843
Tel: 1 207 236 6060
Fax: 1 207 236 9032

NEW ENGLAND / MASSACHUSETTS - CAPE COD

The Whalewalk Inn

220 Bridge Road, Eastham (Cape Cod),
Massachusetts 02642
Tel: 1 508 255 0617
Fax: 1 508 240 0017

NEW ENGLAND / MAINE - GREENVILLE

Greenville Inn

Po Box 1194, Norris Street, Greenville, Maine 04441
Tel: 1 207 695 2206
Fax: 1 207 695 0335

NEW ENGLAND / MASSACHUSETTS - LENOX

Cranwell Resort, Spa & Golf Club

55 Lee Road, Route 20, Lenox, Massachusetts 01240
Tel: 1 413 637 1364
Fax: 1 413 637 4364

NEW ENGLAND / MAINE - GREENVILLE

The Lodge At Moosehead Lake

Upon Lily Bay Road, Box 1167, Greenville, Maine 04441
Tel: 1 207 695 4400
Fax: 1 207 695 2281

NEW ENGLAND / MASSACHUSETTS - MARBLEHEAD

The Harbor Light Inn

58 Washington Street, Marblehead,
Massachusetts 01945
Tel: 1 781 631 2186
Fax: 1 781 631 2216

NEW ENGLAND / MAINE - KENNEBUNKPORT

The Captain Lord Mansion

6 Pleasant Street, Kennebunkport, Maine 04046-0800
Tel: 1 207 967 3141

NEW ENGLAND / MASSACHUSETTS - MARTHA'S VINEYARD

Hob Knob Inn

128 Main Street, po box 239, Edgartown,
Massachusetts 02539
Tel: 1 508 627 9510
Fax: 1 508 627 4560

Condé Nast Johansens are delighted to recommend over 190 properties across North America, Bermuda, The Caribbean, Mexico, The Pacific.
Call 0800 269 397 or see the order forms on page 487 to order guides.

NEW ENGLAND / MASSACHUSETTS - MARTHA'S VINEYARD

Thorncroft Inn
460 Main Street, PO Box 1022, Vineyard Haven,
Massachusetts 02568
Tel: 1 508 693 3333
Fax: 1 508 693 5419

NEW ENGLAND / RHODE ISLAND - NEWPORT

The Agincourt Inn
120 Miantonomi Avenue, Newport, Rhode Island 02842
Tel: 1 401 847 0902
Fax: 1 401 848 6529

NEW ENGLAND / MASSACHUSETTS - MARTHA'S VINEYARD

The Victorian Inn
24 South Water Street, Edgartown,
Massachusetts 02539
Tel: 1 508 627 4784

NEW ENGLAND / RHODE ISLAND - NEWPORT

The Francis Malbone House
392 Thames Street, Newport, Rhode Island 02840
Tel: 1 401 846 0392
Fax: 1 401 848 5956

NEW ENGLAND / MASSACHUSETTS - MARTHA'S VINEYARD

The Winnetu Inn & Resort at South Beach
31 Dunes Road, Edgartown, Massachusetts 02539
Tel: 1 978 443 1733
Fax: 1 978 443 0479

NEW ENGLAND / VERMONT - CHITTENDEN

Fox Creek Inn
49 Dam Road, Chittenden, Vermont 05737
Tel: 1 802 483 6213
Fax: 1 802 483 2623

NEW ENGLAND / MASSACHUSETTS - NANTUCKET

The Pineapple Inn
10 Hussey Street, Nantucket, Massachusetts 02554
Tel: 1 508 228 9992
Fax: 1 508 325 6051

NEW ENGLAND / VERMONT - CHITTENDEN

Mountain Top Inn & Resort
195 Mountain Top Road, Chittenden, Vermont 05737
Tel: 1 802 483 2311
Fax: 1 802 483 6373

NEW ENGLAND / MASSACHUSETTS - ROCKPORT

Seacrest Manor
99 Marmion Way, Rockport, Massachusetts 01966
Tel: 1 978 546 2211

NEW ENGLAND / VERMONT - LOWER WATERFORD

Rabbit Hill Inn
48 Lower Waterford Road, Lower Waterford,
Vermont 05848
Tel: 1 802 748 5168
Fax: 1 802 748 8342

NEW ENGLAND / NEW HAMPSHIRE - ASHLAND

The Glynn House Inn
59 Highland Street, Ashland, New Hampshire 03217
Tel: 1 800 637 9599/1 603 968 3775
Fax: 1 603 968 9415

NEW ENGLAND / VERMONT - MANCHESTER VILLAGE

1811 House
PO Box 39, Route 7A, Manchester Village,
Vermont 05254
Tel: 1 802 362 1811
Fax: 1 802 362 2443

NEW ENGLAND / NEW HAMPSHIRE - JACKSON

The Inn at Thorn Hill
Thorn Hill Road, Jackson Village, New Hampshire 03846
Tel: 1 603 383 4242
Fax: 1 603 383 8062

NEW ENGLAND / VERMONT - NEWFANE

Four Columns Inn
PO Box 278, Newfane, Vermont 05345
Tel: 1 802 365 7713

NEW ENGLAND / NEW HAMPSHIRE - JACKSON

The Wentworth
Jackson Village, New Hampshire 03846
Tel: 1 603 383 9700
Fax: 1 603 383 4265

NEW ENGLAND / VERMONT - STOWE

The Green Mountain Inn
18 Main Street, Stowe, Vermont 05672
Tel: 1 802 253 7301
Fax: 1 802 253 5096

NEW ENGLAND / RHODE ISLAND - BLOCK ISLAND

The Atlantic Inn
Po Box 1788, Block Island, Rhode Island 02807
Tel: 1 401 466 5883
Fax: 1 401 466 5678

NEW ENGLAND / VERMONT - STOWE

The Mountain Road Resort At Stowe
PO Box 8, 1007 Mountain Road, Stowe, Vermont 05672
Tel: 1 802 253 4566
Fax: 1 802 253 7397

MINI LISTINGS NORTH AMERICA

Condé Nast Johansens are delighted to recommend over 190 properties across North America, Bermuda, The Caribbean, Mexico, The Pacific. Call 0800 269 397 or see the order forms on page 487 to order guides.

NEW ENGLAND / VERMONT - WEST TOWNSHEND

Windham Hill Inn
West Townshend, Vermont 05359
Tel: 1 802 874 4080
Fax: 1 802 874 4702

NEW YORK - GENEVA

Geneva On The Lake
1001 Lochland Road (Route 14 South), Geneva,
New York 14456
Tel: 1 315 789 7190
Fax: 1 315 789 0322

NEW ENGLAND / VERMONT - WOODSTOCK

Woodstock Inn & Resort
Fourteen The Green, Woodstock, Vermont 05091-1298
Tel: 1 802 457 1100
Fax: 1 802 457 6699

NEW YORK - LONG ISLAND

Inn at Great Neck
30 Cutter Mill Road, Greak Neck, New York 11021
Tel: 1 516 773 2000
Fax: 1 516 773 2020

NEW MEXICO - SANTA FE

The Bishop's Lodge Resort & Spa
PO Box 2367, Santa Fe, New Mexico 87504
Tel: 1 505 983 6377
Fax: 1 505 989 8739

NEW YORK - MT TREMPER

The Emerson Inn & Spa
146 Mount Pleasant Road, Mount Tremper,
New York 12457
Tel: 1 845 688 7900
Fax: 1 845 688 2789

NEW MEXICO - SANTA FE

Hotel St Francis
210 Don Gaspar Avenue, Santa Fe, New Mexico 87501
Tel: 1 505 983 5700
Fax: 1 505 989 7690

NEW YORK - NEW YORK CITY

The Inn at Irving Place
56 Irving Place, New York, New York 10003
Tel: 1 212 533 4600
Fax: 1 212 533 4611

NEW MEXICO - SANTA FE

Inn of the Turquoise Bear
342 E. Buena Vista Street, Santa Fe,
New Mexico 87505-2623
Tel: 1 505 983 0798
Fax: 1 505 988 4225

NEW YORK - NEW YORK CITY

The Kitano New York
66 Park Avenue New York, New York City,
New York 10016
Tel: 1 212 885 7000
Fax: 1 212 885 7100

NEW MEXICO - TAOS

Fechin Inn
227 Paseo del Pueblo Norte, Taos, New Mexico 87571
Tel: 1 505 751 1000
Fax: 1 505 751 7338

NEW YORK - NORTHERN CATSKILL MOUNTAINS

Albergo Allegria
#43 Route 296, Windham, New York 12496
Tel: 1 518 734 5560
Fax: 1 518 734 5570

NEW YORK - CAZENOVIA

The Brewster Inn
6 Ledyard Avenue, Cazenovia, New York 13035
Tel: 1 315 655 9232
Fax: 1 315 655 2130

NEW YORK - SARATOGA SPRINGS

Saratoga Arms
497 Broadway, Saratoga Springs, New York 12866
Tel: 1 518 584 1775
Fax: 1 518 581 4064

NEW YORK - CHESTERTOWN

Friends Lake Inn
963 Friends Lake Road, Chestertown, New York 12817
Tel: 1 518 494 4751
Fax: 1 518 494 4616

NORTH CAROLINA - ASHEVILLE

The Wright Inn & Carriage House
235 Pearson Drive, Asheville, North Carolina 28801
Tel: 1 828 251 0789
Fax: 1 828 251 0929

NEW YORK - EAST AURORA

Roycroft Inn
40 South Grove Street, East Aurora, New York 14052
Tel: 1 716 652 5552
Fax: 1 716 655 5345

NORTH CAROLINA - BEAUFORT

The Cedars Inn
305 Front Street, Beaufort, North Carolina 28516
Tel: 1 252 728 7036
Fax: 1 252 728 1685

Condé Nast Johansens are delighted to recommend over 190 properties across North America, Bermuda, The Caribbean, Mexico, The Pacific.
Call 0800 269 397 or see the order forms on page 487 to order guides.

NORTH CAROLINA - BLOWING ROCK
Chetola Resort
PO Box 17, North Main Street, Blowing Rock,
North Carolina 28605
Tel: 1 828 295 5500
Fax: 1 828 295 5529

NORTH CAROLINA - RALEIGH - DURHAM
The Siena Hotel
1505 E Franklin Street, Chapel Hill,
North Carolina 27514
Tel: 1 919 929 4000
Fax: 1 919 968 8527

NORTH CAROLINA - BLOWING ROCK
Gideon Ridge Inn
PO Box 1929, Blowing Rock, North Carolina 28605
Tel: 1 828 295 3644
Fax: 1 828 295 4586

NORTH CAROLINA - ROBBINSVILLE
Snowbird Mountain Lodge
275 Santeetlah Road, Robbinsville,
North Carolina 28771
Tel: 1 828 479 3433
Fax: 1 828 479 3473

NORTH CAROLINA - CASHIERS
Millstone Inn
119 Lodge Lane, Hwy 64 West, Cashiers,
North Carolina 28717
Tel: 1 828 743 2737
Fax: 1 828 743 0208

NORTH CAROLINA - TRYON
Pine Crest Inn
85 Pine Crest Lane, Tryon, North Carolina 28782
Tel: 1 828 859 9135
Fax: 1 828 859 9135

NORTH CAROLINA - CHARLOTTE
Ballantyne Resort
10000 Ballantyne Commons Parkway, Charlotte,
North Carolina 28277
Tel: 1 704 248 4000
Fax: 1 704 248 4005

NORTH CAROLINA - WILMINGTON
Graystone Inn
100 South Third Street, Wilmington,
North Carolina 28401
Tel: 1 910 763 2000
Fax: 1 910 763 5555

NORTH CAROLINA - CHARLOTTE
The Park
2200 Rexford Road, Charlotte, North Carolina 28211
Tel: 1 704 364 8220
Fax: 1 704 365 4712

NORTH CAROLINA - WINSTON-SALEM
Augustus T. Zevely Inn
803 South Main Street, Winston-Salem,
North Carolina 27101
Tel: 1 336 748 9299
Fax: 1 336 721 2211

NORTH CAROLINA - DURHAM
Morehead Manor Bed & Breakfast
914 Vickers Avenue, Durham, North Carolina 27701
Tel: 1 919 687 4366
Fax: 1 919 687 4245

PENNSYLVANIA - HANOVER
Shepphard Mansion
117 Frederick Street, Hanover, Pennsylvania 17331
Tel: 1 717 633 8075
Fax: 1 717 633 8074

NORTH CAROLINA - HENDERSONVILLE
Claddagh Inn
755 North Main Street, Hendersonville,
North Carolina 28792
Tel: 1 828 697 7778

PENNSYLVANIA - LEOLA
Leola Village Inn & Suites
38 Deborah Srive, Route 23, Leola, Pennsylvania 17540
Tel: 1 717 656 7002
Fax: 1 717 656 7648

NORTH CAROLINA - HIGHLANDS
Inn at Half Mile Farm
PO Box 2769, 214 Half Mile Drive, Highlands,
North Carolina 28741
Tel: 1 828 526 8170
Fax: 1 828 526 2625

PENNSYLVANIA - NEW BERLIN
The Inn at New Berlin
321 Market Street, New Berlin,
Pennsylvania 17855-0390
Tel: 1 570 966 0321
Fax: 1 570 966 9557

NORTH CAROLINA - MANTEO
The White Doe Inn & Whispering Bay
PO Box 1029, 319 Sir Walter Raleigh Street, Manteo,
North Carolina 27954
Tel: 1 252 473 9851
Fax: 1 252 473 4708

PENNSYLVANIA - PHILADELPHIA
Rittenhouse Square European Boutique Hotel
1715 Rittenhouse Square, Philadelphia,
Pennsylvania 19103
Tel: 1 215 546 6500
Fax: 1 215 546 8787

MINI LISTINGS NORTH AMERICA

Condé Nast Johansens are delighted to recommend over 190 properties across North America, Bermuda, The Caribbean, Mexico, The Pacific. Call 0800 269 397 or see the order forms on page 487 to order guides.

PENNSYLVANIA - PHILADELPHIA
The Thomas Bond House
129 South 2nd Street, Philadelphia,
Pennsylvania 19106
Tel: 1 215 923 8523
Fax: 1 215 923 8504

TEXAS - SAN ANTONIO
Havana River Walk Inn
1015 Navarro, San Antonio, Texas 78205
Tel: 1 210 222 2008
Fax: 1 210 222 2717

SOUTH CAROLINA - CHARLESTON
Ansonborough Inn
21 Hasell Street, Charleston, South Carolina 29401
Tel: 1 843 723 1655
Fax: 1 843 577 6668

VIRGINIA - CHARLOTTESVILLE
200 South Street Inn
200 South Street, Charlottesville, Virginia 22902
Tel: 1 434 979 0200
Fax: 1 434 979 4403

SOUTH CAROLINA - CHARLESTON
Vendue Inn
19 Vendue Range, Charleston, South Carolina 29401
Tel: 1 843 577 7970
Fax: 1 843 577 2913

VIRGINIA - CHARLOTTESVILLE
Clifton - The Country Inn & Estate
1296 Clifton Inn Drive, Charlottesville, Virginia 22911
Tel: 1 434 971 1800
Fax: 1 434 971 7098

SOUTH CAROLINA - NORTH AUGUSTA
Rosemary & Lookaway Inn
804 Carolina Avenue, North Augusta,
South Carolina 29841
Tel: 1 803 278 6222
Fax: 1 803 649 2404

VIRGINIA - CULPEPER
Prince Michel Restaurant & Suites
Prince Michel de Virginia, HCR 4, Box 77, Leon,
Virginia 22725
Tel: 1 540 547 9720
Fax: 1 540 547 3088

SOUTH CAROLINA - PAWLEYS ISLAND
Litchfield Plantation
Kings River Road, Box 290, Pawleys Island,
South Carolina 29585
Tel: 1 843 237 9121
Fax: 1 843 237 1041

VIRGINIA - MIDDLEBURG
The Goodstone Inn & Estate
36205 Snake Hill Road, Middleburg, Virginia 20117
Tel: 1 540 687 4645
Fax: 1 540 687 6115

SOUTH CAROLINA - TRAVELERS REST
La Bastide
10 Road Of Vines, Travelers Rest, South Carolina 29690
Tel: 1 864 836 8463
Fax: 1 864 836 4820

VIRGINIA - STAUNTON
Frederick House
28 North New Street, Staunton, Virginia 24401
Tel: 1 540 885 4220
Fax: 1 540 885 5180

TENNESSEE - KINGSTON
Whitestone Country Inn
1200 Paint Rock Road, Kingston, Tennessee 37763
Tel: 1 865 376 0113
Fax: 1 865 376 4454

VIRGINIA - WILLIAMSBURG
Legacy of Williamsburg Inn
930 Jamestown Road, Williamsburg,
Virginia 23185–3917
Tel: 1 757 220 0524
Fax: 1 757 220 2211

TEXAS - BOERNE
Ye Kendall Inn
128 West Blanco, Boerne, Texas 78006
Tel: 1 830 249 2138
Fax: 1 830 249 7371

WYOMING - CHEYENNE
Nagle Warren Mansion
222 East 17Th Street, Cheyenne, Wyoming 82001
Tel: 1 307 637 3333
Fax: 1 307 638 6879

TEXAS - GLEN ROSE
Rough Creek Lodge
PO Box 2400, Glen Rose, Texas 76043
Tel: 1 254 965 3700
Fax: 1 254 918 2570

MEXICO - BAJA CALIFORNIA
Casa Natalia
Blvd Mijares 4, San Jose Del Cabo,
Baja California Sur 23400
Tel: 52 624 14 251 00
Fax: 52 624 14251 10

Condé Nast Johansens are delighted to recommend over 190 properties across North America, Bermuda, The Caribbean, Mexico, The Pacific.
Call 0800 269 397 or see the order forms on page 487 to order guides.

MEXICO - CANCUN

Villas Tacul Boutique Hotel
Boulevard Kukulkan, KM 5.5, Cancun,
Quintana Roo 77500, Mexico
Tel: 52 998 883 00 00
Fax: 52 998 849 70 70

MEXICO - GUANAJUATO

Casa de Sierra Nevada Quinta Real
Hospicio 35, San Miguel de Allende, Guanajuato 37700,
Mexico
Tel: 52 415 152 7040
Fax: 52 415 152 1436

MEXICO - ISLA MUJERES

Secreto
Sección Rocas, Lote 11, Punta Norte, Isla Mujeres,
Quintana Roo, 77400 Mexico
Tel: 52 998 877 1039
Fax: 52 998 877 1048

MEXICO - ISLA MUJERES

Villa Rolandi
Fracc. Laguna Mar SM 7, MZA 75 Lotes, Isla Mujeres,
C.P. 77400, Quintana Roo, Mexico
Tel: 52 987 7 07 00
Fax: 52 987 7 01 00

MEXICO - MERIDA

Hacienda Xcanatun Casa de Piedra
Km 12 Carretera Mérida-Progreso, Mérida, Yucatán,
Mexico 97300
Tel: 52 999 941 0273
Fax: 52 999 941 0319

MEXICO - NUEVO VALLARTA

Grand Velas All Suites & Spa Resort
Av. Cocoteros 98 Sur, C.P. 63735, Nuevo Vallarta,
Nayarit, Mexico
Tel: 52 322 226 8000
Fax: 52 322 297 2005

MEXICO - OAXACA

Hacienda Los Laureles
Hildago No. 21, San Felipe del Agua, Oaxaca, Oax.
Mexico c.p. 68020
Tel: 52 951 501 5300
Fax: 52 951 520 0890

MEXICO - PUERTO VALLARTA

El Careyes Beach Resort
km 53.5, Carretera barra de Navada, Puerto Vallarta,
Costa Careyes, Jalisco 48970, Mexico
Tel: 52 315 351 0000
Fax: 52 315 351 0100

MEXICO - PUERTO VALLARTA

El Tamarindo Golf Resort
km 7.5 Carretera, Nelaque, Puerto Vallarta, Cihation,
Jalisco 18970, Mexico
Tel: 52 315 351 0000
Fax: 52 315 351 0100

MEXICO - PUERTO VALLARTA

Las Alamandas Resort
km 83.5 Carr, Barra de Navidad, Puerto Vallarta,
Jalisco 48980, Mexico
Tel: 52 322 285 5500
Fax: 52 322 285 5027

MEXICO - ZIHUATANEJO

Hotel Villa Del Sol
Playa La Ropa S/N, PO Box 84, Zihuatanejo 40880,
Mexico
Tel: 52 755 555 5500
Fax: 52 755 554 2758

BERMUDA - DEVONSHIRE

Ariel Sands
34 South Shore Road, Devonshire, Bermuda
Tel: 1 441 236 1010
Fax: 1 441 236 0087

BERMUDA - HAMILTON

Rosedon Hotel
PO Box Hm 290, Hamilton Hmax, Bermuda
Tel: 1 441 295 1640
Fax: 1 441 295 5904

BERMUDA - PAGET

Fourways Inn
PO Box Pg 294, Paget Pg Bx, Bermuda
Tel: 1 441 236 6517
Fax: 1 441 236 5528

BERMUDA - SOMERSET

Cambridge Beaches
Kings Point, Somerset, MA02 Bermuda
Tel: 1 441 234 0331
Fax: 1 441 234 3352

BERMUDA - SOUTHAMPTON

The Reefs
56 South Shore Road, Southampton, SN02 Bermuda
Tel: 1 441 238 0222
Fax: 1 441 238 8372

BERMUDA - WARWICK

Surf Side Beach Club
90 South Shore Road, Warwick, Bermuda
Tel: 1 441 236 7100
Fax: 1 441 236 9765

CARIBBEAN - ANGUILLA

Frangipani Beach Club
PO Box 1378, Meads Bay, Anguilla, West Indies
Tel: 1 264 497 6442/6444
Fax: 1 264 497 6440

MINI LISTINGS NORTH AMERICA

Condé Nast Johansens are delighted to recommend over 190 properties across North America, Bermuda, The Caribbean, Mexico, The Pacific.
Call 0800 269 397 or see the order forms on page 487 to order guides.

CARIBBEAN - ANTIGUA
Blue Waters
PO Box 256, St. John's, Antigua, West Indies
Tel: 1 268 462 0290
Fax: 1 268 462 0293

CARIBBEAN - JAMAICA
The Tryall Club
PO Box 1206, Montego Bay, Jamaica, West Indies
Tel: 1 800 238 5290
Fax: 1 876 956 5673

CARIBBEAN - ANTIGUA
Curtain Bluff
PO Box 288, Antigua, West Indies
Tel: 1 268 462 8400
Fax: 1 268 462 8409

CARIBBEAN - JAMAICA
Grand Lido Negril
Norman Manley Boulevard, PO Box 88, Negril, Jamaica, West Indies
Tel: 1 876 957 5010/8
Fax: 1 876 957 5517

CARIBBEAN - ANTIGUA
Galley Bay
Five Islands, PO Box 305, St John's, Antigua, West Indies
Tel: 1 268 462 0302
Fax: 1 268 462 4551

CARIBBEAN - JAMAICA
Sans Souci Resort & Spa
PO Box 103, Ocho Rios, St Ann, Jamaica, West Indies
Tel: 1 876 994 1206
Fax: 1 876 994 1544

CARIBBEAN - ANTIGUA
The Inn at English Harbour
Po Box 187, St Johns, Antigua, West Indies
Tel: 1 268 460 1014
Fax: 1 268 460 1603

CARIBBEAN - NEVIS
The Hermitage
Nevis, West Indies
Tel: 1 869 469 3477
Fax: 1 869 469 2481

CARIBBEAN - BARBADOS
Coral Reef Club
St. James, Barbados, West Indies
Tel: 1 246 422 2372
Fax: 1 246 422 1776

CARIBBEAN - NEVIS
Montpelier Plantation Inn
Montpelier Estate, PO Box 474, Nevis, West Indies
Tel: 1 869 469 3462
Fax: 1 869 469 2932

CARIBBEAN - BARBADOS
The Sandpiper
Holetown, St James, Barbados, West Indies
Tel: 1 246 422 2251
Fax: 1 246 422 0900

CARIBBEAN - NEVIS
Nisbet Plantation Beach Club
St James Parish, Nevis, West Indies
Tel: 1 869 469 9325
Fax: 1 869 469 9864

CARIBBEAN - CURAÇAO
Avila Beach Hotel
Penstraat 130, Willemstad, Curaçao, Netherlands Antilles, West Indies
Tel: 599 9 461 4377
Fax: 599 9 461 1493

CARIBBEAN - ST KITTS
The Golden Lemon
Dieppe Bay, St Kitts, West Indies
Tel: 1 869 465 7260
Fax: 1 869 465 4019

CARIBBEAN - GRENADA
Spice Island Beach Resort
Grand Anse Beach, Box 6, St George's, Grenada, West Indies
Tel: 1 473 444 4423/4258
Fax: 1 473 444 4807

CARIBBEAN - ST KITTS
Ottley's Plantation Inn
Po Box 345, Basseterre, St Kitts, West Indies
Tel: 1 869 465 7234
Fax: 1 869 465 4760

CARIBBEAN - JAMAICA
Half Moon
Montego Bay, Jamaica, West Indies
Tel: 1 876 953 2211
Fax: 1 876 953 2731

CARIBBEAN - ST LUCIA
Anse Chastanet
PO Box 7000, Soufriere, St Lucia, West Indies
Tel: 1 758 459 7000
Fax: 1 758 459 7700

NORTH AMERICA

Condé Nast Johansens are delighted to recommend over 190 properties across North America, Bermuda, The Caribbean, Mexico, The Pacific.

CARIBBEAN - ST LUCIA
Windjammer Landing
Labrelotte Bay, P.O.Box 1504, Castries, St Lucia,
West Indies
Tel: 1 758 452 0913
Fax: 1 758 452 9454

CARIBBEAN - THE GRENADINES
Palm Island
St Vincent & The Grenadines, West Indies
Tel: 1 954 481 8787
Fax: 1 954 481 1661

CARIBBEAN - TOBAGO
Being - Villa Experience
Arnol Vale, Tobago, West Indies
Tel: 1 868 625 4443
Fax: 1 868 625 4420

CARIBBEAN - TURKS & CAICOS
The Sands at Grace Bay
PO Box 681, Providenciales, Turks & Caicos Islands,
British West Indies
Tel: 1 649 946 5199
Fax: 1 649 946 5198

CARIBBEAN - TURKS & CAICOS
Turks & Caicos Club
PO Box 687, Providenciales, Turks & Caicos,
British West Indies
Tel: 1 649 946 5800
Fax: 1 649 946 5858

CARIBBEAN - TURKS & CAICOS
Point Grace
PO Box 700, Providenciales, Turks and Caicos Islands,
British west indies
Tel: 1 649 946 5096
Fax: 1 649 946 5097

PACIFIC - FIJI ISLANDS (LABASA)
Nukubati Island
PO Box 1928, Labasa, Fiji Islands
Tel: 61 2 93888 196
Fax: 61 2 93888 204

PACIFIC - FIJI ISLANDS (LAUTOKA)
Blue Lagoon Cruises
183 Vitogo Parade, Lautoka, Fiji Islands
Tel: 679 6661 622
Fax: 679 6664 098

PACIFIC - FIJI ISLANDS (SAVU SAVU)
Jean-Michel Cousteau Fiji Islands Resort
Lesiaceva Point, Savu Savu, Fiji Islands
Tel: 679 885 0188
Fax: 679 885 0340

PACIFIC - FIJI ISLANDS (TOBERUA ISLAND)
Toberua Island Resort
PO Box 3332, Nausori, Fiji Islands
Tel: 679 347 2777
Fax: 679 347 2888

PACIFIC - FIJI ISLANDS (YASAWA ISLAND)
Turtle Island
Yasawa Islands, Po Box 9317, Nadi Airport, Nadi,
Fiji Islands
Tel: 61 3 9823 8300
Fax: 61 3 9823 8383

PACIFIC - FIJI ISLANDS (YASAWA ISLAND)
Yasawa Island Resort
PO Box 10128, Nadi Airport, Nadi, Fiji Islands
Tel: 679 666 3364
Fax: 679 666 5044

PACIFIC - HAWAII (HILO)
Shipman House
131 Ka'iulani Street, Hilo, Hawaii 96720
Tel: 1 808 934 8002
Fax: 1 808 934 8002

PACIFIC - HAWAII (HONOMU)
The Palms Cliff House
28-3514 Mamalahoa Highway 19, P.O. Box 189,
Honomu, Hawaii 96728-0189
Tel: 1 808 963 6076
Fax: 1 808 963 6316

PACIFIC - HAWAII (KAMUELA)
The Jacaranda Inn
65-1444 Kawaihae Road, Kamuela, Hawaii 96743
Tel: 1 808 885 8813
Fax: 1 808 885 6096

PACIFIC - HAWAII (LAHAINA)
Lahaina Inn
127 Lahainaluna Road, Lahaina, Maui, Hawaii 96761
Tel: 1 808 661 0577
Fax: 1 808 667 9480

PACIFIC - HAWAII (LAHAINA)
The Plantation Inn
174 Lahainaluna Road, Lahaina, Maui,
Hawaii 96761, USA
Tel: 1 808 667 9225
Fax: 1 808 667 9293

PACIFIC - HAWAII (WAILUKU)
Old Wailuku Inn at Ulupono
2199 Kaho'okele Street, Wailuku, Maui, Hawaii 96793
Tel: 1 808 244 5897
Fax: 1 808 242 9600

PACIFIC - SAMOA (APIA)
Aggie Grey's Hotel
PO Box 67, Apia, Samoa
Tel: 685 228 80
Fax: 685 236 26 or 685 23203

special offers

websites

places to visit

maps

www.
johansens.com

special offers

guest surveys

questionnaires

prize draws

email
updates

Visit the Condé Nast Johansens website for:

Up-to-date special offers

Detailed road maps

Hotels' own websites

Places to visit nearby - historic houses, castles, gardens, museums and galleries

Become an Online Member and receive regular e-mail special offer updates

CONDÉ NAST
Recommended by **JOHANSENS**

INDEX BY PROPERTY

461

Champagne for the Independently Minded

CHAMPAGNE
TAITTINGER
Reims

**Condé Nast Johansens
preferred Champagne partner**

INDEX BY LOCATION

INDEX BY LOCATION

INDEX BY LOCATION

≋ Hotels with heated indoor swimming pool

▼

≋ Outdoor pool

♪ Fishing on-site

☼ Golf course on-site

⤴ Shooting on-site

SPA   Dedicated Spa facilities

England

M²⁵⁰ Conference facilities for 250 delegates or more

England

Index by Consortium

NORTH WEST ENGLAND

Hotel location shown in red with page number

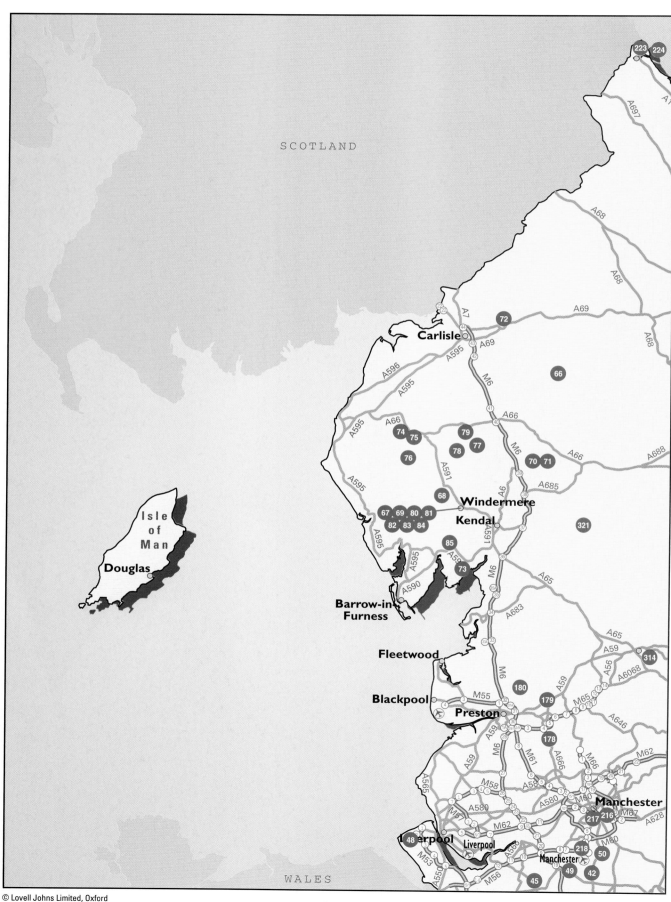

SCOTLAND

Isle
of
Man

Douglas

Carlisle

Windermere

Kendal

Barrow-in-
Furness

Fleetwood

Blackpool

Preston

Liverpool

Manchester

Manchester

WALES

© Lovell Johns Limited, Oxford

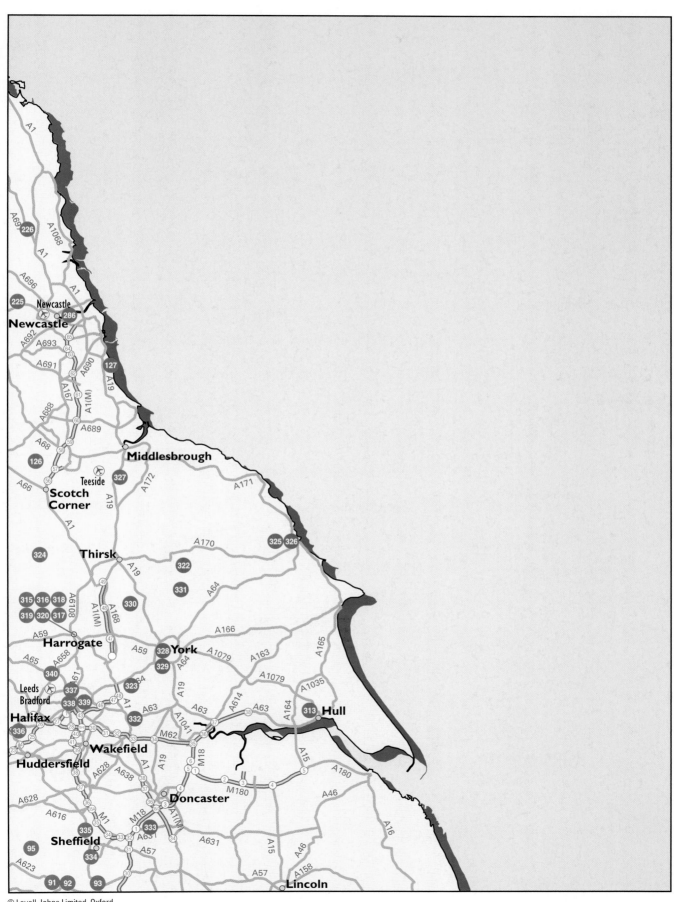

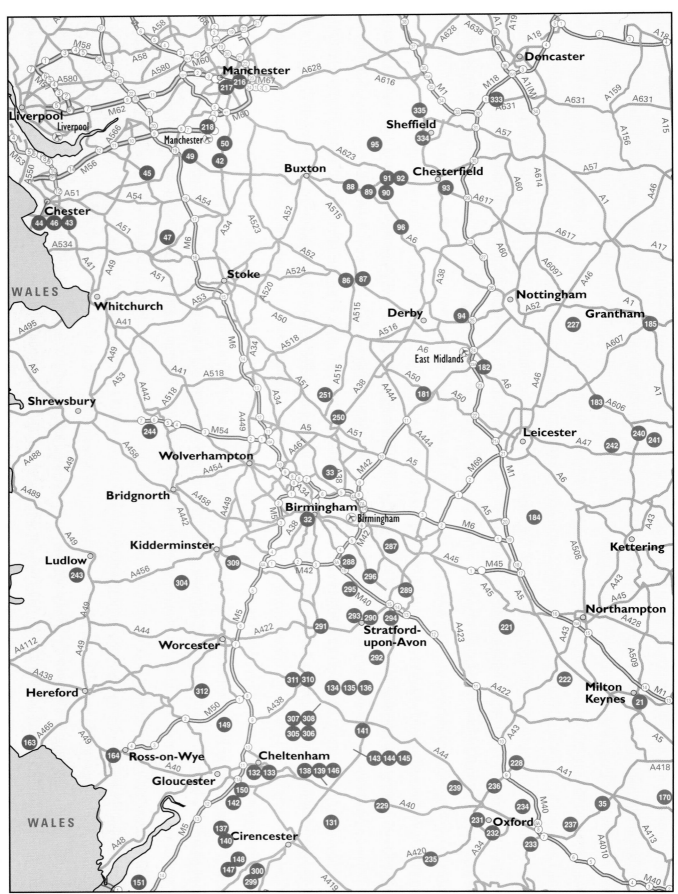

© Lovell Johns Limited, Oxford

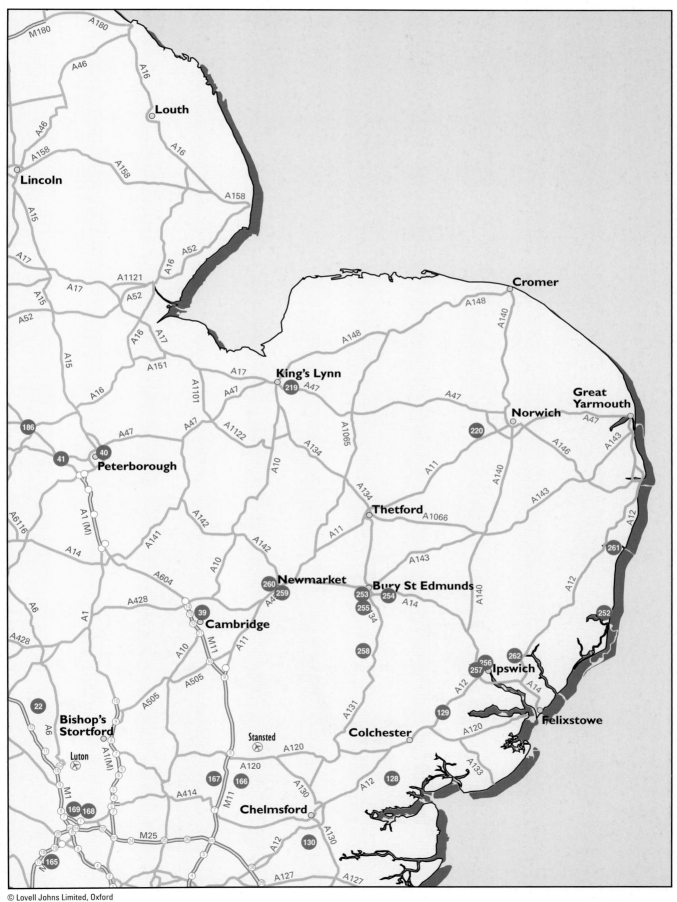

CHANNEL ISLANDS & SOUTH WEST ENGLAND

Hotel location shown in red with page number

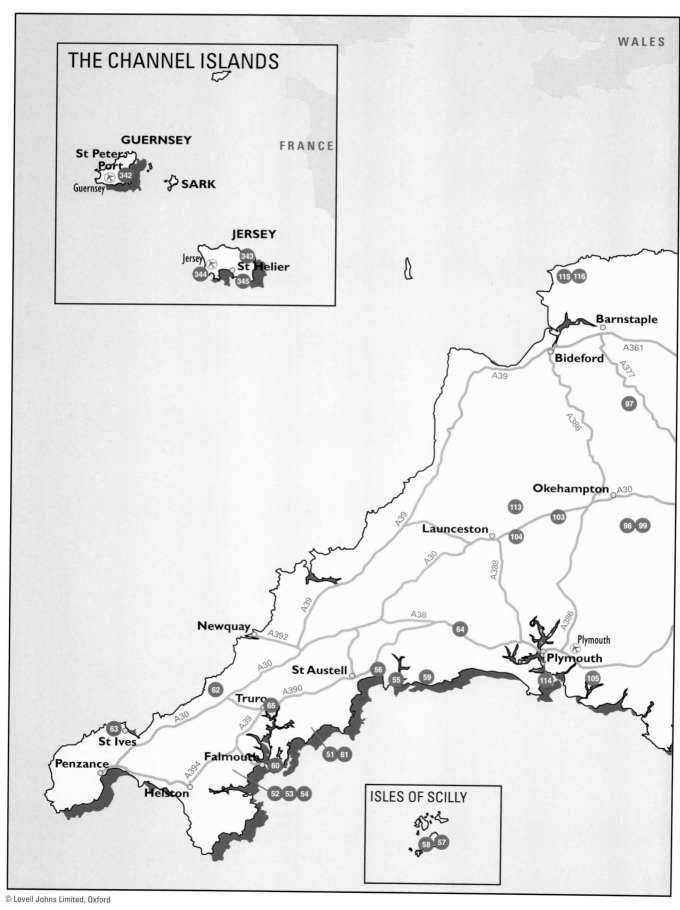

THE CHANNEL ISLANDS

GUERNSEY
St Peters Port
342
Guernsey
SARK

JERSEY
Jersey
344
343
St Helier
345

WALES

115 116
Barnstaple
Bideford
A361
A377
A39
A386
97
Okehampton
A30
113
103
98 99
Launceston
104
A388
A30
A386
A38
64
Plymouth
Plymouth
Newquay
A392
St Austell
56
105
A30
55 59
114
Truro
A390
65
St Ives
63
51 61
Falmouth
60
Penzance
A394
52 53 54
Helston

ISLES OF SCILLY
58 57

© Lovell Johns Limited, Oxford

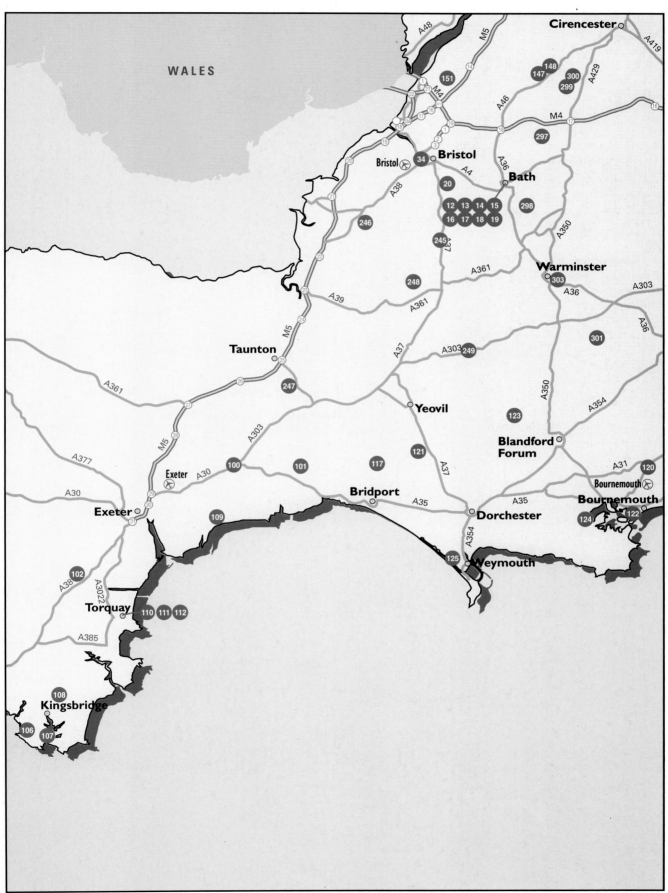

© Lovell Johns Limited, Oxford

Southern England

Hotel location shown in red with page number

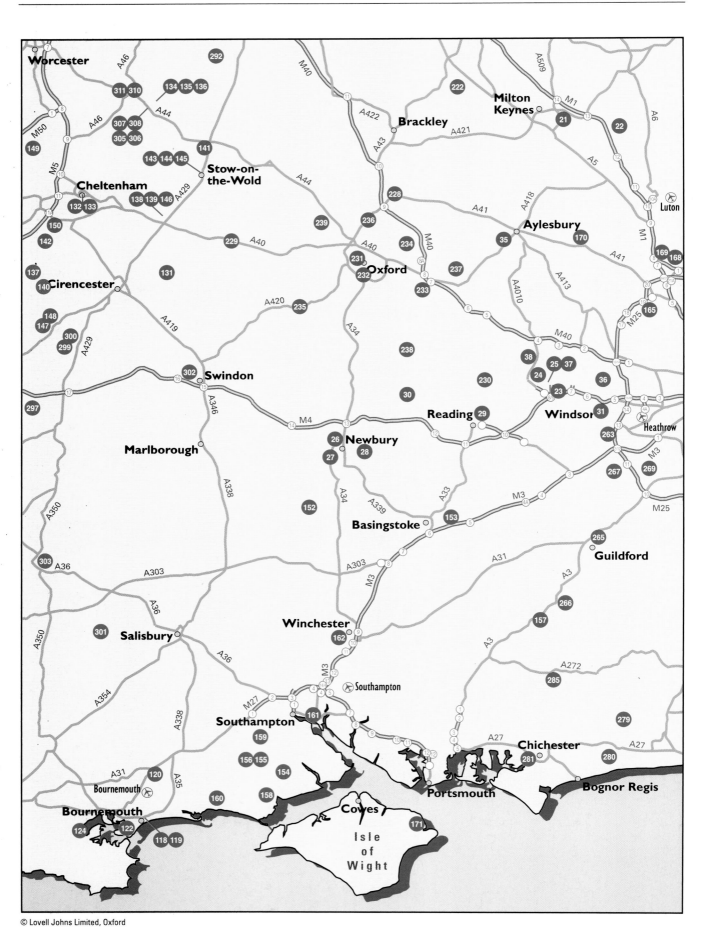

© Lovell Johns Limited, Oxford

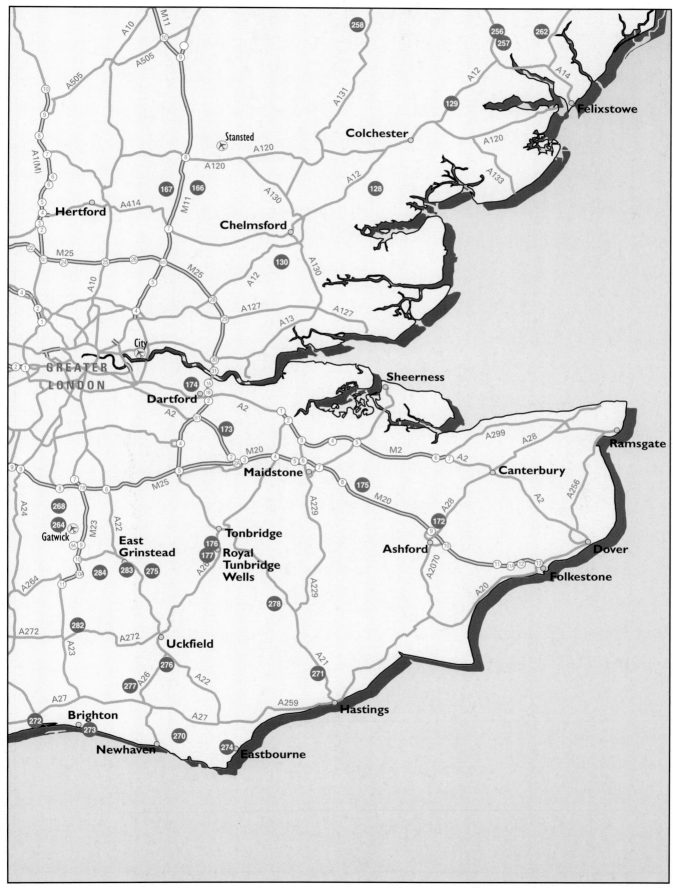

LONDON

Hotel location shown in red with page number

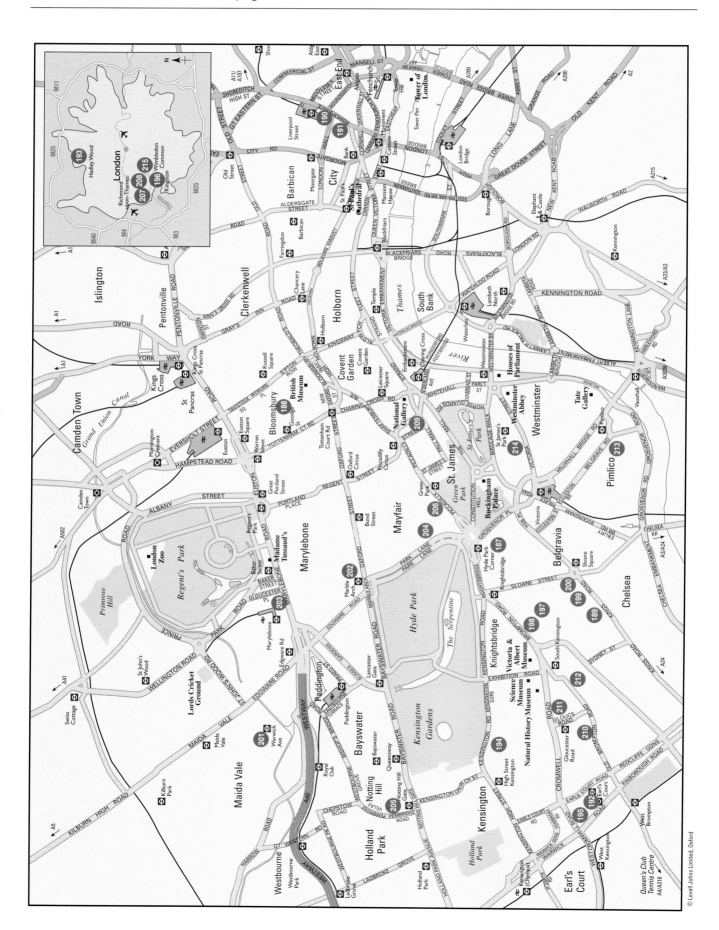

© Lovell Johns Limited, Oxford

Scotland

Hotel location shown in red with page number

Hotel location shown in red with page number

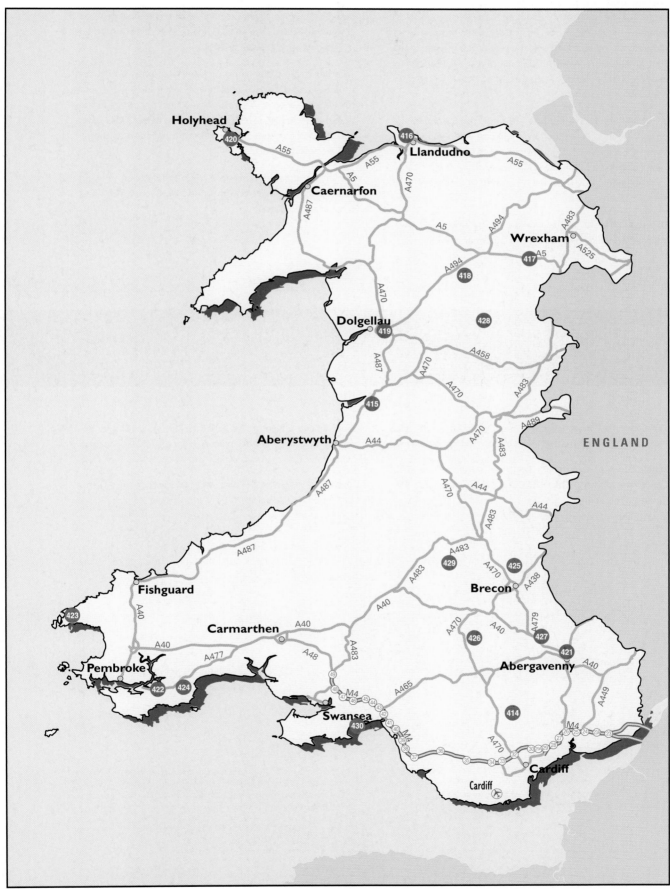

£5 VOUCHER FOR JOHANSENS 2005 GUIDES

We want to ensure that you continue to only stay in the finest hotels, those currently recommended by Condé Nast Johansens. Our team of inspectors visit thousands of properties every year with only the very best receiving Condé Nast Johansens recommendation. Each year there are many newly recommended properties whilst others are rejected for not maintaining standards.

We would like you to use only the latest Guides and so are pleased to offer a contribution to the cost when you update each year. As a 2004 Guide owner, when you order Guides from Condé Nast Johansens 2005 range, please use the order form on page 487 and we will be pleased to reduce the total amount payable by £5.

This reduction will be in addition to any savings you will already have made by ordering two Guides or more.

This offer only extends to orders for 2005 Guides using an order form from a 2004 Guide and must be received by us by 30th August 2004. These 2005 Guide orders will be dispatched upon publication in October 2004.

To order 2005 Guides simply complete the order form in the usual way, enclose a copy of this voucher and reduce your total final payment by £5 (only one voucher per order). **Please note that if you wish to order further copies of the *2004 Guides* you need only return the completed order form as the £5 voucher will not apply.**

For further information call 0800 269 397 and we look forward to keeping you updated with Condé Nast Johansens latest recommended hotels.

JOIN OUR FREE MAILING LIST PLUS WIN ONE OF 20 "CHAIRMAN'S COLLECTIONS"

Join Condé Nast Johansens free mailing list and receive regular information on hotel special offers, promotions and free prize draws.

Simply complete your details below and return this form to **Condé Nast Johansens Ltd, FREEPOST (CB264), London SE25 5BR** (no stamp required)

Your name: ....

Your address: ....

....

....

Postcode: ....

Your telephone: ....

Your E-mail: ....

The details provided will be used to keep you informed of future products and special offers provided by Condé Nast Johansens and other carefully selected third parties. If you do not wish to receive this information, please tick this box ❑ (Your telephone number will not be used for marketing purposes)

E203

Recommend a friend to be added to our free mailing list and qualify for entry in our free prize draw for one of 20 Condé Nast Johansens "Chairman's Collections".

PLEASE REMEMBER TO COMPLETE YOUR OWN DETAILS IN THE LEFT HAND PANEL IN ORDER TO BE INCLUDED.

Friend's name: ....

Friend's address: ....

....

....

Postcode: ....

Friend's telephone: ....

Friend's E-mail: ....

The details provided will be used to keep you informed of future products and special offers provided by Condé Nast Johansens and other carefully selected third parties. If you do not wish to receive this information, please tick this box ❑ (Your telephone number will not be used for marketing purposes)

E204

Prize Draw Terms and Conditions: 1. All entries must be received by 29th August 2004. 2. Entries recommending a friend will go into a prize draw on 1st September 2004. 3. The prize is one of twenty 2005 edition "Chairman's Collections", as described on the order form in this Guide. 4. The winners will be the first 20 names drawn by an independent observer. 5. The 20 winners will be notified in writing as soon as possible after 1st September 2004. 6. No cash alternative is available. 7. Entrants must be over 18. 8. Only one entry per household. 9. Employees of Condé Nast Johansens Ltd., its recommended hotels, agencies and suppliers are not eligible to participate in this promotion. 10. Condé Nast Johansens reserves the right to feature and photograph the winners for future publicity purposes. 11. No responsibility can be taken for entries lost, damaged or delayed. 12. For a list of winners please send an SAE to Condé Nast Johansens, FREEPOST (CB264), London SE25 5BR. 13. No purchase necessary. 14. Entry into the prize draw will be deemed as an acceptance of these rules.

ORDER FORM
Choose from our wide range of titles below

CONDÉ NAST JOHANSENS

Order **2** Guides get **£5 off** · Order **3** Guides get **£10 off** · Order **4** Guides get **£20 off**
Order the Chairman's Collection worth over £90 for just **£70**

Simply complete the form below, total the cost and then deduct the appropriate discount. State your preferred method of payment and mail to Condé Nast Johansens Ltd, FREEPOST (CB264), LONDON SE25 5BR (no stamp required). Fax orders welcome on 020 8655 7817

ALTERNATIVELY YOU CAN ORDER IMMEDIATELY ON FREEPHONE 0800 269 397, please quote ref: E006

Hotels Great Britain & Ireland *410 Recommendations*	Country Houses Great Britain & Ireland *240 Recommendations*	Hotels & Spas Europe & Mediterranean *350 Recommendations*	Hotels, Inns & Resorts N America, Caribbean *200 Recommendations*	Business Venues *230 Recommendations* *(published Feb 2004)*
I wish to order	I wish to order	I wish to order	I wish to order	I wish to order
QUANTITY	QUANTITY	QUANTITY	QUANTITY	QUANTITY
copy/ies at £19.95 each. Total cost	copy/ies at £16.95 each. Total cost	copy/ies at £16.95 each. Total cost	copy/ies at £14.95 each. Total cost	copy/ies at £25.00 each. Total cost
£	£	£	£	£

 Condé Nast Johansens Gold Blocked Slip Case priced at £5 each

Condé Nast Johansens Luxury Luggage Tag priced at £15 each

To order these items please fill in the appropriate section below

The Chairman's Collection
Order the complete collection of
Condé Nast Johansens Recommended Guides for only £70
PLUS FREE *Luxury Luggage Tag worth £15*
PLUS FREE *Slip Case worth £5*
The Chairman's Collection contains all five titles pictured above. The Recommended Venues guide will be dispatched separately on publication in February 2004.

Now please complete your order and payment details

tick

I have ordered 2 titles - **£5 off**	−£5.00
I have ordered 3 titles - **£10 off**	−£10.00
I have ordered 4 titles - **£20 off**	−£20.00
Total cost of books ordered minus discount (excluding the Chairman's Collection)	£
Luxury Luggage Tag at **£15** Quantity and total cost:	£
Gold Blocked Slip Case at **£5** Quantity and total cost:	£
I wish to order the Chairman's Collection at **£70** Quantity and total cost:	£
Packing & delivery: (All UK orders including Chairman's Collection) add **£4.90** per order (Outside UK) add **£6.00** per Guide or for Chairman's Collection add **£25.00**	£

GRAND TOTAL £

I have chosen my Condé Nast Johansens Guides and (please tick)
I enclose a cheque payable to Condé Nast Johansens ☐
Please debit my credit/charge card account ☐
☐ MasterCard   ☐ Visa   ☐ Switch (Issue Number) [ ]

Card Holders Name (Mr/Mrs/Miss)
Address
Postcode
Telephone
E-mail
Card No.   Exp Date
Signature

NOW send to
Condé Nast Johansens Ltd, FREEPOST (CB264), LONDON SE25 5BR (no stamp required)
Fax orders welcome on 020 8655 7817

The details provided may be used to keep you informed of future products and special offers provided by Condé Nast Johansens and other carefully selected third parties. If you do not wish to receive such information, please tick this box ☐.
(Your phone number will only be used to ensure the fast and safe delivery of your order)

SPECIAL OFFER UPDATES
Receive free monthly E-mail updates of hotels' special offers

In order to keep travellers up to date with the latest developments, we have created an Online Membership scheme. FREE to join, Online Membership gives the user a number of complimentary benefits, including monthly E-mail notification of the latest hotel Special Offers. If you would like us to sign you up, please complete the form below.

Alternatively visit **www.johansens.com** today and take a look for yourself.

Title .... Your name: ....

E-mail ....

Password .... Password Reminder ....

Your Address ....

Postcode .... Telephone ....

Example areas of interest (please tick as applicable)

○ Great Britain & Ireland   ○ Europe   ○ North America   ○ Golf   ○ Gourmet

○ Honeymoon   ○ Skiing   ○ Weekend   ○ Midweek   ○ Business use

The details provided may be used to keep you informed of future products and special offers provided by Condé Nast Johansens and other carefully selected third parties. If you do not wish to recieve such information please tick this box ☐ .

Please return completed form to **Condé Nast Johansens, FREEPOST (CB264), LONDON SE25 5BR** (no stamp required). Alternatively send by fax to 020 8655 7817

SPECIAL OFFER UPDATES
Receive free monthly E-mail updates of hotels' special offers

In order to keep travellers up to date with the latest developments, we have created an Online Membership scheme. FREE to join, Online Membership gives the user a number of complimentary benefits, including monthly E-mail notification of the latest hotel Special Offers. If you would like us to sign you up, please complete the form below.

Alternatively visit **www.johansens.com** today and take a look for yourself.

Title .... Your name: ....

E-mail ....

Password .... Password Reminder ....

Your Address ....

Postcode .... Telephone ....

Example areas of interest (please tick as applicable)

○ Great Britain & Ireland   ○ Europe   ○ North America   ○ Golf   ○ Gourmet

○ Honeymoon   ○ Skiing   ○ Weekend   ○ Midweek   ○ Business use

The details provided may be used to keep you informed of future products and special offers provided by Condé Nast Johansens and other carefully selected third parties. If you do not wish to recieve such information please tick this box ☐ .

Please return completed form to **Condé Nast Johansens, FREEPOST (CB264), LONDON SE25 5BR** (no stamp required). Alternatively send by fax to 020 8655 7817

Order **2** Guides get **£5 off** • Order **3** Guides get **£10 off** • Order **4** Guides get **£20 off**
Order the Chairman's Collection worth over £90 for just **£70**

Simply complete the form below, total the cost and then deduct the appropriate discount. State your preferred method of payment and mail to Condé Nast Johansens Ltd, FREEPOST (CB264), LONDON SE25 5BR (no stamp required). Fax orders welcome on 020 8655 7817

ALTERNATIVELY YOU CAN ORDER IMMEDIATELY ON FREEPHONE 0800 269 397, please quote ref: E006

Hotels Great Britain & Ireland *410 Recommendations*	**Country Houses** Great Britain & Ireland *240 Recommendations*	**Hotels & Spas** Europe & Mediterranean *350 Recommendations*	**Hotels, Inns & Resorts** N America, Caribbean *200 Recommendations*	**Business Venues** *230 Recommendations* *(published Feb 2004)*
I wish to order	I wish to order	I wish to order	I wish to order	I wish to order
QUANTITY	QUANTITY	QUANTITY	QUANTITY	QUANTITY
copy/ies at £19.95 each.	copy/ies at £16.95 each.	copy/ies at £16.95 each.	copy/ies at £14.95 each.	copy/ies at £25.00 each.
Total cost	Total cost	Total cost	Total cost	Total cost
£	£	£	£	£

Condé Nast Johansens Gold Blocked Slip Case priced at **£5** each

Condé Nast Johansens Luxury Luggage Tag priced at **£15** each

To order these items please fill in the appropriate section below

The Chairman's Collection
Order the complete collection of
Condé Nast Johansens Recommended Guides for only £70
PLUS FREE *Luxury Luggage Tag* worth £15
PLUS FREE *Slip Case* worth £5

The Chairman's Collection contains all five titles pictured above. The Recommended Venues guide will be dispatched separately on publication in February 2004.

Now please complete your order and payment details

tick

I have ordered 2 titles - **£5** off	☐	−£5.00
I have ordered 3 titles - **£10** off	☐	−£10.00
I have ordered 4 titles - **£20** off	☐	−£20.00

Total cost of books ordered minus discount (excluding the Chairman's Collection) £

Luxury Luggage Tag at **£15** Quantity and total cost: £

Gold Blocked Slip Case at **£5** Quantity and total cost: £

I wish to order the Chairman's Collection at **£70** Quantity and total cost: £

Packing & delivery: (All UK orders including Chairman's Collection) add **£4.90** per order
(Outside UK) add **£6.00** per Guide or for Chairman's Collection add **£25.00** £

GRAND TOTAL £

I have chosen my Condé Nast Johansens Guides and (please tick)
I enclose a cheque payable to Condé Nast Johansens ☐
Please debit my credit/charge card account ☐
☐ MasterCard ☐ Visa ☐ Switch (Issue Number)

Card Holders Name (Mr/Mrs/Miss)

Address

Postcode

Telephone

E-mail

Card No. Exp Date

Signature

NOW send to
Condé Nast Johansens Ltd, FREEPOST (CB264), LONDON SE25 5BR (no stamp required)
Fax orders welcome on 020 8655 7817

The details provided may be used to keep you informed of future products and special offers provided by Condé Nast Johansens and other carefully selected third parties. If you do not wish to receive such information, please tick this box ☐
(Your phone number will only be used to ensure the fast and safe delivery of your order)

GUEST SURVEY REPORT
Evaluate your stay in a Condé Nast Johansens Recommendation

Dear Guest,

Following your stay in a Condé Nast Johansens recommendation, please spare a moment to complete this Guest Survey Report. This is an important source of information for Johansens, to maintain the highest standards for our recommendations and to support the work of our team of inspectors.

It is also the prime source of nominations for Condé Nast Johansens Awards for Excellence, which are made annually to those properties worldwide that represent the finest standards and best value for money in luxury, independent travel.

Thank you for your time and I hope that when choosing future accommodation Condé Nast Johansens will be your guide.

Yours faithfully,

Tim Sinclair
Sales & Marketing Director, Condé Nast Johansens

p.s. Guest Survey Reports may also be completed online at www.johansens.com

1. Your details

Your name: ....

Your address: ....

....

....

Postcode: ....

Telephone: ....

E-mail: ....

2. Hotel details

Name of hotel: ....

....

Location: ....

Date of visit: ....

3. Your rating of the hotel

Please tick one box in each category below (as applicable)

	Excellent	Good	Disappointing	Poor
Bedrooms	○	○	○	○
Public Rooms	○	○	○	○
Food/Restaurant	○	○	○	○
Service	○	○	○	○
Welcome/Friendliness	○	○	○	○
Value For Money	○	○	○	○

4. Any other comments

If you wish to make additional comments, please write separately to the Publisher, Condé Nast Johansens Ltd, 6-8 Old Bond Street, London W1S 4PH

....

....

....

....

....

....

The details provided may be used to keep you informed of future products and special offers provided by Condé Nast Johansens and other carefully selected third parties.
If you do not wish to receive such information please tick this box ☐.

Please return completed form to **Condé Nast Johansens, FREEPOST (CB264), LONDON SE25 5BR (no stamp required)**.
Alternatively send by fax to 020 8655 7817

ORDER FORM

CONDÉ NAST JOHANSENS

Choose from our wide range of titles below

Order **2** Guides get **£5 off** · Order **3** Guides get **£10 off** · Order **4** Guides get **£20 off**

Order the Chairman's Collection worth over £90 for just **£70**

Simply complete the form below, total the cost and then deduct the appropriate discount. State your preferred method of payment and mail to Condé Nast Johansens Ltd, FREEPOST (CB264), LONDON SE25 5BR (no stamp required). Fax orders welcome on 020 8655 7817

ALTERNATIVELY YOU CAN ORDER IMMEDIATELY ON FREEPHONE 0800 269 397, please quote ref: E006

Hotels
Great Britain & Ireland
410 Recommendations

I wish to order

QUANTITY

copy/ies at £19.95 each.
Total cost

£

Country Houses
Great Britain & Ireland
240 Recommendations

I wish to order
QUANTITY

copy/ies at £16.95 each.
Total cost

£

Hotels & Spas
Europe & Mediterranean
350 Recommendations

I wish to order
QUANTITY

copy/ies at £16.95 each.
Total cost

£

Hotels, Inns & Resorts
N America, Caribbean
200 Recommendations

I wish to order

QUANTITY

copy/ies at £14.95 each.
Total cost

£

Business Venues
230 Recommendations
(published Feb 2004)

I wish to order

QUANTITY

copy/ies at £25.00 each.
Total cost

£

Condé Nast Johansens
Gold Blocked Slip Case
priced at £5 each

Condé Nast Johansens
Luxury Luggage Tag
priced at
£15 each

To order these items please fill in the appropriate section below

The Chairman's Collection

Order the complete collection of
Condé Nast Johansens Recommended Guides for only £70

PLUS FREE Luxury Luggage Tag *worth £15*

PLUS FREE Slip Case *worth £5*

The Chairman's Collection contains all five titles pictured above. The Recommended Venues guide will be dispatched separately on publication in February 2004.

Now please complete your order and payment details

tick

I have ordered 2 titles - **£5 off**   −£5.00

I have ordered 3 titles - **£10 off**   −£10.00

I have ordered 4 titles - **£20 off**   −£20.00

Total cost of books ordered minus discount
(excluding the Chairman's Collection)   £

Luxury Luggage Tag at **£15**
Quantity and total cost: £

Gold Blocked Slip Case at **£5**
Quantity and total cost: £

I wish to order the
Chairman's Collection at **£70**
Quantity and total cost: £

Packing & delivery: (All UK orders including
Chairman's Collection) add **£4.90** per order

(Outside UK) add **£6.00** per Guide   £
or for Chairman's Collection add **£25.00**

GRAND TOTAL   £

I have chosen my Condé Nast Johansens Guides and (please tick)

I enclose a cheque payable to Condé Nast Johansens ☐

Please debit my credit/charge card account ☐

☐ MasterCard   ☐ Visa   ☐ Switch (Issue Number)

Card Holders Name   (Mr/Mrs/Miss)

Address

Postcode

Telephone

E-mail

Card No.   Exp Date

Signature

NOW send to
Condé Nast Johansens Ltd, FREEPOST (CB264), LONDON SE25 5BR (no stamp required)
Fax orders welcome on 020 8655 7817

The details provided may be used to keep you informed of future products and special offers provided by Condé Nast Johansens and other carefully selected third parties. If you do not wish to receive such information, please tick this box ☐.
(Your phone number will only be used to ensure the fast and safe delivery of your order)

GUEST SURVEY REPORT

Evaluate your stay in a Condé Nast Johansens Recommendation

Dear Guest,

Following your stay in a Condé Nast Johansens recommendation, please spare a moment to complete this Guest Survey Report. This is an important source of information for Johansens, to maintain the highest standards for our recommendations and to support the work of our team of inspectors.

It is also the prime source of nominations for Condé Nast Johansens Awards for Excellence, which are made annually to those properties worldwide that represent the finest standards and best value for money in luxury, independent travel.

Thank you for your time and I hope that when choosing future accommodation Condé Nast Johansens will be your guide.

Yours faithfully,

Tim Sinclair
Sales & Marketing Director, Condé Nast Johansens

p.s. Guest Survey Reports may also be completed online at www.johansens.com

1. Your details

Your name: ....

Your address: ....

....

....

Postcode: ....

Telephone: ....

E-mail: ....

2. Hotel details

Name of hotel: ....

....

Location: ....

Date of visit: ....

3. Your rating of the hotel

Please tick one box in each category below (as applicable)

	Excellent	Good	Disappointing	Poor
Bedrooms	◯	◯	◯	◯
Public Rooms	◯	◯	◯	◯
Food/Restaurant	◯	◯	◯	◯
Service	◯	◯	◯	◯
Welcome/Friendliness	◯	◯	◯	◯
Value For Money	◯	◯	◯	◯

4. Any other comments

If you wish to make additional comments, please write separately to the Publisher, Condé Nast Johansens Ltd, 6-8 Old Bond Street, London W1S 4PH

....

....

....

....

....

Please return completed form to **Condé Nast Johansens, FREEPOST (CB264), LONDON SE25 5BR** (no stamp required).
Alternatively send by fax to 020 8655 7817

Order **2** Guides get **£5 off** · Order **3** Guides get **£10 off** · Order **4** Guides get **£20 off**

Order the Chairman's Collection worth over £90 for just **£70**

Simply complete the form below, total the cost and then deduct the appropriate discount. State your preferred method of payment and mail to Condé Nast Johansens Ltd, FREEPOST (CB264), LONDON SE25 5BR (no stamp required). Fax orders welcome on 020 8655 7817

ALTERNATIVELY YOU CAN ORDER IMMEDIATELY ON FREEPHONE 0800 269 397, please quote ref: E006

Hotels
Great Britain & Ireland
410 Recommendations

I wish to order

copy/ies at £19.95 each.
Total cost
£

Country Houses
Great Britain & Ireland
240 Recommendations

I wish to order

copy/ies at £16.95 each.
Total cost
£

Hotels & Spas
Europe & Mediterranean
350 Recommendations

I wish to order

copy/ies at £16.95 each.
Total cost
£

Hotels, Inns & Resorts
N America, Caribbean
200 Recommendations

I wish to order

copy/ies at £14.95 each.
Total cost
£

Business Venues
230 Recommendations
(published Feb 2004)

I wish to order

copy/ies at £25.00 each.
Total cost
£

Condé Nast Johansens
Gold Blocked Slip Case
priced at £5 each

Condé Nast Johansens
Luxury Luggage Tag
priced at
£15 each

To order these items please fill in the appropriate section below

The Chairman's Collection
Order the complete collection of
Condé Nast Johansens Recommended Guides for only £70
PLUS FREE *Luxury Luggage Tag* worth £15
PLUS FREE *Slip Case* worth £5

The Chairman's Collection contains all five titles pictured above. The Recommended Venues guide will be dispatched separately on publication in February 2004.

Now please complete your order and payment details

tick

I have ordered 2 titles - **£5 off**   −£5.00

I have ordered 3 titles - **£10 off**   −£10.00

I have ordered 4 titles - **£20 off**   −£20.00

Total cost of books ordered minus discount
(excluding the Chairman's Collection)   £

Luxury Luggage Tag at **£15**
Quantity and total cost: £

Gold Blocked Slip Case at **£5**
Quantity and total cost: £

I wish to order the
Chairman's Collection at **£70**
Quantity and total cost: £

Packing & delivery: (All UK orders including
Chairman's Collection) add **£4.90** per order

(Outside UK) add **£6.00** per Guide
or for Chairman's Collection add **£25.00**   £

GRAND TOTAL   £

I have chosen my Condé Nast Johansens Guides and (please tick)

I enclose a cheque payable to Condé Nast Johansens ☐
Please debit my credit/charge card account ☐

☐ MasterCard   ☐ Visa   ☐ Switch (Issue Number)

Card Holders Name   (Mr/Mrs/Miss)

Address

Postcode

Telephone

E-mail

Card No.   Exp Date

Signature

NOW send to
Condé Nast Johansens Ltd, FREEPOST (CB264), LONDON SE25 5BR (no stamp required)
Fax orders welcome on 020 8655 7817

The details provided may be used to keep you informed of future products and special offers provided by Condé Nast Johansens and other carefully selected third parties. If you do not wish to receive such information, please tick this box ☐.
(Your phone number will only be used to ensure the fast and safe delivery of your order)

HOTEL BROCHURE REQUEST

Find out further information on the hotels of your choice

The Condé Nast Johansens Hotel Brochure Request Service has been established to give guests the opportunity to obtain more information about a Recommendation, additional to that contained within the Johansens guide.

Condé Nast Johansens will pass your request to the Recommendation specified who will directly send you a brochure.

Hotel name(s) and location(s) (BLOCK CAPITALS)   Page in guide

1 _____   _____

2 _____   _____

3 _____   _____

4 _____   _____

5 _____   _____

The Recommendation(s) you have chosen will send their brochures directly to the address below

Your name: _____

Your address: _____

_____ Postcode: _____

Telephone: _____   E-mail: _____

The details provided may be used to keep you informed of future products and special offers provided by Condé Nast Johansens and other carefully selected third parties. If you do not wish to recieve such information please tick this box ☐.

Please return completed form to **Condé Nast Johansens, FREEPOST (CB264), LONDON SE25 5BR** (no stamp required). Alternatively send by fax to 020 8655 7817

HOTEL BROCHURE REQUEST

Find out further information on the hotels of your choice

The Condé Nast Johansens Hotel Brochure Request Service has been established to give guests the opportunity to obtain more information about a Recommendation, additional to that contained within the Johansens guide.

Condé Nast Johansens will pass your request to the Recommendation specified who will directly send you a brochure.

Hotel name(s) and location(s) (BLOCK CAPITALS)   Page in guide

1 _____   _____

2 _____   _____

3 _____   _____

4 _____   _____

5 _____   _____

The Recommendation(s) you have chosen will send their brochures directly to the address below

Your name: _____

Your address: _____

_____ Postcode: _____

Telephone: _____   E-mail: _____

The details provided may be used to keep you informed of future products and special offers provided by Condé Nast Johansens and other carefully selected third parties. If you do not wish to recieve such information please tick this box ☐.

Please return completed form to **Condé Nast Johansens, FREEPOST (CB264), LONDON SE25 5BR** (no stamp required). Alternatively send by fax to 020 8655 7817

ORDER FORM
Choose from our wide range of titles below

CONDÉ NAST
JOHANSENS

Hotels
Great Britain & Ireland
410 Recommendations
I wish to order

copy/ies at £19.95 each.
Total cost

Country Houses
Great Britain & Ireland
240 Recommendations
I wish to order
copy/ies at £16.95 each.
Total cost

Hotels & Spas
Europe & Mediterranean
350 Recommendations
I wish to order
copy/ies at £16.95 each.
Total cost

Hotels, Inns & Resorts
N America, Caribbean
200 Recommendations
I wish to order
copy/ies at £14.95 each.
Total cost

Business Venues
230 Recommendations
(published Feb 2004)
I wish to order
copy/ies at £25.00 each.
Total cost

Condé Nast Johansens Gold Blocked Slip Case priced at £5 each

Condé Nast Johansens Luxury Luggage Tag priced at £15 each

To order these items please fill in the appropriate section below

The Chairman's Collection
Order the complete collection of
Condé Nast Johansens Recommended Guides for only £70
PLUS FREE Luxury Luggage Tag worth £15
PLUS FREE Slip Case worth £5
The Chairman's Collection contains all five titles pictured above. The Recommended Venues guide will be dispatched separately on publication in February 2004.

Now please complete your order and payment details

tick
I have ordered 2 titles - **£5 off** −£5.00
I have ordered 3 titles - **£10 off** −£10.00
I have ordered 4 titles - **£20 off** −£20.00
Total cost of books ordered minus discount (excluding the Chairman's Collection) £
Luxury Luggage Tag at **£15** Quantity and total cost: £
Gold Blocked Slip Case at **£5** Quantity and total cost: £
I wish to order the Chairman's Collection at **£70** Quantity and total cost: £
Packing & delivery: (All UK orders including Chairman's Collection) add **£4.90** per order
(Outside UK) add **£6.00** per Guide or for Chairman's Collection add **£25.00** £

GRAND TOTAL £

I have chosen my Condé Nast Johansens Guides and (please tick)
I enclose a cheque payable to Condé Nast Johansens ☐
Please debit my credit/charge card account ☐
☐ MasterCard ☐ Visa ☐ Switch (Issue Number)
Card Holders Name (Mr/Mrs/Miss)
Address
Postcode
Telephone
E-mail
Card No. Exp Date
Signature

NOW send to
Condé Nast Johansens Ltd, FREEPOST (CB264), LONDON SE25 5BR (no stamp required)
Fax orders welcome on 020 8655 7817

The details provided may be used to keep you informed of future products and special offers provided by Condé Nast Johansens and other carefully selected third parties. If you do not wish to receive such information, please tick this box ☐.
(Your phone number will only be used to ensure the fast and safe delivery of your order)

HOTEL BROCHURE REQUEST
Find out further information on the hotels of your choice

The Condé Nast Johansens Hotel Brochure Request Service has been established to give guests the opportunity to obtain more information about a Recommendation, additional to that contained within the Johansens guide.

Condé Nast Johansens will pass your request to the Recommendation specified who will directly send you a brochure.

Hotel name(s) and location(s) (BLOCK CAPITALS)   Page in guide

1 _____   _____

2 _____   _____

3 _____   _____

4 _____   _____

5 _____   _____

The Recommendation(s) you have chosen will send their brochures directly to the address below

Your name: _____

Your address: _____

_____ Postcode: _____

Telephone: _____ E-mail: _____

The details provided may be used to keep you informed of future products and special offers provided by Condé Nast Johansens and other carefully selected third parties. If you do not wish to recieve such information please tick this box ☐ .

Please return completed form to **Condé Nast Johansens, FREEPOST (CB264), LONDON SE25 5BR** (no stamp required). Alternatively send by fax to 020 8655 7817

HOTEL BROCHURE REQUEST
Find out further information on the hotels of your choice

The Condé Nast Johansens Hotel Brochure Request Service has been established to give guests the opportunity to obtain more information about a Recommendation, additional to that contained within the Johansens guide.

Condé Nast Johansens will pass your request to the Recommendation specified who will directly send you a brochure.

Hotel name(s) and location(s) (BLOCK CAPITALS)   Page in guide

1 _____   _____

2 _____   _____

3 _____   _____

4 _____   _____

5 _____   _____

The Recommendation(s) you have chosen will send their brochures directly to the address below

Your name: _____

Your address: _____

_____ Postcode: _____

Telephone: _____ E-mail: _____

The details provided may be used to keep you informed of future products and special offers provided by Condé Nast Johansens and other carefully selected third parties. If you do not wish to recieve such information please tick this box ☐ .

Please return completed form to **Condé Nast Johansens, FREEPOST (CB264), LONDON SE25 5BR** (no stamp required). Alternatively send by fax to 020 8655 7817